AF516301

Elementary Education in India

Elementary Education in India

Status, Issues and Concerns

D. Jagannatha Rao

Former Director of Public Instruction
Karnataka

Viva Books
New Delhi | Mumbai | Chennai | Kolkata
Bangalore | Hyderabad | Kochi | Guwahati

Publisher's note

First Published 2010

Viva Books Private Limited

4737/23, Ansari Road, Daryaganj, New Delhi 110 002
Tel. 42242200, 23258325, 23283121, Email: vivadelhi@vivagroupindia.net

76, Service Industries, Shirvane, Sector 1, Nerul, Navi Mumbai 400 706
Tel. 27721273, 27721274, Email: vivamumbai@vivagroupindia.net

Jamals Fazal Chambers, 26 Greams Road, Chennai 600 006
Tel. 28294241, 28290304, Email: vivachennai@vivagroupindia.net

B-103, Jindal Towers, 21/1A/3 Darga Road, Kolkata 700 017
Tel. 22816713, Email: vivakolkata@vivagroupindia.net

7, GF, Sovereign Park Aptts., 56-58, K. R. Road, Basavanagudi, Bangalore 560 004
Tel. 26607409, Email: vivabangalore@vivagroupindia.net

101-102, Moghal Marc Apartments, 3-4-637 to 641, Narayanguda, Hyderabad 500 029
Tel. 27564481, Email: vivahyderabad@vivagroupindia.net

First Floor, Beevi Towers, SRM Road, Kaloor, Kochi 682 018
Tel. 0484-2403055, 2403056, Email: vivakochi@vivagroupindia.net

232, GNB Road, Beside UCO Bank, Silpukhuri, Guwahati 781 003
Tel. 0361-2666386, Email: vivaguwahati@vivagroupindia.net

www.vivagroupindia.com

ISBN: 978-81-309-1474-9

Published by Vinod Vasishtha for Viva Books Private Limited
4737/23 Ansari Road, Daryaganj, New Delhi 110 002

Printed & bound by Sanat Printers, Kundli 131 028

Contents

Preface

India's progress in education since independence has been unprecedented by all standards through increase in the number of educational institutions, teachers and other infrastructure facilities. In spite of this growth, the country faces a number of challenges. Nearly one-third of the population is illiterate. Critical gaps exist in educational attainments across regions as well as among different social groups.

The progress in education has also been uneven across states and even within states. Accessibility to schools, quality of educational infrastructure, performance levels of students and various other educational indicators are not uniform across the country. If the mean years of schooling is taken as an indicator of retention, then current levels of completion fall well below the expected objective and constitutional mandate of providing eight years of universal education for all children up to the age of 14.

Free and compulsory elementary education is now a fundamental right of every child in the age group of 6-14 years in the country. This significant milestone (albeit on paper) was achieved after nearly six decades of the country's independence. Lack of political will and inadequate provision of funds for 'universalizing elementary education' are cited as some of the reasons for such an inordinate delay in converting the intent into law. It took another six years for the central government to pass the 'Right to Education Act' in Parliament. We are still not sure how, in what format and with what speed the intent of providing the 'Right to Education' will be implemented in letter and spirit.

In this context, the book tries to analyse the status of elementary education in India. Different dimensions pertaining to elementary education – current status, important initiatives taken up by the centre and the states, various policy perspectives, equity issues, financing of education, community participation, role of private sector in elementary education, quality concerns, and future challenges in the field – are discussed in detail in this book.

I am grateful to numerous academicians, colleagues and friends who gave valuable inputs, comments and suggestions in the preparation of this book. I also wish to thank Smt. Shanti Srikanth for her valuable inputs by way of copy editing this book.

It is hoped that this book will enable teachers, academicians, educational planners and administrators to get a holistic view of the current elementary education scenario in the country.

D. JAGANNATHA RAO
(Email djrao303@yahoo.com)

Abbreviations and Acronyms

ADB	Asian Development Bank
AEO	Assistant Educational Officer
AIE	Alternative and Innovative Education
AIR	All India Radio
ALIMCO	Artificial Limb Manufacturing Corporation of India
ANM	Auxiliary Nurse cum Midwife
AP	Andhra Pradesh
APF	Azim Premji Foundation
AREF	Amylase Rich Energy Food
ASER	Annual Status of Education Reports
AWC	Anganawadi Centre
AWP	Annual Work Plan
AWW	Anganawadi Worker
BAS	Baseline (learning achievement) Assessment Survey
BCM	Backward Classes and Minorities
B.Ed.	Bachelor of Education
BEO	Block Education Officer
BiMaROU states and	Bihar, MP, Rajasthan, Orissa UP (includes Jharkhand & Chhattisgarh)
BPL	Below Poverty Line
BRC	Block Resource Centre
BRP	Block Resource Person
CABE	Central Advisory Board of Education
CAL	Computer Aided Learning
CARE	Cooperative for American Relief Everywhere
CBSE	Central Board of Secondary Education
CCRT	Centre for Cultural Resources and Training
CEC	Continuing Education Centre
CEP	Continuing Education Programme
CFTRI	Central Food Technological Research Institute, Mysore
CIFL	Central Institute of Foreign Languages, Hyderabad
CIIL	Central Institute of Indian Languages, Mysore
CLEP	Continuing and Life-long Education Programme
CPE	Compulsory Primary Education
CRC	Cluster Resource Centre
CRP	Cluster Resource Person
CSS	Centrally Sponsored Scheme
CTE	College of Teacher Education
D.Ed.	Diploma in Education
DEO	District Education Officer
DEEP	District Elementary Education Programme
DIET	District Institute of Education and Training
DFID	Department of International Development
DPO	District Project Office
DISE	District Information System for Education
DPEP	District Primary Education Programme
DRC	District Resource Centre
DRU	District Resource Unit
DWCD	Department of Women & Child Development
ECCE	Early Childhood Care and Education
EDI	Educational Development Index
EE	Elementary Education
EFA	Education for All
EFC	Eleventh Finance Commission
EFT	Electronic Funds Transfer
EGS	Education Guarantee Scheme
EMIS	Education Management Information System
EVS	Environmental Science
FGD	Focus Group Discussion

FCI	Food Corporation of India
FYP	Five Year Plan
GDI	Gender (related) Development Index
GDP	Gross Domestic Product
GEI	Gender Equality Index
GER	Gross Enrolment Ratio
GIS	Geographical Information System
GMR	Global Monitoring Report (of EFA)
GNP	Gross National Product
GPI	Gender Parity Index
GOI	Government of India
HDI	Human Development Index
HDR	Human Development Report
HP	Himachal Pradesh
HRD	Human Resource Development
IASE	Institute of Advance Studies in Education
ICDS	Integrated Child Development Services Scheme
ICMR	Indian Council of Medical Research
ICT	Information and Communication Technology
IDDs	Iodine Deficiency Disorders
IEDC	Integrated Education for Disabled Children
IGNOU	Indira Gandhi National Open University
I.Q.	Intelligence Quotient
ISCE	Indian Schools Certificate Examination
ISKCON	International Society for Krishna Consciousness
ISRO	Indian Space Research Organization
IT	Information Technology
J&K	Jammu and Kashmir
JRM	Joint Review Missions
JSS	Jan Shikshana Sansthan
KGBV	Kasturba Gandhi Balika Vidyalaya
KSQAO	Karnataka School Quality Assessment Organization
LGP	Learning Guarantee Programme
MAS	Mid-term (learning achievement) Assessment Survey
MDGs	Millennium Development Goals
MDM	Midday Meal Programme
MHRD	Ministry of Human Resource Development
MLLs	Minimum Levels of Learning
MMS	Midday Meal Scheme
MP	Madhya Pradesh
MS	Mahila Samakhya
MTAs	Mother Teacher Associations
MVF	M. Venkatarangayya Foundation (of AP)
NAEP	National Adult Education Programme
NAFRE	National Alliance for the Right to Education
NCERT	National Council of Educational Research and Training
NCF	National Curriculum Framework
NCLP	National Child Labour Project
NCPR	National Commission for Protection of Child Rights
NCTE	National Council for Teacher Education
NDC	National Development Council
NEEM	National Elementary Education Mission
NER	Net Enrolment Ratio
NER	North-eastern Region-states
NFE	Non Formal education
NFHS	National Family Health Survey
NGOs	Non Government Organizations
NHDR	National Human Development Report
NIEPA	(NUEPA) National Institute (University) of Education Planning & Administration, New Delhi
NIN	National Institute of Nutrition, Hyderabad
NLM	National Literacy Mission
NLMA	National Literacy Mission Authority

NPE	National Policy on Education (1986)
NP NSPE	National Programme of Nutritional Support to Primary Education
NPEGEL	National Programme for Education of Girls at the Elementary Level
NSS	National Sample Survey
NSSO	National Sample Survey Organization
NUEPA	National University of Education Planning & Administration
OB	Operation Blackboard
OBC	Other Backward Castes
OfSTED	Office of Standards in Education (UK)
OLS	Open Learning Systems
PIs	Performance Indicators
PLC	Post Literacy Campaign
PLP	Post Literacy Programmes
POA	Programme of Action (1992)
PPP	Public Private Partnership
PPU	Policy Planning Unit (Karnataka)
PRIs	Panchayat Raj Institutions
PSE	Pre-school Education
PTA	Parent Teacher Associations
PTR	Pupil-Teacher Ratio
R&D	Research and Development
RCI	Rehabilitation Council of India
ROT	Receive only Terminal
SAC	Space Application Centre
SBC	School Betterment Committee
SC	Scheduled Caste
SCERT	State Council of Educational Research and Training
SDMCs	School Development and Monitoring Committees
SEB	State Education Board
SHGs	Self-Help Groups
SIDA	Swedish International Development Authority
SIE	State Institute of Education
SIEMAT	State Institute of Education Management and Training
SITE	Satellite Television Experiment
SLEC	State Level Empowered Committee
SMC	School Management Committee
SPD	State Project Director
SPO	State Project Office
SRC	State Resource Centre
SSA	Sarva Shiksha Abhiyan
SSLC	Secondary School Leaving Certificate
ST	Scheduled Tribe
TAS	Terminal (learning achievement) Assessment Survey
TIMSS	Trends in International Mathematics and Science Studies
TLC	Total Literacy Campaign
TLM	Teaching Learning Material
TQM	Total Quality Management
TN	Tamil Nadu
TTI	Teacher Training Institute
UEE	Universalization of Elementary Education
UGC	University Grants Commission
UN	United Nations
UNDP	United Nations Development Programme
UNESCO	United Nations Educational, Scientific and Cultural Organization
UNFPA	United Nations Family Planning Association
UNICEF	United Nations Children's Fund
UNMDG	UN Millennium Development Goals
UP	Uttar Pradesh
UPA	United Progressive Alliance (led by the Congress)
UPE	Universalization of Primary Education
UTs	Union Territories
VECs	Village Education Committees
WB	West Bengal (Contextual)
WB	World Bank (Contextual)
ZPs	Zilla Panchayats/Parishads
ZSS	Zilla Saksharata Samitis

1

Status of Elementary Education in India

Elementary Education forms the very foundation on which society, its values and its characters are built. In India, elementary education means schooling of children in the age group of 6-14 and comprising of classes from 1 to 8. Universalization of Elementary Education (UEE) aims at providing universal, free and compulsory elementary education of satisfactory quality to all children. It has two components, numerical and qualitative, which involve:

- Universal enrolment and retention of children in the age group of 6-14 years at the elementary stage, and
- Universal attainment, i.e., children achieving the specified minimum levels of learning (MLLs) with emphasis on inculcation of essential values.

Considerable progress has been achieved in terms of access to basic education and enrolment in schools in the country. The increase in school participation, especially of girls, has been significant in many erstwhile educationally backward states like Madhya Pradesh(MP), Rajasthan, Andhra Pradesh(AP) and even Uttar Pradesh(UP). For a number of reasons, (ranging from persistent poverty to social prejudices) however, many enrolled children do not complete primary school. There are also concerns regarding the quality of education in elementary schools in the country. This chapter discusses the status of elementary education in the country in terms of access, enrolment, retention, completion, participation and achievement of children.

PRIVATE SECTOR PARTICIPATION IN ELEMENTARY EDUCATION

The government schools constitute 80 per cent of all elementary schools in India. However, the number of private aided and unaided (and also unrecognized) schools in the country has increased rapidly in the last few years. India has over 2.44 lakh private schools (constituting 20 per cent of all elementary schools in the country).

Table 1.1 Percentage of Government and Private Primary Schools in India

Type of Schools	Number of Schools	Percentage
Government Schools	1,002,915	80 per cent
Private Schools	243,895	20 per cent
Total	1,246,810	100 per cent

Source: DISE 2007-08, NUEPA

For people who can afford, these schools provide an alternative to government ones. Even though they charge higher fees, they cater to a sizeable elite/middle class and try to satisfy their demand for quality education. The all-India figures for the 6-14 age group enrolled in private schools has shown a marked increase from 16.4 per cent in 2005 to 22.5 per cent in 2008, with a significant increase in many states.

The Indian middle and upper middle class households will continue to spend a large part of their income on funding the education of their children. Hence this, along with budget allocations, will encourage faster growth of private sector schools in the country. Presently however except in the case of a few, the quality of education provided by most of these schools is hardly satisfactory. (For details please refer Chapter IX).

UNIVERSAL ACCESS

The goals of 'Education for All' (EFA) with respect to 'Universal Access' focus on providing schooling facilities to all children including girls, disabled children, children belonging to Scheduled Castes (SC)/Scheduled Tribes (ST) in primary and upper primary classes and, provision of non-formal education (NFE) centres for school dropouts, working children and girls who cannot attend formal schools.

Definition of Universal Access

The basic requirement for achieving universal education is to ensure that all children have access to a primary school within a reasonable distance. 'Universal Access' originally meant making a primary school available within walking distance of the child – a lower primary school in habitations with a population of 300 (the norm is 200 in some states) or within 1km from the residence of the child, an upper primary school within a distance of 3km. This objective also included construction of school buildings/classrooms and provision of adequate teachers.

Extent of Access

In order to assess the extent of provisions made according to these norms, periodic surveys were conducted. The number of rural habitations not served by primary schools in 1993 was 16.64 per cent. Even though this percentage started decreasing, about 40,000 school-less habitations with population more than 300 were still to be provided with primary schools in 2000.

Several states initiated a number of schemes to increase coverage of primary schools. Prominent among them were the 'Education Guarantee Scheme' (EGS) of MP, and 'Lok Jumbish' of Rajasthan. The District Primary Education Programme (DPEP) also focused on improving access in remote and unserved habitations in project districts in all the states. As a result, a dense network of primary schools was set up across the length and breadth of the country, and now, there are more than a million elementary schools. As per the National Human Development Report (NHDR) 2001, there were 5.7 primary schools/1000 school going children in the age group of 6-11 years in 1982-83 as against 5.04 schools in 1997-98. This marginal decline was somewhat made up by improved availability of upper primary or middle schools, from 2.44 schools/1000 children in 1982-83 to 2.75 schools in 1997-98. In 2007-08, 98.5 per cent of the rural population (and 87 per cent of habitations) was served with a primary school within 1km of their habitations. During the Tenth Plan, 1,30,000 primary schools were sanctioned and it is estimated that over 98 per cent of the habitations were served with a primary school within 1km of the habitations.

Table 1.2 Increase in Number of Primary Schools in India (2006-07) (In lakhs)

Year	No. of Primary Schools	No. of Upper Primary Schools	Total No. of Schools
1990	5.60	1.51	7.11
1997	6.11	1.86	7.97
2000	6.41	1.98	8.39
2002	6.64	2.19	8.83
2004	7.10	2.62	10.41
2006	7.72	2.88	10.60

Source: MHRD Reports

Establishment of Smaller Schools

The objective of the central and state governments was to provide primary school facilities with easy access to children. This led to the establishment of smaller schools with relatively less facilities. Since several small habitations across states were in remote and inaccessible areas or had physical barriers (like rivers, hillocks, forest, accident-prone highways, etc.) that prevented easy mobility, a number of states relaxed these norms and provided schooling facilities in such habitations. This was also done based on the belief that barrier to school participation did not consist of physical distance alone as it is also closely linked to cultural and economic factors. It is encouraging to note that this helped improve enrolment and participation considerably.

Access to Upper Primary Schools

However, providing access to schooling at the upper primary level has not been that satisfactory. In most states, it is comparatively less accessible compared to primary level facilities. As in 2006-07, there were 7.72 lakh primary schools and 2.88 lakh upper primary schools in the country. 78 per cent of habitations had access to upper primary classes within a vicinity of 3km in 2002-03. But it improved to 86 per cent in 2007-08. This indicates not only a considerable demand for upper primary education but improvement in transition from lower primary to upper primary classes as well.

Increase in the number of upper primary schooling facilities is also indicated by an improvement of the ratio of upper primary schools to primary schools. In 1957, there was only one upper primary school for every six primary schools. In 1987 this ratio improved to 1:4, and it further improved to 1:3 in 1993. The ratio of primary to upper primary schools stood at 2.7:1 in 2006-07 (against the Sarva Shiksha Abhiyan (SSA) norm of 2:1). About 50,000 new upper primary schools/sections were required to be established to bring the ratio down to 2:1.

Provision of Human Resources

The policy of the Government of India (GOI) was to provide two teachers to every primary school initially. In upper primary schools, the teachers were provided on the basis of subject teaching and teaching workload. But wherever the GOI assistance was not forthcoming, the states continued to run single-teacher primary schools to cater to smaller habitations and remote areas.

The annual average growth rate of teachers between 1951 and 2001 was 2.57 per cent in case of primary and 5.67 per cent in case of upper primary teachers. The percentage of women teachers increased from 17.19 to 34.24 in case of primary schools, and from 15.76 to 36.08 in upper primary schools in the same period.

As per seventh All India Education Survey Report 2002 there were 17.73 lakh primary and 14.88 lakh upper primary school teachers (Annexure VIII – Table 22) in India. Out of this, 5.22 lakh primary and 2.60 lakh upper primary teachers were untrained (Annexure VIII – Table 23).

Table 1.3 Increase in Number of Teachers

Year	Primary Schools			Upper Primary Schools		
	Total in Lakhs	% of Trained Teachers	% of Female Teachers	Total in Lakhs	% of Trained Teachers	% of Female Teachers
1990-91	16.16	85.25	29.24	10.73	88.02	33.24
1997-98	18.72	87.00	34.24	12.12	88.00	36.08
2005-06	21.83	86.00	65.00	16.71	87.00	67.00

Source: EFA 2000 and 2008 Assessment Reports

Several programmes like Operation Blackboard (OB), DPEP and SSA helped improve the number of teachers in schools. Thus, it increased from 19.19 lakh in 1999-2000 to 21.83 lakh in 2005-06 at the primary level and from 12.98 lakh in 1999-2000 to 16.71 lakh in 2005-06 at the upper primary level. In 2005-06, thus, there were an estimated 38.5 lakh elementary school teachers in India. As can be seen in Table 1.3, there are also a large number of untrained teachers in the country. Majority of them are in the north-eastern region of the country, with qualifications ranging from a pass in class 8 to a degree.

Universal Enrolment

India now has the largest student population in the world, with over 1847 lakh pupils at the primary level followed by China (with over 1210 lakh pupils). With considerable progress in access, it is logical for enrolment figures to show a significant improvement. But it is also a fact that mere access does not guarantee participation. This is borne out by the fact that large variations exist across states/Union Territories (UTs) with respect to access and enrolment. It is particularly true of several states with low literacy rates (notably Bihar) which suggest that a large section of the population is not participating in education even though facilities exist.

Table 1.4 Growth in Enrolment (In millions)

Year	Classes 1 to 5 Primary	Classes 6 to 8 Upper Primary	Total
1951	19.30	3.65	22.95
1961	39.10	7.48	46.58
1971	58.82	13.68	72.50
1981	76.11	21.95	98.07
1991	100.94	35.65	136.59
2001	113.80	42.80	156.60
2003	122.40	46.90	169.30
2005	131.70	51.70	183.40
2006	132.00	52.20	184.74

Source: MHRD Reports

Enrolment in primary classes increased by about six times between 1951 and 2001, while in upper primary classes, it increased by about eleven times during the same period. The annual compound growth rate was 3.76 per cent in primary classes and 4.06 per cent in upper primary classes. According to 'Annual Status of Education Report' (ASER) 2008, 24.75 per cent of an average class 1 in India had children under six years of age. Though the total enrolment seems apparently impressive, one must not miss the fact that the population growth in those decades was also very high; hence, several million children were still outside the schooling system. The original target under SSA was that all eligible children were to be enrolled in schools by 2003. Since this was not met, the target was shifted to 2005; but even by then, it could not be achieved.

The 'District Information System for Education' (DISE) data for 2007-08 (Table 1.5) gives the latest picture of the total number of government and private primary schools and enrolment pattern in government and private schools in the country.

Table 1.5 India – Schools and Enrolment

Type of Schools	Number of Schools	Enrolment Classes 1 to 5	Enrolment Classes 6 to 8	Total Enrolment
Government Schools	1,002,915 (80%)	101,153,429 (76%)	32,498,650 (64%)	133,652,079 (72%)
Private Schools	243,895 (20%)	32,736,432 (24%)	18,353,943 (36%)	51,090,375 (28%)
Total	1,246,810	133,889,861	50,852,593	184,742,454

Source: DISE 2007-08, NUEPA,

The ASER Study on School Enrolment

The ASER 2008 study indicated that 95.7 per cent of children (in rural India in the 6-14 years age group) were enrolled in school. Six states – Kerala, HP, Uttaranchal, MP, Maharashtra, and TN – had less than 2 per cent out-of-school children (in the age group of 6-14 years). The distribution of enrolment of children by type of school is indicated below:

Table 1.6 Enrolment by Type of School in Rural India (6-14 age group) (In percentage)

Government	Private	Others	% Out-of-school	Total
71.9	22.5	1.3	4.3	100.00

Source: ASER 2008

Over the years, Bihar showed the steepest drop in the proportion of out-of-school children (more than 7 per cent), with girls recording a drop from 20.1 per cent in 2005 to 8.8 per cent in 2008.

Enrolment in Private Schools

According to ASER reports, the percentage of children in the 6-14 age group attending private schools steadily increased from 16.4 per cent in 2005 to 22.5 per cent in 2008. This increase was particularly striking in Karnataka, UP and Rajasthan. Half of all school going children in Kerala and Goa went to private schools. According to DISE, 95 per cent of private schools in Kerala and 70 per cent in Goa were government aided schools. 32-42 per cent of all school going children in Nagaland, Punjab, Haryana, UP and Rajasthan went to private schools which were mostly unaided.

Gross Enrolment Ratio (GER)

As per the definition of 'Universal Enrolment', all children of school-going age are to be enrolled in primary/elementary schools in the country. GER and 'Net Enrolment Ratio' (NER) are education indicators used to capture the picture of universal enrolment.

GER is a key ratio for assessing the actual extent of access to children. It is defined as the ratio of gross enrolment to the proportion of total number of children in the relevant age group. GER for elementary level is thus the ratio of the number of children enrolled to the actual number of children in the 6-14 age group.

There has been noticeable improvement in GER over the years. It increased progressively since 1950-51 from 32.1 to 94.0 in 2005-06 for the elementary stage.

Table 1.7 GER over the Years

Year	Primary (1 to 5)			Upper Primary (6 to 8)			Elementary (1 to 8)		
	Boys	Girls	Total	Boys	Girls	Total	Boys	Girls	Total
1950-51	60.6	24.8	42.7	20.6	4.6	12.6	46.4	17.7	32.1
2002-03	97.5	93.1	95.3	65.3	56.2	60.8	85.4	79.3	82.4
2005-06	112.8	105.7	109.4	84.2	76.3	78.6	98.5	91.0	94.0

Source: MHRD Reports

Table 1.8 GER at Primary & Upper Primary Levels

Year	Primary GER (%)	Upper Primary GER (%)	Elementary GER (Classes 1 to 8)
1999-2000	94.9	58.8	81.3
2001-02	93.0	69.6	85.6
2003-04	98.3	62.5	84.9
2005-06	109.4	78.6	94.0

Source: MHRD Reports

GER was over 100 per cent in cases where there were repeaters or where some enrolled children were either over-aged or under-aged. In many states, it exceeded 100 per cent. In 2003-04, 16 per cent of children in primary classes were under or over-aged, whereas the figure for upper primary classes stood at 23 per cent. This improved slightly to 14 per cent and 20 per cent respectively in 2004-05. Only when enrolled students are retained in successive classes, the enrolment indicators become useful in capturing the educational progress. The GER declines sharply as we move to higher classes. This indicates a low transition rate particularly on completion of elementary education.

As per Karnataka EMIS 2006-07, 10.1 per cent of children dropped out between class 7 and class 8 for the simple reason that they had to join a new school, as class 8 was not available in a majority of upper primary schools in Karnataka.

Net Enrolment Ratio (NER)

Though GER is a good indicator, it may not reveal the complete status of the enrolment scenario of a particular level and area. Thus, NER has an advantage over it, in that it indicates enrolments of the classes at the prescribed level and in the prescribed age group.

NER overcomes the shortcomings of both GER and age-specific enrolment ratio, as it captures age-specific enrolment of students in the classes they ought to be, as per the prevailing norms for school enrolments.

NER is defined as the number of students enrolled in a level of education, belonging to the relevant age group as a percentage of population of that age group. In other words, it is calculated as a percentage of net enrolment of children of the right age group to the total children in the relevant age group, implying the extent of access of children in the target age group.

In 2003-04, NER was 82.5 per cent for primary and less than 40 per cent for upper primary classes. In 2004-05, it improved to 94.3 per cent and 50.7 per cent respectively. This clearly reflects the need to have greater focus on upper primary education.

Mean Years of Schooling

Only when the enrolled child is retained in successive classes does the enrolment data become useful in capturing current educational progress. In this context, 'the mean years of schooling' acquires a strong significance in reflecting the educational progress.

According to NFHS II survey, the mean years of schooling in India was 5.5 years. But several states are below this national average: Bihar (3.5), Assam (4.5), WB (4.5), MP (4.7), AP (4.7), UP (4.8), and Rajasthan (4.8). Most of the major states of the country that have over six years of schooling are in the south or west of the country.

Intensity of Formal Education

Another useful educational indicator is 'Intensity of formal education' which is based on class-wise enrolment rates. This indicator takes care of dropout rates across all classes. In constructing it, a weighted average of the share of class-wise enrolment in the total enrolment is taken, the weights increasing over successive classes from 1 to 12. This is then adjusted by the GER for the population of children in the age group of 6-18 years, to correct for those in the school-going age group who are not enrolled.

The indicator has a better value for states which are able to have a higher level of enrolments in higher classes. This means that these states are able to retain children in schools for a longer duration and, consequently, have a higher proportion of children of school-going age enrolled in schools.

At the national level (as per NHDR 2001), the intensity of formal education was 4.03 years for students enrolled in 1978. It increased to 4.64 years in 1993. Among the major states, it varied between 3.97 years for Bihar and 5.44 years for Kerala.

UNIVERSAL RETENTION

'Universal Retention' means retaining children throughout the primary/elementary stage through provision of incentives (which vary from state to state) such as competency-based textbooks, free uniforms, school bags, notebooks, hot cooked midday meals, scholarships, health checkups, separate toilets for boys and girls, etc. Several states also follow a no-detention policy in primary classes for this purpose.

The GOI enunciated five indicators to assess the completion of schooling at the primary stage – rate of dropout, rate of repetition, rate of survival from class 1 to 5, efficiency index in terms of average number of years taken by a child to complete the five year cycle and, rate of transition from primary to upper primary stage. Even though the figures published for most states pertaining to the primary stage shows improvement in retention and completion during the past decade, they continue to be a cause for concern at the upper primary stage.

SSA had set a target for all children to complete five-years of primary schooling by 2007. This goal was later deleted as 7 million were still out-of-school even by 2006-07. Another goal of SSA – 'Universal Retention in the primary stage by 2007' was also later modified to 'Universal Retention by 2010'.

Involvement of Panchayati Raj Institutions (PRIs), provision of nutritional support to children in the form of Midday meals, innovations in curriculum, flexibility in scheduling of school terms in rural areas in some states, have largely contributed to improvement of enrolment and retention of children in primary schools.

Out-of-School Children

Table 13 in Annexure VIII gives a detailed picture of the percentage of out-of-school children in various categories and age groups. As per one MHRD sponsored study, 70 per cent of such children in 2005 were concentrated in five states: UP, Bihar, MP, Rajasthan and WB.

In addition there were some districts in states like Uttarakhand and J&K, where girls contributed to more than 60 per cent of the total out-of-school child population. As on 31st March, 2006, 72.8 lakh were still estimated to be out-of-school.

As per another survey carried out in 2006 by the Social and Rural Research Institute, IMRB International, 13.46 million children in the age group of 6-13 years, (6.94 per cent out of 194.03 million children) were out-of-school. About 68 per cent of these children were never enrolled, while the rest were dropouts. MHRD 2008 report placed the number of out-of-school children in March, 2006 at 7.05 million.

Independent studies done by 'ASER' revealed that the all-India percentage of out-of-school children has not decreased from 2007. States like Bihar saw a drop from 6.5

per cent to 5.7 per cent whereas in UP, the percentage of such children increased from 3.9 per cent to 5.6 per cent, and in Rajasthan from 6.5 per cent to 7.1 per cent in 2008.

As per ASER 2008 study, the proportion of out-of-school children in the country in the age group of 7-10 years was 2.7 per cent, for the group of 11-14 years, it was 6.3 per cent. For girls in the age group of 11-14 years, it was 7.3 per cent. With the exception of UP and Rajasthan the percentage of these children in most states decreased since 2007.

Table 1.9 Percentage of Out-of-School Children (6-14 years) in Major States of India

State	2006	2007	2008
Uttar Pradesh	6.0	3.9	5.6
Bihar	12.8	6.5	5.7
Rajasthan	10.8	6.5	7.1
Tamil Nadu	2.1	1.2	0.6
Madhya Pradesh	3.8	2.2	1.9
Chhattisgarh	7.3	4.6	4.6
Karnataka	4.9	3.5	3.5
Jammu & Kashmir	4.7	3.6	2.7
Himachal Pradesh	1.3	1.0	0.6
Uttarakhand	2.4	2.2	1.0
Punjab	3.2	2.9	2.7
Haryana	3.2	3.6	2.9
West Bengal	7.8	4.8	5.7
Orissa	9.1	8.0	7.2
Gujarat	5.6	3.7	4.2
Maharashtra	3.8	1.8	1.5
Andhra Pradesh	4.2	4.3	3.4
Kerala	0.4	0.4	0.2
All-India	6.6	4.2	4.3

Source: ASER 2008

Dropouts

A variety of reasons cause a significant number of children to exit the mainstream education system over time after enrolment in class 1. A child may be reported as enrolled in a certain class, but he/she may not be attending school regularly. Even if attending, he/she may dropout by the end of the year. Under normal circumstances, dropout indicates continuous absenteeism of the child at school. But the duration of absenteeism varies from state to state, according to the adopted time frame. There are various factors affecting dropout and repetition of children at the school level.

The overall dropout rates have been consistently witnessing a declining trend over the years. Though it is declining at the national level, there are considerable regional disparities in states across the country. While most children entering primary schools complete at least 4-5 years of schooling in states like Kerala, Goa and Mizoram, dropout figures continue to be high in many other states. Dropout data provided by most states are often found unreliable due to a number of reasons.

A National Sample Survey Organization (NSSO) survey (for 1995-96) found that dropout increases cumulatively with the level of education. It was least for those belonging to the highest expenditure class and maximum for those belonging to the lowest expenditure class. Children from the poorest sections of society dropout in the early stages of education, while those from better-off sections do so at later stages.

Education indicators such as dropout and school attendance rates can supplement the use of enrolment indicators. The former is an indicator of the efficiency of the school system in the country, since it presents an overview of the wastage of human resources. It measures the percentage of children who dropout from a particular level of education in a particular year. Along with students repeating a class, the dropout rate gives an indication about the wastage of school education and tends to undermine the benefits of increased enrolments.

The dropout rate was as high as 60 per cent in the eighties and an estimated 35.06 million children (in the age group of 6-11 years) were out-of-school in 1997. However, it has been showing a declining trend across the country over the past decade.

Table 1.10 Declining Trends in Dropout Rates

Year	Dropout Rate Primary (Classes 1 to 5)	Dropout Rate Elementary (Classes 1 to 8)
1999-2000	40.3	54.5
2001-02	39.0	54.6
2002-03	34.9	52.8
2004-05	28.5	50.4
2005-06	25.5	48.7

Source: MHRD Reports

According to MHRD reports, the gross dropout rate (which is significantly higher than the dropout rate discounting for repeaters) at the primary stage reduced from 40.3 per cent in 1999-2000 to 25.5 per cent in 2005-06. The decline in the rate for girls was 11.44 per cent against 4.7 per cent for boys. For the entire elementary stage (classes 1 to 8), there was a slow decline from 54.65 per cent in 1999-2000 to 48.7 per cent in 2005-06. The overall dropout rate estimated by National Institute of Educational Planning & Administration (NIEPA) based on DISE data for 2003-04 and 2004-05 was only 10.4 per cent. It must be noted here that greater standardization in methodology and consistency of data is required. Incidentally, one of the objectives of the central government was to reduce the dropout rate to less than 10 per cent for classes 6 to 8 by 2007.

States which have shown significant improvements in literacy and enrolment at primary level have been able to bring down their dropout rates significantly. Rajasthan, MP, TN, Haryana, Punjab and Maharashtra are notable cases in point. Karnataka recorded a fairly high level of dropout – nearly 50 per cent (2004-05), – in classes 1 to 8; hence, it compares poorly with Kerala (0 per cent), TN (24 per cent) and Maharashtra (28 per cent).

The Dropping Enrolment

Children progress at the primary level due to the no-detention policy followed in most states. The following table shows that while there were 30.5 million children enrolled in class 1, at the end of the primary stage (class 5) only 16 million progressed to the upper primary stage, and 10.2 million to the secondary stage. The dropping enrolment indicates that inadequate learning is taking place in schools. It also means that most children do not complete classes in which they are enrolled.

Table 1.11 The Dropping Enrolment (In millions)

Class	Boys	Girls	Total
1	17.1	13.4	30.5
2	13.4	10.4	23.8
3	12.2	9.6	21.8
4	11.0	8.6	19.6
5	10.2	7.8	18.0
6	9.4	6.6	16.0
7	8.3	5.9	14.2
8	7.6	5.0	12.6
9	6.2	4.0	10.2
10	5.4	3.4	8.8
11	2.4	1.6	4.0
12	2.1	1.4	3.5

Source: MHRD Selected Educational Statistics 2000-01

Reasons for Dropouts in Elementary Schools

Dropout is influenced by a series of independent factors, namely school environment, socio-economic and socio-psychological factors, prevalence of child labour, age of the child, negative attitude of parents towards education and the need to earn livelihood at an early stage of life among the disadvantaged children. Coupled with the above, family migration and frequent changes in residence are also responsible.

Some of the other reasons for dropout and non-attendance of children in schools are listed below:

1. Poverty, which forces parents to engage their children in work rather than in schooling.
2. Lack of parental support and motivation due to low education among them.
3. Early marriage of girls among several communities.
4. Utilizing girls for household work and sibling care.
5. Distance of the school from the habitation.
6. Lack of attractive atmosphere in schools.
7. Inadequate infrastructure and overcrowded classrooms.
8. Lack of separate toilets for girls.
9. Lack of drinking water facility.
10. Teacher teaching multiple classes at the same time resulting in lack of individual attention.
11. Poor instructional quality.
12. Teacher absenteeism.
13. Repetition of the class on the part of students.
14. No linkage between education and the job market.

The above factors individually or collectively are responsible for lack of enrolment in or dropping out-of-school. Invariably, more girls than boys discontinue schooling in all the classes because the average rural family treats boys as socio-economic assets, and hence, considers that investing in their education enhances their own economic status.

Poverty forces many children to dropout-of-school. Parents engage the young ones in productive work as the opportunity cost involved in the latter attending schools is substantial for the former. Some other reasons relating to the issue are an unresponsive curriculum, an uninteresting classroom environment, etc. DPEP and SSA tried to solve these problems through introduction of innovative methods like joyful learning, use of activity cards and colourful teaching learning material (TLM).

UNIVERSAL PARTICIPATION & ACHIEVEMENT

'Universal Participation' means that all children who are enrolled in a primary/elementary school continue until the end of that stage with active and regular participation. To ensure universal participation, various programmes made provision for providing TLMs, furniture and equipment, laboratory, library, sports equipment, etc.

'Universal Achievement' means that all children attending elementary school achieve certain MLLs at the end of this stage. This envisaged provision of improved pre-service and in-service training of teachers, resource support to teachers through Block Resource Centres (BRCs)/Cluster Resource Centres (CRCs), provision of TLM, Continuous and Comprehensive Evaluation of Children, etc.

Learning Levels as Reported by ASER

While on the one hand, enrolment figures have been encouraging, the learning levels are found to be disappointingly low. In fact, ASER 2008 noted that the learning levels appeared to be stagnant or declining as only 41 per cent of children across classes 1 to 8 were able to read simple stories in 2008 as against 43.6 per cent in 2005. Similarly, only 27.9 per cent children across the grades could do simple division sums in 2008 as compared to 30.9 per cent in 2005. The quality of performance also decreased as students moved to higher classes. The decline was observed both in government and private schools, even though the latter continued to maintain a marginally higher level than the former, at least on an all-India basis. Some of the major assessment studies on the learning-achievement levels are detailed in Annexure VII.

Performance of Children

The National Curriculum Framework (NCF) emphasizes the need to move beyond scholastic competence to measure quality. Thus, performance of students is a major indicator of the quality of education provided in schools.

The following table gives the performance of students in various classes as per a National Council of Educational Research and Training (NCERT) survey.

Table 1.12 Performance of Students (Average scores in per cent)

Class	States Covered	Maths	Language	Science	Social Science
3	29	58.3	63.1	NA	NA
5	27	46.5	58.6	NA	50.3
7	10	29.9	53.0	36.0	33.0
8	17	38.5	52.5	40.5	45.0

Source: NCERT Survey, NA- Not Applicable

This survey as well as several others (Refer Table 16 – Annexure VIII) point out the dismal academic performance of children, as a large number complete primary school with less than 60 per cent marks. Such children are unlikely to complete even the upper primary stage since academic load increases as they climb higher levels. The achievement levels of children are discussed in more detail in Chapter VI on 'Quality Concerns in Elementary Education'.

STRATEGIES ADOPTED FOR UEE IN THE COUNTRY

Initiatives of the Centre

There have been a large number of initiatives in basic education since 1986 but they were not meant for achieving universalization. Some of the efforts that have been made by the centre include providing technical support to the states through national institutions like NCERT and NIEPA, framing of National Policy of Education (NPE) 1986, Constitutional Amendments, passing of the Comprehensive Education Act in Parliament, and so on.

Major initiatives of the centre in the education sector include the Total Literacy Campaign (TLC), Operation Blackboard (OB), District Primary Education Programme

(DPEP), the National Teacher Education Programme (wherein DIETs/CTEs were created), the Mahila Samakhya and, more recently, the SSA.

SSA was the first national attempt that aimed at planning for every child. GOI sought to implement SSA through decentralization of planning and management, substantial financing through direct transfer of funds, cost effective strategies for UEE, appropriate curricula, textbooks and pedagogical inputs, suitable strategies (including incentives) for learners from disadvantaged groups so as to provide them equal educational opportunities in real terms, suitable academic and resource support to the teachers, full involvement and school monitoring by the community with increased focus on girls, marginalized groups and minorities. Through the SSA, several population-specific programmes [including National Programme for Education of Girls at Elementary Level (NPEGEL)], EGS and Alternative Innovative Education (AIE), inclusive education for children with special needs, Kasturba Gandhi Balika Vidyalaya (KGBV) were initiated for achieving the goals of UEE.

National Programme of Nutritional Support to Primary Education (NP-NSPE) – commonly known as the Midday Meal Scheme – was another major programme launched in 2005 for improving the nutritional needs of children with the aim of retaining them in school.

With the expansion of the education system in the country, the administrative machinery expanded tremendously at all levels. NPE 1986 had also proposed decentralization as a fundamental requirement for improving the efficiency of educational planning and management system along with creating a meaningful framework for accountability.

Strategies Devised by the States for UEE

Several strategies were adopted in different states to improve enrolment and attendance of children:

(a) In states like AP, MP and Karnataka which have a high proportion of smaller habitations, schools were opened to serve such regions by relaxing population and distance norms.
(b) Participatory school mapping and micro-planning, which were started as part of the 'Lok Jumbish' project in Rajasthan, were extended to most states through the DPEP and other EFA projects.
(c) Recognizing the presence of wide disparities within each state, DPEP which covered 200 districts, adopted a decentralized planning and district-specific approach. It was later extended to the entire country when district elementary education plans were made an integral part of SSA.
(d) Out-of-school children constitute the most difficult and hard-to-reach group in terms of socio-economic and cultural backgrounds. Hence, state governments devised several innovative, customized strategies and programmes to tackle the issue. Residential camps, bridge courses, alternative schools were organized (in collaboration with several NGOs) to mainstream these children.

As a result, there was a significant improvement in the last few years in enrolments in states like UP, MP, Rajasthan, AP, WB, Orissa and even, Bihar. Recent studies involving Rajasthan, north Karnataka, and Chhattisgarh reveal that the hot cooked meal scheme, among other factors, has brought about significant improvement in girls' enrolment.

Kerala – A Success Story

Kerala is an educationally forward state in terms of most of the educational indicators. It has achieved the goal of retaining all enrolled children. In 2005, the dropout rate was just 0.03 per cent. Further, the state has achieved parity in enrolment levels not only of girls and boys but also of children from marginalized groups and the general category. Thus, enrolment, retention and dropout figures reveal the absence of gender and social gaps and a strong presence of community ownership of schools.

There is significant improvement in the quality of learning. At the class eighth level, the percentage of children securing 60 per cent and above marks increased from 40 in 2002-03 to 60 in 2004-05. As far as inclusive education is concerned, every year about 100,000 children are identified and, assistive aids and appliances are given to about 15,000 of them. 895 severely disabled children, who could not attend school, have been covered by home-based education.

Bridging of Gender and Social Gaps

One of the important objectives of SSA was to bridge all gender and social gaps in enrolment, retention and learning achievement at the primary stage as well as reduce the gap to 5 per cent at the upper primary stage by 2007.

According to an MHRD report, the gender gap declined from 18 percentage points in 2001-02 to 4.2 percentage points in 2005-06 at the primary stage, and from 15 percentage points in 2001-02 to 8.8 percentage points in 2005-06 for the upper primary stage. Dropout rates for girls have declined more significantly from 39 per cent to 24 per cent (15 percentage points) compared to that of boys (4.7 percentage points).

While the GER differential between SC and general students was 1.45 per cent in 2003-04, it was 1.26 per cent between ST and general students. However, the differential for dropouts was significantly higher – for SC students, it was 5.13 per cent in 2003-04 and for ST students, it was 17.43 per cent. The NCERT class fifth study (2003) indicated that achievement levels for SC/ST students was lower than that for the general category.

Strategies for Reducing Dropouts

With a view to reducing wastage and stagnation as well as improving attendance in primary schools, the states developed various strategies which included back-to-school campaigns, summer bridge courses and formation of School Management Committees (SMCs).

In a majority of states, teachers posted to schools in remote areas are reluctant to work for various reasons. Due to irregularity in teaching, children tend to dropout. To solve this problem, Rajasthan tried the 'Shiksha Karmi' project. Several other states also adopted this model on a fairly large scale.

A number of schemes were implemented by the states to reduce dropouts, such as provision of free uniforms and textbooks, attendance scholarship for children from socio-economically deprived sections of the community, introduction of various incentive schemes, etc. In order to assist children of migrant population (nomadic groups and agricultural labour) and people from inaccessible areas in the country special residential schools (ashram schools, KGBVs) were started through various programmes.

Implementation of Midday Meal Scheme

Education is directly related to health and the nutritional status of children. It was with this in view that the government of TN started the nutritious noon-meal scheme for all school going children more than two decades ago. Following the significant impact that this programme made on children participation in school, the central government implemented the 'National Programme of Midday Meal' in all the states from 1995. With substantial assistance from GOI, many states are running the hot cooked midday meal scheme for all children of elementary schools since 2002. Several states have extended it to children of aided schools also. (For details refer Annexure III).

Promotion of Education of Girls

Considering that girls continue to be at a disadvantage, special attention was given to the issue of their education. Cultural factors also played an important part in their participation in schooling. Innovative efforts were made by states to retain girls in the system. Special scholarships were given to them in several states. Education of girls was made free at all levels. Almost all the states ensured 50 per cent reservation for women in teacher recruitment. SSA in all states has initiated a number of projects for promotion of girls' education. (For details see Chapter IV).

Promotion of Pre-school Programmes

Many children from rural areas and urban slums are first generation learners coming from poor socio-economic backgrounds. Being unable to adjust to the formal schooling system, they dropout in large numbers. Studies have shown that pre-school programmes create greater readiness among such children and help them adjust to the primary school set-up. In this context both the centre and the states promoted the pre-school programmes including Early Childhood Care Education (ECCE) and Integrated Child Development Scheme (ICDS) with cooperation from the NGO sector (For details refer Annexure IV).

FACTORS AFFECTING PARTICIPATION OF CHILDREN IN ELEMENTARY EDUCATION

Health Factors

High levels of malnutrition, particularly among growing children, are directly and indirectly associated with high morbidity and mortality. Iron deficiency in school-going children affects their learning ability and concentration power. Even mild deficiencies of micro-nutrients (Vitamin A, iron, folic acid, zinc, etc.) affect their growth, development and immunity. Malnourished children tend to have lower IQ and impaired cognitive ability, which not only affects their school performance but their productivity in later life as well.

A detailed discussion of the 'health factors' affecting participation of children in elementary education has been made in Annexure II of this book.

Issue of Single-Teacher Schools

Before independence, many states had a large number of single-teacher schools, with a majority of them having not more than 15-20 children. A single-teacher was supposed to teach more than one class. With the introduction of compulsory primary education schemes in many states, the strength in such schools increased considerably.

The OB scheme, implemented in phases, helped convert many single-teacher schools into double-teacher ones. However, they often used to revert to single-teacher status when one teacher went on long leave or one post became vacant due to transfer/ retirement, etc. The teacher could hardly teach and, at best, could maintain a semblance of discipline. A fair number of single-teacher schools still exist in the country. According to seventh All India Education Survey 2002, out of a total of 6,51,381 primary schools in the country, 8,465 schools were without a teacher and a staggering 97,670 schools were single-teacher schools.

The Issue of Multigrade Schools

The multigrade system has become an unavoidable reality at the elementary level. Even advanced countries like Switzerland, Netherlands, Belgium, Canada, Japan as well as China and Sri Lanka have a sizeable percentage of multigrade schools. Many of these countries have local-specific approaches in these schools, even though they broadly conform to the national curriculum.

In India, the implementation of UEE has added more and more dimensions to this multigrade issue. It is necessary to recognize that multigrade teaching continues to be an inevitable phenomenon as we continue to improve access, and open schools in smaller and smaller habitations.

The issue of multigrade schools arises from the norm of fixing the number of teachers per school. In many states, the present norm for a lower primary school is a minimum of two teachers and two classrooms for five classes. For a higher primary school, it is a minimum of four teachers and four classrooms covering seven classes. This has resulted in multigrade situations in a majority of schools, thus severely affecting the quality of classroom transaction.

In India, as many as 54 per cent of primary schools have only one or two teachers. The number of primary schools with three or less teachers is a staggering 1.5 per cent. Also, a significant 31 per cent of primary schools have enrolment which is less than 60. These schools have a total student attendance of 40-50 spread over five classes.

Multigrade schools face the following problems:

1. The teacher has to play different roles simultaneously.
2. The teacher has to handle more than one class at the same time.
3. The teacher is ill equipped and not sufficiently trained to handle multigrade situations.
4. Single-teacher schools do not work when the teacher goes on leave/transfer/ training, etc.
5. Academic support to teachers is poor.
6. When the student strength increases beyond a particular level, the teacher can only try to maintain a semblance of discipline rather than do any effective teaching.
7. Most of the textbooks and teacher training programmes are designed for mono-grade teaching situations.

[For a detailed discussion on this issue please refer to my book 'A Comprehensive Study of the Progress of Education in Karnataka' (pages 357-64).]

Student Attendance

Irregular student attendance is a major issue, especially in several educationally backward districts in a number of states. It is noticed that though students are enrolled in schools through various enrolment programmes, the daily average attendance in most schools in several states rarely exceeds 80 per cent. Please refer to Annexure VIII – Tables 41 and 42 for an estimate of student attendance across states.

Poor student attendance is due to lack of awareness among parents and community, seasonal migration of agricultural labour, sibling care by elder children, entrusting household duties to elder children, specially girls, and social customs, like not sending girls to school after they reach puberty. Under parental pressure, teachers often resort to fake attendance which has, however, been minimized after the introduction of the hot cooked midday meal programme. Nevertheless, poor students' attendance continues to be a major problem in several states of the country.

Pupil-Teacher Ratio (PTR) The number of teachers and institutions per se do not give a true picture of the situation in the classroom. The PTR is a more reliable indicator in judging the adequacy of the system capacity. A higher PTR impacts the quality of teaching as each teacher would have less time to devote to the individual student. Further, a higher PTR in a multigrade situation compounds the problem as the quality of learning of students is adversely impacted.

A high PTR is also correlated with low enrolment and higher dropout rates. The Learning Guarantee Programme (LGP) initiated by Azim Premji Foundation (APF), in

Karnataka, found that all the higher performing schools in North Karnataka had a PTR of less than 30 which was lower than the local average of 43.

The PTR which was 43:1 in 1999-2000 at the primary level in the country, actually increased to 46:1 in 2004-05, whereas it declined from 38:1 in 1999-2000 to 35:1 in 2004-05 at the upper primary level. However, there is significant scope for improving the PTR at both the levels. 9 out of 35 states and UTs have a PTR higher than 40:1 in primary schools, the highest being in Bihar (64:1) followed by UP (53:1), WB (51:1), and Jharkhand (48:1). (Please refer Annexure VIII – Table 30).

School Infrastructure

Infrastructure is a key area of concern in elementary education. Poor infrastructure facilities have a definite bearing on the quality of education provided in schools. (See Annexure VIII – Table 15). All the data available is with regard to infrastructure in government schools in the country. As regards private schools, no data is maintained at any level. Excluding some of the elite schools, it is common knowledge that majority of the private schools lack basic infrastructure facilities.

As per DISE data (2003-04), around 18 per cent of rural primary schools were without buildings and another 20 per cent of schools were functioning out of only one room. 4.5 per cent of schools did not have any drinking water facility. As per SSA norms there was a gap of 3,26,656 toilets in schools in 2005.

Table 1.13 Educational Infrastructure Targets and Progress

S. No.	Items	Cumulative Targets till 2005-06	Progress till 2005-06	Percentage of Progress
1.	Opening of new schools	1,57,967	1,29,863	82%
2.	Construction of school buildings	1,20,629	77,342	58.0%
3.	Construction of additional classrooms	3,29,690	1,55,814	47.0%
4.	Drinking water facilities	1,51,907	90,165	59.3%
5.	Construction of toilets	2,22,405	1,20,710	54.3%
6.	Supply of free textbooks	61.4 million children	53.5 million children	87%
7.	Teacher appointment	7,72,345	5,87,388	76%
8.	Annual in-service training of teachers	32,52,785	21,79,366	67.0%

Source: EFA 2005-08 Reports

According to DISE, 3.81 per cent of primary schools and 2.4 per cent of upper primary schools did not have any building in 2005-06. Even in those that had, there was severe shortage of classrooms. (Average number of instructional classrooms in the country was only 2). Table 28 in Annexure VIII gives a comprehensive picture of infrastructure position in elementary schools in the country.

As per estimates made in 2006-07, the country still needed about 6 lakh classrooms. This requirement is bound to increase by another one lakh on account of upgradation of EGS centres and additional enrolments.

Similarly, 44.6 per cent of primary schools and 15.3 per cent of upper primary schools did not have any toilet facilities (2005-06). Drinking water facilities were not available in 15.1 per cent of primary and 4.8 per cent of upper primary schools. Hence, shortage of such facilities is bound to have an impact on enrolment and retention of children. A study conducted by APF in the LGP (Karnataka) goes further when it says that lack of infrastructure facilities in schools has a bearing on quality of learning as well. (Refer Annexure VIII – Table 15).

Infrastructure Index – Karnataka Example

Price Waterhouse Coopers, in its report 'Position Paper on School Education', computed an Infrastructure Index to assess the infrastructure position of elementary schools in Karnataka across the following eight basic infrastructure requirements giving equal weightage to each – ramp, girl's toilet, playground, compound wall, electricity, general toilet, drinking water and library.

For example, if a school has all the basic infrastructure requirements except the playground, it gets a weightage of 0.875. According to this computation, Karnataka with an Infrastructure Index of 0.577, had a long way to go to reach the magical figure of 1.0 (a condition where basic amenities are said to be available in all elementary schools). Similarly, deficient infrastructure is a major problem in all the states across the country.

Even here, reports of fulfillment of these basic necessities have to be examined with caution. For example, a school may report having a library (by definition), but lack the basic functional components– essential reading materials, newspapers, reference books, etc. More importantly, it must be seen whether it is accessible or always kept under lock and key.

Issues at the Upper Primary Stage

Near complete enrolment at lower primary stage has led to enhanced enrolment and attendance at the upper primary stage, which has brought greater pressure on this stage. The number of upper primary schools, has steadily increased from 1.98 lakh in 1999-2000 to 2.88 lakh in 2005-06 and the ratio of upper primary schools to primary schools has steadily decreased from 3.2 to 2.7 during the same period. This means there is additional demand for classrooms as well as other basic requirements like additional infrastructure, additional teachers, etc. Substantial upgradation of laboratory and library facilities is also required for schools having upper primary sections.

There are many upper primary schools which are so small that maintaining good quality infrastructure and academic resources is simply not viable. In most states, lack of graduate subject teachers to teach upper primary classes is another major issue. Presently, general teachers with qualification of PUC-TCH (or D.Ed.) are unable to meet curricular requirements of upper primary classes as curriculum becomes subject specific, and these teachers find it difficult to teach difficult concepts. A few states have already switched to graduate teachers at the upper primary level.

The three-language formula is introduced at this stage. But in most states, there are no qualified teachers to teach the third language (e.g., hindi in southern states). A majority of upper (higher) primary schools in the country lack physical education teachers as well.

Delays in Teacher Recruitment and Transfers

Vacancies of teachers in elementary schools, which are already facing staff shortage, is a serious problem. Delay in recruitment against vacancies takes several months/years in some states, causing a cascade effect on access, retention and quality in schools.

When a vacancy (due to promotion, retirement, death, transfer, etc.) arises during the academic year, it mostly remains unfilled during that year. Delay in recruitment of teachers is a common phenomenon in almost all the states. Sometimes in several states, the gap is managed by employing part-time/para-teachers.

Clause 26 of the 'Right to Education Act', 2009 provides that vacancies of teachers in a school shall not exceed 10 per cent of the total strength of teachers. But even this small percentage is found to directly impact the quality of classroom transaction. It is also not clear how 'vacancies below 10 per cent' can be ensured in a school.

Every year the transfer policies are framed by states, keeping in mind only the needs of teachers and not those of schools. Transfers are also carried out throughout the year on political considerations. As a result, schools suffer from a number of unfilled vacancies. The use of political influence in transfers has reached alarming proportions, which reduces the morale of those who seek the same on genuine grounds. Teachers also prefer to get transferred to schools situated near towns or the roadside, thus neglecting remote schools and blocks. Posting teachers near their home towns causes a major problem since they tend to neglect school-work and engage in local politics, additional professions like agriculture, shopkeeping, running private schools, taking private tuitions, etc.

A World Bank Report, using the case study of Karnataka makes the following observation: 'A closer look revealed that the problem was concentrated in the Education Department, which registered a total of 19,374 transfers alone (8 per cent of its sanctioned strength). Transfers of teachers continued well beyond the transfer season, with teachers accounting for 8,350 out of 9,700 transfers (roughly 86 per cent) in August and September, and outside the framework of the newly established cadre management authority. Other departments were in line with the 5 per cent annual norm for transfers (World Bank, 2006: 62)'.

Very few states have adopted manpower planning and scientific forecasts of teacher requirements, which will help them take up teacher recruitment periodically and well in advance (i.e., before the commencement of the academic year itself).

Teacher Absenteeism

Teacher absenteeism is a major factor affecting quality of classroom transaction in elementary schools in the country. According to a World Bank Study (2004) '25 per cent of teachers were absent from school, and only about half were teaching, during unannounced visits to a nationally representative sample of primary schools in India'. The report estimated that 'teacher absence' varied from 14.60 per cent in Maharashtra to 42 per cent in Jharkhand. (Annexure VIII – Tables 6 & 17,18,19,20). This problem was noticed across the spectrum – older teachers, more educated teachers, head teachers, (who were all well paid), as well as contract teachers who were paid much less.

Private school teachers were found only slightly less likely to be absent than public school teachers in general. Absence rates were generally higher in low-income states. While it was considerably lower in schools with better infrastructure facilities, multigrade schools had a slightly higher rate. Other working conditions that affected teacher absence were teaching conditions and schools being situated in remote areas.

While 45 per cent of teachers were actively engaged in teaching at the time of the team's visit, in some states it was a mere 20-25 per cent. Absence rates were considerably higher than could be accounted for by official non-teaching duties which accounted for only 4 per cent of total absences. 8-10 per cent could be attributed to annual or medical leave and other officially sponsored reasons.

This means that nearly one out of four or five teachers in every school was found to be absent at work on any given day. Even when present, they spent only 68 per cent of their time in academic work, while the remaining 32 per cent was spent on non-academic work. Taking the teachers' absence also into consideration, the 'Organization Study Report (2006) on Karnataka' (by Price Waterhouse Coopers) estimated that the time spent on academics gets reduced to 53 per cent (117 days out of 220 school working days in Karnataka). Please also refer to Annexure VIII – Table 42 which contains results of a more recent study across states.

The reasons for teacher absenteeism are many. Teachers are entitled to casual leave, earned leave, medical leave and maternity leave/paternity leave. Besides, there is also the problem of unauthorized absence and lack of public awareness. With women teachers forming nearly 50 per cent of the teacher population in primary schools in many states, their going on long leave and maternity leave compounds the problem.

The annual deputation of teachers to newly started schools and against vacant posts is also another reason for teacher absence. In several cases, teachers are deputed to work as Cluster Resource Persons (CRPs) and Block Resource Persons (BRPs). Other external factors, such as teachers being deputed for election work, census, revision of electoral rolls and teacher training, also impact teacher attendance in school.

Since a majority of teachers live in urban areas (for various reasons including education of their children)/in their native places/or other central locations (from where both husband and wife can travel to their places of work), and commute to schools through public transport such as buses or private vehicles and jeeps, there are instances of teachers not coming to schools on time as well as instances of habitual absenteeism in remote/rural schools. This problem can only be tackled by effective monitoring by SMCs. Local community monitoring would be more meaningful when parents are more educated and could bring teacher absence to the notice of all concerned.

Challenges Facing Elementary Education Sector in the Country

The elementary education sector faces a number of challenges which have a direct impact on the outcomes relating to UEE. Some of them are listed below:

- In spite of considerable efforts under various programmes, a small percentage of children still remain unenrolled in different states of the country. Even among those who are enrolled, a significant number do not attend school regularly.
- The issue of dropouts remains a matter of concern. The country still has a high level of dropouts at the upper primary stage, especially of girls. One of the reasons for this is the practice of child marriage and girls being taken out-of-school with the onset of puberty in several backward areas of the country.
- Those who do not complete elementary education are mostly girls and children from rural areas, migratory population, deprived classes and from urban slums.
- Retaining children who are enrolled and ensuring that they acquire the basic knowledge and skills prescribed is also a challenge which most of the states are facing today.
- Quality improvement efforts (teacher training, textbooks, curriculum and improvement of school infrastructure) have to be the focus of various initiatives under UEE.
- GER indicates the major challenge the country faces in bringing all children to school. Though female enrolment has shown a significant improvement, the gender differential in enrolment is still a cause for concern in several states particularly Bihar, J&K, Rajasthan and UP. This calls for innovative strategies to bridge the gender gap.
- The government's own assessment of resources needed (in the financial memorandum to Parliament for the Constitutional Amendment Act) to make elementary education a fundamental right was Rs98,000 crores spread over ten years. However, this commitment is not being honoured in the annual allocations, and it is a serious cause of concern. It must be noted that the Parliament had approved the amendment, including the financial memorandum.
- In most of the states, teacher cadres continue to be centrally managed – needless to say that, to a large extent, it is done inefficiently, with many service matters remaining unresolved. Management of service records needs to be streamlined. And that will be possible only by effective

decentralization. Unfortunately, the matter has not been receiving the required attention (i.e., decentralization) because the education departmental functionaries would feel threatened as they would stand to lose powers and control.

Addressing problems of regional disparities and social inequities is another challenge facing the country. Mainstreaming the children of the most marginalized among the traditionally disadvantaged social groups and minority communities will be a long term agenda which the country will have to pursue as a part of achieving the goal of 'Education for All'.

2

Towards Education for All (EFA)

INTRODUCTION

India is an active participant in the worldwide movement for universal education that began in Jomtien in 1990 and continued at Dakar in 2000. The Framework for Action to meet the basic learning needs was adopted by the World Conference on EFA at Jomtien, Thailand in March, 1990, which brought the political leadership of the world together for the first time in the cause of EFA. This meeting envisaged the need for an end-of-decade assessment of progress as a basis for a comprehensive review of policies concerning basic education. To take this commitment forward, it demanded a greater political will among the governments within each country.

Goals of EFA

The ultimate goal affirmed by the World Declaration on EFA was to meet the basic learning needs of all children, youth and adults. These needs were further classified to consist of:

(a) Essential learning tools such as literacy, oral expression, numeracy and problem solving, and
(b) The basic learning content such as knowledge, skills, values and attitudes.

Towards fulfillment of these learning needs, the Declaration of EFA took a broadened view of basic education that consisted of formal schooling, non-formal education(NFE) and open learning systems, which cumulatively attempted to reach all children as well as adults.

Challenges Relating to EFA

The main challenges in education in the 1990s relating to EFA were the following:

(a) Access to basic education for the inaccessible segments and uncovered habitations.
(b) Qualitative improvement in content and process of education, i.e., to make them more responsive to individual learning needs.

(c) Consolidation and orientation in different areas of education through innovative programmes.
(d) Community participation in education, i.e., making education a people's movement.
(e) Evolving effective and efficient management structures in education.

Steps Taken to Achieve the Goals of EFA

EFA in India is characterized by a collective vision, decentralized planning and multi-level management including community ownership and capacity building. All goals and targets of EFA – aimed to be fulfilled in the 1990s – were assessed in terms of the nature of the programmes and the degree to which they could be successfully met.

The approach adopted for planning and implementation of EFA programmes was characterized by:

(a) A holistic view of basic education with greater linkages and integration between pre-school, primary education, NFE and adult education.
(b) Relating educational programmes to national concerns such as nutrition, health care, environment, small family norms, environment and life skills education.
(c) Collaboration of different departments and sectors of development with primary education.
(d) Decentralization, i.e., shift in strategy from considering the state as a unit of planning to the district, and moving to sub-district levels wherever feasible.
(e) Increase in community involvement in implementation and monitoring of programmes.
(f) Participation of PRIs and urban local bodies in planning and management of education.

During the past two decades, the country took certain significant steps to achieve the goals of EFA. The actions of successive governments at the centre and the states are indicative of the positive political will towards the cause of education in the country.

(a) Legislative measures were taken to make elementary education a fundamental right of every citizen, with some states having implemented additional ones. Another legislative measure adopted related to the constitutional amendment on PRIs following which many states took radical steps to decentralize management of primary education. A third measure was making special provisions for education of educationally backward classes and SCs/STs. The Right of Children to Free and Compulsory Education Act was also passed by Parliament in 2009.
(b) The second important factor was the increased allocation for EFA and UEE programmes. Efforts made under various programmes like DPEP and SSA to

provide increased allocation to elementary education (in comparison to other sectors of education) was really significant, and flowed out of the political will of all political parties to improve educational standards.

EFA 2000 Assessment

The International Consultative Forum on EFA, consisting of UNDP, UNICEF, UNFPA, UNESCO and the World Bank, coordinated the EFA 2000 Assessment at the global level. The EFA 2000 assessment aimed at enabling the participating countries to:

(i) Construct a comprehensive picture of their progress towards their own EFA goals.
(ii) Identify priorities and strategies for overcoming obstacles and accelerating progress.
(iii) Revise national plans of action accordingly.

The Framework for Action towards EFA adopted by the World Education Forum in Dakar, Senegal, in April, 2000 committed the participating countries, including India, to a number of initiatives towards attainment of six major goals within a reasonable time frame. These goals were:

(i) Expansion of comprehensive ECCE, especially for the most vulnerable and disadvantaged children.
(ii) Universal access to and completion of primary education of good quality – ensuring that by 2015, all children, particularly girls and those in adverse circumstances and belonging to ethnic minorities, are assured of the same.
(iii) Improvement of learning achievement – ensuring that the learning needs of all young people and adults are met through equitable access to basic and continued education.
(iv) Reduction of adult illiteracy rate – achieving a 50 per cent improvement in levels of adult literacy by 2015, especially for women, and equitable access to basic and continuing of education for all adults.
(v) Eliminating gender disparities in primary and secondary education by 2005, and achieving gender equality in education by 2015, with a focus on ensuring girls' full and equitable access.
(vi) Improving every aspect of the quality of education and ensuring excellence so that recognized and measurable learning outcomes are achieved by all, especially in literacy, numeracy and essential life skills.

This essentially meant expansion of provision of basic education, training in essential skills required by the youths and adults, increased acquisition of knowledge, skills and values (for a better living) by individuals and families, special provisions for girls and ethnic minorities for equitable access to appropriate learning and life skills, improved levels of adult literacy, elimination of gender and regional disparities, and overall improvement of the quality of education imparted.

Recommendations of Central Advisory Board of Education (CABE)

CABE is the highest advisory body relating to education in India. It plays a lead role in the evolution and monitoring of policies and programmes. It also provides a platform for the centre and the states to share their common concerns, review their experience and frame future policies and programmes. Thus, the partnership implied in the concurrency of education in a federal structure acquires importance and makes it a meaningful one.

CABE endorsed the World Declaration on EFA and the Framework for Action to meet basic learning needs and called for strengthening the processes initiated as a part of NPE 1986. To achieve the goals of EFA, it highlighted the need for increased financial inputs and formulated a broad operational framework for receiving assistance from international agencies so that large-scale projects (like DPEP) could be undertaken.

CABE emphasized that additional resources generated through external assistance should be utilized for educational reconstruction which should go beyond conventional measures such as opening of new schools, constructing school buildings and appointing teachers.

The goals, targets and strategies were included in subsequent Five Year Plan proposals. This also saw the launching of major projects and literacy campaigns under the National Literacy Mission (NLM). Besides, the country began vigorously pursuing the goal of UEE enunciated in the Dakar Declaration through national programmes like the DPEP and SSA.

Improvement of Access for Deprived Children

Though there was tremendous expansion in terms of basic educational facilities, large gaps in terms of access still existed – children from remote and inaccessible areas, and several social and cultural groups in the country were still outside the school system.

Hence, in order to ensure full accessibility in terms of not only availability of schools but also conditions for participation of children, the strategy adopted for EFA involved the following:

(a) Household surveys
(b) Surveys of educational status of specific social and cultural groups
(c) School mapping and micro-planning
(d) Provision for alternate schooling – residential camps, bridge courses, camps for special children including girls and dropouts, NFE programmes, etc.
(e) Support to community-based, innovative and experimental projects by voluntary agencies.

Community Participation

Community participation was seen as an essential prerequisite for ensuring sustainability of government initiatives. DPEP districts set up Village Education Committees (VECs) for monitoring and management of schools. States such as AP and Karnataka set up School

Management/Monitoring Committees to oversee functioning of schools. The promotion of Public-private Partnership (PPP) and local community participation were aimed help enhance the quality of schooling.

Campaign Approach

It was recognized that mobilizing the society to participate in education programmes was essential for achieving the goals of EFA. In order to advocate and promote EFA activities, major efforts were made to use all means including mass media.

Mass campaigns were launched for creating awareness about the educational needs of children, youth and adults. By reaching the common stakeholders thus, an appreciation of the role of education in improving the quality of life was brought about. It was also decided to implement basic education programmes under DPEP/Janashala in mission mode, effectively involving the community through Zilla Saksharata Samitis (ZSS), VECs, Parent Teacher Associations (PTAs), etc. Literacy campaigns were also taken up to strengthen the efforts.

Planning for EFA

Basic education in India is a shared responsibility between the central and state governments. Decision-making for EFA was, therefore, done at both the levels. The central government essentially dealt with national policy and programmes as guided by MHRD, CABE, Parliament, expert committees and commissions.

Within the framework and guidance provided by these bodies, long-term plans (Five Year Plans) for education development were drawn by the Planning Commission with the help of specialized working groups involving educationists, educational administrators and representatives of NGOs. Keeping in view the parameters specified in these plans, specific programmes and projects were formulated for central funding to states, usually on a matching basis.

Following NPE 1986, a number of centrally sponsored schemes were initiated in the last two decades in consultation with the states. The availability of external assistance enhanced the scope of such projects. Some of the states launched their own programmes for expanding the outreach of primary education.

Decentralized Planning

Though finances were provided by the central government, districts were visualized as the basic units for micro-planning and management of EFA. The State Project Office (SPO) provided broad parameters for organization and management of SSA at district and sub-district levels.

A District Project Office (under SSA) operates in every district. Blocks, clusters and villages are reached through BRCs, CRCs and VECs respectively. Besides these well-defined structures, several types of grass root level community-based organizations and NGOs play a responsible role in planning and monitoring activities pertaining to elementary education. But in spite of the constitution of district and sub-district structures, decentralization has not really taken off in the country, as district plans are prepared at the state level under the supervision of the SPO in most of the states.

Major nationally funded projects such as NLM, OB, NFE and those funded by the international agencies such as DPEP and 'Lok Jumbish' devised their own monitoring systems.

Adult Literacy

The census of India describes 'Literacy' as 'the ability of a person aged seven and above to both read and write with understanding, in any language'. UNESCO describes the adult literate as 'a person aged 15 and above, who can both read and write, short and simple statement in his or her everyday life'. Although the test for literacy is similar to Census 2001, UNESCO excludes the 7-14 age group. Hence, the Indian census figures show a higher literacy rate.

From a low threshold of 18.33 per cent in 1951, the literacy rate for the country increased to 64.84 per cent in 2001. During the 1990s, the absolute number of illiterates declined for the first time in India. With serious thrust to adult education programmes, the literacy levels are estimated to improve to 80 per cent by 2015.

Following NPE 1986, a National Literacy Mission (NLM) was initiated in 1988 with a campaign approach in TLC and PLC programmes. On finding that its impact was not very encouraging, it intensified its efforts to hitherto uncovered and inaccessible areas. NLM adopted an integrated approach to make basic literacy, post-literacy and continuing education phases a learning continuum.

Social mobilization generated by the literacy campaigns has had an impact on other social sectors – education, health, women's empowerment, democratic participation and environmental awareness. A more detailed discussion on 'Adult Education and Literacy' has been made in Annexure V.

The EFA Declaration and Curriculum

The EFA strategy also called for qualitative improvement in content and processes of education so as to make them more responsive to the learning needs of individuals, families and the community, apart from facilitating development in different sectors of social and economic life. The state school curriculum largely meets the requirements of EFA with regard to formal schooling.

Efforts to Translate Vision into Action

The goals of EFA were sought to be translated into action through:

(a) Goal 1: Ensuring ECCE and basic pre-school services to all children aged from 0 to 6 years, especially to the disadvantaged sections – The ICDS scheme is being universalized to cover all blocks of the country. ECCE is an important component of the scheme.

(b) Goal 2: Ensuring UEE through a comprehensive flagship programme – SSA launched in 2000-01, aims at providing eight years of quality education to all children aged 6-14 years, by the year 2015.
(c) Goal 3: Education for adolescents and youth: vocational, academic and life skills are sought to be provided through secondary schools, colleges, and technical institutes. A comprehensive plan is being implemented for meeting the educational needs of adolescents, especially girls and those from socially marginalized groups.
(d) Goals 3 & 4: Adult education and literacy that was developed as a people's movement, and carried out by volunteers and governments in every state – NLM aims at bridging gender and regional disparities in adult literacy levels by achieving a 80 per cent literacy rate by 2011-2012.
(e) Goal 5: Girls' education and women's empowerment: Initiation of special programmes like NPEGEL, Mahila Samakhya and Kasturba Gandhi Balika Vidyalayas, towards removal of gender disparities in elementary schools by 2010. This will be accompanied by special provisions for girls at secondary and higher education levels along with a wide range of women development programmes with a view to achieving gender equality at all levels and sectors.
(f) Capacity building and teacher training – ensuring adequacy of the number of trained teachers by giving importance to both pre-service and in-service components.
(g) Data streamlining – meticulous mapping of conditions, gaps and needs in different parts of the country. Data was collected by DISE and GIS to facilitate planning, implementation and monitoring.

Towards Right to Education

The Constitution made a commitment to provide free and compulsory education to all children up to the age of 14 years. The task of providing this received priority only after the adoption of NPE 1986 and POA 1992. It was reflected in the allocation of higher resources as well as clearly defined strategies to achieve the goals of EFA. The EFA Declaration of 1990 gave further fillip to the national commitment.

Further, receiving basic education came to be viewed as a fundamental right of every child. Following the Supreme Court judgment in 1993, (in the case of Unnikrishnan vs State of Andhra Pradesh) the 86th Constitution Amendment Act, passed by Parliament, added Article 21A to the Constitution, which requires the state to provide free and compulsory education to all children from the age of 6-14 years. It also modified Article 45 (directive principles) instructing the state to provide early childhood care and pre-school education.

The Right of Children to Free and Compulsory Education Act, 2008 passed by Parliament in July, 2009 seeks to give effect to the constitutional amendment. It details the responsibilities of the central and state governments, teachers, parents, and community in ensuring that all children between the age of 6-14 years receive free and compulsory education. The details of the legislative measures and policy initiatives so far undertaken are discussed in Chapter III of this book.

Innovative Interventions

Policies and programmes in recent years have gone beyond mere enrolment to focus on quality concerns in basic education, education of girls and children of disadvantaged sections of the society, community participation and educational management. India launched a satellite (EDUSAT) dedicated exclusively for education. Having the potential to create visual (virtual) classrooms, it has facilitated education of children as well as training of teachers.

The EGS-AIE programmes aim at bringing education to the door step of every child, particularly those in remote and inaccessible habitations. Several important initiatives such as SSA, cooked midday meal programme, Kasturba Gandhi Balika Vidyalaya scheme, are working towards achieving EFA goals.

Through various strategies (non-formal centres, bridge courses, remedial classes, summer camps, residential camps and so on), the government wants to reach basic education to all disadvantaged children.

EFA Development Index (EDI)

The Global Monitoring Report (GMR) 2006 on EFA has indicated an improvement in India's EDI value from 0.696 in 2001 to 0.741 in 2002. This reflects progress made by the country in various areas of education. EDI is the arithmetic mean of four components – total primary net enrolment ratio, adult literacy rate, gender-related EFA index and survival rate to grade V. The GMR points out that India is likely to achieve gender parity in elementary education by 2005, although greater efforts will be required to achieve it at the secondary education level as well.

Sarva Shiksha Abhiyan (SSA)

SSA is the most important initiative of the GOI to meet the commitments made under EFA. SSA or the 'Education for All Programme' launched in 2001-02 is an umbrella programme and is an effort to universalize elementary education through community ownership of the school system. It is a response to the demand for quality basic education all over the country, and seeks to ensure access, retention and quality improvement. It reiterates the need to focus on girls' education to equalize educational opportunities and eliminate gender disparities. The programme is implemented in a mission mode. In order to ensure that the priority of EFA is translated into action, the Prime Minister of India heads the National Mission for SSA which monitors the progress made under SSA.

The SSA covers all states and union territories and reaches out to 209 million children in 1.1 million habitations. The scheme encompasses more than a million schools. It is discussed in detail in Chapter IV of this book.

Achievements under EFA

The programmes implemented under EFA helped improve the school education sector in the country substantially. Following are the achievements as per the EFA document 2005 and Mid-decade Assessment 2008:

1. A strong network of over one million schools had been created by 2005. 98 per cent of the rural population had a primary school within 1km walking distance for the child (2008).
2. The number of out-of-school children dropped from 32 million in 2001 to 7.05 million in 2006.
3. GER increased from 32.1 in 1950-51 to 94.9 in 2005-06 in the age group of 6-14 years.
4. Gender Parity Index improved from 0.88 in 2002-03 to 0.95 in 2005-06 at the primary stage, and from 0.78 to 0.88 at the upper primary stage during the same period. Some states could also achieve gender parity.
5. The gender gap at the primary level reduced from 5.5 percentage points (pp.) in 2002-03 to 4.2 pp. in 2005-06 and at the upper primary level from 10.7 pp. to 8.8 pp. during the same period.
6. Dropout rate at primary level fell from 40.7 per cent in 2000-01 to 25.47 per cent in 2005-06, as compared to a decline of just 3 percentage points over the previous decade. During the same period dropout rate fell from 53.7 to 48.71 per cent at the elementary level.
7. Significantly, the decline in dropout rate for girls was higher than that for boys. At the primary level, the dropout rate among girls came down from around 70.9 per cent in 1960-61 to 39.88 per cent in 2001-02 to further 24.82 per cent in 2004-05.
8. PTR improved to 40:1 as 770,000 additional posts of teachers were sanctioned.
9. 98 per cent of rural population had a school within 1km of their habitation. 120,000 new schools were opened since 2001.
10. From a low of 18.33 per cent in 1951, the literacy rate for the country rose to 64.84 per cent in 2001. Absolute number of non-literates came down from 328 million in 1991 to 296 million in 2001. There was also significant improvement in female literacy from 39.2 per cent in 1991 to 53.67 per cent in 2001. The growth rate in female literacy at 14.39 per cent was higher than that for males at 11.13 per cent.
11. 1.62 million (1.24 million in primary and 0.38 in upper primary) children with special needs were enrolled in schools in 2005-06.
12. Provision was made for more than 310,000 additional classrooms, around 115,000 school buildings, 2,20,000 toilets and 150,000 drinking water facilities.

13. Free textbooks were distributed to all girls and children belonging to marginalized groups. Every year, some states distributed free textbooks to all children studying in government elementary schools.
14. Greater convergence was initiated between various governmental programmes to promote elementary education – ICDS for early childhood care. Total Sanitation Programme for school toilets and Accelerated Drinking Water Supply Programme for schools as crucial inputs to the larger mission of EFA.

The nation is eagerly looking forward for EFA Assessment 2010.

The Millennium Development Goals (MDGs)

In AD 2000, the UN General Assembly declared eight MDGs (that included goals for education) with a target date for most of them set at 2015. These goals provide tangible benchmarks for measuring progress in eight areas. Progress towards MDGs reflects progress towards human development. These MDGs represent the most comprehensive and detailed set of human development goals ever adopted. They embody basic indicators for human development in its many dimensions, including income, poverty, education, gender equity, progress in combating infectious diseases and access to clean water and sanitation.

The goals pertaining to education are:

1. Goal 2: 'Achieve universal primary education. Ensure that all children are able to complete primary education'.
2. Goal 3: 'Promote gender equality and empower women. Eliminate gender disparity in primary and secondary schooling, preferably by 2005 and not later than 2015'.

It appears that these targets will be missed by the country and by a wide margin at that.

Table 2.1 Achievement under Various Goals

Goals	Area	Target	Year	Outcome
Universal Elementary Education (UEE)				
1. UN Millennium Development Goal (UNMDG)	Elementary Education	UEE	2015	Concerns are: GER and NER out-of-school children and dropouts
2. GOI	Elementary Education	UEE	2007	Yet to be tackled

Literacy				
1. GOI National Literacy Mission	Literacy	Full literacy (Threshold value of 75 per cent)	2007	Even though recent data for literacy rates are not available, the nation has still a long way to go to reach full literacy.
Remove Gender Disparity				
1. UNMDG	Primary & Secondary Education	Remove gender disparity.	2005	Gender disparity at the secondary level needs to be tackled.
2. GOI (Tenth Plan)	Literacy	Reduce gender gap by half	2007	
Provide Better Inputs				
1. GOI Eleventh Five Year Plan (Also National Common Minimum Programme of the UPA)	Education Sector	Raise public spending to 6 per cent of GDP with at least half the amount being spent on primary and secondary education	2012	Even as late as 2009-10, there was no evidence of increase in GOI spending to 6 per cent of GDP.

Apart from these perspectives, this book discusses the various aspects of elementary education in successive chapters.

3

Legislative and Policy Initiatives for Development of Education in India

HISTORICAL PERSPECTIVE

Concept of National Education

The concept of 'national education' evolved from the freedom movement in the early part of the twentieth century. Immediately after independence, India's education policy was based on the structure provided in 1944 by Sir John Sergeant, educational advisor to the British Government, in his 'Post-War Plan of Educational Development in India'. The objective of the plan was to achieve for India the standard of education that prevailed in England then.

The plan provided for eradication of illiteracy, facilitating UEE, higher education for 20 per cent of students completing secondary school and, vocational, technical and professional education to a limited degree. Provision for compulsory physical education, milk and midday meals for undernourished and, special schools for the physical and mentally handicapped were also part of the plan.

UN Resolutions

Education was declared as a fundamental right by the UN as far back as in 1948. Article 26 of the Universal Declaration of Human Rights adopted by the United Nations declares that 'every one has a right to education'. Subsequently, the UN General Assembly passed the 'Convention on the Rights of the Child' in 1989 which added a new dimension to the development of education all over the world. India signed the convention in 1992.

Article 28 of this Convention states: *'State parties recognize the right of the child to education and with a view to achieving this right progressively, they shall in particular*

(a) make primary education compulsory and available free to all...'

As a part of this agreement, India committed to review its laws and bring them in line with the Convention.

The Constitutional Mandate

The Indian Constitution emphasized the importance of education and enjoined on the state to provide, within a time frame of ten-years, free and compulsory education for all children until they complete the age of 14. This Directive Principle of State Policy played an important role in the development and management of education in post-independent India. Education was a state subject when the Constitution of India came into being and, it was only in 1976 that at the school level, it was brought into the 'Concurrent List'.

THE CONSTITUTIONAL PROVISIONS

The Constitution contains several provisions for the promotion and management of educational development in India. They are:

Article 45 enjoins that the state will endeavour to provide, within a period of ten years from the commencement of this Constitution, free and compulsory education for all children until they complete the age of 14. The priority given by the Constitution to this provision was clearly evident from the time frame specified therein. (No other clause in the Constitution carries this sense of urgency.)

Under Article 15(4) (which was inserted in the 1st Amendment in 1951) reservation of seats for backward classes in educational institutions is provided.

Under Article 46 the state is obliged to promote with special care the educational and economic interests of the weaker sections of the people and, in particular, of the SCs and STs and protect them from social injustice and all forms of exploitation.

Article 29(1) provides that any section of citizens residing in the territory of India and any part thereof, having a distinct language; script or culture of its own shall have the right to conserve the same.

Article 29(2) lays down that no citizen shall be denied admission to any state-owned or state-aided educational institution on grounds of only religion, race, caste, language or any of them.

Article 30(1) enjoins that all minorities, whether based on religion or language, shall have the right to establish and administer educational institutions of their choice.

Article 30(2) lays down that the state shall not, in granting aid to educational institutions, discriminate against any on grounds of their being managed by a religious or linguistic minority.

Article 350A lays down that, it shall be the endeavour of every state and local authority within the state to provide adequate facilities for children of linguistic minority groups to receive instruction in the mother tongue at the primary stage of education.

In compliance with and continuation of these provisions, several state governments and UTs introduced new legislations for providing free and compulsory primary education in their respective jurisdiction.

Recognition of the Right of the Child

Three Articles in the Indian Constitution – 24, 39 and 45 – specifically focus on the child.

Under Article 24, no child below the age of 14 shall be employed in any factory or mine, or be engaged in any other hazardous employment.

Article 39 states: 'The state shall direct its policy toward securing that the tender age of children is not abused and that citizens are not forced by economic necessity to enter a vocation unsuited to their age or strength and that children are given opportunities and facilities to develop in a healthy manner and in conditions of freedom and dignity and that childhood and youth are protected against exploitation and against moral and material abandonment'.

We have already discussed Article 45 which enjoins on the state to provide free and compulsory education for all children up to the age of 14.

Legislations on Child Labour

India has the dubious distinction of having the world's largest force of child labour (an estimated 17 million). The first legislation relating to child labour was the enactment of 'Children (pledging of labour) Act', 1933. Since then, there have been many similar attempts to set a higher age limit for children to involve in work, to improve their conditions of work, and bring about other positive changes to protect children.

The Constitution of India explicitly addressed this problem in Articles 24, 39 (e) and (f) and 45 by incorporating specific provisions to secure compulsory education and labour protection for children. Following these provisions and directives, a number of Acts were formulated, enacted and modified from time to time:

1. The Child Labour (Prohibition and Regulation) Act, 1986
2. The Factories Act, 1948 (Section 67)
3. The Plantation Labour Act, 1951 (Section 24)
4. The Merchant Shipping Act, 1951 (Section 10-9)
5. The Mines Act, 1952 (Section 45)
6. The Motor Transport Workers' Act, 1961 (Section 21)
7. The Apprentices Act, 1961 (Section 3)
8. The Bidi and Cigar Workers' (conditions of employment) Act, 1966 (Section 24).

'The Child Labour (Prohibition and Regulation) Act', 1986 is a comprehensive statement that prohibits employment of children in certain occupations and processes that are listed as hazardous. It also regulates working conditions of children in non-hazardous work spheres. All the legislations listed above, however, were basically flawed in that they tried to unreasonably relate child labour and poverty, perceiving poverty to be a 'necessary evil'. Much water has flowed down the bridge; while legislations were framed and they exist on paper, the evil of child labour has persisted and continued through generations.

Despite constitutional provisions and the various Acts that emanated from them, there are problems in the implementation and monitoring of the preventive framework of laws that regulate the child labour market in the country. A major factor is the structure of the economy and segmentation of the labour market. More than 90 per cent of the labour market is unorganized, including household as well as tiny segments of agriculture and industrial sectors.

There is also a close relationship between child labour and primary dropout rates. It is hoped that the 'Right to Education Act', passed by Parliament, will eradicate the issue of child labour as the right to elementary education has now become legally enforceable.

The Disabilities Act, 1995

The enactment of 'The Persons with Disabilities (Equal opportunities, Protection of Rights and Full Participation) Act, 1995 and 'The Rehabilitation Council of India (RCI) Act', 1992 provided the basic policy framework for addressing the issue of disability among children. The central and state governments were expected to ensure that every child with disability had access to free and adequate education up to the age of 18. It also required setting up of integrated education and special schools to meet the educational needs of such children.

The 1995 Act defines the responsibilities of the central and state governments and seeks:

- To take steps towards the prevention of disabilities, protection of rights, as well as medical care, education, training, employment and rehabilitation of persons with disabilities.
- To create a barrier-free environment for them.
- To remove any discrimination in their sharing developmental benefits, and to counteract all instances of their abuse and exploitation.
- To lay down a framework for comprehensive development of strategies, programmes and service for equalization of opportunities and, to make special provisions for their integration into the social mainstream.
- To provide for better protection of their rights, social security and matters connected therewith.

The RCI Act

The RCI Act regulates the manpower development programmes in the field of education and skill formation for children with special needs. Its main features are:

- To regulate the training policies and programmes concerning rehabilitation of people with disabilities and, to standardize training courses for professionals/ people dealing with them.
- To prescribe minimum standards of education for training institutions in the said field, and their uniform regulation throughout the country.
- To recognize on a reciprocal basis, institutions/universities (including foreign institutions) running degree/diploma/certificate courses in this field.
- To maintain a Central Rehabilitation Register of persons possessing recognized rehabilitation qualification.

- To collect on a regular basis from institutions in India and abroad, information on education and training in this field.
- To encourage continuing rehabilitation education by collaborating with organizations working in this field.

Reservations for Backward Classes

The constitutional provisions, (inserted by the Constitution's 1st Amendment Act 1951) for backward classes were made under Article 15(4) for seats in educational institutions, and under Article 16(4) for services under the state.

However, reservation was limited to 50 per cent seats in the Balaji Case (AIR 1963 SC 649) as the Supreme Court did not favour caste and class being considered at par in this case. It held, 'The criterion for determining the backwardness must not be based solely on religion, race, caste, sex or place of birth, and the backwardness being social and educational, must be similar to the backwardness from which the SCs/STs suffer.'

Though reservation in services is applicable at both levels of the union and the states, it was not applied in the case of the former. Also, there were political movements demanding higher percentage of reservations for backward classes.

The question of reservation, though a constitutional goal, was politicized when the union government sought to implement the recommendations of the 'Mandal Commission', which were made on the basis of the 1931 census – something that did not have much relevance in 1990. The Supreme Court, in a landmark judgment reiterated that 'the overall reservation contemplated under Article 16(4) should not exceed 50 per cent' and that 'reservation shall not apply to promotional posts' (AIR 1962 SC 36).

The Compulsory Primary Education Acts enacted by States and UTs

Even though the central government had made a commitment towards elementary education as per the constitutional mandate, it did not think of passing a 'Central Act on Compulsory Education'. It was the Kothari Commission (1964-66) which observed: 'Education should be given a statutory basis everywhere and in all sectors, and Education Acts should be passed in all states and UTs'. The overall power to regulate education by the states is derived from entry 25 of List III of the seventh schedule to the Constitution.

Kerala was the first state in the country to bring out the 'Kerala Education Act' in 1958.

With the primary objective of providing compulsory education to all children under 14 years, several states (notably, AP, Bihar, MP, UP, Maharashtra and Karnataka) modelled their Education Acts with an emphasis on the Directive Principle of State Policy under Article 45 of the Constitution.

Most of the state Acts for compulsory education in force were drafted in the 1960s and 1970s, and were applicable to that period. 14 states and 4 UTs passed them making education compulsory either in their states or in certain notified areas. These states were Assam, AP, Bihar, Gujarat, Haryana, J&K, Karnataka, MP, Maharashtra, Punjab, Rajasthan, TN, Kerala and WB. The UTs were Chandigarh, Delhi, Pondicherry and, Andaman & Nicobar Islands. Sikkim passed its Act in 2000.

The Compulsory Education Acts enacted in these states and UTs largely remained unenforced due to socio-economic compulsions. Nevertheless, states took some pro-active steps in this direction. They abolished tuition fee in government and local body schools up to the upper primary level. In order to provide incentives for children from the poor and deprived segments, they started bearing other costs of education such as textbooks, uniforms, school bags and transport fee. The criteria for such incentives, however, varied from state to state. Recently, the hot cooked midday meal scheme was also found to be playing a significant role in bringing enrolled children to school. Notable is the fact that some states like the north-eastern ones and HP made rapid strides in improving literacy rates without the support of such Acts.

The Commitment towards 'Compulsory Primary Education'

Regretfully, the enthusiasm of the states in this direction turned out to be a damp squib as resources provided were meager, resulting in a half-hearted implementation. The budget speeches of finance ministers to Parliament during 1951-1961 (which included the first two five year plans) reveal that there was not even a passing reference to 'education', let alone to Article 45 of the Constitution.

The Union Education Minister's address to CABE was full of apology and despair: 'I must confess that I was considerably disappointed when this revised plan was drawn up… it is my resolve that we must try to provide a reasonable allocation for education in the second plan…' (Maulana Abdul Kalam Azad, 23rd meeting of the CABE).

The reason for this laid back attitude on the part of the Cabinet was that, it took the view that only subjects which had the potential of giving quick returns were to be considered. Since education did not fit their bill it was left out of the draft plans. This brought a halt to all attempts at enforcing compulsory primary education in the country.

The 31st meeting of CABE (1964) recommended:

'… in regard to legislation or compulsion at the primary stage, the Board was of the view that whereas statutory provisions may be necessary for such purposes as collection of cess, the really effective method of achieving universality in education in this age group would be extension of facilities in areas not yet covered and use of persuasion incentives'.

Thus the national education goal of 'introduction of free and compulsory education' was changed to 'achievement of the goal of universal education'. Even the national policies of 1968 and 1986 as well as POA did not speak of making education 'compulsory'.

THE REPORTS OF VARIOUS COMMISSIONS

In January, 1948, in his inaugural address to the All India Education Conference, Jawaharlal Nehru observed: 'Whenever conferences were called to form a plan for education in India, the tendency, as a rule, was to maintain the existing system with slight modification. This must not happen now. Great changes have taken place in the country and the education system must also be in keeping with them. The entire basis of education must be revolutionized'.

Radhakrishnan Commission

Nehru's dream could not be realized immediately due to a variety of reasons induced by the partition of the country. A University Commission under the chairmanship of Dr S. Radhakrishnan was constituted in 1948 to restructure university education in India. The recommendations of the commission had wide implications covering all aspects of university education in India. An emphasis on the 10+2 structure up to the pre-university stage, establishment of a central University Grants Commission, autonomy to the universities, recommendation of placing university education in the concurrent list were some of the important recommendations.

The Mudaliar Commission

In 1952 the Secondary Education Commission was appointed under the chairmanship of Dr A.L. Mudaliar; it consisted of one British, one American and seven Indian members. The aim of the government was to consolidate secondary education so as to bring some uniformity into it, provide a common syllabus, content and curricula, and to prepare students for a future 'University Education'. The Commission submitted its report in 1953.

The Commission observed: 'The end of Secondary Education at seventeen plus should mark a terminal stage in education and prepare students in life, and it should also be of a standard which enables them to participate with profit in the three years of degree course'.

It reduced the duration of school education from 12-11 years and transferred the control of the secondary school leaving examination from the universities to the newly constituted 'Boards of Secondary Education'. Another major recommendation was the establishment of multi-purpose schools that would provide terminal courses along with vocational education. The Report also helped the states in reorganization of teachers' certificate examination and the secondary teacher education courses.

The Impact of the Commission Reports

Both the Radhakrishnan Commission and the Mudaliar Commission dwelt on exclusively two sectors of education in which the ruling elite class was interested.

Both these sectors received huge allocations of funds and underwent rapid, unplanned and uncontrolled expansions, resulting in deterioration of standards and creation of severe problems of unemployment. Even the Supreme Court did not hesitate to comment thus: 'In this context we feel constrained to say the allocation of available funds in India discloses an inversion of priorities'. (Unnikrishnan vs The State of Andhra Pradesh 1993).

Apart from an attempt to introduce basic education, not much was done to tackle burning issues in the areas of elementary education and literacy. Programmes of adult education and removal of illiteracy continued to be neglected just as elementary education remained stagnant. The aim of providing free and compulsory education for all children up to the age of 14 years (as envisaged in the constitution) still seemed far fetched.

Kothari Commission

The vision of a national system of education envisaged in 1948 remained a distant dream for several decades. In 1964, an 'Education Commission' was appointed under the chairmanship of Dr D.S. Kothari to recommend policies for development of education at all stages in order to build a national system of education. The commission submitted its report in 1966.

The following recommendations constituted the highlights of the report – qualitative improvement of standards, quantitative expansion of educational facilities on the basis of manpower needs, equal educational opportunities for all, importance to science education, emphasis on vocational education both at the lower as well as higher secondary stages, a common school system with equal access to children from all classes of society, retention of the three-language formula up to the lower secondary stage and, study of only two languages at the senior secondary stage.

The Commission accepted the 10+2+3 pattern up to the first degree level. It recommended providing effective primary education and eradicating adult illiteracy as the main focus areas.

The Commission visualized that total enrolment would rise from 70 million in 1965 to 170 million in 1985 along with an increase in expenditure on education from 2.9 per cent of GDP in 1965 to 6 per cent in 1985. The recommendations along with a report of the parliamentary committee were discussed in both Houses of Parliament. Out of these discussions emerged the first national policy in independent India in the form of a resolution on education in July, 1968.

Even though the recommendations of the Kothari Commission were diluted at every stage, they remained the basic framework on which important decisions on education were taken by successive governments.

The Language Policy

The Kothari Commission had recommended a three-language formula (a regional language, English and Hindi) to be introduced at the school level; this was later recognized by the 1968 Education Policy. Accordingly, one south Indian language (as a modern Indian language) in the northern Hindi speaking states and Hindi in the southern non-Hindi speaking states were to be introduced.

Though this formula was aimed at promoting national integration, certain states like WB and TN refused to fall in line. The northern states could hardly find the utility of introducing a south Indian language. Thus, the three-language formula came to be implemented only in a few states like AP, Karnataka and Kerala.

Towards a National Policy on Education

The first national policy on education conceived in 1968 based on the recommendations of the Kothari Commission, envisaged that education should be an instrument to promote a sense of common citizenship and culture and further, to strengthen national integration.

However, with the change in the socio-political environment and with increased opportunities, it was felt that education should also be perceived as a unique investment for the present and the future. With this principle was born the National Policy of 1986 which recognized education as fundamental to all-round development – especially manpower development – at different levels of the economy.

Both the national policies of 1968 and 1986 emphasized the importance of elementary education for all. The goals, targets and strategies enunciated in the NPE 1986 and endorsed by CABE were incorporated in successive Five Year Plan proposals. These goals were pursued during the Eighth and Ninth Plans which also involved the launching of major projects supported by external funding and literacy campaigns under the NLM.

THE NATIONAL POLICY ON EDUCATION (NPE 1986)

The rising level of illiteracy jerked the central government out of slumber, and that expedited the NPE. In May 1986, Parliament adopted a new national policy of education and in August of that year, it approved a detailed 'Programme of Action' for implementation. It envisaged a national system of education based on a national curriculum framework with specific MLLs for each stage of education.

The NPE expressed in no uncertain terms that education must play a positive and interventionist role in not only correcting gender gaps, social and regional imbalances but also in securing a rightful place for the disadvantaged and minorities. It also stated: '.... up to a given level all students should have equal access to education of comparable quality, that whatever the socio-economic background of the children, they get opportunities to achieve success of a level, which is equal to the level of the children from comparatively better off sections of society and the country moves pace in the direction of a common school system'.

The NPE 1986 also envisaged autonomy and accountability as two guiding considerations for educational institutions:

(a) 'decentralization and creating a spirit of accountability for educational institutions' and
(b) 'establishing the principle of accountability in relation to given objectives and norms'.

NPE interpreted the role of education as: 'Education has an accumulating role. It refines sensitivities and perceptions that constitute national cohesion, a scientific mind and independence of mind and spirit – thus furthering the goals of socialism and secularism and democracy enshrined in our constitution'.

The NPE 1986 was divided into 12 parts. The significant aspects of the policy, which essentially comprised the concept of a national system of education, are given below:

Concept of a National System of Education

- Providing for equal access to education of comparable quality for all, (irrespective of class, caste, creed, or sex and areas) which would be based on the principles enshrined in the Constitution.
- Adopting a common educational structure in terms of the duration of various stages of education, such as 10+2+3.
- Adopting a national curriculum framework with a common core in the curricular programme along with other flexible components.
- Removing disparities and equalizing educational opportunities to educationally deprived classes, i.e., women, SCs/STs, minorities, people living in rural/ remote/inaccessible areas.
- Organizing programmes for adult education that are linked to national goals to ensure the participation of the masses in the development programme of the country.
- Involving local community in ECCE.
- Enriching the cultural current of the curricula and process of education.

Focus on Elementary Education

NPE 1986 emphasized three important aspects in relation to elementary education:

(a) 'Universal access and enrolment'.

(b) 'Universal retention' of children up to 14 years of age.

(c) Substantial improvement in the 'quality of education' to enable all children to achieve essential levels of learning.

The policy further made a significant shift in emphasis, from enrolment to participation and retention. The goal of UEE was enlarged to include providing education of a satisfactory quality to all children. The NPE emphasized the fact that all eligible children were to be exposed to mainstream learning activities; those who were non-enrolled were to be given alternative learning processes that were to be designed to suit the varied needs of various types of children.

The NPE also envisaged a coordinated network involving the non-formal system so that by 1990, all children attaining the age of 11 years would have had five-years of schooling and by 1995, all children up to 14 years of age would have been provided free and compulsory education.

Introduction of Vocational Courses

Even though vocational courses were to be introduced after the secondary stage, there was flexibility to do so after class 8. By 1990 they were to cover 10 per cent, and by 1995, 25 per cent of the higher secondary students.

In the sphere of higher education, the NPE envisaged improving quality, developing autonomous colleges, promoting research in science and technology, inter-disciplinary research in social sciences, setting up of autonomous national research facilities, encouraging the Open University system, etc.

The NPE made a series of observations on cultural perspectives, value education, languages, books and libraries, media, educational technology, work experience, education and environment, teaching of mathematics, science education, sports and physical education, role of youth and, reforming the examination system to ensure a reliable and valid method of student assessment.

It also envisaged:

(a) Better deal to teachers with greater accountability.
(b) Provision of improved students' service and insistence of acceptable norms of behaviour.
(c) Better facilities to institutions.
(d) Creation of a system of performance appraisals of institutions at national or state levels based on predetermined standards and norms.

The NPE committed the government to gradually increase the expenditure on education till it 'uniformly exceeded 6 per cent of the National Income'.

The schemes introduced under the NPE were Operation Blackboard (OB), starting of DIETs and Colleges of Teacher Education (CTEs) under the 'Teacher Education Programme', programmes relating to 'Vocationalization of Education' and 'Technical Education'.

As far as higher education is concerned, the NPE paved the way for the following important decisions to be made:

1. Setting up of centralized agencies to improve quality:
   (a) National Assessment and Accreditation Council (NAAC)
   (b) National Council for Teacher Education (NCTE)
   (c) All India Council for Technical Education (AICTE)
2. Introduction of National Eligibility Test (NET) by UGC to regulate the entry of candidates into the teaching profession in colleges and institutes of higher learning and setting up of Administrative Staff Colleges in important universities for reorienting college and university faculty.

National Curriculum Frameworks (NCF)

The NPE 1986 proposed the periodical preparation of an NCF as a means of evolving a national system of education. It recommended that the core component be derived from the vision of national development enshrined in the constitution. The POA 1992 elaborated this further by laying emphasis on relevance, flexibility and quality.

In order to carry out the directives in the policy, the NCERT prepared the first NCF in 1988 that tried to address some of the emerging curricular concerns based on the socio-cultural, political and economic considerations prevailing at that time. NCERT has been bringing out NCFs periodically so as to give a suitable orientation to the curricular policies and programmes followed by the states. But it is to be noted that some of these NCFs were also prepared with hidden agenda to please the political party in power.

Acharya Ramamurthi Committee Report 1990

After the Congress government was replaced by the National Front government headed by V.P. Singh, a review committee was set up under Acharya Ramamurthi in May, 1990.

The committee called for recognition of the right to education as a fundamental right: 'Now time has come to recognize 'Right to Education' as one of the fundamental rights of the Indian citizens for which necessary amendments to the constitution may have to be made and more importantly, conditions to be created in society such that this right would become available for all children of India.'

The recommendations of the committee also pertained to issues like equality, social justice and education, ECCE, UEE, adult and continuing education and 'education and the right to work.' The redeeming feature of the report was that it suggested developing all educational programmes based on the requirements of the society.

The Programme of Action (POA) 1992

In 1991, the new Congress government headed by P.V. Narasimha Rao took steps to review the NPE 1986. In July of the same year, a Central Advisory Board of Education on policy was constituted under the chairmanship of the chief minister of AP comprising six education ministers from major political parties and eight educationists. The recommendations resulted in the 'POA 1992'

On the recommendation of the POA the District Primary Education Programme (DPEP) was initiated to promote UEE in the country. By May, 1995 education projects were prepared in 42 districts spread over seven states of Assam, Haryana, MP, Karnataka, Maharashtra, TN and Kerala. They were identified based on the following criteria:

(a) Educationally backward districts, with female literacy below national average
(b) Districts where TLCs were successful leading to an enhanced demand for primary education.

EFFORTS OF GOI TOWARDS IMPLEMENTATION OF UEE

The GOI made conscious efforts to achieve the goal of UEE through various measures such as:

(1) The NPE 1986 helped to focus better on efforts of central and state governments in providing free and compulsory education of comparable quality to all children up to the age of 14 years.

(2) The political commitment to make the right to elementary education a 'Fundamental Right' and enforcing it through necessary statutory measures reflected in the passing of the Constitutional (86th Amendment) Act in 2002.

(3) Enactment of 73rd and 74th constitutional amendments for greater decentralization helped enhance the role of local bodies, community organizations as well as voluntary agencies in efforts towards UEE.

However, the central government had to take the blame as well for its failure to achieve the goal for the following reasons:

- Inability to translate into a reality the constitutional mandate (Article 45) of providing compulsory primary education for all children up to 14 years of age.
- Inability to provide expenditure on education exceeding or equal to 6 per cent of the national income, as suggested by the Kothari Commission.
- Rapid and unplanned expansion of higher education which resulted in neglect of primary education.
- Enormous increase in the number of the educated unemployed.
- Failure to reach targets in vocational education.
- Failure to fully implement several schemes like OB which was due to apathy and inherent corruption in the implementation systems.

Nevertheless, the strategy for UEE (or at least for UPE as DPEP and other earlier programmes aimed at) as spelt out by NPE and POA involved the following elements:

(a) Strengthening and expansion of the system of ECCE.

(b) Adoption of a child-centred and activity-based teaching-learning processes at the primary stage.

(c) Provision of primary schools in all habitations with a certain minimum population.

(d) Universal provision of essential facilities in primary schools – essential equipment under the programme of OB, a minimum of two classrooms, and two teachers one of whom would be a lady.

(e) A large and systematic programme of NFE for school dropouts, children from school-less habitations, working children and girls who were unable to attend regular schools.

(f) Micro-planning (to ensure that every child in the relevant age group regularly attended a primary school or an NFE centre) and involving the community in the educational process, especially in the programme of school improvement.

(g) Special measures for UEE among children of disadvantaged groups (like girls, SCs/STs, minorities and children with disabilities), which included –

  (i) Location of schools or NFE centres in their habitations.

  (ii) Provision of incentives like scholarships, uniforms, textbooks, etc.

  (iii) Supplementary remedial instruction to cater to the needs of first generation learners.

(iv) Development of good quality instructional materials in tribal languages.
(v) Suitable training of teachers for integrated education of special children (children with disabilities) and setting up of special schools for children with severe handicaps.

(h) Laying down MLLs for the primary stage and working towards their attainment.
(i) Continuous and comprehensive learner evaluation.
(j) Revision of curricula and textbooks and other TLMs so as to bring them in line with the national system of education, the national core curriculum and MLLs at the same time making them locally relevant.
(k) Use of educational technology for qualitative improvement.
(l) Implementation of a meaningful system for monitoring progress towards the goals of UEE.
(m) Reorganization of the system of planning and management of education with special reference to:
    (i) Decentralization and accountability,
    (ii) Full involvement of the community and NGOs,
    (iii) Promotion of school complexes.
(n) Strengthening of the teacher education system, i.e., in-service and continuing education of elementary school teachers and NFE personnel through DIETs and school complexes.

Education of Girls

The NPE 1986 as revised in 1992 articulated the stand of the GOI that 'Education will be used as an agent of basic change in the status of women; in order to neutralize the accumulated distortions of the past, there will be a well conceived edge in favour of women... This will be an act of faith and social engineering. The removal of women's illiteracy and obstacles inhibiting their access to, and retention in elementary education will receive overriding priority, through provision of special support services setting time targets and effective monitoring...'

The GOI and the states devised and implemented several programmes in support of education of girls which are discussed elsewhere in this book.

The Commitment towards Basic Education

As we have already seen, Article 45 directed the state to ensure provision of basic education for all children up to the age of 14 years. While the struggle to achieve this commitment began immediately and lasted nearly six decades, it has still not been achieved for the following reasons:

- The state failed to comprehend the sense of urgency since Article 45 was placed in Part IV of the Constitution (Directive Principles of State Policy) and, therefore it was not justiciable.

- The time frame of ten years was considered too unrealistic considering the fact that in 1950, the population of free India was about 356 million with hardly 16 per cent literacy.
- The framers of the Constitution failed to consider the financial implications of implementing such a policy at the cost of economic development – the country had meager resources.
- The directive failed to take into account the social conditions existing at that time – poverty, socio-cultural attitudes of the masses towards education, etc.

This Constitutional inaction resulted in disheartening conditions that led to educational backwardness of the masses and imbalances in educational opportunities. It boosted the private sector's initiatives at establishing a large number of private schools with a profit-making motive. However, UNESCOs declaration of EFA, the NPE's drive towards UEE and finally, the Supreme Court's declaration that education up to the age of 14 was a fundamental right helped maintain the pressure on the centre to take proactive steps in making education up to the age of 14 free and compulsory.

Nevertheless, the state was constitutionally obliged to 'endeavour' to provide 'free and compulsory education' to all children until the age of 14. However, it has been deferred time and again. Further, the Tenth Plan (2002-07) set a target for all children to complete five years of schooling by 2007; even this has not been met.

Empowerment of the Community in the Management of Education

The move towards decentralization and empowerment of the community got a further fillip with the 73rd/74th Amendments to the Constitution involving PRIs. Since 1992 these amendments, have provided for delegation of powers and responsibilities thus bringing into the fold a third-tier of PRIs. The basic purpose of this democratic move was to ensure that development was planned to become more responsive and adaptable to regional and local needs of the population.

The Eleventh and Twelfth schedules of the 73rd and 74th Amendments to the Constitution recommended that education should be one of the subjects that needed to be transferred to PRIs. Accordingly, development and management of education – primary and secondary schools, vocational education, adult education and NFE – were to come under their purview. This was an important move in recognizing the inevitability of community participation in all social sectors.

The 73rd Amendment included provisions for devolving authority to local self-governing bodies (panchayats in villages) in various areas of service delivery. The responsibility of management and monitoring of primary education was transferred to local bodies in rural and urban areas. Some manifestations of these can be seen in the formation of the Parent-Teacher Associations (PTAs) [e.g., under the EGS] and the VECs.

The Panchayat Raj Act of 1993 enabled the village panchayats to utilize the VECs to create public awareness, involve the community in the management of primary and secondary education, ensure total enrolment and retention in primary schools and, promote adult literacy.

In this context, Karnataka (and later AP) took a significant step in 2001 by creating a democratic institution – the School Development and Monitoring Committee (SDMC) – which would manage the affairs of the school. The committee was visualized to overcome the limitations of the School Betterment Committee (SBC) and the VEC, and motivate the community to believe that it owned the school. Further, by involving parents, it helped break the monopoly of a few dominant individuals over the affairs of the school.

Education as a 'Fundamental Right'

Education is no longer viewed as a service provided by the state but as a right of every individual. It was only in 1994 that the situation changed dramatically and another significant development took place to reinforce this view. The Supreme Court of India, in a landmark judgment, recognized education as a fundamental right in as much as it flowed naturally from the rights to life and liberty. This judgment thus transformed the perception from education being an obligation (created by Article 45 of the Constitution) into asserting itself as an enforceable right.

J.P. Unnikrishnan Case

The Supreme Court in the case of 'Unnikrishnan and others vs State of Andhra Pradesh and others', categorically pronounced that the child has a fundamental right to free and compulsory education up to the age of 14 and stated that this right flows from Article 21 (Right to Life).

The Supreme Court observed: 'It is noteworthy that among the several articles in Part IV, only Article 45 speaks of a time limit, no other article does. Has it no significance? Is it a mere pious wish, even after 44 years of the Constitution?' asked the Hon'ble judges.

They agreed with the statement in the Bandhua Mukti Morcha case that right to education is implicit in and flows from the right to life guaranteed by Article 21. They further ruled that it is inconceivable to provide right to life without the right to basic education. They dismissed arguments about the economic capacity of the state as far as education up to the age of 14 was considered.

The Supreme Court further ruled that, after the age of 14, the fundamental right to education continues to exist but is 'subject to limits of economic capacity and development of the State'.

The Supreme Court's ruling in the Bandhua Mukti Morcha case and subsequently in the J.P. Unnikrishnan case, brought the debate on right to basic education to centre stage. It clearly placed the onus of UEE on the central and state governments. The Unnikrishnan case was followed by the spirited efforts of Satyapal Anand holding the Indian state accountable in its obligation to children. Accordingly, the states were directed by the Hon'ble Supreme Court to report on the progress made in making elementary education a fundamental right.

This landmark judgment transformed an incremental developmental goal set by the NPE 1986 – of 'universal elementary education of satisfactory quality by the turn of the century' – into an entitlement of all children up to the age of 14. By clearly rejecting arguments for elementary education based on economic capacity, the apex court demanded from the state a sense of urgency, as defined in Article 12 of the Constitution.

It was with this in view that the Indian Constitution recognized education to be a fundamental right of all children up to the age of 14 such that participation of all children becomes a state and parental obligation as well as a legal requirement. It envisages area-specific and population-specific planning to ensure that enough attention is paid to educationally backward pockets and groups not only in the educationally backward states but also throughout the country by a shift of emphasis from mere enrolment to retention and quality of education.

The Report of the Saikia Committee

As a response to the Supreme Court's proactive espousal of the fundamental right to elementary education, political parties included it in their manifestos. In 1996, the 'Common Minimum Programme' of the United Front government resolved to make the right to free and compulsory education a fundamental right and enforce it through suitable statutory measures.

It set up a committee of education ministers under the chairmanship of M.R. Saikia with education ministers of states as its members. The Committee proposed to amend the Constitution through a legislation making elementary education up to 14 years of age a fundamental right. The Committee also recommended amendment of the existing state legislations on compulsory education. The report of the Committee recommended: 'The Constitution of India should be amended to make the right to free elementary education up to 14 years of age a fundamental right. Simultaneously an explicit provision should be made in the Constitution to make it the fundamental duty of every citizen who is a parent to provide opportunities for elementary education to all children up to 14 years of age'.

In 1997, the United Front government introduced the 83rd Constitution Amendment Act that proposed to make free and compulsory education for children aged 6-14 years a fundamental right. The draft Act was scrutinized by a Parliamentary Standing Committee which invited suggestions from the civil society. The 165th Report of the Law Commission of India also endorsed the proposed constitutional amendment and placed a draft proposal for the central legislation to enforce it.

It was during this period that the influential 'Public Report on Basic Education' was published (1999) and released by Amartya Sen, making a strong case for the fundamental right to elementary education, given the strong demand for education from the poorest households. NGOs like the National Alliance for the Right to Education (NAFRE) held the issue centre stage through a series of national and regional consultations.

Report of the Tapas Majumdar Committee

The Tapas Majumdar Committee, in its report in 1999, emphasized that the financial implications of the fundamental right to elementary education was well within the national commitment of 6 per cent of GDP for the education sector. It took into account the overall projections of the 6-14 population and computed norm-based requirements for UEE. This was done 'in order to ensure that quality schooling was available to all children, irrespective of the number of out-of-school children'.

The assessment of schooling facilities required for 200 million children was made on the basis of a set of norms for minimum amenities that were essential for providing quality education to all. The committee concluded that the additional expenditure for achieving the goal of UEE (based on the norm of minimum of two classrooms and two teachers per school with a PTR of 30:1 and, calculating the teachers' salary at the rates revised by the Fifth Central Pay Commission) would be Rs136,922 crores over a ten-year period from 1998-99 to 2007-08.

The financial memorandum for the resubmitted Constitutional Amendment Act that was approved, indicated a requirement of Rs98,000 crores over a ten-year period for elementary education. It was a pragmatic assessment, as the actual requirement of resources was lower since teacher deployment was taken at a PTR of 40:1.

The Constitution (86th Amendment) Act

After a prolonged delay, the 83rd Amendment Bill was again amended and reintroduced as 'Constitution (93rd Amendment) Bill 2001' in Parliament. It was finally passed by the Parliament as the 'Constitution (86th Amendment) Act, 2002'. With this, a 'Fundamental Right' was added to the Constitution of India for the first time since its framing, The Constitution now guarantees eight years of free and compulsory education to each and every child in the country.

The 86th Amendment Act incorporated the following changes:

1. Insertion of Article 21A: 'The State shall provide free and compulsory education to all children of the age 6-14 years in such manner as the State may, by law, determine'.
2. Revision of Article 45: ''The State shall endeavour to provide early childhood care and education for all children until they complete the age of six years.'
3. Amendment of Article 51A bestowing responsibility on parents or guardians: 'who is a parent or guardian to provide opportunities for education to his child or as the case may be, ward between the age of 6-14 years'.

Thus, the state was now to determine, by law, the manner in which free and compulsory education was to be provided to all children in the 6-14 age group. However, the intent of the Supreme Court judgment was diluted by the exclusion of children from their right to ECCE/pre-primary education.

The importance of having a law is based on the assumption that it would result in adequate provisioning of public resources for education, increase resource availability, and bring in sharper public focus. This would improve school enrolment and retention over successive classes by deterring parents from prematurely withdrawing their children from schools. It would also encourage interested social groups to take proactive steps to motivate children to attend schools.

Apart from the above, the Act would help bring in attitudinal changes – those of parents towards their children's education, of the public towards provision of educational facilities, of the state towards out-of-school children/dropouts etc. To put it in the right perspective, compulsory schooling makes it obligatory for the child to attend school and for the parents to send the child to school.

The Constitution (93rd Amendment) Act, 2005

This amendment has inserted a new Clause (5) (in place of the old one) in Article 15 which states: '(5) Nothing in this article or in sub-clause (g) of clause (1) of Article 19 shall prevent the State from making any special provision, by law, for the advancement of any socially and educationally backward classes of citizens or for the Schedule Castes or the Schedule Tribes, in so far as such special provisions relate to their admission to educational institutions including private educational institutions whether aided or unaided by the State, other minority educational institutions referred to in Clause (1) of article 30'.

This amendment has further helped the state to regulate the admission of students belonging to socially and educationally backward classes in private institutions also.

Towards a 'Right to Education Act'

The 86th Amendment Act set the stage for the 'Right to Education Act'. The need for such an Act is obvious from the fact that 70 per cent of the children in the relevant age group (6-14) dropout before class 8.

The provisions of Article 21A itself state that they are to be implemented in such manner as the state may, by law, determine. Hence, a legislation that has the potential to give effect to the provisions of this clause is bound to play a significant role in determining the future of Indian education. The Constitutional Amendment to make elementary education a fundamental right was one such occasion when a lot of debate was generated.

The criticism was mainly on four counts:

(a) The 0-6 age group was being left out.
(b) The commitment of financial resources was far short of the 6 per cent public investment promised by the Kothari Commission.
(c) The obligation on parents/guardians was not desirable.
(d) Quality was seen to suffer as many low cost alternatives were now being proposed for alternative education.

The Parliamentary Standing Committee of HRD that considered the Constitution Amendment Bill made two significant recommendations on the follow-up legislation:

- The central legislation (with some skeletal framework) should indicate the central share in the financial burden.
- The compulsion to provide essential facilities for UEE should be on the state governments rather than parents; hence penal provision on parents is to be avoided.

The other recommendations of the committee were:

- Emphasise on quality and improve capacities of teachers.
- Find ways and means to face challenges from litigation to follow the justiciable 'right to education'.
- Provide formal certification after class 8.
- Along with providing free education, include provision of various other components such as textbooks, stationery, uniform, one meal and, transportation wherever necessary, etc.
- Let the states be made responsible for administrative implementation, according to their convenience.
- Follow directive principles, wherever possible.

The NDA government made public three drafts of the Bill; however, general elections took place before the Bill could go to the Parliament. The first draft of the Bill was prepared in 2003. It ran into rough weather due to issues relating to sharing the financial burden as well as due to banning capitation fees and donations during admission. Apart from the private school lobby, which had reservations in accepting the 'neighbourhood theory' of admitting disadvantaged children of the locality, the states also expressed their inability to share the financial burden for implementing the legislation.

Report of the CABE Committee

The CABE Committee was constituted by the UPA government in September 2004 to draft the revised 'Right to Education Act' as required under Article 21A of the Constitution. A committee, chaired by Shri Kapil Sibal, Union Minister of State, finalized a draft Act in June 2005 which was then circulated.

After considering a financial estimate of the centre and states' expenditure for the period 2006-12 prepared by NIEPA, the CABE Committee concluded that the implementation of the Act by the end of 2005 would lead to an additional outlay of about 1.1-1.5 per cent of GDP (this figure would vary depending on the PTR and teacher salaries that were assumed). The Committee mentioned that this may have to be borne by the central government. The CABE report also pointed out that persistent under-provisioning for elementary education in the past had resulted in a cumulative gap; hence, a substantial part of the financial burden of UEE should be borne by the central government as the finances of all state governments were in a precarious condition.

In May 2006, the central government decided that the proposed 'Right to Education Bill 2005' would not be tabled in the Parliament at all. Instead, it sent a Model Bill, not approved by the Parliament, to the state governments who were asked to formulate a legislation of their own.

However, this did not materialize and the Bill, in its final phase, was referred to the 'Group of Ministers' led by the HRD Minister, Arjun Singh. Finally, the Union Cabinet cleared it in October 2008 with all the controversial sections intact. While making parents responsible for sending their children to school, it did not provide for any penal provision for non-compliance. It finally saw the light of day after six years of tug-of-war between different stakeholders as well as between the centre and the states regarding sharing the financial burden.

The Bill sought to guarantee elementary education to every child between the age 6-14 years. It also stated that every child in the specified age would be able to get enrolled in a school in the vicinity of his/her domicile. It promoted the use of the regional language as the medium of instruction by stating that as far as possible, a child should be instructed in his/her mother tongue at least for the first five years of the elementary stage.

The Right of Children to Free and Compulsory Education Act, 2009

This Act seeks to give effect to the '86th Constitutional Amendment Act', 2002 and implement the fundamental right to elementary education. However, there is no specific provision in it for penalizing any violation of this right.

It detailed the responsibilities of the centre and the state governments, teachers, parents, and community members in ensuring that all children between the ages of 6-14 receive free and compulsory education.

The Act was anchored in the belief that the values of equality, social justice and democracy and the creation of a just and humane society can be achieved through provision of inclusive elementary education to all. 'Compulsory Education' creates an obligation on the state to take all necessary steps to ensure that every child enrols, participates and completes elementary education.

The Act places the onus on the government to ensure enrolment of all children, but does not identify which government agency will be responsible for the task. It is also unclear how the appropriate authority will monitor and ensure that working children and children living on the streets without a parent or guardian will be enrolled in school. It is silent on making the government/parent/guardian accountable for non-implementation of any of the clauses of the Act. There are no specific penalties in case of authorities failing to provide the right to elementary education. It provides the right to schooling and physical infrastructure, but does not guarantee that children will learn. It exempts government schools from any consequences if they do not meet the specified norms.

Highlights of the Act

The Act seeks to focus on the following matters:

(a) Every child has a right to be provided full-time elementary education of satisfactory and equitable quality in a formal school; also, it must satisfy certain essential norms and standards. (The norms and standards prescribed in the Act are given in Table 21 in the Annexure VIII).

(b) Compulsory education casts an obligation on the appropriate government to provide and ensure admission, attendance and completion of elementary education.

(c) Free education means that no child (other than the one who has been admitted by his/her parents to a school that is not supported by the appropriate government) shall be liable to pay/incur any kind of fee/charges/expenses which may prevent him/her from pursuing and completing elementary education.
(d) No child shall be held back, expelled or required to pass a board examination until completion of elementary education.
(e) Schools may not screen applicants or charge capitation fees during admission.
(f) A child who completes elementary education shall be awarded a certificate.
(g) The duties and responsibilities of the appropriate governments, local authorities, parents, schools and teachers in providing free and compulsory education are prescribed.
(h) A person who wants to file a grievance claim shall submit a written complaint to the local authority. Appeals shall be decided either by the State Commission for Protection of Child Rights or a specified authority.
(i) Kendriya Vidyalayas, Navodaya Vidyalayas, Sainik schools and unaided schools shall admit at least 25 per cent of students from disadvantaged and economically weaker sections.

Key Issues

PRS Legislative Branch analysed the key issues pertaining to the Act as follows:

- There are no specific penalties if the authorities fail to provide the right to elementary education.
- Both the state government and local authority are duty-bound to provide free and compulsory education. Thus, sharing of this duty may lead to neither party being held accountable.
- The Act provides for the right to schooling and physical infrastructure but does not guarantee that children will learn. It exempts government schools from any consequences if they do not meet the specified norms.
- The Constitutional validity of reservation of seats in private schools for economically weaker sections could be challenged.
- Minority schools are not exempt from the provisions of the Act. It is possible that this will conflict with Article 30 of the Constitution, which allows minorities to set up and administer educational institutions.
- The Act legitimizes the practice of multigrade teaching. The number of teachers shall be based on the number of students rather than by grade.

Important Provisions

The important provisions of the Act are given below:

Right to Free and Compulsory Education

- Every child from 6-14 years of age shall have the right to free and compulsory education in a neighbourhood school till the completion of elementary education.

- The government shall ensure that all children including those with disabilities including mental illness, mental retardation, blindness and hearing loss, shall enjoy this right.
- Special provisions to be made for children not admitted to or who have not completed elementary education for direct admission to a class appropriate to their age; special training to be given to such children.
- Elementary education shall be free for such children until completion.

Duties of Government and Local Authorities

- The Act demarcates the functions of the central and appropriate governments as well as the local authority.
- The appropriate government and local authority shall establish within such area or limits of neighbourhood, a school within a period of three-years.
- Both the centre and the states shall have concurrent responsibility for providing funds for the implementation of the Act. However, the centre shall prepare the estimates of expenditure and provide a certain percentage of funds to the states for carrying out the provisions of the Act.
- Apart from ensuring availability of a neighbourhood school, every local authority should ensure that children belonging to weaker sections are not discriminated against or prevented from pursuing and completing elementary education on any grounds.
- These authorities are expected to not only maintain records up to the age of 14 years of children residing within their jurisdiction but also ensure and monitor their admission, attendance and completion of elementary education.
- The Act has made it mandatory for the authorities to provide infrastructure including school building, teaching staff and TLM, provide special training facility for teachers and decide on the academic calendar.
- It is also the responsibility of the states/local authority to provide good quality elementary education conforming to certain standards and norms.

Duties of Parents/Guardians

- It should be the duty of every parent and guardian to admit or cause to admit his or her child in a neighbourhood school for elementary education.

Responsibilities of the School and Teachers

- The Act requires all schools to comply with PTR norms. Additionally, all private schools must comply with infrastructure norms failing which they shall lose their recognition.
- A school providing compulsory elementary education shall be reimbursed to the extent of per-child-expenditure incurred by the state or the actual amount charged from the child, whichever is less.
- Schools shall constitute SMCs which shall monitor their running and utilization of government grants, prepare a school development plan, etc.

- A child shall not be denied admission. A child required to move shall have the right to transfer to any state or local government or aided school.
- No child admitted to a school shall be held back in any class or expelled from school till the completion of elementary education.
- No child shall be subjected to physical punishment or mental harassment.

No Capitation & Screening Procedure for Admission

- No school or person shall, while admitting the child, collect any capitation fee and subject the child or his parents or guardian to any screening procedure. Any contravention of this provision shall be punishable with fine which may extend to 10 times the capitation fee charged.
- Any school or person subjecting a child to a screening procedure shall be punishable with fine which may be extended to Rs25,000 for the first contravention and Rs50,000 for each subsequent contravention.
- Penalty has also been prescribed for any person who establishes or runs a school without obtaining certificate of recognition or, continues to run the school after withdrawal of recognition.

School Management Committees

- The school shall constitute an SMC consisting of elected representatives of the local authority, parents/guardians of children admitted in such school and teachers. Three-fourth members of such committee shall be parents/ guardians.
- The SMC shall perform the following functions:
  - (a) monitor the working of the school,
  - (b) prepare and recommend the school development plan,
  - (c) monitor the utilization of grants received from appropriate authorities, and
  - (d) perform such other functions as may be prescribed.

Prohibition of Deployment of Teachers for Non-educational Purposes

- No teacher shall be deployed for any non-educational purpose other than the decennial population census, disaster relief duties or duties relating to elections to the local authority or the State Legislatures or Parliament as the case may be.
- No teacher shall engage in private tuition.

Curriculum and Examinations

- The curriculum and evaluation procedure shall be laid down by an academic authority specified by the appropriate government.
- No child shall be required to pass any Board examination till completion of elementary education.
- Every child completing elementary education shall be awarded a certificate.

Protection of Rights of Children

- The responsibility of monitoring the Right to Education has been vested with the National Commission for Protection of Child Rights (NCPR). But NCPR at present has only three members including the chairperson.
- The Appellate authority under the Act is the State Commission for Protection of Child Rights which is non-existent till date.

Constitution of National Advisory Council

- The central government shall constitute a National Advisory Council consisting of a maximum of 15 members to advise the centre on implementation of the provisions of the Act in an effective manner.

Comparison of the 2005 Draft Bill with the 2009 Act

The 2005 Draft Bill had certain provisions which were absent in the 2009 Act. They were:

- If a parent or guardian does not enrol his child in school, the SMC shall require the parent to perform compulsory community service by providing child care in school. There is no penalty provision in the 2009 Act.
- Teachers in state schools shall be appointed to a school by the local authority or SMC and will not be transferred to another school. There is no such provision in the 2009 Act.

Recommendations of the Parliamentary Committee

The Parliamentary Standing Committee on HRD presented its report on the Bill in 2009. Some of the important observations of the committee were:

- The experiences of the states in implementing the legislations already existing are not very encouraging and, to a large extent, they have remained unimplemented.
- Problem areas and shortcomings in the implementation of the state laws should be taken into account so that they are ameliorated in the present legislation.
- Community involvement and participation is an essential ingredient for the successful implementation of the provisions of the Act.
- The term 'neighbourhood school' has to be defined appropriately to include distance/time for commutation so that young children are spared from commuting very long distances which may cause exertion.
- A formula for sharing of funds between centre and states should be finalized and reflected in the financial memorandum attached to the Act as many states have expressed their inability to bear the huge financial burden estimated for the implementation of the Act.
- Mass awareness is to be created about this social legislation and regular monitoring of its implementation should be ensured.

- The mechanism for ensuring the admission of eligible students to private schools under this provision has to be adequate and appropriate.
- Expenditure incurred on 25 per cent of under-privileged children should not be passed on to the remaining 75 per cent of the children.
- Aided and unaided schools should give 25 per cent of their admissions from the nursery class to under-privileged children.
- A fool-proof monitoring mechanism must be in place to ensure effective implementation of penalties so that no school denies admission to any child.
- In case age proof is not available, there should be provision for parents to produce an affidavit or an age certificate from the chief of Village Panchayat/ local counsellor.
- A minimum level of grading should be fixed for the child for promotion to the next class instead of blanket promotion.
- In the matter of awarding a certificate to a child for completion of elementary education, a standardized assessment of that child should be done periodically to enable the child to know his own level and improve accordingly.
- A provision must be made enabling appeal against orders passed by the NCPR.

However the Act was passed by Parliament in July, 2009 without any major changes. The Central and State governments have the concurrent responsibility for providing funds for carrying out the provisions of the Act. The states have made it clear that they do not have the needed resources to implement the provisions of the Act. Hence, there is apprehension that the good intention of the law would get entangled in financial wrangles between the centre and the states.

With the passage of the Act, (w.e.f. 1.4.2010) education has become a fundamental right as well as a legally enforceable duty on the part of the centre and the states to provide free and compulsory education to all children aged between 6-14. But will this Act secure 'elementary education of a satisfactory quality', for every child and help him/ her to complete it successfully, time alone will tell.

4

Important Government Initiatives in Elementary Education

A large number of initiatives were attempted by the central and state governments as well as by several NGOs in the area of 'Elementary Education' since 1986. Some of these were Centrally Sponsored Schemes (CSS) while some others were partially funded by external agencies. These initiatives resulted in substantial improvement in access, enrolment, retention and participation of children in elementary education. Some of the important initiatives undertaken under 'Access and Retention' are discussed here. Part A deals with those undertaken by the centre and Part B, those by the states.

PART A

CENTRAL GOVERNMENT INITIATIVES

Some of the major central government initiatives profiled in this section are:

1. Operation Blackboard (OB)
2. Non-formal Education (NFE)
3. District Primary Education Programme (DPEP)
4. The Mahila Samakhya (MS)
5. Sarva Shiksha Abhiyan (SSA).

The following major central government initiatives are discussed elsewhere in this book:

1. The National Programme of Nutritional Support to Primary Education (NP-NSPE) in Annexure III.
2. Central Scheme of Restructuring and Reorganization of Teacher Education in Chapter V.

1. Operation Blackboard (OB)

The OB scheme was introduced as a sequel to the NPE 1986. It attempted to define basic norms at the national level for a primary school. As a CSS, it was launched to equip every primary school with certain basic infrastructure and human resources. In addition to the efforts of the state governments, the OB was meant to augment infrastructure and human resources in primary schools.

Small schools located in remote areas and serving mainly the marginalized sections of the population had suffered from severe inadequacies like lack of adequate infrastructure, single-teacher handling multigrade classes, etc. Through this scheme, the GOI specified that every primary school will have a minimum of two classrooms and two teachers irrespective of the number of children. The package included provision of certain basic set of instructional material. This measure helped improve the infrastructure position of schools in rural areas in the country.

Based on the fifth All India Educational Survey (1986), the scheme provided for a second teacher in all the 1.53 lakh identified single-teacher schools and a one time 'teaching-learning equipment' worth Rs10,000 per school for all the 5.23 lakh primary schools. It also provided for two rooms and a verandah from the funds of the Ministry of Rural Development. In turn, the states had to commit to setting up new schools albeit with these minimum provisions. In 1993, the scheme was expanded to provide a third teacher in primary schools with enrolment more than 100, an additional teacher in upper primary schools and teaching-learning equipment for all the upper primary schools at the rate of Rs50,000 per school in tribal areas and Rs40,000 per school in other areas.

The OB scheme was implemented in eight phases from 1987-88 to 1994-95, with four extension phases from 1994-95 to 1999-2000. The first six phases covered lower primary schools while the seventh and eighth phases covered the upper primary schools. The scheme financed construction of additional classrooms, appointment of additional teachers and supply of TLMs. Salary grant for the additional teachers appointed under OB was 100 per cent till the end of the Ninth Plan. In addition to the amounts released under OB, the ZPs utilized their own funds as well as those under 'Jawahar Rojgar Yojana' for construction of classrooms.

Between 1990 and 2000, GOI spent on an average Rs40 crores per year under the scheme. More than 1.82 lakh classrooms were built and 1.49 lakh teachers were recruited. Besides, 42,000 posts of teachers were sanctioned so that a third teacher could be sanctioned to primary schools having more than 100 enrolled children. The OB scheme was evaluated during 1998-2000 in all the states by reputed institutions with the coordination of NIEPA. The evaluation studies pointed out that:

- Utilization of resources had been unsatisfactory in many states as it took years for the same to reach schools.
- Many of the identified single-teacher schools continued to remain so, on account of redeployment of the teaching staff.
- The quality of classrooms was unsatisfactory, also, there was no provision for maintenance and repair.
- No attention was given to the learning needs while designing school buildings.

- Centralized procurement of teaching-learning equipment had got mired in vigilance inquiries.
- Teacher recruitment through OB had been the only step taken towards adding teacher posts due to lack of initiative on the part of many states to create posts on their own.

On the positive side, however, the assessments pointed out to (1) large-scale teacher recruitments which happened due to OB, (2) teaching-learning equipment reaching a large number of schools for the first time, and (3) facilities in schools showing a marginal improvement. All in all, it was found that many states utilized the OB scheme reasonably well. For example in Karnataka, the achievement was 79.2 per cent in classroom construction, 98.33 per cent in recruitment of teachers and 100 per cent in respect of supply of TLM. However, there were several complaints over the quality of construction and quality of TLMs purchased; enquiries relating to these matters dragged on for more than a decade.

2. Non-formal Education (NFE)

In the last two decades, NFE emerged not only as an alternative to formal schooling but also as an answer to the rigidity and inflexibility of the formal system. As a programme, it was designed to cater to the learning needs of those children who were not able to avail of regular schooling facilities. Though it was originally meant for only 10 educationally backward states, it was later extended to cover urban slums, hilly, tribal and desert areas; additionally, it was involved in projects for working children.

Prominence was given to establishing low cost NFE centres in unserved habitations or for out-of-school children who included school dropouts, those from school-less habitations, working and non-enrolled children, etc. The primary objective of the programme was to deliver 'literacy, numeracy and awareness' to such children. Over 800 NGOs were given the responsibility of running these centres. Under the innovative component, assistance was extended to some reputed NGOs like the MV Foundation, Rishi Valley Experimental Project, Eklavya Foundation, etc.

The important features of the NFE programme were:

(a) A condensed course of about two years' duration for lower primary and three-years for upper primary levels.
(b) Part-time instruction to learners in small groups at a time and place convenient to them.
(c) The village community to provide space and other facilities for running the NFE centre with a part-time local teacher.
(d) Emphasis placed on flexibility and decentralization of management.
(e) Curriculum and teaching material to be comparable to that used in the formal system apart from being relevant to the local environment and learners' needs.
(f) Testing and certification of NFE students to enable their entry into the formal system.

Though the programme was started in the Sixth Plan period, it was revised and expanded in 1987-88. Since its inception, it grew consistently in size and coverage. By 1997, there were 2.79 lakh NFE centres covering 7 million children in 21 states. Of these 2.41 lakh centres were run by state governments and 38,000 by NGOs/voluntary agencies. Five states – UP, Bihar, AP, MP and Orissa – accounted for 81 per cent of NFE centres. However, coverage was very limited in J&K and the north-eastern states.

Despite several difficulties faced in the implementation of the programme, NFE provided access to primary education for millions of children from remote and inaccessible areas, urban slums, girls and children from the disadvantaged sections of society. The contribution of the programme comprised 3.5 per cent of total enrolment at the primary stage and, a reduction of over 1 per cent in the overall dropout rate.

In spite of making a palpable dent in primary education, the NFE centres invited one constant criticism – that of their non-performance (PROBE study). Upon evaluation, certain deficiencies were noted in various inputs, monitoring, infrastructure and quality. While NFE was perceived to be a low cost alternative to formal primary schooling, the children seemed to be denied the quality of experience they would have got in a formal school. This observation brought in its wake some concerted efforts to improve the internal efficiency of the system.

The Planning Commission also evaluated the scheme and suggested improvements. Accordingly, it was completely revised firstly as the 'Education Guarantee Scheme (EGS) and subsequently as 'Alternative and Innovative Education' (AIE) scheme in 2000 under the SSA. The revised programme was built on successful innovations like the EGS in MP, residential bridge courses in MV Foundation, Bal Sakhis in Pratham, etc.

The EGS and AIE schemes were designed to provide access to elementary education to out-of-school children and those who lived in school-less habitations. The scheme supported flexible educational strategies such as bridge courses, residential camps, drop-in centres, summer camps and remedial schools.

Alternative and Innovative Education (AIE)

The AIE strategy under SSA involved two approaches – the bridging and the non-bridging. With a choice of being residential or non-residential, the bridge course approach focused on mainstreaming the out-of-school child. The non-residential bridge courses were long-term (for older children) and short-term (ranging from 2-6 months) for children in the 6-8 age group. The non-bridging approach included a variety of innovative practises – seasonal/worksite hostels, mobile schools, etc. During 2005-06, 3.08 million children were enrolled in AIE interventions. Both EGS and AIE centres worked for about four hours a day.

A number of NGOs participated in the innovative and experimental education component of the AIE. In 2005 there were 2785 NGOs actively involved in it. The EGS was another programme meant to set up alternative schools in habitations where there was no formal school within a radius of 1km, and with at least 15 children of the primary school-going age group. Some of the EGS centres addressed very specific local needs

– educating the children of sex workers in Kolkata, children of migratory families in the sugarcane fields of Maharashtra, children of tribal families in remote habitations in many states, etc. Education volunteers, selected by the village, ran these centres. They were trained initially for 30-days and subsequently, received continuous training with CRCs providing academic support.

As of 2005-06, there were 111,416 EGS primary centres catering to 4.04 million children, 4763 upper primary EGS centres (with 2 teachers) catering to 337,756 children from habitations without access to upper primary schooling in Chhattisgarh, Maharashtra, Uttarakhand and WB. The budget per child was Rs845 at the primary level and Rs1200 at the upper primary level.

However, enrolment under the EGS came down from 49.8 lakh children to about 24 lakhs in 2006-07, since relaxation of norms for small schools facilitated the upgradation of many of these centres as primary schools in several states (MP, Jharkhand, Bihar and Rajasthan).

3. District Primary Education Project (DPEP)

The DPEP was launched in 1994 with assistance from the World Bank. It targeted universalization of primary education (UPE) through decentralized planning and management, community mobilization and, district and population specific planning. The districts selected were those where female literacy was below the national average and where the TLC had been successful, leading to greater demand for elementary education. Though DPEP was a project, its goals were actually sectoral and achievement of the same depended not only on the project activities but also on the performance of the entire elementary education sector.

Besides providing access to primary education, the DPEP aimed at reducing dropout rates to below 10 per cent. It was designed to augment the state's efforts at achieving UPE by providing access to all children through formal and non-formal systems, ensuring universal participation of children and improving the quality of teaching-learning transactions at the lower primary stage. The focus was also on mainstreaming children belonging to marginalized groups, particularly girls and SC/ST. Started in 42 districts of seven states, the programme eventually expanded to 273 districts in 18 states. States which were receptive to change (like Gujarat, MP, AP, Kerala, and TN) gained immensely from it. DPEP ended in 2002.

The main objectives of DPEP were:

- Universalization of access (for primary education).
- Universalization of retention.
- Universalization of learning achievements – to increase the learning levels by at least 25 per cent over a measured baseline achievement level.
- Capacity building – to increase the capacity of teachers and other administrative personnel through training.
- Reduction of the gap in achievement levels between the general category, female children and other socially backward groups (SCs & STs) to less than 5 per cent over the measured baseline achievement.

In the first four years, there was progress in many areas. This included strategies and activities for people's mobilization and their participation in the education process through a variety of programmes such as Kala Jathas, Chinnara Melas, VEC Melas and microplanning. These programmes aimed at enlisting the services of the community for universalizing primary education in their area.

DPEP also initiated:

- School surveys and district plans.
- Household surveys to track out-of-school children.
- Alternate schooling facilities in unserved habitations.
- Residential and non-residential bridge courses.
- District level information systems and EMIS database.
- Teacher and school grants.
- Quality community – led development of school facilities using new technologies and local materials.
- Establishment of Block and Cluster Resource Centres.
- Development and availability of attractive textbooks for children.

DPEP had some significant achievements to its credit:

1. Project districts were able to tackle the problem of access more effectively by opening schools in school-less habitations and upgrading lower primary to higher primary schools, wherever required.
2. Awareness programmes boosted the enrolment of children in schools.
3. The participatory mode of teacher training programmes and improvement in curriculum transaction skills helped teachers tackle multigrade situations with confidence.
4. The concept of MLLs helped improve learning levels among children. Competency – and activity – based textbooks and workbooks created a conducive learning environment that had a visible impact on the quality of classroom transaction.
5. Some states like Karnataka conducted radio lessons which were very popular as they provided academic support to rural teachers.
6. Education resource materials, teachers' guides and TLMs contributed to the quality and effectiveness of classroom transaction as the teacher had previously depended solely on the textbook for teaching.
7. Efforts to involve the community in school management brought both parties closer to each other with the community contributing substantially towards improvement of the school infrastructure.
8. DPEP constructed additional classrooms that helped the states to overcome the shortage to some extent.
9. Creation of BRCs and CRCs enabled regular and periodical teacher training apart from providing teacher support and motivation.
10. Holding of regular VEC meetings ensured community participation in enrolment drives, providing additional facilities in the school, monitoring progress of learning, etc.

11. There was a reduction in dropout and repetition rates through enrolment drives, Kala Jathas and other programmes.
12. States that undertook institutional reforms while implementing holistic programmes like DPEP gained significantly from it as DPEP became the harbinger of change that was to bring about a much needed improvement in the system.

Deficiencies noticed in DPEP

DPEP suffered from several deficiencies. The progress in implementation of DPEP was uneven across districts and states. NFE systems for out-of-school children never really took off in several districts. Some of the issues that remained even after DPEP effort were:

- Large number of out-of-school children.
- Quality concerns in achievement levels of children (Please see Tables 34 and 35 in Annexure VIII).
- Issues in providing continuous resource support to teachers.
- Neglect of issues at the upper primary stage.
- Lack of consolidated efforts to tackle the problems faced by multigrade systems that existed in a majority of schools in the country.

With the completion of DPEP in many states, the ongoing programmes under it in the remaining nine states were merged with SSA.

4. Mahila Samakhya (MS)

Consequent to NPE 1986, a need was felt to redress traditional gender imbalances in educational access and achievement. The MS programme designed for education and empowerment of women in rural areas (particularly women from socially and economically marginalized groups) was launched as a Dutch-assisted project in 1987-1989. The programme recognized the centrality of education in empowering women to achieve equality. The MS programme did not set any targets as it adopted an innovative approach that emphasized the importance of processes rather than mechanical fulfillment of targets.

The effectiveness of the MS strategy in mobilizing women for education resulted in its being adopted by other basic education projects. The programme revolved round village level women's collectives, which raised a number of issues relevant to livelihood, education, health and other societal concerns. The initial focus was on enabling greater access to and generating a demand for education, building capacities and strengthening women's abilities in order to get them to effectively participate in the village level processes for educational development.

Mahila Sanghas endeavoured to create an environment for women to learn at their own pace, set their own priorities and, seek knowledge and information to make informed choices. This involved enabling women to deal with problems of isolation, lack of self-confidence, oppressive social customs, struggle for survival, all of which inhibited their learning. The focus was also on transforming gender-biased social attitudes, beliefs and roles.

The programme emphasized the crucial link between women's empowerment and their education. From 2004-05, it was funded through GOI resources and was implemented in nine states – AP, Assam, Bihar, Jharkhand, Karnataka, Kerala, Gujarat, UP, and Uttarakhand. In 2006-07, it covered 5.76 lakh women members in 19,979 villages spread over 63 districts. It was further extended to MP and Chhattisgarh in 2006-07. While the Tenth Plan outlay for the programme was Rs98.48 crores, it was envisaged to cover more than half the country by the middle of the Eleventh Plan.

Successive evaluations of the programme, including one at the national level in 2004-05, pointed to its success in empowering women at the grass roots level through the Mahila Sanghas. Some of its achievements were:

- Generating a demand for literacy and education.
- Increasing recognition and visibility of women within the family and the community.
- Increasing women's participation in PRIs.
- Demanding accountability from delivery systems.
- Mainstreaming girls who had dropped out-of-school.
- Increasing the economic empowerment of women through varied vocational training.

5. Sarva Shiksha Abhiyan (SSA)

Introduction

The single largest initiative undertaken in India for the cause of education, popularly known as SSA, is also one of the largest such programmes in the world. Launched in 2001-02 in mission mode, SSA was the flagship elementary education programme of the GOI. It aimed at achieving the long cherished goal of UEE through a time-bound integrated approach in partnership with the states (and with some funding support from external agencies). It was designed based on the experience of earlier primary education programmes including DPEP, Shiksha Karmi and Lok Jumbish. It incorporated several kinds of interventions in the elementary education sector and was intended to be an umbrella programme.

SSA encouraged local specificity and promoted local need-based planning through a district level decentralized management framework involving PRIs, VECs and women's groups. Each state and district had to set target dates, not later than 2010, for the goals of SSA to be achieved in their specific context.

SSA was also used for channelizing all central government initiatives in school education through a single agency in order to achieve concurrence at the field level. It was funded first on an 85:15 sharing basis between the centre and the states (during the Ninth Plan), then on a 75:25 basis till the end of the Tenth Plan, and on a 50:50 basis thereafter. 33 per cent of the expenditure was earmarked for civil works and the programme management cost was fixed at 6 per cent.

Goals and Objectives of SSA

SSA originally sought to achieve the following goals:

(a) Provision of access to all children in the age group of 6-14 years through formal primary schools or alternative delivery means by 2003.
(b) Completion of primary education of all children by 2007.
(c) Completion of eight years of elementary education of all children by 2010.
(d) Provision of education of satisfactory quality for all by 2010.

Since some of these objectives could not be achieved within the prescribed time frame, the states revised them from time to time.

Focus Areas of SSA

The focus of the programme was on:

(a) Out-of-school children.
(b) SCs, STs, minorities and other deprived classes.
(c) Education of girls and children with disabilities.
(d) Ensuring smooth transition from primary to upper primary stage.
(e) Ensuring adequate learning achievement.
(f) Improving the performance of the school system through a community-owned approach, with specific focus on the provision of quality education.
(g) Bridging gender and social gaps by 2010.

Coverage

SSA covered the entire country. It tried to refine and fine tune the process of identifying educationally backward districts and blocks through the construction of an index that incorporated educational indicators related to inputs, equity and outcomes. This innovative approach also supported decentralized planning by the states.

In recent years, SSA has tried to target districts with specific problems and issues. In 2006-07, 314 districts were selected: 48 with more than 50,000 out-of-school children, 113 with more than 25 per cent SC or 50 per cent ST, 99 with significantly higher minority populations and 105 special focus districts. Preferential allocation of funds followed such identification, with 76 per cent of the 2006-07 outlays being allocated to districts with a high percentage of out-of-school children and SC/ST/minority groups.

Mode of Implementation

The programme was so planned as to pave the way for NGOs and private sector players to significantly contribute towards the achievement of these goals and lead towards a community-owned initiative for UEE. It sought to open new schools, strengthen existing school infrastructure through provision of additional classrooms, toilets, drinking water, maintenance grant and school improvement grant. Existing schools with inadequate teacher strength were to be provided additional teachers. Capacity building of teachers, development of new TLMs and academic support were part of the overall plan.

SSA adopted a community-based approach with the habitation as a unit of planning and monitoring. In order to create a sense of ownership among stakeholders, the planning process was expected to be participatory in nature. Thus, education plans at the village level were supposed to form the basis for elementary education plans at the district level.

The EMIS correlated school level data with community based information obtained from microplanning and surveys. Every school was encouraged to share all information with the community, including the grants received.

Programmes under SSA

In order to realize the objectives of SSA, 10 major interventions and 104 programmes/ activities within these interventions were designed. Some of the important interventions are detailed below:

In-service Teacher Training

A 20-day in-service training for all teachers every year, a 60-day refresher course for untrained teachers already employed as teachers, a 30-day orientation for freshly trained recruits were the SSA norms for teacher training. On an average 77 per cent of teachers receive the in-service training every year. The in-service programmes are discussed in detail in Chapter V. A few states like Tripura and Chhattisgarh collaborated with IGNOU to develop distance education modules to clear the backlog of untrained teachers.

Computer-aided Learning (CAL)

The SSA focused on the use of ICT and CAL to enhance the quality of classroom transactions. Several states which adopted them received partial coverage under the programme head 'innovation' that had a budget of Rs15 lakhs per year per district. These interventions also incorporated PPPs with NGOs that supported education. Also, 14 states developed their own strategies following the national guidelines of the SSA.

Inclusive Education for Children with Special Needs

SSA aimed at ensuring that all children with special needs were provided education in an appropriate environment. Accordingly, it adopted a zero rejection policy and implemented a multi-option model for them. This included mainstreaming in regular schools, provision of AIE/EGS centres or home-based education. Flexibility was also accorded for adopting suitable alternative approaches wherever necessary. This was done through NGOs (as in the case of HP and Uttarakhand), or through resource teachers (as in the case of Kerala). Some states like TN and Haryana had special model schools innovated extensively through ideas like play parks at the BRCs.

As of 2006, about three million children had been identified and 1.83 million were enrolled. The states showed a variety of responses to the multi-option model. AP and UP focused on innovative residential bridge courses in order to prepare the children for school. NGOs specially recruited teachers and trained them to run these courses. Several states also opted for EGS centres. A special grant of Rs1,200 per child per year was envisaged for meeting the special learning needs of these children. 14.24 lakh children were enrolled in regular schools, 61,161 in EGS centres, 74,170 were provided home-based education in 15 states. Central assistance sanctioned for inclusive education was Rs190.45 lakhs.

Other forms of support included provision of assistive devices and barrier-free access. Many states like HP, Kerala, AP and Gujarat converged their activities with the District Disability Rehabilitation Centres like the Red Cross and governmental corporations. The Artificial Limb Manufacturing Corporation of India (ALIMCO) which functions under the Ministry of Social Justice and Empowerment, met 60 per cent of the cost of assistive devices and the balance was borne by the respective states.

Education of Girls

The SSA's approach in making the education system responsive to the needs of girls had two components. The 'pull' strategy – that involves creating platforms that help people to reach out, find and access appropriate resources – included better access to schools (including toilets for girls, free uniforms and textbooks, 'back to school' camps and bridge courses for out-of-school girls, residential facilities and the NPEGEL in 3427 blocks and urban slums), recruitment of more women teachers, teacher training that focused on gender sensitivity, appropriate TLM and interventions like ECCE centres.

The community dimension included creating conditions fostering women's participation, providing women with a specific role in the management of school-related activities and strengthening the linkages between the school and communities.

National Programme for Education of Girls at Elementary Level (NPEGEL)

NPEGEL is an important sub-component of SSA, was launched in September 2003, to enhance the education of girls at the elementary stage. The objective was to provide additional support to girls' education over and above the investments for the same through normal SSA interventions.

It focused on promoting schooling for girls through a range of strategic interventions in educationally disadvantaged pockets, where the female literacy rate was less than the national average and the gender gap was more, or where the population and characteristics of marginalized groups met certain specified criteria. It was also implemented in urban slum areas. It provided additional components through an intense community mobilization and through development of model cluster schools. It also provided for teacher training, development of gender sensitivity and support material.

NPEGEL provided for development of one model girls' school in each cluster, and included incentives such as stationery, additional interventions like awards, remedial teaching and bridge courses. The supplementary teaching material included stories on women achievers and lessons on nutrition, sanitation, environment, gender and legal aid. Curricular enhancement included classes in self-defence and self-image building. Provision of need-based incentives like escorts, stationery, workbooks and uniforms were some of the endeavours under this programme.

NPEGEL also gave thrust to girls' education through community mobilization and local specific interventions to improve the school environment, as well as support services like childcare centres. Teachers and teacher educators were trained in gender sensitization. Short-term residential courses, distance education and open schooling were included to bring learning opportunities to girls who were unable to attend regular schools.

NPEGEL was implemented in 3427 educationally backward blocks in 397 districts in 25 states. The following groups of girls were specially targeted – out-of-school, dropout, working ones, those from marginalized groups, those with low attendance and with low achievement levels. Close to 34,590 schools were in operation and 80,000 ECCE centres were supported in non-ICDS areas in 2006.

A variety of bridge courses and flexi-systems built around remedial teaching (Bihar), condensed course inputs (UP), course for Muslim girls (Orissa), open schooling through the state open school system (MP) were designed in many states under the NPEGEL.

Kasturba Gandhi Balika Vidyalaya (KGBV) Scheme

Launched in July 2004, this scheme was designed to encourage greater participation of girls at the upper primary level. Attempts were made to reach girls living in hard-to-reach, small and scattered habitations that lay at a considerable distance from the nearest school. The scheme was implemented in educationally backward districts of the country where the female rural literacy was below the national average and gender gap in literacy was above it.

Finances were shared on a 75:25 basis between the centre and the states during the Tenth Plan. The total amount released was Rs316.87 crore in the Tenth Plan. The scheme was eventually to be merged with SSA in the Eleventh Plan.

It aimed at setting up residential schools at the upper primary level in 3,073 identified educationally backward blocks in 25 states in the country. 60.6 per cent of these blocks are in special focus districts of SSA. Three-fourths of the seats were reserved for girls from marginalized or minority communities while the rest are given to girls from families below the poverty line. Of the 2,180 KGBVs sanctioned, 270 were opened in blocks with predominantly minority populations, 622 in SC blocks and 583 in ST blocks. Established NGOs and other non-profit-making bodies were also involved in running these schools.

Initial assessments indicated that these residential schools and hostels did make an impact in retaining girls at the upper primary stage. The per-girl cost under a residential intervention was obviously high, and it was bound to be higher when the state tried to reach the hardest-to-reach girls. 63,900 girls were covered under the scheme.

Distance Education

The country's first satellite dedicated exclusively for education, 'EDUSAT', was launched in September 2004. It revolutionized the way in which distance education was carried out in the country. The initial focus was on teacher training at the BRCs. The SSA supported distance education initiatives in seven states: MP, Chhattisgarh, Bihar, UP, TN, Karnataka and Haryana. Karnataka was the first state in the country to use the EDUSAT facility for teacher training and classroom support.

Under the pilot phase of the project, one district in each state was taken up for creation of infrastructure in schools and academic support structures to receive satellite signals, and for the development of educational content. The total financial outlay was Rs14.18 crores of which Rs0.83 crores was provided by the SSA.

In addition, the SSA was also involved in training for the purpose of developing distance education inputs and materials like District Reception Set Systems, down-linking facilities at the state and district levels, orienting teachers to IT-supported elementary education, and facilitating teleconferences.

Electronics Funds Transfer (EFT)

A streamlined fund flow system through electronic transfer was introduced in the country from 2004 to meet the needs of SSA. Under this scheme, selected banks were designated as centres for direct remittance of funds from the state capital to district and sub-district levels.

In accordance with it, the State Project Office (SPO) hands over a single cheque to each bank along with the list of amounts and district-wise accounts where the funds are to be credited. These banks then transfer the funds electronically from the SPO account (maintained in their branch) to the District Project Office (DPO) without delay. This process gets percolated from the district level to the sub-district levels. This system not only speeded up funds transfer but also expedited programme activities and improved fund utilization to a large extent. Several states like Karnataka and Maharashtra implemented 'Computerization of Financial Management System' for effective financial management of the activities of SSA.

Impact of SSA

The implementation of SSA led to significant achievements in the field of elementary education. Alternative strategies for mainstreaming children who were left out of the schooling process were implemented. School infrastructure improved. There was qualitative enhancement of teaching methods and in learning outcomes. As per published reports of GOI, there was significant achievement in several areas such as those detailed below:

- The number of out-of-school children dropped from 23 million in 2003-04 to 9.5 million by 2005-06.
- Dropout rates at the primary level stood at about 12 per cent, and 190 out of the 400 districts (2005-06) showed declining dropout trends.
- The gender gap in enrolment stood at 4.2 per cent at the primary level and 8.8 per cent at the upper primary level. In 2005-06 there were only 22 districts (out of 400 districts for which data was available) with a gender gap of more than 10 per cent. At the upper primary stage, however, there were 82 districts with a gap of more than 15 per cent and 50 with a gap of more than 20 per cent.

- The percentage of SC/ST children at the primary level (2004-05) was also greater than that of the proportion of their population: while the SCs constituted 20.73 per cent against a total population share of 16.2 per cent, the STs stood at 10.69 per cent against a population share of 8.2 per cent.
- Over 400,000 additional teachers were recruited across the country under SSA till October, 2005.
- More than 73,000 academic resource centres were established at the block and cluster levels to provide academic support to primary and upper primary teachers.
- All teachers were provided grants for developing TLMs, leading to improved teaching-learning methods and learning outcomes.
- A majority of teachers (on an average 77 per cent) received in-service training (some for 20-days in a year and others with varying duration).
- Free textbooks were distributed to all girls and children belonging to SCs/STs.
- In addition to maintenance grants, annual grants to improve infrastructure were provided to schools leading to visible and concrete benefits.

However,

- Achievement levels continued to be low as per NCERT and ASER survey assessments.
- Quality of education provided by the non-formal systems, especially in disadvantaged regions, remained a big question mark.

Nevertheless, the trend of the outcomes, except in the area of learning achievement, were indeed encouraging. Apart from the significant impact of national policies and guidelines, individual states madc thcir own choice of activities that needed to be introduced. Another positive feature of these interventions was that they were fairly large in scale and were implemented quite effectively. They also revealed a high degree of involvement of the SSA functionaries at the sub-district levels.

Joint Review Missions conducted by GOI, World Bank and DFID found that:

(a) SSA generated considerable interest and commitment in all the states and helped bring elementary education closer to the centre stage of the developmental agenda. Different states adopted the national framework but adapted it to suit their individual contexts.

(b) SSA generated an intense school-community interface that would serve as the foundation for sustained progress towards UEE. While community participation in school development visibly improved, enrolment went up as did the attendance of students and teachers There was better maintenance of school buildings and accountability in the system was markedly enhanced.

(c) SSA significantly improved access to schooling by opening schools and setting up EGS centres in remote areas and for inaccessible populations. The natural outcome was that the number of out-of-school children reduced drastically.

(d) As a result of recruitment of additional teachers, PTRs came down to 40:1 in several states.

(e) Effective and appropriate TLM was developed, schools became more child-friendly and teachers were trained in child-centred activity-based pedagogy. As a part of capacity building and sustaining reforms, teacher training became an integral part of the planning process.

(f) Several interventions to reduce gender and social gaps like remedial instruction, residential schools, vocational skills development, uniforms and midday meals were introduced in almost all states.

(g) SSA brought in greater convergence between various programmes. States began to view schemes like ICDS, total sanitation and water supply as crucial inputs to UEE.

(h) An increasing number of NGOs and civil society partners were brought into a collaborative relationship.

Progress against Key Targets

The GOI had set aggressive targets which included setting up of new schools, increasing the number of classrooms, recruiting additional teachers, training of existing teachers, etc. SSA largely succeeded in supporting states (in not only improving the existing but also creating new infrastructure) to improve education delivery mechanisms. Even though there was a significant growth in infrastructure, the implementation in other areas was quite slow, in spite of the very nature of implementation being in mission mode.

Table 4.1 Achievement under SSA (Up to 2007-08)

Item	Target	Achievement	% of Achievement
Opening of new schools	1,57,967	1,29,893	82%
Recruitment of teachers	7,72,345	5,87,388	76%
Construction of school buildings	1,20,629	71,143	58%
Construction of additional classrooms	3,29,690	1,55,814	47%
Enrolment in EGS/AIE centres	87,00,000	63,00,000	71%
Children given free textbooks	6,14,00,000	5,35,00,000	87%
Functional BRCs	7,422	7,201	97%
Functional CRCs	70,735	66,140	94%
Teachers trained	30,53,285	23,47,017	77%

Source: MHRD Reports

As per SSA estimates, there was a shortfall of approximately 1.25 lakh upper primary schools in India. It was estimated that the demand for upper primary schools would be greater than that for primary schools in future. Each state also created sizeable parallel structures of administration at the state level (and in several instances at the district level also) under SSA, even when such administrative machinery already existed.

PART B

INITIATIVES OF THE STATES

Under this section, the following state initiatives are profiled:

1. Shiksha Karmi Project of Rajasthan
2. Education Guarantee Scheme of Madhya Pradesh
3. 'School Mapping' in 'Lok Jumbish'.

Shiksha Karmi Project

The Project was started with the collaboration of Swedish International Development Agency (SIDA) in 1987. It aimed at UPE along with qualitative improvement in primary education in remote and socio-economically backward villages of Rajasthan. In addition, it had a special focus on girls.

The novelty of the project approach lay in its engaging local persons who had passed classes 5th and 8th as 'Shiksha Karmis' with intensive support through NGO partnerships for capacity development, further education, and improvement of emoluments based on performance. Special efforts were made to prepare women teachers to take on responsibilities in remote regions through NGO-managed 'Mahila Prashikshan Kendras'.

With teacher absenteeism being identified as a major obstacle to UEE, regularly absent and non-resident teachers were replaced by local ones who were less qualified but specially trained.

The rationale behind the project was that:

(a) A 'barefoot teacher' belonging to the local community can work effectively to reach every child in the locality.

(b) If a person is willing to work as a social worker, the lack of formal training may be made good by intensive in-service training.

(c) Education must have community support and local ownership in order to meet the needs of the deprived sections of the rural areas.

The project expanded to provide flexible learning centres for out-of-school children, children of migrants, etc., and covered 31 out of the 32 districts of Rajasthan. Evaluation of the project indicated a significant achievement in bringing children from remote regions, especially girls, to schools, flexi-schools and low cost hostels.

Learning achievement assessments were significantly positive, thus dispelling the myth that under-educated local youth would not be able to provide quality education.

Development of systems of training along with on-site academic support, monitoring, and capacity development were taken up with large-scale NGO participation.

Education Guarantee Scheme (EGS) of Madhya Pradesh

The government of MP introduced this scheme in 1997 as a community-centred initiative for UPE .The salient features of this scheme were:

(a) Sharing of responsibility between the local community and the state.
(b) Focusing on hitherto unserved sections of society in school-less habitations (having not less than 25 children in tribal areas and 40 children in non-tribal areas).
(c) Fixing a time limit of 90-days within which the demand from the community had to be met by the government.
(d) Utilizing PRIs for non-academic monitoring of school teachers and, CRCs, BRCs and DIETs for academic monitoring.
(e) Creating parity for tribal areas in terms of access to primary education and thereby contributing to equity.

The demand for EGS schools was so large that 19,289 of them came up in the first 18-months of the scheme with a majority of them being in tribal areas. The scheme evoked overwhelming interest in the country and several states tried to emulate it.

School Mapping in 'Lok Jumbish'

Undertaken from 1992 in Rajasthan and sponsored initially by SIDA, the 'Lok Jumbish' project aimed at attaining UPE through people's mobilization and participation, women's empowerment (through female education), providing equal opportunities in education, making education more relevant, etc.

'School Mapping' as a strategy was evolved by Lok Jumbish specifically to enlist people's support and services for the cause of education. The local NGO/education worker built rapport with such members of the community as were interested in improving education standards in the village/habitation. These members called the 'Prerak Dal'(inspirational group) were given training for a short duration after which they undertook school mapping in the village/habitation.

'School Mapping' referred to the exercise of depicting every household in the village visually on a simple map. Small symbols indicated the schooling status of every household member in the 5-14 age group. The whole exercise was an occasion for interacting with the community. When the map was ready, the special educational needs of particular households and the schooling facility required in the village became evident.

Based on the mapping data, the 'Prerak Dal' and the local community drew up a set of proposals that included the need for new schools and non-formal centres and improvement of the existing ones.

These proposals were sent to a block level committee which was the sanctioning authority. The school mapping allowed the ordinary, even non-literate villagers, to not only participate in a field survey but actually come out with viable proposals. Prompt follow-ups to these proposals further built up the confidence of the community and awareness about education grew to a large extent. In fact, the school mapping exercise became so popular that it was taken up by other national programmes like DPEP and implemented across the country.

Apart from some of these governmental initiatives, several NGOs and local society groups have made important contributions to achieve UEE. Some of these NGO initiatives are discussed in Chapter VII.

5

Elementary Teacher Education in India

INTRODUCTION

The teacher is an important and indispensable entity in the teaching-learning process, notwithstanding advances in technology. He/She is expected to play a crucial role in transforming the children into responsible citizens, in the face of several constraints. In fact, a teacher is the pivot around whom our entire education system revolves.

It thus goes without saying that teacher performance is the most critical input in the field of education. Policies laid down by the state become meaningful only when the teacher delivers them in the classroom. Hence, teacher selection, training, capacity building, motivation and performance assume immense importance. But this again depends on the quality of training and academic support that is given to them.

Various education commissions have also emphasized the importance of teachers' role and their proper training that would equip them with basic skills of teaching. The Kothari Commission observed: 'Of all the factors that influence the quality of education, the quality, competence and character of teachers are undoubtedly the most significant'.

The National Commission on Teachers (1985) observed: 'With the explosion in knowledge, the revolution in media, with contemporary issues demanding urgent attention with values getting eroded, the need for helping teachers to keep abreast of things cannot be questioned'.

Both the NPE 1986 and the POA 1992, emphasized the importance of teacher education. 'It is envisaged that selected institutions would be developed as District Institutes of Education and Training both for pre-service and in-service courses of elementary school teachers and for continued education of the personnel working in non-formal and adult education programme'.

The education system in the country has expanded tremendously at all levels. Several important initiatives and innovative strategies in the elementary education sector have been tried out. Yet, teacher education as a sector, has largely remained stagnant since independence. Another important point is that even today, out of nearly 53 lakh full-time school teachers in the country, (See Annexure VIII – Tables 22 and 23), nearly 10 lakh remain untrained. 14 per cent of primary teachers in the country are untrained (Table 45).

The GOI also realized that the goal of achieving UEE would remain elusive unless the centrality of the teacher was recognized in the whole process of educational reforms. Hence it tried to strengthen its 'Teacher Education Programme' that was meant not only to provide training facilities but to undertake curriculum development as well.

Teacher Accountability

In this era of globalization and liberalization of the economy, and implementation of systems relating to measurement of school quality, there is an increasing demand (both from the government as well as the community) on teachers to perform, produce results and also be accountable for them.

POLICY INITIATIVES IN TEACHER EDUCATION

As early as 1949, the University Education Commission observed: 'It is extraordinary that our school teachers learn whatever subject they teach before reaching the age of 24 or 25 and that their further education is left to experience, which in most cases is another name for stagnation. We must realize that experience needs to be supplemented by experiment, before reaching its fullness and that a teacher to keep alive and fresh should become a learner from time to time'.

Teacher education gained recognition as a crucial component of quality in education after the report of the Kothari Commission was brought out. Hence it would be appropriate to examine the opinions, suggestions and recommendations of the various Commissions, Committees and Reports which impact teacher education:

The Kothari Commission (1964-66) recommended a sound and holistic programme of professional education for teachers to bring about qualitative improvement in the professional, academic and social aspects of education. It famously stated 'The destiny of the nation is being shaped in our classrooms'. It further emphasized the need for teacher education to be 'brought into the mainstream of the academic life of the universities on the one hand and school life and educational developments on the other'. Recognizing 'quality' as the essence of such a programme, the Commission recommended the introduction of 'integrated courses of general and professional education in universities... with greater scope for self-study and discussion... and...a comprehensive programme of internship'.

The Chattopadhyay Committee of the National Commission on Teachers (1983-85) felt that teacher education needs to be relevant to the new roles and responsibilities of the teacher. It envisioned a new teacher as one who conveys to his pupils '... the importance of and the feeling for national integrity and unity; the need for a scientific attitude; a commitment to excellence in standards of work and action and a concern for society'. The Commission recommended a four-year integrated course for the secondary as well as the elementary teacher.

The Commission further suggested the following steps to make in-service education more effective:

(a) The needs of teachers to be identified at institutional and other levels, and in-service education to be so customized to directly meet those needs.

(b) The training to be remedial in nature – updating the teachers' knowledge in their respective subjects, dealing with classroom problems, using media effectively, etc.

(c) Teachers to be made aware of the problems affecting modern life: population explosion, environmental hazards, deforestation, alternate sources of energy, proliferation of nuclear problems and so on.

(d) Programmes to be planned well ahead of time and resource persons to be selected carefully.

The Commission also asked national and state level training institutions to evolve a mechanism by which their feedback from the school and training institute was constantly made available. It wanted the 'school inspector' to enquire into the in-service education availed by the teacher, reasons for not availing if any, then insist on the continual education of the teacher as a part of service conditions.

The NPE (1986), while assigning importance to teacher education as a whole, laid emphasis on giving quality training to primary teachers. It recognized that 'teachers should have the freedom to innovate, to devise appropriate methods of communication and activities relevant to the needs of and capabilities of and the concerns of the community'. It further stated: 'Teacher Education is a continuous process and its pre-service and in-service components are inseparable. As the first step, the system of teacher education will be overhauled'.

The Acharya Ramamurthy Committee (1990) also felt that there was need for revamping existing teacher education programmes. It further recommended 'an internship model firmly based on the primary model of the actual field experience in a realistic situation, on the development of teaching skills by practice over a period of time.' It was in favour of internship teaching spread over a long duration.

The Yashpal Committee Report (1993) on 'Learning without burden' noted that '...inadequate programmes of teacher preparation lead to unsatisfactory quality of learning in schools... The content of the programme should be restructured to ensure its relevance to the changing needs of school education. The emphasis in these programmes should be on enabling the trainees to acquire the ability of self-learning and independent thinking'.

The NCF 2005 visualized a major shift in the conceptualization of learning and, accordingly, that of teaching. It had two important concerns – connecting knowledge to life outside school and, enriching the curriculum by making it less textbook centred. While emphasizing the primacy of the active learner, the curriculum framework viewed teaching as a process that enables learners to construct knowledge. The teacher is a 'facilitator who encourages learners to reflect, analyse and interpret in the process of knowledge construction'.

This shift in the conceptualization of the role of the teacher has crucial implications for the aims, content and methodology of teacher education. The teacher must shift the focus of the children away from 'rote learning' and help them to derive meaning from personal experience, i.e., from what they read, see, hear and experience. Thus, emphasis is laid on role modelling, observation, reflection and practice.

In a **Focused Group Report on Teacher Education for Curriculum Renewal** constituted by NCERT (2005) it was observed that the exercise of revising school curriculum with the aim of revitalizing school education cannot be achieved without addressing the need for creating reflective teacher practitioners.

Factors affecting the Teacher Education Sector in India

A number of internal and external factors that are affecting the elementary teacher education scenario in the country are outlined below:

- Teachers working in primary, upper primary and secondary schools have varied qualifications, training, experience, and backgrounds which naturally impact their knowledge of content and pedagogy.
- The minimum educational qualification for recruiting primary (elementary) teachers varies from state to state.
- In the north-eastern states a large number of teachers are under-qualified.
- Many states have appointed a large number of para-teachers.
- More than 60 per cent of schools are multigrade having just one/two teachers.
- In a large number of schools, infrastructural facilities are inadequate – in terms of availability of classrooms, physical facilities and TLM.
- In many schools, the class size is large which is a constraint to effective teaching.
- In the past few years, there is a shift in the school-going population – from state schools to private ones, in search of quality.
- There is also a proliferation of sub-standard and unregulated schools, and teacher training institutions (TTIs) in the private sector.
- Further, there is acute shortage of science and mathematics teachers in many states.
- The teacher education curriculum is outdated and more theory-based.
- The quality of teacher education has seen a decline. Even the level of training of pre-service teachers varies from state to state.

All these factors are found to directly impact not only the teacher education sector but also the elementary education sector.

PRE-SERVICE ELEMENTARY TEACHER EDUCATION

Historical Perspective

It is still a matter of concern that teachers are not considered to be front line professionals and that teacher education institutions continue to exist in seclusion, severely isolated from centres of higher learning, academic colleges and universities. The Education Commission (1966) had envisaged that all teacher education programmes irrespective of their status should be at the collegiate level. In educationally advanced countries, the entire teacher education forms a part of the university system and is characterized by equal rigour as in other disciplines. This view has been supported by several commissions that have followed.

The pre-service teacher education scenario in the country from the beginning was beset with many problems such as:

(a) Mushrooming growth of sub-standard institutions.
(b) Malpractices and irregularities in many private institutions.
(c) Serious mismatch of demand and supply of trained teachers in some states.
(d) Large backlogs of untrained/unqualified serving teachers in most states.
(e) Existence of a large number of trained unemployed teachers in several states.

All matters relating to pre-service teacher education programme were regulated by the concerned examination bodies in the states, with the curricula being prescribed by the SCERTs in most states. The national norm of minimum academic qualification for admission was higher secondary (+2 stage). Some states followed the one-year pre-service course but switched to the two-year course with about 220 working days in each year. Annual intake per section varied from 30 to 50 depending on the norms prescribed by the states.

Below the state level, there were elementary TTIs but their activities were confined mostly to pre-service teacher education. Several districts across the country did not have even this facility. Even where the institutions existed, the inadequate physical, human and academic resources limited their reach and role in improving the quality. The teaching practices adopted by them were also far outdated and not conducive to the fast changing elementary education scene where majority of children attending primary classes were from families of first generation learners and depressed classes.

By the time the NPE was adopted in 1986, the elementary education system in the country had grown into a vast system without any systematic academic support base at the ground level. Hence, decentralization of academic support structures from the national and state levels became imperative.

National Council of Teacher Education (NCTE)

The NPE 1986 and the POA there under, envisaged a National Council for Teacher Education with statutory status and necessary resources as a first step towards overhauling the system of teacher education.

As a statutory body, the NCTE came into existence on the 17th August, 1995 in pursuance of the 'National Council for Teacher Education Act, 1993 (No. 73 of 1993)'. The Act visualized a planned and coordinated development of quality teacher education in the country, and enjoined upon NCTE to ensure that norms and standards are maintained in all TTIs in the country. The NCTE has laid down 'Norms and Standards' for recognition that are specific for every category of TTI. It acts as a regulatory body for all the teacher education institutions in India and since 1995, every such institution is bound by law to seek its recognition.

The main objectives of the NCTE are to:

1. Achieve planned and coordinated development of the teacher education system throughout the country.
2. The regulation and proper maintenance of 'Norms and Standards' in the teacher education system and for matters connected therewith.

The mandate given to the NCTE is very broad and covers the entire gamut of teacher education programmes. This includes research and training of persons for equipping them to teach at pre-primary, primary, secondary and senior secondary stages in schools, and handle NFE, part-time education, adult education and distance (correspondence) education courses as well.

As envisaged in Section 20 of the NCTE Act, there are four regional committees looking after its statutory responsibilities in the eastern, western, northern and southern regions. These are located at Bhubaneswar, Bhopal, Jaipur and Bangalore respectively. The main functions of the regional committees are considering applications of teacher education institutions for recognition of permission for starting a new course or training in teacher education, of increase in annual intake of an institution, withdrawal of recognition of an institution for contravention of provisions of the NCTE Act and other matters connected therewith.

Initially, the NCTE did commendable work by pulling up both government and private TTIs having inadequate infrastructure and insufficient qualified staff. Even though it has prescribed norms regarding staff, equipment, buildings and other infrastructure for various types of TTIs, it could not enforce them due to insufficient staff for monitoring and the presence of a large number of institutions in each state.

The NCTE confined itself to a licensing role by only giving recognition to existing and new TTIs. It totally failed to check the proliferation of unscrupulous private TTIs which exploited the situation by establishing training shops rather than training institutions. As a professional body, it also failed to raise the standards of these institutions. Even after more than ten-years of its existence, the NCTE has not been able to fulfil its broader goal of developing quality teacher education in the country.

Pre-service Courses through the 'Distance Mode'

IGNOU and other universities/distance education institutions also play an important role in the pre-service teacher education sector by offering courses to untrained working teachers. To ensure quality, a two-year 'Diploma in Primary Education (DPE)' course is conducted by IGNOU for untrained elementary school teachers of Orissa, MP, and Jharkhand. Similarly, on request of the government of Bihar, NCTE approved a one-year training course through the distance mode for 43,000 untrained teachers in Bihar.

Pre-service Teacher Education Curriculum

Developed over a century, the present teacher education system in the country has been serving a very limited purpose of narrow pedagogy-related classroom teaching. If the education system and the teachers have to meet the challenges of a knowledge-driven global community, the curriculum needs a thorough overhaul.

Teacher Education Curriculum is a multi-disciplinary area which draws from other disciplines such as psychology, sociology and philosophy, bringing in more comprehensiveness and inclusiveness. This ought to make the curriculum vibrant and relevant to the present day needs. There is a growing need to shift away from traditional practices like acquisition of knowledge, concepts, skills, etc., which isolate the learning mind from the actual experience. Integrating theory and practice as well as content and pedagogy will provide a definitive solution. Frameworks that would be relevant to field level realities must be evolved. At the end of the day, one should be able to answer questions such as, 'Why are millions of children enrolled in schools not learning?' Educational research and practice thus take on a very crucial role in addressing these issues.

The issue of quality in teacher education is closely tied with the duration of initial teacher preparation (pre-service) programmes. The emphasis is on a long duration internship that provides enough opportunity for self-study, reflection and involved engagement with children, the school, the classroom, and pedagogic activities along with theoretical study. Suitable convergence between the NCF and teacher education goals, strategy and instruments needs to be brought about. There should be appropriate linkage between pre-service and continuing in-service teacher education programmes. Hence there is need for revision of 'Teacher Education Curriculum', the course content and materials so as to bring them in consonance with the NCF 2005.

The recommendations of various committees cover various aspects of teacher preparation such as pre-service and in-service education – their duration, curriculum content and practice. The NCF 2005 brought into focus the needs of the child, classroom and the teacher.

NCTE prepared a 'Draft Revised Curricular Framework' for teacher education in 2004 and disseminated it for discussion throughout the country. It also constituted the following expert committees on different aspects of teacher education :

(a) Expert Committee on Evaluation
(b) Expert Committee on ECCE
(c) Expert Committee to 'Develop Models of Course Contents, Mode of Curriculum Transaction and Evaluation Procedures'.

Though subsequently this curricular framework was revised in 2006, not many states adopted it to prepare their teacher training curricula.

Quality Issues in Pre-service Teacher Education

Improvement in the quality of schooling is directly dependent upon the teacher's performance. Over the years, the profile of children entering school has changed radically. Due to the states' efforts at UEE, children who are entering school are first generation learners from economically weaker sections and urban slums, belonging to the migrant population; in short, those who had no access to education previously.

The present day teacher is not equipped to handle such children because the training methods have by and large remained stagnant over the past several decades. Dominated by theory, the pre-service curriculum continues to be far flung from ground realities. The teaching practice sessions hardly enable the teacher to handle multigrade, multilevel situations in the classrooms. Neither can he/she engage students in the creative learning activities which are emphasized by modern experiments.

Apart from the above, the rising aspirations of parents to provide good quality education (especially English education) to their children has made the task of the teacher more demanding.

The states have treated teacher training courses on par with other general courses instead of treating them as professional ones. Over the years, the knowledge base and skill sets that teachers need in order to be effective have changed and expanded tremendously. The student-teacher is unable to use technology to enhance his teaching skills as majority of the elementary TTIs in the country lack computers and other multimedia aids.

Thus, the infrastructure in these institutions needs to be revamped to include computers, internet, LCD projectors, digital libraries, etc. Student-teachers must be trained to imbibe skills that are required to develop computer-based lesson plans. Every training institution should compulsorily have one faculty who can impart computer education and also computer-based education.

The large proliferation of private unaided TTIs has also created a host of problems. In several states, giving permission to a large number of them has not been based on the principle of demand and supply. Also in several states, there are not enough experienced teacher educators to service the institutions and hence, a majority of them are providing sub-standard education. If teacher education has to meet the challenges of the present day, the nature and structure of pre-service training has to be completely transformed.

From an analysis of the types of teacher training programmes being run in a majority of states, it is noticed that teachers need to be trained in:

(a) Development of reference and study skills among students.
(b) Development of reading, language improvement and independent study habits in students.
(c) Use of additional teaching and support materials from electronic media like CDs, TV, internet, etc.
(d) Development of life-skills in students.
(e) Preparation of question papers as per a blue print.
(f) Enrichment of co-curricular activities in school.

Key Concerns in Pre-service Teacher Education Sector

1. The state governments and NCTE permitted/recognized (in spite of NCTE norms) hundreds of private sub-standard TTIs in states where there was actually no need.
2. Poor quality in teacher education has been the outcome of outdated curricula, poor professional preparation of teachers and teacher educators.
3. There is total isolation of TTIs from the school system and institutions of higher learning and universities.
4. NCTE lacks manpower, resources and capacity to monitor and regulate standards.
5. Due to heavy workload, the NCTE is unable to finalize the list of recognized institutions (with intake) before June, every year, for transmission to the state governments. This delays the entire admission process by a few months which, in turn, affects the 'practice teaching' calendar of the institutions.
6. The NCTE norms for selection of teacher educators are very rigid. As a result, the newly started institutions are unable to maintain a PTR of 12:1. In some cases, a teacher educator finds his name on the rolls of several institutions.
7. In respect of elementary TTIs, as per the present norms, the faculty should have a minimum qualification of an M.Ed. degree. Since there are no institutions in several states offering M.Ed. (Elementary Education) course, the faculty after completing B.Ed. and M.Ed. courses pertaining to secondary education, become teacher educators in elementary teacher education institutions with no experience of teaching in elementary schools at all. Hence, they confine themselves to teaching theory resulting in poor standards in student-teachers.
8. Student-teachers who pass out of these training institutions get appointed in remote rural schools and encounter first generation learners, heavy dropouts in upper primary schools, large number of children with special needs, a majority of children belonging to disadvantaged groups, a variety of departmental programmes aimed at enhancing enrolment and participation, lack of effective community support, and above all a multi-cultural and multi-lingual environment which baffles them. The teachers are least prepared to handle such situations.
9. Existing graduates, even from central universities are poorly prepared for teaching jobs.

IN-SERVICE TEACHER EDUCATION IN INDIA

In-service education is a requisite professional support for teachers during their career; in fact, it ought to be indispensable. During a teacher's long service, requirements keep changing continuously as they are influenced by changes in policy, priorities, technology, society, etc. Hence, providing timely and continuous in-service education was felt to be a necessity in order to keep the teachers abreast of the changes taking place in their professional environment as well as to develop their skills and attitudes to keep step with these changes.

The objectives of in-service teacher education are:

(a) To develop knowledge, skills and attitudes required by a teacher to function as a competent professional.
(b) To afford the teacher opportunity for professional growth suited to his individual background, aptitude, talent and choice.

Periodic in-service programmes provide the required support in improving the teachers' knowledge and skills in addition to improving their motivation levels. As teachers get exposed to new techniques of teaching and evaluation, the health of the school system too gets toned, thus bringing about more efficacy into it as a whole.

Out of 53 lakh full-time teachers (in primary, upper primary, secondary and senior secondary sectors), in-service training programmes are needed to be designed for at least 15 lakh teachers who have completed ten-years of service and would continue in the system for a long time.

Recommendations of Various Commissions

The University Education Commission and Secondary Education Commission emphasized the need for quality improvement and diversification of teacher training courses. The Kothari Commission felt the 'need for the organization of a large-scale, systematic and coordinated programme of in-service education in every five-years of a teacher's service'.

Until NPE 1986, support to the teacher in the area of in-service elementary education was largely provided at national and state level institutions like NCERT, NIEPA and SCERTs. But they could do very little in the area of in-service education, as they had very limited reach as well as resources. Also, no clear cut policies and priorities for in-service education were in place. There was no systematic identification of teachers' needs. The content and quality of programmes offered were generally poor. Several states experimented with the concept of 'Teacher's Centres' by establishing them in larger towns. However, these centres turned out to be meeting places for teachers of neighbouring schools.

The coverage under the in-service education programmes was found to be extremely limited. In view of the huge number of teachers as well as logistical and financial constraints, the states organized programmes for durations and in limited frequencies that was feasible with the resources available to them. In the case of many states, in-service education was not a priority at all.

Central Scheme of Restructuring and Reorganization of Teacher Education

After adoption of NPE 1986 in pursuance of its provisions of teacher education, a CSS of 'Restructuring and Reorganization of Teacher Education' was approved in October, 1987, by the GOI. The five components of this scheme were:

(a) Setting up of DIETs to organize pre-service and in-service courses for elementary school teachers and for personnel working in non-formal and adult education sectors.

(b) Strengthening of about 250 secondary teacher education institutions – about 50 of them as Institutes of Advanced Study in Education (IASE) and the remaining 200 as Colleges of Teacher Education (CTEs).
(c) Mass orientation of about five lakh school teachers annually to make them aware of their role in the context of the new policy thrusts, and to improve their professional competence under the supervision of NCERT.
(d) Strengthening and revitalization of SCERTs.
(e) Establishment and strengthening of 'Departments of Education' in universities through the UGC.

The programme of Mass Orientation of School Teachers (MOST) was commenced immediately after adoption of NPE in May, 1986. About 13.5 lakh teachers were covered under it during the first three-years. The programme was also geared towards child-centred education and use of materials supplied to primary schools under OB.

District Institutes of Education & Training (DIETs)

As a part of the policy of overhauling the teacher education system, the NPE and POA envisaged a district level academic structure in the form of a DIET. This was meant to provide adequate functional autonomy – academic, administrative and financial – to teacher education institutions. It was expected that DIETs would cover the entire country, be accountable to clearly defined objectives and norms, and provide better quality academic support to teachers positioned in districts. This was designed as a 'Central Sector Scheme' with 100 per cent central assistance.

A draft of the guidelines for implementing the programme was circulated to the states in 1987. When DIETs were envisaged, data from the fifth All India Education Survey was taken into consideration. According to it, the total elementary teacher population in the country was 27.9 lakhs (1986 figures), which yielded an average per district population of 6,200. However, after taking into consideration, the smaller districts in north-eastern states, Kashmir, Sikkim and some of the UTs, the GOI chose to fix a minimum norm of 2,500 elementary teachers in a revenue district for purposes of establishing a DIET.

It was also stipulated that to become eligible for central assistance under this scheme, the states had to phase out sub-standard elementary TTIs. They were also asked to launch time bound action plans for training of untrained teachers and stop recruitment of untrained and under-qualified teachers.

The DIET scheme was very ambitious in its vision that comprised a team of 21 well-qualified professionals, housed in well-equipped and spacious training institutions, giving academic leadership to the district. Different states approached the DIET scheme with different levels of speed and priority. Hence, the establishment of these institutions was uneven across states. While states like Kerala, TN, AP utilized the support effectively, others like Bihar and UP were slow in setting up these institutions. In the first three-years, a total of 216 DIETs were set up in the country.

DIETs – Mission and Role

DIETs were expected to play a pace-setting role in the areas of elementary and adult education, involving three major functions – training (both induction level as well as continuing varieties), resource support and action research. They were envisaged to provide academic resource support at the grass roots level for the success of various strategies and programmes with the following objectives:

(a) Universalization of Primary/Elementary Education.
(b) NLM targets with respect to functional literacy in the 15-35 age group.

DIETs were supposed to function in a cohesive and comprehensive manner towards teacher development and undertake curriculum and material development in close co-ordination with other state institutions, BRCs, CRCs and schools. As far as curriculum transaction was concerned, they were expected to design programmes that were based on the needs of participants and with a child-centred approach. Participants were to be enabled to experiment, discover, learn, practice and innovate for themselves in addition to making use of the local environment in the learning process.

DIETs – Linkages

DIETs were expected to establish close linkages with:

(a) 'The field', i.e., elementary schools, teachers, head teachers, school complexes, supervisors, project officers of AE and NFE along with district level officers working in these sectors.
(b) National level institutions like NCERT (including the Regional Institutes of Education), NIEPA, CCRT, CIIL, Regional Institutes of English/IASE, etc.
(c) State level academic institutions – SCERT, SRC for Adult Education, Directorate of Adult Education, etc.
(d) District level institutions such as those involved in higher education and secondary teacher training, CTEs, local radio networks, university departments of education, NGOs working in the area of elementary education and AE, etc.

The linkages were to be established through a close, meaningful and continuous dialogue in which institutions shared problems, experiences, achievements, information and resources. Additionally, DIETs could contribute as an agency for implementing programmes of some of the national and state level institutions.

Functions of DIETs

The major task of the DIETs was to offer superior quality in-service and pre-service programmes for primary school teachers and personnel of AE and NFE. Accordingly, they were required to take up initial and incumbent teacher training, plan and manage all training programmes in the district, take up research and development (R&D) projects, curriculum and material development work, coordinate innovative activities, provide support to schools in conducting work experience activities, train teachers in use of education technology, develop low cost and no-cost gadgets, undertake evaluation, action research, etc.

Organizational Structure of a DIET

The DIET guidelines suggested the following seven branches for greater operational convenience and manageability:

(a) Pre-service Teacher Education (PSTE)
(b) Work Experience (WE)
(c) District Resource Unit (DRU) for AE and NFE
(d) In-service programmes, Field Interaction and Innovation Coordination (IFIC)
(e) Curriculum, Material Development and Evaluation (CMDE)
(f) Education Technology (ET)
(g) Planning and Management (P&M).

The principal of the DIET was expected to coordinate the activities of all the seven branches that were supposed to work closely to realize the goals and performance norms of the entire DIET. The inter-dependence of branches was very necessary because generally, most programmes and activities of a DIET would involve more than one branch. States were given flexibility to design different models by regrouping disciplines that might give rise to larger or smaller number of branches in the DIET. However, not all states followed this seven-branch set up.

The DRU was given a special status in the scheme of things as it was accorded functional autonomy within the DIET. It was supposed to establish direct linkages with national, state and district level organizations working in the field of AE/NFE.

The DIET guidelines suggested three-weeks of a 'main' in-service programme along with a number of shorter duration theme-specific programmes. DIETs were supposed to identify the training needs of teachers of different categories, i.e., primary, upper primary, subject-teachers, language teachers, etc.

The state governments were given central assistance for starting the DIETs, which was as follows:

(a) In districts where government elementary TTIs existed, one such institution was to be upgraded as a DIET.
(b) If no such institution existed, a new DIET could be started in that district.

Table 5.1 Average Norms of Central Assistance Rs (In lakhs)

Category of Projects	Average Norms of Central Assistance		
	For civil works	For equipment	Total
Upgradation of Institutions	40.00	10.00	50.00
New Institutions	64.00	13.00	77.00

Source: DIET Guidelines MHRD

In order to implement the above scheme, the states/UTs were asked to:

(a) Constitute a task force for establishing DIETs in their respective states.
(b) Prepare a 'Perspective Plan' for elementary teacher education.
(c) Estimate the demand for and supply of trained elementary teachers.

(d) Identify and phase out sub-standard elementary TTIs.
(e) Finalize the model and organizational structure of DIETs to be established.
(f) Prepare a complete 'Project Document' for each DIET and 'Action Plan' for establishing DIETs.
(g) Prepare an 'Action Plan' for conducting in-service programmes.
(h) Approve proposals put forth in the 'State Level Empowered Committee' (SLEC).
(i) Establish 'State Level Steering and Monitoring Committees' for reviewing the implementation of DIET proposals.
(j) Get an external evaluation of the performance of selected DIETs by NCERT and SCERTs.

Important Issues relating to DIETs

Spread over two decades and four plan periods, as many as 556 DIETs and District Resource Centres (DRCs) were set up across the country for overall quality improvement in elementary education in the districts. But, only 446 institutions came to be functional. In most of the states they were strengthened by upgrading existing elementary TTIs. The following were important issues relating to DIETs:

- Uneven development of DIETs across the country and large variations among them within states.
- Even after many years, DIETs, BRCs and CRCs did not become statutory institutions in most of the states. This diluted their impact on teachers because they were perceived to be toothless when it came to questioning teachers' accountability in innovation, student assessment or learning outcomes.
- In many states, absence of qualified teacher educators in adequate numbers led to a routine placement of 'Education Service Officers' in these institutions.
- DIET guidelines only provided for teacher educators and hence, primary school teachers could not become members of the DIET faculty.
- Understaffing and lack of several requirements – state government's priority and ownership of DIETs, rigours in the selection process, a defined role through the 'State Education Acts', mobility and linkages with cluster, block and state level institutions – interfered with the effective functioning of DIETs in most states.
- The existing TTIs (in the districts) for primary education came to be neglected with all the focus shifting to the new institutions.
- Very few states created separate cadres of 'education service' for research and training.
- In most states, administrative and academic posts were interchangeable, which resulted in academic institutions like SCERTs, DIETs and BRCs becoming a dumping ground for unwanted officers from the field.

Hence, DIETs could not emerge as fully empowered institutions as envisaged by NPE. The CSS of teacher education, revised in 2004, intended to improve the quality of programmes undertaken by DIETs, CTEs, IASEs and SCERTs which, in turn, were supposed to play a nodal role in improving quality of education. These efforts were to be supported by national level apex institutions like NCERT, NIEPA and NCTE.

According to the revised scheme, states formulated plans for the Tenth Plan in accordance with their actual needs, and central funding was made available as per these plans. During all these plan periods, a total of 556 DIETs, 124 CTEs and 31 IASEs were set up till 2006 for overall quality improvement in education.

Evaluation Studies on the Functioning of DIETs

The scheme was evaluated in all the states under the coordination of NIEPA. DIETs could be classified into three categories – fully operational, partially operational and non-functional. Evaluation studies undertaken on the activities of these institutions indicated that:

- The objectives with which they were started had not been realized. There were no clear perspectives about their roles and functions.
- They lacked vision; also, states did not have a sense of ownership as these institutions were seen essentially as central government initiatives.
- Very few state governments followed strict criteria for selection. Large-scale vacancies continued in many states even many years after the programme was initiated.
- These institutions failed to emerge as centres of academic excellence in most districts.
- Wherever DIETs were operational, the seven branches considered themselves to be water-tight departments. Some branches like Curriculum and Material Development, P&M, WE, did not have any well-defined tasks at the DIET level.
- Though most of the DIETs offered pre-service and in-service programmes for elementary teachers, other tasks were either absent or not the focus activity of these institutions.
- DIETs also failed to effectively establish interdependent and mutually reinforcing vertical and horizontal working relationship with reputed professional organizations and institutions at various levels.

Thus almost all the DIETs in the country fell short of achieving the mission set out for them. The Eleventh Plan document noted that 'DIETs have been facing an identity crisis' as 'Centres of Excellence'. The academic ethos of most of them continued to be depressing and unsatisfactory in spite of effecting structural changes in their administrative functioning. The Planning Commission stated that they 'have not justified their existence in terms of outcomes in spite of their existence for over two decades'.

Tenth Plan Review of 'Teacher Education Scheme'

The Tenth Plan 'Working Group Report on Education' identified 'Teacher Education' as a specific focus area. Though the plan emphasized teacher education as a whole, the thrust was on expanding facilities for in-service training of teachers. Institutional development, qualitative improvements in teacher training, professional development of teacher educators, enhanced learner achievement levels, and increased involvement of resource institutions in qualitative development of teacher education were the highlights of the scheme.

Gaps in Teacher Education Sector

The mid-term review identified the following gaps in the sector:

- Absence of a specialized cadre of teacher educators in teacher education institutions.
- Appointment of teacher educators with academic qualifications in violation of norms prescribed by NCTE.
- Low academic profile and capacity of DIET faculty.
- Replacement of DIETs' in-service programmes by in-service programmes for para-teachers, thereby decimating the future potential for quality education in concerned states.
- Annual intake of D.Ed. students being doubled without simultaneous enhancement of faculty strength.
- Lack of coordination between multiple authorities – SCERT, DIET, SSA, NIEPA, NCERT, NCTE, etc.
- The vision of DIETs, CTEs and IASEs as was articulated in MHRD scheme being realized only to a limited extent due to various reasons.

The review identified a series of interventions that had to be undertaken immediately:

- Establishing a separate cadre of teacher educators with university-based designations in SCERT/CTEs/DIETs.
- Modifying policy guidelines to enable direct recruitment of teacher educators.
- Giving top-priority to filling up of vacant posts of teacher educators in DIETs, CTEs and IASEs.
- Restructuring SCERTs, IASEs, CTEs and DIETs so that they could perform their perceived roles and functions.
- Establishing networking and coordination mechanism between teacher education institutions at state/national level institutions.
- Instituting professional development mechanisms for teacher educators.
- NCTE to evolve a mechanism to stop proliferation of poor quality private TTIs in various states.

Redesigning of the Organizational Structure of DIETs

The Eleventh Plan document visualizes DIETs as transformative learning institutions in the area of elementary education and elementary teacher education. It calls for reformulating the branches of the DIETs to meet the present needs of elementary schools and teachers. Each DIET faculty would have to acquire skills and knowledge to play multiple roles of a researcher, a pre-service and in-service trainer, material developer, district level decision-maker, etc.

Hence, the Eleventh Plan envisages upgrading DIETs to the status of undergraduate colleges (with a new vision, mission and a clearly-defined role and function), on par with secondary teacher education colleges. This step would attract individuals with a good academic record towards elementary teacher education apart from strengthening the R&D role of the DIETs. It would also provide greater autonomy to these institutions. Additionally, it is necessary to identify the critical need to develop a separate cadre of teacher educators in DIETs.

Proposed Structural Reorganization of DIETs

According to the Eleventh Plan document, the proposed revised structure would have the following units:

- Teacher Development and Foundation of Education (Pre-service, in-service and extension).
- Curriculum/pedagogic studies (science, mathematics, environmental and social studies, language, arts, heritage crafts and resource centres).
- Survey and Technological support services.
- Library, Documentation and Material Development.

Further, the document proposes distribution of the academic staff of the DIETs in terms of disciplines (proposed staff number given in brackets):

- Foundation of Education (psychology, sociology, philosophy, political science and linguistics – 06)
- Language (English, regional and mother tongue – 04)
- Science (natural science and physical science – 04)
- Mathematics (03)
- Social Science (03)
- Art Education and Theatre (02)
- Visiting faculty (02).

Establishment of Academic Resource Centres: BRCs and CRCs

The process of decentralization of the academic support structures was further extended through the establishment of BRCs and CRCs that are of recent origin. Having started with the Andhra Pradesh Primary Education Programme in the early 1990s, it expanded to the 252 districts of the DPEP (between 1994-2003), and then was universalized through the SSA. The main function of these sub-district level institutions was capacity building of teachers.

BRCs were set up for planning, management and supervision of in-service training of primary school teachers and other functionaries at the grass roots level. They helped in creating groups of resource persons and subject experts in each education block. Being active participants, they were able to organize various types of training programmes for head teachers, teachers cluster coordinators, members of SDMCs and NGOs under the overall direction of the DIETs. Some BRCs also acted as an academic bridge between DIETs and teachers.

CRCs were set up to provide direct academic resource support to primary teachers in a cluster of schools. Originally, each cluster consisted of 10-15 schools with 40-50 teachers. The CRC provided information about the extent to which departmental programmes were being implemented.

During the DPEP period, 414 BRCs and 5,224 CRCs were set up across the country. Since DPEP and other EFA projects were not in operation in all the districts of the country, the non-project districts were denied such sub-district level academic structures. SSA remedied this situation by establishing them in the remaining districts so that ultimately, the number of BRCs and CRCs in the country rose to 7,422 and 70,735 respectively. These centres played a crucial role in conducting teacher training, monthly teacher meetings, school visits, action research and school improvement initiatives in their areas.

However, in almost all states, the BRC locations are based on revenue blocks instead of education blocks. In several cases, one BRC caters to more than two education blocks resulting in heavy work load. In many states, the CRCs have been further burdened with administrative issues and collection of school data, thereby reducing their effectiveness as academic teacher support structures.

The block and cluster centres in most of the states are managed by teachers and therefore pose the challenge of peer group extending academic support.

In-service Training in DPEP Districts

DPEP made an earnest attempt to get feedback from teachers on gaps in the existing training programmes and the type of training they require. During the experience – sharing workshops, questions raised by primary school teachers helped trainers develop new methodologies.

The salient features of DPEP training programmes were:

- Evolving of a participatory mode of training.
- Evolving a standard design for teacher training workshops.
- Priority given to capacity building of teachers.
- Institutionalizing in-service training.
- Covering most of the government school teachers in DPEP districts under these programmes.
- Developing several innovative training packages.

SSA Training Programmes

SSA started supplementing the teacher education programme by enhancing their skills, knowledge, attitude and performance on a continuous basis through a wide range of training programmes, academic support mechanisms and exposure to a variety of educational resources. These included:

(a) Teacher Training: Annual refresher training for all in-service teachers (up to 20 days), induction training (up to 30-days) of newly recruited teachers , training of professionally untrained teachers (up to 60 days). Subject-specific training based on innovative practices and distance mode training through EDUSAT satellite system were also taken up.

(b) Teacher Grants: Each teacher was provided an annual grant of Rs500 for developing locally relevant teaching-learning aids.

(c) Access to Resources: Teachers and teacher educators were given access to a wide range of resource centres, resource persons, resource materials, on a continuous basis through seminars, workshops and academic visits.

(d) Constitution of Resource Groups: Resource groups were constituted at different levels for planning quality improvement strategies and their sustenance.

Distance Education Programmes

DPEP started distance education projects aimed at reaching out to teachers and teacher educators through radio and satellite-based teleconferencing networks. These were operated through cooperation of various national and state level institutions like IGNOU, NCERT, SAC and SCERTs. Distance education is slowly emerging as an effective means of providing academic support to school teachers on a continuing basis.

State Councils of Educational Research & Training (SCERTs)

State Institutes of Education (SIE)/SCERTs were set up in different states/UTs to improve the quality of school education. At present there are 24 SCERTs and 9 SIEs. (Refer Annexure VIII – Table 24). Only the recently created state of Jharkhand, and UTs of Daman & Diu, Dadar & Nagar Haveli, and Lakshadweep, have neither an SCERT nor an SIE. Academic functions in these states and UTs are performed by the Departments of Education.

SCERTs are expected to plan and organize in-service education programmes and extension programmes for all categories of educational personnel. The other functions include development of curriculum, instructional material, textbooks, supplementary material as well as undertaking research programmes.

The NPE and POA envisaged additional roles and functions for these state-level apex organizations in order to make them state-level nodal agencies. They were expected to guide, support and assist state departments of education and function as state resource institutions to provide academic support to all stages of education. They were expected to coordinate all academic matters relating to school education and maintain appropriate linkages with other educational organizations. Apart from these, they were supposed to look after, supervise and support the district and sub-district level academic institutions.

Funds were provided under various Five Year Plans to strengthen the SCERTs and help them discharge the above roles and functions.

Autonomy of SCERTs

Most of the SCERTs do not enjoy autonomy. However, those of Gujarat, HP, Kerala, Delhi and MP states are presently autonomous, and have shown better results in academic matters.

A majority of SCERTs do not have the liberty to function freely; the purpose for which they have been established is hardly served. Functioning as branches of respective government departments, their freedom to take up academic programmes that the states need is curbed. Some SCERTs like the one in West Bengal do not even have permanent academic faculty except the Director. There is a proposal to convert them into autonomous and apex bodies – it is hoped that this move will enhance their accountability as they will be able to carry out their functions professionally.

Key Concerns in In-service Teacher Education Sector

A majority of the in-service teacher education programmes in the country face a number of problems. Some of them are detailed below:

1. Need assessments are not made before organizing in-service programmes.
2. No opportunity is provided for professional development of working teachers, supervisory staff and educational administrators.
3. There is a need to enhance the content knowledge of in-service teachers.
4. Content and pedagogy are taught separately.
5. The in-service programmes have little impact on teaching-learning and classroom processes.
6. There is no scientific basis for evaluation of the current in-service programmes as well as the assessment of their impact on the quality of classroom transactions.

Vision and Strategy for the Eleventh Plan

In order to reform the process and delivery of the teacher education programme, the Eleventh Plan envisages bringing the various programmes in the context of school education under one umbrella called the 'national system of teacher education'. This calls for a relook into the structures, systems and training processes of DIETs, CTEs, IASEs, and SCERTs.

The shift in the conceptualization of the role of the teacher by NCF 2005 has crucial implications for the aims, content and methodology of teacher education. The following matters need to be addressed:

- Restructuring of SCERTs/CTEs/DIETs/IASEs so that they will play a more active role in the academic institutions in their respective areas.
- Revamping the entire teacher education programme to make it more relevant to teachers' needs in the classroom.
- Providing adequate on-the-job support to new teachers.
- Formulating special strategies to train para-teachers and other unqualified teachers to attain professional standards.

- Empowering teachers and teacher educators to use ICT as a tool. Easy electronic access to curriculum and TLM ,and use of ICT in training of student-teachers are necessary.
- Augmenting the infrastructure and resources of teacher education institutions.
- Establishing a separate cadre of teacher educators in SCERTs/CTEs/DIETs.
- Establishing institutional twinning arrangements with university/college departments and teacher education institutions.
- Addressing teacher specialization in crucial areas such as science, mathematics and languages.
- Taking a policy decision to increase intake of student-teachers in certain subjects to combat the shortage of candidates.
- Introducing innovative models in pre-service education programmes.
- Formulating long-term internship in pre-service teacher education programmes, which is an urgent necessity.
- Periodically evaluating the impact of in-service programmes on students' learning achievement.

Scheme of Establishing Schools of Education

The Teacher Education Scheme document for the Eleventh Plan has pointed out the following important issues with regard to IASEs:

- Since 1987 only 31 IASEs were established against the proposed target of 50. While their distribution was disproportionate in some states, not a single IASE was established in 10 states.
- They were basically perceived as institutions providing in-service training to teacher educators but a majority were not involved in any such activity.
- A majority did not undertake systematic annual planning. In-service training programmes were organized at short notice and were not need based.
- The research function of an IASE – expected to be of an advanced level and interdisciplinary in order to contextualize training and other inputs – had become the weakest component with a majority undertaking very few research studies. Even those that were undertaken were found to be inadequate in terms of nature and quality.
- Lack of capability and academic/technical support, limited linkages and interactions with DIETs, CTEs and other educational institutions associated with primary, elementary and secondary stages of education – these could be the reasons behind poor attempts at research.
- Even though majority of IASEs had programme advisory committees, they did not have functional autonomy and rarely met. They simply endorsed the activities chalked out by the departments.
- The fund flow from the centre to the state and from the states to the IASEs continued to be a problem area. In many cases, funds reached IASEs by the financial year end, hardly serving the purpose.

- Variation in staff pattern (only some IASEs had full-time staff) and vacant posts in teaching and staff positions affected the quality of teacher training in most states.

Hence the document proposed that all existing IASEs, 5 RIEs of NCERT and Education Departments of 25 selected universities were to be converted into Schools of Education, (60 in number) which were expected to perform the following functions:

- Experiment with and design innovative programmes for teacher educators at post graduate (M.A. in Education/M.Ed.) and M.Phil levels.
- Undertake R&D with a focus on policy research, evaluative studies and research in the areas of curriculum, pedagogy, evaluation and assessment.
- Design innovative models of in-service and continuing education for teacher educators.
- Develop textual materials and conduct integrated courses in the area of elementary and secondary teacher education.
- Function as a school of continuing education for the faculty of DIETs/CTEs and IASEs.

The document proposed the Schools of Education to have four following centres:

- Centre for Education of Teacher Educators and Pre-service Teacher Education.
- Centre for Curriculum and Pedagogic Studies.
- Centre for In-service and Continuing Education.
- Centre for Educational Technology and ICT.

Apart from undertaking pre-service teacher education (PG/Diploma/Certificate Courses) and research programmes, they were expected to take up interdisciplinary and multidisciplinary collaborative research programmes.

The document also proposed establishment of an 'Inter-school Centre' at the national level under the UGC to help coordinate the activities of Schools of Education for redesigning the curricula for teacher education at different levels. The mandate of this centre was to provide a level specific yet integrated focus on elementary and secondary stages of education.

Strengthening In-service Teacher Training Programmes

The Eleventh Plan focuses on upgrading the content and pedagogical knowledge of teachers, and expose them to newer perspectives on pedagogy. According to various reports, there are serious deficiencies in basic mathematical concepts and skills, language abilities and especially, communication skills of teachers. The document expects every state to take immediate measures for providing in-service training to all teachers, and strengthening the ongoing programmes under SSA as well as other in-service training programmes.

Improvement of Quality of Teacher Education

Some of the recommendations for improving the quality of practising teachers were:

- Providing grants to school improvement projects
- Providing incentives to better performing schools
- Setting standards for teaching performance
- Evaluating teachers
- Raising the pay of teachers
- Establishing a system of incentives to good teachers
- Establishing subject teacher groups.

Some form of performance assessment of the present day teachers is required. This will go a long way in not only identifying good teachers but also motivating them to rise above themselves. This necessitates a study and analysis of present day practices, identifying good ones and emulating them. In-service professional development needs to be provided to all teachers depending on their requirements.

Policies that address problems of teachers need to be established: improving working conditions (PTRs, providing TLM, in-school support, etc.) providing professional development and promotional opportunities which satisfy teachers emotionally, and improving their compensation package from time to time.

Special Training Programmes in Languages

NCF 2005 emphasized the significant role that language and communication skills play in teaching. There is overwhelming support for education in the mother tongue as it is considered best for the mental and overall development of children. It has been observed that acquisition of skills in English would be strengthened in the later primary years by the acquisition of early literacy skills in the mother tongue. However, a significant improvement in the teaching and learning of English in all schools is crucial for bringing about quality in education.

NCF 2005 strongly recommended multilingual classrooms, reflecting the social reality of a rapidly changing economy, which encouraged mobility. Hence, the Eleventh Plan proposed a CSS for enhancing language competencies and skills in general. It recommended a minimum three-week in-service training programme to be designed in collaboration with CIIL-Mysore, CIFL-Hyderabad, IGNOU and other national and state institutions.

Professional Development of Para-teachers

The concept of para-teachers has been accepted by several state governments due to the policy of several states appointing untrained teachers with varied qualifications. Though a 60-day training programme has been proposed for para-teachers under SSA, there is a dire necessity to enhance their professional development as such a programme cannot compensate the knowledge, pedagogy and practice that a student-teacher gains in a two-year teacher training course.

Hence, the Eleventh Plan visualized all open universities to collaborate with TTIs to evolve a distance-cum-contact mode of training para-teachers professionally.

Teacher Education Programmes for North-eastern Region

The status of teacher education is very depressing in the north-eastern region. A majority of SCERTs/CTEs and DIETs are neither operational nor functional. Some of the existing DIETs offer only in-service training programmes with no provision for pre-service teacher education programmes. The Eleventh Plan document advocated strengthening SCERTs and DIETs in this region. It proposed taking up training of teachers through teleconferencing using EDUSAT to clear the backlog of untrained and under-qualified teachers, particularly in the areas of language, science and mathematics.

IGNOU in collaboration with NCERT had developed and introduced a primary teacher education programme for these teachers from 1999. Since the study material was in English, it was not a success. Hence, the Eleventh Plan proposed to develop the study material in local-specific languages to reach out to more teachers so that they could enhance their competencies. Programmes for upgrading the content and pedagogical knowledge were also planned.

Having discussed in detail the status of teacher education in India in the course of this chapter, one realizes that this sub-sector is the weakest link among all other sub-sectors and it cannot work in isolation – it needs proper and sustainable linkages with other sub-sectors contained within the education sector. Qualitative improvement of the teacher education sub-sector will certainly have a beneficial impact on other sub-sectors as well.

6

Quality Concerns in Elementary Education

INTRODUCTION

The sixth goal enunciated at Dakar aims at 'Improving every aspect of the quality of education, and ensuring excellence so that recognized and measurable learning outcomes are achieved by all, especially in literacy, numeracy and essential life-skills.'

'Quality' is an attribute, which is distinctive and connotes excellence. It is based on diverse parameters all of which must be individually and collectively ensured for high levels of attainment. Quality concerns in education have assumed immense importance in the light of poor academic achievement by students. This along with lack of proper training in soft skills reduces the employability of those who step out of the system seeking employment.

There is unanimous agreement among educationists today that the quality of elementary education in almost all parts of the country is questionable. The large-scale expansion of primary education facilities across the country has led to varying quality not only among students passing out but also in terms of institutional infrastructure and teaching-learning processes. Significant variations in quality are found at various levels between government and private schools; at the inter state and intra state levels, between forward-backward regions, rural-urban areas, and so on. Massive efforts to create a vast network of primary schools in the country had not initially taken into consideration quality concerns and achievement of learners.

Factors Influencing a Child's Learning

The quality of a child's learning depends on several factors:

- The child – its innate ability, intelligence, age, gender, etc.
- The teacher – his/her age and gender, qualification, experience, training, etc.
- The school – the type of school, infrastructure and quality of facilities available, quality of learning, learning ability of the peer group, collective performance of all the students, etc.

- The family – its background, the socio-economic condition, parents' education, their contribution to the child's learning, etc.

Perception of 'Quality'

Education accounts for a significant proportion of public and private sector spending in the country with the extent of employment that it generates being substantial. School education is also considered to be an element of micro-economic reform as there is a constant need to meet the ever changing demands of the workplace in the context of globalization of the world economy. Hence, the public as well as governments find it necessary to continually assess the performance (or effectiveness) of school education. This calls for finding out how effective our education system is, what quality of education is it delivering, how it can be improved so that the gains can be harvested by the beneficiaries in real life.

The assessment of quality in education has both objective and subjective dimensions. In assessing the quality of educational services, inputs and processes, long-term objectives are found to be more relevant than short-term ones not that the latter can be ignored. Views, opinions and individual perceptions are as valuable as conclusions based on quantitative information. For instance, in the perception of parents, private schools generally score over government ones and 'English medium' schools over other language medium ones. Such a large-scale perception needs to be taken note of by the authorities concerned when they frame policies or try to infuse efficacy into the system.

'Quality' defies definition. It is relative in nature and cannot be absolute. However, one can arrive at certain indicators or criteria to determine quality. An important indicator of 'quality' of a student as perceived by parents, teachers, educational administrators and the society at large, is the 'marks' (or 'grade' in some states) scored by a student or the 'class' obtained by him/her in an examination. However, this cannot be taken in isolation as a measure of quality. Similarly, an indicator of 'quality' of a school, as it is discerned by many, is the percentage of passes/percentage of first classes obtained by it in a 'public' examination. Thus, learning achievement becomes an important measure of quality education. It is closely linked to school efficiency because the promotion, repetition and school dropout rates are directly linked to the learning achievement of the students.

Other popularly perceived indicators of quality are – the discipline in an institution, quality of teaching, infrastructure facilities provided, reputation enjoyed by the institution, the qualification and reputation of teachers, the number of prizes won by students in co-curricular activities, etc.

Thus, one can see that arriving at a clear cut definition of an 'effective school' or a 'system' is rather challenging, probably impossible. Notwithstanding this aspect, one must still persevere and discuss what constitutes 'quality schooling' and find ways of measuring and improving it. Concerns about quality of school education as well as its monitoring and assessment has been a high priority issue of late.

Quality of Learning in Government Schools

Following the 'World Declaration of Education for All' at Jomtein in 1991, the country prepared a 'Plan of Action' in order to achieve the EFA goals: universal primary education and literacy, policies to promote basic and primary education, and attainment of education for all. However, in its single-minded efforts to expand the school system and provide access to every child, the government to a considerable extent overlooked quality aspects. This resulted in standards deteriorating over a period of time in government schools. While the reasons for this are many, some of them are mentioned below:

- Progress of children in government schools at the primary stage is mostly due to the no-detention policy. Though little learning takes place, they are simply pushed through grades. In fact, a number of studies reveal that children in classes 3 and 4 are not even able to read and write simple sentences.
- The social composition of government school children indicates that they are mostly from families of first generation learners and belong to the poorest of households and socially disadvantaged groups.
- Quality schools require constant on-site support for teacher development, student assessment and academic innovation. Institutions have been established at national, state, district, block and cluster levels to meet this need for institutional excellence. But these institutions are mostly managed by teacher educators who themselves do not have experience in primary school teaching.

Despite a number of programmes including SSA, data shows that student performance in government schools is far from satisfactory and the norm of 80 per cent of children attaining mastery levels remains a distant dream.

'ASER' data reveals that at the national level, the percentage of children in classes 3 to 5 in government schools who can read class 2 texts has hardly changed in the last three-years – 35 per cent in 2006, 37 per cent in 2007 and 36 per cent in 2008. ASER also found that:

- Children whose mothers did not attend school achieved a far lower level of reading proficiency than children whose mothers did,
- Within the category of children whose mothers did not attend school, girls achieved consistently less than boys.

Issues at the Upper Primary Stage

As one progresses to the upper primary stage, one senses the need for more serious attention to various pressing matters. Subject diversification along with an enriched curriculum is the focus at this stage. A third language (usually hindi in non-hindi states) is introduced and teachers are not equipped to handle it. The dropout rates at this stage are still high. The elementary teachers (who are general teachers as opposed to subject teachers) with class 10 or class 12 qualification are unable to handle individual enriched subjects. Several states have attempted to induct graduate teachers at this stage to overcome this problem.

Important Factors Affecting 'Quality'

If publicly funded institutions are to be made more accountable, it would require a stronger thrust on assessment of quality. The quality of a school depends on a variety of factors:

- Quality of school infrastructure
- Quality of students at the entry level
- Social and family backgrounds of students
- Quality teachers who are highly motivated
- Regular teacher attendance in the school
- Quality of curricular content
- Competency-based textbooks, workbooks and quality TLM
- Minimum teaching standards and classroom transaction processes
- Minimum achievement levels of pupils
- Quality and level of evaluation systems
- Quality of supervision prevalent in the system
- Pupil-teacher ratios
- The inevitable multigrade teaching that is rampant in a majority of government schools.

The outcome of all this has to be seen in students when they complete their stay in the school. Thus, the quality of a school can also be estimated by the extent of knowledge, skills and the kind of attitudes the students acquire during their stay in it.

The sub-sector study report on Elementary Education in Karnataka (2001) listed some more factors affecting quality:

1. Low quality of teaching that affects retention of children especially in government schools.
2. Inadequate teacher preparation and lack of quality training to handle all subjects in multigrade situations.
3. Inadequately qualified and trained teacher-educators with no experience of handling primary classes are today training our student teachers, thus affecting the quality of teachers coming out of the elementary training institutions.
4. Low quality of textbooks and inadequate instructional materials that have affected the quality of classroom transactions.
5. Poor performance of students in English, science and mathematics in upper primary and secondary classes is also a factor affecting quality.
6. Unreliable examination system and improper evaluation procedures for assessment of students' performance.
7. Teacher absenteeism and lack of instruction in a particular subject for long periods of time when teachers go on a long leave.
8. Low achievers opting for teachers' jobs which affects quality of education in schools.

Infrastructure and Human Resources

Adequacy and appropriateness of infrastructure and human resources determine the quality of an education system to a very large extent. Unfortunately a majority of states suffer from a lack of basic infrastructure and human resources. The PROBE (1999) survey, for instance, made the following observations with respect to government schools:

(a) Only a fourth of the sample schools had at least two teachers, two all-weather classrooms, and some teaching aids.

(b) At the time of the investigator's visit, one-third of the headmasters were absent, one-third of the schools had a single-teacher present, and about half of the schools had no teaching activity.

(c) In many schools students were systematically neglected.

These observations indicate serious flaws and deficiencies in the schooling process. Several initiatives under SSA have made attempts to remedy them.

Pupil-Teacher Ratio (PTR)

A high PTR means less time for a teacher to provide individual attention. It may also result in one teacher handling more than one class at a time, thus resulting in multigrade situations.

It has been observed that PTR varies widely across the country. (Refer Annexure VIII – Table 45). Even within a state, the PTR may not be uniform across districts or even within a district. For example, in a state like Karnataka, even though the state PTR is around 30, four educationally backward districts – Yadgir, Raichur, Koppal and Bellary– have a high PTR which is again higher than the state average. This shows the inefficiency in the distribution of teachers' posts across districts. Even within a district, usually urban schools have a lower PTR as teachers prefer to work here and tend to get transferred accordingly. Teacher position in remote and rural areas is generally not very encouraging.

High teacher absenteeism is also a factor affecting the daily teacher strength in a school. The 2004 World Bank Survey (Refer Annexure VIII – Table 6) has analysed this issue of teacher absenteeism in schools across states. According to it, even when teachers are present in a school, the percentage of teaching activity is only to the extent of 50 per cent on an average. Lack of motivation and positive/negative incentives is an important reason for teacher absenteeism.

Impact of No-detention Policy

The no-detention policy is followed in the lower primary classes in most of the states and is also recently enunciated in the 'Right of Children to Free and Compulsory Education Act', 2009. This could result in children reaching class 8 without achieving the expected learning outcomes at any level or class. The present policy of no-detention followed by most state governments at the primary level often conceals the actual progress of pupils as, irrespective of their achievement, children are promoted.

Assessment of Quality

During the last few decades, education systems throughout the world have been subject to considerable reforms and change in an effort to improve quality. The major emphasis has been on the assessment and monitoring of student learning outcomes. Since the 1960s, the students' academic performance is being assessed on a regular basis in many developed countries.

The primary function of education is to facilitate the all round development of the individual. Hence, learning in schools should encompass the development of the desirable cognitive and non-cognitive aspects of the child's personality. Learning outcomes refer to acquisition of both cognitive and non-cognitive competencies which are necessary for the child's overall development. Even though the quality of education is certainly not limited to learning outcomes, achieving high mastery levels is the ultimate objective of any school system.

Assessment of Learning Achievement

In India, assessment of learning achievements began rather late, beginning with the 1990s. The last two decades witnessed a high level of importance and attention given to assessment of learning achievement as a sequel to the guidelines set forth by NPE 1986.

A majority of these assessment programmes employed achievement tests for assessing quality. However, these tests have limitations as they often test facts based on memory rather than a complete understanding of a concept.

In India, schools by and large lay emphasis on the cognitive domain. Cognitive outcomes assessed in achievement surveys refer to a package of knowledge and skills to be attained at a particular stage. They were further elaborated to include competencies which the child was expected to achieve at each level in three subject areas. These competencies were outlined in the MLL document. For children at the primary stage, it became essential that they gain mastery over competencies in reading, writing and numerical operations; otherwise, they would have serious problems at higher levels. Learning achievement surveys have thus focused only on assessing the acquisition of basic skills of literacy and numeracy. There is no systematic effort as yet to assess the non-cognitive areas even though it was stressed by NPE 1986.

One of the first attempts to take up learner assessment was made by Dave's study in 1988, which conducted evaluation of achievement levels of children in classes 1 and 4 in 22 states and UTs in the country. The government's real concern on learner assessment began in 1991 with the specifying of MLLs, followed by limited efforts to assess the status of learner achievement in the country. A large-scale national survey was conducted by NCERT in 1994. A handful of studies with smaller samples were conducted intermittently in different parts of the country.

After 1990s, policy planners realized the importance of assessment data and incorporated the assessment of learning achievement in all the EFA projects in an effort to bring about quality improvement in primary education. Several projects under EFA, notably DPEP, carried out baseline studies to assess the achievement of learners in various primary classes. These surveys tried to assess the basic competencies of children in three curricular areas under the broad framework of MLLs. (Annexure VIII – Tables 16, 34 and 35). While DPEP and Lok Jumbish carried out periodic surveys, DPEP set targets of raising the achievement levels by 25 per cent during the project period. It was found that the improvement in learning levels was not uniform across states or even within a particular state or in a particular subject area. However, not many evaluation studies were undertaken in non-DPEP districts.

Many states focused on grading schools as well as the learning of their children. Examples are the 'Learning Achievement Tracking System' of Orissa, the 'Educational Quality Improvement Programme' of Maharashtra and the 'School Grading Exercise' of Uttarakhand. Often student assessments were linked to remedial teaching as in the case of Maharashtra. A few states like Karnataka took up large-scale programmes for annual assessment of learning achievement among children in selected elementary classes. However, no such regular system of assessment exists at the national level even today.

An Analysis of Some Studies in Learning Achievement

A list of some major studies in learning achievement undertaken across the country and in several states is given in Annexure VII of this book. Generalizations from these studies may be difficult to draw as most of the studies have been conducted at different points in time and in different parts of the country. This was prior to ASER's annual studies – no study was carried out on an all-India basis. However, the findings were illustrative of the existing levels of learning achievement.

Several studies point to the fact that learning achievement in India is generally rather low. Most of the recent studies show that achievement levels at the terminal grades of the primary school are disappointingly low compared to the standards of achievement prescribed by the MLLs. Some of the studies also reveal that achievement levels of class 1 children are reasonably high and their performance tends to decline sharply as they move to higher classes. While tests in class 1 are oral, those in higher classes are written. Children can express themselves orally, but they have difficulty in written communication which affects their achievement levels. Moreover, poor learning levels at a higher stage are also the result of poor quality of classroom transactions.

Several studies exhibit a poorer performance in maths in comparison to language. This was also the case in all these studies where the students were found to perform poorly in maths, irrespective of the state or the medium of instruction.

Rural-Urban Variations

In some states (Arunachal, Orissa, Punjab, Sikkim and UP) there was little variation in the performance between rural and urban students. While in some states like MP, rural children performed better than their urban counterparts, states like AP, Haryana, J&K, Karnataka, Kerala, Maharashtra, WB and Delhi showed exactly the opposite – urban children outsmarted their rural friends. The general tendency was a higher achievement in capital cities than in other parts of the state. However, another set of studies revealed a contrary trend.

Gender Disparities in Learning Achievements

Studies have shown that a common practice followed by parents in urban areas was to send sons to private schools and daughters to government schools. Thus, the share of girl students was found to be greater than that of boy students in many urban government schools. Empirical studies have come up with diverse findings on gender variations in achievement scores.

Several studies showed that even with a high pass percentage in primary classes, the learning outcomes among students of classes 4 and 5 were much below expected levels. Independent studies by Vimala Ramachandran in AP, Karnataka and UP pointed out how children in classes 3 and 4 in many of the schools surveyed could hardly read or write. Pratham's work in urban schools in Maharashtra, Delhi, Patna, Vadodara, etc., also pointed out the inability of a large number of boys and girls in primary classes to read and write simple sentences.

NCERT Assessment Surveys

NCERT also conducted periodic assessment surveys for various primary classes in collaboration with state institutions (like SCERTs and SEBs). One such survey for children of class 5 was conducted in 2000 and another for class 3 in 2003. These surveys constituted a representative sample of students covering 29 states, 111 districts, 5293 schools, 8533 teachers and 92,407 children. Utilizing competency-based achievement tests, they took up three areas for their studies – mathematics, language and EVS.

In class 3, the mean achievement was 58.25 in mathematics and 63.12 in language. In class 5, it was 46.51 in maths, 58.57 in language and 50.30 in EVS. Boys performed significantly better than girls in rural areas whereas in urban areas, girls outshone the boys. In all the three subjects, urban students performed significantly better than rural students.

The class 7 and 8 study was taken up in 2003-04 in 30 states/UTs and covered 105 districts, 4124 schools, 17,139 teachers and 1,01,066 students. The mean achievement in class 7 was 29.87 in maths, 53.00 in language, 35.98 in science and 32.96 in social studies. The class 8 study showed the following figures: 52.45 in language, 38.47 in mathematics, 40.54 in science and 45 in social science.

The NCERT study conducted in 2007 indicated that performance of most of the children was below mastery levels indicating a serious gap in the understanding levels of children. The table given below highlights the achievement levels of class 5 students (NCERT study 2007).

Table 6.1 Average Percentage of Achievement of Class 5th Students in Selected States in India

State	Language	Mathematics
Andhra Pradesh	55	44
Arunachal Pradesh	61	53
Assam	49	40

Bihar	65	63
Chhattisgarh	50	38
Delhi	63	48
Gujarat	56	48
Haryana	60	53
Himachal Pradesh	50	34
Jammu and Kashmir	50	36
Karnataka	59	46
Kerala	55	36
Madhya Pradesh	58	49
Maharashtra	62	44
Orissa	61	47
Punjab	58	50
Rajasthan	61	49
Sikkim	50	41
Tamil Nadu	71	58
Uttar Pradesh	50	38
West Bengal	71	60

Source: NCERT Study: (July 2007) 'Quality Related Interventions under SSA'

Under SSA, learning achievement levels have usually been equated with learning quality. The SSA approach provides for a national sample survey of pupil learning levels to be conducted every three-years for classes 3, 5 and class 7 or 8.

The Annual Status of Education Report (ASER) Studies

The lack of 'current, country-wide, reliable, and independently measured information that was easy to understand' provided the impetus for taking up through ASER the challenging task of measuring children's progress in learning across the country from 2005. The aim of the surveys was to understand whether the country was moving towards UEE – whether all the children were attending school regularly, whether they continued to stay in school and whether they were learning well.

The ASER surveys were carried out by local groups consisting of nearly 20,000 trained volunteers drawn from universities, colleges, NGOs, women's groups, SHGs, etc. The surveys tried to assess the pre-school status, schooling status and children's progress in learning through testing skills in basic reading, basic arithmetic, ability to tell time, writing and comprehension.

The assessment survey covered children of 6-14 age group in 20 randomly selected villages in each district in 2005. In subsequent surveys, assessment was carried out among children of 3-16 age group in 30 randomly selected villages in each district in the years 2006, 2007 and 2008. In 2008 ASER covered 7,04,241 children in 3,30,000 households and 16,198 villages in 564 districts (out of 583 districts) across the country.

The ASER 2005 assessment indicated that 35 per cent of all children in the elementary school age group could not read simple paragraphs (Level I text) and close to 52 per cent could not read a short story, and that about 41 per cent could not carry out a two-digit subtraction problem.

The ASER 2006 assessment revealed that only 31 per cent of children completed education up to class 10 and 42 per cent up to class 8. The study highlighted the fact that one out of three children in class 5 was unable to read and write.

The NCERT conducted a Mid-term Assessment Survey (MAS) of learning outcomes of class 5 children in 2007. It reported a 'facility value' for comprehension which was based on a child reading a story followed by reading questions based on the story, and finally writing answers. ASER 2007 conducted a test where regardless of their reading ability and the class in which they studied, children were asked to answer orally, questions based on a class 2 level story. The comparison shown in Table 7.2 is quite close considering that one test required written answers and the other oral.

Table 6.2 Comparison of ASER 2007 with NCERT-MAS Comprehension

States	NCERT 2007 Class 5 Comprehension Facility Value	ASER 2007 Class 5 Children Who Can Answer Questions Based on Class 2 Text Orally	NCERT/ ASER
Jammu & Kashmir	37.97	32.79	1.16
Himachal Pradesh	51.50	74.71	0.69
Uttarakhand	42.90	64.18	0.67
Punjab	46.86	67.29	0.70
Haryana	46.69	63.61	0.73
Rajasthan	42.29	44.29	0.95
Uttar Pradesh	47.03	41.62	1.13
Bihar	--	64.14	--
Jharkhand	48.96	53.52	0.91
West Bengal	55.19	61.48	0.90
Assam	41.07	51.43	0.80
Gujarat	43.99	52.05	0.85
Maharashtra	49.95	71.08	0.70
Madhya Pradesh	48.77	74.57	0.65
Chhattisgarh	39.48	54.15	0.73
Orissa	51.90	55.34	0.94

Andhra Pradesh	35.59	68.28	0.52
Karnataka	39.71	48.08	0.83
Kerala	51.93	74.83	0.69
Tamil Nadu	44.39	37.08	1.20
India	45.30	57.10	0.79

Source: ASER (Rural) 2008

ASER 2008 compared rural female literacy (Census 2001 figures) with the ability of women in the age group of 7+ or 17+ as recorded by ASER 2006. Over 5,50,000 older women and nearly 2,50,000 school-age girls from over 16,000 villages from all the states and rural districts formed the sample. The national rural female literacy of India (46.13 per cent) matched closely with ASER's figure of 47.7 per cent women in the relevant age group being able to read simple sentences. ASER 2008 revealed that even in class 5, there were children (1.9 per cent) who could not read at all and only 56.2 per cent of children could complete the class 2 test.

Table 6.3 Reading Ability (Figures in percentages)

Class	Nothing	Letters	Words	Class 1 test	Class 2 test
1	34.9	41.9	16.4	4.1	2.7
3	6.0	18.1	25.6	28.1	22.2
5	1.9	6.2	11.1	24.6	56.2

In mathematics, even in class 5, only 20.7 per cent of children could count up to 99, only 32.8 per cent of children could do sums involving subtraction and 37 per cent of children could do division sums.

Table 6.4 Mathematics Ability (In percentages)

Class	Nothing	Recognize Nos.		Subtract	Divide
		1-9	10-99		
1	34.7	43.3	17.6	3.1	1.3
3	5.6	21.4	34.3	27.9	10.8
5	1.8	7.9	20.7	32.8	37.0

Source: ASER 2008

At the all-India level, only 46.4 per cent of children could tell time and 66.6 per cent could do currency tasks. Even at the class 8 level, 14 per cent could not tell time and 5.4 per cent could not do currency tasks.

Table 6.5 Percentage of Children Who Can Tell Time & Do Currency Tasks

Class	Tell Time	Do Currency Tasks
1	7.0	21.4
2	17.6	42.6
3	32.9	61.9
4	47.6	75.0
5	60.9	83.2
6	72.1	89.3
7	79.5	92.3
8	85.9	94.6
Total	46.4	66.6

Source: ASER 2008

Chhattisgarh and MP were the two states which showed dramatic improvement in children's reading ability as well as basic mathematical skills. MP topped the ASER scale of reading among all the states where 73-74 per cent of children could read a class 2 text in government schools. Along with MP and Chhattisgarh, Kerala, Maharashtra, and HP states lead the country in terms of children's basic reading fluency. (Also see Annexure VIII – Tables 31 and 32).

The World Bank Study on Completion of Primary School by Poor Children

The World Bank commissioned a qualitative study to identify factors that facilitate/ impede successful completion of primary school by children from diverse poverty situations in UP, Karnataka and AP. Some of the findings of this study were:

(a) Enrolment was not a big issue anymore; attendance, transition, completion and learning outcomes were emerging as an issues that needed more attention.

(b) In all the three states the learning outcomes of children emerged as an area of grave concern. For example, in UP, most children in classes 3, 4 and 5 were neither able to read fluently from their textbooks nor could they solve simple addition or subtraction sums. 'Earlier class 2 pass children could read postcards, now they cannot even write their names', complained a father during a 'focus group discussion' (FGD) in urban Sitapur. Those who could read/write either had literate parents (especially mother) and/or attended private tuition classes. First generation school goers barely managed to recognize the alphabet and could, at best, read a few words. Teachers were not made accountable for the learning outcomes of children, especially in the light of the no-detention policy.

(c) The cohort study done on the basis of school records gave a fairly positive picture. As the midday meal was linked to attendance, official records did not always reveal the truth with respect to regularity of attendance. Teachers were reluctant to admit that children dropped out and hence many children were merely present in the registers while some of them were marked as long absentees. Children from poor households were not very regular.

(d) The governments of Karnataka and AP had ensured that teachers reach schools and made efforts to address cadre management concerns to rationalize teacher deployment. Conversely, lack of sustained mobilization and corresponding governmental efforts (especially in UP) to ensure functioning of schools was a matter of deep concern.

(e) Actual teaching time in class emerged as another important issue. Classroom observations and discussions with children revealed that actual teaching time was indeed well below the expected norm. In multigrade teaching situations, barely 20 minutes of each period was spent on actual teaching. Children were left to do their own work when the teacher was busy with another group. Teaching and learning materials used in schools did not lend themselves to multigrade teaching or self-learning.

(f) When there were three or more teachers, they took turns to come to school and simply left a leave letter to explain their absence. This problem was more pronounced when the teacher commuted from urban centres to rural/tribal areas.

(g) The Supreme Court (2001) judgment on serving cooked meals in school instead of distributing dry rations was welcomed by parents and children. The experience of Karnataka was quite impressive – not just in ensuring regularity in school, but in making a significant difference to children from the surveyed households.

(h) Incentives like textbooks, uniforms and scholarships though welcome generated mixed reactions, mostly to do with regularity of distribution.

(i) If payment for schooling became necessary, parents opted for private schools. Perceived poor quality and poor learning outcomes in government primary schools seemed to be instrumental in the emergence of private schools/tuition classes.

(j) Both children and parents were categorical that teachers treated poor children very differently (more so if they were dalits or tribals), that they did not understand or appreciate the predicament of children who had to work before and after school.

(k) The DPEP programme introduced VECs, SDMCs, PTAs and MTAs. However, these groups were not found to be very effective in the surveyed villages.

Quality Improvement Initiatives

The 'National Plan of Action for EFA' stipulated a five-fold strategy for qualitative enhancement of education:

(a) Improving infrastructure and human resources for primary education

(b) Providing improved curriculum and TLM

(c) Improving the quality of the teaching-learning process through child-centred pedagogy
(d) Capacity building of teachers
(e) Specifying and measuring learner achievement levels.

The centre and the states have taken some important initiatives on the above lines.

Measures Undertaken by the Centre and the States to Improve Quality

A holistic approach was adopted to achieve quality improvement in elementary education through improvement in infrastructure, human resource and the teaching-learning processes. Several policy guidelines and quality programmes were initiated both by the centre and the states for this purpose.

NPE 1986 redefined UEE as consisting not only of enrolment and attendance but also of learner achievement. This along with periodical EFA declarations brought the focus on quality concerns and improvement in learner achievement to the centre stage of policy-making in elementary education in the country. In order to improve quality, the NPE also called for improving the unattractive school environment, unsatisfactory condition of buildings, inadequacy of instructional material and laying down MLLs that all children completing different stages of education should achieve.

Some of the initiatives undertaken by the centre and the states to improve quality were:

- The concept of MLLs was introduced at the national level in order to bring about an improvement in learner achievement levels. The NCERT played a key role in specifying learning competencies in language, mathematics and EVS to be mastered by every child at the end of a particular class of the primary stage.
- This prompted a series of actions in all the states resulting in revision of curriculum and textbooks as well as preparing child-friendly TLM. It also led to massive retraining of teachers. This heightened the awareness of all people working in the field of education towards improvement of learner achievement levels.
- Basic norms for school provision were specified through the OB scheme – physical, human and academic in each school which helped create additional schooling facilities for primary education,
- Teacher capacity building: Massive expansion of the schooling system impacted the quality of teachers and the academic support systems. Hence district and sub-district academic structures (DIETs/BRCs) were created for in-service training of teachers.
- Adult education & literacy programmes: NLM envisaged focusing on imparting functional literacy to non-literates in the productive 15-35 age group. It provided facilities for skill development to improve their economic status and well-being. It encouraged imbibing values of national integration, conservation

of environment, women's equality and observance of small family norms. NLM also envisaged the active participation of the population in this age group in the development process.

- The states took several steps to improve teachers' quality – fixing higher entry qualification (twelve-years of schooling) for elementary teachers, converting the certificate course in teacher training to a Diploma in Education (in several states) through enrichment of curriculum content, revising salaries of teachers to attract better talent, conducting entrance tests to select merited candidates as teachers, taking up improvement of in-service teacher training programmes, etc.
- After the implementation of SSA, a computerized District Information System for Education (known as DISE) was made operational which looks into several quality related parameters –PTR, teachers' profile, evaluation results, etc.
- In addition, MHRD has recently operationalized a quarterly quality monitoring system to monitor student attendance, teacher availability in schools, classroom practices and academic supervision provided by BRCs/CRCs. These tools are supposed to provide grade, subject, gender and social category-wise quarterly data on pupil achievement levels.

In spite of several large-scale initiatives, quality functioning of schools has remained far from satisfactory. On the basis of the results in assessment studies, there have been efforts by the states to improve the quality of school education in the country, to ensure reasonable learning outcomes at the elementary level, especially in literacy, numeracy and life skills.

Eleventh Plan

The Eleventh Five Year Plan has placed a lot of emphasis on the quality of education.

The schemes implemented in this direction aim at:

1. Increasing the number of schools to improve access
2. Improving infrastructure of existing and new schools
3. Increasing enrolment, retention, completion rates and reducing dropout rates
4. Reducing gender and other social inequities
5. Recruiting and training more teachers to impart education more effectively
6. Improving the content and quality of curriculum, textbooks and classroom transaction processes.

Profiles of Some Quality Improvement Initiatives

A number of programmes and schemes were initiated by the central and state governments to improve quality aspects in elementary education. National programmes like DPEP and SSA also took up important quality improvement initiatives in the country on a large-scale. Some of them are discussed here:

(a) Improvement of teaching-learning processes
(b) Child-centred approach
(c) MLLs
(d) The Nali-Kali experiment of Karnataka
(e) Gujarat's single-teacher schools
(f) Use of radio for teacher support
(g) The SITE programme
(h) The EDUSAT project
(i) The LGP of APF
(j) Quality assessment in Karnataka.

a. Improvement of Teaching-learning Processes

The most important factor in improving the quality of education is the teaching-learning process. Several studies have pointed out that some of the important reasons for children dropping out-of-school are the unattractive classroom environment that includes teaching-learning process. Many schools continue working with minimal infrastructure and inadequate support material and equipment. Majority of the schools in the country (in several states up to 80 per cent) are also multigrade which poses a bigger challenge to the classroom teacher, as he/she has to handle more than one class simultaneously.

It is in this context that the states took up a number of projects to bring in quality in classroom transaction. There were also several important individual initiatives in this regard. MP started a major project initiative 'Shikshak Samakhya' (teacher empowerment) in the 1990s with the support of UNICEF. It emphasized teacher creativity and autonomy in the classroom to make learning joyful for the children. 'Anandadayi Shikshan' in Maharashtra, 'Gurumitra Yojana' in Rajasthan, 'Nali-Kali' in Karnataka, are some of the important quality improvement initiatives in this regard. There were also efforts to share these experiences and disseminate them beyond state boundaries through several workshops. DPEP took a major lead in this regard.

b. Child-centred Approach

Para 14 of Chapter II of the POA states: '...by making elementary education child-centred, we would be introducing a long awaited reform in the system. The most important aspect of this reform will be to make education a joyful, innovative and satisfying activity, rather than a system of rote and cheerless authoritarian instruction'.

DPEP and other programmes introduced several innovations and experiments specifically designed to improve the quality of education in the country. Several of these focused on generating and encouraging child-centred pedagogical approaches that provided children with opportunities for learning through friendly, playway methods. Their cognitive and non-cognitive skills were sought to be developed in an integrated process and they were encouraged to enjoy the process of learning. Children were expected to become active learner-partners in the educational process.

The child-centred approach necessitated a fundamental change in the manner of curriculum transaction. The teacher was expected to perform the roles of a facilitator of knowledge and learning experiences, a manager of learning resources and an active contributor to the all round development of the child. All pre-service and in-service teacher education programmes were to be so designed as to train teachers in transacting the curriculum, with the child at the centre of the teaching-learning process.

c. Minimum Levels of Learning

The government's concern regarding improvement of quality in primary education began in 1980s. NPE 1986 emphasized the need for focusing not only on quantitative aspects but also on quality in terms of learning levels. It also emphasized the need for laying down MLLs for each stage of school education as a prerequisite for setting performance goals for teachers.

These MLLs were visualized as effective guides for organizing teaching-learning experiences and evaluating pupil achievement. It was also a step taken towards achieving a comparable standard of education throughout the country. The MLL approach became an integral part of programmes like the DPEP.

A committee was constituted by MHRD under the chairmanship of Prof. R.H. Dave to study afresh the learning outcomes defined in the existing curriculum and accordingly lay down the required MLLs. The committee, in 1991, specified the basic competencies that all children at the primary stage across the country were to achieve in the form of MLLs in selected scholastic areas.

The Concept of MLL

The MLLs were conceptualized as a three-dimensional model encompassing the three key aspects – competency, mastery and equity.

1. They laid down learning outcomes in the form of a set of identified competencies that were essential for all children to acquire at each stage of primary education and in three curricular areas – maths, language and EVS. With this, conventional syllabus-based teaching gave way to learning and developing skills on the part of all children.
2. They further specified that these competencies and skills were to be acquired at the level of mastery, where these would become sustainable and would not allow the pupils to relapse into illiteracy. Mastery was defined as a child acquiring 80 per cent of the specified competencies. Further, 80 per cent of the children were expected to reach this level.
3. The element of equity implied that all children irrespective of their social and economic background should be able to acquire the mastery level; the curriculum and TLM had to be designed accordingly.

The MLLs were designed to equip all children completing primary education with the minimum/essential learning outcomes that would enable them to understand their environment more meaningfully and to function as socially useful adults. The recommended curriculum aimed at substantially reducing the load of information, thereby, aiming at relevance, functionality and achievability of the learning outcomes. It was expected that the learning outcomes would be mastered by all students within a specified time limit and with a reasonable input of facilities. Along with the development of a comprehensive evaluation system, these MLLs aimed at providing the teacher and the system an indication of performance effectiveness.

Implementation of MLLs

The MLLs were intended to be used as a guideline in classroom teaching as well as for evaluation of learner achievement. As an evaluatory tool, they served as a standard against which the performance of the children could be assessed in terms of essential learning outcomes. Based on these concepts, academic and pedagogic interventions were worked out. Almost all states adopted the MLLs and took up curriculum revision, redesigning of textbooks, improvement in classroom transactions, evaluation and teacher orientation as part of programme activities.

Under this scheme, financial assistance was provided to the states for a wide range of activities such as conduct of workshops to list grade-wise competencies, preparation of competency-based textbooks, teacher training, preparation of TLM, orientation of education functionaries and undertaking benchmark surveys.

A majority of the states implemented the MLLs by adapting them to suit their local needs. In several states, the programme was up-scaled to cover higher classes. Programmes were initiated for measuring learner achievement on a regular basis. The GOI supported sixteen large-scale projects to study and streamline this process and work out processes needed for all children to achieve the desired competencies.

Since the content and context of schooling varied from state to state, it is difficult to generalize the impact of MLLs in improving the learning levels of children across the country. Performance of learners does not depend only on inputs provided in the classroom as there are several other socio-economic factors that influence it. MLLs were used to assess baseline, middle and terminal attainment levels of students studying in DPEP districts.

Criticism of MLLs

The MLL programme has been criticized by various educationists from three angles – conceptualization, formulation and implementation. MLL limits children to developing basic concepts in curricular areas rather than training them to become complete, independent, motivated and rational learners. It was also felt that the MLL should have been implemented with a child-centred approach, which would be more humanistic and would have led to the overall development of the child.

Several educationists felt that the MLLs concentrated only on the cognitive traits at the cost of affective traits. The conscious decision to give priority to cognitive areas created a biased perspective of the primary education curriculum. It was also felt that the rigidly defined competencies to be mastered within a given time (grade-wise) by all children was not a viable or desirable idea. Since MLLs were prescribed for only three of the six curricular areas (language, maths & EVS), the other three equally important areas got consciously neglected.

The terms of reference of the committee specified MLLs for two levels (classes 3 and 5) and not for each of the five primary grades. The intention was that it would allow spacing of learning according to a child's ability. But, competencies were prescribed for all the five grades instead of two levels as originally contemplated. Specifying MLLs for all the five grades was not in tune with the original idea of 'mastery learning'. Further, the MLL approach got reduced to teaching of only the three R's (reading, writing and arithmetic). The arts and skills were not accorded any place in the curriculum.

Vast regional and cultural diversities were overlooked in an attempt to specify uniform standards. The standards set were unrealistic given the conditions of the schools and the school environment. Although a provision was envisaged by the committee for 'regional and preferably district adaptation of the MLLs', it was not implemented. The result was that in most schools, students could not achieve the stipulated levels of mastery.

Even the implementation had several shortcomings. These were brought out by Jangira in his study of the implementation of MLLs:

1. Lack of systematic and sustained institutional support resulted in implementation of MLLs without adequate preparation and professional backup.
2. Although the phasing of MLLs – into initiation, extension, expansion and consolidation phases – was contemplated, its implementation had gaps. For example, the expansion phase was not preceded either by a systematic and objective review or with adequate preparation.
3. The implementation of monitoring students' learning progress continuously was not completely effective since neither teachers were provided guidelines nor were they provided the necessary skills.
4. Maximum priority was placed on revision and re-revision of competency-based textbooks rather than on training and classroom practice.
5. The implementation was mostly mechanical in nature using the MLL document sequence as the 'teaching sequence', which was not the intention.
6. Although continuous and comprehensive evaluation is the crux of the MLL approach, it turned out to be the weakest component as is evident from field studies.
7. Despite remedial teaching – which is logically linked to evaluation – being a part of the programme, it was rarely seen at the field level. Even the NCERT stated that the area of remedial teaching did not get enough attention.

In spite of the several flaws in its conceptualization and implementation, the MLL approach still was a serious and sincere attempt to improve quality of primary education for the first time in the country.

d. Nali-Kali Experiment in Karnataka

Nali-Kali was one of the effective initiatives aimed at providing support to the teacher handling multigrade situations. This experiment derived its inspiration from a small experiment conducted by the Rishi Valley Education Trust, Madanapalli, AP. It was taken up in 1995 in 270 schools of the educationally backward HD Kote Block of Mysore district in Karnataka.

The strategies developed were:

(a) Improved classroom instruction through a graded curriculum, replacing text books through activity cards to make learning individualized, child-centred and interactive and, bridging attainment gaps to enable all children to achieve the expected levels of learning.
(b) Promoting teacher commitment and involvement through development of all TLM including activity cards. This helped in enhancing the creativity and competence of the teacher that would motivate him/her to take greater interest in classroom transaction.

The major strengths of the programme were:

(a) Since teachers were involved in all aspects of material development, it created a sense of ownership among them.
(b) All educational personnel including the monitoring and inspecting staff were acquainted with the methodology.
(c) CRPs were carefully selected to provide constant support and guidance.
(d) The methodology was based on sound principles of learning and was appropriate to multigrade situations.

The programme resulted in significant improvement in enrolment and retention rates as well as an appreciable increase in learning achievement. Nali-Kali was later upscaled to cover all six educational blocks of Mysore district with DPEP assistance in 1998. However, when the programme was attempted to be upscaled across the state, it failed to make an impact due to various other factors.

e. Gujarat's Single-teacher Schools

In Gujarat, a three-phased project was taken up to provide assistance and specific guidance to the 7000 single-teacher schools. In the first phase a survey was taken up to investigate the specific problems of these schools. In the second phase, the school teachers were oriented for multiple class teaching – a schedule of guidelines was drawn up to help them. In the third phase, auto-instructional programmes in arithmetic and language were prepared by SIE and given to each school. It was felt that a programmed learning method was helpful in engaging the children of other classes in study while the teacher himself/herself taught students of a particular class.

f. Use of Radio Lessons for Teacher Support

During 1975-76, the Centre for Educational Technology (of NCERT) with the assistance of Government of Rajasthan conducted a series of radio programmes for primary school children in Rajasthan to learn the mother tongue. These lessons were used for the improvement of listening skills and for language development. The programme covered 500 schools from 2 districts. The radio programmes were supplemented by specially prepared materials for teaching, reading and writing. This was a first-of-its-kind effort and helped identify valuable contributions the radio could make in enriching the classroom experiences of the child.

In Tamil Nadu the SCERT in collaboration with CIIL, Mysore and AIR, Madras launched a course for Tamil teachers handling multiple classes. In 1983-84 about 15,000 teachers of class 7 were covered. However these experiments were short-lived as they could not be sustained over a period of time.

'Keli-Kali' Radio Lessons – The Karnataka Experiment

Karnataka has used the medium of the radio rather effectively and has sustained the effort over a decade. Being an innovative programme for primary school children, its objectives are to provide the benefit of expert teachers to the students, promote student-teacher interaction and inculcate in children an awareness of joyful learning. Songs, local dialects, folklore, sound effects and dramatization of lessons contribute to the attractiveness of the programme. The programme aims at quality improvement through empowering teachers to use popular media in academic work and enable them to use innovative teaching methods to sustain the interest of the child in learning.

In 2000-01, the programme started on a pilot basis for children of class 3 and was broadcast from Dharwar and Gulbarga stations of AIR. In the second phase, it was introduced in 11 DPEP districts for children of classes 3 and 4. In the third phase, in 2002-03, classes 3,4 and 5 were covered throughout the state and lessons were broadcast from 10 stations of AIR daily from 11.30 AM to 12.30 PM covering nearly 50,000 primary schools and 70,00,000 children. The lessons were based on concepts, activities and hard spots taken from the textbooks of the respective classes. The aim was to bring in some novelty in the teaching methodology that would ultimately make the child understand the lessons with ease.

While developing radio lessons, care was taken to retain the original ideas and the objectives of teaching these lessons. The teachers were also supplied a handbook which contained information on the objectives and scope of each radio lesson, pre-broadcast activities which the teacher had to undertake to motivate the children, and post-broadcast activities along with an annual timetable giving the exact date when a particular lesson would be broadcast.

The popularity of these radio lessons could be gauged from the fact that after every radio lesson about 10,000 postcards were received as feedback from students, parents and the public. Periodic audio-video conferencing was also held to find out the impact of the programme. It was extended to cover children of classes 6 and 7 in 2005-06 and class 8 from 2006-07. EDC stepped in and produced interactive radio programmes and covered children of classes 1 and 2 as well from 2005-06. The programme was first supported by DPEP and then by SSA.

g. Satellite Television Experiment (SITE) Programme

The SITE programme of 1975-76 was launched to conduct TV programmes through a satellite (ATS-6). Through this, the children in village primary schools received 22 ½ minutes of lessons on every school working day. The programmes were planned for all the five classes of primary school covering 2,400 villages of MP, Bihar, AP, Orissa and Rajasthan. Approximately 50 per cent of the programmes were produced in Base Production Centres in Delhi, Cuttack and Hyderabad in Hindi, Oriya and Telugu. Another 50 per cent that comprised science programmes were produced by ISRO. The lessons were relayed through the Space Application Centre, Ahmedabad. About 50,000 primary school teachers were trained through SITE programmes on science teaching using multimedia.

The second major experience of TV lessons was through INSAT-1 which later covered the entire country. These programmes were produced in Delhi and could be received anywhere in the country with the help of relay stations. It was a major advantage that a large number of teachers and children could be reached simultaneously.

h. The EDUSAT Project

EDUSAT is a satellite dedicated to education. Launched in September 2004, it has a capacity of 74 channels offering regional and national spot beams. The ground level network consists of uplink stations at national and state levels and reception facilities in DIETs/BRCs and selected schools. The network offers interactive virtual classrooms and data transmission through a computer network. The software is produced by IGNOU, NCERT and SCERTs of several states. ISRO is responsible for the hardware design and implementation.

EDUSAT was a major initiative in the use of satellite technology for strengthening the outreach and quality of education. Two-way video interactive technologies were also set up, creating virtual classrooms for continuous improvement of teachers as well as providing education directly to children.

EDUSAT has been functional since early 2005. It allows expert resource people to be accessed directly by learners in remote parts of the country. There is no loss of information as programmes can be recorded and transmitted repeatedly as and when required. Although infrastructural costs of satellite education are high, running costs are relatively low since a large number of programmes can be produced and relayed centrally.

i. Learning Guarantee Programme (LGP)

The Learning Guarantee Programme was a joint venture between the Karnataka Education Department and the Azim Premji Foundation. It was launched in the seven backward districts of north-east Karnataka in 2002-03. LGP aimed at identifying and encouraging good primary and higher primary schools in the region. The objective was also to spread the good practices followed by these schools among all the schools in the region. It was not an intervention but a methodology to identify schools that could guarantee certain MLLs in children. It aimed to provide accountability in the educational system for equity and excellence through assessment-driven reforms. It invited schools to join in the evaluation process.

LGP aimed at creating willingness among schools and communities to volunteer and be evaluated on the three criteria of enrolment, attendance and learning achievements of children. The schools that got evaluated and satisfied all the three criteria became eligible for suitable monetary awards by APF.

All government lower primary and higher primary schools in 48 education blocks in the 7 districts (numbering around 9,000 schools) were invited to participate in the scheme. In the first year over 1,900 schools in the region volunteered to participate. A preliminary survey of a small sample of these schools in one district indicated significant levels of heightened interest and enthusiasm for accepting and meeting the challenges posed by the scheme.

The objectives of the scheme were:

(a) All the children (of school-going age) within the habitation had to be enrolled in school.
(b) All enrolled children had to attend the school regularly.
(c) All the children attending regularly had to attain the expected levels of achievement. In other words, the school guaranteed the learning of every child in the school.

The APF volunteers assessed schools that had volunteered for getting evaluated under this scheme. Even though the number of schools which finally became eligible under this scheme was quite small, the scheme created a significant impact among all the schools of the region. It turned out to be a pilot scheme for the state to launch the 'State-wide Assessment Surveys' through the newly constituted Karnataka School Quality Assessment Organization (KSQAO).

j. Assessment of Quality in Karnataka

Prior to 2005, Karnataka did not have a comprehensive programme for testing students' attainments. Hence, it initiated the Karnataka School Quality Assessment Organization. In January 2006, the organization evaluated 21.62 lakh children studying in class 2 (4 schools per cluster), and all children studying in classes 5 and 7 in all the 19,518 lower primary schools and 24,073 higher primary schools which included both government and aided schools in the state.

The students were evaluated in 55 competencies in kannada, EVS and mathematics in class 2 and, 115 competencies each in kannada, science, social science and mathematics in classes 5 and 7. The overall performance was 67 per cent in class 2, 49 per cent in class 5 and 48 per cent in class 7. Girls performed marginally better than boys.

Table 6.6 Performance in KSQAO Evaluation

Subject	Class 2	Class 5	Class 7
Overall	67	49	48
Kannada	65	51	54
Mathematics	61	46	40
Science (EVS)	78	53	50
Social Science	–	47	46

Source: KSQAO, Karnataka

The performance in 18 (out of 33) educational districts was below the state average of 50 per cent. 12 districts were in the 40-45 range and 6 districts were in the 46-49 range.

In 2006-07, KSQAO assessed about 13 lakh students for subject knowledge in classes 3, 5 and 7. The results indicated that attainment levels went down as the students moved to higher classes. Attainments below 70 per cent in classes 5 and 7 indicated that a large number of students in these classes had not attained the desired MLLs.

Other Initiatives Undertaken by the States

A few more programmes are listed below and the details of these initiatives may be seen in the document prepared by 'Shiksha Sangam'.

Learning Improvement

1. Children's Language Improvement Programme, AP
2. Integrated Learning Improvement Programme, WB
3. Vachan Lekhan Hami Prakalap, Maharashtra
4. Learning Achievement Tracking System, Orissa
5. Education Quality Improvement Programme, Maharashtra
6. Grading Schools for Monitoring and Planning, Uttaranchal.

Computer-aided Education

1. Computer-aided Learning, AP
2. CALTOOZ, Delhi
3. Computer-assisted Learning Centres, Karnataka
4. Head Start, MP

Workbooks, Primers and Learning Enrichment

1. Multilingual Approach, AP
2. Yuva, Delhi
3. Accelerated Reading Programme, Karnataka
4. Preparation of Workbooks, Kerala
5. Interactive CD-ROM, Kerala
6. 'Aas Paas Ki Khoj', MP

Incentive and Convergence Approach

1. 'Education through Wheels', Haryana
2. Vocational Education for Girls, TN

Special Programmes

1. Chinnara Karnataka Darshana
2. Exposure Trips for Girls, Orissa
3. Puppets as 'Handy Tools', Gujarat
4. Pratibha Karanji, Karnataka
5. 'Mukham', Kerala
6. Bridge Courses for Muslim Girls, Orissa

Future Efforts Needed to Improve 'Quality'

Some of the issues that must be considered for improvement of quality are listed below:

1. Implementing the recommendation of the NPE 1986 in the creating of a National Testing Service that will facilitate comparing the achievement levels of pupils of a certain class across states.
2. A sensitive and progressive regulatory framework for maintaining and improving educational standards at the state level throughout the country.
3. Efforts to improve the internal management of schools.
4. Streamline the regular management practices within schools through institutional planning and monitoring mechanisms.
5. Improve the quality of teaching-learning and classroom processes.
6. Academic teacher support structures to be made locally available for teachers to function effectively which calls for strengthening of CRC structures.
7. Monitoring quality of output in schools.

7

Community Participation and Role of NGOs in Education

Community occupies a prime position in all societal activities including education. Involvement of the community increases public awareness, helps in better and more transparent administration, and brings in better accountability in all spheres of public life. Lack of community involvement can create a vacuum and an atmosphere of indifference which distances people from government efforts and initiatives.

In India community participation and empowerment in primary education has been perceived to be essential to the success of UEE. The Dakar Framework laid out six broad goals for EFA and formulated twelve strategies for achieving them. One of the strategies stated: 'Ensure the engagement and participation of civil society in the formulation, implementation and monitoring of strategies for educational development'. In the Indian context, this strategy was considered a key to the success of EFA.

An analysis of district-wise disparities in education and other attainments in many states reveals that there is a nexus between poverty, backwardness, gender disparity and education disparity within and across districts. This implies that low participation of certain sections of the community is responsible for disparities to creep in. Hence, community participation in effective school management was felt to be crucial to UEE in the state.

The NPE 1986 stated: 'Local communities, through appropriate bodies, will be assigned a major role in programmes of school improvement'. The SSA Framework (2000) stressed: 'While SSA is formulated on the premise that the community can plan, it also accepts the tremendous requirement for developing capacities in communities to do so'.

Though the concept of community participation in education has been recognized through various government initiatives, it has not yet taken off at the desirable level.

WHAT IS COMMUNITY?

Communities are defined by characteristics that the members share, such as culture, language, tradition, law, geography, class, and race. As Shaeffer (1992) argues, communities are homogeneous or heterogeneous, united or conflictive. Some communities are governed and managed by leaders chosen democratically who relatively enjoy autonomy from other levels of government, and some are governed by leaders imposed from above and represent central authorities.

Community Participation in the Context of Education

Communities value education both for its inherent value and for the immense possibilities it has for development of the individual, the society and the country. Hence, their participation would add value to the process of education. The term 'participation' is interpreted differently depending on the context. Shaeffer (1994) defined different degrees or levels of participation and provided seven possible definitions of the term, including:

- Involvement through the mere use of a service (such as enrolling children in school).
- Involvement through contribution (or extraction) of money, materials, and labour.
- Involvement through attendance (e.g., attending parents' meetings at school) implying passive acceptance of decisions made by others.
- Involvement through consultation on a particular issue.
- Participation in the delivery of a service, often as a partner with other actors
- Participation as implementers of delegated powers.
- Participation in real decision-making at every stage, including identification of problems, study of feasibility, planning, implementation, and evaluation.

As already indicated, one of the indicators for measuring community involvement is regular participation of children in the school. If all the children of a specific age group are attending school and learning regularly, then one can infer that the involvement of the community does exist (either in active or passive form); however, this cannot be a guarantee for total participation of the community.

In this context the school as an agency must transform itself and ensure community participation by responding to the diverse needs of the society and interests of all the stakeholders within the community. It must take into consideration several key factors responsible for contributing to the effective participation of community. Some of them are listed below:

- An open and democratic environment.
- A decentralized policy with greater emphasis on local initiatives.
- Reform in public and educational administration.
- Democratization of supervision with involvement of professional experts and officials.
- Training for community members to take active part in school affairs
- Involvement of committed NGOs.
- Creation of collective decision-making structures at various levels.
- Linking participatory activities with policy frameworks.

Many research studies have identified various ways in which communities can participate in education. Also, specific channels have been provided through which they can be involved in children's education. They can help identify and address factors that contribute to educational problems, such as low participation and poor academic performance. Being concerned about children's education, parents are often willing to assist in improving the educational delivery. One cannot underestimate the fact that parents and communities are powerful resources that can be utilized by the school for ushering efficiency in the functioning of the school.

Types of Community Participation

Community participation can be varied with all of them making significant contributions to education delivery. The following is a list of ways through which they can promote the cause of education:

1. Contributing to Infrastructure Requirements
   - Contributing through labour, materials, land, and funds.
   - Raising money for schools.
   - Constructing, repairing, and improving school facilities.
   - Collecting more resources from and solving problems at the bureaucratic level.

2. Supporting Academic Activities
   - Scheduling school calendars.
   - Identifying factors contributing to educational problems (low enrolment, and high repetition and dropout).
   - Advocating enrolment and education benefits.
   - Ensuring students' regular attendance and completion.
   - Actively attending school meetings to learn about children's learning progress and classroom behaviour.
   - Helping children with studies.

3. Contributing to School Management
   - Forming SMCs and/or PTAs to manage schools.
   - Boosting morale of school staff.
   - Recruiting and supporting teachers.
   - Making decisions about school locations and schedules.
   - Monitoring and following up on teacher attendance and performance.
   - Advocating and promoting girls' education.
   - Providing security for teachers by preparing adequate housing for them.
   - Handling the budget meant for operating schools.
   - Preparing children's readiness for schooling by providing them with adequate nutrition and stimuli for their cognitive development.

Tackling the Issue of Teacher Absenteeism in Schools

Community participation in education enhances the quality of monitoring of schools to a great extent. It brings in all round involvement, commitment and accountability in the functioning of schools. Some of the most important teacher-related issues facing government schools in the country are their absenteeism, poor performance and lack of punctuality in attending classes even when they are present in school. Lack of a credible monitoring system is one of the critical factors contributing to these problems. The involvement of communities in monitoring and supervision gives rise to regularity in teacher attendance and better performance. Feedback from parents and the community can be a strong incentive to motivate teachers.

Promotion of Girls' Education

'Community participation can contribute to promoting girls' education' (UNICEF, 1992). Participating in school activities and frequently communicating with teachers creates awareness among parents and communities that girls' education improves various aspects of their lives, such as literacy in the family, economic productivity and, family health and nutrition. Further, it reduces fertility and child mortality rates.

Development of Accountability

Parental involvement in education, particularly in school governance, is seen as a means of making schools more accountable to the society which funds them. The notion of parental involvement in accountability derives from a more market-oriented concept in which school-family partnerships are viewed rather like business partnerships, through which the two parties receive mutual and complementary benefits which enable them to operate more effectively (OECD, 1997).

Accountability is also developed through routine parents' meetings and reporting systems on student progress. As parents contribute their time, labour, materials, land, and funds, they become more involved in school activities, including participating in meetings with teachers and monitoring their performance. Teachers, in turn, feel more obliged to deliver better education in a bid to be more responsive to the needs of parents and communities. Community participation can thus greatly help develop accountability, which contributes towards the quality of education provided by schools.

Improvement of Home Environment for Children

The community can be involved in preparing a conducive home environment and making it more education-friendly for children. A World Bank Study (1997) which analysed primary education in India discovered that families that are aware of the importance of education can contribute more to their children's learning achievement, even in disadvantaged sections of the communities. It also showed that students from families that encouraged children's schooling by allocating time at home for study, encouraging reading and supporting children's educational aspirations scored significantly higher on tests of learning achievement.

In order to understand the concept of community participation in education, it is important to understand what constitutes the whole process in India. Some of the questions one needs to answer in this context are:

- Historically, how did communities deal with education?
- How do they contribute to the process of education?
- What are the benefits of community participation?
- How can several local issues be effectively tackled with the involvement of the community?
- What are the challenges facing active community participation?
- What are the efforts made by government to sustain community participation?

Historical Overview of Community Involvement in Education in India

Historically, education was under the purview of communities (though in the hands of a privileged and select few) because education then was not treated as a compulsory function of the state. However, as the state began to actively participate in the promotion of the modern system of education in the nineteenth and twentieth centuries, the involvement of communities became more and more passive until they started feeling that this was a state responsibility.

After independence, however, as the central and state governments took on themselves the task of introducing compulsory primary education, it became increasingly evident that community participation was inevitable for achieving success; in fact, it would help achieve the objective faster. The Compulsory Primary Education Acts of several states envisaged partnership with parents to ensure success of the compulsory primary education programmes. Hence, states started catering to those who voluntarily participated by sending their children to school.

In the beginning, the community involvement was visible only to the extent of its providing the basic infrastructure – land and building – for starting primary schools and other education facilities like non-formal centres. In almost all the states, the norm for starting a primary school in a school-less habitation was that the habitation should have a minimum (size) population and the community should provide a temporary/permanent accommodation to start the school. As a result, several thousand primary schools were started in the decades between the 60s and 80s. The grant-in-aid systems followed by most states also enabled many local communities to start schools across the country.

Later, NPE 1986 recognized the importance of community participation in achieving the goals set forth under UEE. Several significant initiatives were taken up under DPEP for enhancing community participation in primary education. In different parts of the country, local communities were mobilized to contribute to effective functioning of schools through Self-Help Groups (SHGs), PRIs, VECs, PTAs, SMCs, and Mother Teacher Councils (MTCs).

Several states set up vibrant local structures such as PTAs in Kerala and MP, ZP institutions in Maharashtra and Gujarat, SMCs in AP, Karnataka, Bihar and Orissa. While PTAs have also been very active in Kerala and TN, women's groups have taken a lead role in HP. School committees have an active role even in selecting teachers in Meghalaya. West Bengal continues to keep primary education outside the purview of panchayats with the District Boards of Primary Education exercising all powers over schools and teachers.

Community owned 'School Registers' are being maintained in MP under the supervision of the Rajiv Gandhi Mission with very effective outcomes. Habitation planning has been taken up in AP. Periodic household surveys are the norm under Rajasthan's 'Shiksha Aapke Dwaar' programme.

There are several well-documented examples of community as well as civil society groups like NGOs, corporate houses, etc., which have significantly contributed to the furtherance of the goals of UEE. Some of the state governments have started school adoption programmes to encourage involvement of donors, NGOs, and corporate sectors.

DPEP Initiatives

During implementation of DPEP, several strategies (such as school-mapping and microplanning) were adopted to ensure that the community participated not only in bringing all children to school but also in articulating its demand for improved social services. Community participation was seen as a prerequisite for securing long-term sustainability of these initiatives.

While VECs were constituted in most states under DPEP, formation of such committees at the school level in urban areas was slow. Even where VECs were formed, the relationship with elected representatives of PRIs was not clearly delineated in many states.

The DPEP tried to involve the community through mass campaigns like enrolment drives, Kala Jathas (cultural processions), Chinnara Melas (children fairs), formation of VECs, periodical training of VEC members, involvement of other elected representatives in education, etc. It roped in the VEC members in microplanning activities and training, motivating parents to send children to school, evolving strategies to reduce dropouts, mobilizing resources to support activities in the school and implementing AE programmes in villages.

The Constitutional Amendments

The move towards decentralization and empowerment of the community got a further fillip through the 73rd/74th amendments to the Constitution. They recommended delegation of authority related to education – primary and secondary schools, vocational education, AE and NFE – to PRIs. This was an important move in acknowledging the inevitability of community participation in development and in all social sectors.

The SSA Initiatives

SSA envisaged a systematic mobilization of the community and creation of an effective system of decentralized decision-making at the school level. It also favoured community-based implementation and ownership of schools. Apart from central and state funds, SSA aimed at motivating the local people to contribute and mobilize local resources (time, knowledge, money or materials) to meet the needs of the school.

Planning at the level of habitations, monitoring of school activities and a number of interventions (like enrolment drives) were to be carried out by VECs or their equivalent local bodies. SSA funds also flowed through local community-based bodies for all school related expenditure – which constituted more than 50 per cent of SSA funds.

Community Participation in Basic Education: The Present Status

Education administrators are still grappling with the issue of effective and efficient management of schools – they feel very reluctant to delegate powers to school committees. Transfer of teachers, deployment of teachers against fake enrolments, non-accountability of school systems to local communities are some of the issues that hinder efficient administration of school systems in the country.

Political involvement and corruption are rampant in matters like teacher employment and deployment. Neither the state governments nor the teachers themselves wish to delegate these matters to school level committees. With the establishment of a huge number of private unaided schools in the country and with the middle class increasingly preferring them, the government schools are now catering largely to the poorer classes of the population. Hence, inefficient running of government schools do not significantly affect those who are responsible for maintaining them. Teachers also resist making them accountable to the local communities.

Community participation in basic education, as it is, has remained a very weak area in the elementary education sector, notwithstanding the large-scale emergence of VECs/PTAs/SMCs, etc. Except Kerala and, to an extent, EGS schools in MP and the habitation-based planning approach in AP, the role of the community in developing a school vision is still very limited. As far as review and sharing of student progress with parents is concerned, apart from Karnataka's effort, it has been less than satisfactory in most other states.

Evidence from the DPEP suggested that the concept of community ownership of the school was still a limited one and the teacher was still not made adequately accountable at the school level. Small grants for committees mentioned earlier and a role in the execution of civil works were some functions that school level bodies managed to undertake in most states. There was still very little done in the area of management of teacher cadres and teacher development using the decentralization framework.

States like AP experimented with elected SMCs who were assigned the responsibility of engaging additional vidya volunteers. Block and district level PRIs were also involved in varying degrees but there was little evidence of their effectiveness.

Teachers continue to be posted and transferred by state education departments, though many states have made efforts to transfer this power to the district level. Some states make it mandatory for a panchayat representative to certify teachers' attendance. Schools in Kerala have been trying to develop School Development Plans through community organizations.

Efforts to involve the community in quality issues through the preparation of School Improvement and School Development Plans have been attempted but they remain largely teacher-led in most states. In the absence of a role in selecting TLM for children or in contributing to teacher development programmes, communities often feel marginalized. In spite of many years of DPEP experience, many VECs remain largely civil works implementation agencies.

However, the teacher continues to be outside the accountability framework of local communities. Many states recruit teachers on less than the prescribed pay scale. Most of these recruitments take place at the district level, as per broad guidelines given by the state education departments. Communities rarely have a role in selection of teachers.

Challenges Facing Active Community Participation

Several negative factors pose serious challenges for active community participation in education. They are mostly from the stakeholders themselves– teachers, parents, community members, etc.

Resistance among Teachers – Not all teachers welcome the community's participation in education. They tend to feel threatened that they would lose their authority within schools as power is snatched by the community. At the same time, they are compelled or feel obliged to involve community members who sometimes are not willing to participate in any school activities.

Parents and Communities – Not all community members are willing to get involved in school activities. Some of them are hesitant as they might have had negative schooling experiences themselves; some are illiterate and don't feel comfortable talking to teachers, while some feel that since they don't have any kind of control over the school, there's no point in getting involved.

Some parents and families are not willing to collaborate with schools by educating their children because they cannot afford to lose the latter's earnings or contribution through labour to the family. Even though they see the benefits in sending children to schools, opportunity costs are sometimes too high to pay.

Communities ought to have the right to plan for the educational needs of their children. Expecting them to play a limited role in merely executing departmental programmes is not the way in which school autonomy and effective decentralization can be nurtured.

Much greater investment on developing skills among teachers and community leaders for effective management of schools is required for decentralized management to be successful. Forms of social audit that allow full transparency in maintenance of school records will be needed if schools have to be owned up by the community.

Role of DPEP in Community Participation in Education

Involvement of the community in the process of education started as an informal initiative. It became more formalized as a 'state planning initiative' in recent years. This was made possible through constitutional amendments as well as programmes like DPEP and SSA. In fact, the SSA framework also states that the success of SSA will depend on the quality of the community-based planning process.

In order to make community participation more meaningful and solid, DPEP strived to develop a formal procedure for community participation. The steps involved were:

1. Creating awareness among parents about the importance of sending their children to school regularly.
2. Adopting persuasion rather than enforcement as a means of universal participation of children in primary education.
3. Awarding various incentive schemes to children that motivated parents to send them to school regularly.
4. Increasing awareness that created a further demand for education, which enabled the concerned to provide educational facilities.
5. Establishing VECs that ensured community support for establishing and managing new schools – this lead to a sense of ownership among the community. VECs also helped sustain community participation through mobilizing physical and financial support to schools.
6. Taking up TLCs that ensured a conducive environment for active participation of the community in school education.
7. Microplanning that involved setting up a core planning team in each habitation including VEC members, NGO representatives, school head teacher, selected teachers and parents. Community planning included special action plans in order to ensure community partnership in the management of the school.
8. Conducting programmes like parent-teacher meetings and 'Samudayadatta Shale' that enabled the community to monitor school functioning and performance of children.
9. Encouraging NGOs working in allied fields – health, child labour, SHGs – to promote an integrated approach to human resource development including education.

Role of SSA in Ensuring Community Participation in Education

The SSA envisaged the role of local communities in schools as follows:

(a) Community ownership of school-based interventions through effective decentralization.
(b) Local management of schools through SMCs as a part of the decentralization process (as decided by the particular state).
(c) Transfer of all school-related funds through these committees to schools to ensure better accountability.
(d) Capacity building of community leaders regarding management of schools, monitoring children's progress, procedure for expenditure of school funds, etc.

(e) Community-based planning – SSA made it mandatory to track the progress of every child in the 0-14 age group, which again called for focused capacity building of members of PRIs and SMCs.
(f) Habitations rather than villages were recognized as units of planning. In urban areas, a cluster of households in a slum settlement was taken as a unit of planning. Schools were supposed to play a critical role in the planning process by involving the community in regular school-related activities.
(g) Community-based monitoring – The Education Management Information System (EMIS) was expected to correlate school level data with the community-based information derived from surveys and micro-planning. All reports on enrolment, attendance, incentives, student performance were supposed to be displayed on the notice board.
(h) SSA encouraged partnership between communities and research institutions in order to improve the quality of monitoring and research. Process and quality indicators were developed to track the quality of programme implementation.
(i) Teacher recruitment, rationalization and management – SSA encouraged decentralized management of teachers. Local governments were encouraged to recruit teachers, thereby enhancing accountability of teachers to the local community.
(j) Improvement of school facilities – community participation was the basic criterion for undertaking any work to improve school facilities.

SDMCs of Karnataka

The Task Force on Education constituted in Karnataka under the chairmanship of Dr Raja Ramanna, (in 2000) recommended monitoring of school level development through facilitation and not inspection and entrusting local level monitoring to stakeholders. Hence, it recommended the constitution of school level monitoring committees consisting of parents of school-going children.

SDMCs were constituted for every school in 2001, as an extension of the PR system. This reflected a shift in the government's position towards viewing each school as a distinct and independent entity. These SDMCs worked under the Civil Amenities Committee, a body constituted under the Karnataka Panchayat Raj Act, 1993.

The SDMC was visualized to overcome the limitations of the SBC and the VEC and motivate the community to treat the school as a community owned institution. The involvement of parents helped break the monopoly of a few dominant individuals over the affairs of the school.

Some of the important functions envisaged for SDMCs were:

(1) Preparation of annual plan for the school.
(2) Monitoring attendance of teachers and students.
(3) Ensuring enrolment of out-of-school children in the village/habitation.
(4) Ensuring hygiene, upkeep and maintenance of the school.

(5) Augmenting infrastructure facilities.
(6) Reviewing performance of students and teachers periodically.
(7) Supervising the hot cooked meal programme.

Though the above functions suggested that SDMCs were significantly empowered, the reality in the field was slightly different. While a majority of them in Karnataka functioned well, there were some negative reports such as those of tensions between teachers and SDMC members. Most of these members were non-literate and unaware of several education issues, and tended to view issues rather narrowly. Several cases of harassment of lady teachers by SDMC presidents and members, (leading to suicides of lady teachers in some cases) were reported in newspapers.

Several SDMCs were not fully functional and sometimes were controlled by one or two dominant members. In many cases, the members were totally indifferent towards the school whereas in other cases, they only wanted to exercise authoritarian control over the teachers. It appeared that the main objective of the SDMCs was to spend the allotted money which, in turn, led to misappropriation in several cases.

The SDMC research study undertaken jointly by PPU, APF and National Law School in 2004 made the following observations:

1. In some cases (about 2 per cent), the monitoring mechanism was ineffective in documenting non-formation of SDMCs and in taking further action.
2. Many SDMCs did not focus on learning achievement of the students.
3. There was wide variation in members' level of awareness regarding objectives, powers and functions of SDMCs.
4. 83 per cent of the presidents and 50-70 per cent of the ex-officio members attended the monthly meetings; many permanent members were found to be rather irregular.
5. Many student representatives were unaware of the meetings because they were not informed and there was no clarity on their role.
6. Five out of eight block level officers felt that the SDMCs were functioning well and they had a positive impact on school development.
7. Teachers were not aware of the happenings in the SDMCs and hence did not appreciate their performance.
8. Most of the SDMCs had prioritized civil works and had made contributions to them.

NGO PARTICIPATION IN ELEMENTARY EDUCATION

'Unlike the public sector which is often accused of inefficiency and non-responsive behaviour, or the private sector which, driven by profit, prices itself out of the reach of the poor, the voluntary sector is perceived to be motivated by altruism, making it a suitable catalyst for promoting sustainable development of the poor in rural areas; an agency capable of giving voice to the needs and aspirations of people enabling the growth of local participatory mechanisms for self-empowerment'. HDR (Karnataka) 2005.

In recent years, NGOs have emerged as key players in social development in the country by supplementing public/government efforts. Many a time, they have involved themselves as important stakeholders in various social development programmes. Having efficient and participatory service delivery systems, they have been instrumental in promoting and supporting education delivery, healthcare, literacy, poverty alleviation through sustainable development, rehabilitation, women and childcare, human development programmes, environmental protection, HIV/AIDs support programmes, agriculture extension services, etc.

The inherent strengths of some of the effective NGOs are – willingness to work in remote areas among the depressed classes, ability to set in motion a participatory process in identification of the needs, the design and implementation of programmes, the readiness to mobilize and use local resources, a non-hierarchical approach in working with people, cost effective service delivery, freedom from red tape and freedom to innovate.

With governments requiring additional support to fulfil their commitments to society, NGO participation enables them to reach out to the most vulnerable sections of the society. NGOs also prefer a role that is markedly different from that of the governments. Most of them have focused on areas neglected by the latter. While most government initiatives have been on the supply side of education, several NGOs have made efforts to work with communities and improve the demand for education.

However a majority of them see themselves in a supportive role for creating a facilitative environment for learning. Some of the thrust areas of focus by NGOs are:

- NFE to working children who do not attend school
- Literacy
- Evolving teaching-learning aids
- Teacher training
- Empowerment of community
- Enrolment and reduction of dropouts
- Improvement of pedagogic techniques
- Midday meal scheme
- Improvement of school infrastructure.

Despite the presence of many NGOs, a majority of the states do not have a declared or a clearly defined policy on their involvement in the education sector. This has naturally led to some of them trying to influence government policies. Transparency, accountability and regular social audit need to be considered as criteria for allowing them to work in sensitive social sectors like education.

Collaboration of Governments with NGOs in Education

Since the government alone could not achieve the goals of EFA and UEE, it was felt that the collaboration of voluntary organizations, the community and NGOs was necessary, especially in the areas of access, retention and achievement.

The GOI laid emphasis on implementation of NFE through local and national NGOs as well as other voluntary agencies. It viewed NGOs as vibrant partners in the process of moving towards the goals of EFA. Hence as a policy, it proposed to promote their role at all levels in the social sector with a view to not only achieving participatory development but also unburdening the unduly loaded government departments with the implementation of development programmes. It gave liberal grants to these agencies to support such activities.

Besides running NFE centres, some of these NGOs implemented innovative programmes for promoting elementary education. The states noticed their involvement in enlarging the network of agencies in the education field, which would bring greater flexibility and innovation into the government programmes.

The last two decades have seen several successful collaborative efforts between government agencies and NGOs on a large-scale like Pratham, APF, Maya, MV Foundation, Akshaya Patra Foundation, etc. Many of them focus on socially and economically backward areas, marginalized sections of society and on education of girls. A number of them are providing health, nutrition and education to working children and those in urban slums.

Many of these NGOs have worked in specific areas in the field of pre-school and primary education, girls' education, in improving access, enrolment, retention, preparation of education materials, organization of bridge courses, supplementing governmental efforts in providing midday meals, testing of educational attainments of children, etc. Some of them have also collaborated in efforts at social mobilization, facilitating formation of VECs/SMCs, providing orientation to members of VECs/SMCs and PRIs, assisting in supervision, training and evaluation, assisting resource units in providing academic support and TLM, providing training in local communication skills to educators, etc. The NLM and SSA have taken measures to strengthen their partnership with NGOs.

More than 1,000 NGOs are at present actively engaged in rendering cooperation and resource support to various ongoing educational projects with assistance from the government. Their participation together with community support has helped improve the physical conditions and environment of several thousand primary schools in the country.

Issues Concerning NGOs

1. The larger NGOs develop hierarchies and start duplicating the government in all their activities which reduces their effectiveness.
2. Many NGOs are dependent on donor funds. The donors in turn impose certain conditions (sometimes with an ulterior purpose) which make the NGOs lose flexibility and independence in operations.
3. There is a certain amount of secrecy regarding donors and use of their funds.
4. The next serious issue is mandate and accountability – professing to speak for the people or acting as alternatives to government structures undermines the credibility of NGOs.
5. Most NGOs are small, lack institutional capacity, have access to limited funds and are capable of dealing with single or isolated issues and in selected small pockets; hence, they are unable to make a substantial difference to the programmes and activities.

6. There are instances of certain NGOs bidding for contracts from government which also undermines their purpose and credibility.

Brief Profiles of a Few NGOs

There are hundreds of NGOs working in diverse sectors in the field of elementary education. Profiles of a few prominent NGOs are discussed here.

Akshaya Patra Foundation

Since 2000, the Akshaya Patra Foundation (under the aegis of ISKCON, Bangalore) has been addressing the issue of hunger and its correlation with education in the country. With a humble beginning of feeding 1500 undernourished children in Bangalore, the programme has since grown to reach one million children in seven states across India, making it the largest charitable midday meal programme in the world.

The programme utilizes the food grains and conversion charges provided by the governments, and supplements them with its own funds to prepare and distribute tasty and nutritious food (prepared hygienically) to school children. Akshaya Patra initiated the concept of mechanization of its urban kitchens. The Foundation plans, implements, operates, maintains and updates the food management systems so as to meet the highest standards of hygiene and cleanliness. Several of its kitchens have received the ISO 22000 certification.

In addition, the Foundation has launched the decentralized kitchen models in remote parts of Rajasthan and Orissa where there are challenges of road connectivity and material supply. These small kitchens are run by women's SHGs, which provide employment to local women and enhance their socio-economic status.

The Foundation also provides a holistic development environment by conducting teacher training programmes to improve quality of teaching in government and corporation schools. The Life Skills Programme aims to inculcate essential skills among children addressing areas of creativity, critical thinking, problem solving and communication.

Pratham's Initiatives

Pratham started its operations in the slums of Mumbai in 1994. Since then, it has reached more than a million children through pre-school, in-school and out-of-school programmes across the country. Together with its sister organizations, it has taken up projects in several states aimed at mainstreaming children who are out-of-school, working, from the slums, etc. Its programmes for children at risk are meant mainly for those who are working and those who live in remand homes. Pratham's instructors conduct classes for these children initially in their work places with the objective of eventually relieving them from labour and mainstreaming them in regular schools.

Since 2005, every year, Pratham and its associates have been bringing out the 'Annual State of Education Report' (ASER) which is a unique survey of the status of learning in rural India. Educational administrators and policy-makers use these reports to evaluate the impact and progress of their own primary education programmes.

MV Foundation (MVF) of Andhra Pradesh

MVF is now well known for the pioneering work done in providing basic education to working children. It emphasized on strengthening government schools rather than creating alternate schools under NFE. It began its efforts by withdrawing children from work and ended by enrolling them in government schools. The strategies adopted by MVF were:

(a) Convincing parents and children about the need for education through advocacy measures.
(b) Developing confidence in children to study in regular formal schools.
(c) Taking the children away from their homes and work places.
(d) Bridging the gap in academic abilities between these children and the school-going children through bridge courses/summer camps on a full-time basis.

The MVF programme began in 3 villages of AP in 1990. It expanded and freed several hundred villages of child labour and enrolled all children below 11 years in formal schools. The programme also brought attitudinal changes among members of the community, parents, employers and teachers. It fostered community support and paved the way for significant social and cultural changes and practices (like girls' marriage). The NGO also puts pressure on the school system to improve school functioning so that children are retained as long as possible. This successful initiative of MV Foundation inspired several such programmes across the country.

Janarth

'Janarth' an NGO-based in Maharashtra runs the 'Shakshara Shala' programme which covers the sugar belt of western India. The programme extends to three states – Maharashtra (11 districts), Gujarat (2 districts) and Karnataka (2 districts). It is estimated that 7.75 lakh labourers migrate from central and western Maharashtra to these areas during sugarcane crushing season every year. Of these 25-30 per cent are estimated to be children below 14 years of age.

'Shakshara Shalas' are alternate short-term schools that run in temporary structures near sugar factories for six to seven months each year during the migration period. Each school caters to 75-100 children. There is one classroom and one teacher for every 25 children. Each school has also a pre-primary centre attached to it.

Currently, the NGO is running 145 such schools in 45 factories covering 15,000 children. 46 per cent of these children are girls. The programme has also convergence with ICDS to cover infants. The NGO sends the attendance and examination records of students back to their respective village schools to help them seek re-admission on their return.

Azim Premji Foundation (APF)

The APF, established with the personal resources of Sri. Azim Premji (of WIPRO) and operational since January, 2001, is a non-profit organization. It has since grown into a large organization having a national footprint with a team of 200 professionals, in addition to several hundred paid volunteers in the field.

Its vision is to – 'significantly contribute to achieve quality universal education that facilitates a just, equitable and humane society'. Its guiding principles are:

- Focus on 'quality of education in rural government elementary schools'
- Contribute to systemic change and not merely create islands of excellence
- Partner with government(s) in quality initiatives
- Implement – not just fund projects
- Significantly invest in people resources and continuously build capability within the organization to work on quality initiatives.

APF aims to concentrate on curriculum, examinations, teacher preparation and support, education management, and ICT as critical factors in improving education systems in the country. With Karnataka as the focus state, it attempted to understand the management of the education system and thereby create a motivating environment for teachers and education administrators as well as build their capability. Some of these initiatives resulted in:

1. Helping GOK to reorganize the education system based on the organization study of the Karnataka education system by Price Waterhouse Coopers
2. Understanding the role and effectiveness of community in education – a pilot was launched in four clusters across six regions of the state
3. Developing a culture of using facts, data, IT and analysis to make decisions within the government – more than 2000 education functionaries were trained with more than 15,000 person-days of training
4. Contributing to the development of education management– 53,000 education functionaries up to head teacher level were taken through an intensive management and leadership capacity development effort.

Some of the successful initiatives of APF so far are:

1. **Learning Guarantee Programme (LGP):** This programme began with the objective of identifying schools that met the enrolment, attendance and learning outcome criteria. With experience, it moved to a hypothesis that reforms in examinations would enable the teacher to move from rote learning to developing competencies among children. Currently, LGP is being implemented across 4 states, after running its course of three-years in Karnataka. The Karnataka government adopted this model for the entire state and set up the KSQAO for the purpose. In the other states where LGP had been taken up, the state governments replaced their traditional examinations with that of the competency-based examination designed under the LGP. (For details regarding LGP in Karnataka refer Chapter VI).
2. **Computer-aided Learning:** The programme was launched to create excitement through a novel approach so as to improve enrolment and attendance. A little later, APF began developing education software aimed at improving learning of the children. The education software developed for elementary children (as in 2008) has 119 titles in 18 languages, including 4 tribal languages, and was used in more than 16,000 elementary schools across 13 states involving more than 2.5 million children.

3. **Technology for Teacher Training:** This effort along with work on 'Teacher Preparation & Support' aimed at reaching out to more than 5.5 million teachers using technology to build their capability to engage children in a meaningful way.
4. **Technology for Effective Management:** APF worked with the Karnataka Education Department to develop the EMIS using the computer network established by SSA in all education offices of the state.
5. **Workbooks for Classes 1-8:** APF developed workbooks (for Rajasthan) in core subjects to supplement the textbooks. This project was undertaken in partnership with Digantar and Vidya Bhawan, two NGOs in Rajasthan. It was aimed at enhancing the teaching-learning process in schools across Rajasthan.
6. **Child Friendly School, Shorapur (Karnataka):** The project was aimed at promoting systemic change at the block level through individual school transformation. It involved a process of intensive work with each school to develop a holistic 'School Improvement Plan'. As at 2008, more than 50 per cent of the schools in Shorapur project were on target achieving the agreed quality improvement norms.
7. **Remedial Teaching:** This programme covered over 36,000 children in north-east Karnataka in 825 habitations (2001-02).
8. **Partnerships:** APF built partnerships with other organizations having a similar vision. This contributed to specific expertise and value in areas such as research, documentation, academics and pedagogy. The organizations were: Agastya Science Foundation, Karnataka; C-Lamps, Bangalore; Education Resource Unit, Delhi; Digantar, Jaipur; IIT Powai – Mumbai; Karnataka State Trainers Collective, Mangalore; College for Leadership and Human Resource Development; National University of Singapore; Quest Alliance – USAID, Pratham, Dr Reddy's Laboratory and others; Rashtreeya Vidyalaya Shikshana Samithi, Bangalore; Sandhan, Jaipur; SIDH Society, Dehradun; Singapore International Foundation – Singapore; Vidya Bhawan Society, Udaipur.

The various activities of APF across the country (as at 2008) are profiled below:

Table 7.1 Nation-wide Activities of APF (December 2008)

Initiatives	Outreach (States)	Coverage
Assessment led Reforms Learning Guarantee Programme	Uttarakhand (6 districts)	1980 schools
	Gujarat (2 districts)	967 schools
	Rajasthan (2 districts)	1,039 schools
	Karnataka	After three-years of running LGP, GOK expanded the concept to all 46,000 government and aided schools under KSQAO

Technology Initiatives Computer-aided Learning	13 states and Uts AP, Chandigarh, Chhattisgarh, Delhi, Gujarat, HP, Karnataka, Orissa, Pondicherry, Punjab, Rajasthan, TN, Uttarakhand	16,017 schools
Child Friendly School	Karnataka (1 block)	350 schools
Education for Children of Migrant Labour	Karnataka (Bangalore)	2 construction sites (schools) in Bangalore city
Workbook Project	Rajasthan	Classes 1-8 for the whole state
Education Management • Management Development Programme • Namma Shaale (Understanding the role of community in education)	Karnataka	Capacity building for all 53,000 + education functionaries
	Karnataka (4 clusters)	74 schools

Source: APF, Bangalore

Thus, as one can see, NGOs to a large extent have been able to contribute substantially in the field of elementary education in the country. They have also been able to provide much needed expertise to state governments in areas of educational research, field studies, survey, assessment and evaluation, software development, data analysis, innovative approaches, etc., which is definitely a welcome development in the elementary education sector in the country.

8

Financing of Education in India

Financing of education in India is a multi-dimensional issue. Education accounts for a significant proportion of public and private sector expenditure with public expenditure being largely seen as a states' commitment to education. Investment in education is also viewed as an investment in 'human capital' as it benefits both the individual and the society. The education sector is a very large employer of teaching and supervisory staff. Further, education is considered a component of micro-economic reform as it is supposed to meet the constantly changing demands of the job market in the context of increasing globalization of the world economy. All this provides for a strong basis for substantial state spending on education.

In a developing country like India, mobilization of resources for primary education on a large-scale has received considerable attention of the governments, in view of their commitment to UEE. However, public spending on education has been limited by several critical factors such as economic meltdown, deficit in balance of payments, rising inflation levels, the states' financial position, financial priorities given to social sectors, demands on finances by other priority sectors, political will and states' commitment to education. One finds that in the budgetary allocations, education has to compete with large and important sectors like defence, irrigation and power on the one hand, and other social priority sectors like health on the other.

Hence, policy-makers, educators, and others involved in the field of education both at the centre and state levels, are constantly exploring ways to utilize the available limited resources efficiently so as to identify and solve problems in the education sector and to provide quality education.

This chapter has tried to examine the various aspects of financing of education in India, especially in view of the country's commitment to UEE.

EXPENDITURE ON EDUCATION AS A PERCENTAGE OF GDP

Many countries, developed as well as developing, spend nearly 6 per cent of their GDP on education. According to 2002 figures, the US spent 5.6 per cent, France 5.8 per cent, Germany 4.6 per cent, Thailand 5 per cent and Kenya 6.2 per cent of their GDP.

The Kothari Commission recommended that at least 6 per cent of GDP should be spent on education. The NPE 1986 had also recommended, '...from the Eighth Plan onwards, it (expenditure on education) will uniformly exceed 6 per cent of the National Income.' However, this did not materialize. The question now is: Are we ever going to achieve this magical figure? The GOI has continued to reiterate that it is committed to raising the allocation as per recommendations of various policy documents. It has also reiterated that half of this amount will be spent on elementary and secondary education sectors. Despite implementation of several large-scale CSS and big externally assisted projects, the magnitude of financial expenditure by the government, has remained far below the expected level of 6 per cent of national income. It must be noted that the figure of 6 per cent of GDP was suggested by the Kothari Commission in the sixties; apparently, with the current size of the population, the figure needs to be reviewed for an increase.

Public Expenditure on Education in India

There has been substantial increase in the allocation of resources for education, if one considers the long-term trend since independence. As a percentage of GDP, it increased from 0.64 per cent in 1951-52 to 4.3 per cent in 1999-2000, but started declining in later years. Thus the target of 6 per cent of GDP has not been achieved so far.

Table 8.1 Expenditure on Education in India

Year	Total Revenue Expenditure on Education (in Rupees Crores)	Percentage of Education Expenditure Compared to Expenditure on all Sectors	Education Expenditure as a % of GDP
1951-52	64.46	7.92	0.64
1960-61	239.56	11.99	1.48
1970-71	892.36	10.16	2.11
1980-81	3,884.20	10.67	2.98
1990-91	19,615.85	13.37	3.84
1994-95	32,606.22	12.95	3.56
1999-2000	77,056.30	14.61	4.31

Source: Select Education Statistics 2000-01, MHRD

The HDR 2005 has given the following estimates regarding the country's public spending on education:

Table 8.2 Public Spending on Education in India

Public spending on education as % of GDP	4.1%
As percentage of total government expenditure	12.7%
Pre-school & Primary Education	38.4%
Secondary Education	40.1%
Tertiary Education	20.3%

Source: HDR 2005 (UNDP)
(Also please refer Annexure VIII – Tables 43 and 44)

Within the total budget expenditure on education in India, revenue expenditure accounts for more than 99 per cent. However, it is surprising to note that the public expenditure on education, as a percentage of GDP as well as a percentage of budgetary expenditure on education has declined in recent years.

Table 8.3 Decline in Public Expenditure on Education in India

Year	Percentage of GDP	Percentage of Budget	Per capita (Rs) (1993-94 prices)
2000-01	4.26	12.23	509
2001-02	3.82	10.80	470
2002-03	3.97	12.60	495
2003-04	3.74	12.31	498
2004-05	3.49	12.27	NA
2005-06	3.58	12.68	NA

Source: India Development Report 2008

External Assistance for Education Projects

Programmes of EFA to bring about quality were visualized to cost more money than what was available to the education sector in the past. Until 1990s primary education in India was almost free from external funding. Hence, the GOI went for international assistance as a part of a larger effort to mobilize more resources for education.

Some of the international agencies supporting the EFA programmes in India were – UN bodies (UNDP, UNESCO, UNPF, UNICEF, UNFPA), the World Bank and the Asian Development Bank (ADB). Bilateral grants were obtained from a number of donors such as the European Commission, DFID, SIDA, NORAD, HIVOS, the Netherlands and Japan. Large programmes such as DPEP were supported and funded jointly by several of these agencies. Five UN agencies supported the development of a joint initiative (Janashala) on community based education with the GOI and state governments.

Assistance from UN agencies and bilateral donors was in the form of grants while the World Bank provided concessional loan assistance through IDA. Matching contributions were provided by central and state governments for such projects. International support was also provided by NGOs such as Action Aid, Aga Khan Foundation, CARE, Save the Children Fund, Plan International, US Aid, etc.

External aid for elementary education rose from Rs37 crores in 1993-94 to Rs1,210 crores in 2001-02 (budget estimates). This was an increase from <5 per cent of the central government's plan expenditure to >20 per cent. As a proportion of the central government's plan expenditure on elementary education, it increased from 10 per cent to >30 per cent. This raised the issue of whether our dependency on foreign aid for financing elementary education was increasing, and how this affected the public education system and the strategies for future expansion.

Central Government Expenditure on Education

Though comparatively small when compared to expenditure incurred by the states, central funds have influenced state policy in the choice of new programmes, prescribing priorities, and so on. Taking plan and non-plan expenditure together, the share of the centre in elementary education has increased steadily from 12 per cent in 2000-01 to 27 per cent in 2007-08. An analysis of sector-wise central expenditure on education is given in Annexure VIII – Table 43.

States have accepted funds from the central government under various schemes for improvement such as financing additional teachers, classrooms, laboratory and library materials, and TLM. Central government funding was done through CSS and special programmes like DPEP and SSA as well as through budgetary support to initiatives and projects like OB, Computer Education, Promotion of Science, Teacher Education, etc.

The most important of the central schemes were the OB which financed additional teachers and classrooms, the Teacher Education Scheme which financed the DIETs and CTEs in all the states, the DPEP funded by the World Bank and the SSA for UEE. Even though these schemes had certain scope for modification to suit states' needs, the states accepted the general parameters set by these schemes. This impacted the planning process as it became a top-down approach rather than a bottoms-up one.

Criticism of Centrally Sponsored Schemes (CSS)

Over the last few decades, a majority of the states depended increasingly on CSS for raising the magnitude of plan expenditure on elementary education. The experience of CSS in improving quality has not been totally satisfactory. Rigidity in norms led to procurement of low quality materials (as in OB) and construction of smaller classrooms in several states.

There were also several issues and problems pertaining to CSS, as pointed out by Praveen Jha & others in their book 'Public Provisioning for Elementary Education in India'. Some of these issues are listed below:

1. Coverage was not universal and need-based under many of these programmes which resulted in sharp variations even at the level of implementation across states and districts within a state.
2. CSS, by design, favoured economically better-off states as they were easily able to contribute matching grants. They also had better capacity to utilize the

central funds. In contrast, the poorer states were at a disadvantage regarding these matters and hence they suffered from delay in release of central funds.

3. The design of the CSS (with rigid guidelines) failed to address problems specific to states with the latter being rarely permitted to amend the norms/guidelines of the programmes.
4. Delays in release of central funds resulted in non-achievement of targets within the prescribed time frames. Also, states were not able to properly utilize funds due to several inherent constraints which resulted in delay or non-receipt of further central grants, thus directly impacting the programmes.
5. Several of these programmes lacked community participation during their implementation. Efforts on this front did not yield encouraging results.
6. Resource crunch resulted in a number of states exploring expansion of schooling facilities through low cost, non-formal alternatives such as appointment of para/part-time teachers which directly impacted quality.
7. Lack of proper accountability, inability to ensure correctness of data reported by the states, indifferent attitude of the states towards central schemes and misuse of funds were some of the major factors impacting the proper implementation of these schemes.

Expenditure Incurred by the States in India on Education

Although the central government plays an important role with education being in the concurrent list, public provisioning of education is primarily a responsibility of state governments. The expenditure incurred by the states is comparatively more than that incurred by the centre. As seen in Table 8.4, states have been spending more than 80 per cent of total budget expenditure on education in India. However, in the last few years, the centre's share has been steadily going up due to implementation of large-scale programmes like SSA and the midday meal programme. As a proportion of the total budget for all sectors, the centre spends about 3 per cent and the states spend about 20 per cent on education.

Table 8.4 Share of Expenditure by the Centre and the States

Year	Share of the Centre to Total Expenditure (%)	Share of all the States to Total Expenditure (%)	Total Budget Expenditure (in Rs Crores)
1995-96	14.3	85.7	38,768.69
1997-98	14.5	85.5	48,954.93
2000-01	12.3	87.7	82,879.16
2002-03	18.8	81.2	85,889.39
2004-05 (BE)	19.2	80.8	99,917.18

Source: Public Provisioning for Elementary Education in India, Praveen Jha & others

The share of education in the budgets of most state governments has declined significantly, (as also per pupil expenditure in less developed states) as their financial policies accorded low priority to social sectors like education.

Within the total budgetary expenditure on education, elementary education gets between 42-52 per cent. A very important aspect of financing elementary education by the states in India is that close to one-fourth of the expenditure is undertaken through the local bodies. However, in states where total decentralization has taken place, it has been higher. For example, AP spent 65-77 per cent of its total revenue expenditure on elementary education through the local bodies whereas in case of Rajasthan, it was only in the range of 32-40 per cent. It must be noted that salaries of school teachers has constituted all or a major portion of this expenditure.

Public expenditure in the education sector in a state comprises two segments: plan and non-plan. The plan expenditure can be further categorized into expenditure on state plan schemes and central plan schemes including CSS. In case of CSS, the state is also required to provide matching grants based on a pre-decided ratio.

Within the total budget expenditure on education in a state, non-plan expenditure typically accounts for a very high share. For example, for a state like Rajasthan, in 2004-05, plan expenditure was only Rs293 crores against a non-plan expenditure of Rs1,932.4 crores. When one analyses the AP budget, one finds that salary alone accounts for 95 per cent of expenditure on elementary education. Less than 1 per cent is spent on teacher training. AP has not spent anything from the state budget over the period 1993-94 to 2002-03, on important items like textbooks, equipment and maintenance of buildings.

Education Expenditure Ratio

NHDR 2001 notes that over the 1980s and 1990s education expenditure ratio, i.e., the percentage of public expenditure on education, to the total public expenditure, has increased consistently at both centre and state levels. In the case of the centre, it increased from 2.7 to 3.9 from 1980-81 to 1998-99. In case of all the states (for which data was available), it increased from 13.89 in 1980-81 to 17.36 in 1991 and further to 17.39 in 1998-99. In the 1990s, this ratio increased considerably in Rajasthan, Orissa and Bihar but declined significantly in AP, Kerala and WB. The increase in spending was probably on account of higher salaries in many states in the wake of the Fifth Pay Commission.

Pattern of Expenditure in the Education Sector

One of the most significant factors related to change in the pattern of expenditure on education in recent years is the gradual increase in proportion of funds for elementary education in comparison to secondary and higher education sectors. In 1950-51, the share of elementary education in GNP was 0.48 per cent which gradually increased to 2.02 per cent by 2002-03. At present elementary education accounts for the bulk of the educational expenditure.

Another important shift in the expenditure on elementary education is a gradual increase in plan expenditure. Plan expenditure allows investment in development activities like improvement of school infrastructure, recruitment of new teachers, preparation and supply of TLM, capacity building of education personnel, etc.

Substantial investments have been made to upgrade the infrastructure and improve teacher availability in primary schools across the country. A large part of the overall investment has been from domestic resources even though external funding for primary education was substantial during the nineties.

Funding for Elementary Education

In the past, elementary education in India suffered from insufficient allocation of financial resources apart from several other factors. But of late, it is being accorded priority in government budgets. Yet, it has been unable to reach 50 per cent of the total central and state government budgets on education. In recent years, there has been a marked increase in central plan allocations – the outlay in the Tenth Plan (2002-07) was Rs43,825 crores, of which Rs28,700 crores was allocated for elementary education which was 75 per cent higher than the allocation in the Ninth Plan.

Table 8.5 Plan Allocation for Elementary Education 2005-06 (Rs in millions)

S. No.	Scheme	2004-05 Expenditure	2005-06 Budget Estimate
	Non EAPs		
1.	Sarva Shiksha Abhiyan	51,397.50	71,560.00
2.	KGBV	925.70	2250.00
3.	Midday Meal	15,838.20	30107.60
4.	Strengthening of TTIs	2025.40	1800.00
5.	NCTE	0.00	45.00
6.	National Bal Bhavan	42.30	45.00
	EAP		
7.	DPEP	5979.10	6000.00
8.	Shiksha Karmi Project	390.40	65.00
9.	Lok Jumbish	294.10	
10.	Mahila Samakhya	148.50	300.00
11.	Lumpsum provision for NE states & Sikkim	5266.50	10245.00
	Total	**82307.70**	**122417.60**

Source: EFA Document (2005) MHRD, EAP: Externally Assisted Projects

Fund Requirement for Implementing EFA Action Plan

The total funding requirement for implementing the National Action Plan for EFA was projected to be Rs94,119 crores.

Table 8.6 Total Funds Required for EFA (In crores)

S. No.	Sector	Centre	States	Total
1.	ECCE	12,247	0	12,247
2.	Elementary Education	39,760	12,520	52,280
3.	Midday Meal	6,600	11,000	17,600
4.	Girls' Education	2,575	375	2,950
5.	Youth & Adolescent Pro.	1,102	650	1,752
6.	Adult Education	6,340	0	6,340
	Total	69,574	24,545	94,119

Source: EFA Document (2005) MHRD

Hence, in order to fulfil its commitment to EFA, GOI is steadily increasing the share of education in the national budget. It has increased from 7.68 per cent in the Tenth Plan to 19.29 per cent in the Eleventh Plan. (Table 8.7).

The major focus of the Eleventh Plan will be on poverty reduction, ensuring access to basic physical infrastructure, health and education facilities for all, along with bridging the regional/social/gender gaps and focusing on the marginalized and weaker social groups.

Table 8.7 Allocation for Education During Tenth and Eleventh Plans

Sector	Tenth Plan BE in Crores	% of Total	Projected Allocation for Eleventh Plan in Crores	% of Total
Education	62,461	7.68	2,74,228	19.29
Total	8,13,778	100.00	14,21,711	100.00

Source: Eleventh Plan Document

Raising Resources – Education Cess

The tremendous increase in allocation for elementary education was possible on account of additional allocation from the receipts of the 2 per cent 'Education Cess' imposed on all major central taxes (income tax, excise and custom duties and service tax) from 2004-05. The funds flowed into a dedicated non-lapsable fund called 'Prarambhik Shiksha Kosh' (or National Elementary Education Fund) that could be used exclusively for elementary education projects like the SSA and the midday scheme. The cess helped to increase central funding under SSA by 3.2 times in 2004-05 as compared to 2002-03.

The collection of cess was an important decision taken by the GOI in order to provide additional funds for elementary education. Through it, the government was able to raise Rs8,500 crores in financial year 2006-07. Even then, this was only 12-15 per cent of the total government (union and states) expenditure on elementary education in the country. The collection helped enhance the implementation of various education schemes

states will continue whereby each of these states contributes only 10 per cent of the approved outlay as the state share.

Financial assistance from external agencies were pooled (along with money collected under 'Education Cess') with budgetary support from the central government. Allocations were made on the basis of Annual Work Plans (AWPs) submitted by the states. The AWPs were supposed to be the outcome of the planning exercise starting from the habitation and the school. In reality, most of the states prepared their AWPs by getting inputs from the district level functionaries.

During the first five years of SSA until 2006-07, the total expenditure in the programme was around Rs36,000 crores (shared both by the centre and state governments). Considering that there were nearly 21 crore children at the elementary school stage, the expenditure worked out to just over Rs1700 per child over five-years in addition to the expenditure that the states had been incurring annually like salaries of teachers and supervisory staff.

Funds Released under SSA

Every year from 2002-03 to 2005-06, the magnitude of funds released for SSA by the centre was significantly lower than 75 per cent of the aggregate approved amounts under AWP for all states. The total expenditure incurred by all the states under SSA during 2002-03 to 2004-05 was only 50.8 per cent of the approved AWPs for these three-years. However, the expenditure in 2005-06 significantly rose to around 78 per cent of the aggregate AWPs approved for all the states.

Several states (notably Gujarat, Maharashtra, Karnataka, WB, Assam, Tripura and Orissa) did not contribute their mandated shares fully which highlighted the lack of ownership of the programme. Inadequate release of funds resulted in delays not only in completion of infrastructure projects but also in release of teachers' salaries. The mid-term review of the Tenth Plan by the Planning Commission pointed out that several states like UP, Bihar, Jharkhand, Orissa, WB, and Punjab, showed a low resource absorption capacity under SSA. Hence, it was felt that institutional arrangements needed to be strengthened so as to build up capacity in these states.

The total outlay on SSA for the Tenth Plan period stood at Rs26,887 crores which was far short of Rs34,600 crores (for meeting requirements of UEE) estimated by the working group on Tenth Plan. The total budgetary allocation for SSA for 2005-06 was Rs7800 crores. This was 51.8 per cent more than the actual funds released for SSA during 2004-05. Every year there was a substantial increase in allocation of funds to elementary education. The union budget for 2008-09 gave a 20 per cent higher allocation for education, increasing it from Rs28,674 crores to Rs34,400 crores. The allocation for SSA was Rs13,100 crores. (Midday meal scheme was allotted Rs8,000 crores).

However the fact that the states have not been able to spend the approved outlays under SSA tells another story. Yet, the expenditure to approval ratio increased steadily from 15 per cent in 2001-02 to just over 70 per cent in 2006-07. This meant that nearly 30 per cent of the approved outlay of SSA remained unutilized by the states. It laid bare the inherent capacity constraints of many states to utilize funds and implement their own AWPs to the optimum.

Table 8.8 Average SSA Expenditure Per-district by the States Over a Three-year Period (2005-2007) (In crores)

State/UT	Average Expenditure/ District
AP	65.0
Assam	38.7
Bihar	36.8
Chhattisgarh	85.9
Goa	8.0
Gujarat	27.1
Haryana	27.8
HP	23.9
J&K	29.7
Jharkhand	45.5
Karnataka	45.4
Kerala	21.2
MP	62.3
Maharashtra	62.2
Manipur	5.3
Meghalaya	13.0
Nagaland	8.6
Orissa	43.0
Pondicherry	6.1
Punjab	19.6
Rajasthan	69.0
TN	40.9
Tripura	53.7
UP	90.3
Uttarakhand	33.3
WB	113.6

Source: ASER 2008, MHRD

The above table indicates a very wide variation in the per-district SSA expenditure of various states. While Manipur spent only Rs5.3 crores per-district, WB was able to spend as much as Rs113.6 crores.

The foregoing analysis shows that public funding of education in general and elementary education in particular needs to be raised substantially in order to meet the stated objectives.

In the Eleventh Plan period the focus of SSA shifted from access and infrastructure to enhancing retention and improving the quality of learning. According to broad assessments made by the Department of Elementary Education and Literacy, GOI nearly Rs60,000 crores additional resources were required from the centre and the states over the next ten-years for implementing the SSA initiative.

Per-child Expenditure under SSA

The per-child expenditure in various states presents a mixed picture as shown in the table given below:

Table 8.9 Central Releases and Per-child Expenditure in SSA (2006-07)

State	Centre's Release Rs in Crores	Share in 00s* Children (2005)	% of Centre's Release	Per-child** SSA Expenditure
Uttar Pradesh	2066.54	22.53	19.25	770
Madhya Pradesh	1108.80	8.16	10.33	1071
Bihar	1081.73	23.89	10.08	429
Rajasthan	758.10	5.98	7.06	918
West Bengal	639.12	9.12	5.95	666
Karnataka	542.06	0.90	5.05	623
Maharashtra	521.59	3.98	4.86	615
Jharkhand	520.86	4.67	4.85	883
Assam	514.18	4.03	4.79	730
Chhattisgarh	511.82	1.92	4.77	1554
Orissa	440.11	4.08	4.10	1030
Andhra Pradesh	388.61	2.50	3.62	474
Tamil Nadu	363.29	1.45	3.38	455
Haryana	256.47	1.31	2.39	712
Jammu & Kashmir	220.83	0.04	2.06	1211
Uttarakhand	169.34	0.88	1.58	1209
Gujarat	148.07	2.86	1.38	292
Punjab	128.80	0.82	1.20	416
Arunachal Pradesh	89.85	0.17	0.84	3379
Himachal Pradesh	62.51	0.17	0.58	1137
Tripura	53.30	0.04	0.50	1869
Kerala	43.82	0.04	0.41	235
Meghalaya	42.94	0.17	0.40	725

Mizoram	34.45	0.01	0.32	2194
Nagaland	23.15	0.24	0.22	994
Manipur	18.90	0.51	0.18	471
Goa	7.24	0.01	0.07	695
Sikkim	4.62	0.03	0.04	647

Source: ASER 2008 (provisional)
* Out-of-school children, ** includes (Centre+State) Expenditure

Although UP accounted for the highest share of central releases, its per-child expenditure was less than that of many states. On the other hand, Chhattisgarh's per-child expenditure was more than double that of WB. Bihar was almost on par with TN. This indicated that even with increased central government's releases of funds under SSA, the gap in per-child expenditure in educationally backward states was significant. However, percentage of out-of-school children was not the only criteria for obtaining central grants by the states.

At present a significant proportion of the SSA allocation goes to non-plan expenditure items – school grants, maintenance grants, TLM grants, teachers salaries, free supply of uniforms and textbooks – which the states have to take over as a committed liability at the end of the programme period.

The concern for the immediate future is to target increased resources on improving quantitative as well as qualitative aspects of educational facilities. Plan funds must be deployed increasingly to building educational capacity and infrastructure. States need to spend greater amounts on important activities like teacher training programmes, training of community leaders, research, evaluation, supervision, monitoring and innovative activities.

Considering the resource constraints of the states, the Mid-term Appraisal (MTA) of the Tenth Plan recommended that the ratio of 75:25 should be maintained till the end of the SSA mission period. The MTA further notes that enough attention has not been given to financing SSA perspective plans with pooling of resources at the district level adequately.

Public Expenditure on Education in Karnataka

A brief analysis of public expenditure on education in Karnataka is discussed here. Karnataka is a median level state in terms of educational indicators. Allocation for education in Karnataka in 2005-06 was just 3 per cent of GSDP. The proportion of education expenditure in total plan expenditure showed a significant drop from 7.3 per cent in Ninth Plan to 4.3 per cent in Tenth Plan. The per-student public expenditure in elementary education in Karnataka in 2006-07 was Rs4150.

The education sector accounted for just 12.2 per cent of the state's budget outlays. Plan expenditure that was typically associated with new initiatives and development accounted for about 21 per cent of the state budget in 2006-07.

At present, Karnataka spends about 6 per cent of the state's GSDP on the entire social services sector. This encompasses several sub-sectors (health, education, rural development, social welfare, women and child development, etc.) hence the actual share of each sub-sector is apparently quite low. The expenditure on general education was only about 3 per cent of the state's GSDP, which was still lower than the country average.

Table 8.10 Expenditure Under Different Heads as a Proportion of GSDP: Karnataka

Sector	1990-91	1998-99	2002-03
Social Services	6.32	6.00	6.01
General Education	3.03	2.78	2.99
Elementary Education	1.63	1.48	1.58
Secondary Education	0.89	0.89	0.93
University and Higher Education	0.45	0.35	0.42
Adult Education	0.04	0.01	0.005
Health and Family Welfare	1.00	0.93	0.88
Water Supply and Sanitation	0.31	0.58	0.42
Nutrition	0.28	0.09	0.08
Housing	0.15	0.21	0.28
Rural Development	1.01	0.45	0.46

Source: HDR, (Karnataka) 2005

The HDR (Karnataka, 2005) estimated that the state will have to spend another 2 per cent of GSDP on social priority sectors in order to achieve the human development targets set for the Tenth Plan. It further estimated that UEE alone required that the expenditure on elementary education as a proportion of GSDP would have to be increased from the present 1.6 per cent to 2.5 per cent.

The HDR further reported that the share of plan expenditure in Karnataka's total expenditure was the highest among all southern states. Even though the state had increased its public spending on education in real terms, in relation to the state income, its educational expenditure had fallen over the decade.

In 2005-06, the state spent about 7 per cent of the state plan expenditure on education. Competing demands on scarce resources made resource allocation to different sectors a complicated exercise.

Table 8.11 Plan Expenditure: Main Sectors by Investment

Year	Irrigation	Energy	Education	Other Social Services	Others	Total
2000-01	34.25	7.94	6.78	25.20	25.83	100.00
2001-02	29.67	12.58	7.16	24.00	26.59	100.00
2002-03	35.73	10.61	4.18	22.71	26.78	100.00

2003-04	28.00	14.80	6.74	24.03	26.43	100.00
2004-05	27.96	13.88	8.14	19.19	30.84	100.00
2005-06	29.08	13.68	7.47	16.19	33.59	100.00

Source: Annual Plan Documents 2000-01 to 2005-06, Figures in Percentages

An analysis of the above table showed that within the priority sectors, investments in irrigation exceeded investments in social sectors in a majority of the years. Also investments in energy exceeded investments in education in all the years. Within the government, the major part of education expenditure is met by the state education department while a small part is met by the social welfare department which finances residential schools, hostels and scholarships.

The drive towards UEE led to a phenomenal increase in the number of students and schools, with corresponding increase in number of teachers, building and equipment, which in turn led to an increase in expenditure on education. The periodical revision of scales of pay and DA of teachers and introduction of midday meals and other incentives were also responsible for increase in expenditure on school education.

Table 8.12 Increase in Expenditure on Primary Education in Karnataka

Year	Expenditure* on Primary Education	Percentage of Expenditure on Primary Education to Total Expenditure on Education
1956-57	520.76	60.90
1960-61	770.68	57.00
1970-71	2,620.41	42.60
1990-91	40,777.00	49.80
1995-96	88,528.32	52.81
2000-01	171,731.22	49.20
2007-08	292,454.61	57.31

Source: Various Budgetary Reports* in Lakhs

The HDR 2005 analysed the percentage of allocation of education outlay in various sub-sectors of education for the year 2002-03.

Table 8.13 Allocation to Various Sub-sectors within Education in Karnataka (2002-03)

Sub-sector	Revenue Expenditure %	Capital Expenditure %	Total %
General Education**	91.4	70.1	91.4
Elementary Education	48.3	NR	48.3
Secondary Education	28.4	26.7	28.4
University and Higher Education	12.8	43.4	12.9

Technical Education	2.4	2.8	2.4
Medical Education	3.4	27.7	3.4
Agricultural Education	2.8	0.0	2.8
Expenditure on Education*	19.8	0.2	16.6

Source: HDR 2005

NR: Not Reported as expenditure was under ZP/TP programmes.

Expenditure on Education (16.6 per cent) was the proportion to total expenditure of the state.
** General Education accounted for 91.4 per cent of total expenditure on education.

Thus, expenditure within the education sector was characterized by the dominant role of:

(a) Revenue expenditure in all types of education.
(b) General education within the education sector.
(c) Elementary education within general education.

The following table gives sub-sector-wise plan and non-plan expenditure on general education in Karnataka in the budget for 2006-07:

Table 8.14 (In crores)

S. No.	Sector	Plan	Non-plan	Total	Percentage
1.	Elementary Education	744.38	2180.17	2924.55	57.31
2.	Secondary Education	190.03	1350.64	1540.67	30.18
3.	University and Higher Education	26.38	485.50	511.88	10.04
4.	Adult Education	7.27	2.09	9.36	0.18
5.	Language development	4.40	9.27	13.67	0.27
6.	Other General Education	100.01	3.12	103.13	2.02
	Total	1072.47	4030.79	5103.26	100.00

Source: Budget Reports (Education) 2006-07

In the 2006-07 budget, the allocation for general education was 12.19 per cent (excluding Medical and Agricultural Education) of the total budgeted outlay.

The HDR commented – 'The non-salary component is low and the expenditure on infrastructure, teaching aids, curriculum development, instructional material, laboratories, libraries, in-service teacher training, in short all the things that contribute to the quality of education is totally inadequate'.

The state government is providing several incentives and subsidies to stimulate demand by offsetting the private costs of education. Education is free up to 10th standard for boys and up to 12th standard for girls in government institutions. The tuition fee in higher education sector (except self-financing institutions) is also heavily subsidized.

Elementary students in government institutions receive free textbooks and uniforms while girls studying in government secondary schools get free uniforms. Students studying in all government and aided (elementary and secondary) schools are covered under the hot cooked midday meal scheme. SC/ST girls in classes 5 to 7 receive free school bags and notebooks. SC/ST students at secondary and higher levels receive subsidized instructional materials and scholarships. Students from SC/ST/Backward/ Minority communities also get free/heavily subsidized hostel facilities. In addition, all students get transport concessions from public sector transport corporations.

Only in unaided and self-financing institutions (at all levels) do the parents finance all the costs of education (fee, educational materials, uniforms, books, etc.) of their wards.

Key Issues in Financing Education in Karnataka

The following were the key issues in financing education in the state:

1. Salary component accounted for nearly 90 per cent of the total outlay in different sectors of education. This implied that very little of the budgeted outlay on education was left for other development purposes.
2. The heavy cost of financing a very large number of private grant-in-aid institutions in the state impacted the pattern of expenditure on education in the state. Every new government brought more and more private institutions under the grant-in-aid scheme. This policy negatively impacted expenditure on the focus areas of education.
3. The World Bank Report advocated restructuring the grant-in-aid mechanism on grounds of efficiency and equity. It pointed that the aid to private schools benefited the higher income groups to a great extent while the poor benefited more from spending on government schools.
4. Hence, the World Bank Report advocated a revised policy to target subsidies to poor students to enable them to access secondary and higher education and encourage the private sector to seek efficiencies without compromising on quality. However, the state government did not consider implementing such a policy.
5. In order to achieve quality and improve learning outcomes, greater emphasis needed to be placed on non-salary components in the government sector such as infrastructure, laboratory and library facilities, TLM, curriculum and teacher training.
6. Every year with increase in salaries and number of teachers, unit costs rose, which further impacted increase of the share of non-salary components.
7. The World Bank Report pointed out that the distribution of expenditures was negatively correlated with educational backwardness of districts – the educationally more backward districts had higher PTRs and lower per-pupil expenditures.

8. These regional disparities in public spending resulted from state level decisions rather than the differing fiscal and economic capacity of the districts.

Apart from some austerity measures and cost cutting exercises, very little financial reforms were implemented in the state. In the context of improving educational performance, a well-defined financing policy which included changing the pattern of devolution and sanctioning resources to the needy areas/sectors was found to be necessary.

Budgetary Subsidies in Education

The Report of the Karnataka Universities Review Commission pointed out:

'.. higher education in universities has been subsidized to a great extent... People who choose to go for graduate, postgraduate and professional courses decide to invest their money anticipating relevant returns from future employment which will be based on such higher education. Higher education cannot be treated as a basic need or social good as much as elementary education... Therefore higher education has to be treated as a private good constituting private wealth'.

A study paper on subsidies in Karnataka (1997) which analysed the nature and volume of budgetary subsidies, noted – 'While provision of primary and secondary education facilities may be considered as provision for basic minimum needs to the population and therefore the expenditure on them cannot be considered as subsidy, there is no reason why the entire expenditure or even a major part of it on technical/higher education should be borne by the state government...'

The HDR (Karnataka 2005) estimated the implicit budgetary subsidy to higher education in Karnataka by using the framework in 'Narayana M.R.': 'Budgetary Subsidies to Higher Education: Evidence from Karnataka State'.

Table 8.15 Budgetary Subsidies to Higher Education

Aggregate Subsidy	2002-03
Rs in lakh at current prices	74464.83
Share of general education	63.06
Share of technical education	10.30
Share of agricultural education	13.80
Share of medical education	12.83
Aggregate subsidy to higher education to	
Total expenditure on	
(a) Primary Education	35.04
(b) Primary and Secondary Education	22.07

Source: HDR (Karnataka 2005)

Of the aggregate subsidy, the largest share (63.06 per cent) went to general education. Subsidy to higher education was 35.04 per cent (22.07 per cent in 2002-03) of the total expenditure on primary (primary and secondary) education.

Challenges in Financing Elementary Education in India

As per the estimates of the CABE Committee (2005), the additional financial requirement for providing free and compulsory elementary education up to the end of the Eleventh Plan (2006-12) was on an average Rs53,467 crores per annum or about 1.1 per cent of GDP. The main reason given by CABE for this financial requirement was that there was persistent under-provisioning for elementary education in the past, which further resulted in a large cumulative gap.

While providing projections, the Tapas Majumdar Committee noted that 6 per cent of national income was the minimum required for financing public expenditure in the education sector in India, and 'that the actual requirements would have to be eventually seen as substantially larger in the near future'. The recommended allocations presupposed formulation of proper plans and setting up of proper mechanisms for spending resources efficiently. Otherwise, increase in allocations would only lead to wasteful expenditure or misuse of resources.

The Committee noted that allocation to education could be increased by

(i) reallocating resources from other sectors, or
(ii) the government raising more resources from common pool resources or specifically for the education sector, or
(iii) by both.

However, the challenge lies not only in providing higher allocations for the elementary education sector but also in efficient and timely use of these resources by the states in order to reach the set goals of UEE.

9

Role of Private Sector in Elementary Education in India

The private sector pertaining to school education in India has witnessed a tremendous expansion in the last few decades. Privatization and globalization of the country's economy has fuelled an unprecedented demand for English medium schools. Further, a greater demand for quality basic education and a perceived decline of the public education system has led to parallel expansion and growth of the private school system in the country.

With the assurance of providing education of a better quality, though with higher fees, these private schools have managed to effect a gradual shift among the economically better-off classes from government schools to private ones, first in urban and semi-urban areas with rural towns and bigger villages catching up soon. A nationally representative survey ('Public and Private Schools in India' – Harvard University, Boston) of rural private schools conducted in 2003 found that 28 per cent of the rural Indian population had access to fee-charging private schools in the same village.

With nearly one-fifth of all elementary schools under private management, and a steady growth in private school enrolment which has reached 28 per cent of all enrolment at elementary level, it is necessary to examine the role of private schools more closely.

THE GROWTH OF PRIVATE EDUCATION INSTITUTIONS IN INDIA

The post-independence era has seen a remarkable growth in private sector educational institutions at all levels. The number of private aided and unaided (and also unrecognized) schools in the country increased rapidly in the last few years. While they have shown an annual growth of 25 per cent, government schools have recorded only 7 per cent during the past decade. India has nearly 2.44 lakh private elementary schools (constituting 20 per cent of all elementary schools in the country – Refer Table 9.1). A trend of increasing enrolments in private schools is also seen though there are wide variations across states.

Table 9.1 Types of Schools and Enrolments in India

Type of Schools	Number of Schools	Enrolment Classes 1-5	Enrolment Classes 6-8	Total Enrolment
Government Schools	1,002,915 (80%)	101,153,429 (76%)	32,498,650 (64%)	133,652,079 72%)
Private Schools	243,895 (20%)	32,736,432 (24%)	18,353,943 (36%)	51,090,375 (28%)
Total	1,246,810	133,889,861	50,852,593	184,742,454

Source: DISE 2007-08, NUEPA

According to ASER reports, the number of children in the 6-14 age group attending private schools steadily increased from 16.4 per cent in 2005 to 22.5 per cent in 2008 (28 per cent as per DISE which also includes urban schools). This increase was particularly striking in Karnataka, UP and Rajasthan. In Kerala, the enrolment in private schools more than doubled between 2005 and 2008 from 22.4 per cent to 49 per cent. Half of all school-going children in Kerala and Goa went to private schools, and 32-42 per cent in Nagaland, Punjab, Haryana, UP and Rajasthan went to private schools which were mostly unaided. According to DISE, 95 per cent of private schools in Kerala and 70 per cent in Goa were government aided.

The states of Nagaland, Kerala, Goa, J&K, HP, Punjab, Rajasthan, and Karnataka have reported the highest increase of private school enrolments. On the other hand, Bihar, Chhattisgarh and West Bengal have very low enrolment in private schools.

The Status of Private School System in India

Most of the states in India have Education Acts/Grant-in-aid Codes/Rules which regulate the establishment and management of private educational institutions. Private institutions are granted permission/recognition by the education departments of the states provided they meet certain prescribed conditions regarding enrolment, qualified teachers, curricula and school infrastructure.

But there are many instances of schools obtaining temporary recognition and functioning in unhealthy surroundings with poor infrastructure and under-qualified/in-experienced staff. Currently as discussed, 20 per cent of all elementary schools are in the private sector along with the country's estimated student enrolment of 28 per cent. However, want of information about these schools has been a problem. Critical information such as level and quality of infrastructure, number of teachers, PTRs, enrolment, proportion of female students, and sources and quantum of funds is not available either with the education departments of the states or with the GOI. Planning for school education is thus incomplete without adequate data in this sector.

Participation of the private sector in education increases as we move from elementary education to higher levels. Table 9.1 shows that the student enrolment which was at 24 per cent at the lower primary stage increased to 36 per cent at the upper primary stage.

In most states, the percentage of enrolment in government schools decreases from a high of 90 per cent in the elementary education sector to less than 30 per cent as we move higher. Private sector participation is also seen to be the lowest in educationally backward states and districts.

Perceptions about the Private School System

One significant advantage a private institution has over a government one is in the area of management. Policy and decision-making processes are faster. This translates into a higher degree of efficiency in management and therefore a higher degree of productivity.

Students, parents and the general public have strong perceptions of quality based on which they rate an institution and generally, private institutions score over government ones. Two important factors an educated parent takes into consideration while admitting his child to a private institution are 'quality' and the 'continuity' as education at all stages is often available in the same institution.

Parents expect a high standard of education and have comparatively higher expectations from these schools in terms of infrastructure, facilities, and teaching. Similarly, they expect better performance from their children also. Hence, these schools are under constant pressure to upgrade their facilities and improve the standard of education that they provide.

Cost of Education in Private Unaided Institutions

Most of the private institutions treat education as a commercial activity with the exception of a few reputed ones. It is common for private managements to charge heavy donations and fees, pay lower salaries to the staff, provide poor infrastructure and disregard government rules and regulations.

The unaided institutions do not receive any direct grants from the governments. However, the income from such institutions, if managed by a public charitable trust, is exempt from income tax. This is a major incentive for the private sector to establish and run educational institutions. In addition, some institutions managed by SC/ST and minority groups get land and other benefits from governments at concessional rates.

Even then, the cost of education in private institutions is relatively high. In fact, it is prohibitive in a majority of the unaided institutions. In spite of several 'Acts and Rules', the states have not been able to curb some of their unethical practices at the school level – heavy fees, imposition of costly uniforms and additional books (to be bought only from the school) apart from prescribed textbooks, collection of additional funds in the form of building fund, school excursions, school day, extra-curricular activities, and so on.

Teachers' Salaries

Teachers' salaries constitute the single largest expenditure (around 95 per cent) incurred by the managements of private institutions. In several states, the aided school teachers are paid salaries directly by the government under provisions of the grant-in-aid codes so as to prevent managements from misusing government grants. In such cases, the managements provide very little additional financial inputs for improvement of infrastructure and other facilities.

In the case of unaided schools, teachers' salaries are determined by market forces. Generally, they are paid far lesser than their counterparts in government institutions. Of late, some of the reputed private unaided institutions in metropolitan cities are trying to adopt corporate practices and are hiring the best talent by paying hefty salaries. But such institutions are very few and far behind.

Recruitment of Teachers in Private Institutions

Government institutions strictly adhere to recruitment rules and guidelines prescribed by the states. Generally, merit-cum-roster is the most important criteria in recruitment. In private aided institutions, recruitment is done locally and not always based on merit. In many cases, the aided school managements make a lot of money by selling the posts to the highest bidders. Even though procedures are prescribed by the state governments, private managements try and circumvent them to appoint those whom they favour.

Unaided institutions largely ignore the government recruitment and reservation policies. The only criteria these schools have to fulfil is to recruit trained teachers having certain minimum qualifications as prescribed by the state governments. In several cases, under-qualified and untrained teachers work in these institutions albeit under different names. Here, the exploitation of the staff is more the rule than an exception. There is a high degree of dissatisfaction among them as they are poorly paid and treated badly. In matters of service conditions too, they are at a serious disadvantage. With no job security, they are at the mercy of the managements as they can be hired and fired at will by the latter. Only in some private institutions, the contributory provident fund or equivalent schemes are in vogue. Other benefits and service conditions enjoyed by the government staff are almost unheard of in private unaided institutions.

This is borne out by the 'Sub-sector Study Report' (2001) on private institutions in Karnataka. The study found that the salaries of teachers in some of the best unaided schools in Udipi district of Karnataka was no more than two-thirds of what their counterparts in government and aided schools got. In most cases it was hardly 50 per cent. In some schools in Bijapur district of Karnataka, the situation was pathetic as the monthly salary paid for a school teacher was a mere Rs500 per month (consolidated). The situation was no better in colleges and other higher education institutions as well.

Thus, meager and unattractive compensation has brought in its wake a high degree of attrition that disturbs the academic work which in turn impacts quality in these institutions.

Minority Institutions

Under the Constitution, only two types of minority institutions are recognized – religious and linguistic – and both are put on par in Article 30. Article 30(1) ensures protection to linguistic and religious minorities, thereby preserving the secularism of the country.

Though the word 'minority' is not defined in the Constitution, literally it means 'a non-dominant group'. Muslims and Christians constitute the two principal religious minority groups in the country.

Government policies also promote the growth of institutions that provide educational opportunities to minority groups. A number of such institutions are found at all levels of education, both in aided and unaided sectors. Many schools run by Christian missionaries popularly known as Convent Schools are popular in urban and rural areas, and there is a very good demand for such institutions.

The roster system and recruitment policies of the state governments do not apply to minority institutions. Aided minority institutions enjoy certain privileges not available to general category ones. This includes a relaxation in the quota for admission of students and recruitment of staff from the respective minority groups.

Voucher system

In order to enforce accountability, the Planning Commission in its 'Approach Paper to the Eleventh Plan', proposed a system whereby parents can choose schools for their children. The concept behind it was to enable people to choose between the available public or private schools by giving them suitable entitlements reimbursable to the school. This was also expected to create competition among schools. Issues of targeting the needy and quality of education provided are often brought up with regard to vouchers.

However, in the current context of inadequate basic infrastructure in government schools, the issue remains quite different from developed countries where such a system has been tried. The question that arises is – should the government focus on building quality public institutions that provide education for all or, should it provide indirect subsidies to private schools through vouchers albeit with the aim of enhancing demand and arresting dropouts? It must be noted that the voucher system has not been tried out on a large-scale any where in the country to check its effectiveness in the Indian context.

Effect of Regulatory Policies on the Private Institutions

The existing regulatory policies are generally found to encourage the participation of the private sector in education. However, there are a number of critical issues which cause friction between the government departments and the private institutions in several states.

The Sub-sector Study Report on private institutions in Karnataka comments: 'Managements of private schools feel that unrealistic policies of the government with respect to (a) fee structure, (b) staff recruitment, (c) medium of instruction, (d) grants-in-aid – are the root causes of the so-called malpractices in private sector schools'.

Private managements have grouses against what they perceive to be restrictions in the growth of private institutions. Some of them are detailed below:

1. The establishment of private schools in several states continues to be generally discouraged or tightly controlled through an elaborate and cumbersome system of recognition, rules and regulations by government departments.

2. There are instances of private schools fighting long drawn legal battles with state governments, just for survival.
3. In some states, there is the issue of medium of instruction, where English medium private schools are discouraged on the basis of language policies of the states.
4. Unrealistically low student fee structures prescribed by some governments at all levels of education affect the quality of services in unaided institutions.
5. Several restrictions are placed on student admissions and staff selection in many states.
6. Inadequate/no representation is given to private institutions in policy-making bodies and decision-making processes, even when they are critical.
7. There are no opportunities for academic staff for further growth as they are not involved in professional/teacher training/orientation programmes at elementary and secondary levels.
8. Instances of harassing the managements of private institutions in matters of granting approvals of admissions/staff appointments (leading to corruption) are frequently reported.

In order to bypass the rigidity of rules prescribed by the states, several private schools opt to get affiliated to ISCE/CBSE Boards.

Criticism of the Private School System

Private schools provide an alternative to those who can afford them. Yet the quality of many is often questionable. Many of these schools are little more than 'teaching shops' run by poorly qualified and untrained staff for whom the school is a little more than a source of livelihood.

Despite this, such schools continue to attract increasing number of children, leading to closure of government schools, especially in urban and semi-urban areas. In other cases, many children are enrolled both in government and private schools, leading to reporting of double enrolment in many states. The government school teachers never report such cases fearing shifting of their (excess) posts and redeployment to needy schools.

Smt. Shantha Sinha of MV Foundation makes another very important point regarding withdrawal of students of elite families from government schools. This reduces the accountability of schools as those who manage the government school system do not suffer since their children study in private schools.

The government departments of several states also hold the following issues against the private managements:

1. Unauthorized collection of heavy donations.
2. Discriminatory practices followed by managements, harassment of staff, disregarding rules and regulations, lack of accountability, unsatisfactory maintenance of records by managements.

3. Inability to pay attractive pay scales to staff and provide secure service conditions.
4. Inability to cater to the professional growth of the academic staff through continuous professional development programmes.

The private school system in the country has also come in for a lot of criticism from different quarters for a number of other reasons:

- Admission into a private school of one's choice is a nightmare for parents, especially in the metropolitan cities. It is more so for the lower middle class which finds it difficult to cope with the demand for high fees.
- Private schools lose out on good and merited students from the modest-means category as the latter too cannot afford the high fees.
- Lack of transparency in many schools with regard to admission as well as management of accounts.
- Lack of basic facilities for games, classes conducted in cramped classrooms, low paid teachers, focus on English medium rote learning, etc.
- Perception that private schools disturb the concept of common schooling and a national system of education.

Thus there is a need for these institutions to ensure equity though they have some freedom in matters of admissions and recruitment of staff. Since they have a constitutional obligation to socially and economically weaker classes of society, they need to follow government policy on reservations. In fact, the Supreme Court has also echoed this view in its judgments.

Grant-in-aid Policies

Grant-in-aid is generally a discretionary grant provided by the states with the states having the discretion to award, refuse or withdraw grants to an institution. Even courts have opined that grants cannot be claimed as a matter of right by any institution.

The grant-in-aid policies followed by several states have evolved over a period of time. Initially, they had both promotional and regulatory objectives. They envisaged encouraging private sector participation in education through provision of grants, as the states then were not in a position to satisfy local needs. On the one hand they aimed at reducing the cost of providing education for the states as otherwise these institutions would become the sole responsibility of the governments. On the other hand, private institutions stood to gain too as the salary of their teaching and non-teaching staff was compensated by the states.

Through the policy, the states try to ensure equity by ensuring the implementation of reservations in recruitment, regulation of admissions and other similar measures. Another important objective is that quality education in aided institutions becomes more affordable and accessible compared to that offered in unaided/self-financing institutions.

Besides, the teaching and non-teaching staff of aided institutions, are treated on par with those in state institutions in terms of pay, service conditions and benefits. This helps private institutions to attract the best of qualified staff.

To start with, states were liberal in extending aid to private institutions. This depended broadly on the following factors:

- The willingness of the state governments (or the party in power) at a given point of time.
- The capacity of the governments to pay, as any commitment would have a long-term impact on the finances of the state.

However, with proliferation of private institutions, the grants started proving to be a heavy burden on the states' finances. Hence, they were given but with certain conditions and restrictions. It is also significant to note that the country does not have a uniform grant-in-aid policy.

The Demerits in the Grant-in-aid Policies

There are several demerits in the grant-in-aid policies as they are subject to the political will of the respective state governments.

In many states, government school teachers (fully paid teachers and not para-teachers) and those from private aided schools get identical salaries. While the former are recruited through strict rules and regulations on a merit-based-roster system, recruitments by private managements are sometimes made on considerations other than merit. This has led to the evil of donations being collected from selected candidates and poor quality of teachers being appointed.

In several states, private aided institutions (especially in the school education sector) in urban areas have a history of declining student strength. Yet, the states are forced to pay salaries to teachers out of political or other considerations. This problem could be overcome if grants are given based on students' achievement and per-pupil cost, instead of paying salary costs of teachers irrespective of student achievement. Several reports of the World Bank have also advocated reformation of the grant-in-aid policies of the states.

Achievement Levels in Private Institutions

Whether private schools provide better education or not is a highly debatable point. Even at the global level, there is no concrete evidence that performance in terms of learning is better in private schools. ASER 2008 reports that in many states, there is little or no difference in the performance of government and private schools and in many, the performance of the latter is far lower than that of the former, especially in some of the more educationally advanced states.

ASER 2008 found that in class 5, the proportion of fluent readers (those who could read the class 2 level text) in private schools was 68 per cent compared to 53 per cent in government schools. ASER 2008 revealed that private schools were doing well in certain states like Assam, Bihar, Jharkhand, Uttarakhand and WB. In states like Chhattisgarh, Kerala, MP, and TN, there was not much difference between the two.

The second most important advantage is the perceived 'quality' of outcomes in private schools. At the elementary level, there is no standardized and well-established mechanism to compare the performance of government schools with private ones. However, at the secondary level, a single common public examination is conducted for both. An example from the SSLC Public Examination in Karnataka shows that over the years there was a minimum 10-15 per cent difference in performance of students from both schools.

Table 9.2 Karnataka SSLC (Class 10) Public Examination Results (In percentages)

Years	1990	1993	1995	1997	2001	2003	2005	2006
Type of School								
Government	45.4	39.8	30.6	32.5	42.5	51.2	58.5	64.8
Private	60.0	56.7	51.5	57.2	56.3	58.6	66.5	74.7

Source: Karnataka Secondary Education Examination Board, Bangalore

The improved performance of private schools was probably due to better quality of students at the entry level, better infrastructure and probably better classroom teaching.

The general observation is that government schooling stands for 'poor quality' in education, typically characterized by poor learning achievement. This is a gross misconception because even some of the elite and top schools are found to be short on some of the parameters that define quality.

In order to understand how well children learn in private schools, a study (Student Learning in the Metros – 2006 by Educational Initiatives and WIPRO) was conducted in some of the 'Top' schools in the five metros (New Delhi, Mumbai, Kolkota, Chennai and Bangalore) of the country.

The 'Top' 40 schools that were identified in each metro through a popular survey were invited to participate. Over 32,000 students from classes 4, 6 and 8 (from 142 schools) were involved and the number of participating schools ranged from 23 in Kolkata to 37 in Chennai. A group of educationists and school principals formed an expert panel which oversaw the study.

Table 9.3 Schools Tested for the Study

	Bangalore	Chennai	Delhi	Kolkata	Mumbai	Total
Schools tested	26	37	24	23	32	142
Students tested (Main study)	3286	4738	2814	2555	3845	17238
Students tested (secondary study)	2996	4424	2610	2529	3889	16448

Source: Student Learning in Metros 2006 by Educational Initiatives & WIPRO (2006)

Students from the participating schools were tested in learning achievement in English, mathematics and science. The tests tried to measure how well they had understood key concepts in each of these subjects. Apart from multiple-choice questions, they were required to write a paragraph (essay) so as to study their writing competencies.

A secondary study was also conducted to understand the progression of learning achievement across classes. In this study a common test was administered to students of classes 4, 6 and 8 to gather insights into the retention and development of knowledge as the students move to higher classes. Additionally 25 per cent of questions in this paper were taken from an international assessment study (TIMSS) for which performance data of students from 40 countries was available.

The results did not present a happy picture. Students seemed to be learning mechanically and were able to answer questions based on recall or standard procedures quite well. However, their performance on questions testing understanding and application was far below what was considered to be acceptable levels.

An analysis of their performance showed that even in these 'Top' schools, students were not learning with understanding. With schools laying disproportionate emphasis on rote and procedural learning, original thinking and creativity were naturally replaced as students struggled to tackle questions that appeared slightly different from what they were taught in the class. The ability to apply whatever they had learnt to new and unfamiliar situations was not very high.

Consider the following example:

The question asked was:

'What is the chemical formula for pure steam?' (class 6)

The choice for response was:

A. CO (9 per cent) **B.** H_2O (16 per cent) **C.** O_2 (8 per cent) and

D. Pure steam does not have a chemical formula (65 per cent)

(Figures in brackets indicate the percentage of students who chose that option)

This meant that even though the students knew the chemical formula for water, its physical and chemical changes, they were unable to link the two facts. Similarly, the students were also found to be weak in certain real life competencies like measurements and problem solving.

Many of these points were also corroborated by the secondary study in which learning levels were compared. While there was improvement in learning from class 4 to 6 to 8, a number of students seemed to be learning concepts of classes 3 and 4 only in class 6 or much later. A number of misconceptions in English, science and mathematics were also identified among students.

One of the most significant findings of the study was the poor performance of students as compared to the average performance of students from 43 other countries. Across the sample of 11 questions in maths and science, our class 4 students performed below international average on all of them.

A comparative analysis of the five metros again threw up some surprises. Kolkata, New Delhi and Mumbai clearly outperformed Bangalore and Chennai. Schools affiliated to ISCE outperformed CBSE schools which in turn outperformed state board schools. Boys outperformed girls by a statistically significant margin in mathematics in all classes and in science in class 8. None of the factors like class size or school facilities seemed to be strongly correlated to student performance in tests. This study clearly indicates that the quality of learning even in our elite and top schools is far from satisfactory.

The Utility of the Private School System

In order to transform the basic education system in India, a robust public-private partnership (PPP) is needed so that a joint attack on illiteracy can be mounted. While the government/local body school systems require an infusion of excellence, the private school system can play an effective part by providing the necessary inputs and impetus. Given the need to expand the base for elementary and secondary education, the involvement of the private sector and acceptance of the differential fee in private unaided schools is unavoidable.

Besides financing, many professional groups in the non-governmental sector can meaningfully contribute towards a more child-centred pedagogy and a more people-centred accountability of the school management system. However, appropriate norms and standards have to be formulated and maintained. Also, the authority of the state to de-recognize private schools that fail to maintain minimum infrastructural or pedagogical requirements needs to be preserved. Such provisions are included in the Right to Education Act. Hence, development of an independent regulatory framework that allows expansion of the private school system and at the same time meets the ends of social justice and equity is needed.

Given the large-scale of investment – partly financed by 'Education Cess' since 2004– that has taken place in the government education system under SSA, the huge expansion of the private school system in the country should cause serious concern among policy-makers and planners. This trend acquires added significance in the context of 'Right to Education Act, 2009' which requires all schools, including unaided ones, to provide for at least 25 per cent seats to children from the neighbourhood who belong to economically weaker sections.

Supreme Court's Rulings on 'Private Educational Institutions'

The Supreme Court of India in its landmark judgment in 1994 in the 'Unnikrishnan Case' acknowledged the role of the private sector by stating that the constitutional obligation 'of free education up to the age of 14 years can be performed not only by state schools, but also by aided voluntary NGOs who are prepared to impart free education to children'.

The Apex Court further observed that unaided private schools have also a role to play. 'They meet the demand of that segment of the population who may not wish to have their children educated in state run schools. They have to necessarily charge fees from students'.

The Supreme Court took up a detailed review regarding the regulation and control of private institutions by the states in another landmark judgment, the 'TMA Pai Foundation and others vs the State of Karnataka' (2002). Further, in the 'Islamic Academy' (2003) and 'Inamdar' (2005) cases, it issued clarifications which helped in promoting private educational institutions in the country. Some of these issues apply more to higher education institutions rather than elementary ones. However, some of the highlights of these judgments are given below:

Rights of Unaided Educational Institutions

The right to establish and administer an institution comprises the following rights:

- to admit students
- to set up a reasonable fee structure
- to constitute a governing body
- to appoint staff (teaching and non-teaching)
- to take action if there is dereliction of duty on the part of any of the employees.

In the case of unaided private schools, maximum autonomy must rest with the management with regard to administration, including the right of appointment, disciplinary powers, admission of students and the fees to be charged.

The Constitution in Part III neither contains nor does it accord any absolute right. The right to administer is not absolute but must be subject to reasonable regulations for the benefit of the institutions. Also, the right does not confer upon the right to maladminister. Neither can the state enforce the policy of reservation nor can it appropriate any quota or percentage of admissions in a minority or non-minority unaided educational institution.

Recognition

The authority granting recognition or affiliation can certainly lay down conditions. These conditions must pertain broadly to academic and educational matters as well as welfare of students and teachers – but, how private unaided institutions are administered is a matter that would come in the purview of the management of those institutions. Conditions laid down for granting recognition should not be such as may lead to governmental control of the administration of private educational institutions.

It would be permissible for the university or the government, at the time of recognition, to require a private unaided institution to provide for merit-based selection, while at the same time giving the management sufficient discretion in admitting students. In such professional unaided institutions, the management will have the right to select teachers as per the qualifications and eligibility conditions laid down by the state/university subject to adoption of a rational procedure of selection.

Minority Institutions

Only two minorities are recognized – religious and linguistic. Article 30(1) gives religious and linguistic minorities the right to establish and administer educational institutions of their choice. This right cannot override national interest, and regulations framed for compliance in the matter are applicable to all educational institutions, whether run by a majority or a minority. While the right under Article 30(1) does not prevent the government from framing any regulation whatsoever, these regulations cannot destroy the minority character of an institution. Such a limitation must necessarily be read in Article 30.

Laws of the land must apply equally to majority and minority institutions. The state has to ensure equal treatment to both. In order to be reasonable and just, a balance has to be maintained between the two objectives – that of ensuring standards of excellence and that of preserving the right of minorities to establish and administer their educational institutions.

State as the 'Unit' for Determining 'Minorities'

A perusal of Articles 350 A and 350 B, which were inserted by the Constitution (VII Amendment) Act, 1956 indicates that the status of linguistic minorities/groups has to be determined at the state level. Protection is conferred not only to religious minorities but also to linguistic minorities on the basis of their number in a state (unit) where they intend to establish an institution of their choice. 'The unit will be the state and not the whole of India.'

Aided Institutions

Educational institutions receiving state aid are bound by various statutory provisions which are enacted to protect the interests of education, students and teachers. They cannot claim to have complete autonomy in the matter of administration. The state can insist on prescribing reasonable regulations to ensure excellence of the institutions that receive aid – provide certain healthy surroundings, ensure that there are competent teachers with requisite qualifications, and maintain fair standards of teaching. Such regulations are permissible – far from restricting the minority educational institutions from exercising their rights, they help in averting maladministration.

Admission to Aided Institutions

While granting aid to professional institutions, it would be permissible for the authority to prescribe the conditions for admission to different aided colleges based on merit, coupled with the reservation policy of the state.

The merit may be determined either through a common entrance test conducted by the university or the government followed by counselling, or on the basis of entrance tests conducted by individual institutions – the method to be followed is for the university or the government to decide.

Powers to Regulate Grant-in-aid Minority Institutions

Private unaided minority institutions are entitled to autonomy in matters of recruitment of staff, charging of fees and admission of students. However, the state has ample power to regulate the method of selection and appointment of teachers if it bears the payment of the entire pay and allowances for the teaching and non-teaching staff.

There could be regulations to ensure uniformity in service conditions for teachers and staff receiving state aid and those not receiving it. After all, a prerequisite to attracting quality teachers is to have good service conditions. But, in matters of disciplinary action, removal or dismissal, no prior or subsequent approval from any of the functionaries of the state would be required. However, principles of natural justice must be observed.

The grant of aid is not a constitutional imperative. Aided minority institutions must be allowed to maintain their minority character despite receiving grants-in-aid. With merit as the foremost consideration, they have the right to admit minority students and a reasonable number of non-minority students as well – what is a reasonable number is for the state government to decide after considering local needs and the type of education.

An institution maintained by the State funds cannot impart religious instruction. Statutory provisions such as labour laws and welfare legislations would also be applicable to minority educational institutions.

Admissions in Minority Institutions

As long as an educational institution – whether belonging to a majority or minority community – does not receive aid, it would have the right and discretion to grant admission to students of its choice.

Article 29(2), however, curtails this discretionary right to a certain extent. By virtue of it, no citizen can be denied admission by an aided minority institution only on grounds of religion, race, caste, language or any of them. It must follow some identifiable or reasonable methodology of admitting students, i.e., any scheme, rule or regulation that does not give the institution the right to reject candidates who might otherwise be qualified though appropriate guidelines/modalities can be prescribed for holding the entrance test in a fair manner.

The minority educational institutions have the right to admit students of their choice and of their community. They can admit students of the non-minority too, but only without prejudice to the rights of the minority students. The grant-in-aid by the State cannot alter the character of a minority institution, including its choice of students.

There is nothing in Clause (2) of Article 30 to suggest that grant-in-aid will result in making a percentage of seats available for non-minority students. The minority educational institutions can admit non-minority students of their choice against the left over seats in each year as Article 29(2) does not override Article 30(1). If the need of the minority is to be given its due, the question of determining the need cannot be left to the state.

Prohibition of Capitation Fee

Collection of capitation fee, being the worst face of maladministration, can very well be the subject matter of regulatory control of a state. Appropriate machinery can be devised by the state to ensure that no capitation fee is charged.

A rational fee structure should be adopted by the managements such that collection of capitation fees is not necessitated. If every institution is free to devise its own fee structure, the same can also be regulated, particularly when it comes to profiteering. Capitation fee need not be charged then. The fee structure fixed under any regulation or enactment will have to be reworked so as to enable educational institutions not only to break even but also to generate some surplus for future development/expansion apart from providing for free seats.

Disputes between Management and Staff

Disputes between the management and the staff of educational institutions must be decided speedily. It would therefore be appropriate that an Educational Tribunal be set up in every district in a state. In the case of aided institutions, the State has ample power to regulate the method of selection and appointment of teachers after prescribing requisite qualifications. The government will be entitled to formulate regulations relating to admission procedures as well as terms and conditions of employing teaching and non-teaching staff whenever the state grants aid for the posts.

10

Equity Issues in Elementary Education in India

Inequity is a fundamental issue in human development which hampers a country's progress. Inequities exist at various levels – between rich and poor, men and women, rural and urban areas, between different regions and among various socially advantaged and disadvantaged groups.

Education is known to bridge some gaps that the disadvantaged sections of society face in everyday life. In the course of developing human potential, it contributes to improving equity. A UN study of 49 countries showed that about a fifth of income inequality is correlated to education inequality. At lower levels, expanding education could possibly throw up sporadic cases of increased inequality, but with development, education is known to promote equity. Therefore creating equal educational opportunities is essential for people to reap the benefits of a knowledge-based society.

Even though there was an impressive expansion of the elementary school system in the country, a closer analysis of basic statistics reveals glaring disparities in the progress made towards equity. Certain sections of the population and certain geographical pockets in almost all states in the country continue to be educationally backward and have failed to benefit from the investments made in education.

Hence, the NPE stressed on equity and quality when it stated '... up to a given level all students should have equal access to education of comparable quality, that whatever the socio-economic background of the children they get opportunities to achieve success of a level, which is equal to the level of children from comparatively better off sections of society and the country moves pace in the direction of a common school system'.

In order to implement this vision, it became imperative for the centre and the states to address the needs of various educationally disadvantaged groups – girls and women, SCs/STs, minorities, and other special groups such as working and physically challenged children, slum dwellers, inhabitants of hilly, desert and other inaccessible areas, etc. They tried to tackle equity issues in education through several innovative programmes and initiatives. They tried to interweave their concern for education of special groups into all policy frameworks. Through a strategic shift in educational planning, they attempted to target inaccessible areas and disadvantaged social groups. But the success was often limited due to various factors.

This chapter makes an attempt to analyse the progress in basic education achieved in the country from a perspective of social justice and equity. The issues discussed here are under four broad areas: education inequities, gender disparities, regional disparities and socio-economic disparities.

EDUCATION INEQUITIES

It is ironical that education is also responsible for creating inequities in society, though to a certain extent. Historically, the rapid growth and expansion of the education sector resulted in inequities in educational opportunities and achievements of various social groups that in turn, left them with the least paid jobs in the job market. An example of education equity is given in Table 10.1. The table analyses the average years of schooling by employment sector:

Table 10.1 Average Years of Schooling by the Employment Sector

Employment Sector	Years of Schooling
Agriculture	1.98
Mining and Quarrying	4.48
Manufacturing I	3.14
Manufacturing II	4.54
Manufacturing III	8.13
Electricity, Water, Gas	2.79
Construction	7.12
Trade	4.79
Transport and Communication	6.05
Services 4	11.36
Services 5	7.46
All	3.21

Source: Sub-sector Study on Equity in Education in Karnataka (2001)

One can notice that even with a massive expansion of the education system in the country, the labour force was found to be poorly educated with an average schooling of a mere 3.21 years. The World Bank report on the labour market in Karnataka also pointed out that employers felt that there was a gross mismatch between skills that candidates passing out of our education institutions possessed and those needed for employment.

Dimensions of Education Inequity

There are several dimensions to education inequity among the marginalized and depressed classes in the country. They are issues of equality of access (provision of schools, infrastructure, scholarships, etc.) equality of inputs (provision of textbooks and

TLM, effective classroom transaction, etc.) equality of processes (classroom transactions, teacher recruitment and training) and finally equality of outcomes (progression, completion and achievement levels).

Income, gender and social grouping continue to be matters of concern with regard to school participation and completion. Information on gaps in enrolment, retention, completion and achievement between the rich and the poor are not collected by the states. Studies show that education inequity between the rich and poor is the greatest.

Education inequities are more pronounced in the educationally backward states in eastern and northern India, and lower in the educationally forward states of southern and western parts of India. Participation of girls at school in general and of minority communities in particular, continue to be much lower than that of general categories in states like UP and Bihar which have a high incidence of poverty. These states also have large social gaps in school participation.

There has been a significant decline in the number of out-of-school children between the period 1999 and 2008. However, completion rates at primary and upper primary levels indicate that large gaps exist between genders, among social groups as also between and within regions. The overall dropout rates have shown a declining trend at the primary level but are still a cause for concern at the upper primary level and above. This trend over the years indicates that the universal goal of achieving zero dropouts cannot be achieved even by 2010.

Equality of Educational Opportunity

Educational opportunity is a cumulative process in which early opportunities lead to further opportunities in life. It starts at the most basic level when a child gets the opportunity of enrolling in class 1. The next step is the opportunity to learn sufficiently in that class so as to complete it with enough command of basic skills that would lead to continued learning in school. Then comes the opportunity to complete each class and eventually, each education cycle. The skills and knowledge acquired in every particular class and cycle helps the child grow and compete for better socio-economic opportunities. Dropout is a serious issue in this regard. Table 10.2 gives an estimation of children dropping out-of-school. It shows that out of every 100 children enrolled in class 1, only 60 reach class 5 and further only 42 complete the upper primary stage (class 8).

Table 10.2 Children Retained at Different Stages of Education

	As % of those who enter Class 1
Enter Class 1	100
Reach Class 2	88
Reach Class 3	82
Reach Class 4	65

Reach Class 5	60
Reach Class 6	53
Reach Class 7	47
Reach Class 8	42
Reach Class 9	34
Reach Class 10	29
Reach Class 11	14
Reach Class 12	12

Source: Extracted from MHRD Selected Educational Statistics 2000-01

The figures indicated in the above table are also in tune with the findings of ASER 2006 which reveal that only 42 per cent of children could complete class 8 and only 31 per cent could further complete education up to class 10. A substantial number of such children dropping out are from underprivileged social groups: SCs/STs/OBCs and minorities studying in government/local body schools.

Several studies have shown that enrolment solely is not a valid indicator as the enrolled child may not attend school, may be irregular or may dropout at various stages due to several factors. The dropping enrolment signifies that little learning is taking place and that most children are not completing classes for which they are enrolled.

There has been a significant decline in the number of out-of-school children in the last decade even though concerns relating to completion and achievement level of these children remain. The gaps are more prominent in educationally backward states of north and east India. School participation among girls, minority communities and depressed classes is still lower than in general categories in UP, AP, Bihar, MP, Rajasthan and Orissa. Districts like Malkangiri in Orissa, Palamu in Jharkhand, Jhabua in MP, Banswara in Rajasthan, Kishanganj in Bihar, Sonebhadra in UP with a high incidence of poverty have larger gender and social gaps in school participation.

Recently, the report of the Sachar Committee on social, economic and religious status of the muslim community of India has among other things pointed out deficiencies in the availability of educational opportunities for certain socio-religious communities. In view of this, the focus of action in the Eleventh Plan is to put in place a growth strategy that promotes social justice, inclusiveness and equity.

Reasons for Education Inequities

Several factors have been detrimental to the educational outcomes of the children of poor and disadvantaged social groups which in turn contribute to the inequality in educational outcomes. They are:

- Poverty, which prevents parents from financially supporting their wards fully.
- First generation learners, as neither parents are educated or have very low education levels.

- Lack of supportive home environment.
- Irregular school attendance as children are frequently withdrawn from schools by parents for paid/unpaid work outside/within homes.
- Poor child health and nutrition which keeps children away from school and affects their concentration while and if at school.
- Seasonal migration of agricultural labour which affects the academic progress and continuation of children in the education system.
- Reluctance of rural parents to send matured girls to school.
- Sibling care by elder girls.

There are also several other factors within the existing system which reinforces the disadvantages these children face in school – indirect harassment by children of higher castes, social attitudes and behaviour, discrimination practised by teachers within the classroom, etc.

This situation has naturally led to:

- Students receiving poor quality instruction within the classroom.
- Students lacking in expression and confidence.
- Teachers tending to have lower expectations from these students.
- Teachers devoting less time and attention to them in the class.
- Poor quality of education system in our government schools.

All these factors in turn lead to dropout of children at various levels of education. Almost all studies point to poverty as a significant factor contributing to inequality. One such study found that below a certain threshold, poverty combined with unattractive schooling facilities, restricted enrolment and retention. (Sub-sector Study Report on Equity in Karnataka 2001).

Gender Disparities

Gender inequality is one of the most important factors impeding human development. Historically, low educational participation of girls has adversely impacted women's empowerment in the country. The 'Gender Development Index (GDI)' measures the level of women's development relative to men. India ranks 98 in GDI which stands at 0.586 and is very low when compared to several Asian countries. The GDI rankings of some Asian countries are as follows: Malaysia (50), Thailand (57), China (64), Sri Lanka (66), Vietnam (83), and Indonesia (87).

Gender disparity also plays a very significant role in perpetuating educational disparities. As it is, the situation of the girl child in several states in the country is a matter of serious concern. An adverse sex ratio, high malnutrition and maternal mortality rates, poor school enrolment levels, high dropout rates and low skill levels with low value work are indicators of a fundamental preference for the male child and a belief that girls are more a liability than an asset. The NFHS noted that preference for sons was fairly strong in most of the states in the country.

The gender gap becomes sharper and wider when comparisons are made of completion rates instead of enrolments. As against 44.4 per cent of 15-49 year old women completing primary education in India in 1998-99, there were 68.9 per cent men in the same category. There is evidence of the gender gap getting bridged in the lower age groups in recent years, yet it continues to be very large.

Table 10.3 shows a significant and direct linkage between female literacy and girls' attendance in schools. States having high female literacy are also those where attendance of girls in schools is high. Similarly, low female literacy states (Bihar, UP and Rajasthan) are also associated with low attendance of girls in schools.

Table 10.3 Girls Attending School and Female Literacy in States

Girls of 6-14 age Attending School Female Literacy	High Girls Attendance (More than 80%)	Medium Girls Attendance (70-80%)	Low Girls Attendance (Less than 70%)
High Female Literacy (More than 60%)	Kerala, Maharashtra, Punjab, Tamil Nadu,	West Bengal	
Medium Female Literacy (50-60%)	Haryana	Andhra Pradesh, Assam, Gujarat, Karnataka, Madhya Pradesh, Orissa,	
Low Female Literacy (Less than 50%)			Bihar, Rajasthan, Uttar Pradesh,

Source: Female Literacy 2001 Census, Girls Attending School-NFHS II 1998-99

In several parts of rural India, parents are more keen on getting their male children educated rather than their female ones. This has naturally led to lower literacy rates among females. There is also a considerable gender differential in enrolment with more girls dropping out than boys at all stages of education as seen from Table 10.4.

Table 10.4 The Gender Disparity in Enrolment in India (In millions)

Class	Boys	Girls	Gender Differential in Enrolment
1	17.1	13.4	3.7
2	13.4	10.4	3.0
3	12.2	9.6	2.6
4	11.0	8.6	2.4
5	10.2	7.8	4.8

6	9.4	6.6	2.8
7	8.3	5.9	2.4
8	7.6	5.0	2.6
9	6.2	4.0	2.2
10	5.4	3.4	2.0
11	2.4	1.6	0.8
12	2.1	1.4	0.7

Source: Extracted from MHRD
Selected Educational Statistics 2000-01

This situation has changed significantly at the lower primary stage since then. The gender disparity at the primary level is low and decreasing consistently. However, gender equality in enrolment at the elementary stage is yet to be achieved. At higher levels, (upper primary and above) it is still quite significant even though it is showing a decrease albeit a little slow.

Table 10.5 Gender Disparity in Education (In per cent)

Level	2002-03	2003-04	2004-05	2005-06
Primary (Classes 1 to 5)	5.5	5.1	5.1	4.2
Upper Primary (Classes 6 to 8)	10.7	9.4	8.9	8.8
Elementary (Classes 1 to 8)	6.8	6.2	6.1	5.4

Source: DISE 2007-08

Though the proportion of working girls is lower than that of boys, the proportion of girls who are neither working nor going to schools is higher than that of boys. The gender gap has declined narrowly in urban areas whereas it has stagnated in rural areas.

There are several reasons for gender gaps in enrolment – parental attitudes, girls engaging in household work, younger sibling care, rural parents unwilling to send mature girls out of their habitations, inappropriate attitudes and behaviour of male teachers towards girls, fear of sexual harassment and of safety. The gender inequality in enrolment is also due to cultural and economic constraints and is known to decline in educationally advanced states with awareness and enhancement of access to education.

Legislative & Policy Initiatives on Girls' Education

Gender sensitivity underpins all activities of educational processes – planning and management, school improvement, pedagogical renewal, strategies for community mobilization and participation or specific interventions for girls' education.

Article 15(2) of the Constitution prohibits any discrimination on grounds of sex, but at the same time Article 15(3) enables the state to make special provision for women and children.

The Kothari Commission observed that 'The education of girls should receive emphasis, not only on grounds of social justice, but also on the ground that it accelerates social transformation. For full development of human resources, the improvement of homes, and for moulding the character of children during the most impressionable years of infancy, the education of women is of even greater significance than that of men...'

The NPE 1986 was a landmark in formulating a policy on women's education since it recognized for the first time the need to redress traditional gender imbalances in educational access and achievement. The policy stated that education would be used as an agent of basic change in the status of women.

The POA 1992 further stated: 'Rural girls are doubly disadvantaged by non-availability of educational facilities and by the work they have to do related to fodder, water, sibling care and paid and unpaid work'.

The Dakar Declaration reflects the critical importance of programmes for girls and women in order to empower them through education. The fifth Dakar goal which states that 'Eliminating gender disparities in primary and secondary education by 2005 and achieving gender equality in education by 2015', gives a greater focus on ensuring girls' full and equal access to and achievement in basic education of good quality.

Implementation of Girls' Education Programmes by the States

The DPEP and 'Lok Jumbish' adopted a holistic approach to reduce gender-based disparities and enhance access, retention and achievement levels. The 'Shiksha Karmi' project helped evolve effective strategies for education of girls. Programmes relating to ECCE, youth and adolescents, adult education and teacher training had special components for girls and women. Community participation was elicited in support of girls' education for enrolment and retention as well as monitoring of performance and progress. SSA up-scaled some of these programmes to cover the entire country.

Ensuring girls' education required changes not only in the education system but also in societal norms and attitudes. Gender mainstreaming through diverse programmes involved gender sensitization as well as training of teachers and educational functionaries at various levels. Classrooms, textbooks and co-curricular activities were monitored and efforts made to identify and remove gender-discriminatory material. Critical interventions to create girl-child-friendly TLM were inherent in the entire range of new educational initiatives. Special incentives were provided for girls from disadvantaged sections to enable their sustained participation in the educational process.

The Tenth Plan (2002-07) recognized the need for special programmes to raise levels of girls' participation in education. A two-pronged gender strategy was adopted to make the education system responsive to the needs of the girls – gender mainstreaming on the one hand and introduction of special schemes for promoting girls' education on the other.

Different states took up multi-pronged approaches to enrol and retain girl children. On the one hand, targeted interventions under the SSA served as a pull factor ensuring access and retention of girls in school and on the other, they generated community demand for girls' education. In addition, the GOI, launched two focused interventions

– the NPEGEL and the KGBV to reach out to girls from marginalized social groups in over 3,000 educationally backward blocks in the country. These programmes helped in promoting enrolment and retention of hard-to-reach girls.

Most of the states took up special enrolment drives. Many incentives like free uniforms and cycles, residential schools, helped improve girls' participation. Some of the strategies were:

- Providing free textbooks.
- Providing separate toilets for girls.
- Recruiting women teachers to the extent of 50 per cent of the total teacher strength.
- Starting of ECCE centres in/near schools.
- Promoting teachers' sensitization programmes to provide equitable learning opportunities.
- Taking up back-to-school camps for out-of-school girls.
- Starting of bridge courses for older girls.
- Preparing and distributing gender sensitive TLM.
- Making intense efforts at community awareness and mobilization .
- Providing special funds for innovative need-based interventions for girls' attendance and retention in schools.

The result of these efforts are reflected not only in the decreasing disparity in male and female enrolment figures but in improving female literacy rates as well in recent years. Various advocacy programmes have aided in overcoming the traditional resistance to girls' education in many states.

The EFA documents brought out by MHRD in 2005 and 2008 list the following achievements:

(1) Female literacy increased from 39.2 per cent in 1991 to 53.67 per cent in 2001. The growth rate in female literacy at 14.39 per cent was higher than for males at 11.13 per cent. Gender gap in literacy declined from 24.89 per cent in 1991 to 21.59 per cent in 2001.

(2) In comparison to the total enrolment, girls' enrolment increased at the primary school level from 28.1 per cent in 1951 to 46.6 per cent in 2005-06.

(3) At the upper primary level, there was a significant jump in enrolment of girls when compared to the total enrolment, from 16.1 per cent in 1951 to nearly 44.60 per cent in 2005-06.

(4) At the primary level, the dropout rate among girls came down from 70.9 per cent in 1960-61 to 24.82 per cent in 2004-05. There was no significant gender gap in dropout rate at the primary level.

(5) At the upper primary level, the dropout rate for girls came down from 85 per cent in 1960-61 to 53.4 per cent in 2002-03. Here the gender gap was below 1 per cent.

(6) Gender disparity in GER at the elementary stage declined steadily. The Gender Parity Index in the elementary stage showed a steady improvement from 0.80 in 2000-01 to 0.92 in 2005-06. (Schedule VIII-Table 39).

(7) In 2005-06, there were 65 female teachers for every 100 male teachers at the primary level and 67 female teachers for every 100 male teachers at the upper primary level.

The 2006-07 Central Budget, in what is known as gender-budgeting made an allocation of Rs28.737 billion for the benefit of women and girls, covering more than 20 dimensions spread across 18 Ministries and departments.

Performance of Girls

The results of various examinations show that girls consistently perform better than boys, even though they lag behind in enrolment. If policy interventions have helped more girls enter the education system, girls who continue education are found to perform better than boys. Even among different social groups, girls are found to outperform the boys.

Socio-economic Disparities

Poor children fail to learn when education policies and practices generate instruction of low quality. The SC/ST children are found to consistently perform below the performance of general category candidates, as is evidenced in class 10 Public Examination results of various states. There is a significant difference in the performance of SC/ST and non-SC/ST students.

The reasons for lower achievement levels of these social groups are –

1. Non-availability of adequate infrastructure facilities and number of teachers.
2. Inability to derive full benefits from available facilities.
3. Language barrier – in most cases, use of a language or dialect slightly different from what is taught in schools.
4. Experience of a subtle form of discrimination from upper caste students and teachers.
5. Challenge of survival in a rigid and unresponsive school system – these social groups sometimes have their own cultural and social identities.
6. Low participation in village level committees and SMCs leading to lower enrolment, participation and achievement.
7. Economically weaker communities fundamentally do not attach much value to education.

As a result of various initiatives taken up by the centre and the states, the share of SC students in total enrolment moved up to 20.72 per cent at the primary stage and 19.42 per cent at the upper primary stage in 2005-06. Similarly, for ST students, share in total enrolment moved up to 11.75 per cent at the primary stage and 9.28 per cent at the upper primary stage.

Positive Discrimination in Favour of Marginalized Groups

As a part of the overall social policy in the country, the 1990s threw up what was considered to be a positive discrimination in favour of marginalized groups. This approach got intensified in all educational programmes initiated during the nineties. In particular, girls' education came in for special treatment in almost all education development schemes. For example, the OB scheme specified that at least 50 per cent of additional teachers appointed must be women. Most of the states agreed to adopt this as a standard feature of their teacher recruitment policy.

In order to ensure participation of people from ethnic minority groups in education, special incentive schemes were given. Almost all states initiated exclusive programmes in regions inhabited by ethnic minority groups. Analysis shows that the principle of selective focus worked well in bringing more girls to school and improving the overall literacy rates among women. However, improvement in the case of socially and economically marginalized groups appeared to be much slower.

Measures to Reduce Socio-economic Inequities

DPEP and SSA designed several interventions and strategies to include girls. Children belonging to various groups – SC/ST, working and, urban deprived ones, those from minority groups, below poverty line, with special needs, as well as migratory and hardest-to- reach ones – were also covered.

As in the case of girls, special incentives and scholarships are provided by states to SC/ST children so as to facilitate their mainstreaming and retention. In states like Orissa, AP, Assam, Gujarat and Jharkhand, primers and TLM were developed in the local tribal languages. Norms for opening of EGS/AIE centres were relaxed for tribal areas. Recruitment of local teachers (para-teachers, contract teachers) in recent years provided a more conducive environment and school climate for children of disadvantaged groups.

Special drives in collaboration with state agencies, NGOs and concerned departments were periodically conducted to identify 'hard-to-reach' children and enrol them in AIE centres. Mapping of migratory children was tried in several states. Work-site schools in brick kilns, long-term infrastructure projects, sugarcane crushing centres, salt panes, etc., were opened to enrol children who either worked in these sites or migrated with family members. Some states like Karnataka tried mobile schools to attract children from disadvantaged groups who were unable to attend regular schools.

Special enrolment drives, starting of EGS/AIE centres in Madrasas and Maktabs, capacity building of teachers of these institutions, preparation and use of TLM in Urdu were steps taken to increase the participation of minority children. As in 2006, 8309 Madrasas and 4867 unrecognized Madrasas/Maktabs received assistance under SSA.

Education of Special Children

Special children are those who suffer from some form of disability/restriction/lack of ability to perform an activity in the manner considered normal for a human being. Disabilities can be related to vision, speech, hearing, locomotor abilities, and so on. Children affected by them are also disadvantaged as they are denied equal opportunities in education. In poorer families, a significant number of special children are subjected to deprivation and hardship.

Data on special children reveals that roughly 1 per cent of the child population suffers from various types of disabilities. This is probably a gross underestimation. In India as per an NSSO survey on disability, there were 16 million persons with some physical disability in 1991 as against nearly 12 million persons in 1981.

The Sub-sector Study on Elementary Education in Karnataka identified the following issues relating to provision of equal opportunities for education of special children:

- Lack of proper infrastructure for identifying physically challenged children and lack of awareness among parents about incentives provided for their welfare and education.
- Need for flexible curriculum in desegregated schools.
- Lack of individualized instruction for all learners with special needs.
- Lack of special support services in collaboration with other departments.
- Absence of compensatory and remedial measures in education to suit the needs of the specially challenged children.
- Lack of adequate training for primary teachers in methods to handle specially challenged children.
- Non-identification of gifted and talented children and lack of suitable programmes to nurture their diverse and creative abilities.

Several state governments have set aside a certain percentage of seats in almost all educational institutions for the physically challenged children. SSA aims to ensure that every child with special needs, irrespective of the kind, category and degree of disability, is provided education in an appropriate environment. It envisages adoption of a zero-rejection policy so that no child is left out of the education system. Steps were taken to make all school buildings barrier-free.

In 2005-06, against a target of 21 lakh identified children with special needs, 15.5 lakh (77.35 per cent) were enrolled in schools. Further, 48,183 children were covered through EGS/AIE centres in 13 states. 50,339 children were provided home based education in 11 states. In all, 82.23 per cent of the identified children with special needs were covered in 2005-06 through various strategies. 3.7 lakh children were provided assistive devices. Resource support was provided through 4052 resource teachers and 530 NGOs in 26 states. 30.3 lakh children with special needs were targeted to be covered in 2006-07.

Building Synergies in Tackling Disabilities

Many government departments are directly engaged in addressing the problem of disabilities through several programmes of their own, some of which are listed below:

- Health & Family Welfare – Implementation of programmes in child immunization, leprosy eradication and blindness control.
- Education Department – Programmes for Integrated Education for Disabled Children (IEDC), teacher training to handle children with disabilities, provision of books, uniforms and other materials to school going disabled children.
- Ministry of Labour – Setting up of 'Vocational Rehabilitation Centres' for the disabled and training for promotion of employment of the disabled.

- Ministry for Urban Development – Prescription of 'Model Norms and Space Standards' for barrier-free in-built environment in all public places.
- Ministry for Rural Development – Reservation of 2-3 per cent benefits in all poverty alleviation schemes for the disabled and for improving their environment by building barrier-free infrastructure.
- Department of Personnel and Training – Implementation of 3 per cent reservation of government jobs for the disabled.
- Department of Women and Child Development – Training of AWWs and ANMs for early detection and timely prevention of disabilities.
- Ministry of Social Justice and Empowerment – Monitoring implementation of the 'Persons with Disability Act', 1995, and the national programme of rehabilitation of persons with disabilities in states, setting up composite resource centres, rehabilitation centres and national trust for persons with various disabilities.

However, synergies between all these departments need to be built and a coordinating agency at the implementation level needs to be set up.

Education of Working Children

As we are already aware, education is a critical factor in building an individual's personality and capability leading to his/her well-being. This presupposes the need for a happy and normal childhood which in turn is essential for leading a healthy and productive life with dignity.

In India, despite a national policy on child labour as well as laws and regulations at national and state levels, millions of children are engaged in work, often in hazardous conditions. Besides being detrimental to their health, it robs them of a normal childhood. This further deprives them of education and becomes a constraint for them to live as normal individuals in society.

As per ILO and Census definitions 'A child is classified as a child labourer if he/she is in the age group of 5-14 years and is economically active'. But this narrow definition runs into problems as it does not include a child who is involved in unpaid work like day-to-day household work and sibling care. These children are classified as 'no-where' children as they are neither part of the work force nor attending regular schools.

Reasons for the Incidence of Child Labour

NHDR 2001 reports that states in which income/consumption levels are lower, there is greater prevalence of poverty, adult literacy rates are lower, are generally those which have higher incidence of child labour and 'no-where' children. Poverty is stated to be the most important reason for children to be engaged as labourers. The NSSO data for 1993-94 showed that children belonging to the bottom 30 per cent (of expenditure class) of households accounted for 36 per cent and 49 per cent of working children in rural and urban areas respectively.

Migration from rural to urban areas encourages child employment. With growing population, mechanization of agriculture operations and limitation of the agriculture sector to absorb the growing labour force productively, a large number of farm labourers are forced to migrate to cities and other urban areas in search of unskilled/semi-skilled employment opportunities. In unfamiliar circumstances and deprivation, the children of these migrant families often end up in the workforce as rag pickers, domestic helps or in construction and such other unorganized sectors. Many studies point out evidence of widespread ill-health, including incidence of TB, bacterial and parasitic diseases, among these children.

School-related problems also result in children seeking employment avenues. Child labour is closely related to school dropout rates. Even when access is not a problem, overcrowding, poor quality of education, unsympathetic teachers, unwelcome school atmosphere, etc., lead children to dropout and end up in the labour market. High dropout rates at upper primary levels are found to be in proportion to high incidence of child labour. Cumulative dropout rates are high in Bihar and AP which also have a high incidence of child labour. Kerala has the lowest dropout rates and the lowest incidence of child labour.

National Policy on Child Labour

Constitutional and legal provisions relating to 'child labour' are discussed in Chapter III. The Indian Constitution requires the State to protect children against being forced by economic necessity to take up vocations which are unsuited to their age and strength. Hence, the problem of working children and their education is not related to a single department like 'Education' or 'Labour', but is a multi-sectoral one. In order to tackle it, the GOI accepted the National Policy on Child Labour in 1987.

This policy formed the framework of action and consisted of three components:

(a) A legislative action plan
(b) Focus on general development programmes for benefiting children
(c) Project-based action plans in areas of high concentration of child labour.

These action plans along with recommendations of NPE 1986 formed the basis for initiating programmes for education of working children.

National Child Labour Projects

As a result, 12 National Child Labour Projects (NCLP) were implemented in areas of high concentration of child labour. They were located in AP (Jaggampet and Markapur), Bihar (Garwah), MP (Mandasaur), Maharashtra (Thane), Orissa (Sambalpur), Rajasthan (Jaipur), TN (Sivakasi), and UP (Varanasi – Mirzapur, Bhadohi, Moradabad, Aligarh and Ferozabad). In all, about 100 such projects were sanctioned in child labour endemic states covering about 1,30,000 children up to the year 2000.

A major activity undertaken under the NCLP was establishment of special schools to provide NFE, vocational training, supplementary nutrition, stipend and healthcare to children withdrawn from employment. Under the grants-in-aid scheme of the ministry of labour, NGOs were also financially assisted to the extent of 75 per cent of the project cost to set up such projects for working children. Besides, MHRD provided assistance to NGOs involved in the education of working children.

Within the education sector, all major EFA projects incorporated specific components to meet the educational needs of working children. The states tried several approaches to tackle the problem of child labour. The 'preventive approach' involved suitable legal provisions including checking and regulating the entry of children in the labour market. The objective was to create a conducive social and economic atmosphere for discouraging children in the target group of 5-14 years from entering the labour market. Special NFE and AE programmes were also taken up for girls involved in domestic work.

At the same time the states took recourse to publicly funded programmes aimed at improving access and enrolment of children in schools – incentives in the form of fee exemptions, free uniforms and textbooks, providing nutritious midday meals, increasing adult wages, etc., to retain children in schools. With a significant decline in the population growth rate along with improvement in overall literacy levels and school enrolment, the incidence of child labour has been on the decline.

Regional Inequities

Within the country, there are inter-regional and intra-regional disparities as far as human development is concerned. Even within a state, disparities in development are found across districts. The presence of inter-district and intra-district variations both at the level of development generally and human development in particular means that people's access to services is shaped by where they live, and their quality of life is determined, to a certain extent, by regional disparities.

Similarly, living in a rural area is always considered a disadvantage for want of quality services including quality educational and health facilities. Poverty rates are also higher in rural areas. In the elementary education sector, regional disparities exist in areas of access, retention, completion and achievement of children.

Disparities in Performance of Students in Urban/Rural Areas

Children from rural areas do not have access to the same quality of educational opportunities as their urban counterparts. With most higher education institutions of quality being concentrated in urban areas, rural students are naturally at a disadvantage when it comes to admission to them. Children in urban areas, specially slums, also suffer multiple disadvantages with regard to nutrition, health, sanitation and access to various facilities and services apart from access to quality education. These problems are further compounded by existing social inequities. Rapid urbanization has deprived urban slum children of food, shelter, education, health and other services. It is estimated that at least 25 per cent of them belong to economically disadvantaged 'at risk' groups.

However, in several states rural-urban education disparities have been on the decline. In Karnataka, 31.36 per cent of students appearing for the class 10 public examination in 1972 were from rural areas. The proportion steadily increased to 53.88 in 2000.

Table 10.6 Class 10 Results

Category	1990	1995	1999	2005	2006
Rural	52.35	40.46	54.08	62.42	71.75
Urban	56.43	48.83	57.97	62.31	69.63
Total	54.33	44.98	56.72	62.51	70.69

Source: Annual Reports (Karnataka)

Previously, the success rate was higher in urban than in rural areas. This trend also got reversed in recent years as is seen from Table 10.6.

PROMOTING EQUITY IN EDUCATION

Various disadvantaged groups strongly articulated the need for education during the last decade. The demand for basic education facility – a school in their own habitation – has become a symbol of social assertion among these communities. Poor parents perceive value in education and are willing to make adjustments to support their children, including girls, in schools.

The state governments in collaboration with the GOI implemented several initiatives to promote equity. Elementary schooling is now completely free across the country. Several SSA initiatives improved the availability of educational (formal/non-formal) facilities in areas with a predominance of marginalized populations.

Several schemes have been funded and implemented by states to cater to the needs of the weaker sections and disadvantaged groups – free uniforms and textbooks, scholarships, hostels for girls and SC/ST children, hot cooked midday meal, establishment of Ashram Schools, Navodaya Residential Schools for merited backward class children, residential schools for minorities and SC/ST girls, AWCs for women and children, special bridge course schools for rehabilitation of child labour, sports schools for backward and minority children, grant-in-aid for pre-metric hostels run by private agencies and NGOs, etc.

Due to these interventions there was a visible improvement in several educational indicators – access, enrolment, retention, participation and achievement. Several states achieved near 99 per cent access in primary education. Along with additional infrastructure, these states were able to provide additional teachers and this led to a beneficial impact on PTRs.

There were also instances when gaps were bridged in some districts through intensive programmes. Some of these districts were: Gadhchiroli in Maharashtra, Bellary in north Karnataka, Panchmahal in Gujarat, Tirunelveli in TN, Mallapuram in Kerala, among others. Recent efforts to expand access to schools in MP and Rajasthan led to increased participation in remote habitations in the schooling process. Even during years with scanty rainfall, schools in remote habitations started attracting children in large numbers and enrolments were not seen to be falling significantly. The 'no-detention' policy in primary classes followed by several states also benefited various social groups.

The Indian Constitution provides for promotion of education and economic interests of the weaker sections of the people and, in particular, people belonging to SC/ST. On the basis of this provision, a certain percentage of seats is reserved for these sections in admission to educational institutions as well as employment in government and aided institutions.

Apart from reservations for SC/ST groups, caste-based reservation has a long history in several states like Tamil Nadu and Karnataka. The reservation policies followed by the states have also been influenced by socio-economic considerations. The socially backward people in each state are classified into various categories and the percentage of seats reserved for them varies from state to state. D. Devaraj Urs, the Chief Minister of Karnataka was a pioneer in implementing the roster system (favouring backward classes) in Karnataka in 1978. This system was adapted by several states with suitable modifications.

Access to education, especially higher education, has been seen as the principal instrument for redressing economic inequalities between castes and social groups. Reservation currently accounts for half the seats in publicly financed educational institutions and in public sector jobs. Quotas in education and in jobs have also been given at various times for students from rural backgrounds and/or those who have studied in the local language media.

A World Bank Study in 2003 undertaken by ERU in the three states of AP, Karnataka and UP points out –

- The recognition of the value of education by poor families and the decision to withdraw children from full-time work and send them to school has not in any significant way reduced the work burden of children.
- Gender relations in the family, community and in the society exert a significant influence on the ability of girl children to access services, nutrition, immunization, healthcare and schooling. If regularity can be assured, girls perform as well in school, if not better, than boys.
- There is a communication gap between the community and service providers. The latter seem unable to look at issue of nutrition and child development from the viewpoint of the mothers and the community.

Obviously, there is a clear need to bridge these gaps. Discussion with service providers (ANM, AWW and even some school teachers) revealed that though their belief systems are rarely in disagreement with those of the community, often there is a lack of conviction in the way they deliver the message.

Additional focus, special local specific programmes and higher budgetary allocations are needed to bring the backward regions and disadvantaged groups to the mainstream of the economic sphere of the country. In the absence of such positive, inclusive steps, these regions/groups would still remain marginalized from society.

11

Concerns in Elementary Education

INTRODUCTION

A good education system needs to have three important considerations, that is, providing high quality education, ensuring equity and catering to the aspirations of different sections of society. Hence, it becomes necessary for it to be based on a good curriculum, be accountable to all stakeholders and have an efficient management system in place along with a participative involvement of the community.

The pace of the country's educational development since independence has been unprecedented by all standards through increase in number of schools, teachers and facilities. In spite of this unparalleled growth, the country faces a number of challenges. Nearly one-third of the population is still illiterate and critical gaps exist in educational attainments across regions as well as among different social groups. Accessibility to schools, quality of educational infrastructure, performance levels of students and various other educational indicators are not uniform across the country. A large section of the disadvantaged social groups is still not served by schools that need to be made available within a reasonable distance.

The progress in education has also been uneven both across and within states. If the mean years of schooling is taken as an indicator of retention then current levels of completion fall well below the expected objective and constitutional mandate of providing eight-years of universal education for all children up to the age of 14.

There exist significant inter state variations with regard to several educational indicators. While states like Kerala, Maharashtra, TN, Karnataka, and Mizoram, have been able to ensure near universal enrolment, some others like AP, Rajasthan, MP and WB are still striving to provide universal enrolment and are yet to achieve significant retention of children at the primary stage. In states like Bihar, Orissa and UP, a significant number of children continue to be out-of-school. Only Punjab, Haryana and HP have recorded performances comparable to southern states in this regard.

As smaller and smaller schools are being opened to provide access to remote habitations, several issues relating to them – infrastructure, teachers, TLM, quality, etc., – remain to be addressed. The country has yet to tackle the gargantuan problem of nearly one lakh single-teacher schools.

Though there are sizable regional differences, large-scale educational programmes undertaken by the centre and the states have ensured significant reduction in inequalities in educational attainments across genders, populations, social categories, income levels and the rural-urban divide. There is an increasing trend in school enrolments with close to 95.7 per cent of the children in the age group of 6-14 years enrolled in some form of elementary school as reported by ASER 2008.

However, a high dropout rate at the upper primary level indicates that the focus will now have to shift from enrolment to retention of children as half of them are likely to leave before completing elementary education. There is a fairly large difference between boys and girls with regard to the respective proportions moving from lower primary and upper primary classes. Multigrade teaching is more a norm in a majority of the elementary schools in the country.

The quality of education has also assumed equal importance in the light of poor academic achievement by students. One out of three children in class 5 is still unable to read and write. The low quality of education as well as a lack of proper training in soft skills has a direct bearing on students' employability.

The country's ever expanding education system has posed several serious challenges – need for an efficient management system, mobilization of sufficient resources for creation and maintenance of infrastructure, professional training of teachers on a large-scale and, above all, the need for maintaining uniform quality of educational services throughout the country. All this calls for a major relook at the present education policies of the centre and the states.

This chapter tries to analyse and flag critical issues and identify future challenges facing the country in the field of elementary education.

Human Development

Human development (as discussed in Annexure I) includes improvement in knowledge and skills of the people, better employment opportunities, greater democratic participation at all levels, and improvement in quality of life among other things.

The HDI as a composite index of three basic issues crucial to human welfare – income, basic health and education – is now widely used to measure a country's development. In the HDI prepared by UNDP, India ranks a dismal 127 (out of 177 countries) and much below several Asian countries. A significant factor impeding the country's progress in human development is found to be education inequity. Hence, improvement of basic education gains importance in order to improve human development in the country.

Literacy

India's literacy rate in 2001 was 64.84 per cent as against 52.21 per cent in 1991, with a 12.63 percentage point increase being the highest in any decade. However, when compared to the average world literacy rate of 80 per cent, the country's record remains depressing, with one-third of the population still being illiterate. Even though all states have achieved a minimum male literacy level of 60 per cent, female literacy is still a serious cause for concern. Similarly, inter state and intra state disparities have continued although the gap between educationally forward and backward states has narrowed considerably.

The Dakar goal aims at achieving a 50 per cent improvement in levels of adult literacy by 2015, especially for women, and equitable access to basic and continuing education for all adults. India has made substantial efforts to achieve this goal. While it aims to improve its literacy levels to 80 per cent by 2015, it has a long way to go before it can reach full literacy. A detailed discussion of the country's literacy scenario along with programmes undertaken to improve literacy is found in Annexure V.

Early Childhood Care & Education (ECCE)

With the Constitutional Amendment Act of 2002, Article 45 was revised to provide ECCE for all children until they complete the age of 6. However, a number of constraints have come in the way of states extending ECCE facilities to all habitations in rural areas. The states also need to relook at the linkage between programmes relating to ECCE and primary education. Even though several states established pre-school centres in primary schools, these were mostly token efforts for lack of a clear cut state policy on the pre-school education sector as a whole.

If pre-school education is to prepare children for primary school in terms of their physical, social and cognitive development, the school itself should be ready to absorb them and facilitate their transition to the primary level. Both these levels need to be integrated by forging stronger links among the health and education components, creating continuity in curriculum, combining multigrade classrooms, and improving teaching methods to respond to varying abilities and interests of students. Also, taking up joint training of pre-primary and primary teachers is a must so as to ensure professional continuity between the two levels.

The pre-school component in the private sector needs to be regulated. Collection of illegal donations, harassment of parents and children through levy of heavy fees and purchase of costly books and uniforms, enforcement of rigorous discipline on children at such a tender age, and use of unsuitable methods of teaching are some of the horrendous problems which the states have not been able to prevent.

Is Elementary Education Adequate?

The tremendous changes that have taken place (since the drafting of the Constitution) in the socio-economic conditions of the people of the country have subsequently brought in new demands which did not exist six decades ago. The eight-years of elementary education is no more adequate as it neither equips children with the necessary knowledge and skills to face the world of work nor does it empower them to deal with the globalization and privatization of the country's economy. Presently, children completing the elementary stage of education have no career options. The minimum that a child requires to start work (paramedical, technical or a primary school teacher) now is completing ten/twelve years of schooling.

Hence it is widely felt that the time has come for the state to declare ten/twelve years of schooling as both free and compulsory, and make it a constitutional obligation for implementing it.

School Infrastructure

A sizable percentage of schools continue to exist without buildings and where there are buildings, there is a shortage of classrooms. An estimate in 2006-07 indicated that the country required over six lakh classrooms. A significant proportion of primary schools and upper primary schools do not have toilet or drinking water facilities. (Table 28 – Annexure VIII). These are priority issues and call for immediate attention. A lackadaisical attitude would only hamper both enrolments as well as the quality of education. Although SSA has been able to significantly contribute towards building of the required infrastructure facilities, much more needs to be done in this direction.

Studies point out that in some cases, either due to a faulty planning process or due to political interference, excess infrastructure facilities were created where they were not required, while a majority of schools continue to languish under denial of the same.

Incentives

The states initiated the system of providing incentives in order to improve access and participation in elementary education. However, policies relating to them vary from state to state. In many states, some incentive schemes like providing textbooks and uniforms cover all categories of children while other schemes like scholarships are targeted towards specific social groups. However, the proportion of families who are in actual need and who are benefiting from these incentives is a big question mark.

A World Bank Study in 1997 pointed out that even though SCs/STs and other backward classes constitute the poorest of the population, only 3 per cent of the beneficiaries were from financially weak households and only 2 per cent received the incentives on a merit plus income criterion.

Hence, there is a need to re-examine all the incentive schemes and formulate policy frameworks such that the creamy layer which constitutes the bulk of the population is excluded from receiving these benefits. Only the deserving and the needy must benefit from them.

Centrally Mandated Decentralization

Under the Constitution, education was on the 'State List' of subjects till 1976. It has since been on the concurrent list, and is therefore the responsibility of both the centre and state governments. Though there has been much emphasis on decentralization in recent years, most of it has been centrally mandated with the direction and policy focus being decided by the centre.

The policy frameworks of large-scale programmes like OB, DPEP or SSA did not provide any flexibility in norms to suit local needs. With a uniform policy framework imposed on all, the states had no option but to follow central guidelines in order to get the benefit of utilizing central funding. Hence, policies with flexible norms must be formulated in order to allow the states to devise programmes to suit local needs.

Equity Issues

As we have already seen, a substantial number of children dropping out are from under privileged social groups studying in government and local body schools. Poor quality of schooling – poor infrastructure, demotivated teachers, significant teacher absenteeism, high PTRs, poor teaching methods, unattractive school environment, low achievement levels of children, high dropout rates, low teaching time, corporal punishment, etc. – are some of the main reasons contributing to inequities in education.

In addition, failure of the education system to respond to the needs of the society contributes to inequalities. There is need for selective discrimination not as a populist measure but as a consciously planned programme that can be actually implemented for purposes of uplifting the disadvantaged sections of society.

Girls' Education

Apart from other equity issues, girls' education assumes special importance due to the significant percentage of dropout of girls at the upper primary stage and above. Child marriages are prevalent in many states – once the girl marries, it is common for the girl to dropout.

Issues regarding girls' schooling that continue to need special attention include:

(a) Enrolment at the upper primary level
(b) Retention in school
(c) Completion of the elementary education cycle
(d) Participation of girls from tribal and other disadvantaged groups.

Several programmes to promote education of girls from educationally backward communities have been launched under SSA. But most of them are token efforts and do not cover all blocks in the country. Proper education and community awareness are also required for the success of these programmes.

The Common School System

No doubt the concept of the common school system that aims at ensuring equity is desirable. But in reality, it is not practical as ground realities are different. Parents have the freedom of choice in providing education best suited to their children. More and more parents, even in rural areas, are veering towards private schools with the appealing idea of providing 'English education' to their children. We are also witnessing the phenomenon of dropping enrolments in government/local body schools in urban and semi-urban areas across the country.

Under the circumstances, states should evolve policies that would strengthen government schools so that they provide quality education for all children. This is the most important step for ensuring social justice, assuming that the poorest of the poor will continue to access government schools in the coming years.

Medium of Instruction

In a multilingual and multi-religious country like ours, the medium of instruction has been a highly debatable question even from the pre-independence days, when there was a demand for adopting one's mother tongue as the medium of instruction as a part of the 'swadeshi' movement. While there is always political pressure on governments to give primacy to the mother tongue and the regional language, most of the middle and upper classes (who are responsible for influencing policies) prefer to send their children to English medium schools as 'English education' is supposed to ensure easier upward mobility.

This is also one of the reasons for a significant reduction of student strength in government schools and the unprecedented growth of private sector schools in the country. The states need to reconsider their policies regarding medium of instruction and rectify some of the defects in order to ensure a healthy growth of the elementary education system in the country. The states should also consider providing English medium instruction in at least selected centrally located government schools in the country.

TEACHER-RELATED ISSUES

The teaching profession has all along attracted persons of average ability as it had been a low paid one. One does hear of cases of several states where teachers are paid fairly well, yet the profession by and large attracts only average talent. Nevertheless, all government and aided institution teachers enjoy the benefits of security and good emoluments.

The Karnataka HDR pointed out that excessive teacher recruitment had taken place in a few politically powerful southern districts, whereas the north Karnataka districts where levels of literacy were much lower had suffered on account of inadequate teachers. Even in districts where the district level PTR looked good at an overall of 40:1, analysis revealed the presence of a high percentage of schools in single and two-teacher categories.

Hence, inter state disparities exist in almost all states, with backward and remote areas deprived of the optimum number of teachers at any given point of time. Even when vacancies occur, they are not filled because of the teachers' unwillingness to work in such schools.

The PTR norm of 40:1 is definitely a diluted version of the PTR norm of 30:1 that has been suggested by the Tapas Majumdar Committee. Taking into consideration the issue of teacher absenteeism which is as high as 25 per cent in many states, the PTR norm of 40:1 will have a serious impact on the number of teachers available (on any given day) to each primary school and on the quality of elementary education in the country.

Para (Contract) Teachers

Large-scale recruitment of locally selected but generally higher secondary pass teachers at lower-than-pay scale has become a reality, even in states like Bihar and UP. The SSA norms are silent on qualifications and unit costs of salaries of new teachers. This has led states to adopt several low cost alternatives with many of them having stopped recruitment of permanent teachers on account of growing salary bills.

In fact, in several states, para-teachers/contract teachers are being preferred to regular ones. Even though the arrangement was visualized to be an interim measure, the practice became a permanent affair in several states due to the limited financial liability the scheme accorded to the states. Also, recruitment procedures and service conditions varied across states.

The issue of para-teachers has affected the quality of schooling due to the absence of professionally qualified and trained teachers. A majority of these teachers are under-qualified and ill-trained. They are not even paid as per the norms of the minimum wages for skilled labourers. The country has an estimated five lakh para and part-time teachers. The Tapas Majumdar Committee observed that while para-teachers may play a useful role in the short run in promoting higher school attendance, in the long run, there is no substitute for fully qualified and properly paid teachers.

While all efforts should be made to streamline selection procedures so as to encourage local persons willing to serve in remote rural locations get selected, there should be no compromise on the criteria of selection, the minimum qualification required and training of teachers.

The Shiksha Karmi Project of Rajasthan provides for experienced Shiksha Karmis to earn as much as regular primary school teachers if they clear the internal assessments designed for them. The performance criteria is strict and rigorous but there is a possibility of Shiksha Karmis drawing as much pay as regular teachers do. Hence para-teachers can become fully paid teachers with all the opportunities to improve their academic qualifications. The other states need to draw on this experience and provide suitable opportunities to them for professional improvement.

Teacher-Related Equity Issues

The issue of violation of equity has taken serious proportions due to the recruitment of local teachers in regular schools at less-than-pay scales. Some states like MP have totally stopped recruitment at the state level and all recruitments involve only Shiksha Karmis at the local level. States like Gujarat see the payment of less-than-pay scale as an interim measure and continue to recruit trained teachers. However, they are paid a lumpsum every month, with an assurance that they will be regularized with the official pay scale within five-years, subject to satisfactory performance. Andhra Pradesh follows the old practice in which regular trained teachers work as apprentices for three-years before drawing the regular pay scale. Karnataka, Kerala and TN are the only states which continue to recruit trained teachers on a regular basis and on full pay scale.

While local recruitments at less-than-pay scale have contributed to the appointment of more than five lakh teachers (many times under-qualified) during the last six-years, serious questions have arisen about the 'principle of equal pay for equal work', teacher training, quality and sustainability of such ad hoc and interim measures.

The opening of a large number of very small primary schools (with student strength of less than 30) has also raised the issue of a large number of single and two-teacher schools and their implications for multigrade teaching, quality and sustainability. Many schools in remote regions in almost all states have remained without adequate number of teachers in spite of regular recruitment of primary teachers.

The next issue is of large number of vacancies and the unfulfilled need. Assuming that there are 200 million children in India in the 6-14 age group, even for a PTR of 40:1, nearly 50 lakh teachers are needed. Even after the large-scale recruitment of para-teachers over the last six-years, the total number of teachers in the country is estimated to be about 40 lakhs. Hence, the country has a shortfall of ten lakh teachers at the elementary level.

Excess deployment of teachers in urban, semi-urban, roadside schools is a reality across the country and this naturally has even worse consequences for schools in remote areas. Hence, states need to have realistic and clear cut policies regarding teacher related issues: PTRs, para-teachers, teacher qualification, teacher recruitment, deployment of excess teachers, etc.

Teacher Education

In order to improve quality of education in schools, it is necessary to improve the quality of pre-service teacher training. The TTIs in the country need to be infused with a sense of purpose in order to achieve excellence and produce teachers of quality.

The states need to develop a system where the intake in pre-service training institutions is directly proportional to the number of projected vacancies in schools. Only candidates from areas where vacancies occur can be selected for training. This will naturally satisfy the needs of schools in remote areas where previously appointed teachers are not willing to work.

The Kothari Commission recommended placing 'Teacher Education' within the 'academic life of the universities'. It is still a matter of concern that teacher education institutions continue to exist in isolation, severely secluded from centres of higher learning, academic colleges and universities. These institutions are also cut off from field level realities and are unaware of issues relating to first generation learners, dropouts, multigrade teaching situations, latest experiments being undertaken in the field, impact of quality initiatives, etc. To put it in a nutshell, teacher education is the most neglected sector in most of the states.

NCTE which is supposed to supervise the functioning of TTIs has failed in its task because it is functioning as little more than a licensing authority. The centre and the states need to take a hard look at the present scenario and formulate policies to weed out numerous ill equipped institutions and improve the quality of existing ones. This will go a long way in getting better equipped and well-trained teachers.

In order to professionally equip the para-teachers already working, the states need to depute them to regular pre-service teacher training courses. These courses should intensively utilize school vacations for their contact programmes as well as the distance mode and on-site support in schools to reinforce the classroom learning by teachers.

Teacher Training

The DIETs, as discussed in the chapter on 'Teacher Education', need a complete overhaul and should be able to respond to the needs of teachers as well as the community. Participation of voluntary agencies in teacher training programmes may be explored in order to make them more responsive to community needs. Each DIET must satisfy the specific needs of the district it is supposed to cater.

Inadequate provisioning and absence of appropriate norms impact the quality of teacher training programmes in the country. Whether the training programmes make a difference to actual classroom transaction or not is a matter that needs to be assessed. Steps must then be taken to improve the quality of these programmes. Meager remuneration to resource persons is hardly motivating and has a direct bearing on the quality of training. Teachers also resent being called for training during school holidays.

The data provided by states regarding training is found to be unreliable in several cases. Misuse of SSA funds at the lower levels has also been noticed and the existing safeguards are found to be grossly inadequate.

Teacher Absenteeism

Teacher absenteeism is a major factor affecting quality of classroom transaction in schools across the country. With one in four government primary school teachers absent on any given day, and only one in two actually teaching, teacher absence has a direct bearing on the quality of learning in government schools and wastage of scarce public resources.

As per a World Bank Study in 2004, on any given day, nearly 25 per cent of primary school teachers in India are absent from schools and only half of those present actually teach. Rates of absenteeism vary from 15 per cent in Maharashtra to 42 per cent in Jharkhand. Table 6 in Annexure VIII gives an idea of teacher absence and the percentage of time spent by teachers in non-teaching activities in different states. Multigrade schools also report a higher incidence of teacher absence. (Also see Table 42).

Even when teachers are present in school, they spend only 68 per cent of their time in academic work, while the remaining 32 per cent is spent on non-academic work. If we take the teachers' absence also into consideration, the 'Organization Study Report (2006) on Karnataka' by Price Waterhouse Coopers estimated that the academic time gets reduced to 53 per cent (117 days out of 220 school working days).

The reasons for teacher absenteeism are many. Teachers are entitled to take different kinds of leave – casual, earned, medical and maternity/paternity leave. Besides, there is the problem of unauthorized absence. Lack of public awareness is also a reason for teacher absenteeism. The formation of SMCs in several states has helped to control this problem. But all the states by and large need to develop efficient monitoring mechanisms in order to tackle this issue and improve the quality of classroom transaction.

Physical Education

Physical Education is an important part of the curriculum that is necessary to develop the all round personality of the child. NPE 1986 stated that it is an integral part of the learning process and will be included in the evaluation of student performance.

The NCERT in its curriculum developed in 1975-76 allotted 10 per cent of the instruction time at the lower primary and upper primary stage and 8 per cent of the time at the secondary stage for physical education. However, these policy initiatives were not matched in implementation at the ground level.

A majority of primary and upper primary schools in the country still do not have physical education teachers. The evaluation of performance of students in this area has not yet become a reality in most states. The states continue to give it low priority when it comes to providing playgrounds, adequate infrastructure, sports equipment and physical education teachers to bigger schools.

PLANNING AND MANAGEMENT OF EDUCATION

Inadequacies in EMIS

EMIS of a high quality is needed if functions of education management at any level are to be carried out effectively. The EMIS also needs to be reliable in order to provide the right information to the right people at the right time for taking the right decisions. Feedback to schools and educational functionaries at various levels is also necessary for identifying strengths and weaknesses and to take up suitable remedial measures as well.

The EMIS in India has become a little more than an expensive data-gathering exercise. Instances of fudging data abound at various levels in several states is an attempt to suppress failures in implementing programmes. Needless to say that the reliability of data provided becomes questionable. Hence, the data must be validated by cross checking the same from various sources. This is again a time consuming procedure.

Besides, the present level of data from EMIS also suffers from several deficiencies and hence does not have the potential to bring about improvements in classroom processes, student learning outcomes and ultimately in system efficiency. The centre and the states have to ensure reliability and timely availability of data for use by educational planners and administrators.

Deficiencies in the Planning Process

District level planning along with autonomous management structures was adopted as a major strategy for designing and implementing primary education projects, such as in literacy campaigns and other EFA projects including DPEP and SSA. Together with emphasis on investing in educationally backward districts, it helped tackle local specific problems and overcome inter-district disparities. It also facilitated faster movement of funds towards project activities.

However, decentralization of educational planning and management also exposed the fragility of the expertise available at these levels. Some of the inadequacies in the planning process are mentioned below:

- Participatory and consultative planning is perhaps the weakest area in the SSA – AWPs of the states. If the process of planning is handled competently, it can ensure successful utilization of SSA funds. However, a majority of the states resort to getting the district officials to the state headquarters and getting the district plans prepared under the direction of state officials and later getting post-facto approvals of the district implementation committees. This defeats the very concept of decentralization in the planning process.
- Another major flaw is that enrolment figures instead of actual attendance forms the basis of all planning. The difference between enrolment and attendance varies considerably – in some states as much as 30 per cent of enrolment. Hence, the states' plans tend to be skewed to that extent. (Refer Table 42 – Annexure VIII).
- Several rural and urban schools try to boost enrolment and attendance figures on one hand and suppress dropout figures on the other. Reasons for this are varied – to retain a larger number of teachers in their schools, get a higher share of food grains under the midday meal scheme, etc. Also, greater vigilance on the part of the monitoring authorities at the local levels is needed to tackle the issue of double enrolment when government/private schools function in the same areas.
- Data mismatch is another major problem in most states. Projection of a flat increase in enrolments in all districts of a state (for example, 5 per cent in the case of Rajasthan AWP 2006-07) indicates that the use of data is limited to costing purposes. In many states, time series data is not available for analysis. In several cases, the district plans do not reflect the actual requirements of a district both in terms of interventions required and magnitude of funds. This impacts the efficient utilization of funds.
- In several states, delay in release of funds is a major problem with the whole process going through a rigmarole. Firstly, there is an inordinate delay in submission of AWPs by the states; then comes the approval by the 'Project Approval Board' at the Central level. This is followed by sanction of funds by the centre, and finally the release of the states' and the centre's shares of funds to the SPD, and from SPD to district and sub-district levels. It is hardly surprising that the officials are left with very little time for utilization of funds.

Issues in Financing of Elementary Education

There are several issues pertaining to financing of education both at the centre and state levels. The amount of government spending on education has remained far below the expected level of 6 per cent of the national income. As seen in Chapter VIII, the financial requirement to cover 'Education of satisfactory quality for all' is quite high. Schools would require higher financing with decentralized management to meet the demands of modern day quality education. Mobilizing additional resources for education to reach the critical mark of 6 per cent remains a challenge before the country.

Even though there has been an incremental increase in the availability of resources for the education sector with central initiatives like collection of education cess, the additional finances required for providing free and compulsory elementary education up to the end of the Eleventh Plan (2006-12) is an estimated Rs53,467 crores per annum or about 1.1 per cent of the GDP. However, the government is yet to commit making allocations of this order to education.

Besides provision of additional resources, another major concern is the efficient use of the same. Rigidity in the norms of central funding is also an issue which has adversely impacted the implementation of programmes at the state levels. Some of the important issues in financing of education are listed below:

- It is the centre's responsibility to ensure equity in financing elementary education across states. This means that states with higher proportion of out-of-school children/dropouts/ deficiencies in infrastructure have to necessarily get higher resources than others. However, ground realities paint a completely different picture.
- In each of the years from 2002-03 to 2005-06, funds for SSA released by the centre was less than 75 per cent of the aggregate approved amounts under AWP for all states. This means a considerable gap exists between availability and release of funds.
- Due to inherent systemic deficiencies, utilization of funds has been inadequate and even inappropriate. Even though the allocation has been planned as per AWPs, a majority of the states have been unable to utilize the funds. In a hurried bid to generate evidence, several states divert funds and merely show the utilization on paper. In addition, the pace of utilization under SSA has varied widely not only across states but also across different activities within each state.
- The utilization of funds has been consistently low in several states. Some examples are given below. The overall expenditure on SSA in Bihar as a proportion of approved AWP was 13 per cent in 2001-02, 9.8 per cent in 2002-03, 32 per cent in 2003-04, 45 per cent in 2004-05 and 53 per cent in 2005-06. In the case of Rajasthan, it was 21.1 per cent in 2002-03, 51.2 per cent in 2003-04, 62.5 per cent in 2004-05, and 77 per cent in 2005-06. In AP, it was less than 20 per cent in 2001-02 and 2002-03, 53.24 per cent in 2003-04, 60.6 per cent in 2004-05 and 81.2 per cent in 2005-06. Hence even

when funding was not an issue, the inability of the state machinery to make optimum use of funds allocated has impacted the implementation of several educational programmes.

- Some of the reasons for under utilization of SSA funds in several states were found to be delay in release of funds, shortage of staff at the supervisory level, delay in appointment of teachers, appointment of teachers at less than pay scales, inability to draw teachers for training, teachers being assigned non-teaching work, teachers' unwillingness to get trained during school holidays, lack of adequate infrastructure at school level, and inadequate technical staff which hampered construction activities at the school level.
- Once the centre implemented the fifth (and now sixth) pay commission recommendations, the states had virtually no choice but to follow suit with regard to their own employees. Since this happens periodically (whenever the centre revises the pay scales of its employees) the finances of the states are bound to get dented.
- Teachers form a major proportion of government employees in all the states. In an attempt to cut costs, several states opt for para/contract teachers in place of permanent ones which in turn has impacted the quality of education.

Concerns Relating to Private Sector Participation

The private sector has shown an impressive growth as the Indian middle class continues to spend a large part of its income on funding the education of its children. But, except for a few, the quality of education provided by most of these private schools is far from satisfactory. Some of the issues that need the attention of the states are:

- Friendly regulations for granting permission/ recognition to schools are needed in order to encourage more private sector participation.
- Regulatory policies for private sector institutions (especially the unaided ones) should be more realistic and unambiguous with respect to fee structure, staff recruitment policy and admissions. The Supreme Court has also advocated such a view in its judgments in a number of cases.
- Issues of equity, salary and service conditions of staff need to be regulated.
- In order to ensure equity, the states need to develop policies that allow the admission of poor children in private schools through a system of cross subsidies. The concept of differential fee in private unaided schools can help such schools in meeting their social obligations. While the unaided institutions may be allowed to charge higher student fees depending on institutional needs, they must have provision for free/subsidized education for the merited and needy students. The 'Right to Education Act', 2009 has tried to remedy this situation to some extent. But how it is implemented remains to be seen.
- Support systems must be created for ensuring high quality education in these private institutions. This includes resource support and teacher training which, at present are not given to teachers of private unaided institutions.

Community Participation

Sustained progress in primary education can be achieved only when states give priority to educational management reforms. Community involvement in planning for educational needs and management of schools is crucial to such reforms.

States which initiated household surveys mainly utilized teachers for the purpose with the involvement of the community being marginal. Even the information generated through such surveys was not adequately utilized in the district plans under SSA. Hence, there is greater necessity to involve community/people's representatives even in preparation of district plans under SSA.

Parents need to take on a larger role in the management of schools as ultimately they are important stakeholders. Similarly, more authority is required for decentralized and transparent decision-making through school committees. The states also need to evolve policies for effective collaboration with NGOs working in the field of education at the village level.

Several state governments have moved towards decentralization of educational administration through empowerment of school management committees for effective school management. Legislative measures were also put in place to speed up the process of decentralization. Some also involved the community in the process. Ultimately schools need to be made accountable to communities.

Quality Issues

Student Learning Outcomes

In today's world, it is necessary but not sufficient, for students to achieve minimum competence, knowledge, understanding and skills in curricular areas. Besides this, students need to develop critical skills necessary for effective functioning in everyday life. Schools are also expected to develop personal and social skills such as leadership, self-confidence, communication and life skills, self-motivation, and group work. Student development is thus multi-dimensional in nature.

Formerly, no reliable data was available on performance of children in elementary schools. The only available data was the achievement surveys of DPEP (BAS, MAS, TAS) which showed less than 50 per cent achievement levels in DPEP districts. (Tables 34 & 35 Annexure VIII). Since 2005, we have survey reports of ASER on students' learning achievement, which reflect poor quality of student learning outcomes in schools across the country.

The decline of the governmental/local body school system in many states has contributed to the poor student learning achievement in these schools. Some of the issues which impact quality of student learning are mentioned below:

- The PTR has a direct bearing on quality. At the national level, the average PTR for primary schools is very much above 40:1, with large inter state, inter-district and inter-school variations. There are still a large number of districts which have a PTR above the national average.

- Several studies have pointed out that considerable gaps exist in quality of learning among students in primary classes. Teachers and children face a large number of problems in classrooms as a result of multigrade situations and teacher absenteeism.
- Curriculum at the upper primary stage becomes subject specific. In several states, for example, often teachers who have not studied science and mathematics at the + 2 level teach these subjects at the upper primary level. Lack of proper laboratory and library facilities is another important factor impacting quality of classroom transaction.
- Quality was compromised when there was a massive expansion of the education system across the country. For example, the Karnataka HDR (1999) reported that 86,000 teachers were appointed in the state (under the OB scheme) during the four-year period 1994-95 to 1997-98. Such a massive exercise (in such a short period) is in itself an indicator of quality being sidelined in recruitment of teachers.
- Efforts to evaluate the performance of teachers or grade them are absent. Even national level institutions like NCERT have done very little to bring out suitable models for teacher evaluation.
- The no-detention policy practiced in most states impacts quality of outcomes, as children move from class to class without learning adequately. Here, progress is not linked to student performance. 'The Right to Education Act', 2009 proposes to extend the policy to the upper primary stage, which is not a pragmatic step, as the elementary education system will be turning out students without achieving the required competencies and skills. This will certainly have a deleterious effect both on the secondary education sector and employability of these students in the job market.
- Inadequate supervising and monitoring mechanisms as well as the existing system of examinations do not in any way contribute to improving quality.

The education systems across states should ensure school level autonomy through meaningful partnerships for quality improvement with the active involvement of parents, teachers, children, NGOs, elected representatives, etc. There is also an urgent need to develop a suitable community owned accountability system for these schools.

Present Challenges in Elementary Education

Despite considerable achievements in the field of elementary education, there are serious concerns and issues relating to this field. Even though expenditure on education has increased, achieving the goals of UEE requires a strong political will, improvement in educational planning and management systems and measures to improve quality at all levels. There are also serious problems of gender, regional, social and cultural disparities in achieving the goals of UEE.

- The main challenge in achieving the goals of UEE is not merely providing physical access but also ensuring participation of all children in the process of primary education. Persistent disparities still exist among different geographical regions as well as between different social groups.
- A sizable number of students continue to dropout due to socio-economic and cultural factors, inadequacy of infrastructure, shortage of teachers, teacher absenteeism and unsatisfactory quality of education being provided in the classrooms.
- Issues of equity continue to challenge educational planners and administrators. Efforts were made to meet this challenge by bringing the school and community closer, and creating a sense of ownership and accountability among stakeholders at the grass roots level.
- Sustenance and upscaling of programmes is a major challenge for any government. For example in Karnataka, the popular 'Nali-Kali' initiative came to a standstill once the DPEP ended. Sustenance of the initiative post DPEP did not happen for lack of integration of 'Nali-Kali' into the larger system. Later, efforts to upscale the programme failed due to a variety of reasons.
- Reforms are needed to effectively decentralize down to the school level, allow for local initiatives, make communities manage the affairs of the school, encourage transparency and social audit, focus on institutional capacity development for quality and excellence, and most of all, develop an accountable public system of schooling.

Challenges Facing Elementary Teachers

Teachers generally tend to work in a challenging environment, as a majority of elementary schools are multigrade and there is the perennial problem of one teacher handling more than one class everyday. This problem is compounded when the existing teacher strength in the school is further reduced due to absence or shortage of teachers; teachers being deputed for official work, etc.

Teachers are sometimes forced to get involved in activities that are related to the broader social, cultural and economic conditions that have a direct impact on the school and the teachers themselves. They must respond to the diverse needs of the children, work with parents, implement social policies (prevention of drug addiction, HIV, etc.) and also involve in campaigns of other social sectors (polio and other immunization programmes, etc.).

Teachers are also expected to take part in other non-classroom-based activities which bring a lot of pressure on them. In a majority of rural areas and some urban pockets too, they are expected to generally conform to the expectations of the community leader. If there is more than one socio/political group in the village, they are constrained to do a tight-rope walk between the groups. There are also instances of some teachers getting involved in local politics, acting as political advisors, etc.

Apart from academic duties, teachers are expected to perform all other tasks entrusted to them by their superiors – children's census, general census, cattle census, revision of electoral rolls and all election-related work. Even though there is a bar on them being involved in such activities during school sessions, it is at best ignored and they are continued to be deployed for all kinds of work.

Future Efforts Needed to Improve 'Quality'

The centre and the states must take a number of steps to ensure quality. Some of them are:

- Ensure that schools compulsorily work for a minimum of 5 hours in a day and a minimum of 220 days in a year.
- Reform the present assessment and examination system at the elementary level.
- Reform the teacher education sector both at the in-service and pre-service levels.
- Provide better academic resource support even at CRP level.
- Ensure a healthier PTR to around 30:1 for effective classroom transaction.
- Address issues relating to teacher absenteeism.
- Train head teachers in leadership and administrative skills.
- Establish a closer link between ECCE centres and primary schools.
- Implement the recommendation of the NPE 1986 in the creation of a 'National Testing Service'. This would facilitate comparing the achievement levels of pupils of a certain class across states.
- Have a sensitive and progressive regulatory framework for maintaining and improving educational standards at the state level throughout the country.
- Make efforts to improve the internal management of schools and streamline the regular management practices within schools through institutional planning and monitoring mechanisms.
- Improve the quality of teaching-learning and classroom processes.

Promotion of Equality of Educational Opportunities in the Country

Some of the policy decisions that help in promoting equality of educational opportunities are mentioned below:

- Enforce a policy of not transferring teachers during the academic year.
- Assign best teachers to the first grade.
- Give some incentives to teachers working in rural and remote schools.
- Ensure a highly trained and motivated supervisory staff.
- Identify low performing schools through EMIS and give them special academic support.
- Decentralize management to the school level.
- Put in place a mechanism for weeding out non-performing teachers from the system at regular intervals, preferably every year.

- Test at least a sample of students at the primary level (class 5) and the upper primary level (class 7 and 8) regularly. Analysis of the results will enable planners and administrators to take up remedial measures and follow up activities.
- Provide suitable library books, TLM, teachers' guides to enhance the quality of classroom transaction.
- Provide quality in-service training regularly to teachers both in content and methodology.
- Enhance the quality of pre-service programmes through suitable quality monitoring mechanisms. Enforce strict quality norms on teacher training institutions. Ensure that the training provided is more field oriented than theory-based.
- Provide pre-school facilities to all children specially in rural and remote areas.

Separate administrative structures are found to be involved in tasks which have a common goal and which comprise a common set of activities. Hence there is need to:

(a) Avoid creation of parallel structures for implementation of similar development programmes.

(b) Re-examine the norms and patterns of operation specified under different schemes and projects to ensure greater convergence.

(c) States must reorganize education management structures so as to achieve greater coordination in planning and effective convergence in implementation of education development programmes.

Annexure I

Education as a Critical Factor in Human Development in India

Different countries have different priorities in formulating policies for economic and general development. Increasing national wealth, improving the well-being of the majority, ensuring freedom, and increasing economic security are some of them. Economic growth no doubt increases a nation's total wealth, enhances its potential for reducing poverty and helps in solving social and other problems. But a look at several countries reveals that economic growth is not necessarily a precursor to progress in human development.

Broadly speaking, human well-being includes not only consumption of goods and services, but also the accessibility of all sections of the population (especially the deprived and those who are living below the poverty line) to the basic necessities of a productive and socially meaningful life. Hence, economic growth should result in sustained human development – improvement in knowledge and skills of the people, better employment opportunities, greater democratic participation at all levels, improvement in quality of life, etc.

As a World Bank report points out, that countries with similar incomes can differ substantially when it comes to the 'Quality of life' of their people that would include access to education and healthcare, employment opportunities, availability of clean air and safe drinking water, adequate housing, availability of sufficient food, and so on.

THE CONCEPT OF HUMAN DEVELOPMENT

Earlier, till the sixties, the economic attainment of a country was measured on the basis of the per capita income. However, it was since realized that economic growth may not reach all sections of the population and that development could not be equated with economic growth per se. Through the eighties and nineties economists experimented to arrive at a formula for measuring human welfare which would take into account not only access to resources and services but also deprivation of the basic facilities required for a comfortable existence.

UN agencies stressed on the importance of 'human development' as measured by life expectancy, adult literacy, access to all three levels of education, as well as people's average income. Finally, UNDP created a reasonably satisfactory measure that could assess people's welfare, and called it the 'Human Development Index'. Similarly, UNDP's identification of human development indicators to assess parameters not normally encompassed by economic criteria (such as rate of growth of GDP) has significantly changed the way we look at 'development'.

The simplicity and universal appeal of this indicator was largely responsible for its acceptance by economists and other social scientists. A major advantage of the index is its applicability to both developed and developing economies. The measure picks up just three basic issues that are crucial to welfare income, basic health and education and puts them together on an equal footing.

While the HDI that is calculated using the UNDP technique throws light upon development disparities in the social sectors at the state and regional levels, gender-related development indices focus upon the unequal access that men and women have to income earning opportunities as well as health and educational facilities.

The HDI computed every year by the UNDP since 1990, measures average achievements in basic human development and assigns ranks to countries. By doing so, the UNDP has been able to bring into sharp focus deficiencies in health and educational facilities in high income countries, apart from drawing attention to success stories in less-developed countries. Consequently, most experts now use HDI to measure a country's development.

Human Development Index

As already discussed, HDI comprises of several social indicators that are used for broad cross-country comparisons or for more specific comparisons across the states within a country. It was first used in UNDP's Human Development Report (HDR)1990. Its purpose is not to give a complete picture of human development but to provide a comprehensive measure that goes beyond income. Thus, HDI is considered to be a barometer of change in human well-being and a tool for comparing progress in different regions. It measures the average achievement in a country in three basic dimensions.

(a) Health and longevity (as measured by life expectancy at birth)
(b) Education (as measured by literacy and combined GER for primary, secondary and tertiary institutions)
(c) Living standards (as measured by GDP per capita in purchasing power parity US dollars).

Achievements in each area are measured by the extent of a country's attaining the following goals: life expectancy of 85 years, 100 per cent adult literacy and enrolment and real GDP per capita of $40,000 in terms of purchasing power parity. Although highly desirable, these goals are yet to be achieved by any country. While one needs to understand that the concept of human development cannot be confined to a single composite index, it must be appreciated that the HDI offers a powerful alternative to income as a summary measure of human well-being.

Since 1993, efforts have been made to make the HDI tangible: accordingly, minimum and maximum values have been prescribed for the variables it employs. The advantage of HDI is that it allows countries to be ranked in order of their achievements in human development. In 1997 the top five countries were Canada, Norway, US, Japan and Belgium. In the HDR 2005 prepared by UNDP, Norway ranked first with an HDI of 0.963, Health Index (Life expectancy index) of 0.91, Education Index of 0.99 and Income Index (GDP index) of 0.99. Over the last decade, the HDI has been rising across all developing nations.

The HDI for India rose from 0.412 in 1975 to 0.602 in 2003. India ranked 127 with an HDI of 0.602, Health Index of 0.64, Education Index of 0.61 and Income Index of 0.56 and was classified as a country with medium human development. It ranked much below Asian countries like Malaysia (Rank 61 HDI: 0.796), Thailand (73 and 0.778), China (85 and 0.755), Sri Lanka (93 and 0.751), Vietnam (108 and 0.704), and Indonesia (110 and 0.697).

Human Development Reports

Since 1990, the UNDP has been regularly bringing out annual HDRs containing assessments of the well-being of people of different countries. The UNDP technique is ideally suited to identifying gaps in social sectors and measuring relative levels of well-being at the district level. According to the HDR 1996 published by UNDP: 'human development is the end; economic growth, the means'.

As UNDP's HDR 2005 notes, 'Overcoming the legacy of decades of under-investment in human development and deep rooted gender inequities poses immense challenges. Political leadership of a high order will be needed to address these challenges. Failure to provide it and to extend health and education opportunities for all, regardless of wealth and gender, will ultimately act as a constraint on India's future prospects in the global economy'.

In a developing country, public expenditure on services and infrastructure is the most desirable channel to improve the quality of life of the poor and the marginalized. By going beyond the provisioning of basic necessities, it paves the way for better access to facilities such as education, basic healthcare, nutrition, safe drinking water, sanitation and housing, all of which make a huge difference to the quality of life. It is in this context that government expenditure on social sectors becomes a crucial factor.

However, most states have other imperatives as well, such as economic growth which is also a prerequisite for human development. For instance, Karnataka invests heavily in irrigation and power.

India has been widely heralded as a growth story for globalization. Over the past two decades, it has moved into the premier league of countries clocking high economic growth, with technology exports booming and India's middle class consumers having become a magnet for foreign investors. The incidence of income poverty fell from 36 per cent in the early 1990s to 25 per cent in recent years. Improvements in child and infant mortality declined. However, education inequities puts a brake on India's progress. As UNDP's HDR points out, 'About 1 in 4 girls and about 1 in 10 boys do not attend primary school'.

Regional imbalance has been a continuing concern in most Indian states. Along with policies to address regional disparities, there is now a greater emphasis on public-private initiative in the social sector. There has also been a thrust on institutional reforms directed at strengthening and empowering PR institutions, thus enabling the emergence of a sustainable, participatory development environment.

States like HP and TN sustained rapid progress in education, not just by increasing budget provision but also by making service providers more accountable as well as creating incentives for poor households to be pro-active in participation. Madhya Pradesh and Karnataka were the first two states in the country to bring out HDRs in the 1990s.

The National Human Development Report (NHDR) 2001

The Planning Commission, GOI took the lead in preparing the NHDR 2001 for the first time. Being an attempt to map the state of human development in the country, the NHDR tracked the quality of life and the level of human well-being across states. (Refer Annexure VIII – Tables 1-3).

It considered three critical dimensions of well-being:

(a) longevity – the ability to live a long and healthy life;
(b) education – the ability to read, write and acquire knowledge; and
(c) command over resources – the ability to enjoy a decent standard of living and have a socially meaningful life.

Subsequently, it estimated the HDI for selected states for 2001 according to which an improvement of 26 per cent during the eighties and by another 24 per cent during the nineties was seen, both in rural and urban areas. Though the rural-urban gap continued to be significant, it showed a decline during the period. At the state level wide disparities were observed. Human attainments appeared to be better and more sustained in states where there was social mobilization for human development and, where female literacy and empowerment encouraged women to have a say in decision-making at the household level.

Status of Gender Equality

The Gender-related Development Index that was introduced in UNDP's 1995 HDR measures achievements using the same dimensions and variables as the HDI, but it is gender sensitive. Thus, GDI is the HDI discounted for gender inequality. NHDR 2001 prepared the 'Index of Gender Equality (GEI)' measuring the attainments in human development for females as a proportion to that of males.

The GEI has shown a marginal improvement as per NHDR. At the national level it increased from 62 per cent in the early eighties to 67.6 per cent in the early nineties. In the nineties, HP had the highest equality whereas Bihar was at the bottom. In general, women were better off in South India. On the whole, gender disparities declined over the period.

Gross Domestic Product (GDP) and Gross National Product (GNP)

GDP is calculated as the value of the total final output of all goods and services produced in a single year within a country's boundaries. In an open economy GDP can be different from GNP because Indian nationals hold assets abroad and foreign nationals hold assets in India. GNP is GDP plus incomes received by residents from abroad minus incomes claimed by non-residents.

Education and Human Capital

Most human capital is built up through education or training that, in turn, increases a person's economic productivity, that is, it enables him/her to earn a higher income. Governments spend public money on education because they believe a better educated population will contribute to faster development. Investing in education contributes not only to building a nation's human capital but also to improving its prospects for economic growth and higher living standards.

Most governments are committed to providing free primary (and often secondary) education because it is believed that the entire country benefits when its citizens can read and write as well as participate in social and economic life. Moreover, economic and social returns to society are known to be higher for primary education than for other levels of education.

In many low income countries, public funds available for this purpose are often insufficient to meet the increasing demand of rapidly growing populations. Primary school enrolments are generally lower for girls than for boys. The gender gap is widest in South Asia, the Middle East and Sub-Saharan Africa. The gap reflects cultural norms, early child bearing, limited employment opportunities and traditional expectations of girls' larger contribution to household work.

The expenditure on education is higher in developed countries compared to developing ones. On an average, the expenditure on education is 3.4 per cent of GDP in low income, 4.4 per cent in middle income and 5.6 per cent in high income countries. In many countries, private spending on education is also significant. Around the world, the difference between public and private spending on education varies enormously.

Primary Education and Literacy

Primary school education helps children to acquire basic literacy and numeracy as well as other knowledge and skills. In low income countries, it often improves the welfare of the poor by making them productive workers and by enabling them to learn new skills as and when required. In addition, primary education – especially for girls and women – leads to healthier and smaller families.

Human Development Reports by Karnataka

Karnataka is the only state in the country to have brought out two HDRs, one in 1999 and another in 2005 with a thematic focus. In 2005, the state occupied the seventh place in human development (behind Kerala, Maharashtra, TN, Punjab, Gujarat and Haryana occupying the first 6 places respectively). Similarly, it occupied the fifth place in the Education Index (behind Kerala, Maharashtra, TN, Gujarat occupying the first 4 places respectively).

The level of human development was much higher in Karnataka (0.650) than in India as a whole (0.621). It increased from 0.541 in 1991 to 0.650 in 2001, showing a 20 per cent improvement. This was possible because of increase of 39 per cent in the Income Index, 18 per cent in the Education Index and 10 per cent in the Health Index.

The status of human development in the districts in Karnataka was first scientifically assessed by the HDR 1999 and reviewed in the HDR 2005. It was found that there was a strong correlation between the economic status and HDI even at the district level in a majority of the districts.

There is a need to bring out HDRs regularly, both at the national and state levels. This would not only facilitate comparative studies between states and identification of gaps but would bring about greater focus for sustained development as well.

Annexure II

Health Factors Affecting Participation of Children in Elementary Education

INTRODUCTION

The importance of health in the well- being of an individual can never be underestimated. A healthy child is not only able to attend school readily but is also likely to be a better learner. A healthy adult has the potential to find work and engage in an economic activity thus ensuring for himself of a better quality of life. NHDR 2001 points out that adult female literacy is directly correlated to life expectancy and infant mortality.

An analysis of data collected (World Bank 1999) from 115 low and middle income countries showed that the education level of adult females had a significant impact on improving health, longevity and demographic indicators.

As UNDP's HDR 2005 notes: 'About one-third of India's children are underweight at birth… The under-five mortality rate is more than twice as high for illiterate mothers as for children of mothers who have completed middle school … As well as depriving girls of a basic right, education inequities in India translate into more child deaths'.

The HDR observed that girls between the ages 1-5 were 50 per cent more likely to die than boys. It was found that four states – Bihar, MP, Rajasthan and UP – accounted for more than half of child deaths.

This report has also estimated the percentage of people and children in India who are affected by health factors (2003 estimates):

(a) Undernourished population 21% (2002)
(b) Children underweight for age 47% (under age 5 years)
(c) Children underheight for age 46% (under age 5 years)
(d) Infants with low birth weight 30%

Data from NFHS-3 carried out in 2005-06 showed that 46 per cent of children under 3 years and 49 per cent under 6 suffered from malnutrition while 79 per cent of children had fallen prey to anemia. The position was equally dismal in the case of adolescent girls. About one-third of India's children were underweight at birth. These national averages mask the huge variations in the incidence of child malnutrition across Indian states. In 2005-06, the incidence of malnutrition varied among major states from 27 per cent in Punjab and 29 per cent in Kerala to 60 per cent in MP. NFHS-3 also estimated that 38.4 per cent of children under 3 years of age suffer from stunted growth.

A World Bank Study 2003 undertaken by ERU in the three states of AP, Karnataka and UP notes: 'Despite the conventional wisdom about regional and inter state variations with regard to availability of resources and provision of social services with the southern states ranked higher than those in north India, there is little difference with regard to access and utilization of services by poor households across the three states. Poverty continues to exert a strong influence on nutrition of children, health seeking behaviour of households, and in overall living standards'.

Overall, there are both tangible and intangible effects of poverty on the lives of children:

- On the overall health status of children.
- On the ability of a child to be regular in school and/or continue and complete primary education.
- Intensity of poverty (acute poverty) influences parental choice of how many children go to school and up to what level (beyond primary).

As per a survey conducted by the National Council for Applied Economic Research (1995), morbidity decreased with increase in education level of the head of a family.

In a country like India, anemic girls under 18 giving birth to children with neither adequate supplementary nutrition during pregnancy nor requisite antenatal care and support continues to be rampant. This is particularly true of backward regions with very high incidence of poverty. The persistent malnourishment in the first three-years of a child's life has a significant impact on his/her learning ability in later years.

Malnutrition

Malnutrition seriously retards human development. Adults who have survived malnutrition in their childhood are less healthy, physically less productive, and have poor intellectual abilities. NHDR 2001 points out that over half of the children under 5 years of age in India are moderately or severely malnourished, 30 per cent of newly born children are underweight and nearly 60 per cent of women are anemic.

Deficiency of protein/energy is the most common cause of malnutrition among children aged 0-4 years. Iron-deficiency anemia is widespread among children as well as women, especially pregnant women. In school-going children, deficiency of iron along with deficiencies of micro-nutrients (Vitamin A, iron, folic acid, zinc, etc.) affect the growth, the physical and mental development, and the immunity levels. A critical consequence of the prevalence of malnourishment is the impact it has on cognitive development and learning achievements – while it reduces productivity and the capacity to work among adults, it enhances mortality and morbidity among children.

Data also reveals that households with lower per capita income had lower calorie and protein intake. NSSO's 50th Round Survey on Nutritional Intake in India reported that nearly 37 per cent of rural and 42 per cent of urban households were consuming less than the recommended average energy levels. Though there was not much variation in the nutritional status of male and female children, there were considerable rural-urban differences. It is significant to note that the nutritional status of children and adults in some of the middle income states (such as Kerala and TN) was better than that in higher income states (like Maharashtra and Gujarat).

Major nutritional deficiencies affecting young children in India are:

(a) Protein-energy malnutrition
(b) Iron-deficiency anemia
(c) Vitamin A deficiency
(d) Iodine-deficiency disorders (IDD).

Protein-energy malnutrition among school-going children assessed through weight deficit for age is the most sensitive indicator of the nutritional status. The percentage of underweight children of elementary school as per Gomez classification is as shown in the table below:

Table II-1

Age	Undernutrition/Underweight Children		
	Mild	Moderate	Severe
6-9 years	31.9	54.0	8.6
10-13 years	18.2	47.8	30.1

Source: NNMB, NIN & ICMR, 2002

Nutritional anemia due to iron and folic acid deficiency is widely prevalent in young children and adolescents, with 67.5 per cent children under 5 years and 69% adolescent girls being afflicted (NNMB 2003). The percentage of prevalence of anemia in school children (6-14 years) as per studies conducted during 1981 to 1996 ranges from 14-96 per cent as seen in the table below:

Table II-2

Location	Percentage of Anemic Children (with Hb<12g/dl)
Baroda	91
Kolkata	96
Hyderabad	60
Chennai	14
New Delhi	67
Varanasi	68

Source: Task Force Report on Micro-nutrients, 1996, DWCD,GOI

Vitamin A deficiency affecting growing children is also a public health problem in the country. Vitamin A is important for promoting growth of the child as well as building immunity and resistance to diseases. Prevalence of Vitamin A deficiency contributes to diarrheal diseases, respiratory infections, measles, etc.

Iodine deficiency during childhood – the period of maximum growth – can result in loss of IQ points, poor physical and mental growth and development. Although, on an average, prevalence of 'goitre' among 6-12 year old children is about 4 per cent, it is 12.2 per cent in Maharashtra and 9 per cent in WB which is much above the WHO cut-off level of 5.0 per cent. It must be noted that no state in the country is free from IDD while 260 out of 321 districts surveyed have more than 10 per cent prevalence of the same.

The table below used the NFHS-II 1998-99 to look at the nutritional status of children, especially those in the severely malnourished category. It brings out the strong linkage between high rates of severe malnourishment and non-participation in schools. Recent studies (Vimala Ramachandran; Jean Dreze) have pointed out that many children come to schools with hunger pangs – surely, this is a major limiting factor in non-participation of those who are out-of-school and lack of learning among those who struggle to remain in the school.

Table II-3 Nutrition Status of Children by States – The Severe Category

State	Weight for Age – Percentage Below – 3SD (Severely Undernourished)	Height for Age – Percentage Below – 3 SD (Severe Stunting)	Weight for Height Percentage Below – 3 SD (Severe Wasting)
Haryana	10.1	24.3	0.8
Himachal Pradesh	12.1	18.1	3.3
Punjab	8.8	17.2	0.8
Rajasthan	20.8	29.0	1.9
Madhya Pradesh	24.3	28.3	4.3
Uttar Pradesh	21.9	31.0	2.1
Bihar	25.5	33.6	5.5
Orissa	20.7	17.6	3.9
West Bengal	16.3	19.2	1.6
Assam	13.3	33.7	3.3
Gujarat	16.2	23.3	2.4
Maharashtra	17.6	14.1	2.5
Andhra Pradesh	10.3	14.2	1.6

Karnataka	16.5	15.9	3.9
Kerala	4.7	7.3	0.7
Tamil Nadu	10.6	12.0	3.8
All India	18.0	23.0	2.8

Source: NFHS-II, 1998-99

15 years after universal childhood immunization was introduced, national health surveys suggest that only 42 per cent of children are immunized. Again, coverage is lowest in states with high child death rates, and less than 20 per cent in Bihar and UP.

At the state level, the problem of nutrition among children is addressed by the ICDS and, National Midday Meals Programmes apart from various micro-nutrient schemes including those targeted at improving intake of iron-foliate, Vitamin A, and iodized salt.

By providing services like supplementary feeding, immunization against preventable childhood diseases, health checkups, health and nutrition education to women and pre-school education for children, the ICDS programme has recorded significant success, particularly in states where primary level healthcare facilities are fairly well-developed. States which have done well include Kerala, TN, Karnataka and AP in the south, Maharashtra and Gujarat in the west, WB in the east and HP, Haryana and Punjab in the north.

The World Bank Study on Completion of Primary School by Poor Children

The World Bank commissioned a qualitative study to identify factors that facilitate/ impede successful completion of primary school by children from diverse poverty situations in UP, Karnataka and AP. Some of the findings of this study were:

Three to six years:

(a) The frequency and quantity of children's eating was observed to be rather inadequate. The majority of children in poor households appeared moderately to severely malnourished, sporting pot-bellies and extremely thin limbs. Though they otherwise appeared active and alert, there was a likelihood of the effects of poor nutrition manifesting themselves later in life. The overall nutritional status of children thus needs urgent attention.

(b) These children were left unattended and unsupervised as they played and wandered around on their own. A few, however, accompanied their older siblings to primary school. Nevertheless, to a large extent, they were found to be active and alert, whether it was in the household or at school.

(c) There was little structuring by adults/parents of children's activities, whether it was in school, play, language or health.

(d) Socio-economic participation in household and productive activity seemed far ahead of age-expectations. Even at such an early stage children were taking responsibility for small tasks related to sibling care, household chores and even cattle care.

Evidence from the ground indicated a rather contrary picture, marked by erratic provision of nutrition by the state and a rather weak and ineffective pre-school component. Politics of caste identity and status too emerged as an important factor in access of very poor households to nutrition supplements and pre-school education. These detrimental practices persisted in the absence of effective monitoring strategies as well lack of positive synergy with other grass roots level social delivery apparatuses – i.e., state-sponsored and NGOs.

Six to eleven years:

(a) Most children in the surveyed households were enrolled in schools. Many of them had been attending school though with varying degrees of regularity.

(b) Children attending government schools reported that they worked before as well as after school hours. The burden of work was most severe for the first-born, especially in case of a daughter. Apart from sibling care, children supported their families by caring for milch cows/goats, fetching wood for fuel, fodder and water, running errands and looking after sick family members. As a result, they were either late for school or missed it altogether.

(c) Gender-based division of work and added responsibility of household work on older girls in the family was marked in all the three states. Engaging in full-time work during weekends and holidays was fairly routine.

(d) Children slogged for long hours everyday. Most children in poor households were deprived of time to revise/read their books, especially girls who were higher up in the birth order. Energy levels were low and impacted children's ability to concentrate in school.

(e) Children had almost no access to story books or any other reading material either in school or at home.

(f) Discussions with children revealed that almost 10-15 per cent of them (majority being girls) came to school without eating on most days. Girls were specially affected because of the time they spent over morning chores. In this context, the provision of a hot midday meal became all the more necessary.

(g) Another significant factor that emerged is one of changing social norms with regard to schooling. Discussions in rural Karnataka and AP revealed that sending children to school has become a community norm while in UP, such an awareness was yet to fully emerge.

(h) Almost all interactions revealed an ambiguity in understanding the value of education. Generally, people agreed that education was important, that it was valuable in itself and that it enhanced self-worth and dignity. Yet, when they observed that formal education had not changed some lives, they wondered whether it was really a stepping-stone to a brighter future – meaning, would it really provide employment or improve one's status and so on. They also pointed out that many children who attended school for four to five years were not able to read or write fluently.

As children in the research sample reached school-going age, one thing they were assured of (despite poor nutrition, health, and sanitation) was a proof of formal enrolment – their names would be recorded in a school register. However, what was not assured was their ability to attend school uninterrupted – not merely due to ill health but also due to compulsions of working or lack of motivation for them or their parents on the part of the existing school.

Attendance was erratic and chronic absenteeism often the norm, especially for older boys and girls. In other instances, both boys and girls also worked before and after school, engaging in a wide range of domestic chores. The research study indicated that this pattern of (non) attendance as well as physical energy expended on work does impact the learning outcomes; however, it was unable to conclusively demonstrate the link.

Despite evidence of universal primary enrolment, a holistic approach to child development is needed. Hence, one needs to come to grips with, rather than merely scratch the surface to tackle the cumulative nature of social, political, and economic exclusion that relentlessly plagues the lives of poor children. Given this context, the ambivalence of the poor with regard to the value of education is hardly surprising.

Annexure III

The Midday Meal Scheme

[NATIONAL PROGRAMME OF NUTRITIONAL SUPPORT TO PRIMARY EDUCATION (NP-NSPE)]

'School feeding helps create literate, educated societies... School feeding programmes often double enrolment within a year and can produce 40 per cent improvement in academic performance within two-years. Children who take part in such programmes stay in school longer. And the expense is minimal'. [World Food Programme 2002].

Several independent studies have highlighted the impact of the midday meal scheme. It is perceived to be an indispensable component of food security initiatives, for children's health and their right to nutrition throughout the world. In India, being a major intervention of the GOI, it has tried to successfully address the issues of dropouts, teacher absenteeism and social discrimination, while providing nutritional support to children at the primary stage in government schools, government aided schools, EGS and AIE centres. It has grown to become the largest school nutrition programme in the world covering 12 crore children in a million schools across the country.

A hungry child is less likely to attend school regularly. As has been discussed in Annexure II, malnutrition also adversely affects retention and participation of children. The school midday meal scheme facilitates enrolment and attendance in schools. Apart from this, it has an important social value in that it fosters equality. As children learn to sit together and share a common meal, there is bound to be some erosion of caste prejudices and class inequalities. Cultural traditions and social structures often impact girls more than boys. However, by encouraging female school attendance, the scheme reduces the gender gap in education. Involvement of parents in school governance is also another beneficial offshoot of the programme.

Objective of the Cooked Midday Meal Scheme

The scheme aims at boosting universalization of primary education (classes 1 to 5) by improving enrolment, retention, attendance and learning levels of children, especially of those belonging to disadvantaged sections while simultaneously improving their nutritional status. It motivates parents not only to enrol their children in school but have them attend regularly as well. Thus, it enhances community involvement in schools.

Since malnourishment is detrimental to concentration and learning, the scheme tries to providing nutritious food and alleviates short-term hunger in malnourished or even otherwise well-nourished school children. It also addresses the problem of specific micro-nutrient deficiencies among this age group.

Historical Background of the Scheme

The midday meal scheme in schools has a long history in India. It was introduced for disadvantaged children in Madras Municipal Corporation in 1925. It was in existence in the princely Mysore state as early as 1946. In 1951-52, the state sanctioned Rs3.70 lakhs for the midday lunch programme in which 9366 children in 1957 middle schools and 25 high schools were covered. The main objective of the programme was to provide nutritious food to children coming from poor and weaker sections and also to improve their attendance.

A midday meal programme was started in 1963 with assistance from 'Cooperative American Relief Everywhere' (CARE) in selected blocks in the country. The coverage reached a peak in 1976-77, when the 'Central Kitchen Scheme' was introduced. The programme supported both pre-primary and primary education till 1984-85, when CARE assistance to the pre-primary sector was discontinued. It was finally wound up in 1993-94.

By the mid 1980s, three states – Gujarat, Kerala and TN – and the Union Territory of Pondicherry had universalized a cooked midday meal programme with their own resources for children studying in primary schools. In 1982 the TN government introduced a cooked meal scheme to cover all rural children in the 2-9 age group. It was then extended to urban areas and to children of ages 10-15 in 1984.

Children in tribal areas in some states like MP and Orissa also benefited similarly. By 1990-91 the number of states implementing the programme with their own resources on a universal or a large-scale had increased to twelve to cover Goa, Gujarat, Kerala, MP, Maharashtra, Meghalaya, Mizoram, Nagaland, Sikkim, TN, Tripura and UP.

In three states – Karnataka, Orissa and West Bengal – the programme was implemented with state resources in combination with international assistance. Another two states – AP and Rajasthan – were implementing the programme entirely with international assistance. At this point, the GOI stepped in and devised a centrally sponsored scheme for the entire country.

Nutritional Support Programme

The 'National Programme of Nutritional Support to Primary Education (NP-NSPE)' was launched as a centrally sponsored scheme on 15th August 1995, initially in 2408 blocks in the country. Under its aegis, the states started distributing 3kg of wheat or rice per child per month through fair price shops. Food grains were given to all children studying in classes 1 to 5 in government and aided primary schools subject to the children maintaining an average 80 per cent attendance per month. The entire cost of the scheme was borne by the central government.

By 1997-98, the NP-NSPE was extended to all the blocks of the country. It was further extended in 2002 to cover not only children in classes 1 to 5 in government, government aided and local body schools but also those studying in centres run under EGS and AIE schemes. When the scheme was introduced, central assistance under the programme consisted of the following:

(a) Free supply of food grains @ 100 grams per child per school day and
(b) Subsidy for transportation of food grains up to a maximum of Rs50 per quintal.

In addition to food grains, the midday meal involved two other major inputs:

(a) Cost of Cooking – which included cost of ingredients (pulses, vegetables, cooking oil and condiments), cost of fuel and wages for cooks.
(b) Provision for infrastructure – which included kitchen-cum-store, adequate water supply for cooking, washing and drinking, cooking devices, containers for storage of food grains and, utensils for cooking and serving.

Initially, the cost of cooking and provision of infrastructure facilities were to be borne by the state governments. Unable to meet these costs, many states resorted to distribution of food grains rather than providing cooked meals to children. The programme continued to suffer due to budgetary constraints in several states.

Revised Midday Meal Scheme 2004

Acknowledging the crucial linkage between education, malnutrition and poverty, the GOI revised the midday meal scheme in 2004 and laid emphasis on providing hot, cooked meals to children, with specified nutritional norms. It aimed at providing 300 calories and 8-12 grams of protein to all children studying in primary classes in government and aided schools and EGS/AIE centres.

In addition to free supply of food grains, the revised scheme provided central assistance to the following:

(a) Cooking cost @ Re1 per child per school day
(b) Transport subsidy that was raised from Rs50 per quintal to Rs100 per quintal for special category states and Rs75 per quintal for other states
(c) Management, monitoring and evaluation costs@ 2 per cent of the cost of food grains, transport subsidy and cooking assistance
(d) Provision of midday meals during summer vacation in areas declared by state governments as 'drought affected'.

Some states took time to make the required logistical arrangements and gradually progressed towards full coverage of the scheme during 2005. Infrastructural requirements continued to be met through convergence of other development programmes for the construction of kitchen sheds. Water supply requirements were met through convergence with Accelerated Rural Water Supply Scheme, Swajaladhara and SSA.

The revised 2004 scheme also provided for a four-tier institutional mechanism for programme management, through the constitution of 'Steering-cum-Monitoring Committees' at the national, state, district and block levels. Coverage of eligible schools was near universal under the scheme. Several states moved towards better management of the scheme and added more variety and value to the meal. Some states also provided for micro-nutrient supplements and regular deworming to help improve the overall health of school children.

Deficiencies in the 2004 Scheme

However, certain critical issues still remained to be addressed: provision of balanced diet-based on national norms, of adequate cooking costs, and of necessary infrastructure – kitchen sheds, safe drinking water, etc. In the absence of kitchen sheds, classrooms were being used for storage and cooking in most schools in the country. Elsewhere, cooking was done in open and unhygienic surroundings.

Some of the major difficulties that came to light in the implementation of this scheme were:

(a) The prescribed cooking cost of Re1 per child per school day was found to be inadequate to meet the cost of a nutritious meal as per prescribed norms.

(b) The existing nutritional norm of 300 calories and 8-12 grams of protein was felt to be inadequate to meet the growing needs of young children.

(c) It was felt that there was a need to provide micro-nutrients and deworming medicines.

The Revised (2006) Scheme

Against this background, a sub-committee of the 'National Steering Committee' was constituted in August, 2005 to go into the above aspects and make recommendations including the quantum of central assistance to meet the enhanced requirements. Based on the recommendations, the GOI revised the scheme with effect from June, 2006.

Table III-1 Revised Norms as per the 2006 Scheme

Nutritional Content	Norm as per 2004 Scheme	Norm as per 2006 Scheme
Calories	300	450
Protein	8-12 grams	12 grams
Micro-nutrients	Not prescribed	Adequate quantities of micro-nutrients like iron, folic acid, Vitamin A, etc.

Source: NP-NSPE Guidelines 2006, MHRD

Provision was made for running of the scheme during summer vacation in drought-affected areas. Accordingly, the GOI enhanced the cooking cost reimbursable by it to Rs1.80 per child per school day in respect of special category states (Arunachal Pradesh,

Assam, Meghalaya, Mizoram, Manipur, Nagaland, Tripura, Sikkim, J&K, HP and Uttarakhand) and Rs1.50 per child per school day in respect of other states. The states were to contribute 50 paise to achieve the overall cost norm of Rs2.

In addition, increased attention was sought on issues of quality (nutrition, hygiene, cleanliness and safety) through sensitization and training of teachers, cooks and helpers. Nutritional experts were involved in planning and testing weekly menus. Use of locally grown and nutritionally rich foods was also promoted.

Some states (notably, AP, TN, Chhattisgarh, Orissa, Uttarakhand) gave eggs and fruits additionally. Several states (Chhattisgarh, Gujarat, Karnataka and MP) gave essential micro-nutrients and deworming medicines. Successful models of centralized kitchens run by NGOs (Nandi Foundation, Akshaya Patra Foundation, etc.) came up mainly in urban areas. The programme generated over one million employment opportunities, mostly for women of disadvantaged sections.

Extension of the Scheme to Upper Primary Classes

In the 2008 budget speech, the Union Finance minister proposed to extend the scheme to the upper primary classes (6-8) in government schools across the country. This was intended to cover an additional 250 lakh children, taking the total coverage to 1390 lakh children. Some states like TN and Karnataka extended the cooked midday meal scheme (on their own) to high school classes too.

Responsibility for Implementation of the scheme

The overall responsibility for implementation of the scheme lay with the state governments and union territories. These included:

(a) Ensuring adequate budgetary provisions and establishing systems for timely flow of funds towards all components of the programme – cooking costs, infrastructure, procurement of materials, etc.
(b) Formulating state norms of expenditure under different components of the scheme.
(c) Formulating safety specifications.
(d) Establishing systems for continuous and uninterrupted flow of food grains to schools.
(e) Ensuring all logistic and administrative arrangements to be in place for effective implementation of the programme.
(f) Formulating guidelines that would promote participation of community, Panchayati Raj institutions and genuine voluntary agencies in the programme.

Monitoring

The GOI assigned the external monitoring of the midday meal programme to 42 universities as well as national and state level institutions on a periodical basis. Appropriate mechanisms for quality check were devised in different areas which were as follows:

- 'Steering-cum-Monitoring Committees' were constituted at block, district, state and national levels.
- Nodal officers were appointed by FCI in all states to ensure smooth supply of quality food grains.
- DISE was upgraded to include data on the midday meal scheme.
- 550 DIETs were also involved in quarterly assessment of district-wise programme implementation.

Financing of the Midday Meal Scheme

The annual budgetary requirement of the programme in 2005-06 was Rs3300 crores. Over 24.6 lakh tons of food grains were allocated for the purpose and the GOI released Rs1200 crores to the states towards cooking costs. The budget and expenditure during the Tenth Plan are given in the following table:

Table III-2 Budget & Expenditure of the scheme (In crores)

Year	Budget Provision	Expenditure
2002-03	1,101.50	1,099.03
2003-04	1,375.00	1,375.00
2004-05	2,907.00*	2,820.55
2005-06	3,345.26*	3,186.33
2006-07	5,348.00*	NA

Source: MHRD Reports * Includes the NER states

An analysis of Food Corporation of India's statement for 2005-06 containing the estimated enrolment, allocation of food grains, and percentage of food grains lifted by the states indicates that on an average, the states were able to lift only up to 80 per cent of the allocated food grains. Further, if one were to consider that the average daily attendance in schools was less than 80 per cent of the enrolment and that schools did not work for the required 220-days in a year due to various reasons, one could easily deduce that usage was far less than 80 per cent.

Akshaya Patra

With the dedicated purpose of liberating poor children from the vicious cycle of hunger & illiteracy, the 'Akshaya Patra Foundation' (ISKCON, Bangalore) came into being in the year 2000. Initially, it started providing free, nutrition-rich midday meals to thousands of underprivileged children in and around Bangalore. By 2008, the coverage had touched one million children across seven states of India. The programme utilized the food grains as well as the conversion charges provided by the central and state governments.

One of the most successful social initiatives in India, the Akshaya Patra midday meals programme has documented benefits such as:

1. Protecting children from hunger and improving their nutrition.
2. Increasing school enrolment, attendance and school performance.
3. Improving socialization among children – the experience of sitting together and sharing a common meal irrespective of caste, gender and status.
4. Empowering the girl child.

A number of NGOs across the country have also been participating in the midday meal programme and enhancing its value.

Evaluation Studies on the Midday Meal Scheme

Evaluation of the scheme was undertaken by several independent as well as government agencies. Some of these studies pointed out the following achievements of the scheme:

- Effective addressing of classroom hunger.
- Significant improvement in enrolment, specially that of girls.
- Improvement in the daily attendance of children from poorer sections and of girls.
- Improvement in retention, learning ability and achievement.
- Reduction in teacher absenteeism.
- Narrowing of social distances because children from all communities sit together to eat.
- Enhancement of parents' (and of the community) participation in school governance.

A 2003 study of the midday meal scheme in three states – Chhattisgarh, Rajasthan and Karnataka – conducted by the Centre for Equity Studies, New Delhi, established the benefits that accrued to student enrolment and retention.

Studies about the cooked meal programmes in several states were conducted by independent agencies. Some findings of a few of these studies are given below:

1. 'Cooked Midday Meal Programme in WB – A study in Birbhum district' 2005; Study by Prof. Amartya Sen's Pratichi Trust:
   (i) It facilitated universalization of primary education by increasing enrolment and attendance of children with it being more marked among girls and SC/ST students.
   (ii) It made a substantial contribution to eliminating classroom hunger.
   (iii) It averted severe undernourishment among many children, particularly those who were socially and economically backward.
   (iv) It narrowed social distances.
   (v) It curbed teacher absenteeism.
2. 'Situation Analysis of Midday Meal Programme in Rajasthan' – University of Rajasthan and UNICEF; Prof. Beena Mathur, 2005.
   (i) Introduction of menu-based midday meal programme resulted in increased enrolment and daily attendance of children.

(a) 75 per cent of teachers said that it boosted enrolment
(b) 85 per cent of teachers said that it enhanced school attendance.

(ii) Cooked midday meal reduced classroom hunger, especially those belonging to underprivileged sections.
(iii) It contributed to the cause of social equity as children, cutting across caste and class lines, sat together to share a common meal.
(iv) It contributed to the cause of gender equity by providing employment opportunities to women in addition to liberating poor working mothers as they could leave early for work.
(v) 67 per cent of the parents interviewed felt that the quality of midday meals was satisfactory.
(vi) 85 per cent parents felt that the scheme should continue.

3. 'Midday Meal in MP' Samaj Pragati Sahayog; Jyotsna Jain and Mihir Shah, 2005

The survey was carried out in 70 most backward villages of MP. The main findings were:

(a) 63 per cent of parents felt that the meal had improved the learning ability of school children while 74 per cent of teachers said that it had definitely benefited the students.
(b) Overall, there was 15 per cent increase in enrolment, with it being more marked in the case of SC and ST children (43 per cent).
(c) The rise in enrolment of girls on the whole was 38 per cent, out of which SC/ST girls recorded an increase of 41 per cent.
(d) While 60 per cent of parents felt that the meal was good/very good, only 10 per cent felt that it was not satisfactory. In Tikamgarh, 45 per cent of parents felt that the meal was bad. Also, there were inter-regional variations.

4. 'Midday Meals: A Comparison of the Financial and Institutional Organization of the Programme in Two States': Farzana Afridi: EPW 2005

The focus of the report was implementation of the midday meal scheme in two states – Karnataka and MP. In MP the findings of the report were:

(a) Improvements were seen in the implementation of the programme though a lot needed to be done, especially regarding the quality of food.
(b) The new initiative 'Suruchi Bhojan' was more attractive and nutritious as it provided more calories in comparison to the earlier 'Daliya' programme.
(c) 80 per cent of parents were satisfied with the 'Suruchi Bhojan' programme with only 30 per cent preferring distribution of dry ration to it.
(d) Parent-teacher associations needed to be strengthened.

In the context of Karnataka the findings of the report were:

(a) 'Akshara Dasoha'– the midday meal programme – was found to be better planned and managed.
(b) Iron and folic acid tablets as well as deworming tablets were regularly provided.
(c) There was good community participation and SDMCs were functioning well.
(d) Meals were provided regularly and quality of meals was satisfactory.

5. 'Midday Meal Scheme in Delhi – A Functioning Programme': Anuradha De, Claire Noronha and Meera Samson, CORD, 2005.

The report said that school children in all schools were getting cooked food and parents were happy with the quality of the meal. However,

(a) Availability of drinking water was a problem; in fact, some children who were found to leave the school premises to drink water did not return to school.
(b) There was need to orient teachers about the scheme as they were instrumental in bringing discipline and order as well as inculcating good habits among children.
(c) There was an urgent need to disseminate information among parents, especially about the nutritional value and the ill effects of poor nutrition and health status.

6. 'Report on Akshara Dasoha Scheme of Karnataka' Dr Rama Naik, University of Dharwar, 2005.

The report states that there was sharp rise in enrolment particularly in rural areas. Schools were supplied with vitamins, deworming and iron tablets. More than 90 per cent of parents were satisfied with the scheme. The findings were as follows:

(a) The programme cut down teacher absenteeism to a large extent.
(b) No discrimination based on caste, etc., was found to be made with respect to serving and eating food.
(c) 72 per cent of parents felt that the children had gained weight because of midday meals.
(d) 59 per cent of parents felt that their children suffered from common ailments like cold and cough.
(e) 95 per cent of children felt that their concentration had improved.

7. NCERT 'Learning Achievement of Students at the End of Class 5', 2005

The NCERT learning achievement survey inferred that children covered under the midday meal scheme had higher achievement levels than those who were not covered under it. It further stated that the scheme was better managed than many others being implemented by states.

Annexure IV

Early Childhood Care and Education (ECCE)

INTRODUCTION

The Global Framework for Education for All (EFA – Dakar 2000) emphasizes that – 'expanding and improving comprehensive early childhood care and education, especially for the most vulnerable and disadvantaged children' is the first goal of EFA.

It is now universally recognized that ECCE has not only a positive influence on the participation of children in primary education but also significantly impacts their cognitive and emotional development by providing a stimulating environment to the children. It is also a significant input for life-long learning and development.

In the poorer sections of the society, ECCE is essential as it provides a stimulating environment and nutritional support and counters the physical, intellectual and emotional deprivation of the child. It also helps in the development of children in a variety of ways – group socialization, inculcation of healthy habits, stimulation of the creative learning process and enhanced scope for overall personality development.

ECCE is also a support for UEE as it indirectly supports enrolment and retention of children in primary schools. A child with pre-school experience adjusts and performs better on entering primary school. ECCE also prepares the children for meeting the demands of the primary curriculum and enhances the enrolment and retention of girls in primary schools by freeing them from sibling care responsibilities.

Several studies have pointed out that exposure to ECCE constitutes the first critical step in the learning process and contributes significantly to the successful completion of primary education. But the ECCE component in almost all states in India is extremely limited in its outreach and is almost entirely in the private sector.

Impact of Governmental Policies on Pre-school Education

The NPE 1986 explicitly spoke of ECCE, emphasizing the need to invest in the development of the young child. It emphasized the importance of ECCE as a crucial input to human resource development and hence was conceived as a feeder programme to strengthen primary education, as also as a human resource development programme. ECCE was seen as a holistic input for fostering health, psycho social, nutritional and educational development of the child.

The Acharya Ramamurthy Committee of 1990 also emphasized that the Constitutional directive of providing free and compulsory education for all children up to 14 years of age should include ECCE. The committee also recommended programmatic and physical linkages with the primary education system.

Though the NPE 1986 gave a good deal of importance to pre-school education, responsibility for pre-school education in the government sector, still remained with the government sponsored ICDS. The coverage under ICDS however was not universal. The pre-school component was also reportedly the weakest.

The Sub-sector Study Report on Early Childhood Education in Karnataka notes – 'In the face of an ongoing situation of scarce resources, increasing public opinion and financial focus on primary education and an all round indifference to pre-school education, the GOK concentrated attention on primary education, relegating pre-school education to the ICDS and its mixed pot of food, health and education. The ICDS is with the Department of Women and Child Development, with it's till recent image of welfare thus taking a step backward, in making the pre-school a matter of welfare and not part of main stream education'. This is almost the current scenario of pre-school education in almost all the states in the country.

A majority of the state governments also do not have a policy on pre-school education. Their fear is that formulating such a policy will bind them to provide facilities in this sector and thereby unduly burden them financially. But such a policy is needed not only for guiding the states' initiatives but also for promoting and monitoring the activities of providers in the private sector.

The Constitutional Commitment

The national commitment to expand ECCE services gained immensely from the Constitution (86th) Amendment Act 2002, which enjoins the state 'to endeavour to provide early childhood care and education to all children until they complete the age of 6 years'.

The ECCE programme for the 3-6 age group is directed towards ensuring a natural, joyful and stimulating environment with emphasis on necessary inputs for optimal growth and development.

ICDS Scheme

To translate its concern for the overall development of children, the GOI initiated a national programme called the 'Integrated Child Development Services Scheme' in 1975 with a modest coverage of the country. It has since grown into one of the world's largest and unique programmes for early childhood development.

The ICDS Scheme was launched to ensure that no child was deprived of education due to hunger. Anganawadis were conceptualized to meet the ICDS objectives which included supplementary nutrition to children, nutrition and health education for women, health cover and non-formal pre-school education among other things.

The Main Objectives of the ICDS Scheme

- Improve the nutritional and health status of children in the age group 0-6 years.
- Lay the foundations for the proper psychological, physical and social development of the child.
- Reduce the incidence of mortality, morbidity, malnutrition and dropping out-of-school.
- Achieve effective coordination of policy and implementation amongst the various departments to promote child development.
- Enhance the capability of the mother to look after the normal health and nutritional needs of the child through proper nutrition and health education.

The ICDS scheme is an inter sectoral programme which seeks to directly reach out to children from vulnerable and remote areas, and give them a head start by providing an integrated programme of health, nutrition and early childhood education. It also reaches out to women through family planning, pre-natal care and nutritional support for pregnant and nursing mothers. Besides, the Social Welfare Boards of the centre and the states are also running pre-schools and balwadis.

Major Components of ICDS Scheme

A package of six services are provided to the beneficiaries through the AWCs that are managed by an AWW and a helper at the village level in rural areas and in slums in urban areas (between 9.30 a.m. and 1.30 p.m. during the day). The package of services rendered under the ICDS consists of:

(a) Nutrition: Supplementary feeding, Growth monitoring and promotion, Nutrition and health,
(b) Health: Immunization, Health checkup, Referral services, Treatment of minor diseases,
(c) Support to pregnant and nursing mothers: Pre-natal care, Nutritional support, and Family planning services,
(d) ECE and Pre-school education: Early care and stimulation for the 0-3 year-old children, Early learning readiness programme for the 3-6 year-old children.

Coverage of ICDS Scheme

Though the ICDS scheme was launched in 1975, it was universalized only during 1995-96 through sanction of projects for all the 5,320 community development blocks in the country along with 310 major urban slums.

Even though the spread of ECCE facilities has been significant in recent years, the out reach and coverage in respect of the early childhood education component has been rather poor. The GER which was just 10.33 in 1990 increased to a mere 16.90 in the next decade. The coverage was also uneven across the different parts of the country. Where as the north east states did well, the educationally backward states (Bihar, UP, etc.) had still poorer GERs (less than 10).

There were efforts to create alternate models of ECCE under different EFA programmes in Assam, MP, Rajasthan, AP and Karnataka. There were also efforts to create convergence between ongoing programmes of ICDS and other childhood education activities.

As per 2001 census, there are approximately 60 million children in the age group of 3-6 years in the country. The target set for this sector was two million ECCE centres to cover about 70 per cent children in the pre-school age group by the year 2000. Despite this, the coverage and progress of ICDS has been tardy. The total number of AWCs in the country stood at 7.98 lakhs. The GOI in 2007 sanctioned 173 ICDS projects, 107,274 AWCs and 25,961 mini AWCs. The number of beneficiaries under ICDS rose from 16.6 million in 1992 to 45.2 million in 2007-08.

In response to a petition on the 'non-implementation of directions' given by the Supreme Court relating to ICDS, the Supreme Court in its order in December 2006, issued the following directive: 'Government of India shall sanction and operationalize a minimum of 14 lakh AWCs in a phased and even manner starting forthwith and ending December 2008. In doing so, the central government shall identify SC and ST hamlets or habitations on a priority basis'.

Though ICDS is a major programme catering to the ECCE needs, several other schemes were also initiated by the central and state governments mainly to supplement the ICDS provisions in content and coverage.

'Crèches and Day Care Centres Scheme' was started in 1975 to provide day care services for children below 5 years. It caters mainly to children of casual, migrant, agricultural and construction labourers. The programme in the scheme is mainly custodial in nature.

'Early Childhood Education Scheme' was introduced as a distinct strategy to reduce the dropout rate and to improve the retention rate of children in primary schools. Under this scheme, central assistance is given to voluntary organizations for running pre-school centres.

In addition to these schemes that reach out to the rural, urban slums and tribal areas there are innumerable private nursery schools charging heavy fees in urban and semi-urban areas. There is no system of licensing and regulating such institutions.

The Report of the Working Group on development of children in Eleventh Plan has recommended the strengthening and full coverage of ICDS services as the main focus in the coming years. In order to introduce PPP, it has recommended to create a public trust under the control and supervision of the government.

Financial Outlay

While the Eighth Plan (1992-97) had an outlay of Rs2,601.28 crores for the scheme, the Tenth Plan (2002-07) had an increased outlay of Rs11,684.60 crores. The annual outlay doubled from Rs1,623 crores in 2004-05 to Rs3,142 crores in 2005-06. The budgetary allocation for ICDS has been raised to Rs4,761 crores in 2007-08.

Convergence between ECCE and primary education has been explored under different schemes and programmes including SSA, DPEP, Mahila Samakhya and NPEGEL. Initiatives for forging linkages between ECCE and primary education was undertaken under DPEP by locating ECCE/ICDS centres together with schools and synchronizing their timings. Key strategies under DPEP included working closely with ICDS, setting up new centres in non-ICDS areas, running school readiness programmes, and starting pre-primary classes in primary schools. Community involvement was an integral part of ECCE centres in DPEP.

SSA Interventions under ICDS

The SSA supports strengthening the pre-school component in ICDS by need based training of ECCE workers, provision of additional playway kits, relocation of AWCs in schools and building advocacy for ECCE.

The SSA seeks to set up ECCE centres where there is no coverage of ICDS. Around 80,173 ECCE centres have been made operational under various elementary education schemes. The SSA provides Rs15 lakh per district per year for opening ECCE centres.

Under NPEGEL, provision of childcare centres, mobilization and community monitoring for ECCE services in under-privileged areas was created. The centres were also run by the local community.

Supplementary Nutrition Programme

Children below 6 years of age, pregnant and nursing mothers and adolescent girls in selected blocks hailing from vulnerable sections of society form the target group of beneficiaries under the Supplementary Nutrition programme. A minimum of 10-12 grams of protein and 300 calories of energy are provided to each beneficiary at a unit cost of Re2.00 per beneficiary/day for normal children and Rs3.00 per beneficiary/day for pregnant and nursing mothers and severely malnourished children and adolescent girls. Children in the age group of 3-6 years are provided local food. From 2005-06, the GOI and the state governments are sharing the cost of the supplementary nutrition programme on a 50:50 basis.

Deficiencies in the ICDS Scheme

It is assumed that the ICDS centre (AWC) will cater to the pre-school needs of the community where it is located and therefore universal provision of ICDS would suffice. The criteria for starting of an AWC itself negates this view. The ICDS has not been able to cover a large number of smaller villages and habitations in the country as they do not meet the criterion of population size for starting an AWC. Hence, children from smaller and remote habitations, who are also from poorer and depressed classes, are deprived of the access to ECCE and the socialization process provided by the AWC prior to primary schooling.

The Sub-sector Study Report on pre-school education in Karnataka has pointed out a number of anomalies in the functioning of the ICDS scheme. Many of the AWCs do not have proper buildings and function in rented buildings, temples, community halls, etc. They lack adequate equipment. Many of the charts/materials used are not appropriate and not meant for the age group. Many AWCs lack basic minimum facilities like toilets and clean drinking water. Supply of rice is also intermittent due to inherent inefficiency in the administrative system. Sometimes the children get only energy powder and sometimes nothing.

The AWW has to take care of many programmes. She has to play multiple roles simultaneously – she is a pre-school educator, she is a health worker and she is also a community worker. She has to maintain about 21 records about birth, death, medical checkups, vaccination, number of children coming to the centre, supply of food and expenditure.

The AWCs need active supervision and monitoring. The Sub-sector Report has pointed out that there is need for reconceptualizing, revitalizing and making pre-school curriculum more realistic. The alphabet and number teaching can be done through child friendly and joyful methods.

In spite of its perceived inadequacies, it is universally accepted that the ICDS programme turns out children who are more sociable and show more school readiness than those children who go directly to the primary school without attending any pre-school centre.

The World Bank Study

The World Bank commissioned a qualitative study to identify factors that facilitate/ impede successful completion of primary school by children from diverse poverty situations in Uttar Pradesh, Karnataka and Andhra Pradesh. Some of the findings of this study relating to ICDS scheme were:

- Existing programmes have not been sufficiently focused on improving overall awareness levels, instruction on supplementary nutrition for pregnant and nursing mothers. The IEC component of ICDS or three generations of maternal and child health programmes (MCH/FP, CSSM, RCH) seem to have made little impact on the overall awareness towards nutrition and hygiene/sanitation.
- Caste is a serious issue with the ICDS teacher and ayah (helper). If both are from the forward caste, then children from dalit families have little access.
- The location of the AWC determines access. Several children profiled did not access ICDS even though they were from very poor families.
- While the team saw pregnant and nursing mothers coming to AWC in Karnataka and Andhra Pradesh, it did not come across even a single woman who came to the AWC in Uttar Pradesh.
- Enrolment does not automatically imply access to services. Some children are merely enrolled and not necessarily benefiting from the ICDS programme – mothers admit that they are not able to reach their children to the centre and the helper does not fetch them either.

- The pre-school education component was non-existent in all but one of the ICDS centres visited.
- The attitudes of the teacher and the helper also leave much to be desired – they were indifferent towards them if not shouting and scolding the children. The ICDS programme does not seem to play any significant role in enhancing the preparedness of children to go to school. Given the urgency of responding to the nutritional and health needs of the 0-3 years age group (especially in the context of securing nutrition for overall development of children) and given ICDS habitation based structure; the programme is best suited to address the needs of this age group. In this context, it would be valuable to re-examine the pre-school component of ICDS programme. ICDS would be more effective if the programme focused primarily on under 3s.
- The mother's committees were introduced to strengthen IEC activities (education and awareness) and make the AWW accountable to the community. In all the villages/slums surveyed, these committees were dysfunctional, even though they existed on paper.
- The ICDS programme does not seem to enjoy the same status as other schemes, more so in the eyes of government. The status of the AWW, as compared to the school teacher or the ANM, is low.

Some of the Recommendations of the Study

- Explore the option of delinking the pre-school education component from ICDS and make it an integral part of primary schools. This would ensure that children in the 3 to 5+ age group benefit from the universal midday meal programme, thereby improving their nutritional status.
- Since not all poor children have access to the ICDS centre (especially in UP where each village has only one centre), the government could consider making ICDS a universal programme for all children in the appropriate age group and for all pregnant and nursing mothers in the catchment area of the ICDS centre.
- It may be worthwhile considering the involvement of the panchayats or educating and empowering the women's committee to play a more effective monitoring role to ensure the programme reaches its stated objectives/goals.

Annexure V

Literacy and Adult Education

Literacy's positive association with improved socio-economic indicators underlines its importance in human development. Literacy is crucial for achieving all the goals of EFA. In India, it has a constructive role in the success of UEE. In comparison to all countries, India is confronted with the biggest challenge of improving literacy as it is home to one-third of the world's non-literate population. Though the country's literacy rate has been increasing steadily, it has not kept pace with the population growth rate. Consequently, the number of illiterates in the country has been rising for several decades.

The objectives of adult literacy, as outlined in policy documents, stressed on individual intellectual growth, entrepreneurial abilities, socio-economic development and empowerment as well as enhancing the quality of life by pro-actively addressing global concerns like poverty, environment, human rights, peace and human values.

India has made substantial efforts to achieve the fourth goal enunciated in the Dakar Framework: 'Achieving a 50 per cent improvement in levels of adult literacy by 2015, especially for women, and equitable access to basic and continuing education for all adults'. Based on the growing trend of literacy since 1991 and projected demographic changes, India seems likely to improve its literacy levels from 64.84 per cent in 2001 to 80 per cent by 2015.

The NLM has intensified efforts to spread the outreach of the literacy programmes to hitherto uncovered and inaccessible areas. It adopted an integrated approach to make basic literacy, post-literacy and continuing education into a learning continuum. 596 out of 600 districts in the country were covered under various adult education programmes – 138 under TLC, 167 under PLC and 291 under CEP. NLM identified regional disparities and low literacy states for special attention – 45 districts with female literacy below 30 per cent were taken up for a multi-pronged strategy to improve the female literacy rate. Nearly 7 million non-literate women were targeted with the involvement of 200 NGOs and ZSS.

Opportunities for life-long learning, skill development and generation of income were provided under the continuing education programmes, taken up in 291 districts (projected to be extended to 400 districts) of the country. Technical support and training was provided by the 'Jan Shikshan Sansthan', and 26 State Resource Centres managed by NGOs provided academic and technical support in the form of training, material preparation, extension activities, innovative projects, research studies and evaluation.

Following is a brief discussion of India's literacy scenario and the various programmes undertaken by the central and state governments for improving it among adults.

INDIA'S LITERACY SCENARIO

The literacy rate in 2001 was 64.84 per cent as against 52.21 per cent in 1991 with the 12.63 percentage point increase being the highest in any decade. An additional 203 million persons became literate during the period. Three out of four men (75.85 per cent) and one in two women (54.16 per cent) in the country were literate in 2001 while, the rural female literacy was rather low at 46.13. Among the SCs it increased from 37.41 per cent in 1991 to 54.69 per cent in 2001 and for STs, there was an increase from 29.60 per cent in 1991 to 47.10 per cent in 2001. Besides, urban-rural literacy differential also decreased during the period.

All states achieved a minimum male literacy level of 60 per cent. However, inter state and intra state disparities continued although the gap between educationally forward and backward states narrowed considerably. Several states – notably Rajasthan, MP, and AP and to some extent Orissa and UP – have made significant progress. The performance of HP, TN, Punjab and some north-eastern states was also quite impressive.

Of the 20 districts recording the largest decadal decrease in the number of illiterate females in 2001, 14 were from the traditionally educationally backward states like MP, Chhattisgarh, AP and Rajasthan. A large number of blocks recording less than 30 per cent female literacy in 2001 were in Bihar, Jharkhand, Chhattisgarh, Orissa, Arunachal Pradesh, UP, AP, Rajasthan and, Jammu and Kashmir.

Decline in Non-literates

For the first time since India's independence, there was a significant decline in the absolute number of non-literates, from 328.88 million in 1991 to 296 million in 2001. India had 562 million literate persons (of age 7+), of whom 337 million were male and 225 million female. In spite of recording such an impressive growth, the following states were found to have more than 10 million non-literates, even in 2001 – Rajasthan (18 million), UP (58 million), Bihar (35 million), WB (21 million), Jharkhand (10 million), MP (21 million), Maharashtra (19 million), AP (31 million), Karnataka (15 million), and TN (15 million).

Improvement in Female Literacy

A desirable factor was that female literacy rate was growing faster than its male counterpart. Since the former recorded an increase of 14.38 percentage points from 39.29 per cent to 53.67 per cent in comparison to the latter's increase of 11.13 percentage points from 64.13 per cent to 75.26 per cent, the female-male literacy rate narrowed from 24.84 per cent in 1991 to 21.59 per cent in 2001. In the same year, the female literacy in Chhattisgarh, AP, Orissa, MP, Rajasthan, Arunachal Pradesh, UP, J&K, Jharkhand and Bihar was lower than the national average of 54.16 per cent. While a very large inter state variation was reflected with 87.86 per cent in Kerala and 33.57 per cent in Bihar, the same was true at the inter-district level as well, with a variation ranging from 96.06 per cent in Aizawl district of Mizoram and 18.49% in Kishanganj district of Bihar. All the twenty districts with the lowest female literacy were found to be in Bihar, UP, Jharkhand, MP, Orissa and Chhattisgarh.

Considering the figures available for 2001 and as per ASER 2006, ASER 2008 compared literacy levels in states pertaining to girls/women in the age group of 7+ or 17+. The sample that covered practically all states and rural districts of the country consisted of over 5,50,000 older women and nearly 2,50,000 school-age girls from over 16,000 villages. The national rural female literacy figure of 46.13 came close to ASER's figures of 47.7 women in the 17-80 age group; this group showed an ability to read simple sentences. The proportion for the 7-80 age group was much higher because school-going girls were able to read better.

Table V-1 Comparison of Rural Female Literacy

States/UTs	Census 2001 Rural Female Literacy	ASER 2006 (Rural)% of Women Who Can Read	
		Age 7-80	Age 17-80
AP	43.5	68.6	62.5
Assam	50.7	62.7	60.4
Bihar	29.6	44.6	32.1
Chhattisgarh	47.0	60.0	54.3
Goa	71.9	76.5	72.6
Gujarat	47.8	57.4	47.0
Haryana	49.3	60.5	48.3
HP	65.7	72.1	66.8
J&K	36.7	60.2	50.2
Jharkhand	29.9	51.7	37.8
Karnataka	48.0	50.9	45.0
Kerala	86.7	89.3	90.3
MP	42.8	54.9	38.5
Maharashtra	58.4	64.1	56.3
Manipur	57.0	69.5	70.8
Meghalaya	53.2	72.3	75.1
Mizoram	77.3	80.9	79.3
Nagaland	57.5	64.3	65.2
Orissa	46.7	57.8	49.7
Punjab	57.7	65.2	61.1

Rajasthan	37.3	68.7	62.6
TN	55.3	55.2	49.9
UP	36.9	45.7	34.3
Uttaranchal	54.7	68.8	59.6
WB	53.2	63.4	54.9
DN Haveli	30.8	53.8	38.6
Daman, Diu	59.3	70.1	62.6
Pondicherry	64.4	59.8	57.6
India	46.1	56.6	47.7

Source: ASER 2008

National Adult Education Programme (NAEP)

Eradication of illiteracy was one of the major national concerns of the GOI since independence. The neglect of education under the British rule combined with social distortions turned out to be an impediment in implementing literacy programmes for the underprivileged sections of the population.

The literacy programmes under the adult education component of the GOI were targeted at the 15-35 age group with the aim of providing functional literacy, which included reading, writing and numeracy skills. Some additional skills were also sought to be developed through these programmes: self-reliance, skill development, values like small family norms, etc. The single decisive result of these campaigns was the awareness created among communities about literacy and the benefits of education that, in turn, would improve the quality of their lives.

In the 1990s, literacy campaigns reached more than 90 per cent of India's villages. The campaign expanded to cover remote parts of the country including the educationally backward states of Bihar, MP, UP and Rajasthan. Even inaccessible districts like Dumka in Bihar and Banswara in Rajasthan (with very low female literacy levels) generated significant social mobilization campaigns. Nearly 50 per cent of the districts in the country moved on to the post-literacy phase and started continuing education centres. 120.35 million persons became literate (as in 2006) under various literacy programmes, out of which 23 per cent learners belonged to SC and 12 per cent to ST groups.

The NAEP contributed considerably to improve enrolment of children in schools. Studies conducted across India showed that enrolment of boys and girls in the age group of 5-15 years was significantly higher in neo-literate households as compared to children from illiterate households. Two out of three boys from neo-literate households were found enrolled in schools as compared to three out of four from illiterate ones. In the case of girls, this difference was found to be even more pronounced – 58 per cent in case of illiterate and 72 per cent in case of neo-literate households. (EFA-India, Year 2000 Assessment Report). This showed that NAEP had a significant impact on girls' education across the country.

The NAEP had a beneficial impact on gender equality as well. With 62 per cent of participants being female, the programme contributed towards women acquiring skills such as reading and writing, increasing their awareness levels which, in turn, empowered them to take independent decisions about themselves, their families and their communities. Thus, they were able to improve their status within their families.

Another major area in which NAEP had a significant impact was on health and hygiene. Raising the functional literacy level of a community led to a demonstrable decline in fertility and infant mortality rates. NAEP also created awareness about healthcare and nutrition, enabling mothers to take better care of their children and families.

Although the impact of NAEP was not uniform across the country, the overall strategy was designed to have a positive influence. This coupled with the initiatives in the primary education sector helped to significantly increase the total literacy rate and literacy levels among people in rural areas, especially women. The effectiveness of the strategy may be assessed in terms of the massive demand created for post-literacy and continuing education.

National Literacy Mission (NLM)

After evaluating earlier programmes, strategies and achievements, the country set up the NLM in May 1988 and adopted the mode of mass campaigning for spreading literacy in the country. Instead of using paid workers, it was decided to take the help of NGOs who would mobilize volunteers to take part in the mass campaigns. Led by people from within the district, these campaigns were designed to be district-specific.

NLM was launched in a mission mode with a clear timeframe to achieve the objective of rendering 100 million people in the 15-35 age group literate by 1999. The success of the Ernakulum (Kerala) model, which was based on a spirit of community voluntarism, was followed for the TLCs launched across the country.

Emphasis was on attainment of relevant standards as per certain pre-determined norms and parameters of literacy, numeracy with comprehension, and functional literacy. Literacy as enunciated in NLM was not an end in itself, but was to be an active and potent instrument of change, ensuring achievement of these social objectives and creation of a learning society. The acquisition of functional literacy was to result in empowerment and a definite improvement in quality of life.

The goal of NLM was to attain a sustainable threshold literacy level of 75 per cent by 2007 by imparting functional literacy to non-literates in the age group of 15-35 years, (which constitutes a major segment of the workforce in the productive and reproductive age group). Besides this group, persons outside it were included in the programme – particularly dropout children in the age group of 9-14 years.

The NLM monitored the programme by periodically organizing campaigns in districts by external groups and generating performance reports. Monthly monitoring meetings were held at the state level involving all ZSSs to assess qualitative aspects such as problems encountered in accelerating the pace of literacy campaigns and planning the future course of action.

Both concurrent and external evaluations were conducted in all the districts and achievements were also assessed through sample surveys. Concurrent evaluation was undertaken when at least 50 per cent of the enrolled learners had completed the First Primer. Final evaluation of the TLC was conducted when at least 60 per cent of the enrolled learners were in the process of completing the Third Primer. Districts in the post-literacy and continuing phases were also evaluated.

Total Literacy Campaigns (TLCs)

The TLC was the principal strategy of NLM for eradication of illiteracy. The TLCs had certain unique features that distinguished them from other government programmes. These campaigns were area-specific, time-bound, participative, cost-effective and outcome-oriented. They were implemented through ZSSs (which had independent and autonomous status with representation from all sections of society). The campaign approach to promoting literacy was characterized by large-scale mobilization through a multifaceted communication strategy.

The survey undertaken at the grass roots level also served as a tool for planning, mobilization and environment building. Apart from imparting functional literacy, the TLC also disseminated socially relevant messages such as enrolment and retention of children in schools, immunization, propagation of small family norms, women's equality and empowerment, peace and communal harmony. These literacy campaigns generated a demand for primary education, which was reflected in the rapidly rising enrolment ratio in schools. Consequently, the number of non-literates entering 15-35 age group started declining.

The skills of attaining literacy were imparted to the beneficiaries in their local dialect as far as possible. NLM prepared the TLM after taking into account the local needs and the specific requirements of the clientele group. Keeping in view the totally different socio-economic and cultural environment of the tribals, primers were prepared in the tribal language or dialect or spoken language to meet the specific requirements of the tribal community.

The basic literacy skills acquired by non-literates were at best fragile. There was a greater possibility of these neo-literates lapsing into illiteracy unless special efforts were continued to consolidate, sustain and possibly enhance their literacy levels. The NLM aimed at ensuring that the TLC and 'Post-Literacy Programmes' (PLP) successfully led one to continuing education which would provide life-long learning.

During the Tenth Plan period, inclusion of 36 new districts under TLC, brought the total number of districts covered under it to 597 while involving 102 districts under PLP increased the total districts covered under it to 487. With a budget of Rs131 crores for these literacy campaigns, about 28.82 million persons became literate during the Tenth Plan period.

The revised parameters and norms of enhanced financial assistance of the schemes under NLM were extended for implementation during the Tenth Plan. The main features of the revised schemes included an integrated approach to literacy, amalgamating all the features of literacy and post-literacy phases. The responsibility of overseeing and running the literacy programmes was entrusted to ZSSs which helped synergize strengths of local youth clubs, mahila mandals, voluntary agencies, PR institutions, small-scale industries, cooperative societies, etc. The expansion of the 'Scheme of Continuing Education' encompassed removal of residual illiteracy.

FINANCING OF ADULT EDUCATION PROGRAMMES

The working group on Adult Education had recommended a budget allocation of Rs6339.50 crores for adult education during the Tenth Plan. However, as against this only Rs1250 crores were allocated. The year-wise allocation and expenditure were as follows:

Table V-2 Expenditure on Adult Education (In crores)

Year	Budget Allocation	Expenditure
2002-03	233.00	216.29
2003-04	233.00	232.50
2004-05	250.00	236.47
2005-06	290.00	249.30
2006-07	235.50	NA
Total	1241.50	1003.07

Source: MHRD Reports

The TLC and PLP were funded on the basis of per-learner cost. This could range from Rs90-180 in respect of TLC and Rs90-130 for PLP projects. The total cost of the project was shared between the centre and the states in the ratio of 2:1 respectively for general districts and 4:1 respectively for tribal districts.

Accelerated Female Literacy Programme

As per the 2001 census, 47 districts in the country had a female literacy rate below 30 per cent dealing with which was of immense concern to the NLM. As most of these districts were concentrated in the states of UP, Bihar, Orissa and Jharkhand, special innovative programmes were taken up for promoting female literacy.

The support of 97 NGOs was enlisted in 2002-03 for a special project in eight districts of UP to cover 25 lakh illiterate women in the 15-35 age group. Need-based primers were designed on female-related issues. External evaluation of the programme conducted by NSSO and the Planning Commission indicated that 6 out of the 8 districts achieved above 60 per cent results.

A similar programme was implemented in 2003 in 13 low female literacy districts of Bihar. In the first phase, it covered 24.03 lakh women learners in the 15-35 age group. Additionally, 10-day residential teaching camps were conducted in some districts. The evaluation revealed that 8 out of the 13 districts showed above 60 per cent results.

In Orissa, 9 districts were covered through a network of 117 NGOs which saw 5.80 lakh persons becoming literate. In Jharkhand, the programme was implemented in five low female literacy districts and covered five lakh illiterate women.

Projects for Residual Illiteracy (PRI)

Although TLC took the form of a mass movement enveloping the length and breadth of the country, in many cases a number of campaigns stagnated due to natural calamities, lack of political will, frequent transfer of key personnel, shortage of resources, etc. In these areas projects for residual illiteracy were taken up only after conclusion of TLCs so as to cover the remaining illiterates. Accordingly, PRIs involved 30 districts in Rajasthan, 10 in AP, 1 in Bihar, 4 in Karnataka, 3 in Tripura, 12 in MP and 8 in WB.

In order to achieve the target of 75 per cent literacy by 2007, NLM took up special literacy drives during 2005-07 in 150 districts (having lowest literacy rates as per 2001 census), mainly in the states of UP, Bihar, Jharkhand, Rajasthan, MP, Chhattisgarh and Orissa.

Continuing Education Programme (CEP)

The CEP provided for a learning continuum to the efforts of TLC and PLP in the country. The main thrust was on providing learning opportunities to neo-literates by setting up Continuing Education Centres (CECs) which provided area-specific, need-based opportunities for basic literacy, upgradation of literacy skills, pursuit of alternative education programmes, vocational skills and also to promote social and occupational development.

One CEC for a population of 2000-2500, and a nodal continuing centre for a cluster of 8-10 CECs were sanctioned. A one-time non-recurring grant of Rs25,000 for each CEC and Rs45,000 for each nodal centre, was also sanctioned. During the Tenth Plan period, 206 new districts were covered under the CEP, bringing the total number of districts under it to 316. An allocation of Rs826.00 crores was made for the programme under the Tenth Plan. The GOI provided 100 per cent funding for the first three-years and thereafter, the funding was shared on a 50:50 basis between the centre and the states. After five-years, the states were expected to take over the entire liability.

Support to NGOs

The NLM fully recognized the potential of NGOs in furthering its objectives and took measures to strengthen its partnership with them. It assigned them an active promotional role in the literacy movement. Apart from imparting literacy, the NGOs were expected to provide academic and technical resource support through experimental and innovative programmes and also conduct evaluation and impact studies, organize workshops, seminars, etc. For the Tenth plan, the allocation for the scheme to support NGOs was Rs110 crores.

The (25) SRCs managed by NGOs provided academic and technical resource support in the form of preparation of training material, extension activities, innovative projects, research studies and evaluation, etc. Some of the SRCs took up several innovative projects – action research projects on life skills education and counselling on HIV/AIDS (SRC, Kolkata), special schools for street children (SRC, TN), conversion of basic literacy primers to Braille script for the benefit of visually impaired illiterates (SRC, Kerala),etc.

Jana Shikshan Sansthan (JSS)

The first JSS in the country was established at Worli, Mumbai in 1967. Gradually the number increased and by 2007, 172 JSSs were known to be functioning in the country. The JSSs offered about 300 different types of vocational courses from candle and agarbatti making, sewing and embroidery to computer courses. About 14 lakh people were trained every year in these institutions with about 65 per cent being women. During the Tenth Plan period, an allocation of Rs130 crores was made for this scheme.

The objective of the JSS was educational, vocational and occupational development of the socio-economically backward and educationally disadvantaged groups of urban/rural population constituting neo-literates, semi-literates, SCs, STs, women and girls, slum dwellers, migrant workers, etc. With the emergence of thousands of neo-literates (through TLCs) in the country, JSS focused not only on them but on unskilled and unemployed youth as well. These Sansthans acted as district level support agencies in organizing vocational training and skill development programmes for the neo-literates and other target groups of CEP.

Directorate of Adult Education

The Central Directorate of Adult Education also provides academic and technical resource support to NLM. It has played an important role in the development of a network of resource support, particularly production of prototype teaching/learning materials/media software, etc. Monitoring of literacy programmes and those conducted by SRCs and JSS is also an important function of this directorate. The allocation for this Directorate for the Tenth Plan was Rs78 crores.

Mid-term Appraisal of the Tenth Plan

The Planning Commission made the following recommendations relating to Adult Education in its Mid-term Appraisal of the Tenth Plan:

- The literacy schemes like TLC, PLP and Continuing Education should be transferred to states along with funds to ensure better participation/involvement and effective monitoring. This recommendation was not accepted as states felt that the scheme should remain with the centre.

- All NGO operated schemes under adult education should be amalgamated into single CSS and funds routed through state governments.
- A new scheme should be launched as a part of literacy programmes, operated through NGOs, to impart functional literacy to 35 plus age group as a sizeable proportion of the 31 crore illiterate persons are in the said age group.

National Literacy Mission Authority (NLMA)

The NLMA was set up as an independent and autonomous wing of the Department of Elementary Education & Literacy, and is vested with executive and financial powers in its sphere of work. The NLMA has a General Council, Executive Committee and Project Approval Committee. The NLMA lays down the policies and programmes in the field of literacy and adult education in the country.

Revised Strategies of NLMA

- Restructuring of ZSSs by integrating them with the PR system
- Literacy programmes at various levels to be brought under the control of PR structures ;'Panchayat Saksharata Samitis' to be set up that will include elected representatives and other stakeholders.
- CE Programme to be replaced by Continuing and Life-long Education Programme (CLEP) which will include TLC, PLC and CE programmes.
- CLEP will offer Diverse Learning Programmes, Functional Skills, Quality of Life Improvement Programmes, Vocational Skills and Equivalency Programmes.
- CLEP will try to integrate issues relating to information, livelihood and governance with literacy programmes.
- CLEP will serve as an information window on all development programmes in addition to creating and organizing convergence with various departments implementing these programmes at the grassroots level.
- Continuing and Life-long Education Centre (CLEC) will be a multi-functional and multi-dimensional centre, seeking to provide a variety of learning programmes to beneficiaries.
- A nation-wide mass mobilization campaign will be taken up to seek the involvement of all sections of the community.

Assessment of the Adult Education Programmes

Since all literacy campaigns were subjected to a rigorous internal monitoring and external evaluation by renowned autonomous institutions, a great deal can be learnt from these findings.

- Broadly, the volunteer-based literacy campaigns displayed enthusiasm across the states, leading to a large-scale participation of dedicated volunteers as instructors. Increase in demand for primary education and improvement in school participation, especially of girls, has been a significant impact of literacy campaigns.

- Some factors that had adversely affected the outcome of these literacy campaigns were: Discontinuous 'Collector' led leadership to literacy campaigns, weak ZSSs and, ineffective management and monitoring structures, excessive bureaucratization, limited civil society partnerships, inability to motivate and build collectives of poor women, weak and non-existent linkages with the formal elementary education system, inability to relate to sustainable livelihoods and life contexts of poor, use of standardized languages and insufficient integration with local dialects.
- While the spirit of voluntarism was effective in sustaining community enthusiasm for a few months, inability to compensate full-time volunteers through a process of community/social audit interfered with success. The significant gains made by the Padhna Badhna Andolan (Movement for Education and Development) in MP suggested stronger social audit-based systems of compensation for education volunteers in difficult and poor regions.
- Greater integration of livelihood and life-related issues in the learning materials used in literacy campaigns appeared to have a positive influence on outcomes (e.g., – the Fourth Primer in MP).
- There was a variance in the effectiveness of decentralized institutions for people's participation. While Panchayats worked very well in literacy campaigns in WB, Padhna Badhna Sanghas (groups of non-literates associated with a 'guruji' through a community process) in MP, Self-Help Groups in AP, and All Women's Groups in Rajasthan with civil society participation worked effectively. Nevertheless, it is extremely important to understand that if efforts at securing literacy must meet their desired objectives, one needs to work out with NGO participation the community structures, their capacity development needs, and the overall management framework so as to infuse more efficacy and value.

The Eleventh Plan Targets

The Eleventh Plan has set the following targets and special focus areas:

- Achieve 80 per cent literacy rate
- Reduce gender gap in literacy to 10 per cent
- Reduce regional, social and gender disparities
- Extend coverage of NLM programmes to 35+ age group
- Special focus on SCs, STs
- Focus also on low literacy states, tribal areas, other disadvantaged groups and adolescents.

Annexure VI

Educational Performance Indicators

Following the 'World Declaration of Education for All' at Jomtein in 1991, every country prepared a 'Plan of Action' in order to achieve the EFA goals: universal primary education and literacy, policies to promote basic and primary education, and attainment of 'Education for All'.

During the last two decades, education systems throughout the world have been subject to considerable reforms and change in order to improve 'quality' in school education. Concern about quality of school education as well as its monitoring and assessment has been a high priority issue.

When judging educational quality, we focus either on what schools spend or what students achieve. Hence, all discussion on 'quality schooling' would centre on how it can be measured and how one could bring about improvements. In the current scenario we expect all children to learn; therefore, we must assess them to understand the extent of their learning.

Here, major emphasis has been placed on the assessment and monitoring of student learning outcomes. 'Learning achievement' is considered to be a significant measure of quality education. It is also closely linked to school efficiency because it has a bearing on promotion, repetition and dropout rates. These are some of the 'performance indicators'(PIs) used in the education sector at various levels.

PERFORMANCE INDICATORS (PIS)

The PIs, in a broad sense, can be considered as 'indices of information' by which the quality of functioning of a system or an institution can be expressed. They may refer to various aspects of the system/institution and hence can serve various purposes such as review of policy, planning, organizing, implementing, evaluating and taking up reforms. Being output oriented, they help in ensuring 'accountability, monitoring of standards, benchmarking, school effectiveness as well as in the reform process.

These indicators further assist in incorporating delivery of educational services into 'public sector accounting' so that the services not only represent 'value for money' but also encourage a system of accountability to ensure efficient and effective utilization of resources.

Type of Performance Indicators

The range and type of input-output indicators in the education sector are many and varied. Every country prioritises their own PIs along with targets that need to be achieved.

The sources from which they may be obtained are also many and at different levels of the system – namely student, class, district, region, state, national and international. The methods of collection of data may be either manual or through the sophisticated computer generated management information systems (EMIS). Some of the 'Educational Performance Indicators' are:

- Indicators for provision of resources and funding at system/institution levels
- Population literacy rates
- Gross/Net enrolment rates
- Access/Participation/Retention rates at different levels – pre-school, primary, upper primary, secondary, tertiary, etc.
- Per capita cost at each level
- Class sizes
- Pupil-teacher ratios
- Teacher qualification and certification
- Provision of teacher training and participation in professional development programmes
- Student achievement outcomes at various levels
- Longitudinal achievement progress and indicators as well as factors affecting student progress rates
- Measures of strategic interventions for students with special needs
- Incentives for those from disadvantaged groups.

Characteristics of Useful Indicators

A useful PI helps in effecting measurable improvements to desired outcomes. The major characteristics of these indicators are – relevance, effectiveness, timeliness, reliability and validity.

(a) Relevance: A PI is deemed to be relevant if it provides useful information for strategic decision-making. This means it should be useful for a specific purpose.

(b) Cost-effectiveness: Even though a PI is useful, its cost-effectiveness and logistic feasibility are important. For example, in case of students' achievement outcomes, obtaining estimates of a large student population may prove very costly in comparison to those obtained from a smaller but well-designed sample.

(c) Timeliness: A PI should be available in time when key informed policy decisions are to be made. Information regarding certain PIs (like student achievement progress rates) require longer periods to collect. In the absence of such timely availability misinformed decisions are likely to be taken.

(d) Reliability: Determining the reliability of an indicator involves evaluating how well or how accurately it has been measured. This goes a long way in bringing about precision in the interpretation of the indicator, and it applies both to smaller samples and national/system-wide testing as well as public examination systems. Evidence about the uncertainty associated with the observed scores is required to minimize the potential 'risk' of misinterpretation of the indicator.

(e) Validity: It is to be noted that an estimate of the reliability of an indicator is not necessarily commensurate with its validity – both content and criterion related. It is possible to have a highly reliable indicator but one that lacks validity (as in assessment tasks). Similarly a valid indicator with low reliability has little value. For example, conclusions about student achievements are valid only when measured reliably and based on evidence about intended and achieved learning outcomes.

Also, there is always a possibility of these indicators being misused. Even if their calculation is flawed, there is a risk that they may mislead potential users.

In UK, the use of the Educational Performance Indicators for educational accountability and monitoring of standards had a notable impact on schools since 1990. The implementation of a national curriculum, national assessment, an external school inspection system administered by the 'Office of Standards in Education' (OfSTED), and the publication of schools' average, unadjusted, achievement scores on tests and public examinations had a significant impact on the quality of schooling in that country.

The publication of the 'league table' of school rankings also had far reaching educational, political and economic impact though in a negative sense. Parents went to the extent of relocating near 'high profile schools' (based on league rankings) in order to enrol their children in them. This had severe consequences on the economy of several households as house prices escalated in localities closer to the high profile schools.

However, school managements took the league rankings seriously and sometimes chose to restrict information to select staff members. They embarked on specific personnel management strategies that included:

- Personal counselling and encouragement of select staff by the school's senior management team.
- Team teaching approaches designed to engender both peer support and goal congruence as well as to maximize and minimize the effects of 'effective' and 'ineffective' teaching practices respectively.
- Specific teacher professional development with the assistance of key personnel from relevant 'Subject Associations'.

The feedback from the project was encouraging as observed by many educational experts.

Misinterpretation and Misuse of Educational Performance Indicators

Several studies have pointed out that there are serious and inherent limitations to the efficacy of several such educational PIs and that they cannot provide reliable judgments about educational institutions and systems. It is increasingly recognized that schools or teachers within schools should not be judged by a single 'cohort' of students, but rather on their performance over time.

There is a possibility that the misuse and misinterpretation of educational indicators may have catastrophic consequences on the school system, some of which are given below:

- Schools and teachers may be constantly subjected to negative comments by public/media which, in turn, may adversely impact their morale.
- A test-dominated curriculum inadvertently lays overemphasis on content-oriented examinations. Hence, students and teachers tend to conclude that passing these examinations is the ultimate goal of the present education system.
- A majority of private schools refuse to admit 'low achievers' as their only aim is to get good results in the examinations. Schools and teachers also tend to concentrate on coaching 'bright' students and tend to pay less attention to 'dull' ones.
- This would also promote malpractices in the examination on the part of students, teachers and schools as the only aim would be to get 'good' results at all costs, sometimes sacrificing honesty and integrity.
- Parents tend to enrol their wards in 'reputed schools' exert all sorts of pressure and are prepared to pay 'capitation' to gain admission.
- States as well as 'authorities' at various levels tend to publish facts and figures that are only favourable to them and suppress other information that may be otherwise vital.

Annexure VII

List of Some Major Studies in Last 10-15 Years on Learning Achievement Levels:

A list of some major achievement studies undertaken across the country and in several states is given in this annexure. Generalizations from these studies may be difficult to draw as most of the studies have been conducted in different parts of the country at different points in time and none of them were on an all-India basis. (This was prior to ASER). However, the findings are illustrative of the existing levels of learning achievement.

Studies done by the NCERT, NIEPA (now NUEPA), and other research institutions underscore that learning achievement in India is very low. Children from poor families are at a greater disadvantage with the dropout rate among the poorest being about four times that of the richest ones. Besides, large gaps are found in their access to education; quality of education; and learning according to gender, social class, and location.

1. A rigorous study of student achievement found that about 70 per cent of class 4 students and 60 per cent of class 5 students from schools in the 'privileged urban zone' in Madhya Pradesh had not mastered competencies in hindi and mathematics that would be expected of class 2 students. And in the 'highly underdeveloped rural zone' no class 4 or class 5 student had mastered the class 2 competencies. (Govinda & Varghese, 1993).
2. A 1991 study conducted in 23 states by the NCERT found that, for a sample of 65,000 urban and rural class 4 students, the average achievement on class 4 curriculum-based skills tests of arithmetic, reading, comprehension and spelling was 46.4 per cent. (Shukla et.al., 1994).
3. Aikara's study (1997) found mean achievement scores of 41.2 per cent for language, 34.7 per cent for maths and 42.2 per cent for environmental studies in Bihar, Maharashtra, Rajasthan and Karnataka.
4. Bashir Sajitha (1994) studied the learning achievement of 113 schools in TN (govt. and private) in maths and Tamil. Average student performance for class 4 was as low as 30-35 per cent of the maximum score.

5. Yash Aggarwal's study of 169 schools in Delhi came up with similar findings: mean score of 40.46 per cent in maths and 56.5 per cent in language.
6. Although the DPEP districts in Karnataka (1997) did indicate significant improvement in maths and kannada, the learning achievements of children from disadvantaged backgrounds remained low. This was despite a quantitative goal of improvement of 25 per cent in learning levels being stipulated in the DPEP.
7. The study of learning achievement at the end of the primary cycle in DPEP states showed that less than 10 per cent children in class 4 scored more than 80 per cent in language and maths tests. (TN was an exception). In class 3 of DPEP II states, only in Gujarat and Maharashtra the mean score in language was above 60 per cent while in Maths it was below 60 per cent (ABL Srivastava, 2004).
8. The PROBE report states that school quality is responsible for pupil achievement, and therefore, needs to be improved. Saxena, Singh and Gupta (1995) studied school level factors that, apart from increasing learning capabilities, decrease differences in learning levels that result from gender, caste, and socio-economic status. The findings revealed that differences between schools were responsible for 20-65 per cent variation in achievement in maths and 14-45 per cent variation in reading achievement in schools of low literacy districts in eight Indian states. (World Bank, 1997).
9. As mentioned in the chapter on 'Learning Conditions and Learner Achievement in Primary Schools' presented in the India Education Report 2002, generalizations from these studies may be difficult to draw as most of the studies have been conducted in different parts of the country and at different points in time (ASER has remedied this situation with its pan-Indian achievement surveys since 2005). However, the findings are illustrative of the existing levels of learning achievement.
10. Only 31 per cent of children complete education up to class 10 and 42 per cent complete class 8. (Annual Status of Education Report (Rural) 2006). Facilitated by Pratham, 2007, Mumbai: Pratham Resource Centre.
11. One out of three children in class 5 are unable to read and write. (Annual Status of Education Report (Rural) 2006). Facilitated by Pratham, 2007, Mumbai: Pratham Resource Centre.
12. Only about 10 per cent primary schools have majority children learning as per expected levels of competencies. (Azim Premji Foundation's evaluation of over 8000 schools and Government of Karnataka's evaluation of about 45,000 schools).*
13. 'Primary Education in India' published by the World Bank (1997) first consolidated the findings of a few empirical studies of learning achievement at the primary level carried out in India. It showed that primary level learning achievement was low, and that it varied across schools and according to the background of the child.

Annexure VIII

Statistical Tables

Table 1 Human Development Index (HDI) in India

(NHDR methodology)

State	1981 Value	1981 Rank	1991 Value	1991 Rank	2001 Value	2001 Rank
Andhra Pradesh	0.298	9	0.377	9	0.416	10
Assam	0.272	10	0.348	10	0.386	14
Bihar	0.237	15	0.308	15	0.367	15
Gujarat	0.360	4	0.431	6	0.479	6
Haryana	0.360	5	0.443	5	0.509	5
Karnataka	0.346	6	0.412	7	0.478	7
Kerala	0.500	1	0.591	1	0.638	1
Madhya Pradesh	0.245	14	0.328	13	0.394	12
Maharashtra	0.363	3	0.452	4	0.523	4
Orissa	0.267	11	0.345	12	0.404	11
Punjab	0.411	2	0.475	2	0.537	2
Rajasthan	0.256	12	0.347	11	0.424	9
Tamil Nadu	0.343	7	0.466	3	0.531	3
Uttar Pradesh	0.255	13	0.314	14	0.388	13
West Bengal	0.305	8	0.404	8	0.472	8
All India	**0.302**		**0.381**		**0.472**	

Source: NHDR 2001

Note: The NHDR has estimated only for a selected few states for which data was available at the time.

Table 2 Comparison of Some States by HDI and GDI 2001

(UNDP methodology)

S. No.	State	HDI	Rank	GDI	Rank
1.	Kerala	0.746	1	0.724	1
2.	Maharashtra	0.706	2	0.693	2
3.	Tamil Nadu	0.687	3	0.675	4
4.	Punjab	0.679	4	0.676	3
5.	Gujarat	0.655	5	0.642	5
6.	Haryana	0.653	6	0.636	7
7.	Karnataka	0.650	7	0.637	6
8.	West Bengal	0.647	8	0.631	8
9.	Andhra Pradesh	0.609	9	0.595	9
10.	Rajasthan	0.596	10	0.573	10
11.	Assam	0.578	11	0.554	12
12.	Madhya Pradesh	0.572	12	0.548	13
13.	Orissa	0.569	13	0.555	11
14.	Uttar Pradesh	0.535	14	0.520	14
15.	Bihar	0.495	15	0.477	15
	India	**0.621**	—	**0.609**	—

Source: HDR Karnataka 2005; GDI: Gender Development Index

Table 3 Comparison of Some States by Education Index 2001

State	Education Index	Rank
Kerala	0.887	1
Maharashtra	0.796	2
Tamil Nadu	0.764	3
Gujarat	0.726	4
Karnataka	0.712	5
India	0.652	—

Source: HDR Karnataka 2005

Table 4 Literacy Rates 2001

S. No.	State	Total	Male	Female
1.	Andhra Pradesh	60.5	70.9	51.2
2.	Assam	63.3	71.9	56.0
3.	Bihar	47.0	60.3	33.6
4.	Gujarat	69.1	76.5	55.6
5.	Haryana	67.9	79.3	56.3
6.	Karnataka	66.6	76.1	56.9
7.	Kerala	90.9	94.2	87.9
8.	Madhya Pradesh	63.7	76.5	50.5
9.	Maharashtra	76.9	86.3	67.5
10.	Orissa	63.1	75.9	51.0
11.	Punjab	69.7	75.6	63.5
12.	Rajasthan	60.4	76.5	44.3
13.	Tamil Nadu	73.5	82.3	64.5
14.	Uttar Pradesh	56.3	70.2	43.0
15.	West Bengal	68.6	77.6	60.2
	India	64.8	75.8	54.2

Source: Census of India 2001

Table 5 HDI and GDI by Social Groups in Karnataka 2001

Index	All	SCs	Gap	STs	Gap
HDI	0.650	0.575	0.075	0.539	0.111
GDI	0.639	0.564	0.073	0.527	0.110
Difference between HDI & GDI	0.013	0.011	—	0.012	—

Source: HDR Karnataka 2005

Table 6 Teacher Absence & Teaching Activity in Schools

State	Teacher Absence Percentage	Non-Teaching Activity – % of Observations
Karnataka	21.70	44.00
Maharashtra	14.60	40.70
Gujarat	17.00	43.10
Madhya Pradesh	17.60	48.90
Kerala	21.20	43.50
Tamil Nadu	21.30	50.40
Andhra Pradesh	25.30	57.00
West Bengal	24.70	53.90

Source: World Bank Survey 2004

Table 7 Reasons for not Attending School by Children (Karnataka)

Reasons for Out-of-School	Impact	Reasons for Out-of-School	Impact
Household work	16%	Sibling care	5%
Earnings because of poverty	16%	Gender related issue	3%
Unwillingness of parents	9%	Tribal life	3%
School is far	5%	School not attractive	1%
Disability	5%	Others (Miscellaneous)	37%

Source: Children's Census 2005 (as reported by PWHC)

Table 8 Expenditure on Education in Five Year Plan
(As percentage of total expenditure in the FY Plan)

Five Year Plan	Total Education	Elementary	Secondary	Higher
Fifth Plan	3.27	0.8	0.4	0.5
Sixth Plan	2.70	0.8	0.7	0.5
Seventh Plan	3.55	1.3	0.8	0.5
Eighth Plan	4.50	2.1	0.8	0.3
Ninth Plan	6.23	3.2	1.1	0.5

Source: India Development Report 2008

Table 9 Population Growth Trends

Year	Population (in million)	Decadal Growth %
1951	361.09	1941-51 :13.3
1961	439.23	1951-61:21.6
1971	548.16	1961-71:24.8
1981	683.33	1971-81:24.7
1991	846.39	1981-91:23.9
2001	1028.61	1991-01:21.5

Source: Census of India 2001

Table 10 Decadal Growth in Female Literacy

State	1991 Female Literacy	2001 Female Literacy	Difference
Andhra Pradesh	32.72	51.17	18.45
Gujarat	48.92	58.60	9.68
Haryana	40.47	56.31	15.84
Karnataka	44.34	57.45	13.12
Kerala	86.17	87.86	1.69
Maharashtra	52.32	67.51	15.20
Punjab	50.41	63.55	13.14
Tamil Nadu	51.33	64.55	13.22
Assam	43.03	56.03	13.00
Bihar	21.99	33.57	11.58
Madhya Pradesh	29.35	50.28	20.93
Orissa	34.68	50.97	16.29
Rajasthan	20.44	44.34	23.90
Uttar Pradesh	24.37	42.98	18.61
West Bengal	46.56	60.22	13.66
All States	39.28	54.28	15.00

Source: Census of India 2001

Table 11 Human Development in India

Indicators	Value
Human Development Index (HDI 2005)	0.619 (ranking India – 127)
Life expectancy at birth	63.7 years
Adult literacy rate 1995-2005	61.0 (% ages 15 and above)
Female adult literacy rate	65 (as % of male rate)
GER (Primary, Secondary &Tertiary)	63.8
NER (Primary) 2005	89%
NER (Primary – Girls)	85%
Children reaching class 5 (2004)	73 (as % of grade I students)
GDP per capita 2005	3,452 (PPP US$)
Life Expectancy Index	0.645
Education Index	0.620
GDP Index	0.591
Human poverty index	31.3 (ranking India – 62)
Children underweight for age Children underheight for age	47 (% under age 5) 46 (% under age 5)
Population below income poverty line	34.3 % ($1 per day)
National poverty line	28.6 %
Demographic trends (2003) Annual population growth rate Population under age 15	 1.9% 32.9%
Public expenditure on education (2002) -,,- on pre-primary & primary education -,,- on secondary education -,,- on tertiary education Public exp. on edn. (% of total govt. exp. 2005)	4.1 (as % of GDP) 38.9 % 40.1 % 20.3 % 10.7 %

Source: Extracted from HDR 2005, 2007, 2008 (UNDP)

Table 12 Differences among States in India

Indicator	India	Kerala	Bihar	Rajasthan	UP
Female share of population (%)	48	52	49	48	48
Under 5 mortality rate (Per 1000 live births)	95	19	105	115	123
Total fertility rate (Birth per woman)	2.9	2.0	3.5	3.8	4.0
Children receiving all vaccinations (%)	42	80	11	17	21

Source: Extracted from HDR 2005 (UNDP)

Table 13 Children Out-of-school (All India) 2005

Out of a child population of 194.03 million in the age group of 6-13 years, 13.46 million (6.94%) were found to be out-of-school.

(Figures in percentages)

	Rural	Urban	Total
All children (6-13 years)	7.80	4.34	6.94
Boys (6-13 years)	6.78	4.33	6.18
Girls (6-13 years)	9.14	4.36	7.92
All children (6-10 years)	6.92	3.51	6.10
Boys (6-10 years)			5.51
Girls (6-10 years)			6.87
Boys (11-13 years)			6.46
Girls (11-13 years)			10.03
All children (11-13 years)	9.58	6.06	8.56
SC children	8.55	6.25	8.17
ST children	10.11	4.21	9.54
OBC children	7.73	3.83	6.90
Muslim children	12.03	7.17	9.97
Other children	4.39	2.44	3.73
Children with disability			0.80
% of children with disability out-of-school			38.13

Source: All India Survey of out-of-school children in the 6-13 years age group, Social & Rural Research Institute, EdCIL, Noida, May, 2006

Table 14 Criticality of PTR in Learning Achievement (Learning Guarantee Programme-Karnataka)

The average pupil-teacher ratio in qualifying lower primary schools was much lower than the non-qualifying (other) lower primary schools.

	No. of Participating Lower Primary Schools	Number of Qualifying Schools	The Other Schools
	766	80	686
Average pupil-teacher ratio	37.4	24:1	39:1

S. Giridhar and D.D. Karopady Azim Premji Foundation, Bangalore

Table 15 Indicators of Quality (Learning Guarantee Programme-Karnataka)

Infrastructure Indicators that do not make a Difference	Infrastructure Indicators that make a Difference (significant or directional)
Bus reaches within 0.5 kms of school	Drinking water
Pucca building	Usable toilets for children
AWC on premises	Separate teacher's toilets
Compound wall	
Avg. number of classrooms	
Electricity	
Playground	
Teacher Related Indicators that do not make a Difference	**Teacher Related Indicators that make a Difference**
Gender	Average experience in this school (yrs)
Caste	Average total experience (yrs)
Age	
Average age (yrs)	
Qualifications	
Married or otherwise	
Live in the same village	
School Practice Related Indicators that do not make a Difference	**School Practice Related Indicators that make a Difference**
Up to date student and teacher register	TLM in classrooms
Multigrade teaching involved	Good school appearance
Average no. of working teachers	Head teacher present/absent
School with shortage of teachers	School with shortage of teachers
Schools with temparary teachers	All teachers present
	Focus on enrolment and attendance
	Extra classes
	Orientation on exams
	Additional reading material

S. Giridhar and D.D Karopady, Azim Premji Foundation, Bangalore

Table 16 Students' Learning
Percentage of Boys and Girls Securing more than 60% Marks

Classes State	4/5 Boys	4/5 Girls	7/8 Boys	7/8 Girls
Andhra Pradesh	59.90	59.12	52.62	54.75
Assam	21.17	18.52	14.72	13.09
Bihar	32.14	31.86	23.87	24.00
Gujarat	53.88	54.29	59.07	63.27
Haryana	29.89	30.11	16.40	17.50
Himachal Pradesh	44.91	46.55	16.98	19.04
Jharkhand	22.89	22.60	19.97	20.19
Karnataka	59.37	60.49	44.26	48.98
Kerala	38.90	42.85	35.92	41.16
Madhya Pradesh	23.73	23.05	18.99	21.96
Maharashtra	63.16	62.38	25.34	26.98
Orissa	10.50	9.52	12.17	11.93
Rajasthan	52.50	51.22	46.97	48.88
Tamil Nadu	44.64	47.63	24.95	26.69
Uttar Pradesh	39.34	38.29	32.56	36.70
Uttarakhand	40.23	36.05	24.22	23.95
West Bengal	40.21	38.40	23.31	21.40

Source: DPEP Report Cards in Sinha. A (2003)

Note: This table shows the dismal academic performance of children, as a large number of Class 4 and 5 children complete primary school with less than 60% of marks. Such children are unlikely to complete the upper primary stage because academic load increases as they climb higher levels of education.

Table 17 Teacher Absence Rates by Country

Country	Teacher Absence %
Peru	11
Ecuador	14
Papua New Guinea	15
Bangladesh	16
Zambia	17
Indonesia	19
India	25
Uganda	27

Source: World Bank Survey 2004

Table 18 Teacher Absence in Public Schools by States

State	Absence %	State	Absence %
Maharashtra	14.6	West Bengal	24.7
Gujarat	17.0	Andhra Pradesh	25.3
Madhya Pradesh	17.6	Uttar Pradesh	26.3
Kerala	21.2	Chhattisgarh	30.6
Himachal Pradesh	21.2	Uttaranchal	32.8
Tamil Nadu	21.3	Assam	33.8
Haryana	21.7	Punjab	34.4
Karnataka	21.7	Bihar	37.8
Orissa	23.4	Jharkhand	41.9
Rajasthan	23.7	**Weighted Average**	**24.8**

Source: World Bank Survey 2004

Table 19 Absence by Type of School

	Public Schools	Non-formal Schools	Private Aided Schools	Private Schools
Weighted teacher absence	24.8%	28.0%	20.1%	22.8%
Rate of teaching activity	44.8%	42.9%	58.8%	48.5%
No. of observations	34525	393	3371	9098

Source: World Bank Survey 2004

Table 20 Absence by Type of Teacher

	Head	Deputy Head	Permanent/ Regular	Contract/ Informal
Absence rate	30.2%	22.2%	23.1%	24.0%
No. of observations	7177	1979	23333	2037

Source: World Bank Survey 2004

Table 21 Norms and Standards Prescribed by Right to Education Act, 2009

<table>
<tr><th>Item</th><th>Description</th><th colspan="2">Norms & Standards</th></tr>
<tr><td rowspan="2">1. Number of teachers</td><td>a) For Classes 1 to 5</td><td>Class enrolment
Up to 60
61-90
91-120
121-200
Above 150
Above 200</td><td>No. of teachers
2
3
4
5
5+1 Head Teacher
PTR excluding Head Teacher shall not exceed 40</td></tr>
<tr><td>b) For Classes 6 to 8</td><td colspan="2">(1) At least one teacher per class so that there shall be at least one teacher each for-
(i) Science & Mathematics,
(ii) Social Studies,
(iii) Languages,
(2) At least one teacher for every 35 children,
(3) Where admission of children is above 100-
(i) a full-time Head Teacher,
(ii) part-time instructors for – Art Education, Health and Physical Education, &Work Education</td></tr>
<tr><td>2. Building</td><td colspan="3">Whether building consisting of –
(i) at least one classroom for every teacher and an office-cum-store- cum-Head Teacher's room,
(ii) barrier-free access,
(iii) separate toilets for boys and girls,
(iv) safe & adequate drinking water facility to all children,
(v) a midday meal kitchen,
(vi) playground,
(vii) arrangements for securing the school building by boundary wall or fencing.</td></tr>
<tr><td>3. Minimum number of working days/ instructional hours in an academic year</td><td colspan="3">(i) 200 working days for Classes 1 to 5.
(ii) 220 working days for Classes 6 to 8.
(iii) 800 instructional hours/academic year for Classes 1 to 5.
(iv) 1000 instructional hours/academic year for Classes 6 to 8.</td></tr>
<tr><td>4. Minimum no. of working hrs/week</td><td colspan="3">45 teaching +preparation hours/week/teacher</td></tr>
<tr><td>5. TLM</td><td colspan="3">Shall be provided to each class as required</td></tr>
<tr><td>6. Library</td><td colspan="3">There shall be a library in each school providing newspaper, magazines and books on all subjects, including story books.</td></tr>
<tr><td>7. Play material, games & sports equipment</td><td colspan="3">Shall be provided to each class as required.</td></tr>
</table>

Source: The Schedule of the Right of Children to Free & Compulsory Education Act, 2009

Table 22 Number of School Teachers* in India

(Figures in lakhs)

Stage	Types of Schools				
	Govt.	Local Body	Private Aided	Private Unaided	Total
Primary	8.65	5.63	1.18	2.27	**17.73**
Upper primary	5.94	3.63	1.52	3.77	**14.88**
Secondary	3.04	0.99	2.76	2.93	**9.72**
Sr. secondary	3.52	0.34	3.73	2.67	**10.26**
Total	**21.17**	**10.59**	**9.19**	**11.64**	**52.59**

Source: Seventh All India School Education Survey(NCERT)
* Full-time teachers

Table 23 Number of Untrained Teachers in India

(Figures in lakhs)

Stage	Number*
Primary	5.22
Upper primary	2.60
Secondary	1.35
Sr. secondary	0.63
Total	**9.80**

Source: Seventh All India School Education Survey

Table 24 SCERTs/SIE s in India

Institution	States/Union Territories	Total
SCERT	AP, Assam, Bihar, Chhattisgarh, Delhi, Gujarat, Haryana, HP, Karnataka, Kerala, MP, Maharashtra, Manipur, Meghalaya, Mizoram, Nagaland, Orissa, Punjab, Rajasthan, TN, Tripura, UP, Uttaranchal, WB.	**24**
SIE	Andaman & Nicobar Islands, AP, Assam, Chandigarh, Goa, Jammu (Tawi), Kashmir (Srinagar), Sikkim, UP.	**9**
Both SIE & SCERT	Assam, UP.	**2**
None	Dadar & Nagar Haveli, Daman & Diu, Jharkhand, Lakshadweep, Pondicherry.	**5**

Source: MHRD Reports

Table 25 Gross Enrolment Ratio (GER)

This table presents GER which represents school enrolment as a ratio of the total population in the respective age groups. In the 1990s there was a decline in the figures at the upper primary stage.

Years	Classes 1 to 5 Primary (6-11 years)			Classes 6 to 8 Upper Primary (11-14 years)		
	Boys	Girls	Total	Boys	Girls	Total
1991	98.12	75.89	87.28	79.82	54.62	67.87
1997	98.50	81.50	90.30	66.50	49.50	58.50
2000	104.90	85.90	96.30	75.70	58.90	67.50
2006	112.80	105.70	109.40	84.20	76.30	78.60

Source: MHRD Reports

Table 26 Per Capita Expenditure on Education in 1997-98

(Rupees at 1981-82 prices)

State	Per Capita Expenditure in 1997-98 (Rupees)
Himachal Pradesh	191
Kerala	164
Maharashtra	158
Tamil Nadu	144
Gujarat	142
Assam	134
Haryana	134
Karnataka	130
Rajasthan	128
Orissa	102
West Bengal	101
Andhra Pradesh	88
Uttar Pradesh	78
Bihar	76
Madhya Pradesh	73

Source: Dr Sajitha Bashir: Government Expenditure on Elementary Education in the Nineties: 2000

Table 27 Poverty Reduction and Basic Education – Poverty in Rural Areas Adjusted Head Count Ratios – Percentage of those below the Poverty Line

State	1987-88	1993-94	1999-2000	Reduction in Percentage Points between 1987-88 and 1999-2000
Andhra Pradesh	35.0	29.2	26.2	8.7
Assam	36.1	35.4	35.5	0.6
Bihar	54.6	48.6	41.1	13.5
Gujarat	39.4	32.5	20.0	19.4
Haryana	13.6	17.0	5.7	7.9
Himachal Pradesh	13.3	17.1	9.8	3.5
Jammu and Kashmir	15.3	10.1	6.1	9.2
Karnataka	40.8	37.9	30.7	10.1
Kerala	23.8	19.5	10.0	13.8
Madhya Pradesh	43.7	36.6	31.3	12.4
Maharashtra	44.3	42.9	31.9	12.4
Orissa	50.4	43.5	43.0	7.4
Punjab	6.6	6.2	2.4	4.2
Rajasthan	35.3	23.0	17.3	18.0
Tamil Nadu	49.0	38.5	24.3	24.7
Uttar Pradesh	34.9	28.6	21.5	13.4
West Bengal	36.3	25.1	21.9	14.4
All India Rural	39.0	33.0	26.3	12.7

Source: Jean Dreze and Angus Deaton: Poverty and Inequality in India, *Economic and Political Weekly*, 7 September, 2002

Table 28 Infrastructure Facilities in the Country

Schooling Facility	Rural	Urban	Total
% of schools with no boundary wall	53.14	26.34	49.45
% of schools without building	4.01	2.33	3.81
% of schools without pucca buildings	30.60	25.48	30.71
Average number of rooms in a school imparting elementary education	3.30	6.70	3.70
% of schools without a classroom	7.86	8.00	8.84
% of schools with only one classroom	11.86	4.96	10.94
Student-classroom ratio	43.00	37.00	42.00
% of schools with student-classroom ratio of 60 and above	22.81	18.01	22.00

Average school size	143.00	250.00	154.00
% of schools with drinking water	77.91	84.75	77.89
% of schools with common toilet facilities	39.44	63.24	41.81
% of schools with separate toilet for girls	25.10	54.26	28.24
% of schools with electricity connection	20.35	64.10	25.23
% of schools without blackboards	8.57	8.59	9.51
% of schools with computers	5.74	22.77	7.68
% of schools with playgrounds	48.81	59.67	49.57
% of schools with attached pre-primary sections	—	—	15.86

Source: DISE Analytical Report 2004

Table 29 Out-of-school Children – All India (6-13 years) 2006

(In lakhs)

Category	Out-of-school Children			% of out-of-school Children		
	Rural	Urban	Total	Rural	Urban	Total
All children	113.53	21.06	134.59	7.80	4.34	6.94
SC children	27.06	3.98	31.04	8.55	6.25	8.17
ST children	15.85	0.71	16.56	10.11	4.21	9.54
Muslim children	15.67	6.85	22.53	12.03	7.17	9.97

Source: SRI – IMRB Survey 2006

Table 30 Pupil-Teacher Ratios

State/ UT	PTR 2005	PTR 2006	PTR 2007
Andhra Pradesh	24	24	22
Assam	26	25	25
Bihar	78	65	64
Chhattisgarh	37	28	27
Goa		25	24
Gujarat	36	35	35
Haryana	36	33	32
Himachal Pradesh	21	20	18
Jammu & Kashmir	19	18	16
Jharkhand	54	48	48
Karnataka	35	30	32
Kerala	28	29	27
Madhya Pradesh	32	36	38
Maharashtra	28	29	28
Manipur	—	20	20
Meghalaya	19	18	17

Nagaland	22	22	22
Orissa	37	35	33
Pondicherry	27	24	24
Punjab	29	33	32
Rajasthan	34	33	31
Tamil Nadu	29	29	27
Tripura	22	23	22
Uttar Pradesh	68	57	53
Uttarakhand	26	26	26
West Bengal	55	54	51

Source: DISE 2006-07/ASER 2008

Table 31 Children in Class 1 Who Cannot Even Read Letters

State/ UT	2005	2006	2007
Andhra Pradesh	30.8	19.8	26.8
Assam	37.5	41.3	25.9
Bihar	47.8	42.5	37.3
Chhattisgarh	33.4	33.5	32.5
Goa	3.2	3.5	4.5
Gujarat	34.9	32.9	30.0
Haryana	37.5	32.4	32.5
Himachal Pradesh	19.0	18.7	12.9
Jammu & Kashmir	13.6	18.8	11.1
Jharkhand	42.8	41.8	33.6
Karnataka	46.1	29.8	23.7
Kerala	9.1	2.2	4.4
Madhya Pradesh	57.1	19.4	11.3
Maharashtra	29.1	19.6	12.2
Manipur	21.3	22.9	4.5
Meghalaya	2.2	6.9	5.0
Nagaland	6.3	4.1	3.1
Orissa	50.7	39.2	36.6
Pondicherry	–	39.7	36.9
Punjab	39.7	24.5	19.9
Rajasthan	58.2	66.5	45.0
Tamil Nadu	44.9	51.1	57.8
Tripura	0.0	5.2	20.9
Uttar Pradesh	52.0	55.7	45.8
Uttarakhand	29.3	19.6	29.5
West Bengal	16.1	13.6	19.4

Source: ASER 2008

Table 32 Children Who Can Read Level 1 (Class 1 Text) +Level 2 (Class 2 Text) at Class 3

(In percentage)

State/UT	2005	2006	2007
Andhra Pradesh	53.1	41.3	58.7
Assam	55.4	56.4	49.0
Bihar	63.2	54.0	53.9
Chhattisgarh	52.8	36.2	31.1
Goa	79.0	73.8	78.5
Gujarat	43.4	46.6	40.1
Haryana	56.8	61.7	54.3
Himachal Pradesh	66.5	58.6	72.7
Jammu & Kashmir	49.7	37.0	37.9
Jharkhand	54.9	49.7	42.6
Karnataka	39.3	38.7	37.6
Kerala	79.1	73.9	69.6
Madhya Pradesh	38.4	65.0	68.4
Maharashtra	65.7	66.0	74.8
Manipur	62.2	51.5	66.3
Meghalaya	81.2	72.0	67.7
Nagaland	76.0	48.3	54.2
Orissa	45.4	47.3	44.5
Pondicherry	–	24.5	27.3
Punjab	46.1	49.5	53.8
Rajasthan	46.7	38.4	35.8
Tamil Nadu	39.5	24.9	28.4
Tripura	70.4	66.0	51.3
Uttar Pradesh	39.4	31.1	32.3
Uttarakhand	68.9	57.6	59.2
West Bengal	74.2	67.9	64.7

Source: ASER 2008

Table 33 Student-classroom Ratio

Year	Primary	Upper Primary
2002-03	48	36
2003-04	45	35
2004-05	44	33
2005-06	41	33
2006-07	40	31

Source: DISE/NUEPA

Table 34 Performance in Class 4 and 5 and Class 7 and 8 Tests Percentage of Boys and Girls Securing More than 60% Marks

State/ UT	*4/5 Boys	*4/5 Girls	*7/8 Boys	*7/8 Girls
Andhra Pradesh	59.90	59.12	52.62	54.75
Assam	21.17	18.52	14.72	13.09
Bihar	32.14	31.86	23.87	24.00
Gujarat	53.88	54.29	59.07	63.27
Haryana	29.89	30.11	16.40	17.50
Himachal Pradesh	44.91	46.55	16.98	19.04
Jharkhand	22.89	22.60	19.97	20.19
Karnataka	59.37	60.49	44.26	48.98
Kerala	38.90	42.85	35.92	41.16
Madhya Pradesh	23.73	23.05	18.99	21.96
Maharashtra	63.16	62.38	25.34	26.98
Orissa	10.50	9.52	12.17	11.93
Rajasthan	52.50	51.22	46.97	48.48
Tamil Nadu	44.64	47.63	24.95	26.69
Uttar Pradesh	39.34	38.29	32.56	36.70
Uttarakhand	40.23	36.05	24.22	23.95
West Bengal	40.21	38.40	23.31	21.40

Source: DPEP 2002 Report Cards: Universal Access and Retention: Yash Aggarwal
* Classes

Table 35 Mean Achievement Scores of Class-4 Students

State/District	Mean Achievement Score in Language for Boys : Class-4	Mean Achievement Score in Language for Girls : Class-4	Mean Achievement Score in Mathematics for Boys: Class-4	Mean Achievement Score in Mathematics for Girls: Class-4
Haryana				
Jind	58.85	55.90	46.82	46.35
Kaithal	45.30	52.66	42.31	48.19
Chhattisgarh				
Bilaspur	53.88	50.52	41.59	38.20
Raigarh	50.12	46.06	33.17	33.93
Madhya Pradesh				
Betul	66.09	67.53	62.09	61.76
Dhar	59.94	59.33	48.13	46.01
Tamil Nadu				
Dharampuri	71.46	69.92	61.50	60.69
Villupuram	68.00	67.56	62.28	62.49

Source: Student Achievement under TAS: An Appraisal in Phase – I DPEP States 2002, NCERT

Table 36 The Dropping Enrolment Scenario

Class	Boys (in millions)	Girls (in millions)	Total (in millions)
1	17.1	13.4	30.5
2	13.4	10.4	23.8
3	12.2	9.6	21.8
4	11.0	8.6	19.6
5	10.2	7.8	18.0
6	9.4	6.6	16.0
7	8.3	5.9	14.2
8	7.6	5.0	12.6
9	6.2	4.0	10.2
10	5.4	3.4	8.8
11	2.4	1.6	4.0
12	2.1	1.4	3.5

Source: Selected Educational Statistics 2000-01 (As on 30 September, 2000)

Table 37 Where Do They Go

Course	Boys (in lakhs)	Girls (in lakhs)	Total (in lakhs)
Teacher Training Schools	0.57	0.60	1.17
Polytechnic Institutes	3.15	0.80	3.95
Technical, Industrial, Arts and Crafts Schools	4.08	0.68	4.76
MBBS	0.88	0.60	1.48
BE/BSc./B.Arch.	3.25	0.93	4.18
B.Ed./BT	0.70	0.52	1.12

Source: Selected Educational Statistics 2000-01

Table 38 Improvement of Access Facilities

	V Survey 1986	VI Survey 1993	VII Survey 2002	2006 (SSA)
Proportion of habitations having primary schools with in 1km.	83.83	83.36	86.96	98.0
Proportion of habitations served by upper primary schools within 3km.	74	76.15	78.11	86.0

Source: EFA Mid-decade Assessment 2008

Table 39 Improvement in Girls' Enrolment

(In percentage)

Stage	2000-01	2001-02	2002-03	2003-04	2004-05	2005-06
Primary (1-5)	43.7	44.1	46.8	46.7	46.6	46.6
Upper primary (6-8)	40.9	41.8	43.9	44.0	44.4	44.6
Gender Parity Index	0.80	0.81	0.85	0.93	0.93	0.92

Source: EFA Mid-decade Assessment 2008(NUEPA)

Table 40 Teacher-pupil Ratios

Year	Primary	Upper Primary
1999-2000	1:43	1:38
2000-01	1:43	1:38
2001-02	1:43	1:34
2002-03	1:42	1:34
2003-04	1:45	1:35
2004-05	1:46	1:35

Source: EFA Mid-decade Assessment 2008 (NUEPA)

Table 41 Attendance Rate of Students by Gender and Social Group

	Primary	Upper Primary
Boys	68.9	75.2
Girls	70.6	78.7
SC	68.7	76.5
ST	70.5	76.5
Minority (muslim)	66.4	79.1
Rural	68.0	73.7
Urban	71.2	79.9

Source: EFA Mid-decade Assessment 2008(NUEPA)

Table 42 Average Attendance Rate of Students & Teachers Based on Headcount During Three Unannounced Visits in 2006-07

	Students		Teachers	
States	Primary Stage	Upper Primary Stage	Primary Stage	Upper Primary Stage
Andhra Pradesh	72.7	76.6	78.1	77.3
Assam	81.3	84.5	79.2	55.2
Bihar	42.2	36.8	75.8	74.9
Chhattisgarh	67.7	75.0	75.7	73.5
Delhi	73.5	NA	95.0	NA
Gujarat	75.0	78.6	70.0	87.6

Haryana	82.2	85.1	86.9	91.9
Himachal Pradesh	94.6	93.2	80.0	88.0
Jammu & Kashmir	78.5	77.5	80.8	83.1
Karnataka	86.2	86.9	83.9	83.9
Kerala	91.4	92.0	84.5	85.3
Madhya Pradesh	72.1	69.8	70.4	67.0
Maharashtra	89.0	89.0	87.8	87.1
Orissa	66.8	69.0	87.4	86.6
Punjab	81.7	74.7	83.5	78.1
Rajasthan	62.7	78.9	81.1	79.8
Tamil Nadu	88.3	87.8	86.6	89.6
Uttar Pradesh	57.4	60.5	77.8	82.6
Uttarakhand	80.0	83.2	83.0	77.7
West Bengal	74.2	70.2	96.3	98.1

Source: EFA Mid-decade Assessment 2008

Table 43 Share of Sector-wise Central Expenditure on Education 2005-06

Sector	Percentage
Elementary	61%
Secondary	9%
Adult Education	1%
University	11%
Technical	9%
General	8%
Others	1%
Total	100%

Source: EFA Mid-decade Assessment 2008

Table 44 Share of EFA Components in Eleventh Plan Outlay (2007-08 to 2011-12)

Component	Share in %
Elementary Education	67%
ECCE	28%
Youth & Adolescents	1%
Adult Education & Literacy	3%
Women Development	1%
Total	100%

Source: EFA Mid-decade Assessment 2008

Table 45 Percentage of Trained Teachers/Female Teachers and PTR, 2005-06 (At Primary Level)

States/UTs	Percentage Of Trained Teachers	Female Teachers Per 100 Male Teachers	PTR
Andhra Pradesh	93	83	32
Arunachal Pradesh	25	51	32
Assam	41	66	45
Bihar	85	26	104
Chhattisgarh	56	40	41
Goa	93	646	32
Gujarat	100	136	34
Haryana	89	99	42
Himachal Pradesh	100	103	23
Jammu & Kashmir	53	69	32
Jharkhand	100	30	79
Karnataka	100	81	26
Kerala	99	283	27
Madhya Pradesh	52	40	49
Maharashtra	96	150	37
Manipur	33	63	31
Meghalaya	45	88	46
Mizoram	58	97	25
Nagaland	34	59	20
Orissa	89	55	42
Punjab	98	167	44
Rajasthan	82	40	47
Sikkim	72	102	22
Tamil Nadu	100	117	34
Tripura	67	103	36
Uttar Pradesh	98	40	57
Uttarakhand	100	114	24
West Bengal	74	37	50
A&N Islands	52	133	19
Delhi	100	308	45
Pondicherry	97	304	26
India	86	65	46

Source: Selected Educational Statistics, MHRD 2008

Bibliography

1. Shariff, Abusaleh, *Human Development Report: A Profile of Indian States in the 1990s*, Oxford University Press, India, 1999.
2. Jacob, Aikara, 'Learner Achievement in Primary Schools', Unit for Research in the Sociology of Education', TISS Mumbai, 1997.
3. Mahal, Ajay, et.al., 'The Poor and Health Service Use in India', March, 2001 paper presented at Fiscal Reforms Conference, organized by the National Institute of Public Finance and Policy, N D. and Political Weekly, 10 March, 2001.
4. Sinha, Amarjeet, Basic Education for All, The Elusive Quest for Social Justice in a Dynamic Society. The Case of India, A DFID Report, (2003).
5. ———, *Primary Schooling in India*, Vikas Publishers, 1998.
6. ———, (Ed.), *Understanding Sustainable Initiatives,* Centre for Sustainable Development, LBSNAA, Mussoorie, 1995.
7. Sen, Amartya Pratichi Trust, '*Cooked Midday Meal Programme in WB: A Study in Birbhum District*', 2005.
8. ———, and Dreze, Jean, (Ed.), *India Development: Regional Perspectives*, Oxford University Press, 1999.
9. Sinha, Amarjeet and Sinha, Ajay Kumar, *Concurrent Evaluation of Poverty Alleviation Programmes*, LBSNAA, Mussoorie, 1995.
10. ———, *Primary Schooling in Northern India: A Field Investigation*, Centre for Sustainable Development, Lal Bahadur Shastri National Academy of Administration, Mussoorie, 1995.
11. Sinha, Amarjeet, '*Feedback on Rural Development Programmes', Some Village Studies*, Lal Bahadur Shastri National Academy of Administration, Mussoorie, 1996.
12. Sen, Amartya and Dreze, Jean, *Economic Development and Social Opportunities*, Oxford University Press, India, 1995.
13. ———, *Development and Participation*, Oxford University Press, India, 2002.
14. Rampal, Anita, 'Development of Curricula, Textbooks and Teaching Learning Materials', Text in Context, An EFA 2000 Review.
15. ———, Education for Human Development in South Asia, *Economic and Political Weekly*, 22 July, 2000.
16. De, Anuradha, Noronha, Claire and Samson, Meera, 'Primary Education in Himachal Pradesh: Examining a Success Story'.
17. ———, Majumdar, Manabi, Noronha, Claire, and Samson, Meera, *Role of Private Schools in Basic Education.*
18. ———, Noronha, Claire, and Samson, Meera, *Midday Meal Scheme in Delhi – A Functioning Programme* CORD, 2005.

19. 'Annual Status of Education Reports', ASER (Rural) Reports from 2005-2008.
20. Bose, Ashis, 'Health for All by 2000: Broken Promises' *Economic and Political Weekly*, 17 March, 2001.
21. Kohli, Atul, (Ed.), *The Success of India's Democracy*, Cambridge University Press, 2001.
22. Mehta, Arun, '*Elementary Education in India: Progress Towards UEE*', NUEPA, New Delhi, 2008.
23. Azim Premji Foundation, Giridhar, (Ed.), 'A Paper on Criticality of Pupil-Teacher Ratios', 2003.
24. Pradhan, Basanta K., Singh, Sulabh Kumar, 'Policy Reforms and Financing of Elementary Education in India: A Study of the Quality of Service and Outcome', NCAER.
25. Sajitha, Bashir, *Achievement Performance at the Primary Level in Public and Private Schools of Tamil Nadu*, Indian Educational Review, Vol. 29, No. 3-4, July-Oct, 1994.
26. Kothari, Brij, Chand, Sherry, P.G., Vijaya, Sharma, Rajeev, '*A Review of Primary Education Packages in Madhya Pradesh*' IIM, Ahmedabad, 2000.
27. Ghosh, Buddhadeb, 'Panchayats and Elementary Education', *Economic and Political Weekly*, 11 May, 2002.
28. 'Budget Reports of Central and Several State Governments'.
29. 'Debating Right to Education Bill'. People's Campaign for Common School System', 2005.
30. Lal, Deepak, et.al., 'Economic Reforms and Poverty Alleviation: A Tale of Two Surveys', *Economic and Political Weekly,* 24 March, 2000.
31. Dewan, H.K., 'Understanding Pedagogical Interventions DPEP in Karnataka', Draft Report, Vol. I, Vidya Bhawan Society, Udaipur, 2002.
32. Jhingran, Dhir and Jha, Jyotsna, 'Elementary Education for the Poorest and other Deprived Groups: *The Real Challenge of Universalization*, Centre for Policy Research, 2002.
33. Nayyar, Dhiraj, 'Role of Good Governance and Constitutional Reforms', *Economic and Political Weekly*, 14 October, 2000.
34. Nawani, Disha, *Role and Contribution of NGOs to Basic Education*.
35. Gupta, Dipankar Das, et.al., 'Growth and Inter-State Disparities in India: Statistical Analysis', *Economic and Political Weekly*, 1 July, 2000.
36. Economic and Political Weekly Research Foundation, 'Finances of State Governments', 19 May, 2001 and 26 May, 2001.
37. 'Educational Initiatives and WIPRO: Student Learning in the Metros', 2006.
38. CIL, (Ed.), 'Programme for Improvement of Secondary Teacher Education Institutions', 1987.
39. CIL, (Ed.), 'All India Survey of Out-of-School Children in the 6-13 Years Age Group', Social & Rural Research Institute, May, 2006.
40. Afridi, Farzana, 'Midday Meals: A Comparison of the Financial and

Institutional Organization of the Programme in Two States,' *Economic and Political Weekly*, 2005.

41. Frankel, Francine R. and Rao, M.S.A., (Ed.), 'Dominance and State Power in Modern India', Decline of a Social Order, Vol. I and II, 1989.
42. ———, Hasan, Zoya, Bhargava, Rajeev, Arora, Balveer, *Transforming India: Social and Political Dynamics of Democracy*, Oxford University Press, 2000.
43. Nambissan, Geetha, 'Equity in Education? The Schooling of Dalit Children in India', Discussion Paper No. 15, Studies on Human Development in India, UNDP, New Delhi, 1996 .
44. Giridhar, S., Karpody, D.D. and Periodi, Umashanker, 'Assessment Reforms Through Voluntary Participation of Schools: Experiences from Learning Guarantee Programme', Paper presented at National Seminar on Assessment, NCERT 20-22 March, New Delhi, 2006.
45. R., Govinda, and Varghese, N. V., *Quality of Primary Schooling in India: A Case Study of Madhya Pradesh*, IIEP Paris and NIEPA New Delhi, 1993.
46. ———, and Divan, Rashmi, *Community Participation and Empowerment in Primary Education*, NIEPA, Sage Publications, 2003.
47. Government of India, 'Approach Paper to the Eleventh Plan', Planning Commission.
48. ———, 'The Apprentices Act', 1961.
49. ———, 'Budget Papers of Selected Years'.
50. ———, 'Census of India', 2001.
51. ———, 'DIET Guidelines', MHRD, 1989.
52. ———, 'DISE Analytical Reports'.
53. ———, 'Education for All Assessment', MHRD/NIEPA, 2000.
54. ———, Policy Document, 'Education for All', MHRD, November, 2005.
55. ———, EFA Mid-decade Assessment, 'Reaching the Unreached', NUEPA, India, November, 2008.
56. ———, 'Education in India' (1949-50 – 1971-72).
57. ———, 'Expert Group Report on Financial Requirements for Making Elementary Education', MHRD.
58. 'A Fundamental Right', Tapas Majumdar Committee, 2000.
59. ———, 'National Programme of Nutritional Support to Primary Education', Guidelines MHRD, September, 2006.
60. ———, 'National Policy on Education', 1986.
61. ———, 'Programme of Action', 1992.
62. ———, 'National Human Development Report', Planning Commission, 2001.
63. ———, 'Right of Children to Free and Compulsory Education Bill', 2008 (Bill LXV of 2008).
64. ———, Dr Mudaliar, A.L., 'Report of Secondary Education Commission', 1952-53.

65. ———, 'Report of the Kothari Commission', 1963-64.
66. ———, Prof. Yashpal, 'Report of the Committee on Learning Without Burden', MHRD, 1993.
67. ———, 'Selected Educational Statistics', MHRD.
68. ———, 'SSA Framework'.
69. ———, 'The Bidi and Cigar Workers' (conditions of employment) Act', 1966.
70. ———, 'The Child Labour (prohibition and regulation) Act', 1986.
71. ———, 'The Children (pledging of labour) Act', 1933.
72. ———, 'The Constitution of India'.
73. ———, 'The Merchant Shipping Act', 1951 (Section 10-9).
74. ———, 'The Mines Act', 1952 (Section 45).
75. ———, 'The Motor Transport Workers' Act', 1961.
76. ———, 'The Panchayat Raj Act', 1993.
77. ———, 'The Plantation Labour Act', 1951 (Section 24).
78. ———, 'The Persons with Disabilities (equal opportunities, protection of rights and full participation) Act', 1995.
79. ———, 'The Rehabilitation Council of India (RCI) Act', 1992.
80. Government of Karnataka – An Approach to Subsidies in Karnataka', 1997.
81. ———, Dr Prasad, Nagendra, (Ed.), 'Dropout Study Report', PPU, 2006.
82. ———, Dr Govinda, R., (Ed.), 'Eduvision-Shaping Education in Karnataka', 2002.
83. ———, 'Evaluation of Study Reports of DIETs/CTEs of Karnataka', DSERT, 2006.
84. ———, 'Human Development in Karnataka', Reports 1999 and 2005.
85. ———, 'Karnataka Education Act', 1983 with Commentary by Prof. B.M., Baliga', 1999.
86. ———, 'Medium Term Fiscal Plan (DMTFP)', DPSE, 2003.
87. ———, Rao, D. Jaganntha, (Ed.), 'Quality Initiatives in Education DSERT', 2006.
88. ———, 'Reports of the Taskforce on Primary Education in Karnataka, 2000-2001.
89. ———, 'School Quality Assessment Reports', KSQAO, 2006, 2007, 2008.
90. ———, 'Sub-sector Study Reports of Karnataka', GOK, 2001.
91. - Smt. Krishnamurthy, Lakshmi, (Ed.), *Education and Child Development.*
92. - Sri. Bhaskar, Vijay, (Ed.), *Elementary Education.*
93. - *Secondary and P U Education,* (Ed.), Sri. K.P. Surendranath, IAS.
94. - Prof. Jayalakshmi, T.K., (Ed.), *Teacher Education,* RV Consortium.
95. - Dr Narayana, M.R., (Ed.), *Collegiate Education.*
96. - Dr Kanbargi, Ramesh, (Ed.), *Education and Equity.*
97. - Dr Seetharamu, A.R., (Ed.), *Structure and Functions of Educational Management and Decentralization,* ISEC.
98. - Prof. Prasad, S.N., (Ed.), *Role of Private Sector in Education.*

99. 'Kerala Education Act', Government of Kerala, 1958.
100. 'Human Development Report', Government of Madhya Pradesh, 1997.
101. Shah, Harit & Agrawal, Sulabh, *India Educating,* Education Sector Report, Angel Broking, 2008.
102. 'A Survey Report on Rural Schools', *Public and Private Schools in India*, Harvard University, 2003.
103. Hom Chaudhuri' S., *EFA in Mizoram. The Dynamics of Success.*
104. Health Watch Trust, *'The Community Need' Based Reproductive and Child Health in India: Progress, and Constraints*, Jaipur, 1999.
105. Dr Humayun, Kabir, *Education in New India*, 1956.
106. 'Evaluation of DIETs in Karnataka,' Institute for Social and Economic Change, Bangalore, 2001.
107. 'IIM Studies on DPEP', 2001-02.
108. Parikh, Kirit and Radhakrishna, R., (Ed.), *'India Development Report 2002'* Indira Gandhi Institute of Development Research, Oxford University Press, Mumbai, 2002.
109. Rao, Jagannatha, D., *A Comprehensive Study of the Progress of Education in Karnataka*, UBS Publishers' Distributors, New Delhi, 2009.
110. Manor, James, *Madhya Pradesh's Experiments with Direct Democracy*, 3 March, 2001.
111. James, K.S., Aitken, Iain W. and Subramaniam, S.V., *Neo Natal Mortality in India: Emerging Paradoxes*, Harvard University, 2000.
112. Alam, Javeed, 'What is Happening Inside Indian Democracy?', *Economic and Political Weekly*, 11 September, 1999.
113. Dreze, Jean and Goyal, Aparajita, *The Future of Midday Meals*, Centre for Equity Studies, 2003.
114. ————, and Deaton, Angus, 'Poverty and Inequality in India', *Economic and Political Weekly*, 7 September, 2002.
115. Sachs, Jeffrey D., Varshney, Ashutosh, Bajpai, Nirupam, (Ed.), *India in the Era of Economic Reforms*, OUP, 1999.
116. Harriss, John, *Globalization and the World's Poor: Institutions, Inequality and Justice*, June, 2001.
117. Jain, Jyotsna and Shah, Mihir, 'Midday Meal in MP', Samaj Pragati Sahayog, 2005.
118. ————, Saxena, K.B.C. and Baxi, C.V., *Management Practices in Elementary Education: A Study of the Existing Practices in Selected States in India*, The European Commission, 2001.
119. ————, 'Education Guarantee Scheme and Alternative Schooling Community Based Initiatives in Primary Education in Madhya Pradesh', 2000.
120. 'Survey and Study of Current Status of Selected D.Ed. Colleges in Karnataka', Karnataka Education Network, 2009.
121. Bhatty, Kiran, 'Educational Deprivation in India: A Survey of Field Investigations, *Economic and Political Weekly*, 11 July, 1998.

122. Kumar, Krishna, et.al., 'DPEP and Primary Education in India', *Economic and Political Weekly*, 17 February, 2001.
123. ———, *Political Agenda of Education*, Sage, 1991.
124. ———, *Social Character of Learning*, Sage, 1998.
125. ———, *What is Worth Teaching*, Orient Longman, 1997.
126. Sangari, Kumkum and Chakravarti, Uma, (Ed.), *Essays on Gender*, Manohar and IIAS Shimla, 1999.
127. Kurian, N.J., 'Widening Regional Disparities in India: Some Indicators', *Economic and Political Weekly*, 12 February, 2000.
128. Lieten, G.K. and Srivastava, Ravi, *Unequal Partners: Power Relations, Devolution and Development in Uttar Pradesh*, Sage Publishers, 1999.
129. Karlekar, Malavika, (Ed.), *Reading the World: Understanding the Literacy Campaigns in India*, Asian South Pacific Bureau of Adult Education, 2000.
130. Mathew, E.T., 'Growth of Literacy in Kerala', *Economic and Political Weekly*, 25 September, 1999.
131. Ahluwalia, Montek Singh, 'State Level Performance under Economic Reforms in India', 2001.
132. Eswaran, Mukesh and Kotwal, Ashok, *Why Poverty Persists in India*, OUP, 1994.
133. Weiner, Myron, 'The Child and the State in India', *Child Labour and Education Policy in Comparative Perspective*, Princeton University Press, 1991.
134. Narayana, M.R., 'Budgetary Subsidies to Higher Education: Evidence from Karnataka State'.
135. 'Concurrent National Evaluation of Integrated Child Development Services', National Council of Applied Economic Research, 2001.
136. 'National Family Health Survey Reports'.
137. National Curriculum Frameworks', NCERT.
138. 'Minimum Levels of Learning at Primary Stage', Report of the Committee set up by MHRD, NCERT, 1991.
139. 'Learning Achievement of Students at the End of Class 5', NCERT, 2005.
140. 'All India Education Surveys', NCERT.
141. 'Teacher Education Curriculum Frameworks', NCTE.
142. Burra, Neera, *Born to Work – Child Labour in India*, Oxford University Press, 1997.
143. Newspaper Articles on Current Issues in Elementary Education in India'.
144. 'Karnataka's Elementary Education System', Summary Report, NIAS, 2006.
145. Aggarwal, Yash, 'Primary Education in Delhi', *How much do the Children Learn*?', NIEPA, 2000.
146. ———, Universal Access and Retention, DPEP 2002 Report Cards, NIEPA.
147. 'Elementary Education in India', NIEPA, 2003.
148. Juneja, Nalini, 'Constitutional Amendments to make Education a Fundamental Right', NIEPA, 2003.

149. 'Survey Reports', NSSO.
150. 'Report of the CABE Committee on Universalization of Secondary Education, NUEPA, 2006.
151. Panchamukhi, P. R., 'Social Impact of Economic Reforms in India: A Critical Appraisal', *Economic and Political Weekly*, 4 March, 2000.
152. Jha, Praveen, Das, Subrata, Mohanty, Siba Shankar, Jha, Nadan Kumar, '*Public Provisioning for Elementary Education in India*', Sage Publications, 2008.
153. 'Public Report on Basic Education in India', Probe Survey, 1996.
154. *Public Report on Basic Education*, Oxford University Press, 1999.
155. Price Waterhouse Coopers, 'Position Paper on School Education' in Karnataka', 2006.
156. Price Waterhouse Coopers, 'Organization Reengineering Study', Karnataka, 2006.
157. *Public Report on Basic Education in India*, Oxford University Press, New Delhi, 1999.
158. Radhakrishnan, P. and Akhila, R., 'Progress Towards Education for All: The Case of Tamil Nadu'.
159. Naik, Rama, 'Report on Akshara Dasoha Scheme of Karnataka' University of Dharwar, 2005.
160. Radhakrishna, R., (Ed.), '*India Development Report, 2008*', Oxford University Press.
161. Ramanathan, G., *The Quest for General Education*, 1968.
162. Rammohan, K.T., 'Assessing Reassessment of Kerala Model', *Economic and Political Weekly*, April 8-14, 2000.
163. Muralidharan, Rajalakshmi and Kaul, Venita, '*Early Childhood Care and Education: Status and Problems*'.
164. 'Report of the CABE Committee on Free and Compulsory Education Bill', June 2005.
165. 'Report on the 'Status of Learning Achievements in India', A Paper by Azim Premji Foundation, 2004.
166. 'Reports of the National Commission of Teachers'.
167. Mukherjee, Rohan, 'Policy Reforms in Primary Education', Centre for Policy Research, 1985-2005.
168. Seshadri, C., *Primary Teacher Training in the EFA Decade.*
169. Seetharamu, A.S., *Status of Elementary Teachers in India.*
170. Shukla, et.al., *Attainments of Primary School Children in Various States*, NCERT, New Delhi, 1994.
171. Jain, Sharada, *Children, Work and Education: Rethinking on Out-of-school Children.*
172. Srivastava, A.B.L., 'Learning Achievement at the End of Primary Cycle in DPEP States', Paper presented at the National Conference on Enhancing Learning in Elementary Schools, 2004.

173. Mukhopadhyay, Sudesh and Mani, M.N.G., *Education of Children with Special Needs.*
174. Sujatha, K., *Education among Tribals.*
175. Chowdhury, Sumitra, 'Universal Elementary Education in Rajasthan: A Study with Focus on Innovative Strategies'.
176. Sundaram, K., 'Employment-Unemployment Situation in the Nineties: Some Results from NSS 55th Round Survey', *Economic and Political Weekly,* 17 March, 2001.
177. Supreme Court of India, 'Judgment in Balaji Case', 1963.
178. ———, Judgment in 'Bandhua Mukti Morcha Case'.
179. ———, Judgment in 'Unnikrishnan & others vs State of Andhra Pradesh', 1993.
180. ———, Judgment in 'TMA Pai Foundation & others vs State of Karnataka', 2002.
181. ———, Judgment in 'Islamic Academy vs State of Karnataka', 2003.
182. ———, Judgment in 'P.A. Inamdar vs State of Maharashtra', 2005.
183. Ghosh, Suresh Chandra, *The History of Education in Modern India,* 1757-1998.
184. 'Human Development Reports', UNDP, 2005, 2006, 2007, 2008.
185. 'Education for All: Framework of Action', Global Conference on Education, UNESCO, 2000.
186. Prof. Mathur, Beena, *Situation Analysis of Midday Meal Programme in Rajasthan*, University of Rajasthan and UNICEF, 2005.
187. Nayar, Usha, *Education of Girls in India: An Assessment*'.
188. Chakrabarty, Vandana, 'Education of the Urban Disadvantaged'.
189. Vaidyanathan, A. and Nair, P.R. Gopinathan, (Ed.), *Elementary Education in Rural India: A Grassroots View*, Sage Publishers, 2001.
190. Ramachandran, Vimala, *Backward and Forward Linkages Case Studies in Primary Education,* Research Supported by DFID India, 2001.
191. ———, 'Community Participation in Primary Education: Innovations in Rajasthan', *Economic and Political Weekly*, 23 June, 2001.
192. ———, et.al., *Bridging the Gap Between Intention and Action: Girls' and Women's Education in South Asia*, 1998.
193. ———, *Gender and Social Equity in Primary Education*, The European Commission, 2002.
194. 'Voluntary Health Association of India: Report of the Independent Commission on Health in India', 1997.
195. Soubbotina, Tatyana P. and Sheram, Katherine, A., *Beyond Economic Growth, World Bank*, 2000.
196. ———, 'Employment Opportunities in Labour Market vis a vis Education in Karnataka', 2002.

197. ———, 'Expanding and Improving Upper Primary Education in India', Report No. 20347.
198. ———, 'Financing Education in the Context of Economic Restructuring Karnataka', 2002.
199. ———, 'Factors that Facilitate/Impede Successful Primary School Completion: A Quantitative Study Educational Resource Unit, 2003.
200. ———, Community Participation in Education: What Do We Know?', 1999.
201. ———, 'Teacher Absence in India: A Report', 2004.
202. Fernando, Reimers, 'Quality Education for All', A Paper for the World Bank Institute.
203. Forster, Margaret, Masters, Geoff and Rowe, Ken, 'Managing Learning Outcomes', A Paper for the World Bank Institute.
204. ———, Beatrice, 'Teachers at the Heart of the System', A Paper for the World Bank Institute.
205. ———, 'India's Future Health Systems', Issues and Options (Draft), 2001.
206. ———, *Primary Education in India*, 1997.
207. ———, *Reducing Poverty in India: Options for More Effective Public Services*, 1998.
208. ———, Dr Bashir, Sajitha, *Government Expenditure on Elementary Education in the Nineties*, 2000.
209. ———, 'Reports of Joint Review Missions'.
210. Yadav, M.S. and Bharadwaj, Meenakshi, 'Learning Conditions for Primary Education: A Review'.

TOWARDS GENDER EQUALITY

India's Experience

TOWARDS GENDER EQUALITY

India's Experience

Editors

Prof. N. Linga Murthy

Prof. T. Jyothi Rani

Prof. G. Rajaiah

Prof. K.V. Narayana

Prof. Mohd. Iqbal Ali

Prof. T. Papi Reddy

SERIALS PUBLICATIONS

NEW DELHI

First Published - 2007

ISBN : 81-8387-084-8

Published by

SERIALS PUBLICATIONS
4830/24, Prahlad Street, Ansari Road
Darya Ganj, New Delhi-110002 (India)
Phone : 23245225. Fax : 91-11-23272135
E-mail: serials@satyam.net.in

Contents

PART - V
GENDER EQUALITY

Preface

Economic Development is expected to show a positive impact on women's control over resources and their participation in decision-making and this has initiated great interest in empowerment studies. Researchers, Policy Makers, Feminist Scholars, Activists, Administrators, Politicians, Bureaucrats, Sociologists, Economists, Anthropologists, Intellectuals, Non-Governmental Organisations (NGOs) and International Institutions, such as the United Nations, etc., have been examining the impact of development on the status of women in general and developing countries in particular. Many of them are inspired by Easter Boserup's path breaking study on "Women's Role in Economic Development" published in the year 1970. Most of the studies conducted by them address the problems of gender discrimination that is beset with the process of development. In the light of this backdrop, the collection of essays in this volume made an attempt to examine the national policies and ideologies which often declared their commitment towards the attainment of gender equality. Though, this book does not seek to offer a definition or meaning of empowerment that will be effective and applicable globally, it speaks about the approach to "Moving towards Gender Equality" at the national and regional levels and further this volume tries to highlight the different implications of empowerment of women in the specific context of development and social change. This volume is divided into five sections. Section-I deals with Women's Status, Section-II with Women's Education, Section-III with Women's Employment, Section-IV with Women's Health and the last and the fifth section deals with Gender Equality. This volume is the outcome of the Two-Day National Seminar conducted in the Department of Economics of Kakatiya University, Warangal, Andhra Pradesh.

Smt. K. Rama Devi in her Keynote Address to the seminar stated that the very essence of Gender equality lies in women being given the same rights as men. She felt that the empowered women socially, economically and politically would add to economic growth and overall development which would in turn bring in more women into the fold of better opportunities and more choices. The process is on, but the pace differs from one state to another state. While analysing it, she cited many success stories of women like M.S. Subbalaxmi, Mangeshkar Sisters, Yamini Krishnamurthy, Kiran Bedi, Bachendri Paul, P.T. Usha, Kalpana Chawla, Karanam Malleshwari and Sania Mirza etc. She opined that what women want is "Emotional Freedom"–the freedom to dream and carve out their future for themselves. If this opportunity is given, they will prove their mettle and will reach higher and higher pinnacles of glory and also to an equal world as well.

SECTION – I: WOMEN'S STATUS

B. Ratna Kumari and A. Rajani in their paper on the "Impact of Women in Governance in BIMSTEC–Changes and Dynamics in the Political Policy", highlighted the importance of gender mainstreaming in governance and women' participation in governance. Further, the authors identified the barriers and constraints for the effective participation of women elected representatives and also suggested some policy implications for their effective participation in governance. Political participation alone does not empower women totally. It needs to be all encompassing according to them. They were of the opinion that the external inputs will help in creating the necessary socio-political environment that will facilitate the women to emerge confident and perform their roles to the optimum level possible.

The paper written by S. Radhakrishna and K. Madhava Rao, analysed the violence against women, more particularly, the domestic or familial violence which is gradually increasing in Andhra Pradesh. The phenomenon of continued violence on the respondents had adverse multiple consequences. It was ranging from acute tension and anxiety, lowering the self-esteem and nervous breakdown to internalisation of shame and guilty. The need of the hour is the conscious classification of wife-beating as an intrinsic and integral part of violation of human rights. The authors felt that creating awareness and enhancing women empowerment by building the social capital in rural areas is yet another area to be concentrated to reduce the domestic violence in our society. They want public services to be more accessible to women.

G. Satyanarayana, M. Reddi Ramu and K. Krishna Reddy's paper on the "Role of Women-A Study of Rural Women Headed Households" made it clear that the services rendered by Madanapalli urban centre and institutional contact of the rural women headed household respondents seemed to be encouraging in improving their living conditions. They observed that a few of the women headed households could effectively check their husbands indulgence in drinking and gambling habits which improved the saving levels and ploughing back of these savings into investments resulting in income-yielding assets among the sample women headed households. The authors feel that if this trend continues for a considerable.

M.E. Swamy & M. Ashok Kumar's paper on "The Status of Women in Rural Areas in the Post-Independent India" has highlighted the problems of rural Dalit women whose problems are more complicated and subject to ignorance and illiteracy. He is of the view that Dalit women's life pattern itself speaks volumes on Dalitism. Dalit Women have all the capacity, power and potential to govern the world but they are denied of the opportunity to realize and express their potentials. The liberation of Dalit women will take place when they organize themselves and fight for their rights.

N.M. Das and S. Vidya Sagar in their paper on "Practical Utility of Gender Study" observed that gender inequality is a global phenomenon. It differs from place to place, country to country depending upon the level of socio-economic indicators. Empowerment of women is not only the duty of the government but every one in the society. P. Sammulal, A. Hari Prasad and P. Ramlal in their paper expressed that the patriarchal values and normative structure established some two thousand years ago hindered women's emancipation and empowerment in general and tribal women in particular.

In their paper on "Muslim Women in India, Problems and Prospects" N.T.K. Naik, Mansoor Rahman and H. Akthar Banu analysed the status of muslim women who are more backward educationally when compared to the women of other communities. According to the 1991 Govt. of India Census, there are over 48 million Muslims in India. They face multifaceted problems and issues which are to be analysed in a proper perspective.

E. Revathi and Burra Ramulu's paper on "Agrarian Distress, Farmers' Suicides and Gender Vulnerability" explored the vulnerability of the women in the deceased farmers' households with the help of select case studies in Warangal district of Andhra Pradesh. They observed that the Farmers' suicides make the household vulnerable to a host of issues. Women from suicide affected households suffer shocks that erode self and alter the self in drastic ways. They have suffered in silence for months and years. Despite such suffering they have entered into new roles with new capabilities and new challenges without much worldly knowledge.

Overall, the papers felt that there is a need to empower women for enhancing their socio-economic status in our country.

SECTION - II: WOMEN'S EDUCATION

T. Jyothi Rani & K. Katyayani in their article made an attempt to examine the gap between policy goals and achievement in connection with women's education since the British rule till today. Despite constituting various committees on the one hand and constitutional guarantees on the other, women's education is still at low levels. Further, they had also discussed the denial of various dimensions of Human Development to Women. They pleaded for some more committed efforts for widening the accessibility of education to women.

C. Sivaramakrishna Rao, N. Linga Murthy & K. Mohan Reddy, in their paepr on "Women vis-à-vis Higher Education: An Analytical Note", highlighted the gender disparity at various levels of education in India. They are of the opinion that, during the last three decades, the gender disparity at various levels of education in India has declined but it still needs to be further reduced. The authors are of the view that there is an imminent need to disseminate the information on the kind of courses they should take at the higher secondary level which will enable them to enter into the portals of higher education courses having more employment potential.

The paper on 'Education of Girls in India' by M. Rukmini, C.V. Naidu and S. Ratnakumari felt that though significant progress has been made in providing of education for all girls, the task is not yet completed. To attain it, they made a mention of the aspects like special focus on enrolment and retention of SC, ST and OBC girls in the educational institutions.

The paper written by S. Vidya Sagar & K. Manuja Devi made an attempt to examine the Gender disparities in the spheres of education and employment. They are of the opinion that the rural women suffer from the increased insecurity of both income and employment in the globalisation era and further they felt that women education is not so much encouraging in India.

Gulam Rabbani and Kunati Rajireddy in their paper on "Analysis of Gender inequality in Literacy Rates-A Study in Andhra Pradesh" primarily discussed the literacy levels in Andhra Pradesh in general and gender wise literacy rates in various districts of Andhra Pradesh in particular with special reference to 1991 and 2001 census. They observed that the rate of literacy increased to 60.47 per cent in 2001 from 44 per cent in 1991. Both and female literacy rates were shown as increased in 2001 over 1991. Though, it is significant but it is not upto the expectations. They want the voluntary organizations also apart from the government to play a key role in improving women literacy.

Vijaya Laxmi Pandit in her paper on "Girls Education in India –A Development Imperative" examined that the main reason for the multi-dimensional nature of the problem of gender inequality it is due to lack of education, skills and economic freedom to women. She wants the involvement of all agencies in eradication illiteracy and gender in equality.

In his paper on "Promoting Gender Equality through Education in the Indian Context" Mohamed Khaiser Ahmed analysed the status of women's education in India and identified the causes for the low level of education despite the significance of women's education for the attainment of development in general and women in particular.

V. Sreedevi and D. Usha Rani, in their paper discussed the perceptions of college going Adolescent Girls regarding various reproductive health issues. They opined that girls should be given health and family life education to help them understand about their bodily functions, menstrual cycle, marital behaviour, personal hygiene, importance of vaccination and preventive medicines etc. Girls should be given informative lectures and training with regard to family life, education, contraception, family size, values, childcare etc., for a quality life and happy civil society. This will also lead to improved human relations in society.

D. Pulla Rao in his paper on "Gender Inequality in Literacy Rates and Education in India analysed the gender inequalities in relation to literacy rates and education in India. He highlighted that they are not given equal opportunities either in education or in employment and hence they are left far behind their male counterparts in almost all fields of life. The overall rate of growth of women employment was recorded less than one per cent during the period 1993-94 to 1999-2000.

Overall, the papers felt that there is a need for increased efforts on expanding education among women in our country.

SECTION – III: WOMEN'S EMPLOYMENT

In their paper on "Gender-wise Labour Absorption in Agriculture –An Empirical Analysis" T. Papi Reddy, G. Mallikarjun and Mohd. Iqbal Ali examined the gender-wise labour absorption in SRSP area in the case of Paddy crop. Their study has thrown light on the gender-wise labour absorption in number of operations involved such as preparation and ploughing of fields, sowing, weeding, applying fertilizers, harvesting and stacking, threshing and winnowing and transporting. They are of the view that gender-wise labour absorption in the commercial crops like cotton is quite distinct as male labourers are preferred in certain operations and female labourers in others and infact this tendency is observed in all the areas under the major irrigation projects of Andhra Pradesh.

K. Padma Latha, in her paper on "Empowerment of Women through Employment–A Review" tried to present a concrete picture of employment status of women in India. She also reviewed the governmental policies under five year policies and their impact on women employment. According to her, the success of our planning process has to be judged only when gender equality is fully achieved.

Gulam Rabbani and M. Ramesh Reddy in their paper on "Gender Disparities in Workforce Participation Rates–A Study in Andhra Pradesh" analysed the availability and utilization of female and male labor workforce participation in Andhra Pradesh. They were of the view that male participation is predominantly high in the total workforce when compared to that of female work participation.

G. Sreedhar in his paper on the "Impact of SHGs on Livelihoods, Income and Household Assets: A Study in Karnataka" analysed the impact of SHGs on various aspects especially, livelihoods, income and household assets. He is of the opinion that the SHG members were better placed when compared to non-members in terms of livelihood sources, income and possession of consumable household assets, even though both had more or less similar socio-economic characteristics. Because the savings habit and access to credit enabled the SHG members to diversify their occupational base and contributed to relatively more secured income when compared to non-members who did not have access to such benefits.

Sita Vanka and N. Linga Murthy in their paper made an attempt to highlight the trends in women entrepreneurship from economic, business and sociological perspectives in general and from a research perspective in particular. To them, there exists an enormous potential for research in women entrepreneurship in the context of liberalization, privatization and globalization to attain gender equality.

In a paper on "Gender Discrimination in Agricultural Wages: A Case Study in Kurnool District of Andhra Pradesh", I. Narendra Kumar, V.K. Reddy and G. Chandrasekhar Rao made an attempt to examine the gender discrimination on the basis of prevalence of male-female wage differentials in agricultural sector. They are of the opinion that the gender based wage differentials are not uniform and vary according to the nature of agricultural operations as well as the regions.

A. Venkateshwarlu and Y. Venkateshwar Rao in their paper on "Gender Inequalities among Marginal Farmer-cum-Agricultural Labour Households–A Study of two villages in Khammam District" examined the gender inequalities and biases. They also analysed by taking the parameters such as duration and nature of work, age of marriage, age at first delivery, decision about family planning operations, gender preferences and educational opportunities, contribution of female income and decision making and gender inequalities in other areas. They suggested that the government should come forward with different schemes to improve the conditions of females.

In their paper on "Gender Equality and Watershed Programmes", K. Ramanuja Rao and M. Narasimha Rao analysed gender equality and watershed programmes in India. They are of the view that Watershed Programmes in India have provided significant platform for women to participate, involve and also to make decision in natural resource management. The women are participating actively in watershed programme because of its combination such as drinking water, fodder development, fire wood and rearing of livestock etc., Most of these sectors are manned by women. They are experiencing immediate results because of their participation and decision making in such programmes. But it is not uniform in all the study villages.

C. Swarajyalakshmi in her paper on "Working Women in the Organised Industrial Sector" analysed the problems of working women which are interwoven with a number of intricate socio-economic and cultural problems in a country, apart from the traditional set up, habits, conventions, philosophy of life and the approaches to various problems facing the society. Hence, the problems of working women are of multi-dimensional in character. It is only a multipronged attack on the problems than can help the working women to come out of the several ills, woes from which the working women are suffering. She is of the opinion that every conceivable effort shall be made to treat them on par with men and strive for their overall prosperity and happiness.

In a paper on the "Role of Micro Finance & Changing Socio-Economic Conditions of Women" K. Harathi primarily made an attempt to study the role of Micro finance through various Central Government sponsored poverty alleviation and self-employment schemes for the reduction of women poverty. Further, her study had also analysed the impact of the Micro finance on the women, especially, in the empowerment process in Khammam district of Andhra Pradesh.

In sum all the above papers emphasized on the need to enhance employment opportunities to move towards gender equality.

SECTION – IV: WOMEN'S HEALTH

In a paper on "Prevalence of Chronic Energy Deficiency and Obesity among Rural Women–An Analysis of Nutrient Intakes in Relation to Plane of Nutrition", D.L. Kusuma and B. Babita examined the prevalence of Chronic Energy Deficiency and obesity among rural women. They observed that the nutrient intake of Chronic Energy Deficiency women showed groups inadequacies and those of normal and obese were satisfactory for some nutrients. Comparison of nutrient intakes with the reference values showed per cent deficits of varying order in all the three states viz., Chronic Energy Deficiency, Obese and the Normal.

D. Usha Rani and V. Sreedevi in their paper made an attempt to examine the perceptions of adolescent girls regarding menarche and related problems. The study was undertaken in various colleges of Chittoor district of Andhra Pradesh. The respondents were girls aged in between 17-20 years. Totally 200 girls, 100 from Junior Colleges and 100 from Degree Colleges in Chittoor were selected using random sampling technique. The authors are of the view that information and knowledge about menstrual cycle, its associated problems and natural process should be given to adolescent girls before menarche itself. This would ensure good physical and mental health to the girls.

The paper on "Nutritional Status and Dietary Profile of Married Pregnant Adolescent Girls and Young Women", was presented by Baby Depur and G. Nagamani, where in they assessed the nutritional status of adolescent rural girls, married pregnant, (n =25), married non pregnant(n=25), and pregnant young women (n=25), non pregnant young women (n=25) aged between 15 to 21 years belonging to rural and rural scheduled caste communities ofTirupati Rural Mandal of Chittoor District (A.P.). The findings of the study revealed that all the girls and young women were far below the ICMR standards for their heights and weights. Teenage pregnant mothers recorded poor weight gain than pregnant young women in 1st, 2nd and 3rd trimester indicating poor foetal growth. The dietary intakes of girls were below the ICMR's recommended dietary allowances. Adolescent married pregnant girls are worst affected. All the subjects are suffering from anaemia, had low levels of haemoglobin less than 12gm/dl. Thus, the results call for an urgent need to initiate intervention programmes and educate rural girls and mothers regarding consequences of early marriage followed by early pregnancy and maternity. Special programmes are necessary for girls in the deprived sections belonging to scheduled castes and tribes.

A paper on "Mainstreaming Gender in Health, Nutrition & Population Stabilization", presented by Padma analysed the holistic state of well-being in consonance with the psychological and social facts with which an analysis of health must go beyond male and female bodies to the institutions, traditions and attitudes that play a crucial role in determining quality of care, and the root cause of poor health. She is of the opinion that Gender plays an important and irrefutable role in life expectancy of women.

Overall, the paper writers felt that there is a need to educate women about their poor health status for improvement of not only their health conditions but also their children who are going to be the active citizens of our country.

SECTION – V: GENDER EQUALITY

A paper on "Empowerment ofWomen and Moving towards Equality –Some Conceptual Issues" was presented by C. Siva Rama Krishna Rao, N. Linga Murthy and K. Mohan Reddy. While analysing the many facets and conceptual issues saddled with the empowerment of women, they were of the view that a woman has the right to be first recognised as a human being before various roles are expected of her in the domestic and public arenas. For this to happen, everyday patterns of gender discrimination that are usually accepted justified as socially legitimate have to be questioned and placed at a centre stage. In the context of the values of democracy and existing discriminatory social norms, feminist ideology should attempt to change current understandings of power and empowerment in such a manner that men are not isolated from the processes leading to equality. There is immense advantage to be gained by both men and women where gender discrimination is effectively countered. Though, this process will take some time for realisation, it is the same pattern for moving towards equality.

B. Ratna Kumari, Tara Kumari and A. Rajani in their paper on "Gender Equality: New Opportunities for Moving Ahead", felt that to influence policy discussions at the local and international levels, women's groups and other NGOs need to become familiar with the Millennium Development Groups (MDC) process and with key international legal instruments and other agreements that commit Governments to action.

The paper of D. Srilatha and B. Sambasiva Rao examined the girl child discrimination in terms of literacy in the two villages of Guntur district in the state of Andhra Pradesh. Their analysis clearly revealed that in the case of age at marriage, the parents perform early marriages to girls compared to boys in all the social groups. Further, they had also observed that the parents are paying much attention to complete the marriage of their daughters before the age of 18 in order to relieve their burden. So, the girl is considered to be a burden to the family in all the groups of people in the study villages.

A. Rajani in her paper examined the causative factors and the implications of declining child sex ratio in Andhra Pradesh. She is of the opinion that the decline in juvenile sex ratio in less developed districts ofTelangana could be due to the higher incidence of poverty and illiteracy which leads to higher child mortality rate, particularly, among female children. Since low overall sex ratio is leading to the low juvenile sex ratio, it implies that children are moving out along with their parents for better employment and other economic opportunities.

P. Tara Kumari and Vijay Prakash in their paper throws light on many ramifications pertaining to the Gender Related Development Index and Gender Empowerment Measure in relation to India and also ASEAN region as well. They felt that India is lagging behind ASEAN region in both GDI & GEM. By improving health facility, life expectancy can be improved and the gross female tertiary involvement is relatively low in India as well as in the ASEAN region. Hence, steps should be taken to improve this by increasing the employment opportunities and through self employment programmes employment of women can be increased. P. Leela's paper analysed the question of gender equality in SAARC countries on the basis of Gender Related Development Index, Gender Empowerment Resources, Gender Inequality in education, economic activity and political participation. Inter-country variations can be found in regard to various aspects of gender equality.

A paper by M. Pushpa Latha and B. Sudhakar examined the gender inequalities pertaining to the working women both at domestic and work place as well. They pointed out that the violence against women at domestic level and at work place have to be removed by creating awareness among the women to fight against the guilty. The phenomenon of acceptance of unequal gender roles are relatively less among educated working women when compared to illiterates in terms of preference for son, personal level decision making and violent physical behaviour of the husbands. The teacher women respondents are a bit more empowered when compared to the nurse women respondents.

S. Vijaya Kuamr in his paper on "Gender Equality through Empowerment of Women in India", stated that there still exists a wide gap between the goals enunciated in the Constitution, legislation, policies, plans, programmes and related mechanisms on the one hand and the situational reality of the status of women in India on the other.

K. Narasimhulu's paper on "Gender Discrimination in India", has thrown light on the status of girl child in India on the basis of sex ratio, infant mortality rate and health status determined by the availability of nutrition levels. The people's perception towards girl child which is rooted in patriarchy is the cause of her low status in our society according to him. Hence, he felt that this situation required immediate attention.

V.V. Reddy and G. Bhaskar in their paper examined the Gender Inequalities in India in retrospect and prospect. They were of the opinion that the Gender Inequality is not a new phenomenon as such and moreover its origin goes back to the emergence of the institutions of the marriages and family. The paper makes an attempt to examine the evolution of present marriage system and family. It observes that the patriarchal family system based on gender inequality did not undergo any change in live with the movement of socio-economic formation from one stage to another. The paper further tries to identify the obstacles for the attainment of gender equality.

The paper of Vijaya Chandra Tenneti and T. Yadagiri Rao highlighted the important dimensions relating to the problems of women and women as victims of crime etc. The authors made certain constructive suggestions for emancipation and protection of women against crimes and atrocities.

M. Sankara Reddi, M. Chandrayya and M. Sunder Rao in their paper "Gender Dimensions among Adivasis of Eastern Ghats–Sharing the Experience of Jana Chetana, an NGO", examined the various ramifications pertaining to the dimensions of gender issue. They were of the view that gender is all about reconciling growth with equitable distribution of benefits among men and women, equality of power-relations between men and women, and most of all to highlight the interdependence and partnership between men and women in any area of development.

K. Sudhakar and M. Ravinder in their paper observed that government programmes introduced from time to time are slowly creating positive impact on women's status and hence there is a need to introduce more and more government interventions especially at gross root level for enhancing women's empowerment.

This book is a part of the activities of the Special Assistance Programme sanctioned by the UGC, New Delhi to the Department of Economics of our university. I am highly thankful to the paper contributors for helping us in bringing out this book which will be of some help to the researchers and also policy makers in India. We are very much beholden to the authorities of the UGC, New Delhi, for their assistance. Our special thanks are due to our honourable Vice-Chancellor, Prof. V. Gopal Reddy, who is always encouraging our Department and constantly promoting the research activity through generous financial help. We are also thankful to the local UGC Unit, Kakatiya University, Warangal for providing us publication grant towards printing of this book. We would like to thank each author and all the participants of the seminar for sparing their valuable time and effort. We would like to especially thank the teaching, non-teaching and the project fellows and research scholars for their untiring effort and assistance in the successful completion of the seminar in the Department.

Our special thanks are due to "Serials Publications, New Delhi", for taking up the publishing work and bringing out the book neatly within a short span of time. Sincere appreciation to all our colleagues and friends' for their support and encouragement.

If any commissions or omissions are there in the book, we are solely responsible for the same and none else.

—Editors

List of Contributors

K. Rama Devi, President, Association of Lady Entrepreneurs of Andhra Pradesh (ALEAP)

B. Ratna Kumari, Centre for Women's Studies, Andhra University, Visakapatnam, A.P.

A. Rajani, Junior Research Fellow, Centre for Women's Studies, Andhra University, Visakapatnam, A.P.

S. Radhakrishna, Asst. Professor, Department of Economcis, UPGC, Khammam, A.P.

K. Madhava Rao, Lecturer in Economics, SR & BGNR Govt., Degree College, Khammam, A.P.

G. Satyanarayana, Professor of Economics, Sri Krishnadevaraya University, Anantapur, A.P.

M. Reddi Ramu, Research Scholar, Department of Economics, Sri Krishnadevaraya University, Anantapur, A.P.

K. Krishna Reddy, Research Scholar, Department of Economics, Sri Krishnadevaraya University, Anantapur, A.P.

M. Erragattu Swamy, Joint Director, SDLCE, Kakatiya University, Warangal, A.P.

M. Ashok Kumar, Head, Department of Economics, Kakatiya University, Wgl. A.P.

N.M. Das *(Rtd)*, Chief Planning Officer, Warangal, A.P.

S. Vidya Sagar, Project Fellow, UGC (SAP-DRS), Department of Economics, Kakatiya University, Wgl.

P. Sammulal, Associate Professor, Department of Political Science, Kakatiya Univeristy, Warangal, A.P.

A. Hariprasad, Assistant Professor, Univ. Arts & Science College, Kakatiya University, Warangal, A.P.

P. Ramlal, Research Scholar, Department of Commerce and Business Management, KU, Warangal, A.P.

N.T.K. Naik, Associate Professor, Department of Economics, SKU PG Centre, Kurnool.

S. Mansoor Rahman Asst. Professor, Department of Economics, Osmania College (Autonomous), Kurnool, A.P.

H. Akther Banu, Asst. Professor, Department of English, Osmania College of P.G. Courses, Kurnool, A.P.

E. Revathi, Fellow, Centre for Economic and Social Studies, Hyderabad, A.P.

Burra Ramulu, Associate Professor, Department of Economics, KU, Wgl., A.P.

T. Jyothi Rani, Department of Economics, Kakatiya University, Wgl, A.P.

K. Katyayani, Department of Telugu, Kakatiya University, Wgl, A.P.

C. Sivaramakrishna Rao, *(Rtd)*, Department of Economics, Kakatiya University, Wgl, A.P.

N. Linga Murthy, Professor of Economics & Co-Ordinator, UGC (SAP-DRS), Department of Economics, Kakatiya University, Wgl, A.P.

K. Mohan Reddy, Asst. Professor, Department of Economics, UPGC, Karimnagar, A.P.

M. Rukmini, Research Scholar, Department of Economics, Sri Venkateshwara University, Tirupati A.P.

C.V. Naidu, Department of Economics, Sri Venkateshwara University, Tirupati, A.P.

S. Ratnakumari, Department of Economics, Sri Venkateshwara University, Tirupati.

K. Manuja Devi, Department of Economics, Kakatiya University, Wgl, A.P.

Gulam Rabbani, Faculty Member, Department of Economics, Kakatiya University, Wgl, A.P.

Kunati Raji Reddy, Asst. Professor of Commerce, Kakatiya University, UPGC, Karimnagar.

P. Vijayalakshmi Pandit, Dean, Student Affairs, Dr. B.R. Ambedkar Open University, Jubilee Hills, Hyderabad. A.P.

Mohamed Khaiser Ahmed, Lecturer in Economics, Al-Ameen Degree College, Bangalore, Karnataka.

V. Sreedevi, Department of Home Science, S.V. University, Tirupati, A.P.

D. Usha Rani, Director, Centre for Extension Studies, S.V. University, Tirupati, A.P.

D. Pulla Rao, Dept. of Co-operation and Applied Economics, Andhra University, Visakapatnam.

T. Papi Reddy, Head, Department of Economics, Kakatiya University, Wgl. A.P.

G. Mallikarjun, Research Scholar, Department of Economics, Kakatiya University, Wgl. A.P.

Mohd. Iqbal Ali, Department of Economics, Kakatiya University, Wgl. A.P.

K. Padmalatha, Associate Professor, Department of Economics, SDLCE, KU, Wgl, A.P.

G. Sreedhar, Department of Economics, Sri Krishnadevaraya University, Ananthapur, A.P.

Sita Vanka, Associate Professor of Management, University of Hyderabad, Hyderabad.

I. Narendra Kumar, Academic Consultant, Dept. of Econometrics, Sri Venkateshwara University, Tirupati. A.P.

V.K. Reddy, Professor & Head, Department of Econometrics, Sri Venkateshwara University, Tirupati, A.P.

G. Chandrasekar Rao Professor of Economics, Sri Venkateshwara University, Tirupati, A.P.

A. Venkateshwarlu, Lecturer in Economics, SSRJ College, Khammam, A.P.

Y. Venkateshwar Rao, Lecturer in Economics, SSRJ College, Khammam, A.P.

K. Ramanuja Rao, Associate Professor, Department of Sociology, Kakatiya University, Wgl. A.P.

M. Narasimha Rao, Research Scholar, Department of Sociology, Kakatiya University, Wgl. A.P.

C. SWarajyalakshmi, Department of Commerce, Sri Padmavati Women's Degree College, Thirupati.

K. Harathi, Lecturer in Economics, SR & BGNR Govt., Degree College Khammam.

D.L. Kusuma, Associate Professor, Dept. of Home Science, Sri Venkateshwara University, Tirupati, A.P.

B. Babitha, Research Scholar, Dept. of Home Science, Sri Venkateshwara University, Tirupati, A.P.

Baby Depur, Professor & Head (Food Science and Nutrition), Dept. of Home science, Sri Venkateshwara .University, Tirupati, A.P.

G. Nagamani, Research Scholar, Dept. of Home Science, Sri Venkateshwara University, Tirupati, A.P.

Padma, Associate Professor, Department of Law, Kakatiya University, Wgl, A.P.

B. Ratna Kumari, Faculty member in Centre for Women's Studies, Andhra University, Visakapatnam, A.P.

Tara Kumari, Associate Professor, Department of Economics, Andhra University, Visakapatnam, A.P.

D. Srilatha, Research Scholar, Department of Economics, Acharya Nagarjuna University, Nagarjuna Nagar, Guntur, A.P.

B. Sambasiva Rao, Professor of Economics, Acharya Nagarjuna University, Nagarjuna Nagar, Guntur, A.P.

A. Rajani, Centre for Women's Studies,. Andhra University, Visakapatnam, A.P.

P. Tara Kumari, Associate Professor, Department of Economics, Andhra University, Visakapatnam, A.P.

P. Vijaya Prakash, Department of Anthropology, Andhra University, Visakapatnam, A.P.

M. Pushpalatha, Asst. Professor, Department of Economics, UPGC, Khammam, A.P.

B. Sudhakar, Lecturer in Economics, SR&BGNR Gov.t Degree College, Khammam, A.P.

S. Vijaya Kumar, Lecturer in Economics, Govt. Degree College, Huzurabad, A.P.

P. Leela, Department of Applied Economics, Andhra University, Visakapatnam, A.P.

K. Narasimhulu, Department of Economics, Sri Venkateshwara University, Tirupati, A.P.

V. V. Reddy, *(Rtd),* Associate professor, Department of Humanities, NIT, Warangal, A.P.

G. Bhaskar, Associate Professor, Department of Economics, Kakatiya University, Wgl, A.P.

Vijaya Chandra Thenneti, Asst. Professor, Department of Law, Kakatiya University, A.P.

T. Yadagiri Rao, Asst. Professor, Department of Public Administraiton, SDLCE, Kakatiya University, Wgl, A.P.

M. Sankara Reddi, Doctoral Fellow, Andhra University Campus, Srikakulam, A.P.

M. Chandrayya, Department of Rural Development, Andhra University Campus, Srikakulam, A.P.

M. Sunder Rao, Special Officer, Andhra University Campus, Srikakulam, A.P.

K. Sudhakar, Associate Professor of Law, Department of Law, Kakatiya Univeristy, Warangal, A.P.

M. Ravinder, Junior Lecturer in Economics, Vivekananda Junior College, Warangal, A.P.

Editors

Dr. Nagishetty Linga Murthy, *Professor of Economics Co-Ordinator, (SAP-DRS) UGC*

Prof. N.L. Murthy started his career as Lecturer in Economics in 1975 at C.K.M.Degree College and worked there for 5 years. He joined in the university service in January 1981. He did his M.A. (Economics) from Osmania University in 1975, M.Phil from University of Hyderabad in 1980 and got Ph.D. in 1984 from Kakatiya University. He was appointed as Reader in Economics in July 1984 and professor in 1992.

Prof. Murthy guided 18 M.Phil Scholars, 7 Ph.Ds. and had undertaken Four Minor and Two Major Research Projects sanctioned by U.G.C. At present 2 M.Phil and 4 Ph.D Scholars are working under his supervision. He published around 30 papers in national and international journals and published 6 books in English and Telugu. Prof. Murthy has attended several national conferences, Seminars and also international conferences and is working as a resource person to several Universities. He is on the Boards of studies of many Universities. He was the Convener of the prestigious project on "Rural Unrest in Telangana" sanctioned by the National Commission on Rural Labour, Govt. of India.

Apart from academic work, Prof. Murthy has also contributed heavily to the university administration for the last many years. He served as the In-charge, Publication Cell, Head, Department of Economics, Chairman, Board of Studies, Special Officer University P.G.Centre, Khammam, Controller of Examinations and Principal, University College, Director of SDLCE, KU, Wgl. He has visited Hongkong, Singapore and South Africa. Prof. Murthy's Research interest areas are Rural Development, Agricultural and Unorganised Labour and Tribal Problems. He is the life member of many professional associations of Economics. At present he is the Co-ordinator, UGC (SAP-DRS) of the Department of Economics.

Dr. Thota Jyothi Rani, *Professor of Economics*

She joined in the University service as a regular lecturer in March 1978 and promoted as Reader in January, 1986. Subsequently she became professor in November, 1994 she has put in 27 years of teaching experience of which 18 years are at PG level and 9 years at UG level. Her research areas of interest are Women's Studies, Political Economy and Industrial Economics.

She has supervised 6 Ph.Ds and 9 M.Phils and published 10 Books and edited 5 books; she has published 103 articles in various regional and National level journals to her credit and has presented papers in 115 regional, national and international level conferences, seminars and symposia. She has completed and submitted reports of 3 Minor Research projects of UGC and 3 Major Research Project. She acted as Director& Co-Director/ Convenor for 3 UGC sponsored National level seminars and One State Level Seminar. She was the writer of the course material for School of Distance Learning and Continuing Education, Kakatiya University, Warangal and Dr.B.R.Ambedkar Open University, Hyderabad. She wrote lessons on Political economy for M.A. Political Science and on Environmental Economics for M.Sc. Environmental Sciences. She acted as a Resource person for various Refresher / Orientation courses organized by the Department of Economics, Kakatiya University, Osmania University, S.V. University, DRDA, Nehru Yuva Kendram, ICDS, Police Training College, ASC for NGO's, Kakatiya University and University college of Law, Kakatiya University.

She held the position of Head, Department of Economics, Chairperson, Board of Studies in Economics, Principal, University PG.College, Khammam, Chair Person Women's Welfare Committee, Kakatiya University. As a Social activist, she is the Convenor of Society for Women's Studies and Development (SOWSTUD) since 1982. She is a life-member of many Academic Associations.

Dr. G. Rajaiah, *Professor of Economics*

Dr. Rajaiah was appointed as Lecturer at Kakatiya University soon after his M.A. (Economics) from Kakatiya University. After having worked as Lecturer at University, upto 1982, he has gone to Delhi in 1982 as a Teacher Fellow under UGC/CAS fellowship. He has completed M.Phil in 1985 and registered for Ph.D to complete the condition of Residential requirement which was a minimum qualification to submit Ph.D at the Delhi School of Economics (DSE), University of Delhi. He has collected the data for Ph.D under Prof. Dharma Kumar, the former editor EISHR and the CEHI, Vol. 2. He has joined, after the fellowship at the Kakatiya University in 1987 and since then he is working in the University. He became the Head, Department of Economics in 1996 and served as Chairman, Board of Studies during the period 2000-2002.

He has attended many seminars conducted at the Delhi School of Economics (DSE), Institute of Economic Growth (IEG, Delhi) and other UGC funded seminars. He has conducted seminars sanctioned by DRDA and other agencies at Kakatiya University.

He has completed his Ph.D in the year, 2000 from Osmania University and got publication grant from ICHR and is shortly publishing his thesis as book through Himalaya Publishing House, Bombay.

He has published one Monograph, 4 books and about 6 articles. He has produced 8 M.Phils on different topics relating to rural artisans. Dr. Rajaiah's interest areas are Micro Economics, Industrial and Labour Economics.

Dr. Kurapati Venkat Narayana, *Professor of Economics*

Dr. Venkat Naryana obtained Master' Degree in Economics from Osmania University and joined as lecturer in 1981 January at the Kakatiya University service and were promoted as Reader in 1990. He got his Ph.D, in 1985 from Kakatiya University and was promoted as Professor of Economics in 1998. He has guided 7 Ph.Ds. 5 M.Phils and published more than Two-dozen papers in various National reputed Journals.

Dr. Naryana has handled 3 Minor Research Projects and 4 Major Research Projects sponsored by the UGC, Ministry of HRD and Planning Commission, Government of India. A part from academic work, Dr. Narayana has served as the Head, Department of Economics and Programme Coordinator N.S.S unit of the Kakatiya University. His major research interest areas are Labour Economics and Developmental issues of Indian economy. He also worked as the president of Association of Kakatiya University Teachers. He is also an activist working for the cause of development ofTelangana, a backward region in Andhra Pradesh. At present, he is working as the Director, School of Distance Learning and Continuing Education, Kakatiya University.

Dr. Mohd. Iqbal Ali, *Professor of Economics Chairman, Board of Studies in Economics*

Mohd. Iqbal Ali, after graduation from Osmania University (1976), did his Post Graduation and M.Phil with first class from Kakatiya University and University of Hyderabad respectively. Subsequently, he has completed his doctoral work from the Department of Economics, Kakatiya University in 1985 on a topic entitled "Irrigation and Agricultural Development–A study in Sreeram Sagar Project Area".

Dr. Ali has so far guided 9 Ph.D Scholars and Thirteen M.Phils completed 5 Minor and One Major Research Projects. He is the Author of a book and also Co-editor for 3 books. He has published 45 research papers in National-level journals, and participated in 17 State and National-level Conferences/Seminars and Chaired a International Seminar and presented papers. He is a life member of All India Economic association, Regional Science Association and AP Economic Association. Dr. Ali led the Department of Economics of Kakatiya University, Warangal for one and a half year and was the Principal for University Post-Graduate College, Kakatiya University, Subedari, Warangal for 3 Years. Earlier to this, he was the Co-ordinator for Non-teaching training centre for Universities of India, KU, Warangal, for three years. At present, he is the Chairman, Board of Studies of the Department of Economics.

Dr. T. Papi Reddy, *Professor of Economics, Head, Department of Economics*

Prof. Reddy has completed M.A. (Economics) in 1977 and M.Phil in 1981 and Ph.D. in 1988 from Kakatiya University. He joined the Kakatiya University service in 1981. He became Reader in 1992 and Professor in 2000 in Kakatiya University.

Dr. Reddy has published 18 papers in national journals and guided 8 M.Phil scholars and about 6 Ph.D scholars are working at present. He has attended a number of seminars and conferences at state and national levels. He authored two books and contributed articles to many books. He completed 3 minor research projects and one major project is in progress. His areas of research interests are Agrarian Unrest, Rural Problems, Regional Studies and

Development issues. Dr. Reddy has been actively associated with teachers' activities of Kakatiya University for the last twenty years in various capacities. He worked as the Head, Department of Economics, Kakatiya University, Waragnal. He is the member of the most prestigious National Labour Research Institute located at Noida. At present he is working as the Controller of Examinations, Kakatiya Univeristy.

Gender Inequalities in India
–Task Ahead

Keynote Address

K. Rama Devi
President
Association of Leady Entrepreneurs of Andhra Pradesh

As we are here today for the National Seminar on "Moving towards Gender Equality-India's Experience", it is an important occasion for us to ponder over the progress achieved towards gender equality and also the unfinished tasks in this regard.

The Preamble to our Constitution refers to the promise of social justice. Right to equality has been enshrined as a Fundamental Right under Chapter III of the Constitution, which also has a provision for affirmative action in favour of women. Despite these Constitutional provisions, special laws enacted to promote gender justice; the status of women continues to be a cause of concern not only in our country but also in most countries of the world.

Gender inequities throughout the world are among the most pervasive, though deceptively subtle forms of inequality. Gender equality concerns each and every member of the society and forms the very basis of a just society. Human rights issues, which affect women in particular, play a vital role in maintaining the peace and prosperity of a just society.

Today as we stand at the beginning of the 21st century, we are still unable to boast of a society where there is total gender equality or gender equity. Until recently, the question of gender equality or gender equity was merely a topic of theoretical discussion. Things are changing but rather slowly.

At the International level, prohibition against sex discrimination was first articulated in the *United Nations Charter of 1945* and later reiterated in the *Universal Declaration of Human Rights* of 1948. Since then, virtually all human rights instruments have reinforced and extended protections against discrimination. The *International Covenant on Civil and Political Rights* adopted in 1966 guarantees equal protection of the law to both sexes. The *International Covenant on Economic, Social and Cultural Rights* also adopted in 1966 promises women *equality of status*. The *Fourth World Conference on Women,* held at Beijing brought us further forward by reaffirming gender equality as a fundamental pre-requisite for social justice.

Perhaps the most important conceptual advance in the international law of women's rights is the *Convention on the Elimination of All Forms of Discrimination Against Women* (CEDAW), effective 1981, which provides that women be given rights equal to those of men on equal terms. The Preamble of CEDAW maintains that "the full and complete development of a country, the welfare of the world and the cause of peace require the maximum participation of women on equal terms with men in all fields."

In India, "WE THE PEOPLE" gave to ourselves a Constitution, which guarantees justice-social, economic and political. In the matter of equality Article 14 confers on men and women equal rights and opportunities in the political, economic and social spheres. Article 15 prohibits discrimination against any citizen on the grounds of religion, race, caste, sex, etc. Article 15(3) makes a special provision enabling the State to make affirmative discriminations in favour of women. Similarly, Article 16 provides for equality of opportunities in matter of public appointments for all citizens. Article 39(a) lays down that the State shall direct its policy towards securing all citizens, men and women, equally, the right to means of livelihood, while Article 39(c) ensures equal pay for equal work. Article 42 directs the State to make provision for ensuring just and humane conditions of work and maternity relief. Above all, the Constitution imposes a fundamental duty on every citizen through Article 51A(e) to renounce the practices derogatory to the dignity of women. The question, however, is: Have the women been able to reap the benefits provided for them under the Constitution of India? The answer, unfortunately is not encouraging. There is a long way to go to achieve the goals enshrined in the Constitution.

Consider the following statistics:

- Two-thirds of world's adult illiterates are women, who number about half-a-billion adult women.
- 70% of the world's poor are women.
- Women now account for 50% of those infected by HIV worldwide. In Africa that figure is now 58%.

Even at the national level, there are several areas of deep concern

- Sharp decline in juvenile sex ratio
- Continuing high maternal mortality rate and infant mortality rate
- High gender gap in literacy at all levels
- High rate of dropouts of girl students
- Increasing incidence of crime against women

With a view to convert the equality of women from *de jure* to *de facto*, educating the female would play an important role. So long as there is disparity between the male and female in education level, the difference between the position of men and women would continue to exist. It is unfortunately true that a woman has, even in her own home given a rather subordinate role to play.

For the emancipation for women in every field, economic independence is of paramount importance. Along with economic independence, equal emphasis must also to be laid on the total development women—creating awareness among them about their rights and responsibilities—the recognition of their vital role and the work they do at home. If necessary, a social system must evolve. The society must respond and change its attitude.

The Heads of State and Government who gathered at the United Nations Headquarters in New York in September 2000, at the dawn of a new millennium adopted a historic Declaration. They recognized that, in addition to their separate responsibilities to their individual societies, they have a collective responsibility to uphold the principles of human dignity, equality and equity at the global level. They recognized that they had a duty to the world's people, especially the most vulnerable. The Declaration affirmed their respect for human rights and fundamental freedoms and respect for equal rights of all without distinction as to race, sex, language or religion.

The Millennium Declaration asserted that no effort would be spared "to free fellow men, women and children from the abject and dehumanizing conditions of extreme poverty, to which more than a billion of them are currently subjected." They affirmed their commitment to making the right to development a reality for everyone and to freeing the entire human race from want."

Specific targets had been laid down under the categories of 'eradication of extreme poverty and hunger, achieving universal primary education, promotion of gender equality and empowerment of women, reduction of child mortality, improvement of maternal health, combating HIV/AIDS, malaria and other diseases, environmental sustainability and a global partnership for development. All 189 United Nations Member States have pledged to meet the above goals by the year 2015.

Though the enrolment of girl children has been growing at an impressive rate in recent years, yet it is said that there exists a gap of about 20 percentage points between the enrolment of girls and boys, be it in primary, secondary or higher education level. This gender gap in education is unconscionable. Studies have shown how education of a girl child has positive impact on infant mortality, maternal mortality, health and hygiene, productivity. Education is key to empowerment, which in turn is key to achieving other millennium development goals.

Women constitute half of the country's population accounting for 495.7 million as per the 2001 census and represent 48.3 per cent of the population. As a result of the space created for women in the local governance structures with the 73rd and 74th Amendments nearly a million women have gained entry at different levels of the grassroots governance body- the panchayat. The policy of reservation of one-third seats for women in these village level panchayats and urban municipalities, has enabled women to hold elected positions in the three tiers of the panchayati raj institutions (PRIs)—the gram panchayat, panchayat samiti and the Zilla Parishad (at the district HQs).

In keeping with the frequently changing paradigms for social development, that is laying greater stress on gender issues at the global and national level now, moving towards more gender equality is a part of the process of governance in the country. Empowerment and development are two sides of the same coin. The basic objective of development, as defined in the Human Development Report (UNDP) is to enlarge people's choices. It is based on three key components:

- Equality of opportunity for all people in society;
- Sustainability of such opportunity from one generation to the next.
- Empowerment of the people so that they participate in, and benefit from, the development process.

These components have many dimensions. They can be articulated as:

- Equal access to basic social services, including education and health;
- Equal opportunity for participating in political and economic decision-making;
- Equal reward for equal work;
- Equal protection under the law;
- Elimination of discrimination by gender and violence against women;
- Equal rights of citizens in all areas of life, both public—as in workplace—and private—as in the homes. And so on.

For too long it was assumed that as the development process unfolded, benefits would trickle down to all income groups. It was also considered as being gender neutral. But, experience has shown otherwise. Moving towards gender equality is now seen as a political process that calls for a new way of thinking, in which the stereotyping of women and men gives way to the philosophy that all people are essential agents of change.

Investing in women's capabilities and empowering them to exercise choices contributes to economic growth and the overall development in the country.

As a result, the importance of investing in women has gown steadily in every successive five-year-plans of the country. In fact, women form a separate category for planning interventions as they have a direct bearing upon the country's total development. Women who represent 90 per cent in the informal sector have been the backbone of the rural economy, but unfortunately their contribution to the development process has remained invisible.

They are, actually being hit the hardest in the wake of the changing development paradigms, especially of economic liberalisation and globalisation apart from suffering of social backwardness. It is therefore that these women are given priority, requiring special attention in several government programming.

Empowered women adorn several tags of success. In performing arts we have Stalwarts like M.S. Subba Lakshmi, The Mangeshkar Sisters, Yamini Krishnamurthi who brought India's Cultural treasure into Lime light. We have tenacious policewomen Kiran Bedi, Mountaineer Bachendri Pal and a variety of sportswomen from P.T. Usha and Karanam Malleswari to today's teen sensation Sania Mirza. All these women opened up new vistas which were previously dominated by Men. Kalpana Chawla entered the Final frontier of human endeavour, Space in 1997-some sentiment echoed, that Women could soar to the same heights as men. In business we have women such as Naina Lal Kidwani who was recently ranked 3rd among Aisa's Top Business Women by Fortune Magzine and Kiran Mazumdar of Biocon. Social activists like Arundhathi Roy, Madhu Patkar achieved victories to the society. Can we ever forget Mother Teresa?

Agreed that we have taken note worthy strides towards gender equality, we are not quite there. But can we bridge the gap just by getting mere words into policies?

The solution for gender equality is much more complex than just that. As a citizen of India let me remind you our Constitution was drafted by visionaries who had impeccable foresight. No where the Constitution discriminate against women. It is only non implementation of these Laws that has hindered the attainment of gender equality. And it is here we need to concentrate and not on roping more women into political circle.

Another very important issue is the sterotype that exists in the minds of people in society even today regarding the capabilities of women.

Women in South Asia are considered among the poorest people in the World. Gender inequality is considered by UN Experts as the primary cause of persistent poverty and the main reason why many developing countries are off track to meet the UN ambitious 'Millennium Development Goals'.

To conclude the very essence of Gender equality lies in women being given the same rights as men. And the one they most crave for today and the one they have most been denied in the past is not political power, but freedom 'Emotional Freedom'. The freedom to dream and crave out their future for themselves. Now if this freedom is given they may exhibit boundless talent, charisma and leadership qualities. They will prove their mettle and will reach higher pinnacles of glory but to an equal World as well.

Empowered women socially, economically and politically would add to economic growth and overall development this would in turn bring in more women into the fold of better opportunities and more choices. The process is on, but the pace may differ from state to state.

PART - I
Women's Status

1

Impact of Women in Governance in BIMSTEC—Changes and Dynamics in the Political Policy

B. Ratna Kumari and A. Rajani

"One is not born a woman, one becomes a woman. No biological, psychological or economic destiny can determine how the human female will appear in society"

—**Simone de Beauvoir**

INTRODUCTION

The BIMSTEC region is unique in many ways. The diversity of people, languages and religions has resulted in a rich cultural heritage and a complex social texture, which is hard to find elsewhere. Breaking the political glass ceiling for women is a gigantic task in a background of patriarchal and hierarchal value based societies. However, the remarkable and positive development in this modern age is the introduction of women's quotas in politics. Several countries in the region have introduced reserved seats for women in local and district councils or at local governance. Logically bringing women into mainstream of development should be one of the main key issues of millennium development goals. Multiple studies have shown that the majority of women politicians can boast of better records than their male counterparts. Hence there is a need to study the impact, of women in governance in this region and the changes and dynamics of the political policy to enhance women empowerment in political sphere.

OBJECTIVES

The main objectives of the study are:

1. To assess the importance of gender mainstreaming in governance.
2. To analyse the women participation in governance.
3. To study the barriers and constraints for the effective participation of women elected representatives and
4. To suggest some policy implications for their effective participation in governance.

GENDER MAINSTREAMING IN GOVERNANCE

Gender mainstreaming is a process to achieve greater gender equality and overcome the costs of women's marginalization. The South Asian Countries have had a long tradition of local government with similar structures and a wide variety in nomenclature. During the British rule in the region the system underwent a long process of evolution through various structural and legal reforms. Even after gaining independence the process continued in all the countries under study, though at varying paces. Nevertheless, the informal institutions have not totally faded away and there are instances where they hold way over the state, the law and the modern local governance structures. Caste and kinship structures have their own form of community decision making, and are heavily influenced by convention and tradition. Often the functioning of these informal local bodies has proved to be detrimental to the cause of women. On the positive side, one of the major achievements of the women's movement in the region is that some form of quota in local bodies has been introduced in all the countries except Sri Lanka (Damyanty and Vesna, 2004)

South Asia presents us with a paradox; it has more powerful women politicians than any other set of countries in the world. Women have been prime ministers, leaders of major parties, heads of state and regional governments Chandrika Kumaratunga in Sri Lanka, Sonia Gandi in India, Benazir Bhutto in Pakistan and Khaleda zia in Bagladesh are the most famous examples. Yet, overall women's political participation is dismal. The membership of women in the parliaments of these countries has ranged between 6 and 8 per cent during the last few decades. The predominance of women political leaders at the highest level seems to have no implication for even the slightly lowest level of the lowest level, village policies have been in the hands of men, with women confined to domestic duties. Even in the areas of greatest community concern to women, for instance, water and forest management, they have little say. (Gail Omvedt, 2005)

The countries of south Asia have taken steps to remedy this situation. The main method chosen is that of reservation (quotas in electoral bodies). India and Bangladesh since 1993, and Pakistan since 2000 all reserve 33 per cent of the seats in local village governmental institutions for women. At the national level in India, a bill for reserving one third seats for women in parliament has been pending for several years; all major parties have expressed commitment to it and it continues to be debated fiercely though it has not yet been passed.

EMERGENCE OF LEADERSHIP IN THE REGION

Historically and in contemporary times, patriarchy governs the status of women across the region. This is reflected in the gender insides for all the countries in the region. Sri Lanka fares much better than other countries-at-least statistically. Since 1995 UNDP has come out with three indices, viz., the Human Development Index (HDI), Gender Development Index (GDI) and the Gender Empowerment measure (GEM), which measure gender inequality across countries. The HDI measures a country's human development attainment and income. The GDI adjusts the measure of human development for gender equality in terms of the same three components relating to longevity at birth, education, and income. The GEM captures women's access to political, economic and social opportunities. The components captured by these indices are not in any way exhaustive but they do provide a yardstick to measure disparities between men and women in opportunities and achievements in the overall development of various countries.(Damyanty Sridharan, Vesna Rodifc 2005). A comparative gender development index in BIMSTEC region is given in table 1.

The above Table presents the values and rank of HDI, GDI and GEM of South and South East Asia. It can be observed from the Table that Thailand, is leading in HDI and GDI with values of 0.778 (73) and 0774(57) respectively. Sri Lanka occupies the second place in both the HDI and GDI with 0.751 (93) and 0.747 (66) respectively. India's position is far behind with HDI value of 0.602 (127) and GDI value of 0.586 (98). Bangladesh occupies the last position with HDI and GDI values 0.520 (139) and 0.514(105).

Table 1
A Comparative Gender Development Index in BIMSTEC Region

	HDI value	*Rank*	*GDI value*	*Rank*	*GEM value*	*Rank*
Bangladesh	0.520	139	0.514	105	0.218	79
India	0.602	127	0.586	98	0.240 (*)	-
Nepal	0.526	136	0.511	106	-	-
Sri Lanka	0.751	93	0.747	66	0.370	72
South Asia	0.628	-	0.555 (*)	-	0.252	-
Bhutan	0.54	134	-	-	-	-
Philippines	0.654	84	0.755	63	0.526	46
Mynanmar	0.578	129	-	-	-	-
Thailand	0.778	73	0.774	57	0.452	63

Source: UNDP: Human Development Report-2005.
*UNDP Human Development Report-2003.

Gender empowerment measure (GEM) is the latest measure of gender equality interims of political and economic empowerment. For many countries the data are not available. Philippines is leading in this index with a GEM value of 0.526(46) and Thailand occupies the second place with GEM value of 0.452 (63). India's position in 2003 was 0.240 which is one of the lowest values nearer to Bangladesh (0.218).

The data reflects that the necessary condition for gender empowerment is faster economic growth along with HDI. Then only any welfare state will be able to design policies for gender equity and implement them effectively.

WOMEN PARTICIPATION IN GOVERNANCE

After the Second World War, long and enduring nationalist struggles took place, which led to the entire South Asia region emerging independent from colonial rule. Simultaneously, the search for ethnic, linguistic and national identity led to unending strife within and between the nations. The region's countries have been alternating between autocratic regimes, military rule and democratic representations. Further the details of women participation in governance of the region is shown in Table 2.

Table 2
Women's Participation in Governance

Indicators	*Bangla-desh*	*India*	*Pakistan*	*Nepal*	*Sri Lanka*
Women in Parliament					
Upper House (total) 1999	-	20.0	2.0	9.0	-
As % of total	-	8.5	2.3	15.0	-
Lower House (total) 1999	41.0	48.0	6.0	11.0	11.0
As % of total	12.4	8.8	2.8	5.4	4.9
Cabinet (total) 1999	4.0	8.0	3.0	1.0	4.0
As % of total	8.9	10.8	10.3	3.1	12.1
Women in Governance					
Female civil servants (As % of total)	10.4	6.8	5.4	7.7	-
Year women received right to vote	1972	1950	1947	1951	1931
Stand for elections	1972	1950	1947	1951	1931
First elected (E) or nominated (N)	1973 E	1952E	1973E	1952A	1947E
Female Voters					
Total no of registered F voters (millions)	27.96	289.19	25.17	6.85	-
Female voters as % of total	49.29	47.73	44.45	50.74	

Source: Human Development in south Asia 2000, Human Development report 2003.

BANGLADESH

Bangladesh has a unitary and a parliamentary form of government, with the Prime Minister as the chief executive flanked by a Council of Ministers. The Bangladesh constitution provides for a unicameral legislature called the Jatiyo Sangsad (National Assembly/Parliament) comprising 300 seats, members of which are directly elected through adult franchise.

Of the 300 seats in National Parliament, 15 were reserved for women in 1970, which was increased to 30 in 1980. In the 2000 elections, there were 37 women in Parliament, as in addition to the reserved seats, seven women were directly elected. The tenure of reserved seats for women has expired since April 2001 due to a parliamentary boycott by the then opposition, the Bangladesh Nationalist Party. As a consequence, there are currently no reserved seats for women in Parliament. The current six women members (including the Prime Minister and the Leader of the Opposition) have been directly elected. Although both the main political parties are under the leadership of women, this has not resulted in larger participation of women in politics, government or at other decision-making levels. At the local level, since 1997 there is a quota of three seats: one fourth of the total number has been reserved for women in union councils which consists of representatives from several villages. This has increased women's representation to over 20 per cent at this level.

INDIA

In the Indian Constitution there is an emphasis on gender equality which enables the state to undertake special measures for women, when it proclaims under Article 15 that "nothing in this article will prevent the state from making any special provision for women and children. "Under this clause the Government in subsequent years could introduce many policies for women.

The democratic politics in India and the women's movement have always believed that the nature and extent of participation of women in the electoral process are important for women's development. The Constitutional Amendment (73rd and 74th) has provided a chance to one million women to enter into politics at local governance.

NEPAL

There are three seats reserved for women in the upper house. Thus, it appears that women citizens get equal rights in the public domain, but the question is whether they get citizenship in the first place. Citizenship rights are recognized only along patrilineal descent or by marriage to a Nepali male citizen. There is a fundamental problem for single women in getting Nepali citizenship for their children.

Women's political awareness and their willingness to participate in the political process increased significantly during the eighties and nineties. A little more than 17 per cent were willing to participate as local representatives as opposed to 15 per cent in 1978. The proportion of rural women who are aware of women's organization has also grown, in fact more than tripled from 1978 to 1992 (from 4.7 per cent to 14.9 per cent). Still, only 15 per cent of rural women are aware of women's organizations and only one per cent actually participate in them. Overall, women have not been able to translate the increase in awareness to positions of leverage or decision-making at the political and administrative levels.

SRI LANKA

As far as women's participation in politics is concerned, Sri Lanka has no constitutional provisions for ensuring women's representation. No reservations have been made for women in Parliament or in local bodes. Although the country had the first elected woman Prime Minister in the world way back in 1960, the proportion of women in Parliament has been dismal. Few women have been appointed to the Sri Lankan Cabinet. From 1960 to mid 1990s there was only one woman in a Cabinet of more than 20 men. After the 2004 elections there are three women out of 36 Ministers in the government. In the Provincial Councils women hold two to three per cent seats. In the local bodes while the total membership exceeds 3000, less than three per cent are women in urban bodies, and in the rural local bodies (Pradeshiya Sabhas) women represent only 1.38 per cent of the total membership.

Women's willingness to participate in the political process by exercising their right to vote in Sri Lanka is quite high. It is seen from the votes cast at polls and observations that female votes cast are around 70 per cent of the registered female voters. The experience of the officials at the polling stations indicates almost equal turnout of males and females. However, there is no disaggregated date collected on votes cast by males and females separately.

BARRIERS TO PARTICIPATION

Despite increased presence of women in local governance and many positive fallouts, certain factors have restricted their performance. These include social constraints lack of political will, criminalisation of politics, conditioning by patriarchy, lack of access to resources and support structures, including education, training and finances.

(a) Social Constraints

Ingrained male attitudes hamper the progress of women in almost all areas–economic, social and political. Women's lack of mobility and interaction with male counterparts puts them at a disadvantage. Their role in decision – making is marginalized since all financial, economic, commercial and political negotiations conducted outside the home have been traditionally male-dominated.

(b) Lack of Political will

Most countries have taken steps in the recent past to reserve seats for women or increase the representation of women in governance through quotas. Yet these steps are only restricted to the lower levels of governance, with very few women being elected t the Parliament. Women play an important role in campaigning but decisions on candidates are made by the party mechanisms and have been unfavorable to women. Most mainstream political parties have women's wings but their membership is low, and funding and infrastructure inadequate.

(c) Criminalization of Politics

Criminalization has been cited as another significant factor due to which women refrain from entering politics. The open use of money and muscle power marks the electioneering process. Criminalization affects women even more adversely and the government and bureaucracy have been helpless in this matter. At times women party workers have been targets of violence to prevent women's political participation even in the process of canvassing and grassroots campaigning.

(d) Lack of Resources

Lack of financial resources is another impediment for women to enter local politics. Lack of economic resources for women has been a major restricting factor in all the countries of the region.

It is evident that quotas have paved the way for women's entry into local politics. Many changes have been witnessed with their increased presence and participation, but inhibiting factors are still restricting women from reaping the full potential of their new found political role.

POLICY IMPLICATIONS

The whole experiment with quotas and reservation for women in politics has often been described as the political empowerment of women. This is only partially correct. Reservation and the consequent participation at the decision-marking level are definitely an aspect of the empowering process. However, this process cannot be restricted to politics. It needs to be all encompassing and involve other aspects. A majority of the women in South Asia, despite their heavy load of work and contribution to family income, are not economically empowered; they neither get a share in the income nor have a share in the property rights. Equally, women in their social life and interaction are bound by taboos and restrictions on behaviour, movement and knowledge seeking. Political participation is thus being attempted in a social environment that is patriarchal and restrictive. In this situation, women in general and elected women in particular, feel the need for extensive support structures providing services like information, training, political education, political and social counseling skills in management, etc. The external inputs will help in creating the necessary socio-political environment that will facilitate the women to emerge confident and perform their roles to the optimum level possible.

(a) Legislation and Implementation

In India, the Panchyati Raj Act, which is powerful on paper, needs to be keenly implemented. Local government should be entrusted with legal powers (judicial and police power) to make it more effective.

In Sri Lanka, credibility and acceptability of policies and actions have increased with women being involved in the decision-making process. Women too, should learn about politics, its impact and its positive consequences.

The political upheavals in Nepal since 1990 have brought women to the centrestage of national politics.

(b) Advocacy, Lobbying and Networking

Promoting exchange of experience and information among women already in local government and women aspiring for positions in local government through regional, country-level and local networks is both desirable and necessary. Women's organizations in the countries across the region need to join hands and network for a greater presence in the political process. There should be more women in the cadre of local administration and village level officials. For every local body headed by a woman, the corresponding official should also be a woman. Regular discussion forums at the block and district levels and interactions between women belonging to various areas within or from different states help women to share experiences. This helps a great deal in improving their performance as Chairpersons and members.

(c) Research and Training

Sustained and continuous data collection and field research on the experiences of women need to be undertaken by research centers and universities and academic institutions. Research should particularly focus on the best practices, successful role models and experiences of empowered elected women, so that it can inspire other elected and aspiring women.

(d) Support Structures

Lack of information, training, security and childcare problems have all been cited as factors that inhibit and restrain elected women from full participation. Legislation and quotas have to be accompanied by support structures that augment women's participation and enable them to play out their roles and responsibilities. Women also need technical advice at times. Gender sensitization training should be given to the bureaucracy, as often they have very unsympathetic views regarding the women Chairpersons and members. Self-help groups, where they exist, have proved to be good support structures for elected women.

(e) Larger and effective participation of women in the higher tiers of governance–and in the economic and social sectors too–leading to equity in all spheres of life.

- Focus of human capital is a key to enable women to move away from low- income, low technology activities to more skilled and paying tasks. Related to this, it is also important to identify assets and skills that are competitive in changing economic contexts and strengthen women's control there in.
- Organizing women appears as a key strategy for helping women gain access to assets- an essential meal for building their confidence, leadership as well as bargaining power. This is because the process of claiming assets implies challenging the status quo with its consequent social risks, which becomes possible only when women have substantial common interest and social support to take such action. Higher cluster level

federations become important for ensuring not just forward and back ward linkages but also structural change.

- Monitoring and evaluation should include quality and process factors and not just for gender as been mainstreamed in each programme component and the performance there in.

REFERENCES

Damyanthy Sridharan, Vesna Rodic (2004), Breaking the Political Glass Ceiling–women and Local Governance in South Asia.

Gail Omvedt (2005), Women in Governance in South Asia Economic and Political Weekly pp. 4746 to 4752, Vol. XLL, No. (44 & 95).

UNDP–Human Development Report–2005.

UNDP–Human Development Report–2003.

Govind Kelkar (2005), Development Effectiveness through Gender mainstreaming–Gender Equality and poverty Reduction in south Asian–Economic and Political Weekly pp. 4690 to 4698, Vol. XL. No. (44 & 45)

Ramakrishna S. and Rangacharyulu (eds.) (1999), Poverty decline and human development factors in some states NIRD, Hyderabad.

David luddess (2005), "Development Regions in South Asia History and the Governance Conundrums" Economic and Political Weekly Vol. XL., No. 37, Sept., 10-16.

Asian Development Bank (1993), Gender Indicators of Developing Asian and Pacific Comprises.

Nithya Rao (2005), Women's Rights to land and assets-experience of Mainstreaming Gender in Development Projects. Economic and Political Weekly, Vol. XL, No. 44 and 45.

2

Violence Against Women—A Study in Khammam District of A.P.

S. Radhakrishna and K. Madhava Rao

Traditionally, the sex ratio in India has always, been biased against women. The latest government report of the Census Survey of India of 2001 indicates that there are 935 women for every 1000 men in the country, making the female population about 48 per cent of the total population. The female working population constitutes around 36 per cent of the total working population. Majority of working women are crowded in the unorganised sector. As per the country report presented at the Fourth World Conference on women in Beijing in 1995–only 4 per cent of all women working are employed in the organised sector. This means that only about 0.005 per cent of India's population comprises of working women in the organised work force (quoted in Ujvala Rajadhyaksha 2004). As per Ujvala Rajadhyaksha & Swati Smita (2004) there is lack of focus on work and family research and part of the reason attributed to this is a gender inequalitarian culture and the low status accorded to women and women's issues in developing countries including India.

The distribution of adult rural women workers (above 15 years) by economic living standard shows that around 47 per cent belong to the low economic standard category, while 45 per cent belong to the medium economic standard category. More than 50 per cent in

A.P. belong to the low standard category (NFHS 1998-99 census) and (quoted in Sundaram 2001).

METHODOLOGY

The study depends on both primary and secondary source of information. To elucit the information from the women respondents, a structured questionnaire schedule is designed and administered. Apart from this technique, the qualitative method includes Focus Group Discussions (FGD), personnel interactions (village elders, women organisations, police personnel etc.) were also held to obtain optimum information. As the sample size is small in number, the FGD played a pivotal part of the study. The secondary source of information is obtained from National and AP state crime Records Bureau and records from District Police Office, Khammam. The information from 30 respondents has been collected in two villages, one from plain area and other from Agency area in Khammam district of A.P. The sample is selected covering all the caste-communities.

STUDIES OF VIOLENCE ON WOMEN

Discrimination and exploitation on the basis of gender constitutes a serious issue which effectively means that half the human race is unable to realise its potential and condemned to sub-optional standards of existence. This problem has received worldwide attention and several efforts have been made to bridge the seemingly ever-widening gap. Yet, even after years of efforts to integrate women into the mainstream development process, the effectivity of the same remains to be questioned owing to a multitude of factors which aid the continued marginalisation of women. Women's access to education, health, employment and political spaces still remain distant goals in many countries of the world. One of the most serious impediments to women's development is the phenomenon of continuing and increasing violence against them. Needless to say, this constitutes a serious violation of women's human rights. Gender violence manifests itself in various forms–female foeticide and infanticide, sexual abuse, incest, molestation, sexual harassment at work and on the streets, marital rape, domestic violence in the form of wife assult and women battering. Of all the forms of violence that women face, domestic violence remains the least reported and largely suppressed.

Table 1
Crimes Against Women – National Trends
(Actual Figures)

Crime head	*1990*	*1991*	*1992*	*1993*	*1994*	*1997*	*1998*	*1999*	*2000*	*2001*	*2002*	*2003*
Rape	9518	9793	11112	11242	12351	15330	15151	15468	16496	16075	16376	15847
Kidnapping & abduction	11699	12300	12077	11837	12998	15617	16351	15962	15023	14645	14506	13296
Dowry deaths	4836	5157	4962	5817	4935	6006	6975	6699	6995	6851	6822	6208
Torture	13450	15949	19750	22064	25946	36592	41376	43823	45778	49170	49237	50703
Molestation	20194	20611	20385	20985	24117	30764	30959	32311	32940	34124	33943	32939
Sexual harassment	8620	10283	10751	12009	10496	5796	8054	8858	11024	9746	10155	12325
Importation of grils												
Sati prevention Act												
Immoral Traffic prevention Act												
Indecent Representation of women												
Total	68317	74093	79037	83954	90843	110105	118866	123121	128256	130611	131036	131318

Source: National Crime Records Bureau, Ministry of Home Affairs.

According to Subadra (1999) domestic violence arises from patriarchal notions of ownership over women's bodies, sexuality, labour, reproductive rights, mobility, and level of autononomy. Deep rooted ideas about male superiority enable men to freely exercise unlimited power over women's lives and effectively legitimises it too. Violence is thus a tool that men use constantly to control women as a result of highly internalised patriarchal conditioning which accords men the right to beat their wives and thus ostensibly perform the duty of chastising them. The unequal and hierarchical gender relations manifest itself clearly in the familial set-up and is accentuated by clear demarcation of sex roles and sexual division of labour.

As per Mahajan, not much research has been done on family violence in India. Sriram and Bakshi (1988) study on battered women found that in the percentage distribution of causes of violence against married women, dowry demands, extra marital affairs and bigamy, alcohol and gambling were the highest. Their analysis revealed that for more than 50 per cent of the cases, regular beating was a fact of life. Gautam and Trivedi (1987) found that the dowry victims were mostly young (18-30 years) less educated than their spouses, dependent on husbands or in-laws for their living and mostly died from burn injuries (Action Aid 1994).

CRIMES AGAINST WOMEN IN INDIA AND ANDHRA PRADESH STATE

According to the available NCRB data from 1990-1994 and 1997-2003, the following patterns were observed at national level. The table shows that the crimes against women during the period 1990-1994 registered a gradual, steady increase of 33 per cent. During 1997-2003 the percentage of increase is at 19. It can be observed from the data that the highest increase was in the area of 'torture' (cruelty by husband and relatives) of women, i.e., harassment for dowry under Sec. 498-A of the IPC.

The proportion of crime against women to total IPC crimes during 1997-2003 at National level presented in table 2. The table reveals that the percentage of crimes against women increased from 6.4 per cent to 7.7 per cent.

The State-wise incidence and rate of crime committed against women depicted in table 3. It can be observed from the data that in both percentage of share in total incidence and rate of total cognizable crimes against women, the state of A.P. is in the first rank. With regard to sexual harassment (eve teasing), Uttar Pradesh has reported 40.3 per cent of cases (4,970) followed by A.P. 18.5 per cent (2,286). The torture cases in the country have been increasing year to year. For instance, this type of cases in the country have increased by 3 per cent in 2003 over the previous year (49,237). The highest rate of 10.5 was reported from Andhra Pradesh as compared to the National rate at 4.7 per cent.

Table 2
Proportion of Crime Against Women (IPC towards total IPC Crimes)

Year	*Total IPC Crimes*	*Crime against women (IPC cases)*	*% to Total IPC crimes*
1997	17,19,820	1,10,183	6.4
1998	17,78,815	1,19,012	6.7
1999	17,64,629	1,23,122	7.0
2000	17,71,084	1,28,320	7.2
2001	17,69,308	1,30,725	7.4
2002	17,80,330	1,31,112	7.4
2003	17,16,120	1,31,364	7.7

Source: Same as table 1.

Table 3
Incidence of Rate of Crime Committed Against Women in States during 2003

Sl. No.	*State*	*Incidence*	*Percentage contribution to all-India total*	*Rate of total gognizable Crimes*	*Rank**	*Rank***
1.	Andhra Pradesh	18382	13.1	23.6	1	1
2.	Aurnachal Pradesh	139	0.1	12.3	15	25
3.	Assam	5312	3.8	19.2	6	12
4.	Bihar	5900	4.2	6.8	27	8
5.	Chattisgarh	3336	2.4	15.4	12	15
6.	Goa	121	0.1	8.5	25	28
7.	Gujarat	5735	4.1	10.9	19	10
8.	Haryana	4170	3.0	18.9	7	14
9.	Himachal Pradesh	729	0.5	11.7	17	21
10.	Jammu & Kashmir	2164	1.5	20.2	4	19
11.	Jharkhand	2488	1.8	8.9	24	17
12.	Karnataka	5834	4.1	10.7	20	9
13.	Kerala	5653	4.0	17.3	8	11
14.	Madhya Pradesh	14547	10.3	23.0	2	2

Sl. No.	*State*	*Incidence*	*Percentage contribution to all-India total*	*Rate of total gognizable Crimes*	*Rank**	*Rank***
15.	Maharashtra	11273	8.0	11.2	18	5
16.	Manipur	137	0.1	5.5	33	26
17.	Meghalaya	69	0.0	2.9	34	29
18.	Mizoram	147	0.1	15.9	11	24
19.	Nagaland	25	0.0	1.2	35	31
20.	Orissa	4946	3.5	13.1	14	13
21.	Punjab	2375	1.7	9.5	23	18
22.	Rajasthan	11812	8.4	19.9	5	4
23.	Sikkim	37	0.0	6.6	28	30
24.	Tamil Nadu	8888	6.3	14.0	13	6
25.	Tripura	537	0.4	16.3	10	22
26.	Uttar Pradesh	12840	9.1	7.4	26	3
27.	Uttaranchal	886	0.6	10.0	22	20
28.	West Bengal	8508	6.1	10.3	21	7
	Total	136990	97.4	10505.9	13.0	

Source: National Crime Records Bureau, Ministry of Home Affairs.

The percentage of crimes against women in A.P. during the period 1995-2004, as per the data available with A.P. Crime Records Bureau depicted in table 4. The percentage of crime against women, to total IPC crimes remaining more or less constant around 10 per cent during this decade.

Table 4
Prcentage of Crimes Against Women in A.P. Against Total IPC crimes 1995-2004

Year	*Total IPC Crimes*	*Crime against women (IPC cases)*	*Per cent increase over previous year*	*Per cent to Total IPC crimes*
1995	91470	9232	—	10.0
1996	93659	9831	6.5	10.4
1997	102620	10561	7.4	10.2
1998	109195	11259	6.6	10.3
1999	108902	12060	7.1	11.0
2000	110124	13061	8.3	11.8
2001	118293	11879	(-) 9.0	10.0
2002	133111	13555	14.1	10.1
2003	141975	14970	10.4	10.5
2004	146043	15008	0.2	10.2

Source: AP Crime Record Bureau, 2004.

The incidence was negative in the year 2001, but shotup by 14.1 per cent in 2002. The phenomenal increase from 2002 could be attributed to a rise in the actual incidence compounded with increased reporting owing to the knowledge of and the access to women police stations.

From Table 5 it is evident that, during the years 1995-2004, there has been an upward movement in the incidence of harassment of dowry followed by dowry deaths, while in other crimes the trend is mixed.

Table 5
Crimes Against Women in A.P.

Year	*Dowry Death*	*Dowry harassment*	*Rape*	*Molestation*	*Bigamy*
1995	419	2725	792	2687	505
1996	390	3367	769	2665	438
1997	464	3539	872	2681	507
1998	458	4181	810	2731	485
1999	420	4441	855	2952	661
2000	450	5107	893	3147	606
2001	397	4681	814	3015	394
2002	413	5280	952	3371	395
2003	450	6415	901	3695	388
2004	488	6746	898	3460	359

Source: Same as table 4.

CRIMES AGAINST WOMEN IN KHAMMAM DISTRICT

The percentage of crimes against women in Khammam district during the period 1999 to 2005, as per the data available with District Police office, Khammam presented in table 6. The percentage of crimes against women to total IPC crimes is gradually increasing. The incidence was negative only in the year 2003, but again an increasing trend can be seen from 2004 onwards.

In table 7, the police/legal action is depicted in terms of the number of cases reported (Rep); convicted (con); acquitted (acq); pending investigation (PT); under investigation(UI). As in apparent from the data, the number of persons convicted of as serious a crime as the dowry death is less than 1 per cent. While the number of persons acquitted is around 7 per cent. This trend may be due to lack of adequate evidence. The guilty manage to suppress the evidence by all means.

Table 6
Proportion of Crimes against Women in Khammam District

Year	*Total IPC Crimes*	*Crime against women (IPC cases)*	*Per cent increase over previous year*	*% to total IPC crimes*
1999	3384	327	–	9.66
2000	3859	430	31.49	11.14
2001	4579	592	37.67	12.93
2002	5271	667	12.66	12.65
2003	4933	570	-14.54	11.55
2004	5620	681	19.47	12.12
2005	5517	820	20.41	14.86
Total	33163	4087	–	12.32

Table 7
Police Action against women in Khammam 1999-2005

Year	*Crime*	*Rep*	*Con*	*Acq*	*PT*	*UI*
1999-2005	Dowry Death	1.4	01	07	83	10
	Dowry harassment	1121	08	160	798	63
	Rape	263	04	28	198	25
	Molestation	1095	55	164	682	32
	Sexual harassment Eve teasing	2079	2079	–	–	–

Note: Rep–No. of cases Reported; Convicted (Con); Acquitted (Acq); Pending investigation (PT); Under Investigation (UI)

In the case of harassment for dowry, 71 per cent of the cases are still pending trial, while about 6 per cent of the cases are still under investigation. With regard to convictions in these cases would also follow a similar pattern. As these cases are under private domestic disputes, it is very difficult to produce the evidences before the court of law. In other cases such as rape and molestation the cases still pending trial are around 75 and 62 per cent respectively. The respondents opined that they are under severe pressure from opponent parties (guilty) while the trial is going on in the court of law.

The incidence of violence against women within the family has been on the increase too for the past 7 years i.e., from 1999-2005 (earlier data is not available). The trends evidence in table 8 and 9 are quite disturbing. Familial violence during the said period formed 63.20 per cent of the total number of crimes against women reported.

The reporting in dowry harassment cases is went up during 1999-2005. This could be due to the levels of awareness created by widespread media coverage and attention on the issue; setting up of women police station, family courts; awareness about the legal amendments like 498-A, D.P. Act. Apart from these sources the structural social capital (especially Self Help Groups, Village Education Committees, Water Users Associations etc. and other women activist groups) in villages for the last one decade has strengthened and playing a crucial role in reducing the domestic violence in the form of suppression by creating social awareness among women.

Table 8
Trends in Family Violence in Khammam

Years	*Dowry Death + Dowry Harassment*	*Rape + Molestation*	*Total Crimes against women*	*Per cent to total crimes against women*
1999-2005	1225	1358	4087	63.20

Table 9
Crimes against Women in Khammam (1999-2005)

Year	*Dowry Death*	*Dowry Harassment*	*Rape*	*Molestation*	*Sexual Harassment*
1999	10	89	38	114	NA
2000	20	95	33	137	467
2001	17	165	45	190	336
2002	13	192	41	188	375
2003	11	157	41	144	341
2004	19	223	44	173	310
2005	14	200	21	149	250

Source: from Table 6-9, office records, DCRB, SP Office, Khammam.

DOMESTIC VIOLENCE (FIELD STUDY RESULTS)

In order to support, the secondary data as it is presented above, the following observations have been made as FGD in relation to domestic violence in the form of oppression.

An environment in which women have experienced violence (physical or mental) or live with the threat of violence is likely to act to undermine empowerment. The researchers asked the respondents about their life time experience of beating and reasons for such behaviour of their husbands.

The main attributable reasons for such a behaviour of their husbands are as follows:

IN RURAL AREAS

1. Ill treatment by the wife of the relations on the in laws side.
2. For not procuring money & gifts from the parents.
3. For going out with out permission from the husband.
4. When the food preparations are not to the satisfaction of the husband.
5. For neglecting household duties and children.
6. For being questioned on abstaining from work getting drunk.
7. For not providing money for liquor.

IN URBAN AREAS

8. Extra dowry demands
9. Extra marital affairs
10. Alcohol and Gambling

One of the most prominent reasons for domestic violence is the evil of dowry demands. In the present day society male chauvinism is more often than not is favoured in villages for sundry reasons. The relatively better education of a husband than his better half and also the unequal division of labour between man and his wife i.e.-mans' hardwork in the fields and also at the other hired labour being greater in proportion than that of his wife-are the main reasons for domestic violence. Quite often the agreement regarding dowry–in cash or in the form of landed property between the gentlemen on either side of the bride and the bridegroom is infringed for several reasons causing disputes between the married couple. It is a general experience that when the accepted dowry is denied to be given directly to the son-in-law keeping his behaviour in view and the fixed deposit of the dowry or the landed property is preferred by the parents to be kept on the name of their daughter, inferiority complex in the son-in-law is evoked resulting in difference of opinion between wife and husband ultimately leading to unpatchable misunderstandings between the couple.

It is obvious that most of the parents in villages abide themselves to the conditions of dowry they make before the marriage alliance. Cases of teasing for more dowry are comparatively less in villages.

As a result of the growth in modern science and technology so many changes are taking place in our life style. Man has become crazy about enjoying all the living comforts bestowed upon him by the so called modernity. As such it is needless to say that most of the newly married husbands whose income is hardly enough to meet both the ends have begun pressurizing their wives to bring more and more money to meet the requirements of the modern life. In this process minute quarrels take place between wife and husband spreading an unbridgeable gap between them, finally leading to divorce.

Some times parents of a girl are very much fond of employees in foreign countries such as doctors and software engineers with a lucrative income as their son-in-laws. In majority of the cases it is not uncommon that the newly wedded brides are subject to lot of mental and physical harassment by their husbands demanding for transfer of the bride's movable and immovable property to his name. It is likely that at such junctures a women who feels delicate of persuading her parents to accept the demands of her husband is prone to commit suicides.

In certain instances, the pressure on woman for extra dowry is caused due to a lot of increase in the financial resources and income of her parents than what they were at the time of her marriage. Such husbands are not only harassing their wives mentally but also take recourse in physical violence of their wives.

EXTRA MARITAL AFFAIRS

In a male dominated society man is free to act according to his whims and fancies while women is restricted to be chaste in her actions. Man who is indulged in extra marital relations naturally does not take care of his wife and children.

Thus, his negligence of family responsibility leads to disharmony of relations between married couple. As man feels that he is superior to his wife, he makes her suffer physically if she interferes in his affairs with other women. In most of the families, the idea of reaching either for police help or seeking redressal of grievance against the wrong done to the women in court of law is considered to be 'infra-dignitatem' of dishonour of the family. As such most of the women have become reconciled with the situation where physical and mental tortures are inflicted upon them.

Though it is appreciable that the Faminist Organisations are putting sincere efforts to champion the cause of women and fight all the injustices done to them tooth and nail, there is no decrease in the rate of autrocities done to the women. In spite of all the measures taken by the government and the women organisations the graphic curve of domestic violence is steadily increasing statistically.

Besides the things that have been cataloged before, today the autrocities on women are not only limited to the physical plane but also extended to the mental plane due to various psychological reasons on the part of the husbands. If the possessive instinct of man runs beyond the level of his control it is likely that he suspects every movement of his wife and harasses her under various pretexts such as her relatives are ill-treating him, they occupy higher positions and so are careless about him, they are highly qualified than himself etc. resulting out of the inferiority complex to which he is subject to.

ALCOHOL AND GAMBLING

One of the evils that has affected some families and has influenced the minds of the youth as the fashion of the day is the consumption of alcohol.

Most of the alcoholics failed to spend time with their wives and children. So is the case with gamblers. This inability ultimately stifles the natural relationships between the members of the families causing ultimate ruin.

CONCLUSION

The above analysis clearly shows that the violence against women more particularly the domestic or familial violence is gradually increasing in A.P. The phenomenon of continued violence on the respondents had adverse multiple consequences as the women ranging from acute tension and anxiety, lowering in self-esteem and nervous breakdown to internalization of shame and guilty. The need of the hour is the conscious classification of wife-battering as an intrinsic and integral part of violation of human rights. Creating awareness and enhance women empowerment by building the social capital in rural areas is another area to be concentrated to reduce the domestic violence. Public services need to be made more accessible especially to women in crisis situations. Establishing more women police stations, and handling the cases of women with human touch and giving moral support is essential. Necessary steps should be taken to reduce the gap between the number of cases reported and convicted and disposal of the cases at a reasonable time by the court of law.

REFERENCES

Andre Beteille (1999), "Empowerment" EPW, Vol. XXXIV Nos. 10 & 11 March 6-13.

Malathi Ramanathan (2004), "Women and Empowerment: Shri Mahila Griha Udyog Lijjat Papad", EPW, Vol. XXXIX No. 17 and 24.

Ujvala Rajadhyaksha, Swathi Sunita (2004), "Tracing a Timeline for Work and Family Research in India" EPW, Vol. XXXIX, No. 17, April 24, 2004.

Subhadra, "Wife Battering in Chennai" EPW, Vol. XXXIV Nos. 16 and 17, April, 1999.

Sunita Kishor, Kamala Gupta (2004), "Women's Empowerment in India and its States Evidence from the NFHS" EPW. Vol. XXXIX No.7, Feb.14.

National Population Policy (2000), 'Department of Family Welfare', Ministry of Health and Family Welfare, GOI.

Quoted in Arvind Pandey and others "Maternal Health Care Services" E.P.W. Feb.14, 2004.

Kavitha, N and N. Audinarayan (1997), "Utilisation and Determinates of Selected Maternal and Child Health Care in Rural Areas ofTamilnadu in Health and Population and Issues.

Bhattacharya R. and J.Tandon (1991), Managerial Gaps in the Delivery of Antenatal Care Services in a Rural Area ofVaranasi in Jounral of Public Health.

Renana Jhavvala, Shalini Sinha (2002), 'Liberalisation and the Women Worker', EPW, May 25-31, 2002.

3

Role of Women: A Study of Rural Women Headed Households

G. Satyanarayana, M. Reddi Ramu and K. Krishna Reddy

INTRODUCTION

Women hold half the sky as such they cannot be ignored in the nation building and their active participation in the economic development, especially, in the context of a developing country, like India.

If one observes recent trends one unfailingly comes to a conclusion that women compete equally with their men folk in every activity, including Software sector, Industry, Administration, Judiciary, Participation political activities and Space excavation ventures. With every Sun rise one is witnessing ever increasing in number of women in diverse activities apart from performing assigned duties as mothers and wives at home. Their active involvement in the diverse sectors of the country has empowered them rendering to improve their stand of living.

It is a widely accepted opinion that development in the case of developing countries like India implies progressive withdrawal of workers engaged in agricultural activities. Because agriculture is over burdened with more than 65 per cent of the people eking out their livelihood from agriculture in India. One is surprised at the skewed distribution of wealth and landed property in India.

It is a bitter truth that the top 20 per cent of the people have command over 80 per cent resources, including land in India. Perhaps it is a because of this reason poverty continued to be unsolved problem in India. Intensity of poverty is felt more in rural India and women are the worst affected victims of poverty in rural areas. This article examines the role of women-headed-households (WHHs) in rural development in Chittoor district. Women headed households refer to those households that are being managed and maintained by women who have assumed the role of head of the households. The women who head the households who are either widows that have lost their husbands or those whose husbands have become too weak to head the households and in our study, the former constitutes 45 per cent and the latter 55 per cent of the sampled households. As rural social change is eagerly anticipated through development efforts the role played by women is grudgingly acknowledged. But before long, how are they influenced, it is by institutional agencies or through their own urban contacts will be very interesting to note.

Empowerment of women has emerged as one the major issues of development after the International Conference on population and development at Cairo and Women's Conference at Beijing, and gender equality has been considered as one of the essential components of human development in recent years. Gender disparity varies among countries depending upon the socio-economic context, which prevails significantly in the SAARC (South Asian Association for Regional Cooperation) region due to the limited efforts of the countries—Bangladesh, Bhutan, India, Maldives, Nepal, Pakistan and Sri Lanka—to equalize the opportunities between males and females. The patriarchal societies of SAARC countries have been influenced by the feudal culture and the age-old image of women keeps her illiterate, economically unorganized, socially inferior and legally helpless and their image in public life have been negatively influenced due to their unvalued and undervalued work in economic terms. Although a modest socio-economic growth was visible in the SAARC countries in the last decade, the problem of gender disparity remains persisting, besides poverty. Despite the fact that empowering women through investing in their capabilities makes greater strides in the economic growth and the overall development of the countries, these governments have not made any serious efforts towards women's upliftment. However, in the recent past, there has been a positive move—a slow change in the mental attitudes and awareness of the economic activity rates of females—in the societies and governments of the region. They have started recognizing the importance of encouraging women to acquire economic opportunities and even establishing some departments in the governments for their progress. Along the sidelines, non-government organizations (NGOs) are also striving vigorously for women's cause especially in the rural sector in these societies. Viewed against this background, this paper aims at increasing the attention drawn in favour of the economic empowerment of women in the SAARC countries and also highlights the need for gender—focused policies and makes a case for a greater social investment in women.

STATUS OF WOMEN

In the SAARC, region women are continuously relegated to a secondary position as they live and work under disadvantaged conditions due to the predominantly agrarian structure of these economies. The problems facing women in these countries are enormous—viz., low levels of literacy, poor enrolment in schools coupled with high drop outs, lack of vocational and technical training, marketing, and credit facilities, low health and nutritional status, low economic activity rates, poor political participation and less involvement in policy making apart from the prevailing customs, traditions and social taboos, as shown in the following Table:1 presents the female male disparity in health and literacy fields; and the share of females in the total labour force.

An overall improvement in life expectancy at birth was registered in these countries from 1985 to 1998 in both males and females. Though female life expectancy was higher than males in the latter year with the exception of Maldives, the life expectancy in the former year was lower in females till recently, defying the fact that women five longer than men due to biological norms reflecting the low nutritional status and the inadequate health facilities available to them. There was a wide, variation between Sri Lanka women and the rest in SAARC owing to the proper extension of health services to the people on the former particularly in rural areas. This country has a better quality of life in the entire developing world even when its income levels are lower. Adult literacy of females was also substantially low in the SAARC countries barring Sri Lanka and Maldives, despite its significant contribution to the decline in infant

Table 1
SAARC: Women in Development

Country	*Life Expectancy at Birth*				*Adult Literacy Rate (% of People 15 and above)*				*Female labour Force (% of total Labour Force)*	
	1985		*1998*		*1990*		*1998*		*1980*	*1999*
	Female	*Male*	*Female*	*Male*	*Female*	*Male*	*Female*	*Male*		
Bangladesh	50	51	59	58	22	47	29	51	42	42
Bhutan	–	–	63	60	–	–	–	–	–	–
India	56	57	64	62	34	62	43	67	34	32
Maldives	–	–	64	66	34	–	96	96	–	–
Nepal	46	47	58	58	13	38	22	57	39	40
Pakistan	50	52	63	61	21	47	29	58	23	28
Sri Lanka	72	68	76	71	83	93	88	94	27	36

Source: World Bank, World Development Report, various years, Oxford Press, New York.

mortality, high acceptance of family welfare, fertility decline, delayed age at marriage, better hygienic conditions and above all women's status in society. The female literacy was less than half of male literacy—through both were at low levels-in Bangladesh, Nepal, Pakistan and was a little over half in India in 1990. Notwithstanding the considerable improvement in the female literacy from 1990 to 1998, the female gap was still high in these countries including India. Sri Lanka with least gender disparity and Maldives with gender equality in adult literacy stand as better examples not only in the SAARC region but also in the entire Asia. Low labour participation rates of females in the region reflect the lack of education and training along with the socio-cultural factors that restrict the entry of women into labour market. A modest increase in the female labour force was noticed only in Sri Lanka and Pakistan from 1980 to 1999. The relatively high rates in Bangladesh and Nepal were attributed to the significant proportion of women in agriculture and allied activities. Interestingly, the rate in India witnessed a slowing down from 1980 to 1999 perhaps due to the problem of enumeration.

An attempt has been made to identifying the areas where woman engaged in economic activities and the returns, which they get as a reward for labour, empowered them to maintain their families.

SAMPLE AREA AND RESPONDENTS

The two villages' viz., Kothapalli and Enumulavaripalli in Madanapalli rural mandal of Chittoor district, each with more than 600 households formed the study area.

The villages were selected in random. These two villages are being located on either side of the Arogyavaram Medical Centre and are within a radius of 8 kms from Madanapalli town.

However, Madanapalli rural mandal was chosen in view of its socio-economic characteristic which is worth studying as most of the rural development programmes are vigorously implemented in this mandal in Chittoor district.

The data relating to 200 women respondents from both the sampled villages were pooled together for the purpose of analysis and presentation. The respondents were purposively selected in order to give due representation to all the vulnerable castes in the study area. The number of households studied on the basis of caste were Kurabas (55 households), Gollas (35 households), Boyas (28 households), Potters (25 households), SCs (30 households), STs

(20 households), Lingayats (7 households). Those households were selected in proportion to their total population in the villages.

SOCIO-ECONOMIC CHARACTERISTICS OF THE SAMPLE RESPONDENTS

The same respondents: Kurabas, Gollas, Boyas, Lingayats and Potters own land in the pattern of 7.5, 7.2, 5.0, 3.9 and 1.8 acres respectively as the caste order presented above and it is significant to note that both SC's and ST's are the landless villagers who solely depended on their labour for livelihood.

As regards to education, 162 respondents (81 per cent) were literates, only 32 respondents (18.5 per cent) illiterates who did not even attend night schools. The family literacy level for females was 37 per cent while it was above 62 per cent for males in the sample households. The household were engaged in varied occupations, such as, agriculture and allied activities; self-employment-basket weaving, silk weaving, stone-breaking, road laying works, petty shops, tailoring, dairying, vegetables, fruits vending, brick laying, house construction workers, food grain processing and domestic servants.

The urban contact by the village men had another repercussion on the family income. Men inclined to reduce their contribution to the family income as they were spending substantial amount of their earnings on liquor and eating out. This has resulted in less income to the household and many women bitterly complained about this practice. This practice also led to frequent bickerings in the family, especially, among the lower income households that we have taken for our study.

Another interesting dimension of urban contact by the rural women has led to a through change in their attitude towards work. Many of the women in the sample villages (Kothapalli and Enumulavaripalli), who were educated up to primary and secondary levels were now looking down upon their family occupation-agriculture. Gone were the days when they would pursue this occupation with a devotion and now most of them were hoping against hope of pursuing gainful employment which would fetch them good income to sustain them. Besides, some of them eagerly migrated to the near by cites and remained non-communicant to their parents. This has added on increased burden on the women in the households in terms of household and farm work.

It may be seen in Table 2 that the sampled households engaged in agriculture and allied activities to earn livelihood. Although the two villages are located nearby the Madanapalli urban centre, self-employment ventures attempted by the sampled women headed households is depressing as it is only 3 per cent of them took up self-employment avenues.

It is significant to notice that 30 per cent of the households find these employment in stone breaking and road laying, brick laying and house construction works. These activities provide work almost throughout the year (Table 2).

Madanapalli is basically fruits and vegetables growing area, the transportation of which gave rise a good demand for basket manufacturing sectors. Here again women find employment during major part of the year. Similarly, women have been engaged throughout the year in silk handloom weaving and a few of them in tailoring works.

Table 2
Occupational Distribution of the Sampled Households

Sl. No.	*Type of Activity*	*Percentage*
1.	Agriculture Labours	15
2.	Dairying	20
3.	Vegetables and Fruits vending	10
4.	Self-employment (Petty Business)	03
5.	Stone breaking and Road laying works	20
6.	Household activities (Basket weaving, Silk handloom weaving, Tailoring)	05
7.	Brick laying	05
8.	House Construction	15
9.	Food grain Processing (Free Food)	02
10.	Domestic Servants (Free Food)	05
	Total	100

Source: Field Survey Data.

As mentioned earlier the villages located on either side of Arogyavaram Medical Centre women find work either as domestic servants or food grains processing workers in the Arogyavaram Medical Centre. Income earned by women workers in other than agriculture sector seemed to be encouraging. As seen from the Table 3 an agriculture labourer gets Rs.50 as a daily wage as against Rs. 60 in vegetables and fruits vending, Rs.70 in stone breaking and road laying works, Rs. 70 as a house construction workers and Rs. 50 as a worker in household activities.

The annual incomes of the women headed households is the highest in the case of dairying activities (Rs. 86400) followed by household activities, self-employment, stone breaking and road laying works, brick laying and house construction works (Table 3).

Income earned through self-employment activities is quite encouraging. There is a lot of scope for women to exploit and to enrich themselves in these activities in the villages.

Table 3
Annual Income of the Sampled Households

Sl. No.	*Type of Activity*	*Daily earning of a worker (Rs)*	*No. of workers per house-holds*	*No. of working days in a year*	*Annual income of house-holds (Rs.)*
1.	Agricultural Activities	50	2	180	18000
2.	Dairying	80	3	360	86400
3.	Vegetables and Fruits vending	70	1	240	16800
4.	Self-employment (Petty Business)	100	1	360	36000
5.	Stone breaking and Road laying works	70	3	240	50400
6.	House Constructions	70	2	210	29400
7.	Household Activities (Basket weaving, Silk handloom weaving, tailoring)	50	3	360	54000
8.	Brick laying	60	2	180	21600
9.	Food grain processing (free food)	30	3	240	21600
10.	Domestic servants (free food)	15	3	360	16200

Source: Field Survey Data.

The illiterate and hard working women who belonged to traditional house construction community-Vadderlu, finding work throughout the year because there are half a dozen stone crushing and quarries units within a distance of 4 kms from these two villages.

In the case of Women who are engaged in food grain processing work, and domestic works of course, have been getting the lowest annual income per household. This is, as reported, they were served free food on all the working days; and in addition they would provide used clothes; hence the wages were lower compared to the wages of workers engaged in other sectors in the villages. It is mostly SCs and STs Women that taken up these two category of works in the villages.

CONTACT WITH INSTITUTIONAL AGENCIES

The most important source of knowledge regarding agriculture an allied activities for the rural people is imparted to through the contacts with the institutional agencies, such as, Agricultural Extension Officers, Veterinary doctors, Health works, Gram sevak etc. They provide them with recent information about the innovations in agriculture, subsidiary occupation, the schemes of rural credit, advice on health problems.

The lack of contact with extension agencies was the reason for many rural women losing touch with technological innovations. The next frequent visit was made by the gram sevak and community health workers situated within easy reach of people, they made only cursory visits as they were forced to show their diaries to their superiors. The lowest number of contacts were made by the Agriculture Extension Officer. It may be mentioned here that the knowledge level of participants regarding the high yielding varieties, pesticides etc. was not an appreciative level. This is mainly because of the neglect of women in the dissemination of knowledge of farm practices.

The most un-cherished contact official for the rural people was the contact with the Agricultural Bank Officer. They felt that the official was not sympathetic towards their problems in repayment of loans and through that they visited them to rob their little possession even, as they were unable to repay the loan amount for one or the other reasons.

The above discussion indicates a wrong identification of the problem and needs of the rural women while trying to help them in their needs. Therefore increased attention to the extension needs of rural women must be paid through the services of the women extension officers. Most of the women expressed that it was especially incompatible for them to freely mix with the male extension agencies.

The extension agencies should take special interest to give importance to the extension needs of the women who have taken up the dairying and silk handloom weaving as a part of rural development schemes.

The neglect of women in developing countries regarding to dissemination of extension knowledge in agronomic research is not uncommon. It is observed that in the study, Women Headed Households who have taken up agriculture have been using traditional methodology of cultivation. Hence, appropriate technology has to be developed and passed on to actual cultivators, so that they may enhance their productivity levels in the rural areas.

URBAN CONTACT OF RESPONDENTS

Owing to nearness to the urban centre of Madanapalli has some effect on the knowledge level and the attitude of women respondents in the villages. The frequent interaction with Agriculture Extension Officer, Veterinary doctor, State bank of India (Agricultural) Field Officer, Sri Venkateswara Grameena Bank Field Officer, Community health workers and primary health centre doctors in the Arogyavaram Medical Centre and Panchayat Extension Officers has richly helped the households to acquaint themselves with the necessary knowledge and to improve their economic well-being in the study area.

The respondents seek more of the services of bankers, Agricultural Extension Officers, Veterinary doctors and Community health workers to increase their efficiency levels in the works that they have taken up of their works.

It is heartening to note that more number of women workers engaged in sectors other than agriculture. More number of women have been engaged in activities, such as, Dairying, Basket weaving, Silk handloom weaving, Vegetables and Fruits wending and House construction than in agricultural sector. As such the women have an opportunity to mix with the outside world, which may help in breaking caste division through marketing their commodities.

Of late, the number of Auto rickshaws have increased in their number and for every ten minutes one Auto rickshaw of either seven seater or three seater would be plying between these two villages and Madanapalli town facilitating the villagers either to buy or sell goods at Madanapalli urban centre.

CONCLUSION

On the whole, the services rendered by Madanapalli urban centre and institutional contact of the rural women headed household respondents seemed to be encouraging in improving their living conditions. Most of the women headed households have complained that they did not have access to bank finances as they lack the required knowledge and their inability to produce co-obligants in availing themselves of bank loans to take up some enterprises, which have a lot of potentials in villages. A few of the WHHs could effectively check their husbands indulgence in drinking and gambling habits which improved the saving levels and ploughing back of these savings may result in income-yielding assets among the sampled WHHs and if this trend continued vigorously for a considerable period it finally ends up in rural development in the study area.

REFERENCES

Lewis, A.W. (1972), The Theory of Economic Growth, George Allen & Unwin Ltd., London.

Reddy, K. Venkata (2001), Agriculture and Rural Development (A Gandhian Perspective) Himalaya Publishing House, Mumbai-400004.

Geraldine Forbes, Women in Modern India, Cambridge University Press, 1998, New Delhi.

Bhai, L. Thara, "Women's Studies in India", A.P.H. Publishing Corporation, 5, Ansari Road, Darya Ganj, New Delhi-110002.

Enarson, E.P., "Woods-Working Women", The University of Alabama Press, University, Alabama, p. 174.

Pandit, S.K., "Women in Society", Rajat Publications, 4/32, Geetha Colony, Delhi-110031.

Hasnain, N., "Weaker Sections the Psycho-Social Perspective", Gyan Publishing House, New Delhi-110002.

4

The Status of Dalit Women in Rural Areas in the Post-Independent India

M. Erragattu Swamy and M. Ashok Kumar

The major asset of a nation on which the hopes of its rapid development rests on its people. The women constitute about half of the total population in our country. The social, economic and political roles of women in the society are essentially structured by the age-old traditions, beliefs, values, and customs and by the process of socialization. The Indian constitution provides for equal rights and privileges for women and men. On the employment scene also, a number of social legislations have been enacted to raise the status of women and eliminate discrimination in payment of remuneration against them. But still it is observed that women's work is invisible and unaccounted for both by our policy makers and implementing agencies, as they are not perceived to be major earners of family but as marginal and supplementary contributions. The approach has been 'work for the man is income for the family', which ignores the reality that one third of all households are supported solely by women, while in another one third, fifty per cent of the financial contribution comes from women only.

The role of women in economic development even at the global level as a subject received attention around seventies with the declaration of the International Women's Year by United Nations General Assembly in 1975. In our country also as a result of transition from traditionalism to modernism, working of women outside the home is being gradually encouraged. In spite of this visible and welcome change, the social problems that a working woman has to face are numerous and her zest and zeal to get herself actively engaged in gainful employment is always dampened.

Majority of women are to be found in vast rural unorganized sector. Employment in this sector is characterized by low wages, longer hours of work, low productivity, low skill and lack of job security. Inability of women to acquire skill and training is responsible for her low employment status and socio-economic conditions. This is attributed to the prevailing social relations between men and women as well as the structure of the economy. Objectives of the Study: The present study is an attempt to examine the status of rural dalit women in the post-Independent India. The main objectives of the study are:

- To analyze the socio-economic, political and cultural status of Dalit women.
- To find-out the difference between the status of High-caste women and Dalit women in Hindu society.

The term Dalit has been derived from Sanskrit, which means broken and downtrodden. Bharata Ratna Dr. B.R. Ambedkar often described the untouchables as broken people. The Dalits are socially and economically weak, culturally backward and politically powerless. Thus, the word 'Dalit' describes a condition of being under-privileged and deprived of basic rights and refers to people who are suppressed on grounds of their lowly birth.

In recent years, various studies on women have appeared with the focal point, ranging from 'abortions of female foetuses' to 'bride-burning' and the ideology of SATI. But amazingly, there is little interest in Dalit women who suffer from dual disadvantages i.e being Dalit and being women.

Most of the women's studies concentrate on middle class women, among whom very few are Dalits, because 5 to 10 per cent of Scheduled Caste and Scheduled Tribe women are able to lead a middle class life. Infact, in the general literature of women, no special attention is paid to the problems of Dalit women.

Dalit women work hard and very often work much more than their men folk. In rural areas they find work as daily-wage agricultural labourers. They undertake the works such as plantation, weeding, harvesting, threshing, manuring etc. The women cultivatior's are found in the hilly areas. They are engaged in the cultivation of their own small holdings in the absence of their husbands who migrate in search of jobs. They go to bed late at night and get up again early in the morning, light the fire to cook the morning meal and send the children to school mostly to government schools). Then they themselves go to work for nearly eight hours in the fields. If they do not find work as field labourers, they walk long distances to collect fire wood and grass to sell and for their use. Majority of the Dalit women are landless and own little productive assets. Hence these women have to be contended with less remuneration and more labour intensive jobs. On the other hand the women belonging to other than Dalit group enjoy high social status and possess productive assets in terms of cultivable land, houses, cattle wealth, consumers' durables etc. Dalit female child labour is also common due to the poverty and low levels of family income.

The education level of Dalit women has a very significant role to play in determining her social and economic status. The incidence of illiteracy is the highest among Dalit women than men.

Data from the census reveals that 20 to 25 per cent of Dalit female children between 5-14 years attend the schools. The majority of the Dalit students avail the schooling facilities provided by the Government and local bodies. Various studies on school enrolment figures suggest that there is a relatively high degree of drop-out rate among Dalit female children than male children. Because schools are not available within easy access even at the primary stage. As per the data provided by NCERT survey, Dalit communities have relatively poorer access to schooling when compared to general population.

Hence, the social and private cost of women's development through education, training and medical care is still considered to be very high vis-à-vis the returns from them. The following are the important factors, which are responsible for low educational status of Dalit women.

- Poverty
- Early marriage
- Social customs that hinder female mobility after puberty.
- Inadequate facilities in the form of school buildings, hostels.

In Dalit families with little or no formal education most female children are married off when they are between 12 and 15 years old. An uneducated girl of 17 is already considered 'old' and has little chance for a good match in the case of rural female children. The legal age for marriage i.e. 18 years for girls and 21 years for boys is hardly ever observed. The problem of dowry also exists even in the Dalit families and it depends upon the girls education and to a smaller extent on her beauty. If a father is too poor or has too many daughters, he must try some how to get them married without dowry to a man who is much older, to a widower with children, to a man who is permanently without work or who has a physical defect or to a man who is known as a notorious drunkard. The girl may also be given as a second wife to somebody who is already married. And even if it is known that the second wife is threatened badly and has to work like a slave, usually nobody bothers to help her. The second-rate weddings are performed without a big feast, mostly the ceremony will be held in temples. Once the daughter is married, the Dalit parents feel often that their obligations are over. In times of quarrel, the wives are taken back by their parents, but frequently they are told, you have another name now, and we have done everything. Neighbours normally donot interfere even if they know that a young women is maltreated. Bride burning for the sake of dowry seems to be more frequent in all communities and Dalits are also no exemption in this regard. Infact, cases of suicide or attempted suicide are becoming common among the Dalits.

Formerly when a wife feels that she is ill-treated by her husband, she could leave him without major problems, returning to her parents house on getting divorce. But, nowadays divorce seems to be much more difficult for the women. A man, who is not interested and to get rid of his wife, sends her home for a festival or for the delivery of her first child or if he is not interested to have female child does not bring her back. In suspecting this type of attitude, the Dalit women are not preferring to leave their husbands they stay with them even if they suffer. When there are quarrels with husband and in-laws (If they are beaten by drunken husbands) she may only hope that everything returns to normal. She is not leaving the house and children for the sake of society and family. Widow remarriage is also a major problem of Dalit families. Particularly for a young woman with one or two children cannot marry again, once the husband has died. It means if a widow is young and her parents permit it she can marry again but if she has children she must not remarry. But in the case of men this is not so within months of his wife's death even with two or more children or above 40 years of age he can remarry. It depends upon his economic status.

As far as the political awareness among the Dalits particularly among the Dalit women is concerned in the villages the men often discuss these matters and decide, together with the heads of political parties concerned mostly with the village Sarpanch, in favour of a political party. Once, the decision has been made, the elections become a family business, the men announce their decision, and the women vote for the party the husband has chosen. Even in the case of reserved seats for Dalit women, they do not have courage to speak in the public meetings and most of the decisions will be taken by their husbands like in the case of other caste women husbands for which the women have no opinion of their own. There is a special name in use for the women political leaders husbands, Sarpanch pati, Mandal President pati, MLA pati, Minister pati etc.

There are differences in the socio-economic, political and cultural conditions of women of other castes and Dalit women. Dalit women in rural areas work as daily-wage labourers. Apart from working in other peoples fields, the Dalit women have to do all the household chores. Dalit women in general have more freedom than women of tradition bound higher Hindu castes. Like Dalit women they can move about rather freely once they are married. Without much difficulty, a woman can leave her husband if she is treated badly in his house and live with another man of the same community.

Traditionally, Dalit women were free in their social, economic and religious sphere. Unlike the upper-caste women who used to remain at home, the Dalit women had to work for their bread mostly outside their home. Hence, the Dalit women are more economically independent than the upper caste women of Hindu society.

But in modern society, the women belonging to upper caste society is being influenced by the lives of Dalit women. For example, the traditional freedom enjoyed by Dalit women is under constraints. When a man is in the house, the woman is always under his control and has a subordinate position. She cannot invite her relatives when she so feels, but has to welcome her husband's relatives during festivals and other occasions or when the in-laws desire to invite them, in addition to attending work in the fields as labour, she has to cook for them, serve them and she will take food whatever is left at the end. If it is not sufficient to her nobody bothers in the family.

The Dalit women cannot keep her earnings for herself. Often the husband takes the money, which she earns to buy cheap liquor and gets drunk. If she is interested to buy a new sari, she cannot do so independently, even if she has earned the money. She has to tell her husband and he will buy her clothes.

In Indian Hindu society, the Dalit's have a low position and they are treated badly by the high-caste Hindus. Then, the men belonging to these communities come home, and at least here they want to be treated with respect. It means that the Dalit men take absolute precedence over their wives. They take the decisions, they take the money and they eat first, if something remains, the women may eat it, sometimes nothing is left and the women go to bed hungry. The main problem that Dalit women face is sexual molestation by high caste men. Generally the Dalit women work for rich men (landlords) and that they are sometimes reped and do not dare to speak or they are given money and everything is hushed up. No police case will be filed against the landlord, sometimes the victims have to leave the village after this incident.

In the rural society, still, there is a lot of difference between Dalit women and of other castes women. Both the castes had to work in the agricultural fields. But Dalit women work in others field and high-caste women in their own fields. When compared to earlier times the caste tensions with the Dalits particularly SC's are some what improved. Formerly, the Dalit women were not permitted to touch the other women for dual purpose as an untouchable and with a fear of high-caste women. And even today, the Dalit women don't dare to take water from the village tank / well and ask women of higher castes to fill up their pots or to help in lifting the pot or vessel. The cases of physical violence against women particularly beating of wife are more frequent among Dalit women and less frequent among higher caste women.

There is a difference between Dalit women and high-caste women with regard to working in the fields. Dalit women mostly work for the wages in other peoples fields while the higher-caste women work in their own fields or they supervise the agricultural operations. Even if the amount of work may be the same, the differences are there and are different in different parts of the country.

The system of joint families are still prevailing in the case of non-Dalit castes who possess plenty of land and other assets whereas the Dalit communities who possess little or no land often live in nuclear rather than in extended families looked after by an aged father or mother. In the joint families, work in the house and fields is divided between the women of the family, sometimes there may even be servants and there is always someone to look after small children. On the other hand, the Dalit women often have to manage all the household work and work in the fields as labour alone or with the help of elder children sometimes the small kids use to be taken alongwith them to the fields.

As far as family planning is concerned still the Dalit women in rural areas is not aware of the advantage of small family norms. But, generally, family planning is more common among the non-Dalit and the number of children are small. During pregnancy higher caste women go in far medical control to determine the sex of the foetus. If the foetus is found to be female and there is already a daughter in the family, the woman often go in for an abortion. Dalit women on the other hand particularly, the SCs due to poverty and illiteracy cannot generally afford medical control, which leads to have a number of daughters, until finally the eagerly expected son is born. The consequences are disastrous for scheduled caste and schedule tribe women. This happens only with the caste traditions and customs and there will be high pressure from the in-laws with regard to male child. In times of quarrel with others, the Dalit women actively participate with her husband when compared to other women. In fact, the Dalit women will be treated equally at the work and also during festivals and ceremonies they enjoy with their menfolk and whenever they get handsome money they celebrates.

In view of the above it can be concluded that the problem of Rural Dalit women is more acute and complicated who are subject to ignorance and illiteracy. Dalit women's life pattern itself speaks volumes on Dalitism. Dalit Women have all the capacity, power and potential to govern the world but they are denied the opportunity to realize and express these potentials. The Dalit women will protest all forms of violence, violations of rights, atrocities and exploitation she will not keep quite. She is able to work more, give more, face the life more courageously than men. She is in the forefront of any struggle. But she is neglected ignored for various reasons. The only panacea seems to lie in putting greater emphasis on the education of women. Investment in education in general and womens education in particular needs to be given top priority, as education plays a vital role in raising the level of social consciousness and political awareness. In this regard the Government of India has introduced National Policy on Education (NPE) during 1986 which was aimed to universal enrolment of all Dalit children in the 6-11 age group and 75 per cent enrolment in the 11-14 age group as well as the successful completion by them of primary and middle school stages by 1990. These targets have been reiterated in the revised programme of action in 1992. In addition to this several other programmes like District Primary Education Programme (DPEP), Sarva Shiksha Abhiyan (SSA), Adult Education Programme, Hostel facilities, Scholarships, Fee concession, Free books, Mid day meals all these helped the Dalits particularly dalit girls to improve their education. The educated girls generally are facing less problems when compared to illiterates.

In the Post-Independent India and with the policies of the government to uplift the Dalits, today the position of Dalit women seems to have changed to some extent. In addition to the developmental activities by the government, the Dalit organizations are also working actively all over the country and are forcefully demanding for their rights of which they have been deprived for centuries. But the Dalit Movement as it exists today has done much for a handful of male Dalit intellectuals, less for the great majority of Dalit men such as improving their position within the family and nothing for Dalit women.

Keeping in view of the attitude of the Dalit men and their organizations towards Dalit women, they have arrived to a conclusion to initiate their own Dalit movement and formed National Federation of Dalit Women (NFDW) at New Delhi on 11th August 1995 to liberate Dalit Women from all oppression. Therefore, we hope that the Dalit women organizations with the help of government Dalit upliftment programmes and to fulfill the dreams of Dr. B.R. Ambedkar, the champion of women development and who has rightly said that the liberation of the Dalits would come not from the educated intellectuals but from the ordinary people. The liberation of Dalits women will come from when Dalit women struggle for the cause of the development of Dalit women to liberate themselves and keep up their dignity in the society as in the case of high-caste women. This will be achieved not merely passing the legislation's and establishment of organizations but will be achieved with proper implementation of the above.

REFERENCES

Pawade, K., The Position of Dalit Women in Indian Society; in B. Das and J. Massey (eds) Dalit Solidarity, New Delhi: ISPCK.

Guru, G. Dalit Women Talk Differently, EPW XXX(41/42), Oct: 2548-50.

Ghanshyam Shaw: Dalits and the State.

Usha Kundu & Raksha Rani, Socio-economic Status of Rural Working Women: A Haryana Study, EPW; Jan-June 1995, Vol. 4, No. 1.

National Sample Survey Organisation, 1999.

5

Practical Utility of Gender Study

N.M. Das and S. Vidya Sagar

Gender inequality is a global phenomenon it differ from place to place country to country depending upon socio-economic indicators. The fundamental purposes of various Gender issues is to raise awareness amongst both men and women to participate in decision making socio-economic activities related to all round development of an economy.

In India the dimension of women empowerment with a focus on Gender empowerment and development needs a very close and careful study more specially in the backward regions. Women have been subjected to discrimination in all walks of life and or deprived of equality of status and opportunities in socio-economic programmes. This is mainly due to deep rooted Gender biased social attitudes and practices.

The word Gender stands for men (masculine) and females (feminine). Many research scholars who made field studies on gender issues opined that women are the fore runners agents of socio-economic change.

One of the problems of first world countries is to maintain Gender equality whereas the third world countries like India is not only to initiate the process of Gender equality but also to adopt various formidable measures through sustained efforts to mitigate the evil effects of gender inequality (if complete eradication is not possible) from the sociological soil of India.

Professor Malini Bhattacharjee, Director School of Women's studies, Jadavpur University (SOWS), says "Gender studies can be a fulfilling career option for those who believe in advocating a free and unbiased society".

The saying behind every successful man there is women has proved in countries like England, U.K, U.S.A, and other countries whereas in India it is a rare one.

In U.S and U.K, Gender studies are given paramount significance. In USA, RICE University in Houston at Texas State conducts programmes in gender studies. The curriculum covers topics like gender and ethnicity in society and provides an inter disciplinary perspective often ignored by traditional scholarship.

In India the need for Gender equality has been the chief objective over a century. It attracted the attention of planner's social reformers development thinkers for the lost five decades. It is increasingly felt that the progress of nation is integrally linked with the empowerment of women. Women constitutes a significant percentage to Indian population. Women are nearing equal to male population. It may be possible that in the next decadal census of 2011 the female and the male population ratio may be 50:50.

The negative effect of Gender in equalities greatly hinders the process of development and undermines the effectiveness of programmes and policies. It is a fact that women are vital and productive workers in Indian economy.

The various reasons for Gender inequalities may be broadly classified under major heads namely social, economic, cultural, religious, institutional, demographic and environmental. All the above may be substantiated in sub heads such as ignorance, illiteracy, unemployment, poverty, unorganized nature of women in different occupations, domestic operation, double burden of work, issue of child girl, differences in the payment of various undertakings, natural resource use, low participation of women in policy making and decision taking, inadequate budgetary provision and insufficient and ineffective government measures.

At International Level: The United national organization which has already recognized the prevalence of Gender inequality has declared 1975-1985 as the first international women's decade. The fourth world conference on women which held at Beijing in 1995 pointed out that the women's participation in development did not bring any qualitative change. As a result the Gender inequality has not shown any significant decrease. This is a warning signal which created a shock to almost all developing and under developed countries.

Glaring Social Evils: Inspite of assuring constitutional safeguards adopting a number of legislative and legal measures women still lag behind. It is seen that the poor sections of rural women are not properly respected and treated in organized mandals and social organizations. The protective measures remained on paper only. This view has been substantiated in the below mentioned cases.

1. The system of dowry gives second status in society. Their structural condition leads them to in a state of social deprivation and mental torture.
2. One of the dominant features of Indian women character is that they never complain openly against the ill treatment and injustice being done to them by males. They feel shy to reveal the facts thinking that it would be disrespect to husband and to the prestige of the family.
3. As per section 498 and 406 Indian penal code if a women is harassed for dowry her in-laws can be arrested. But in actual practice the number of such complaints lodged with police stations or in courts is very limited and they may be hardly counted on fingers.
4. The right of women in parental property is not ensured. It remained on paper only.
5. So far as reservation of seats to women weaker sections minorities are concerned, are not enforced as per the promise and assurance given.
6. Discrimination against the girl child is a still exist in major governments of all types of verbal and physical abuses not only from the members of the family but also from her employer.
7. It is seen that women are often subjective double burden of earning from the family and caring from the children. They are not leading quite independent life.
8. Domestic violence as a form of oppression is another handicap to the uplift of women.

SUGGESTIONS MADE TOWARDS ACHIEVING GENDER EQUALITY

Gender identity women's empowerment personality development and promotion of gender studies has been a common feature not only in India but in foreign countries as well. Indian experience is that the efforts made by the government hither to through legislative constitutional and legal measures have no doubt proved to some extent but have not totally succeeded in fulfilling the cherished expectations and aspirations of the poorest of the poor of women section on rural front in particular. What is being done is not enough and sufficient cause for the welfare of women must more remains to be done to achieve Gender equality.

Amongst many remedial measures the following suggestions with a special reference to environmental planning and Gender budget initiatives are made here with

1. Environmental Planning

This has not received sufficient and required attention of the planners and administrators. The surroundings greatly affect the human life. Awareness on (i) Conservation (ii) Management (iii) Protection of Environment (iv) health and sanitation and (v) Natural Resource Use are to be examined very seriously to create a healthy and congenial atmosphere. Environmental issues right from the grass roots level to be higher level are to be studied thoroughly and suitable measures through action oriented peoples participation are to be taken up accordingly. The environment measures should ensure civil amenities and win the most popular and good will of the public.

Prof. Justinesaws in his paper "Women men an environmental change policies and programmes contributed to the institute of National Rural Development, Rajendranagar, Hyderabad has focused on gender dimensions. He says that to understand how Gender shapes the activities that affects the environment it is necessary to examine women and men's role and responsibilities, access to land control over resources, knowledge of resource and authority to make decision about the resource use.

Understanding women and men's relationship to the environment plays an important role in developing solutions, for more sustainable use of natural resources for example in Zimbabwe, Burkinafaso and Cameroon women have the legal right to own land and trees but in actual practice men control nearly all of the property.

Knowledge Base: Gender knowledge also varies by class age and ethnicity under scoring its complexity an old man from a indigenous group may have different ways of working with land and forest then an a young man living outside his native community the same is applicable to women. Understanding the difference knowledge of women and men in different socio-economic circumstances helps to determine appropriate and suitable interventions.

Women's Participation in Decision Making: The fourth world conference an environment management held at Bejing 1995 proposed actions to strength women's role in decision making but this has not being materialized since women involvement into formulation planning and execution of environmental policy remains low at all levels from local position to the ranks where national and international environmental policies are determined. Of course women in some countries such as Ukraine, Bangladesh, Russia and Mexico have being involved in planning the management of fresh water resources. At international level women are not properly represented in environmental management.

A number of actions have been proposed by policy makers and planners to improve the integration of Gender concerns in the environmental planning.

The following points have been highlighted:

1. Improve data collection on women's and men's resource use, knowledge of access to and control over resources, and opportunities to be involved in decision making.
2. Train staff and management on the relevance of gender issues to environmental outcomes.
3. Establish procedures for incorporating a gender perspective in planning, monitoring and evaluating environmental projects.
4. Ensure opportunities for women to participate in decisions about environmental policies and programmes at all levels, including roles as designers, planners, implementers and evaluators.
5. Foster commitment at all levels–local, national and international–that the integration of gender concerns into policies and programs leads to more equitable and sustainable development. Continued commitment and increased capacity at all levels of society are essential for achieving these goals.

2. Gender Budet Initiatives

This has been discussed by United Nations General Assembly special session on women held in June, 2000 and by the sixth conference of Common Wealth Ministers ofWomen Welfare held at New Delhi, in April 2000. Australia is the first country to adopt a Gender sensitive budget. Later on the women budget exercises are taken up by South Africa and other developing countries.

In India it is Eighth Five Year Plan 1992-97 that highlighted for the first time the need to ensure a definite flow of funds for gender developmental sectors to the women. The plan document made an express treatment that the "benefit of development from the different sectors should not by pass women and special programmes on women should complement to general development programmes". This could not make much dent in ensuring advocate timely flow of funds and benefits the women.

The Ninth Five Year Plan (1992-97) and the Tenth Five Year Plan (2002-2007) while reaffirming the earlier committees adopted women's component plan as one of the major strategies and directed both the central and state governments to ensure not less than 30 per cent of the funds/benefits are ear marked in all the women related sectors. The budgetary provisions made for the welfare of women under any circumstance should not be diverted to other programmes. It should be strictly used for the welfare of women programmes only.

3. Three Point Formula

(i) The first and foremost requirements is to reform all the institutions to establish rights and opportunities for both men and women on equal footings.

(ii) Fostering the all round development to strength more equal resource and participation.

(iii) Taking very strong and effective measures to redress persistence disparities in all the spheres such as socio-economic and cultural fields.

4. Welfare Measures

In Germany and U.K the feminist scholars of the welfare made a case study for social state policy impact on the material status of women. They argue the core policies of the welfare state are basically patriarchal, because they reaffirm the gendered division of labour in society. In India such similar cases should be examined by research scholars on women welfare programmes which have a greatre significance to achieve Gender equality.

5. Mal Ladies in Socio Economic and Cultural Pattern

The Gender based division of labour, domestic violence and oppression are prevalent in Indian rural society. Besides this there are a number of anti social and un progressive cultural elements are also existing. Therefore it is necessary to take preventive measures and implement them effectively.

6. Need For Fresh Thinking

The process of change for the all round development of Indian economy needs a fresh thinking, strong and efficient administrative machinery to implement the programmes and policies and sincere commitment on the part of political parties and NGO's and women's participation in decision taking etc, are the need of an hour.

7. Academic Strategy

Academic institutions such as colleges and universities should play pivotal role in promoting Gender studies. In order to attract a good number of research scholars all the universities in India may open Post Graduate Courses in Gender Studies leading to M.Phil and Ph.D.

Gender study had employment potential and a promising future. It one who is employed on foreign sponsored project is assured of a salary ranging from Rs.12,000 to 15,000 per month.

In Andhra Pradesh it is given to understand the Tirupathy University is only one academic institution that started Gender Studies course. Therefore it is suggested that all other universities in the state may also take up such institutions.

As it is said that our learning should have some earning power, Gender studies assure employment to educated youth in sponsored projects.

In view of practical utility of Gender studies the University Grants Commission may be requested to make a special budgetary provision to the various academic institutions that start gender study after graduation.

8. Human Approach

Empowerment of women is not only the concern of government alone but also the bounden duty of one and all more specially males to encourage and back women in various undertakings.

6

Status of Tribal Women: Some Issues & Concerns

P. Sammulal, A. Hari Prasad and P. Ramlal

The tribal communities are at various stages of development in our country due to their inaccessibility, living in rigorous habitats, large scale illiteracy and ignorance, lack of suitable areas specific and group focused strategies of development etc., At the national level among STs for every 1000 males there are 972 females where as in the general population the sex ratio is 927 as per 1991 census. The relevant information is shown in table 1.

Table 1
Females Male Ratio

Sl. No.	*Year*	*General Population*	*Tribal Population*
1.	1961	941	-
2.	1971	930	-
3.	1981	934	983
4.	1991	927	972

Women are very industries in tribal communities when compared to men and she is an economic asset. It is said that if a man has more land, he marries more than one wife, as all his wife/ wives could assist him in all kinds of agricultural operations in addition to their regular household duties, but still tribal women is not given part of bread in development.

STATUS OF WOMEN IN TRIBALS

We are in the ages of digitalisation and still the position and development aspects of women remained as such.

1. Most of the tribal communities treat their sons and daughters alike and there is no disparity in bringing them up. The parent of girl never faces any kind of difficulties in marrying them. Even woman as daughter-in-law occupies respectable position.
2. As per traditional customary laws women are not allowed to sit in the traditional panchayats and they are prohibited from becoming traditional village or community heads or even members, which is against constitution of India.
3. They play dominant role in traditional colourful dances and they behave and act as priestess to the goddesses in tribal areas. This definitely indicates superior status of women in tribal areas when compared to the social status enjoyed by their counter parts in rural areas.
4. A tribal woman is considered as an economic asset. She attends to all kinds of economic activities except ploughing. [A Lambada women even do ploughing].
5. The occupational pattern of tribal women as per 1991 census reports.

   Cultivators - 32.2%
   Agricultural Labourers – 59.1%
   (Male constitute only 37.2%)
   Women working in primary sector 96.2%.

PROBLEMS OF TRIBAL WOMEN

1. Inspite of good socio-economic status enjoyed by tribal women, women folk are steeped in ignorance & illiteracy.
2. Inspite of good personal hygienic conditions among tribal female population they are found to be deteriorating due to inaccessibility of medical and health facilities. Tribal women sleep on the floor without any kind of mats during nights, sometimes sharing the space with goats, sheep, which are considered as immovable property to them.

3. The women works in the fields and forest till the last days of her advanced pregnancy and again resumes her regular duties soon after purificatory bath is performed, by which her health is under check.
4. The following proverb means a lot for tribals towards women.

   "A women, after all is the cleaner of utensils in the house of others"

   Which is why women are not permitted to plough lands.
5. The girl's education is totally neglected by parents since they believe that investment on girl is not rewarding and early marriage and various peculiar types of matrimonies are great obstacles for the development of education among girls.
6. During menstruation period, in certain tribal areas woman is confined to separate hut or they have to live in the near by forest till the period is over by which she may suffer from various health hazards.
7. With regard to sanction of various kinds of inputs and loans, specially male members are given and seldom a female is sanctioned the benefits except when a particular women is a head of the family and she is also deprived of skill full training courses on agricultural practices.
8. They are deprived of equal share in family and ancestral property, which is her constitutional right.

NEED FOR EMPOWERMENT

In view of various debilitating problems faced by women folk as discussed, empowerment of tribal woman is sine-qua-non for not only improving their quality of life styles but also improving the conditions of tribal families & tribal villages. This process encompasses social, cultural, financial, skill and knowledge empowerment. Unless all these vital aspects are integrated and greater vision is developed in local female population, the sustainable development among tribals cannot be ensured.

These are some of the areas of important concern for empowerment of tribal women.

1. Functional literacy and education has to be carefully formulated to suit changing scenario in tribal areas.

- Gender education and strengthening Sanghas (Women's groups) through workshops, meetings and a mutually aided co-operative society (MACS).
- Education for adolescent girls.
- Technical training for women as well as adolescent girls.
- Support of administrative activities like documentation, monitoring and evolution and training of staff.
- Educational scholarships for individual women as motivation tool.
- Night schools for working women.

2. Local dietary patterns, availability of low cost food items have to be taken into consideration while recommending nutrition's diets to tribal clients.
3. Their skills should be developed to take up new income generating schemes like DWCRA; Self Help Groups mutually aided co-operative society, Anganwadi Centres, Girijana Mahila Sanghas etc. Through this woman should be trained in masonry, carpentry, and black smithy, activities. Encouraged to raise nurseries, grafting, crafting, embroidery etc.
4. Social and cultural development should be achieved through melass, exhibitions etc. As tribal dances, arts and crafts are enriching and empowering aspects of their life styles; these vital aspects have to be further encouraged in every tribal settlement.
5. The local organisations have to be empowered and guided properly in functioning and maintenance by women liasion workers and community coordinators.
6. Tribal women-folk have to be specially trained to take up the responsibilities as envisaged to in the gramsabhas. They should be also enlightened about various regulations pertaining to protective regulations.
7. Entrepreneurship among tribal women should be encouraged.
8. The traditional village institutions and development organizations of tribal villages should become modern pillars for achieving foundation for self-reliance and progress of tribal women.

9. Focus should be on generation of awareness on education, health and nutrition and participation by women particularly in productive sector encompassing savings, grain banks and other economic activities.
10. The system of women reservation specially is to be brought out for the upliftment of these people.
11. The concept of social justice includes principles like emancipation, equality, dignity, is to seriously concerned.
12. The special component plan (SCP) and the tribal sub-plan (TSP) needs to be made on par with women are to be developed.
13. Supervising survey for identification of atrocity prone areas towards woman.
14. Due to the advent of technology woman have to be educated through various technical tools.
15. Usage of Internet, personal computer and computer literacy should be provided.
16. Various government policies, programmes should be facilitated and reached to the tribal areas.

GOVERNMENT POLICIES AIMED AT TRIBAL WOMEN

The Ministry of Tribal Affairs implements two specific schemes, namely, Educational Complexes in Low Literacy Pockets for the educational development of tribal women and construction of hostels for tribal girls.

In addition to these schemes, the Ministry through State Governments/UT Administrations and Voluntary Organisations are implementing a number of Central and Centrally-Sponsored Schemes. Out of these schemes, such as:

- Special Central Assistance to Tribal Sub-Plan;
- Grants under First Provision to Article 275 (1) of the Constitution;
- Ashram Schools in Tribal Sub-Plan areas;
- Vocational Training Centres in Tribal Areas;
- Grant-in-aid to Voluntary Organisations;
- Research and Training;
- Investment in TRIFED;

- Price Support to TRIFED;
- Grants-in-aid to State Tribal Development Corporations;
- Establishment of Village Grain Banks;
- Development of Primitive Tribal Groups, the Tribal women also get benefits for their upliftment.
- The Government has amended its rules to provide employment on the post of LDC/Class IV to a woman who has been incapacitated by her in-laws on account of dowry torture.
- To protect the workingwomen from harassment, the women Rajasthan Civil Service Conduct Rules have been amended to deal sternly with those male employees who harass or misbehave with women employees.
- Various women policies are announced on May 8, 2000 for various states.
- In certain State's Women Commission constituted on May 15, 1999 and accorded constitutional status.
- Rajasthan in the first state where maintenance allowance for women has been raised from Rs. 500 to Rs, 2500 per month.
- Widows, divorced, deserted and other exploited women shall be helped for self-employment through loan facilities of Khadi and Gramodyog.
- In the handicrafts sector about 32.5% of the outlay of the identified Central Sector Schemes is earmarked for the benefit of the scheduled caste, scheduled tribe and women artisans with an allocation of 15%, 7.5% and 10% respectively. The major schemes are
    - Baba Saheb Ambedkar Hastshilp Vikas Yojana,
    - Design and Technology Up gradation Scheme,
    - Marketing Support and Services Scheme,
    - Export Promotion Scheme,
    - Research & Development and
    - UNDP Project.

  These schemes play a vital role in the empowerment and upliftment of women artisans and particularly those belonging to scheduled caste and scheduled tribe.

- In Handicraft sector, women constitute 47.42% of workforce and of these 37.11% belong to scheduled caste and scheduled tribe category (Source: NCAER survey, 1995-96). There are certain crafts, which are practiced predominantly by women like embroidery, beadwork, appliqué, durries, shawls, Cane and Bamboo, artistic textile, weaving, mat weaving etc. can be marketed by government support.
- Special attention is being paid to ensure that a large number of women artisans get benefit of all the development schemes such as training, marketing related programmes, National Awards, exhibitions etc., which are being implemented by the Office of the Development Commissioner (Handicrafts).

Denial of equal participation, access and control of productive resources had placed women as unequal partners in developmental process. Despite enactments of several socio-economic legislations and the Indian Constitution declaring gender equality, the patriarchal values and normative structure established some two thousand years ago hindered women's emancipations and empowerment. Very specifically tribal women are adversely effected and are deprived of opportunities, which has been highlighted here may become a source towards the urgent realization of tribal women empowerment which will add to the total empowerment of women marching towards gender equality.

REFERENCES

Bhowmick, P.K. (1991), Tribes in the Changing Circumstances of India, Man in India, Vol. 71, No. 1.

Janah, Sunil (1993), The Tribals of India, Calcutta, Oxford University Press.

Mohan Rao K. (1999), Tribal Development in Andhra Pradesh, Problems Performance and Prospects, Book links Corporation, Hyderabad.

Mohan Rao K., Socio-Cultural Profile of Tribes of Andhra Pradesh, TCR & TI, Hyderabad.

7

Muslim Women in India–Problems and Prospects

N.T.K. Naik, S.Mansoor Rahman
and H. Akther Banu

STEREOTYPING is usually a necessary precondition for social discrimination, and all the more so when various social and cultural realities are sought to be hardened into "identities". That is probably why, over the past decade especially, certain stereotypes have been systematically developed about the minority communities (especially Muslims, but also Christians).

In such a context, it is refreshing to come across a study that seeks to go beyond the sociological veil spread by a focus on *purdah* and actually examines the conditions faced by different categories of Muslim women in the country. There is widespread perception that Muslim women are among the most backward, illiterate and oppressed in the world. In media they are always shown clad in burqa or wrapped in hijab (veil). They are also perceived to be confined to the four walls of their homes totally cut off from outside world. While partly it is true but reality is much more complex and also not static.

A new book by Zoya Hasan and Ritu Menon (presents the results of a national survey covering around 10,000 Muslim and Hindu women. This is the first such survey of this magnitude, covering the whole country, and obviously therefore, the findings deserve attention. But perhaps even more interesting than the results themselves are the insights that are drawn into the interplay of various factors that determine the conditions of Muslim women's lives.

One of the standard assumptions about Muslim women is that religion prevents them from getting more equal access to education. It is certainly true that Muslim women are more likely to be illiterate than Hindu women (in the survey, 59 per cent had never attended school and less than 10 per cent had completed school). Across the survey, among all communities and caste groups, financial constraints and gender bias dominate over other factors in determining levels of education. Indeed, in those regions where Muslims are better off (as in the south and to a lesser extent in the west), Muslim women also have higher levels of education.

The question of Muslim women, their social status and rights cannot be understood without keeping these things in mind. First of all it must be kept in mind that Quran makes clear pronouncement in favor of equal rights for both sexes (2:228). However, this vision of Islam for sexual equality could not find practical implementation for number of reasons. Those who embraced Islam, however sincere they might have been, were product of a fiercely male-dominated society.

The Quranic pronouncement on the other hand, was an ideal which required very different cultural milieu. From sociological viewpoint it was not immediately implementable. However, two other features that are more specific to the Muslim community may have operated to devalue continuing education for girls. The first is that Muslim men also have very low educational attainment in general. The study found that 26 per cent of educated Muslim women had illiterate husbands. In addition, the low age of marriage is a major inhibiting factor. At the national level, the mean age of marriage of Muslim girls is very low at 15.6 years, and in the rural north it falls to an appalling 13.9 years.

Some of this is due to straightforward control over women's agency by male members of the household. Seventy five per cent of the women in the survey (both Hindu and Muslim) reported that they need permission from their husbands to work outside the home. Interestingly, the study revealed that across the board women in India tend to have relatively less autonomy of decision-making within the household.

Less than 10 per cent of the respondents took any decisions on their own in major or minor matters, and among the 30 per cent who took decisions jointly with their husbands, Muslim women reported greater consultation than Hindus for all categories of decisions. Clearly, however, patriarchal control remains one important constraint upon the outside work of women, among Muslims as well as certain other social categories.

But in addition, most of the outside work that the representative Muslim woman has access to falls in the lowest paid and most exploited categories of labor. Such activities-self-employed in low-productivity activities in the informal sector, as casual laborers and domestic servants-imply poor working conditions and low wages. It is, therefore, possible that Muslim women are kept out of the paid workforce not only by religious or *purdah* type motivations, but perhaps more significantly by low education, lack of opportunity, low mobility and the inability to delegate domestic responsibilities.

Orthodox Muslims uphold the low position of women as a symbol of cultural identity. Muslims hold conformist ideals and beliefs from the Quran and the Hadis. Although Indian women live under the Hindu Code Bill that gives equal rights to women, most Muslim women are restricted under the Muslim Personal Law. Muslims who are ignorant of the Quran are unaware of the allowances in the Shariat for social adjustment, change, and accommodation. In fact, Indian Muslim communities follow four different Shariats: the Hanafi, the Shaafi, the Hambali, and the Maliki. Islamic scholars state that the Shariat is not unchangeable. There is also disparity between the actual practice of polygamy and the Quran's strict provision that all wives must be treated equally. Islamic practices have been manipulated to suit male interests. Indian Muslims are either Ashrafs or non Ashrafs. Ashrafs are the upper social class and are made up of the Sayyads, the Sheikhs, the Mughals, and the Pathans, in descending order of hierarchy. There are differences in the treatment of women within this stratification. For instance, many nonAshraf women do not observe purdah, but the tendency among the Ashraf is to impose purdah.

There exist 110 million Muslims in India-which, with the exception of Indonesia-is the largest population of Muslims in a single country in the world. Muslim communities in India are geographically scattered, culturally diverse and economically disparate. A majority of Muslims in India live in Uttar Pradesh, Bihar and West Bengal. According to the 1991 Government of India Census, there are over 48 million Muslim women in India.

Like women from other communities, Muslim women are differentiated across gender, class, caste and community, and are subject to the interface between gender and community within the Indian social, political and economic context. At the same time, Muslim women's location in modern India also derives from their status as a minority which colours their life experience and self-perception in distinct ways, and in this respect they differ from women belonging to other communities.

After five decades of independence the majority of Muslim women are among the most disadvantaged, least literate, economically impoverished and politically marginalized sections of Indian society. The social and economic issues confronting women in Muslim communities mandate attention as does the violation of their rights as citizens of India.

Women in India do not constitute an undifferentiated, homogenous category, yet, little information exists on Indian Muslim women. However, the perception that Muslim women's social status in India can be ascribed to a certain intrinsic, immutable feature of Islam or that their legal status derives solely from reference to Muslim laws is widely prevalent. As a result of this misconception, Muslim women are often considered as 'separate' or 'different' from Indian society, reinforcing cultural stereotypes and obscuring their contemporary realities. Mainstream historical narrative with its emphasis on the rise and fall of the Muslim empire excludes Muslim women. Although Muslim women were generally absent from public life during this period, several women from royalty were authors and poets-or even a Sultan as in the case of Raziya Sultana.

At the turn of the twentieth century the topic of female education was taken up by Muslim communities. Several Muslim women made pioneering contributions to female education. Figures for Muslim girls' participation in educational institutions during the early decades of the twentieth century surpassed figures for the national average. Muslim women also participated in campaigns against female seclusion and legal discrimination, and played an active part in the emerging women's movement. This trend suffered a setback due to the social, political and economic upheavals in, during and after the partition of India in 1947. In the wake of the trauma and large-scale migrations during 1947, and a subsequent lack of political presence, it was extremely difficult for Muslim women to articulate their concerns, both within the community and as citizens of India.

Higher levels of women's education are strongly associated with both lower infant mortality and lower fertility. A literate mother is more prone to be embedded with appropriate future generations, dexterous in achieving higher economic growth and productivity than an illiterate mother. Better-educated women are also able to communicate better with their spouse about family size decisions, family planning programmes more effectively, and have higher potentialities to save and protect their children with special emphasis on girl children who are the usual victims of social evils like gender bias, ill treatments, sheer manipulations and so on beyond their limits of tolerance.

Muslims still remain backward in the education. A number of radical steps need to be taken on priority basis if they are to come on par and overtake their more advanced brethren. The increasing incidence of dropouts as one climbs the educational ladder, and the occupational structure of the Muslim society is partly responsible for this. As soon as the male child is strong enough to help his father, he is withdrawn from the school to supplement the meagre earnings of the family. Similarly as soon as the female child acquires marriageable age they give first preference to perform marriage only.

Table 1
Literacy Among Muslim Women in Selected States

Category	*Andhra Pradesh* (%)	*Tamil Nadu* (%)	*Utter Prades* (%)
All Women	50.4	64.4	42.2
Muslim Women	59.1	76.2	37.4

Source: Muslim Education in India, Yojana, September, 2005.

Linking education with employment is a common trait which acts sharply as a disincentive in the case of Muslims who some how come to believe that their prospects of getting a job in the public sector or the organized private sector are slim. Many Muslim children do not get at home either the benefits of inherited learning or academic support, as most of them are first generation learners and by and large there is a lack of awaremess and academic interest.

Many orthodox and well-to-do parents are reluctant to send their daughters to co-educational institutions. Another important factor is the economic condition. With a majority working as petty shop-keepers, crafts men or landless labourers their middle class base is extremely low.

The influence of recent communal conflicts exhorted the parents started to give importance to modern education in order make their daughters self reliant. Many schools were opened and enrolment campaigns were organized with education getting impetus. However, despite this awakening, Muslims continue to be educationally backward community in the country. The correlation between education and development is universally accepted. The impact of education on the weaker sections whose economic condition has improved in the process and self confidence augmented is all too evident.

MUSLIM WOMEN'S SOCIO-ECONOMIC AND POLITICAL STATUS

In modern-day India, the socio-economic status of women in Muslim communities, along with their political participation rates and the need for legal reform, are causes for concern and need attention. A central feature of this 'backwardness' is the appalling educational and socio-economic status of Muslims in India, particularly Muslim women.

In a study of 39 districts in 1981-where the population of Muslims ranged from 20 per cent to 95 per cent (which could be considered a fairly representative sample of the Muslims in India)-the literacy rate of Muslim women was found to be 21.91 per cent, which was lower than the average of 24.82 per cent for the whole country. Muslims' share in public employment in All-India and Central Services is less than 3 per cent. Within this picture of poor overall employment statistics, it is a predictable certainty that the corresponding figures for Muslim women are still lower.

Equally importantly, it is crucial for members of Muslim communities-Muslim women and men-to introspect and debate among themselves as to the reasons and remedies for their economic vulnerability and poor educational and employment status, and to consider possible remedies. There is also a need for debate and mobilization by Muslim women on legal reform in order to overcome patriarchal structures with Muslim communities. The debate on legal reform is linked to debates on women and Islam. Muslim women in India need to participate in the contemporary debate on Islam and women's rights. It is imperative for Indian Muslim women to reclaim their right to religious knowledge, enter the discourse on the Shari'a and challenge their historic marginalization from religious knowledge as well as its discriminatory interpretations.

This session on 'socio-economic and educational status of Muslim women in India' is wide and complex. However, in normative terms the status of Muslim women is quite high. This status is amply supported by Quranic injunctions. It is widely realized that Quran confirms high place to women and supports decent and equal treatment to men and women. Secondly, the status may be ascertained on the basis of their power of decision making in matters of socio-cultural importance. Decisions in matters of marriage, festivals, entertaining guests, use of social interacting channels etc. are subject to approval of the lady of the house. And, as she grows old, she is more powerful. But, in actual terms of facts and figures, the condition of Muslim women is bad. This situation causes a concern and challenge to both the Islamists and secularists in terms of analyzing scientifically the reasons and to drawing an action plan in view of the positive emerging context for amelioration of condition of Muslim women.

There are multiple causes responsible for bad condition of Muslim women particularly in northern and eastern parts of the country. Social, cultural, religious, legal, economic and political reasons are broad areas, which are generally talked about.

Archana Chaturvedi in her compilation "Encyclopaedia of Muslim Women," concludes "Muslim women remain largely backward and deprived. They continue to be uneducated, resourceless and victimised in spite of reformative attitude of Islamic movement."

Muslim women are not the exclusive agent, they share operational space with all other sections of Indian society. They should be taken as part of Indian women folk, who have multiple roles to play in different capacities as economic, social, cultural and political actor. She is participant in all processes and suffers of all ills. She is to be taken beyond marriage, divorce and guardianship syndrome.

Even the Personal Law Board has organized open sessions with women representatives. Muslim women's Forum is also active. Muslim reform movements like those of Nadwatul Mujahidin, Jamaat-e-Islami floated their own women organizations and are trying to unleash a new awareness. Processes are on, and results will follow. In many Muslim countries, women are on the move.

There are both kinds of Islamic and secular movements in Muslim world but reflecting a change. In some Muslim countries, Muslim women theologians have also emerged with thorough knowledge of the Quran, Islamic theology and Sharia. There are well-recognized women theologians like Fatima Mirsani from Morocco, Amina Wadood and Riffat Hassan from USA. There are a number of famous women organizations also like 'Sisters in Islam' in Malaysia, Shirkatgah in Pakistan and so on. Iran has very active women's movement.

They are active in practically all field of work and represent in considerable number in Iranian Parliament as well. Another success story may be taken from Indonesia where women have made their presence felt in higher education.

There are large number of Islamic universities and a strong movement for women's rights. As per figures of 2000, Saudi women also outnumbered men as graduates making up 58 per cent of nearly 3200 students. Jordan has amended its law to give equal rights to men and women. These trends are visible in many countries like Pakistan, Bangladesh etc. as well. Hence, the women world is not static. They are on the move. Their efforts in finding place in economic and educational sectors must be properly channelized.

To sum up, there are scores of problems and issues relating to Muslim women in India, but these are to be analyzed in a proper perspective. Their status and conditions are related to their economic and educational advancement. Secondly, a strong movement is to be built in order to open a dialogue within the community for providing space and choice of opportunity to Muslim women unleashed by emerging positive context.

8

Agrarian Distress, Farmers' Suicides and Gender Vulnerability

E. Revathi and Burra Ramulu

INTRODUCTION

The recent unprecedented and large-scale incidence of farmers' suicides has drawn the attention of policy makers, academics and activists. There are number of studies that focused on identifying causes of these suicides which reveal the multi dimensional and complex nature of the problem of agrarian crisis in general and its specificities to the context of Andhra Pradesh that has been pursuing economic reforms.

Suicides by cotton farmers were reported from Andhra Pradesh in the second half of the decade of eighties from the district of Prakasam. Suicides as a phenomenon have started from the early years of the 1990 decade starting with the state of Punjab which has continued in the decade of nineties and well into the 21st century. The overall instances of suicides across the nation show a concentration around dry land tracts. Nevertheless irrigated tracts have not been exempt from the occurrence, which manifest a different set of issues. States like Andhra Pradesh, Karnataka and Maharashtra have manifested suicides from mid 90's which mostly revolved around the dry tracts like the Bidar (Karnataka) Vidarbha (Maharashtra) and Rayalaseema and Telangana (Andhra Pradesh) pervading the macro effects of the phenomenon (Vasavi, 1999

Deshpande 2005, Mohanty 2001a, Mohanty and Shroff 2003, Reddy and Rao, Revathi 1998, Aware 1999, Assadi 2001). Studies have explored the causative factors but the resultant effects remain less explored. Studies in this area focused on the economic dimension of the tragedy at household level or the agrarian crisis in general at the macro level and have often missed to understand the implications the tragedy has to the women. A gender perspective of the crisis has been conspicuously missing in the studies so far made on the subject. The manifestation of loss of the head of the household is not only rooted in the economic domain but also in social, psychological, realms that are closely interrelated. Farmers' suicides make the household vulnerable to a host of issues.

The present paper explores the vulnerability of the women in the deceased farmers' household with the help of select case studies in the district of Warangal. Suicides that have occurred before the year 2000 make the sample for the study. This paper examines nine case studies of the deceased farmers' households.

FRAMEWORK OF THE PAPER

Case study method has been adopted essentially to document in detail the post suicide situation as well as the implications of the tragedy to the women of these households. An attempt is made to identify forces that affect the efforts at relating to the post suicide situation faced by these women.

The paper addresses the consequences of farmers' suicides in the different domains viz economic; social; and psychological. The economic parameters considered are the indebtedness, shifts occurred in the livelihoods, the social parameters include the loss of status of women and the children, the psychological factors include the trauma faced, the emotional loss. The paper centers on the two issues viz., the impact of the crisis and the coping mechanisms. The involuntary changes in the household manifest the impact of the shock. The coping mechanisms include processes of how the affected women negotiated the challenges posed by crisis/ trauma situation and how they have taken up voluntary action to mitigate the crisis. The differential impact with respect to the factors of age, class, and social group of the women is the basis for analysis. Age becomes a crucial factor in adjustment where young women seek to have protection in the form of children. Adjustment to shocks varies across class and social group determined by cultural and social construct of patriarchy. Section I deals with the voluntary and involuntary changes in the households and section II gives the summary and conclusions.

Warangal has registered the largest number of farmers' suicides beginning from the last quarter of 1997. The intra district distribution of suicides shows two patterns. Firstly the incidence is characteristic of divisions, which are tube well dependent for farming like Jangoan, Narsampet and partly Mulugu. Secondly areas characteristic of irrigation through canals but which form the tail end parts and also partly irrigated under tanks (Revathi 2005). Irrespective of the irrigation sources in both the areas, there is heavy dependence on ground water for irrigation. The sample cases are drawn from both types of areas representing high and low stakes of the farmers. While details of the incidence of suicides in Warangal district vis-à-vis the state are furnished in Table 1 distribution farmers' suicides by revenue division in Warangal district are furnished in Table 2.

Table 1
Distribution of suicides in Andhra Pradesh

State/Region/district	*1998*	*1999*	*2000*	*2001*	*2002*	*2003*	*2004*	*Total*
Andhra Pradesh	190	180	220	357	328	347	1795	3416
Telangana	169	149	163	230	221	201	1084	2217 (64.90)
Warangal	69	100	98	119	123	92	88	689

Table 2
Incidence of Suicides by Division in Warangal District between December 1997 and August 2004

Revenue Division	*No. of suicides*
Jangaon	105 (15.24)
Mulugu	242 (35.12)
Mahabubabad	49 (7.11)
Narsampet	76 (11.03)
Warangal	217 (31.49)
Total	689 (100.00)

SECTION - I

SOCIAL PROFILE OF THE DECEASED

Studies show that farmers' suicides took place mostly in the age group of 30-50 (Bhushan and Reddy, 2004). The age of the respondent is generally between 25-45, which implies two groups of age, as to that of young widows with young children, and women with older children along with responsibilities.

All the cases are nuclear families. In fact studies show that 90 per cent of the deceased cases have been separated from the joint family on average around 7-10 years. The family cycle is evident. For the first 5-7 years they are generally joint families during which time the couple have children, but after they get separated they try to set up independent farming during which time the investment soars up. Generally some additional land, bullocks, cart, and other implements, are purchased. Land is taken on lease in which high value crops are cultivated, to improve the income levels. The process of falling into debt trap too is almost the same. Though most of the deceased have farming experience they have for the first time become cultivators or have scaled up the cultivation by leasing in land. For the women, it is almost getting out of joint family after the childbirth cycle is completed, into the phase of self-cultivation which amounts to more work in terms of labour, and supervision. Though women were part and parcel of work they were not part of decision-making nor were they aware of financial affairs of the agriculture. Women who were well into the cultivation process knew about their debts, their sources and they could stick on to cultivation even after death of husband.

"He never told me anything about the farm needs or the money (debt) he brought in. I had no idea at all of the monetary matters of farming. I could not think of farming after his death. Those who lent him still harass for repayment". (Jalgoori Lakshmi)

DEBT- LEVELS AND DEGREE

One of the major factors leading to suicides is indebtedness. Social and psychological factors may appear to be the causative factors but they act more as stressors often the underlying cause being indebtedness. Often debt was incurred for setting up cultivation. For the cash starved farmers private sources were the only means. The average debt of the farmers who committed suicide is around a lakh rupees. Causes for the debts in all the eight cases are predominantly because of agricultural investment, capital and current investment, then for marriage of daughters and house construction. The composition of debt shows the interest component to be higher than the principal. While drought, lack of rainfall, hence less yield, pest attack have depreciated their earnings, low and fluctuating prices increased cost of production have eroded their paying capacity. In the case of Hymavathi debt is large, she belongs to upper caste and it is because of marriage of daughter. The degree of debt varies only slightly across the cases, in the two upper caste cases it is high because of marriage expenses. All suicides have a history of debt accumulation for the past 3-4 years.

Sambaiah made two attempts to dig well for irrigation. Both these attempts failed and only brought him into debts. As he was a close associate of the Telugu Desam Party leader, he could get institutional loans easily. He borrowed from the co-operative society bank (PACS), Corporation bank, and Land Mortgage bank to purchase oil engine costing Rs. 6600 for lifting water from the rivulet and purchase of a bullock cart for Rs. 10,000. Besides these institutional loans he also incurred debts at high interest rates from Warangal adtidars (commission agents) and traders of neighboring Dwarakapet village. He also took three acres of land on lease to cultivate cotton crop for a period of two years, for which the rent was Rs. 4000 per acre. He was already in debts and in order to get out of these debts he extended area of cultivation by taking additional land on lease. (Sarojana)

The investment for the bore well, pipe lines, motor regularized service connection was between Rs. 40,000 and 50,000. All this investment was brought on loans, of course not from the banks. We did not know much of the bank loans or anybody to support in getting it. The debts at the time of my husband's death came to Rs. 96,000. We brought it from our relatives. (Nirmala Reddy)

Krishna Reddy had two attached labourers. Good margins made him to take land on lease and cultivate it in large extent. Insufficient rains continuously for 3-4 years resulted in depletion of ground water. In the year 1997-98 pest attack was severe and expenditure on pesticide also rose up very much. Krishna Reddy had to borrow for the inputs from *adtidars* of Warangal at high interest rates. (Hymavathy Reddy)

'We never leased out our land when Yadagiri was alive. We had full-fledged agriculture with a plough, a pair of bullocks, and an attached labour or the jeetha. When there was no sufficient water in the well then Yadagiri went for deepening it spending between Rs. 20,000 to 30,000. The well was deepened by another two golas, still it did not yield sufficient water. Mostly loans were brought from outside, he was not telling anything to me regarding the debts, or crops; I used to say this is not good but he never listened. I lost all my jewellery given at the time of my marriage except for this pair of ear tops. Debts soared up in just three years before his death. (Akkapally Lalithamma)

We started our life with one acre of dry land and some sheep. My husband took land on lease as we had insufficient land for cultivation. With the help of the income on the sheep we were able to buy 4 acres of land. As there was no irrigation source for the land we dug a well. We spent about Rs. 37,000 for the well. We spent another Rs. 3000 for sanction of power, or the service connection, and another Rs. 7,000 for purchase of motor. At that juncture we incurred an expenditure of Rs. 80,000 for purchase of land and also for the well. All this could not be from our own savings, and we incurred debt. (Karra Rajamma)

SPECTER OF INDEBTEDNESS HAUNTS–POST SUICIDE CHALLENGES

"Shakuntalamma, the Kapu lady from Hanamakonda town, has given an acre of her land on lease and also Rs. 15000 for farm needs to Sambaiah. But she has been pressing for repayment of the loan. Whenever she visits she calls me to remind the loan to be repaid. I beg her to give time and just fall on her feet praying mercy. What else can I do, without anybody to stand by me? We performed marriage of our eldest daughter a year before he committed suicide. We paid only half of the amount of dowry to my son-in-law. My son-in -law harasses my daughter to get the remaining amount of dowry. How can I pay it now when my man has died leaving me in the sea? My daughter has regular nuisance at home because of the dowry that we could not pay and any little help that she extends to us. Her life is ruined because of my poverty. That's constant worry to me. (Jalgoori Lakshmi)

The pressure for repayment was so high even after the suicide that Vijaya from Issipeta had to put all her land to sale.

"After the death of Sudhakar Reddy I could not face the pressure of the debtors. Then I sold off the whole of 2.5 acres. Actually the land was divided among the debtors, fertilizer dealer took one acre under debt, three other debtors took one acre, 20 guntas (half acre) was given to debtors from my natal village. They tried to sell the land but nobody purchased it. There was 2.5 lakh debt totally. The Sarpanch and village elders made a settlement regarding the debts. Still I have to repay debts to my sisters" (Yara Vijaya).

When he died the debt was Rs. 1,10,000 from relations and friends and aditidars in Warangal. On some debts the interest rate was as high as 36 per cent. Sammaiah was an active worker in the CPM party. I also attend the party meetings. The arty people helped in reducing the interest rates on our debts. After his death the party people in the village negotiated the interest rate and fixed it at 24 per cent (L. Prameela).

The pressure of unpaid debts remained on the women persistently. Delayed payment of relief though was useful in settlement of debts but in most cases it also witnessed sale of assets unable to bear the pressure of debts. Indebtedness, an individualized problem is treated the same even in the post suicide situation. Kinship, community, local governance, political parties intervened to some extent in settlement of debts and in reducing the pressure of repayment, phasing it and also waiving or standardizing the interest rate. Often the debtors could wait also in the hope that the women are receiving the relief package and hence their debts be cleared. There was connivance on part of debtors, the middlemen who pursued for the package on behalf of the victim and also the revenue officials.

SHIFTS IN LIVELIHOODS AND MIGRATION: LOSS OF STATUS AND INCREASING HARDSHIP

Women surviving in the deceased households faced lot of hardship in terms of shifts in livelihoods, migration, incomes, assets, debt repayments in the post suicide times. The loss of husband affects the family economy in adverse manner. Inevitably the woman has to take up the responsibility of running the family that was not so smooth sailing either when the husband was alive. She is also required to clear the loans and also take care of the children. New challenges and pressures put the woman to great stress. The woman is often a victim of greater work and less time to rest or take care of her health and personal needs. Often women in these situations are forced to work for extra hours or do a variety of works. Most women used to work in the farm as wage labour or in their own farm and had occasional free days as the work was not available or there was another member who could do something to feed the family while one would do domestic works. But in the post suicide situation as cultivator they had to own up the entire responsibility of running it or as agriculture labour had to diversify to casual wage work to support the family. Women belonging to the middle and lower social groups wound up most of the debts with help of government relief package, leased out land and took to wage labour thereby slipping into unstable occupations and incomes. Where they took up cultivation as in the case of Hymavathi, Rajamma, Nirmala, it was a difficult task in terms of lack of extension, information of markets, interface with markets etc. Besides, the insufficient infrastructure in terms of power, irrigation also puts them to innumerable difficulties.

"I worked as farm labour all my life but for a few years before my husband died I was working in the lands that we took on lease. But after Sambaiah's death, we did not do cultivation again. How can I do farming with a girl and small boy and no money to get grains for the next day? I became a wage labour again. Now I do whatever work I get, *vuppari pani* (construction work), *baayi pani* (farm labour). I cannot sit idle. (Jalgoori Lakshmi)

'On March 1 1998 Yadagiri consumed pesticide and died in the cotton fields. After the death of my husband my occupation remained as a casual agricultural labour, the land we have is leased out, as I could not manage cultivation single-handed. (Akkapally Lalithamma)

'I get tensed up looking after domestic as well as outside works. Sometimes the power is gone it comes at night times and we have to water the fields I have to get things done somehow. Sometimes I also go to the market with the attached labour to sell the produce' (Hymavathy Reddy).

'When we were working as labour though social status was low we were tension free but from the time we took to cultivation there is always a worry not for one thing but for so many things, how to cater to the needs of cultivation, is the major problem'. (Nirmala)

'I work in others' fields as we have sold most of our land for clearing the debts. Now we have very little land, which cannot provide enough work or income for us. Now I have no prestige problems and I work less as exchange labour and more as casual labour. I go for work whoever calls me. I even take my daughter for work on Sundays. We get 40 rupees each which is so important for us now. I also learnt sewing on the machine. This I learnt when I was at my parents' house. I stitch clothes during night times. I also bought a second hand sewing machine. (Yara Vijaya)

'After the death of my husband, when there was no work available in the village, I went Hyderabad along with my two sons in search of work. First time in life I had to go out of the village. My sister living there asked me to come there instead of starving here. There I worked as casual labour in construction industry for two months. I was earning Rs. 60 as daily wage then. I was not happy living in Hyderabad away from my home and the people here.

I thought that I cannot continue cultivation and therefore gave the land on lease to one of our brothers-in-law. From that time onwards my occupation has become multifarious. I work as farm labour in the peak season, and then get into selling seasonal fruit like the custard apples, guavas, and mangoes and vegetables. This year I purchased two goats costing Rs. 3000 each and along with these we are also rearing a few goats belonging to my brother-in-law. My younger son looks after the goats. I have to do so many works to survive in harsh times'. (L Prameela).

There is an increase in the work burden for the women in the post suicide situation, integrating two roles, besides the household work, it is almost triple burden. Some women have become workaholics to support the household taking up extra work. They hardly take a break because there is no second person to look after the affairs in her absence. 'I cannot go anywhere, if I go the work here gets stuck up and I have to be back by the evening. All social relations come only after my work'. (Nirmala)

LOSS OF ASSETS

Loss of an earning family member disturbs the family emotionally and shatters the family organization in multiple ways. It has severe impact on the well being of the members. Often the family stands to lose the earnings of the member who has died and puts extra burden on the remaining members to clear the liabilities, loss of workdays and additional costs of death. It affects their earnings and erodes their economic strength. The situation of lesser earnings and higher needs put the family under greater stress and compels them to borrow to tide over the situation of growing marginal credit needs.

In some cases it aggravates the situation by reduced period to clear the loans and eroded sources of credit. In situations where cultivation is continued by the women it becomes a Herculean task to cater to the credit needs. Affected families tend to complete the social responsibilities with the belief that it may become more difficult in future with the fragile family situation and the risks a family has to run with single woman as the head of it. All these factors further dispossess the family and assets are often sold to honor the commitments.

"I lost all my gold ornaments one by one. Whenever there is need or there is no food, I sold off ear tops, silver anklets to the komati Seth (Vysya trader) in the village. I even sold kitchen utensils. I mortgaged these for a paltry amount or sold them way for a cheap price. Seth gave me Rs. 500 for 14 tolas of silver anklets and Rs. 500 for two grams of ear tops. All our assets are with the Seth in the village. In the end I also sold rice storage tin for fifty rupees that I bought for hundred and fifty rupees when I needed money to take my daughter to hospital for delivery. (Jalgoori Lakshmi)

We had buffaloes, bullocks' and bullock cart when we had full fledged agriculture when he was alive. Everything was sold off after he left us. Now it is a small patch of land we cultivate and daily wage is the only source for living. (Yara Vijaya)

After his death I continued with the agriculture on our own land. I sold off the cattle, a pair of bullocks, bullock cart, and one buffalo and repaid the immediately pressurizing debts. My son worked for two years as attached labour for grazing sheep after death of his father. We took to cultivation with rented tractor as we sold off everything. (Karra Rajamma)

'Now our economic position is deteriorated. I am the only working hand, and how much do I get it is only Rs. 25 a day. Only this year my younger daughter has also started working with me in the farm. And that is some relief for me. She is also now learning how to roll beedis, this work is just now picking in the village. (Akkapally Lalithamma).

I abandoned the house where my husband took his life. We now live in rented house as I don't like to go to that house again. The government has sanctioned housing scheme under which a house plot was given. I started house construction with Rs. 10,000 borrowed amount but could not complete and finally I had given the house to those who lent me money. (Nirmala)

Loss of major earning member cannot be compensated in any way, the effects are that shift of roles, and children pulled out of school and put to work. There is desperate need for additional hands for work and income. Where children are not of working age it is not possible for the woman alone to feed the entire family.

HUMAN CAPITAL: EDUCATION AND HEALTH OF CHILDREN AND WOMEN

Children of these families are affected adversely. Their future is put to a rude shock. The plight of the children further disturbs the strength of the woman. Often the children are pulled out of school. They are put into labour to supplement the family. Girls are married off earlier than normal in a hurry to complete the responsibilities early. In some cases the families settle for lesser than best alliance for fear of expenses and newly perceived vulnerability of the family. Developmental opportunities of the child are affected in a big way. A few families also witness threats to survival or growth of the kids. Children age faster in these troubled times with early entry into labour force, marriage and from 'security' to single woman.

"My son is 14 year old and he is in 10th class. The MRO asked me to join him in the residential school away form the village. How do I survive all alone if I send him away? His studies suffer now and also cost me a little more. I cannot send him as I will not have anybody to help me and just be there with me. I know he is a kid but that still makes me feel that I am not all alone. (Jalgoori Lakshmi)

My younger daughter dropped out of college to help in farm wage labour and beedi work. My brothers help me in expenditure on clothes and expenditure of child's studies. My brother asked me to let my daughter continue with her studies. I was reluctant because of the burden and I also have to send my son to the school. I was spending Rs. 1000 per annum on his schooling as he was going to a private school in the village. But this year I put him in the government school, now he is in the 6th class. My elder daughter rolls beedis at her in –laws place. She had to give up studies from Intermediate though she was good at studies. She is also now learning how to roll beedis. And that is some relief for me. (Akkapally Lalithamma).

My son was studying 10th class when we were in severe debt conditions. Then my husband stopped his studies and put him to graze the cattle, whereas he has gone to work outside the village to earn to pay off the debts. My son was 16 years when his father died, after that for one year he could not work at all. He was under depression, and was unstable mentally. My youngest daughter was also going to school then, with the help of the MRO I put her in hostel at Ghanpur in the sixth class but she could not stay there. That was the first time she was away from me. She would cry everyday that her father came in the dreams. I had to bring her back. She stopped with 7th class and next year I got her married. (Karra Rajamma)

'The only happy event for me is my younger son, Srinivas, is able to study. At the time of his father's death Srinivas was working as attached labour. With the help of MRO Srinivas could get admitted to Social Welfare residential high school. He passed out in first division, later completed plus two and now is in the second year of under graduation'. (Sarojana)

'After his death help was offered to put my children in school. I wanted my younger son to study but he cried at the idea of sending him to hostel, moreover people around chided me at the idea, so I put him to graze the goats' (L. Pramila).

Often the women are not able to access the facility extended for the education of their children especially the girl child because of the fears of 'society' and 'neighbourhood'. Also because of the trauma faced neither the mother nor the girls are able to withstand separation to be educated in residential schools.

Loss of a male member and head of the family affects the capacities of the family in many ways. Earnings and ability to borrow or extent of help from the community also erodes with the loss of man in the house who is seen as head of the family. Loss of earnings further accentuates the process of immiserisation and the single women headed family suffers malnutrition and deteriorating health.

"After the death of my husband we had nothing to eat. For several days we used to go with barely one meal a day. Then my eldest daughter gave her silver anklets to be sold and to buy provisions fearing that otherwise we would starve to death. Knowing this her husband thrashed her for silver selling anklet to feed us. He beats her regularly for this help she did to us" (Jalgoori Lakshmi)

Often the medical care of the woman is the first casualty. But it also extends to the children in extreme cases. It could lead to loss of earning abilities of the woman and severely affecting her ability to provide medicare to children. It also affects the mental health of the woman. In some cases the women in such serious situations have also died within a few months of the loss of husband.

"My second daughter aged 14 year old was not well. She was suffering from vaginal bleeding. I could not take her to the doctor in the town for fear of money required for fee and medicines. She died within a few days in the village. What more a mother can lose after losing the husband? (Jalgoori Lakshmi)

After the death of my husband, I divided the land among my sons, I was working on my youngest son's land (1 acre) and also as casual labour, till my arm had a fracture last year. Now my work is only regular work of washing clothes and when there is work on farm I do it'. (Ch Sammakka)

Unable to meet the pressure of the debtors my husband put my son into attached labour for Rs. 3000. My elder son worked there till last year, when he had a major accident and fractured his hand carrying a large wooden plank last year (2004). He has not recovered and cannot handle any heavy objects. We had to incur the expenses of medicare. (L. Prameela)

Women and children from poor households belonging to lower social groups had the worst impact of the suicide of the head of the household. Lack of food to eat and medicare besides loss of assets eroded their earning capacity further. The future of children was put to jeopardy as they were pushed out of school into work.

SOCIAL SECURITY: STATE INTERVENTION

State has declared the compensation package for the suicide victims as a policy in 2004. Though suicides took place earlier from 1997 onwards the then government did not identify it as social calamity[1]. The relief package came after a lag of 7-8 years either freshly or in the form of matured 5 year bonds[2]. However the award of compensation was wrought with problems, where the opportunity and transaction costs were high.

'My brothers in law looked after all the work of compensation. I did not go around the offices. Because my family is politically connected, it was not a great difficulty otherwise I may not have got the government support. My husband was an important member of Communist Party (Marxist) as was my father. The CPI (M) party also helped monetarily. I was also going to meetings of the party. My co-daughter-in-law is sarpanch of the village. All this helped me to get government package. I received the relief package of

Rs. 1 lakh after three months. Rs. 25,000 was used to repay debts and Rs. 75,000 was put in bank in the name of two daughters' (A Lalithamma).

'As I cannot live alone with a young child, my brother-in-law stays with us although he is not of much help. But his presence is a big solace. He went round the mandal office for the sanction of government grant. Sometimes he abuses and I bear all that. I felt low when my sister-in-law quarreled for her share in the land that we had been cultivating' (Nirmala).

'My younger brother-in-law took all the responsibility of meeting the expenditure of burial and death ceremony. As Sambaiah was an active TDP follower the local MLA took personal interest and facilitated early disbursement of the ex-gratia and all other benefits'. About Rs. 25000 was spent on the last rites, the rest Rs. 50,000 was kept in the bank in the name of my younger son and Rs. 25000 on me. (Sarojana).

'Let the Sarkar (government) be blessed it gave us Rs. 1,00,000 in 1998. They helped with a cash ex-gratia of Rs. 25,000 and Rs. 75,000 as Indira Vikas Patra bonds locked in for five years. Bonds worth Rs. 25,000 were put on my name and worth Rs. 50,000 were put on the name of my daughter, which matured to Rs. 1.5 lakh by 2003. I performed the marriage of my daughter in the same year and gave Rs. 1.2 lakh as dowry to my daughter. Part of the amount I received (Rs. 50,000) also I gave as dowry (Rs. 20,000) and the rest I spent on marriage expenses. My sons asked for a share in this but I said that the girl's marriage is important. How we can perform the marriage if the sons take away the money? Of course my sons did not oppose me on this". (Ch Sammakka)

'My father-in-law helped me a lot in getting government support. He took me to the mandal offices at Ghanpur. My brothers-in-law do not help me for anything. I have to struggle for everything. The government helped me and our Sarpanch also helped me in getting the money. I repaid some loan amounts. I used Rs 50,000 for my daughter's marriage. I performed the marriage of my daughter last year. I have agreed to give Rs. 60,000 dowry, I made partial payment. My sister, brothers helped me to perform the marriage (L. Prameela).

'I received Rs. 25,000 in cash from the mandal revenue officer, this I paid it off for the adtidar in Warangal. My brothers and brothers-in-law looked into the settlement issues and also dealt with the officials. We also incurred some expenses for accessing the relief package. The rest of Rs. 75, 000 was put as fixed deposit on my name'. As it matured to Rs. 1.5 lakh last year (2004) I used it to pay off part of the promised dowry amount to my daughter, some amount of debts also were repaid (Hymavathy Reddy).

'Last year when I received Rs. 50,000 from the government, my daughter's in-laws pressurized for the dowry due to them. I could not give it and they ill treat her and she was sent away twice from the house. When I could not pay the dowry amount for the second daughter she took away a buffalo last year costing Rs. 7000. She even attempted suicide unable to bear their harassment. That disturbed us a lot and we brought her here after treatment'. (Karra Rajamma)

POLICY INSENSITIVITY

Policy denying assistance to those affected by it in the name of 'rules' can not be viewed as a lesser curse than the death that befallen those poor widows. Government assistance is dismal as it failed to look the situation from the gender sensitivity. Technicalities like a cut off date for the award of compensation denied the same in the case of Yara Vijaya.

'We spent a lot of money for the sake of compensation, nearly 30,000 rupees I spent but all in vain[3]. My brother-in-law squeezed a lot of money in the name of expenses for getting the compensation'. Women farmers and farmers who have no land titles have been denied the status of a 'farmer' and hence compensation package.

"Only help I received after my husband's death is 3000 rupees from the Rythu Seva Samithi immediately after the death. They also gave us a bag of rice that was used for the death ceremony. I did not receive any money from the government. The MRO says that our name is sent to the higher officers but nothing happened. I also spent money to go to the mandal office". (Jalgoori Lakshmi)

STRUCTURED AND LAISSEZ FAIRE KINSHIP

Vulnerability to the shock is high in certain cases like those belonging to lower social groups, a loose knit or laissez faire kinship, where often women say *'all our people are economically weak and how can they support others or how long will they help anybody else'*. Even among the family this gets reflected for the close kith and kin too where they cannot support another family for too long a time. Whereas in the case of upper castes, the kinship relations which came to the rescue of women in. Social groups with their economic, social and political space in the village economy serve as an important recourse to shocks and vulnerabilities. While structured kinship relations help in absorbing shocks relatively easily laissez faire kinship has no capacity for cushioning any shock and hence these groups are more prone to vulnerability. There is willingness but lack of ability to support deters any collective action on part of such kinship.

One of my brother-in-law (distant) has a tractor and with his help I get to do market related works, purchasing the inputs required and transporting the output to the Warangal market yard. My co-daughter-in-law stays by our side, she too is a widow, my sister-in-law is also there who is well versed in agriculture works as her husband passed away very early. With the help of these women who are my close relations I carry on the work (Hymavathi Reddy)

My sister, brothers helped me to perform the marriage of my daughter. (L Prameela).

The case of Lakshmi shows the magnitude of vulnerability in the absence of structured kinship and any monetary compensation from the government.

CIVIL SOCIETY

The response of civil society to social calamity of suicide can be witnessed by the initial support given by farmer organizations even before the state could reach out the people. Solidarity in the form of self help groups is an effective way of coping with shocks where it could act as cushioning to the vulnerable.

'Local MLA was very friendly to my husband and my brother-in-law. MLA helped get all the benefits due in the farmer's suicide case. I got Rs. 14,000 for the house. As we already had *pucca* house it was used by my elder son for the farm inputs. We also got loan for setting up a tent house in the mandal headquarter. That was a failure and luckily that loan was waived off. We also got loan from Corporation Bank for sheep that we reared for a year. We did not have much experience in this work we had to sell of after a year. It was a loss of Rs. 16,000. The outstanding loan in the banks was waived off with the help of MLA. At the time of Sambaiah's death the total debt was Rs. 1.12 lakh. (Sarojana).

The Rythu Sahaya Committee also has given Rs. 3,000 as instant help when no government help came forth. I receive widow pension of Rs. 75 a month, I also have Antyodaya Annayojana card on which

I get 35 kg of rice per month. I also worked under the Food for Work (FFW) programme (L Prameela).

'I joined a thrift group three years back. I am paying 30 rupees a month. Each member took 3000 rupees as loan and so now I am paying 150 rupees per month since past 7 months to clear the loan. The thought of how to make a living haunts me, especially with two daughters and with no money and no land. Whatever I get is not enough for me and my two daughters. What can I give them? (Yara Vijaya)

EMOTIONAL TRAUMA

The psychological stress and emotional trauma experienced by the woman is immense in the early period but the inevitability to support the family made them to stand up and cope with the tragedy. The 'farm widows' carry a stigma of being widows by debt, and the burden to clear the debt. These women become vulnerable as at times their own members start to rob off the remaining assets or deprive her needs from the resources and her own labour. The laissez-faire kinship plays foul. The process of coping becomes relatively easy where there is structured kinship, responsible civil society and flexible state policy. Women's status as widows is voiceless and helpless; often men take the role of protector though they do not turn to be provider.

'But for me none would have faced so many difficulties in life. After his demise it only problems and nothing else. We were very good to each other. He had no bad habits at all. All what he was saying was that we should live a good life, the wish to be economically stable and not to live in poverty. He was not doing anything without my knowledge and it was the same with me. The only thing we knew was work and work. My son and I had psychological problems after his death (Karra Rajamma).

'Our kins, all those sharing my husband's family name have 10-15 acres of land. We planned to take up cultivation in our land collectively and become successful agriculturists. But that dream died with his death. We all have only hands to work and no money to invest. And we are all in debts. I have to do both man and woman's jobs which puts lot of pressure physically and psychologicaly, in such times I feel for my husband a lot. My fate is not good and I cannot blame anybody for this'. I am only 31 years now I am suffering from pain in the leg and not able to work like earlier. (Nirmala)

'I do not go anywhere, where will I get the money for travel? Sometimes I stay with my daughter and with my brothers that is the only relief for me. In the village I very much go to social gatherings, functions etc. (Ch. Sammakka)

'Everybody has their own works and preoccupations, who will come to our rescue? My mother-in-law and sister-in-law are very quarrelsome; they wanted a share in the money I received. They suspect that I received lakhs of money, if people like you come she definitely shouts after you go and abuses me' (Rajamma). Rajamma's health deteriorated after the death of her husband. Stress and worry resulted in temporary memory loss, feelings of fear, confusion is there.

SHOCK & RECOVERY

The shock suffered by the women is severe and the period to recover is varying form months to years to manage simple tasks of running the household work. Some women have not recovered completely even after five years of the crisis. The loss in terms of the social and emotional balance and strength is of a different nature and not many have been able to reestablish normal equations with the kin and community. The duration required to recover varied with the degree of support they receive from the parents and siblings and also the age of kids.

'Unable to carry on with agriculture, I kept the lands fallow two years back. We have also changed the crops now, last year I cultivated red gram, and maize the other year it was castor, nuvvulu (sesame) and red gram, only one year we planted cotton. At present my daughter-in-law and I work on our lands and also as casual labour. Even at this age and in spite of ill health I work as casual labour without which there is no survival'. (Karra Rajamma)

'After the death of my husband I could not work for one year. For two years after his death I stayed with my parents. They took care of me. There was so much of harassment from the lenders and there was not much help from my husband's brothers. Now I go out for work'. (Yara Vijaya)

'There is no one who is good to the farmer, in the market it is nothing else but cheating. I was 40 year old when my husband passed away, though I was not that much into the outside affairs earlier; I had to get into them. I was inside the house weeping for six months. The first two years was a big puzzle and everything was ridden with crisis for me. But then I picked up myself and slowly prepared for looking after the affairs, otherwise everything was going uncontrolled. My brothers and his brothers help me whenever I ask for'. (Hymavathy Reddy)

CHANGED ROLES AND NEW BURDENS

'Till the suicide took place I was more of helping hand to my husband. I used to join him occasionally and it was more of a casual work doing what he asked me to do. After his suicide the whole burden fell on me. After the disaster slowly I gathered myself and started to take hold of the agriculture, cotton crop failed that year, we had heavy debts. For a few months I could not work at all. There was no alternative but to get into work again, I do light works, like the co-ordination between the various works, watering the chilli fields, weeding etc. I think women do not get to know the latest trends and happenings in agriculture unlike men. With the help of the attached labour, the jeetha I try to know the things and act accordingly. I go for the same seed variety or the pesticide as my neighbours. I invested Rs. 23,000 on the agricultural well in 2004. I cannot go for deepening because of the rock so we went for side drilling to tap additional water sources. Agriculture is like snakes and ladders. It is suffocating. Yet can we get away from it? (Hymavathy Reddy)

'When ever I asked about the debts, investments and the like he never told me anything. He would simply brush me aside saying why do you bother when you don't get the loans or repay them? He has put the entire burden on my head. Now I have to bear this, there is no other go. I cannot stand if people talk ill of me. I keep my credibility high that is the reason people do not hesitate to lend me money. I repay debts on time'. My sister and brothers are financially better than me, I don't feel like going to their houses, I am afraid that they look at me cheap. (L. Prameela)

My younger son, Srinivas, who is studying works on holidays and earns about Rs. 50 per day. He also works in his part of the farm that he got after splitting form his elder brother. We could retain only one buffalo which was purchased by my husband. I get some income from sale of milk in the village. I get Rs. 30 by way of wages in the peak time and only Rs. 20 during lean season. (Sarojana)

We did not have land of our own for some time after our marriage. Since the time that we set up our own agriculture I worked on our fields and after the demise of my husband I became an agriculturist. I started doing a variety of farm workers only after coming to my husband's place. I learnt all the activities related to crops like tobacco. In the beginning I did not know the work in tobacco field. Slowly I learnt and now I am fast in making the leaves into a garland which is put for drying. There is hardly any farm work not done by me. After Aaga Reddy's death I am doing both male jobs as well as female jobs. My brother-in-law supervises the work, but he cannot deal with the management either financial or work. Now I take care of marketing of farm produce and I go to the Warangal market for sale of cotton, groundnut, and til. My work load only increased to that which is done by at least two people.(Nirmala)

It is taking up new roles for all the women, the men roles additional roles in order to set the household economy in place. In this process they are innovative, search for ways of having assured income sources. Women do not tend to take risks, as experience deters them to do so, instead they consolidate and attempt to make a safe living. This is reflected when Rajamma says that she changed the crops and does not invest much on pesticides and fertilizers as in earlier times.

SECTION - II

CONCLUSIONS

Vulnerability emanates from and relates to a region, a class, and the social group. Suicides of farmers have thrown open a number of causative and resultant issues to the fore, although the latter remained less explored. Loss of spouse, considered as head of the household, is not only an economic burden to the women but also debilitating life in a complex way with direct implications to her status in social, psychological, occupational spheres. Farmers' suicides make the household vulnerable to a host of issues.

Women from suicide affected households suffer shocks that erode self and alter the self in drastic ways. The loss of husband and the new image of a widow impose several limitations and taboos on the behaviour and alter the status of women in the household and the community. Under normal circumstances women 's priorities often take a secondary place because of the patriarchal social construct, this is more so in case of tragedies like death of husband due to suicide. They cease to be the centre of the world which is now more defined around the needs and priorities of the children. Their alienation results in the loss of self and is a 'social death' (Erich Fromm 1955). Their pain is 'disenfranchised grief' affecting the person's social interactions. Some of the women have suffered inability to go with regular life and work for months and years. It is suffering in silence.

Despite such suffering they have entered into new roles with new capabilities and new challenges without much worldly knowledge. The urge to look to the needs of the children, keep up the family honour, the credibility, and the word made them to rise to the occasion and put things together. This process becomes easier for the women when support from the community is forthcoming. Examples of community action in terms of reduction of interest rates settlement of pay back mechanisms for the heavy debts are signs of positive collective actions which need to be replicated. Collective institutions could be one way forward where the voice of many could come to the rescue of one. More space for such institutions could be an effective way forward to build a good and resourceful human capital. The social tragedy of farmers' suicides once again emphasise the need for this.

NOTES

1. A few cases were awarded compensation as ex-gratia but not as a policy by the Telugu Desam Govt.
2. Relief packages are of two types-(a) Rs. 1 lakh at the time of suicide during 1997-98 that was split as Rs. 25,000 cash as ex gratia, and (b) Rs. 75,000 Indira Vikas Patra bonds of 5 years in the name of the woman and girl child.
3. The GO (government order) says that the compensation package gets executed from October 1997. Sudhakar Reddy committed suicide in July 1997 hence his family became ineligible for the compensation.

REFERENCES

Anitha Gill and Lakhwinder Singh (2005), "*Crisis of Agrarian Capitalism, Farmers' Suicides and Response of Public Policy: Evidence, Diagnosis and Alternatives*, Working paper 5 GAPS Series.

Assadi, Muzaffar (1998), "Farmers Suicide: Signs of Distress in Rural Economy", *Economic and Political Weekly*, Vol. 33, No.14.

Assadi, Muzaffar (2005), "*Agrarian Crises/Distress and Farmer's Suicide in Karnataka: State, Market and Identity*", Paper presented at National

Seminar on Farmers' Suicide and Agrarian Distress in India held at Nagarjuna University under GAPS Project.

AWARE (1998), *Report on Farmers Suicides in Andhra Pradesh,* Development Research Advisory Group, Hyderabad.

Chowdary, P.A., "Commission Report (2002) on Agriculture in Andhra Pradesh", GoAP: Ministry of Agriculture.

Chandrasekhar, C.P. Jayati Ghosh (2005), "The Burden of Farmers' Debt" *Business Line.*

Deshpande, R.S. (2002), "Suicide by Farmers in Karnataka: Agrarian Distress and Possible Alleviatory Steps", *Economic and Political Weekly.*

Doka, Kenneth J., ed. (1989), *Disenfranchised Grief: Recognizing Hidden Sorrow,* New York, Lexington Books.

Gopal Iyer, K. (2005), *"A Comparative Study of Farmers Suicides in Punjab and Andhra Pradesh",* Paper presented at National Seminar on Farmers Suicide and Agrarian Distress in India held at Nagarjuna University under GAPS Project.

Fromm Erich (1955) *The Sane Society.*

Mohana Rao R.M. (2004), *"Suicides among Farmers: A Study of Cotton Grower",* Concept Publishing Company, New Delhi.

Mohanty, B.B. & Sangeeta Shroff (2004), "Farmers' Suicides in Maharashtra" *Economic and Political Weekly,* Vol. 39.

Mohanty, B.B. (2005), We are Like the Living Dead': Farmer Suicides in Maharashtra, Western India, *The Journal of Peasant Studies,* Vol. 32, No. 2, pp. 243-276.

Parthasarathy, G. (1998), "Suicides of Cotton Farmers in Andhra Pradesh: An Exploratory Study", *Economic and Political Weekly,* Vol. 33, No. 13, March 28, pp. 720-726.

Ramulu Burra (1998), "Why Farmers Suicides" paper presented in AP Economic Association Conference, January, 1998, Published in Conference Volume, APEA, 1999.

Revathi E. (1998), "Farmers' Suicides: Missing Issues", *Economic and Political Weekly,* May 16, 1998.

Revathi, E. (2006), *"Suicide as Vulnerability: Some Dimensions of Agrarian Distress in Andhra Pradesh",* Centre for Economic and Social Studies, Hyderabad.

Vasavi A.R. (1999), "Agrarian Distress in Bidar Market, State and Suicides", *Economic and Political Weekly,* August 7, pp. 2263-2268.

Vasavi, A.R. (2005), *"Individualization of Agriculture: Suicides and the making of Agrarian Distress",* Paper presented at the National Seminar on Farmers Suicides and Agrarian distress in India, held at Nagarjuna University under GAPS Project.

Annexure 1
Social Profile of the Deceased Farmer

Name/ Village/ Mandal	*Caste*	*sex*	*age*	*Debt (Rs in lakh)*	*Source*	*Cause*	*Land holding (acres)*	*crops*	*Type of family*	*Number of children*
Samabaiah Keshavapuram Duggondi	BC Chakali	M	48	1.12	PACS Corporation bankLMB CAtraders	Agr inv. Borewell marriage	6	Maize, chillicotton	N	1D 2 S
A Yaadagiri Timmampet Duggondi	BC Padma shali	M	47	0.8	PACS, Villagers	Borewells	2	chillicotton	N	2 d 1 S
Krishna Reddy Nachinepally Duggondi	OC Reddy	M	48	2.00	C A Relations Peer farmers	Marriage Borewells	63 LI	Paddy, Cotton,	N	1 D 1 S
Aaga Reddy Raghavapur Ghanpur	OC Kapu reddy	M	31	0.96	Relations Family members	Borewell Lease of land Agr inv.	1.5 2.5 Ll from FM	Tobacco Cotton paddy	N	1 S
Ilamallu Lingampally Ghanpur	BC Golla	M	47	2.10	Relations Trader CA	Land purchase Agr. invborewells	6 2 LI	Paddy Cotton	N	3D 1S
Sudhaker Reddy Issipet Mogullapally	OC Reddy	M	26	2.5	Relation Traders CA	Inherited debt Borewells Agr inv	2.5	Cotton	N	2 D
Sambaiah Jookal Chityal	SC Madiga	M	28	0.8	Relations friends	Agr. inv. health	1	Cotton	N	2D 1 S
Sammaiah Ippagudem Ghanpur	BC Mudiraj	M	36	1.10	Relatives, friends	Agr. inv. borewells	3 3 LI	Cotton chilli	N	2S 1D

Contd...

Name/ Village/ Mandal	Caste	sex	age	Debt (Rs in lakh)	Source	Cause	Land holding (acres)	crops	Type of family	Number of children
Yellaiah Mohammadapuram Duggondi	BC Chakali	M	50	0.7	PAC, relations, friends traders	Purchase of land borewells	4	Cotton chilli	J	4 S 1D

PACS = primary agr cooperative society, LMB= land mortgage bank,
CA = commission agents
Agr inv = agricultural investment
LI = leased in land
N = nuclear family, D = daughters, S = sons

Annexure 2

Negotiation of survivors (women) with the challenges

Name /Village/ Mandal	*Age*	*Debt repayment*	*Occupa-tional changes*	*Migration/ Relocation*	*Sale of assets*	*Changes in family*	*Kinship/family, other support systems*	*Ex-gratia*
Sarojana Keshavapuram Duggondi	48	Old debt settled debts distributed to sons	no	no	gold B cart oil engine bullocks	Son resumed studies son migrated	Yes TDP	R
Lalitamma Timmampeta Duggondi	46	Repaid	no	no	gold	Daughter stopped studies	Yes RCS MCPI	R
Hymavathi Nachinepally Duggondi	47	Old debt settled Dowry to be settled	House wife to self agr	no	no	no	Yes, brothers	R
Nirmala Raghavapur Ghanpur	26	Old debt repaid 0.5 outstanding	no	no	no	no	yes	R
Rajamma Lingampally Ghanpur	48	Old debt settled 1.5 outstanding dowry to be settled	Self agr to wage labour to agr and farm labour	yes	Cattle Bullocks B cartBuffalo	Son stopped studies went to Dubai	No RCS	R
Vijaya Issipet Mogullapally	28	Part settlement Yet to be repaid	Self agr to wage labour	no	Land Bullocks Cart buffaloes	no	Yes, natal family	N R
Lakshmi Jookal Chityal	32	Debts repaid to some extent	Agr wage lab to non farm labour	no	Gold Household articles	Daughter died Son stopped studies	no	N R

Contd...

Name /Village/ Mandal	*Age*	*Debt repayment*	*Occupa-tional changes*	*Migration/ Relocation*	*Sale of assets*	*Changes in family*	*Kinship/family, other support systems*	*Ex-gratia*
L Pramila Ippagudem Ghanpur	34	Settled by MRO	Self agr to wage labour	no	Goats and sheep	Sons stopped studies	No RSC	R
Sammakka Mohamadapuram Duggondi	56	Debts settled by MRO	Self agr to wage labour	no	Land, gold	Sons got separated	Yes brothers	R

RSC= Rytu Sahaya Committee, MCPI= Marxist communist party of India.
R= received ex-gratia, NR not received.

Annexure 3
Social and Psychological Aspects and Pressures the Respondents Encounter

Name	*Response of In laws*	*Pressures on assets*	*Emotional loss*	*Health disorders*	*Burdens*	*New conflicts, if any*	*Present condition*
Sarojana	Too old to help	No distributed land between sons	Difficulty for food imme diately after death	Poor health	Debt shifted to sons, Younger son settlement	With elder son, further debts	Elder son migrated to Hyderabad
Lalitamma	favourable	No	For first two years	Poor health, nutrition	Daughter marriage	no	Less income at present
Hymavathi	favourable	no	For first one year	no	Sons settlement	Pressure to pay dowry	Status quo
Nirmala	Don't exist Brother-in-law is favourable	no	Not much	appendicitis	Sons education	Sister-in-law pressure for land as dowry	Status quo
Rajamma	Don't exist	Pressure from debtors to sell land	Herself and son psycho Logically affected	Appendicitis to son asthma poor health	To look after sons family as he migrated to Dubai	Pressure to pay off dowry	Low economic status
Vijaya	No help	Pressure to sell land	For 2 years could not work, depen-dent on parents	Poor health	Daughters' education	With in laws	Low economic status
Lakshmi	No help	Pressure to sell all assets	Not much	anemic	Son s settlement	Conflict with son-in-law	Slipped into poverty
L Pramila	Help from Father in law	no	For 2 years could not work	anemic	Sons settlement	With brother in law	Slipped into poverty
Sammakka	Don't exist	Pressure to sell for repayment	None to take care	Ill health due to old age	Youngest sons settlement	no	Slipped into poverty

PART - II
Women's Education

9

Women's Education as an Unfinished Agenda–India's Experience

T. Jyothi Rani and K. Katyayani

The education is identified as a vital source of raising consciousness to fight against all sorts of discrimination, inequalities and oppression in human relations. It is a historical reality that the privileged sections of the society always create obstacles for the spread of education to the oppressed sections. While the latter struggle hard to create a favorable environment where the deprived sections get an access to education. Thus, the history of education particularly the accessibility of education to all moves around this contradiction and conflict.

Education as a system institutionalized in the process of emergence and development of State. Initially, there were two types of education – one was Vedic education, which was confined to male members of Brahmins with some exceptions and second was arts of war for which warrior class alone was eligible to learn. Thus, initially, the education was under rigid class, caste and gender limitations. In the process, it was not available to women.

The emergence of patriarchy during the period of Rigveda gradually developed and reached a stage by the time of Upanishads and would establish a concept where women's efficiency must always be developed in relation to the maintenance of household. The concept is strongly rooted in the structure of patriarchy and continued even in the period of British rule though they could introduce liberal education.

However, a small change in the attitude towards women's education can be noticed in recent years. The expansion of opportunities for the entry of women to show their talent even in technical and science education would be an indication for it. Nevertheless, Sthree Dharma-doing domestic work continued to be the ultimate goal of women irrespective of their level of education. Under this complex and contradictory social situation, a serious analysis is required to examine the extent of qualitative effect of woman's education on her status.

I

The English colonial liberal education created an opportunity for Indian women to enter into social education fold. In the early period, the colonial government did not show any serious interest in women's education. But, the religious institutions like Missionaries and Brahma Samaj could put serious efforts on women's education. Consequently, as early as in 1854, the schools exclusively for girls were 624 in number and could provide education to as many as 21,755 girls. Meanwhile, the East India Company could show some interest in women's education. Lord Dalhousie, the Governor General of India (1848-1856) declared that 'no single change was likely to produce more important and beneficial consequences than female education'. The Indian Education Commission which was popularly known as Hunter Commission reviewed the progress of education in India and recommended to develop primary schools and Teachers Training Institutions for girls. Faced with the fact that 98 per cent of school age girls were not in schools, the authors of the Hunter commission Report recommended more liberal grants and aid for girls' schools than for boys and special scholarships and prizes for girls. Panditha Ramabhai who worked for the cause of women's education gave evidence before the Hunter Commission in Poona and stressed the urgent need for women doctors and teachers. It is relevant to mention the opinion of Jyothi Rao Phule of Maharashtra who was seriously working at that time for the cause of education for Backward Classes and Women, expressed his dissatisfaction in regard to the methods followed by Hunter Commission in the preparation of its report. He made an allegation that the commission had a discussion only with rich people and missionaries. Moreover, the Commission did not consult the poor, farmers and working class who were the actual sufferers. In view of this limitation, it can be assessed that the education of majority of women folk in India did not come under the purview of the Hunter Commission.

The nature of English liberal education system was uniform education for all irrespective of the gender. However, Indians did not accept it and strongly expressed the opinion that the education provided to women should be different. The patriarchal society assigns certain role models to women as mother, wife, daughter and daughter-in-law. Therefore the Indian society expected that through education women should learn skills to perform her role models effectively. From this viewpoint, the syllabus was prepared to develop womanhood. The syllabus so prepared was not uniform for all the women and vary according to their martial status. In this context, D.K. Karve, himself had set up "Mahila Vidyalaya' to develop 'good wives, good mothers and good neighbors'. He believed that widows needed education that would make them economically independent and would enable them to think for themselves while unmarried girls need an education that would reinforce their dependence. This form of education received well appreciation from the Indian society. However, Panditha Ramabhai differs with this opinion to some extent and states that the primary nature of education is to give knowledge to women in regard to their bodies and about the society in which they live. In addition, the education should train women in different occupations so as to make them economically independent.

Annie Besant, an English woman, had strong appreciation for Indian culture and past. Therefore, her opinion in regard to women's education did not vary with the opinion of social reformers. In 1901, she wrote an article on 'Education of women' for the Indian Ladies magazine. In this article, she warned that 'India's fate would be sealed if women were not educated, but western education was not an answer, it would "unsex" women.' Indians should look to their own ideal of womanhood, the Godess Durga.

In the beginning of the 20th century, educated women directly entered into the field of women's education. They could recognize that the obstacles to women's education were rooted in the patriarchal family and social structures.

The speech of Bandaru Atchamamba which was published in 'Hindu Sundari' in June 1903 clearly stated that the negligence on the part of women themselves, child marriages, Purdha system for married women, lack of women teachers in girls' schools were the obstacles to women's education. Further, she felt that the timings of girls' schools should be in the afternoon as they find leisure during that period. Further, she requested educated women to come forward voluntarily to teach girls and every mother should take care of her daughters' education. "Bharat Sthree Mahamandal", a national level organization (1910) identified purdah system as an obstacle to women's education. The women's association felt that they should put efforts to create a favorable social environment for women's education. In their Annual Conference, they took resolutions for the promotion of women's higher education. The 5th conference of Andhra Mahila Sangam held at Vijayawada during 11-12 April 1914 resolved that:

(i) In each district, at least one girl school should be established;

(ii) Women teachers to be appointed in girls schools;

(iii) More wages to be paid to women teachers;

(iv) Marriage should not be done to a girl until she attains 16 years;

(v) Scholarship system to be continued for poor widows to encourage their education.

This kind of resolutions clearly indicate increasing consciousness and zeal of women towards women's education.

The intensification of Nationalist movement and consequent increasing participation of women in it could raise their level of awareness with which they demanded for civil, political rights and to recognize them as individuals on par with men. This demand transformed into a constitutional right in the Post-Independent India.

II

On the eve of departure of British from India, Jawahar Lal Nehru declared that the task ahead includes "the ending of poverty and ignorance, disease and inequality of opportunity". The Preamble of the Indian Constitution declares that the aim of the State is to achieve equality in states and opportunities. The 45th Article of the Directive Principles of Indian Constitution suggested that "State shall endeavor to provide within a period of 10 years from the commencement of this constitution for free and compulsory education for all children until they complete the age of 15 years". Consequently, since the beginning of the First Five-year Plan, the action had been initiated in this direction. However, this did not yield expected results in the promotion of girls' education. A National Committee on Education for Girls was set up in 1958 under the leadership of Mrs. Durgabai Deshmukh, which recommended concentrated attention on this vital problem and allocation of resources for greater facilities to girls at primary and secondary levels. It also recommended the setting up of National and State level councils for the promotion of female education. This has resulted in the issue of "National Policy on Education," in 1968. However, the goal of compulsory primary education for all children was slightly modified in 1978 when the government stated that "every child shall continue to learn, in the age group of 6-14 years on a full time basis if possible and on a part time basis if necessary" In National Policy on Education, 1986, the goal of compulsory primary education has been reiterated and extended to girls. Moreover, this goal had been emphasized in every Five Year Plan since 1951. The National Development Council report on Literacy in 1992, gives importance to female education.

All these developments in regard to education in India have emerged as a part of International environment on this vital issue. The UNESCO constitution, as early as in 1950's identified 'Education For All' (EFA) as a key aspiration and the goal to be achieved by all countries. In 1990, the International Community renewed its commitment to 'Education For All' at the Jomtien Conference, which initiated a decade of intense activity, at both global and national levels, to promote the development of basic education. Further, education came to be seen not simply as an instrument of social and economic development, but as a basic human right. In continuation, 2nd International meet was held in 2000 at Dakar. Learning from the experience of Jomtien Conference, the Dakar forum was more deliberate in settling out quantitative goals, precise deadlines and a detailed strategy for achieving EFA. The UNESCO was asked to be the co-ordinator and catalyst of an international effort to be conducted over the first 15 years of the New Millennium. The Dakar Forum set global targets but the action to achieve must take place at the national and grassroots levels. To this effect, an Education Report in India is prepared in 2002 to make realistic assessment of the current situation not only in quantitative terms but also in the analysis of trends, of causes and effects and of previous policies. In this context, a serious discussion is needed to examine the accessibility of education to women and its effect on their status.

III

The government has initiated various policy actions to promote women's education because it is being recognized as a basic human right. The extent of realization of these efforts can be ascertained on the basis of statistics available on women's education. The effect of the policy of compulsory primary education for a period of 50 years from 1951 to 2001 can be seen in Table 1.

Table 1
Census-wise Literacy rates 1951-2001

Year	*Total Population in lakhs*	*Literacy rate in percentage*		
		Male	*Female*	*Total*
1951	4,392.30	27.16	8.86	18.33
1961	5,481.60	40.40	15.34	28.31
1971	6,833.30	45.95	21.97	34.45
1981	8,463.00	56.50	29.85	43.67
1991	8,463.00	64.13	39.29	52.21
2001	10,270.15	75.85	54.16	65.37

Source: Census Reports, Registrar General and Commissioner, Census Operations, Government of India, New Delhi, various years.

Table 1 indicates that there is a continuous rise in the percentage of literate women over a period of 50 years from 8.86 in 1951 to 54.16 in 2001. Nevertheless, it did not exceed 55 per cent even in 2001 and further, gender disparity can be noticed in regard to male-female literacy rates in all the period under study.

The data in regard to gender-wise, rural-urban literacy rates have been depicted in Table 2.

It can be observed from Table 2 that rate of growth of female literacy rate over a period of 50 years is more than six times and it is higher when compared to the rate of growth of male literacy during the same period. Similar trend can be noticed in rural as well as in urban areas. However, gender disparities prevalent in both rural and urban literacy rates. The rural-urban variation in female literacy is very sharp where urban female literacy is relatively higher than the rural female literacy. Thus, gender disparities in literacy rates and sharp rural-urban divide continued to be the serious problems.

Table 2
Gender-wise Rural-Urban Literacy Rates
(in percentage)

Particulars		1951	1991	2001
Male				
	Rural	19.02	57.87	66.13
	Urban	45.06	81.09	83.21
	Total	24.95	64.13	70.85
Female				
	Rural	4.87	30.62	44.36
	Urban	22.33	64.05	69.34
	Total	7.93	39.29	51.17

Source: Selected Education Statistics, Ministry of Human Resource Development, Dept. of Education, New Delhi, 1997 and Census Report, Govt. of India, New Delhi, 2001.

The data pertaining to enrolment ratios in schools are shown in Table 3.

Table 3
Gross Enrolment Ratio

Year	*Boys*			*Girls*		
	I-V	*VI-VIII*	*I-VIII*	*I-V*	*VI-VIII*	*I-VIII*
1951	60.6	20.6	46.4	24.8	4.6	17.7
1991	114.0	76.6	100.0	85.5	47.0	70.8
1997-98	97.5	66.5	NA	81.2	49.5	NA

Source: Selected Education Statistics, Ministry of Human Resource Development, Department of Education, New Delhi, 1997.

It can be seen from Table 3 that the enrolment ratio of girls is always less when compared to the enrolment ratio of boys in primary as well as secondary level education. However, it is significant to note that the enrolment ratio has increased from 24.8 in 1951 to 85.5 in 1991. But this trend did not continue in 1997-98. The enrolment ratio of girls in VI-VIII class indicates a continuous rise from 4.6 in 1951 to 49.5 in 1997-98. It is to be noted that the enrolment ratio of girls in secondary stage education inspite of rise did not exceed 50 per cent.

The information in regard to drop-out rates in primary and secondary level education has been shown in Table 4.

Table 4
Drop-out rates at Primary and Middle levels

Particulars	*1961*	*1998-99*
Class I-V		
Boys	61.7	38.62
Girls	70.9	41.22
Class VI-VIII		
Boys	75.0	54.40
Girls	85.0	60.09

Source: Selected Education Statistics, Ministry of Human Resource Development, Department of Education, New Delhi, 1997 and Govinda R. (Ed): India education Report, NIEPA, Oxford University Press, New Delhi, 2002.

Table 4 indicates a decline in dropout rates of boys as well as girls in primary and secondary level education over a period of 38 years from 1961 to 1998-99. Inspite of this decline, the drop out rate of girls is always higher when compared to boys in all stages of education and in all the period under study. Further, the drop out rate is high in secondary level education when compared to primary level education among girls. Thus, gender disparity can be observed even in dropout rates. Further, the drop-out rate is not uniform in all the levels of education and it vary according the stage of education.

The data about the enrolment of girls in degree, PG technical and professional courses have been illustrated in Table 5.

Table 5 reveals that there is a rise in the enrolment rates of girls in all types of higher education from 33.2 in 1990-91 to 35.5 in 1996-97. However, the rate of growth is not uniform in all types of higher education. The enrolment rate of girls in B.Ed./BT and PG courses shows a decline in spite of a rise in the absolute numbers of girls in these courses. The percentage share of girls in B.Ed. is relatively higher when compared to other courses in all the period under study. The percentage share of girls did not exceed 44.2 in B.Ed. in 1990-91 and 43.1 in B.Ed. in 1996-97. thus gender disparity has clearly been observed in the enrolment ratios in higher education.

Table 5
Enrolment of Girls at Graduate/Post-graduate/ Professional courses

Levels	*1990-91*		*1996-97*	
	Girls	*Total*	*Girls*	*Total*
Graduation Level (B.A., B.Sc., B.Com.)	11.40 (34.7)	32.87	18.20 (37.4)	48.72
Post-graduation (M.A., M.Sc., M.Com.)	1.16 (32.8)	3.54	1.65 (30.5)	5.41
B.Ed. /B.T.	0.40 (44.2)	0.92	0.50 (43.1)	1.16
B.E., B.Sc. (Engineering), B.Arch.	0.26 (10.9)	2.41	0.49 (14.9)	3.28
MBBS	0.28 (34.3)	0.84	0.43 (35.4)	1.21
Ph.D./D.Sc. /D.Phil.	0.10 (26.2)	0.33	0.12 (29.2)	0.41
Total	13.60 (33.2)	40.91	21.39 (35.5)	60.19

Source: Selected Education Statistics, Ministry of Human Resource Development, Dept. of Education, New Delhi, 1997.

Several studies have proved a correlation between women's literacy and their status. Moreover, rise in the female literacy is closely associated with rise in their life expectancy at birth; fall in child mortality rate and resultant decline in birth rate, reduction in material mortality rate and a rise in the age of marriage. Thus, accessibility of education to women will be a pre-condition to move towards the attainment of rise in the status of women.

IV

A.K. Sen and Jean Dreze opine that the education is valuable to the freedom of a person in several distinct ways.

(i) The education will have an intrinsic importance in which they state that being educated and healthy are valuable achievements in themselves and the opportunity to have them can be of direct importance to a person's effective freedom;

(ii) It has a instrumental personal role because it helps a person to do many things. The Education is important for getting a job and more generally for making use of economic opportunities. The resulting expansion in incomes and economic means can, in turn, add to a person's freedom to achieve functioning that a person values;

(iii) Greater literacy and basic education can facilitate public discussion of social needs and encourage for collective demands. These in turn can help expand the facilities that the public enjoys and contribute to the better utilization of the available services;

(iv) The expansion of schooling can reduce the distressing phenomenon of child labor schooling also brings young people in touch with others and there by broaden their horizons and this can be particularly important for young girls; and

(v) Greater literacy and educational achievements of disadvantaged groups can increase their ability to resist oppression, to organize politically and to get a fairer deal.

The appropriation of all these benefits of education by all the people will result in the emergence of a real democratic, civil society. But, in-built obstacles that are rooted in the basis of the social-economic formation will come in the way of realization of the benefits of education. In fact they are determined in the relativity of needs, opportunities, nature and level of education interests and individual's consciousness. This is doubly applicable in the case of women. Nevertheless, few women could get an access to education, which has resulted in the rise in their level of consciousness and made them active in the process of social decision-making.

Since the period of social reform movement, educated women were in a position to express their love for freedom and worked hardly to achieve that end. As a result of social reform movement, initially, at least widowed women could lead economically independent life. By the beginning of the 20th century, educated women were in a position to run their own journals and could organize themselves for the cause of women.

The benefits of education reflects in their level of consciousness which encouraged them to participate in on-going social and political movements. They could demand for civil rights on par with men.

These achievements of pre-independence era could continue even in post-Independence period. By 1960s, educated women who were conscious of their individuality could fight for recognition. They could pressurize households as well as society for their identification. All these efforts took a qualitative form and transformed as feminist movement. No doubt, accessibility of education to women resulted in the widening of their opportunities. Consequently, women could enter into various fields and could depict their efficiency. It appears, as sky is the only limit for their growth.

In reality, this is half-truth only. In large part of Indian society, all these developments are not traceable in the lives of women. An examination of women's lives on the basis of Human Development Index will prove it clearly.

V

The prime component of Human Development Index are…

- To lead long and healthy life
- To be educated and
- To have Decent standard of living.

In addition, to have political freedom and to live with self-respect are also part and parcel of Human Development. Thus, one of the component of Human Development Index is education. Several studies have proved a direct positive relationship between women's literacy levels and their life expectancy. Still, female literacy rate did not exceed 55 per cent so far. To be educated itself is a vital index of development. But it is a fact that more than 50 per cent of school going age children are out of schools. Thus, the majority of women are marginalized and will not come under the definition of development of Human Development index. Keeping apart all the qualitative changes in the lives of women, even quantitatively, Human Development will not indicate Women's Development.

Women did not have access to health facilities and therefore, it is critical to expect a rise in their life expectancy. In patriarchal families, intra-household distributive rules that are in operation are against to women in general and health of women in particular. Even educated women did not find time and chance to think about their own health condition. The needs, opportunities and priorities of the patriarchal family always ignores and neglects women's health.

The corporation and privatization of health facilities is a natural phenomenon under globalization. Consequently, the cost of medical facilities increase to the extent where it is very difficult for a common man to afford. In these conditions, accessibility of medical facilities to women cannot be imagined as they are marginalized by the patriarchal family and social structures. Thus, access to health facilities is not gender-neutral and will be determined by structures of patriarchy in addition to economic causes.

In India, the institution of marriage is dictated and determined by dowry. The violence against women for dowry spread over to all the castes and classes. The dowry harassment became a regular feature in many households. The conditions are so created with in the family in which either women commits suicide or husband or in-laws kills her. Thus, women forgo her right to live itself. Then, the question of long life does not arise. Moreover, social crime and violence are on the rise where women have been harassed, humiliated, some times victimized through acid attacks and murdered. In certain cases, all this happens on the name of love. All the young girls experience this kind of situation in one form or the other from high school level to higher education. In this tragic context, women are denied the opportunity to live long and healthy life.

Usually, any one can hardly imagine about women's independent economic life. Therefore, men's economic living standards are the basis for assessing women's economic living standards. Only 28.58 per cent of women in India have independent earnings. In 1991 and of them as low as 4.2 per cent are working in organized sector. Even these women hardly exercise any control over their earnings. Therefore, the question of decent standards of living for women is debatable.

Another aspect of Human Development is political freedom in India, women's active participation in political sphere is marginal. In 1992, the reservation of 33 per cent seats for women in the institutions of Panchyat Raj and Local Self Government came into existence with 73,74 Constitutional Amendments. But the women Reservation Bill in Parliament is still in pending on one or the other pretext. Further, women who could enter into political field did not take any independent decisions and their husbands will take decisions on their behalf. Thus, women's representation is only quantitative one.

Another important dimension of Human development is the guarantee of human rights. However, this cannot be seen even in the lives of men owing to various socio-economic and cultural causes. Therefore, the denial of human rights for women will be quite common, as they do not have any independent identity owing to the patriarchal familial structure. Thus, life with self-esteem is impossible for women. Therefore, 'women's development through education' will be a difficult task owing to the prevalence of imperialist, patriarchal social-economic relations.

International pressures for 'Education for All' (EFA) on the one hand, National Policies and Programmes on these lines on the other did not achieve the goal in regard to women. The in-built misconception in these programmes is that they find solution in the allocation of more economic resources for the issue of women's education. Consequently, the policies are confined to the provision of concessions and scholarships and did not address the socio-cultural obstacles that come in the way of women's education.

As early as in Social Reform Movement, reformists could identify the familirial and social obstacles for women's education. At present, feminists could question and prove the forms of oppression of patriarchal structures. On the basis of this knowledge, now it is being identified that gender politics itself is a giant obstacle for women's education. All this knowledge did not find any space in the programmes of women's education itself is a tragedy.

The National Policy of Education (NPE) 1986 and its programme of action (revised in 1992) give education a mandate to work for women's equality and empowerment. It further states that "Education will be used as an agent of basic change in the status of women. The National Education System will play a positive, interventionist role in the empowerment of women. It will foster the development of new values through redesigned curricula, text books, the training orientation of teachers, decision makers, administrators and the active involvement of educational institutions. This will be an act of faith and social engineering. The removal of women's illiteracy and obstacles inhibiting their access to and retention in elementary education will receive overriding priority, through provision of special support services, setting of time targets and effective monitoring".

All these issues are not materialized so far in spite of their identification not less than two decades ago.

The SAARC has declared 1991-2001 as the Decade of the Girl Child. The National Plan of Action for this states that "Rights can be declared and policies can be formulated to express our collective liberal and humanistic concern, but unless the real life of the girl child in her family and community is touched by tangible efforts and action, nothing can be achieved. Therefore, a climate has to be created in which she can exercise her rights freely and fearlessly. One has to work for the transformation of those social and cultural values that shackle and constrict the girl child and mould her into stereotypical roles. For this, every forum and every platform should be used to create awareness and stimulate positive action. Along with this effective implementation of the long for protecting her and provision of opportunity for her to benefit from them has to be insured". Only committed efforts in this direction would result in the accessibility of education to women and it will be expected to pave the way for attaining improvement in the status of women in the real sense.

REFERENCES

Brockway K.N. and Marjorie Sykes (1973), Unfinished Piligrimage – The Story of some South Indian Schools, Saint Christopher's Training College, Golden Jublee Volume, Madras.

Geraldine Forbes (1998), The New Cambridge History of India – Women in Modern India, Cambridge University Press, New Delhi.

Govinda R. [ed.] (2002), India Education Report, NIEPA, Oxford University Press, New Delhi.

Joanna Liddle and Rama Joshi (1986), Daughters of Independence– Gender, Caste and Class in India, Zed Books Ltd, Kali for Women, New Delhi.

Jean Dreze, Amartya Sen (1997), India–Economic Development and Social Opportunity, Oxford University Press, New Delhi.

Jyothi Rani Thota, Katyayani Vidmahe (etal) (2005), Swathantrayanantara Bharatha Desam–Sthree Sthithigathi (Telugu), Society for Women's Studies and Development, Warangal.

Michel Chossdovsky (2001), The Globalization of Poverty, Madhyam Books, Delhi.

Mira Seth (2001), Women and Development–The Indian Experience, Sage Publications Pvt. Ltd., New Delhi.

UNDP: Human Development Report, 2005.

10

Women vis-à-vis Higher Education: An Analytical Note

C. Sivaramakrishna Rao, N. Linga Murthy and K. Mohan Reddy

Education is catalyst of physical intellectual and moral development in a human being. To Swamy Vivekananda "nothing can be done to improve the state of things unless there is a spread of education among the women". Education has been of central significance to the development of human siciety[1]. Our country is not an exception to this sort of trend-setting. Thus, education has been a very important part of Indian social and cultural fabric from the times immemorial. There is hardly have any evidence about the educational system and opportunities for women's education in the Indus civilization of Mohenjodaro and Harappa. However, there was a great deal of evidence about the status of women's education in Vedic literature right from the Rigveda onwards[2]. Manu in his famous Manusmruti states that women needed to acquire knowledge for running a good household, managing the home economy and inculcating the knowledge of medicine as well as crafts[3]. Buddhism and Jainism were great agents of change and they gave much importance to the status of women, as they sought change in so many other fields of social activity[4]. As a matter of fact, the modern economy of the 21st century, certainly the knowledge economy requires highly educated people for accelerating the process of economic development. The higher education system of a country plays a significant role in the creation of skilled human resources[5].

Women empowerment has become a prime concern all over the world due to the growing tendencies of victimising women and committing social crimes on them making them weak, destitute and rescue prone. The situation is grave and formidable, where the women are poor and illiterate. Thus, the only remedy to overcome this horrible malpractice is to make them literate by providing them education at any cost through both formal and informal systems so as to attain a balanced socio-economic development because any attempt to develop a society will be a futile effort unless and until the women are brought to the forefront of the society through proper education, training and social as well as economic rehabilitation. In fact, it is often said that female access to education can be improved through physical proximity to the school system. But a study conducted by the Women Studies Department in twenty-two universities of the country has stated that this is not an important reason for entry into the schools[6].

In the light of the growing importance of higher education as an instrument of equality and vertical mobility especially in this era of knowledge, the present paper is intended to examine the growth of women's enrolment in higher education. It is also devoted to examine the inter-state variations regarding the access of women to higher education. Another objective of the paper is to analyse the male female differentials in literacy rates in India. To ascertain the said objectives researchers of the paper have primarily based their analysis on the macro-level data.

Since 1951 in India the female literacy rate had increased to almost six fold. This can be seen from the Table 1. While looking at the table, it had been observed that the female literacy rate in the year 1951 was worked out to be 8.86 per cent, which had increased to 54.16 per cent in the year 2001.

As a corollary to the aforesaid documentation, the most significant aspect of the data presented in Table 2 on literacy reveals the male female hiatus.

The male-female combined literacy rate in 1901 was 5.9 per cent, the female literacy rate being only 0.60 per cent. Right upto the 1941census, it had increased only upto 7.3, which was a little less than 50 per cent of the total literacy rate of 16.10. The gender gap worked out to be 100 per cent. Over the five census conducted

Table 1
Female Literacy Rates in India since 1951

Year	*Female Literacy Rate (%)*
1951	8.86
1961	15.35
1971	21.97
1981	29.76
1991	39.29
2001	54.16

Source: India Development Report, 2002.

Table 2
Census-wise Literacy Rates: 1901-2001

Year of Census	*Total population (lakhs)*	*Literacy Rates (per cent)*			*Difference between Male-Female Literacy rates (col.3-col. 4)*	*Percentage of Male-Female gap in literacy rates (col.3-col.4) / col. 5 × 100*
		Male	*Female*	*Total*		
(1)	(2)	(3)	(4)	(5)	(6)	(7)
1901	2,520.90	9.83	0.60	5.39	9.23	171.24
1911	2,513.20	10.56	1.05	5.92	9.51	160.64
1921	2,789.80	12.21	1.81	7.16	10.40	145.25
1931	3,186.60	15.59	2.93	9.50	12.60	133.26
1941	3,610.90	24.90	7.30	16.10	17.60	109.31
1951	4,392.30	27.16	8.86	18.33	18.30	99.83
1961	5,481.60	40.40	15.34	28.31	25.06	88.52
1971	6,833.30	45.95	21.97	34.45	23.98	69.60
1981	8,463.00	56.50	29.85	43.67	26.65	69.02
1991	8,463.00	64.13	39.29	52.21	24.84	47.57
2001	10,271.00	75.85	54.16	65.38	21.69	33.19

Source: Various Census Reports of India, Registrar General and Commissioner, Census Operations, Government of India, New Delhi.

in India since Independence, the literacy rate in the case of females has increased from 8.86 to 39.29 which means that only since 1981 the gap is less than 50 per cent. Furthermore, since 1951 one can observe that there had been a decelerating trend in male female differentials in literacy rate in India, despite, it is still quite large. In the year 1951 male-female gap in literacy rate was worked out to be 18.30, which had increased to 21.70 in the year 2001. Thus, it can be surmised that the gap between literacy and education levels of men and women is mainly due to patriarchal society and its hierarchical stand with clear prescription of the roles of women. In the light of this scenario, it is very much apt to quote the 1990's World Development Report that "in India education is heavily biased in favour of urban dwellers and males as well". The same had also been reported in Human Development Report, 1997.

There has been a phenomenal growth in the number of women's enrolment in higher education since Independence, which can be seen in Table 3.

Table 3
Women's Enrolment to total Enrolment in Higher Education

Year	*Total Enrolment*	*Women Enrolment*	*Percentage of Women Enrolment*
1995-96	65,74,005	23,63,607	36.00
1996-97	68,42,598	25,14,511	37.00
1997-98	72,60,418	27,22,062	37.00
1998-99	77,05,520	29,32,993	38.00
1999-2000	80,50,607	31,12,090	39.00
2000-2001	83,99,443	33,06,410	39.40
2001-2002	88,21,095	35,14,450	39.84

Source: (i) Annual Report of UGC, 2001-2002.
(ii) Selected Educational Statistics for Various years, Ministry of Human Resource Development, Department of Education, Govt. of India, New Delhi.

Women have been receiving much attention right from the very first plan[7], women enrolment was less than 10 per cent at the time of Independence and it has increased to 39.84 per cent in 2001-2002. During 1995-96 their per centage was worked out to be 36 and this has increased to 39.84 during 2001-2002. Thus, while looking at the Table, it can be inferred that there had been a marginal increase of only about 3 per cent from 1995-96 to 2001-2002 year, which reflects a decimal enrolment of them in the case of higher education. Thus, it can be said that the progress of women in higher education is far from satisfactory. Therefore, to raise the access it is necessary that the pre-higher education for girls must receive utmost attention.

Access, relevance, quality, equity and parity have always been the major concern of higher education system in India. India has a massive system of higher education[8]. So far as the higher education of women is concerned a large difference between male and female enrollment is found. The higher education programme in India is categorised in terms of faculty. The faculty-wise distribution of women enrollment during 2001-2002 and 2002-2003 can be seen in the Table 4.

Table 4
Faculty-wise Distribution of Women's Enrolment in Higher Education during 2001-2002 and 2002-2003

Sl. No.	*Faculty*	*Enrollment*	
		2001-2002	*2002-2003*
1.	Arts	18,20,134 (5179)	18,89,799 (51.13)
2.	Science	6,99,376 (19.90)	7,36,890 (19.94)
3.	Commerce/ Management	5,81,993 (16.56)	6,08,949 (16.48)
4.	Education	59,394 (1.69)	67,096 (1.81)
5.	Engineering/ Technology	1,31,792 (3.75)	1,54,041 (4.17)
6.	Medicine	1,23,006 (3.50)	1,34,364 (3.63)
7.	Agriculture	9,137 (0.26)	9,332 (0.25)
8.	Veterinary Science	3,163 (0.09)	2,982 (0.08)
9.	Law	56,934 (1.62)	61,947 (1.68)
10.	Others	29,521 (0.84)	30,564 (0.83)
	Total	35,14,450 (100.00)	36,95,964 (100.00)

Source: (i) Annual Reports of UGC, 2001-2002 & 2002-2003.
(ii) Selected Educational Statistics, Ministry of Human Resource Development, Department of Education, Govt. of India, New Delhi, 2001-2002, 2002-2003.

Note: Figures in parentheses indicate the percentages.

While looking at the above table, it can be observed that approximately 90 per cent women were enrolled in general education consisting of Arts, Science and Commerce. Only 10 per cent were enrolled in technical disciplines, which focus upon practical and occupational skill and opportunities. This clearly reveals that there is a need of an effective policy to attain higher enrolment in higher education and more so particularly in the case of technical disciplines. Furthermore, it had also been observed that there was only slight change in the percentage of women enrolled in any faculty in the year 2002-2003 as compared to 2001-2002 except the faculty of Engineering/Technology, where the percentage of enrolment has increased by only 0.42 per cent.

State-wise women's enrolment to total enrolment has been depicted in Table 5.

Table 5
State-wise Women's Enrolment to Total Enrolment
2001-2002

Sl. No.	*State*	*Total Enrolment*	*Women Enrolment*	*Per centage of Women's Enrolment to total Enrolment*
(1)	(2)	(3)	(4)	(5)
1.	Andhra Pradesh	7,04,075	2,75,276	39.1
2.	Arunachal Pradesh	5,832	1,732	29.7
3.	Assam	1,94,245	78,602	40.5
4.	Bihar	4,79,035	1,10,178	23.0
5.	Chatisgarh	1,43,906	52,526	36.5
6.	Delhi	1,66,039	76,046	45.8
7.	Goa	19,245	11,278	58.6
8.	Gujarat	4,88,129	2,16,241	44.3
9.	Haryana	2,39,217	96,882	40.5
10.	Himachal Pradesh	86,319	36,858	42.7
11.	Jammu & Kashmir	55,603	26,133	47.0
12.	Jarkhand	1,91,413	58,381	30.5
13.	Karnataka	5,37,025	2,14,272	39.9
14.	Kerala	2,40,038	1,44,023	60.0
15.	Madhya Pradesh	4,50,745	1,66,776	37.0
16.	Maharashtra	1,22,0167	4,99,048	40.9
17.	Manipur	35,424	15,705	44.3

Sl. No.	*State*	*Total Enrolment*	*Women Enrolment*	*Per centage of Women's Enrolment to total Enrolment*
(1)	(2)	(3)	(4)	(5)
18.	Meghalaya	27,271	13,063	47.9
19.	Mizoram	10,345	4,836	46.7
20.	Nagaland	11,460	4,431	38.7
21.	Orissa	3,41,761	1,18,249	34.6z
22.	Punjab	2,33,745	1,23,651	52.9
23.	Rajasthan	3,41,198	1,11,230	32.6
24.	Sikkim	3,808	1,534	40.3
25.	Tamilnadu	6,97,343	3,13,107	44.9
26.	Tripura	19,215	7,840	40.8
27.	Uttar Pradesh	11,00,887	4,22,758	35.4
28.	Uttaranchal	1,08,594	43,437	40.0
29.	West Bengal	6,20,372	2,43,806	39.3
30.	Andaman & Nicobar Islands	1,943	1,123	57.8
31.	Chandigarh	30,882	17,140	55.5
32.	Daman & Diu	536	252	47.0
33.	Pondechery	15,278	8,036	52.6
	Total	88,21,095	35,14,450	39.84

Source: (i) UGC Annual Report, 2001-2002.
(ii) Annual Report 2001-2002, Ministry of Human Resource Development, Department of Education, Govt. of India, New Delhi, 2002.

It had been observed that there is a wide variation from one State to another regarding the access of women's higher education. While looking at the data it can be said that Kerala with 60 per cent, Goa with 58.6 per cent and Chandigarh with 55.5 per cent women's enrolment in higher education are leading other states, but on the other hand, there are States like Arunachal Pradesh with 29.7 per cent, Jarkhand with 30.5 per cent and Bihar with only 25 per cent women's access to higher education. While looking at the data, it had been observed that 18 states had higher enrolment of women than the national percentage of 39.84, while in the rest of the States the percentage of women's enrolment was less than the national average. While looking at the table it can be surmised that

Table 6
Sex-wise Rural-Urban Literacy Rates and Gender Differentials: 1951-2001

(in terms of percentages)

Year	*Area*	*Male*	*Female*	*Persons*	*Gender Differential*
1951	Rural	19.02	4.87	12.10	14.15
	Urban	45.60	22.33	34.59	23.27
	Total	27.16	8.86	18.33	18.33
	RUD*	26.58	17.46	22.49	–
1961	Rural	34.30	10.10	22.50	24.20
	Urban	66.00	40.50	54.40	25.05
	Total	40.40	15.35	28.30	25.05
	RUD*	31.70	30.40	31.90	–
1971	Rural	48.60	18.50	27.90	30.10
	Urban	69.80	48.80	60.20	21.00
	Total	45.96	21.97	34.45	23.99
	RUD*	21.20	30.30	32.30	–
1981	Rural	49.60	21.70	36.00	27.90
	Urban	76.70	56.30	67.20	20.40
	Total	56.38	29.76	43.57	26.62
	RUD*	27.10	34.60	31.20	–
1991	Rural	57.90	30.60	44.79	27.30
	Urban	81.10	64.00	73.10	17.10
	Total	64.10	39.29	52.20	24.81
	RUD*	23.20	33.40	28.31	–
2001	Rural	71.40	46.70	59.40	24.70
	Urban	86.70	73.20	80.30	13.50
	Total	75.85	54.16	65.38	21.69
	RUD*	15.30	26.50	20.90	–

Source: (i) Selected Education Statistics, Ministry of Human Resource Development, Department of Education, New Delhi, 1997.
(ii) Economic Survey, 2001-2002, Govt. of India, New Delhi.
*RUD: Rural Urban Differentials

the large Hindi speaking States of Arunachal Pradesh, Bihar, Rajasthan, Uttar Pradesh and Madhya Pradesh have a female literacy rate of less than the national average. One region for such a phenomenon could be that the cultural perception of women here is different from the cultural norms applied to women in the south.

This affects the status of women in several ways[9]. Within the country census-wise data shows greater variation in literacy rates for rural and urban areas. Only 46.70 per cent women living in rural areas were literate in 2001 though most of the developmental efforts were directed towards them. The sex-wise rural-urban literacy rates since 1951 has been depicted in the Table 6.

Lower literacy rates in rural areas are primarily due to the more conservative nature of the Indian village society. The low female literacy rates here bring down the total literacy rate of the country. Lower male literacy rates in the village are primarily due to the physical nature of work agricultural labour and migration of literate men to towns.

By and large, it can be concluded that during the last three decades the gender disparity at various levels of education in India has declined but it still needs to be further reduced. In the developed regions of the world, the male-female differentials in education are almost negligible. In the case of higher education women outnumbered men in many countries of the developed world. In the developing country like India, to attain the parity in the higher education nearly giving free education to women upto graduation level will not help much. Therefore, there is an imminent need to disseminate the information on the kind of courses they should take at the higher secondary level, which will enable them to enter into the portals of higher education courses having high employment potential. Thus, girls need motivation as well as vocational counseling with much greater involvement of teachers and employing agencies to empower them for higher employment potential as well as higher income earning jobs through gender equality in the higher education system.

NOTES AND REFERENCES

1. Harsh Gandhar, "Gender Disparity in Higher Education in Independent India", *University News*, Vol. 43, No. 42, Oct, 17-23, 2005, PP. 1-6.
2. Mira Seth: "Women and Development the Indian Experience, SAGE Publication, India, Pvt. Ltd. New Delhi, 2001. P.115.
3. Ibid..., P. 115.
4. Ibid..., P. 115.
5. Ibid..., PP. 120-121.

6. S. Anand Lakshmi (ed): "The Girl Child and the Family – An Action Research Study", Sponsored by the govt. of India, Executed by the UGC, Centres for Women's Development Studies in the University system in India, 1994, P. 111.
7. Nalini Srivastava: "Empowerment ofWomen through Higher Education *University News* Vol. 43, No. 47, Nov 21-27, 2005, P. 13.
8. Mridula Bhadauria: "Access of Women to Higher Education", University News Vol. 43, No. 06, February, 7-13, 2005, P.13.
9. Ibid..., P. 13.

11

Education of Girls in India

M. Rukmini, C.V. Naidu & S. Rathna Kumari

Education of girls has been high on the national agenda. Since Independence special commissions and committees were set up from time to time to assess the progress of girls. Education and propose suitable interventions to promote their participation in education. Several strategies were adopted to promote education of girls as an integral part of the planned socio-economic development of the country. A major conceptual shift is noticed in the last decade in the approach to the education of girls and women. Education of girls is increasingly being seen as a basic human right and a crucial input for national development. Yet gender disparities within the education sector are far from having been over come. This chapter reviews the progress of girl's education in India during the last five decades with special focus on developments during Jomtien period of the 1901 (1999-2000) and within the framework of education for all (EFA).

THE POLICY FRAME WORK

Investment in female education is now considered a development imperative rather than a moral commitment, thus lifting it from the plane of pure thought to that a sound economics. The problem of girls education however does not stand alone, but is inextricably linked with the status of women and the under development of rural areas.

The constitutional guarantees and policy mandate: The constitution of India not only grants equality to women and forbids any discrimination based on religion, race, caste, sex or place of birth but also empowers the state to practice protective discrimination in favour of women. Under the protective discrimination clause, the State has passed several social and labour legislations and drawn up special programmes and schemes for the protection, welfare and development of women and children. Additionally, women have reservations in many educational and training institutions, development schemes local bodies and certain categories of government jobs. Theoretically women have gained equality. India has one of the most impressive sets of laws for women and children girls and get little is known about them either by women themselves or by men.

EDUCATION OF ALL GIRLS PROGRESS AND SHORTFALLS

India has the second largest educational system in the world after China with 610,763 primary 185,506 upper primary and 107,100 higher secondary schools, 7199 colleges for general education 2075 colleges of professional education and 229 universities. In addition there are 290,000 non-formal education (NFE) centers for out-of-school children in the age group 6-14 and a massive volunteer-based literacy programme for adults in the age group 15-35. there are 109 million children enrolled in the primary grades, classes I-V 39.5 million in classes VI-VIII 27.3 million in classes IX-XII and close to 6 million in institutions of higher learning.

Yet, Universal Elementary Education (UEE) a constitutional directive remains unfulfilled six of ten female above 7 years of age were illiterate at the last census count. Secondary and higher education started as an urban-middle-class phenomenon and continues to be so even after fifty years of educational development in independent India. Rural females and urban poor form bulk of the illiterate and out of school population. The National Sample Survey (NSS) 1997 however indicates a break through in literacy with male-female and rural-urban gaps getting reduced.

FEMALE LITERACY

Female literacy is considered to be a more sensitive index of social development. Compared to overall literacy rates. Female literacy is negatively related with fertility rates, population growth rates infant and child mortality rates and show a positive association with female age at marriage life expectancy participation in modern sectors of the economy and above all female enrolment. Female literacy rate has grown from 8 per cent in 1951 to 39 per cent in 1991 and the corresponding increase in male literacy during this period was from 25 to 64 per cent. Rural-urban and inter group disparities were sharp. The rural urban divide was the sharpest amongst females urban females were twice as well off in literacy as compared to their rural counterparts. Scheduled Caste (SC) and Scheduled Tribe (ST) females were at the bottom of the heap.

FASTER GROWTH OF GIRLS PARTICIPATION

In fact the growth rates for girls have always been higher than those for boys, not only because of starting from a much lower base but also on account of sustained state effort to promote education of girls as an important part of planed development.

PERCENTAGE SHARE OF GIRLS TO TOTAL

The percentage share of girls in the total has shown a steady increase since independence at all levels of education.

Table 1
Percentage of Girls in School Enrolment of Elementary Stage (1950-51 to 1997-98)

Sl. No.	*Year*	*Primary Stage Classes I-V*	*Middle Stage Classes VI-VIII*
1.	1950-51	28.1	6.1
2.	1960-61	32.6	23.9
3.	1970-71	37.4	29.3
4.	1980-81	38.6	32.9
5.	1990-91	41.5	36.7
6.	1997-98	43.6	40.1

Source: Development of Education (Various Years), Ministry of Human Resource Development, Government of India.

Table 1 shows that the percentage of girls in school enrolment of elementary stage. During 1950-51 to 1997-98 the percentage share of girls among the children enrolled at primary stage went up from 28 per cent to 44 per cent from 16 per cent to 40 per cent at middle stage.

ENROLMENT AT THE ELEMENTARY STAGE

A fairly strong gender focus has resulted in greater participation of girls in elementary schooling but the male-female gap in enrolment ratios and share of girls in total enrolment is below part for the country as a whole and is very marked at middle stage. Intra-female disparities as between rural urban areas among general populations SCs, STs, Other Backward Castes (OBCs) and some minorities are sharp.

Due to persistent efforts, the enrolment of girls at the elementary stage has grown steadily over the last five decades. Table 2 reveals that the percentages share of girls in total elementary groups at elementary stage. The number of girls at primary stage has gone up from 5.38 million in 1950-51 to 47.45 million in 1997-98. The number of girls at middle stage has increased from 0.53 million in 1950-51 to 15.84 million in 1997-98.

Table 2
Percentage Share of Girls in Total Enrolment by Groups at Elementary Stage (1997-98)

Sl. No.	*Category*	*Primary Stage Classes I-V*	*Middle Stage Classes VI-VIII*
1.	All Communities	43.62	40.12
2.	Scheduled Castes	42.59	38.49
3.	Scheduled Tribes	42.82	37.09

Source: Development of Education MHRD, GOI.

PERCENTAGE SHARE OF SC/ST CHILDREN IN TOTAL ENROLMENT AT ELEMENTARY STAGE IN 1997-98

The percentage share of SC, ST girls to total SC, ST children is not very remarkably different from the overall percentage share of girls in the general population at primary stage. At middle stage SC, ST girls are way behind it is perhaps pertinent to state that the percentage share of SC, ST children at the total is similar to proportion of these groups in the total population at primary stage but the situation is not satisfactory for both ST boys and girls at middle stage.

Table 3 provides that percentage share of SC/ST children in total elementary at elementary stage in 1997-98. The SC and ST population constituted 16.33 per cent and 8.01 per cent respectively at the 1991 census.

Table 3
Percentage share of SC/ST Children in Total Enrolment at Elementary Stage in 1997-98

Sl. No.	*Category*	*Primary Stage Classes I-V*			*Middle Stage Classes VI-VIII*		
		Boys	*Girls*	*Total*	*Boys*	*Girls*	*Total*
1.	SC's	17.27	16.60	16.96	14.99	14.01	14.59
2.	ST's	8.40	8.13	8.28	6.26	5.52	5.96

Source: Department of Education , MHRD, GOI.

ENROLMENT RATIO

Enrolment ratios moved up constantly up to 1990-91 giving gross figures of 86 for girls and 114 for boys at primary stage and 47 for girls and 77 for boys at middle stage. The enrolment ratios appear to be moving towards set figures in 1997-98 being 81 for girls and 98 for boys at primary level and 50 for girls and 67 for boys at upper primary stage.

Table 4 and 5 explores that the gross enrolment ratios by stages and sex from 1950-51 to 2002-03. Enrolment ratio moved up constantly up to 1990-91 giving gross figures of 86 for girls and 114 for boys at primary stage and 47 for girls and 77 for boys at middle stage and 71 for girls and 100 for boys at elementary stage. The enrolment ratio's appear to be moving towards net figures in 1997-98 being 81 for girls and 98 for boys at primary level and 50 for girls and 67 for boys at upper primary stage and 71 for girls and 87 for boys at elementary level.

The enrolment ratio's appear to be moving towards net figure in 2002-03 being 93 for girls and 98 for boys at primary level and 56 for girls and 65 for boys at upper primary level and 79 for girls and 85 for boys at elementary level. The enrolment ratios appear to be moving towards net figures increase in every year. A provision of Rs.489 crore has been made for the Tenth Five Year Plan and Annual Plan allocation for the year 2004-05 is Rs.100 crore. 525 KGBVS have been approved by the department of elementary education involving an amount of Rs.123.03 crore for 2004-05.

An education less of 2 per cent on all direct and indirect central taxes has been imposed through the finance (No. 2) act, 2004. Soon after the relevant bill was introduced in parliament on July 8, 2004. Action was initiated for creation of a separate, dedicated, no lapsable fund to be named as Prath Mik Shiksha Kosh and maintained by

Table 4
Gross Enrolment Ratios (GER) by Stages and Sex
1950-51 to 2002-03

(in Per cent)

Sl. No.	*Year*	*Primary Stage Classes I-V*			*Upper Primary Classes VI-VII*		
		Boys	*Girls*	*Total*	*Boys*	*Girls*	*Total*
1.	1950-51	60.6	24.8	42.6	20.6	4.6	12.7
2.	1960-61	82.6	41.5	62.4	33.2	11.3	22.5
3.	1970-71	95.5	60.5	78.6	46.5	20.8	33.4
4.	1980-81	95.8	64.1	80.5	54.3	28.6	41.9
5.	1990-91	114.0	85.5	100.1	76.6	47.0	62.1
6.	1991-92	112.8	86.9	100.2	75.1	49.6	61.4
7.	1992-93	95.0	73.5	84.6	72.5	48.9	67.5
8.	1993-94	90.0	73.1	81.9	62.1	45.4	54.2
9.	1994-95	96.6	78.2	87.7	68.9	50.0	60.0
10.	1995-96	97.1	79.4	88.6	67.8	49.8	59.3
11.	1996-97	97.0	80.1	88.8	65.8	49.2	58.0
12.	1997-98	99.3	82.2	91.1	66.3	49.7	58.5
13.	1998-99	100.9	82.9	92.1	65.3	49.1	57.6
14.	1999-00	104.1	85.2	94.9	67.2	49.7	58.8
15.	2000-01	104.9	85.9	95.7	66.7	49.9	58.6
16.	2001-02	105.3	86.9	96.3	67.8	52.1	60.2
17.	2002-03	97.5	93.1	95.4	65.3	56.2	60.9

Source: 1. Selected Educational Statistics (relevant years), DOE, MHRD, GOI.
2. Economic Survey, 2004-05.

Table 5
Gross Enrolment Ratios (GER) by Stages and Sex
1950-51 to 2002-03

(in Per cent)

Sl. No.	*Year*	*Elementary Classes I-VIII*		
		Boys	*Girls*	*Total*
1.	1950-51	46.4	17.7	32.1
2.	1960-61	65.2	30.9	48.7
3.	1970-71	75.5	44.4	61.9
4.	1980-81	82.2	52.1	67.5
5.	1990-91	100.0	70.8	86.0
6.	1991-92	101.2	73.2	87.7
7.	1992-93	87.7	65.7	77.2

Sl. No.	*Year*	*Elementary Classes I-VIII*		
		Boys	*Girls*	*Total*
8.	1993-94	80.2	63.7	72.3
9.	1994-95	87.2	68.8	78.4
10.	1995-96	86.9	69.4	78.5
11.	1996-97	85.9	69.4	78.0
12.	1997-98	87.4	70.7	79.4
13.	1998-99	87.6	70.6	79.4
14.	1999-00	90.1	72.0	81.3
15.	2000-01	90.3	72.4	81.6
16.	2001-02	90.7	73.6	82.4
17.	2002-03	85.4	79.3	82.5

Source: 1. Selected Educational Statistics (relevant years), DOE, MHRD, GOI.
2. Economic Survey, 2004-05.

the ministry of HRD(Human Resource Development), department of elementary education and literacy. The proceeds would be available on a rollover basis for the schemes of basic education and the mid-day meal scheme. Budget provision for the mid-day meal scheme during 2004-05 is Rs.1,675 crore. In addition Rs.1,232 crore has been provided to the states. VTS as Additional Central Assistance (ACA) under state sector as earmarked outlay for meeting cooking cost.

Table 6
Enrolment Ratios by Stages Sex, Scheduled Castes and Secluded Tribes (1998-99)

Sl. No.	*Groups*	*Primary Stage Classes I-V*			*Upper Primary Classes VI-VIII*		
		Boys	*Girls*	*Total*	*Boys*	*Girls*	*Total*
1.	All Groups	97.5	81.2	89.7	66.5	49.5	58.5
2.	SC's	102.25	81.60	92.36	75.84	37.59	56.17
3.	ST's	102.93	78.34	90.73	50.03	32.93	43.24

Source: Selected Educational Statistics (relevant years), DOE, MHRD, GOI.

Table 6 reveals that the enrolment ratios by stages sex, scheduled castes and secluded tribes. Enrolment ratios were 81 girls and 97 for boys at primary stage as well as 49 for girls and 66 for boys at upper primary stage in the year 1998-99.

DROUPOUT RATE

Over the period 1960-61 to 1997-98 both enrolment and retention have registered improvement. The dropout rate for primary stage classes (I-V) has gone down from 62 to 38 per cent for boys and from 71 to 41 per cent for girls. At middle stage the dropout rate has come down from 75 to 51 per cent for boys and from 85 to 59 per cent for girls.

Table 7
Dropout Rate at Elementary Stage in India
1960-61 to 1997-98

Sl. No.	*Year*	*Primary Classes I-V*			*Middle Classes VI-VII*		
		Boys	*Girls*	*Total*	*Boys*	*Girls*	*Total*
1.	1960-61	61.7	70.9	64.9	75.0	85.0	78.3
2.	1970-71	64.5	70.9	67.0	74.6	83.4	77.9
3.	1980-81	56.2	62.5	58.7	68.0	79.4	72.7
4.	1990-91	40.1	46.0	42.6	59.1	65.1	60.9
5.	1997-98	38.2	41.3	39.6	50.7	58.6	54.1

Source: Selected Educational Statistics (relevant years), DOE, MHRD, GOI.

CRITICAL ISSUES AND INTERVENTION

Theoretically all formal and non formal education and training prgrammes are open to women. In addition, provision exists for opening of separate institutions or separate wings for women girls exclusively education is free for girls up to the higher secondary stage and several states have made education free for girl's right up to university level. Besides free education for all children up to the age of 14, there are incentive sachems like free noon meals, free books, free uniforms and attendance scholarships for girls and children from disadvantaged groups.

ISSUES THAT REMAIN

Though significant progress has been made in the provision of education for all girls, the task is not yet complete. There are several issues that need to be seriously addressed by educational planners and policy makers in the years to come. Some to these are:

- Special focus on enrolment and retention of SC, ST and OBC girls.

- Absence of data in case of educationally backward minorities.
- Education of out-of-school girls in the age group 10-18.
- Improvement of quality of state and state aided schools.
- Lack of regular inflow of rural-urban statistics on girls education.
- Improvement of quality of state and state aided schools.
- Higher proportion of women teachers in rural areas.

INTERVENTIONS NEEDED

1. As already pointed out, the situation with respect to girls education varies considerably across the country. Therefore, interventions have to be worked out in a contextual manner. However, following are some general proposals that may help in tackling the various issues confronting girls education in the country.
2. A large number of girls from remote and small rural habitations continue to get excluded from primary education. It is necessary to create part or alternative schooling in small unsorted habitations.
3. Make all whether motorable roads to all villages as a first charge and provide free school bus service to all elementary school children and to girls up to higher secondary level.
4. Girls primary-level boarding schools or ashram shale's are needed for scattered populations in forests, deserts, mountains, for instance.

The problem of education of muslim girls needs to be specially addressed.

REFERENCES

Aggarwal Y.P. (1999), Access and Retention in District Primary Education Programme Districts, A National Overview Paper Presented at the International Seminar on Researches in School Effectiveness at Primary Stage, National Council of Educational Research and Training, New Delhi.

Govt. of India (1995), Country paper India presented in Fourth World Conference on Women, Bejing Ministry of Health and Family Welfare (1997-98), Annual Report, New Delhi.

National Council of Educational Research and Training (1998) Sixth All-India Educational Survey, New Delhi.

Srivastava-ABL (1999), Internal Efficiency of Primary Education in Phase I District Primary Education Programme, District Paper Presented at the International Seminar on Researches in School Effectiveness at Primary Stage, NCERT, New Delhi.

Economic Survey, 2004-05, HRD, GOI, www.finmin.nic.in.

12

Gender Disparities in Education and Employment

S. Vidya Sagar and K. Manuja Devi

Women in the world in both the industrially advanced and less advanced countries have been suffering with cumulative inequality and such inequalities are more serious in the third world countries like India. Women in India have been denied equality of status and opportunities in the social, economic and political spheres despite their significant contribution to the social and economic progress of the country. The low status of women has been resulting in low levels of education and employment. Education is the basic input for bringing about the social and economic transformation of any community. It is much more for women who are socially and economically depressed for centuries. Apart from literacy, economic dependence of women is the major factor of their deplorable social and economic conditions. It has been observed from several studies that the economic activity rates for women are lower than men in our country.

The present paper, therefore, aims to examine changes in women's educational status and their work participation rates in rural and urban areas in India. Basic data for this study have been drawn from the secondary sources. Periodical rounds of socio-economic surveys conducted by the NSSO and population census have been used to analyse various aspects of education of women and female workforce in India.

WOMEN AND EDUCATION

Education is one of the most crucial instruments of empowerment of women. It is generally accepted that literacy and education helps in enlarging the capability of a person and it serves as the first defense in the struggle towards existence. According to notable economist Amartya Sen "Education may enhance a young women's decisional power in the family in many ways. These include its effect on her social standing, her ability to be independent, her power to articulate, her knowledge of the outside world and her skill in influencing group decisions". Empirically strong linkages have been established between education and improvements in levels of human well being. Through education, learning and skill formation, women can be much more productive over a period of time, which adequately contributes to the process of economic expansion.

In India women folk during the colonial rule was a largely neglected affair as the rulers at that time showed their interest in formal education of only men. Even at the time of independence women literacy rate in India is very low i.e., about 9.0 per cent only. After independence the government of India and state governments adopted steps to improve women's literacy and education. The constitution of India is giving equal rights to women in every aspects including education. As a result women's literacy started to improve after Independence. The table 1 presents the literacy rate by sex in India since Independence.

Table 1
Disparity in Literacy Rate in India

Year	*Persons*	*Male*	*Female*	*Female/Male Disparity Index*
1951	18.33	27.16	8.86	32.62
1961	28.30	40.40	15.35	38.00
1971	34.45	45.96	21.97	47.80
1981	43.57	56.38	29.76	52.78
1991	52.21	64.13	39.29	61.27
2001	65.38	75.85	54.16	71.40
Percentage increase in 2001 over 1951	47.05	48.69	45.30	

Source: Computed from various issues of Census of India.

Table 1 shows that there is high gender inequality in literacy levels in India. When compared to male, the literacy rate among female is low in all the years from 1951 to 2001. An encouraging fact is that the literacy rates both male and female have risen after independence. However, the female literacy is rising faster than that of male literacy. Percentage increase in 2001 over 1951 in persons, males and females was 47.05 per cent, 48.69 per cent and 45.30 per cent respectively. In the year 1951 the female literacy rate was only 8.86 per cent and the female-male disparity index was 32.62. This disparity index is rising gradually upto 2001, and this rising trend is more pronounced after globalization era. Hence, the index shows that over years female literacy rises relatively to male. The female literacy is faster than the male literacy indicating reduced disparity over a period of time. However, the increase in male literacy in 2001 over 1951 (48.69 per cent) is three percentage points higher than that of female literacy (45.3 per cent) thus, the difference in male/ female literacy at national level is prevailing more according to 2001 census.

The literacy rates by sex in some of the major states and in India can be seen in table 2.

Table 2 presents state-wise male, female literacy rates in India during the year 1981, 1991 and 2001. In all the major states, disparity index is in increasing trend, that means male-female gap in literacy is declining gradually from the year 1981 to 2001, but if varies from state to state. The literacy is highest in Kerala in general and also female in all the years when compared to other states. The disparity index shows that the male-female gap in literacy is less in Kerala, followed by Punjab in all the years. The disparity index is low that means gap between male-female is highest in Rajasthan followed by Bihar in 1981 and 1991, but in 2001 Bihar stands in least disparity index, (male-female gap is more), than Rajasthan is the next place. We can observe in this table that the female literacy is higher in the developed states like Punjab (63.55 per cent) Maharashtra (67.51 per cent), Tamil Nadu (64.55 per cent), Kerala (87.86 per cent) and lower in the backward states like Bihar (33.57 per cent). In Andhra Pradesh it is much lower (51.17 per cent) than that of national average (54.16 per cent). At the state level the differentials in the level of literacy by sex are quite enormous except for states like Kerala.

The progress of female literacy is uneven throughout the country. Female literacy in rural areas continues to be lower than

Table 2
Disparity in Literacy Rates in some Major States before and after Reforms Period

States/ Union Territories	*1981*				*1991*				*2001*			
	Persons	*Male*	*Female*	*D.I*	*Persons*	*Male*	*Female*	*D.I*	*Persons*	*Male*	*Female*	*D.I*
India	43.57	56.38	29.76	52.78	52.21	64.13	39.29	61.27	65.38	75.85	54.16	71.40
Andhra Pradesh	35.66	46.83	24.16	51.59	44.09	55.13	32.72	59.35	61.11	70.85	51.17	72.22
Bihar	32.03	46.58	16.58	35.55	38.48	52.49	22.89	43.61	47.53	60.32	33.57	55.65
Gujarat	52.21	65.14	38.46	59.04	61.29	73.13	48.64	66.51	69.97	80.50	58.60	72.88
Jammu & Kashmir	32.68	44.18	19.55	44.25	NA	NA	NA	NA	54.46	65.75	41.82	63.60
Karnataka	46.20	58.72	33.16	56.47	56.04	67.26	44.34	65.92	67.04	76.29	57.45	75.30
Kerala	81.56	87.74	75.65	86.22	89.81	93.62	86.13	92.00	90.92	94.20	87.86	93.27
Madhya Pradesh	34.22	48.41	18.99	39.23	44.20	58.42	28.85	49.38	64.11	76.80	50.28	65.47
Maharashtra	55.83	69.66	41.01	58.87	64.87	76.56	52.32	68.34	77.27	86.27	67.51	78.25
Orissa	40.96	56.45	25.14	44.53	49.09	63.09	34.68	54.97	63.61	75.95	50.97	67.11
Punjab	48.12	55.52	39.64	71.40	58.51	65.66	50.41	76.77	69.95	75.63	63.55	84.03
Rajasthan	30.09	44.76	13.99	31.26	38.55	54.99	20.44	37.17	61.03	76.46	44.34	57.99
Tamil Nadu	54.38	60.05	40.43	67.33	62.66	73.75	51.33	69.60	73.47	82.33	64.55	78.40
Utter Pradesh	33.33	47.43	17.18	36.22	41.60	55.73	25.31	45.42	57.36	70.23	42.98	61.20
West Bengal	48.64	59.93	36.07	60.19	57.70	67.81	46.56	68.66	69.22	77.58	60.22	77.62

*Source:*Census of India, 1981, 1991, 2001.

that in urban areas. Table 3 shows the literacy rate of female in rural and urban in India since 1961.

Table 3
Rural-Urban Disparity in literacy among the Women

Year	*Rural*	*Urban*	*Rural/ Urban Disparity Index*
1961	9.10	37.4	24.33
1971	13.08	42.05	31.10
1981	17.96	47.82	37.56
1991	24.60	53.70	45.81
2001	N.A	N.A	N.A

Source: Census Reports.

Table 3 shows that in all the years since 1961 rural female literacy is lower than that of urban female literacy. In both the areas female literacy rate is in increasing trend. The Rural-Urban disparity index in 1951 was 24.33 per cent. It rose to 31.1 per cent in 1971. In 1981, and 1991 the respective indices were 37.56 and 45.81 per cent. It means the gap in the Rural-Urban literacy is decreasing gradually. Thus, we can conclude that the rate of increase in female literacy, in rural areas is faster than that of urban areas. Yet the gap between rural/ urban literacy is more in India.

WOMEN AND EMPLOYMENT

The economic reforms in India which were initiated in early nineties aims at improving efficiency, productivity and integrating the economy with world trade and capital movements. Given the nature of reforms these are likely to have significant implications on employment especially female employment. Generally the nature of unemployment in under developed countries is different from the advanced countries. Majority of women workers are engaged in the unorganized sector particularly in agriculture sector and allied activities. Their access to ownership of land and other productive resources remain negligible. They are paid lower wages than male workers and they have to work under very poor working conditions and longer hours. They suffer from increasing job insecurity. The poor economic conditions of the family compel the women workers to accept more and more inferior conditions of work and it leads to feminization of informal sector which has not favourable to women in terms of employment pattern, work conditions and wage rates. To analyse the employment pattern we should see the changes in the labourforce participation rates. Table 4 shows the labourforce participation ratio in India.

Table 4
Trends in Female Labourforce Participation Ratio in India

(Percentage of Population)

	1983	*1987-88*	*1993-94*	*1999-2000*
Rural Male	55.5	54.9	55.3	53.1
Rural Female	34.2	33.1	32.8	29.9
Urban Male	54.0	53.4	52.0	51.3
Urban Female	15.9	16.2	15.4	13.9

Source: Various NSS Rounds.

According to this table there is a progressive decline in the labour force participation ratio in male workers as well as female workers. In rural male workers, there is a slight increase after 1987-88 i.e., from 54.9 per cent in 1987-88 to 55.3 per cent in 1993-94, but this ratio is declined to 53.1 per cent in 1999-2000. While in rural female workers we can see gradual decline since 1983 and after 1987-88 this declining trend is more significant. Reduction in female rural workforce participation ratio in liberalization decade is more when compared to rural male workforce and also urban male and female workforce. The declining trend in female workforce in rural areas is mainly due to excessive dependence on agriculture sector and the employment in this sector is inversely affected by globalization policy.

It is observed that about 80 per cent of female workers are engaged in agriculture sector itself leaving 20 per cent in the household industries and other type of work. On the other 70 per cent of rural men are engaged in agriculture sector. Thus, agriculture is the single most important contributor of employment in rural sector and more so to the rural women (table 5).

Table 5 shows that the share among the two major categories viz., that of agricultural and non-agricultural workers are considered for looking at the changes in the occupational structure of India and state of Andhra Pradesh during 1961 to 2001 by sex and location. The share of female agricultural workers are in dominant position at all India level as well as in state of Andhra Pradesh, while for non-agricultural workers, the share is dominant in urban areas.

Table 5
Female-Male Labourforce Participation Ratio or Gender Composition of Workers

	Persons					*Male*					*Female*				
	1961	*1971*	*1981*	*1991*	*2001*	*1961*	*1971*	*1981*	*1991*	*2001*	*1961*	*1971*	*1981*	*1991*	*2001*
All India (Rural)															
Agriculture Workers	82.15	82.47	81.68	81.26 (-0.51)	73.34 (-9.75)	79.65	81.18	79.08	77.52 (-1.97)	69.67 (-11.27)	86.95	87.16	88.11	89.12 (+1.15)	79.86 (-10.39)
Non-Agriculture Workers	17.85	17.53	18.32	18.73 (+2.24)	26.67 (+42.39)	20.35	18.81	20.91	22.48 (+7.51)	30.32 (+34.88)	13.04	12.84	11.89	10.88 (-8.49)	20.14 (+85.11)
Total	100.00	100.00	100.00	100.00	100.00	100.00	100.00	100.00	100.00	100.00	100.00	100.00	100.00	100.00	100.00
All India (Urban)															
Agriculture Workers	10.97	11.23	11.8	12.45 (+5.51)	7.92 (-36.39)	8.3	9.87	10	10.41 (+4.1)	6.41 (-38.42)	25.92	22.15	23.87	24.65 (+3.27)	15.29 (-37.97)
Non-Agriculture Workers	89.03	88.77	88.21	87.55 (-0.75)	92.08 (+5.17)	91.7	90.13	90	89.59 (-0.46)	93.59 (+4.46)	74.08	77.85	76.14	75.35 (-1.04)	84.7 (+12.41)
Total	100.00	100.00	100.00	100.00	100.00	100.00	100.00	100.00	100.00	100.00	100.00	100.00	100.00	100.00	100.00
Andra Pradesh (Rural)															
Agriculture Workers	77.2	79.34	81.02	81.37 (+0.43)	75.15 (-7.64)	72.77	75.53	76.56	76.41 (-0.20)	69.76 (-8.70)	83.46	86.68	87.85	88.3 (+0.51)	82.58 (-6.48)
Non-Agriculture Workers	22.8	20.66	18.97	18.63 (-1.79)	24.85 (+33.39)	27.23	24.47	23.44	23.58 (+0.6)	30.24 (+28.24)	16.54	13.32	12.15	11.7 (-3.7)	17.11 (+46.24)
Total	100.00	100.00	100.00	100.00	100.00	100.00	100.00	100.00	100.00	100.00	100.00	100.00	100.00	100.00	100.00
Andra Pradesh (Rural)															
Agriculture Workers	21.08	16.52	16.09	16.54 (+2.80)	8.33 (-49.64)	15.75	12.95	12.08	12.62 (+4.47)	6.3 (-50.0)	36.78	32.59	33.86	33.26 (-1.77)	16.8 (-49.49)
Non-Agriculture Workers	78.91	83.48	83.91	83.47 (-0.52)	91.67 (+9.82)	84.26	87.05	87.92	87.38 (-0.61)	93.69 (+7.22)	63.23	67.41	66.13	66.13 0	83.19 (+25.80)
Total	100.00	100.00	100.00	100.00	100.00	100.00	100.00	100.00	100.00	100.00	100.00	100.00	100.00	100.00	100.00

Source: Census of India and Census of Andhra Pradesh.

Note: 1. Agriculture workers include cultivators and Agricultural Labourers. 2. Non-Agriculture Workers include Household industry Workers and other Workers. 3. Figures in Bracket indicate rate of change over previous period.

This contrast position is because of the rural areas are agriculturally dominant and urban areas are non-agriculturally dominant in sources of employment.

The share of rural female agricultural workers were increased gradually upto 1991, under in economic reforms decade i.e., from 1991 to 2001, there is a fall in their share both in all India level as well as in Andhra Pradesh. Likewise the share of urban female agricultural workers was declined gradually from 1961 to 2001 but a drastic fall can be seen in 2001 in All India as well as Andhra Pradesh. This declining trend of work participation rate in agriculture sector is because of introduction of technology like threshers, tractors in agriculture sector under reform period and all the traditional jobs done by women which are more labour intensive and has been replaced by machines which are mostly controlled by men. As a result of these displacements, dropout of the labour force engaged in household industries is badly affected to rural women.

Percentage distribution of usual status workers by status of employment in rural and urban areas can be seen in table 6.

Table 6
Percentage Distribution of Usual Status Workers by Status of Employment in Rural and Urban Areas

Employment Status	*1983*	*1987-88*	*1993-94*	*1999-2000*
Rural Males				
Self Employed	60.5	58.6	57.9	55.0
Regular Employed	10.3	10.0	8.3	8.8
Casual Labour	29.2	31.4	33.8	36.2
Rural Females				
Self Employed	61.9	60.8	58.6	57.3
Regular Employed	2.8	3.7	2.7	3.1
Casual Labour	35.3	35.5	38.7	39.6

Source: NSS Rounds.

National Sample Survey classified workers into employment statuses-self-employed, regular wage/ salaried and casual labourers. Table 6 shows that the changes in the nature of employment in India. It shows that self-employment among female in rural areas was declined from 60.8 per cent in 1987-88 to 58.6 per cent in 1993-94 and it has further declined to 57.3 per cent in 1999-2000. Regular employment among rural female also declined from 10 per cent in 1987-88 to 8.8 per cent in 1999-2000. The share of casual wage employment among female in rural areas has increased from 35.5 per cent in 1987-88 to 39.6 per cent in 1999-2000. Casual labourers include all form of wage laboureres other than those with assured full time jobs with an employer. Casual labourers are thus exposed to greater uncertainty about getting work, duration of employment and the wage they can get. Increase employment for women is mostly of casual type. The casualization trend, therefore, supported by the increasing trend of women employment in irregular, temporary than regular status. As evident from the secondary data, thus rural women suffer from the increase insecurity of both income and employment in the reform decade. The women who are participating in the feminization process have neither experienced any favourable shift in the employment pattern, nor acquired skill any nor absorbed in jobs, nor getting high wages.

Table 7 shows the per cent share of female workers in total workforce across States by location in all NSS surveys from 1983.

Table 7
Percentage share of UPS Female Workers in total UPS Workers in 17 Major States

State	*Rural*				*Urban*			
	1983	*1987-1988*	*1993-1994*	*1999-2000*	*1983*	*1987-1988*	*1993-1994*	*1999-2000*
Andhra Pradesh	40.9	41.4	42.6	42.0	23.0	24.8	23.3	23.2
Assam	11.3	10.7	14.0	13.9	9.4	7.7	11.3	14.3
Bihar	24.4	20.1	19.4	20.0	13.7	10.0	9.9	11.6
Gujarat	36.7	34.5	29.9	34.0	16.2	13.8	14.4	16.4
Haryana	20.7	18.0	9.8	5.8	11.5	9.6	10.6	9.3
Himachal Pradesh	45.8	41.8	41.5	36.3	18.6	19.2	20.5	15.3
Jammu & Kashmir	8.0	15.5	14.6	7.7	8.7	10.7	15.7	7.5
Karnataka	35.0	35.3	35.2	36.8	24.0	23.9	20.0	23.4
Kerala	28.7	28.1	23.4	23.8	23.9	22.0	22.5	23.3
Madhya Pradesh	39.6	37.9	33.7	37.0	18.6	18.1	18.8	18.7
Maharashtra	44.1	43.7	42.2	42.1	19.0	19.0	18.8	20.4
Orissa	28.8	27.4	27.3	27.1	15.9	12.7	16.7	17.5
Punjab	6.2	11.2	5.7	6.4	10.3	8.8	8.4	10.7
Rajasthan	37.5	42.5	34.3	33.6	23.2	21.8	16.6	14.5
Tamil Nadu	39.3	40.9	40.3	40.1	14.0	25.0	25.4	25.4
Uttar Pradesh	20.6	23.0	18.6	18.8	11.0	10.8	11.2	10.8
West Bengal	14.3	15.8	12.8	17.1	13.8	12.2	14.4	14.1

Source: NSS Rounds.
Note: UPS: Usual Principal Status.

Irrespective of the years, the female participation rate in rural areas in all states was more than urban areas. The share of rural women workers in 1983 was the highest in Himachal Pradesh (45.8 per cent) and it declined to 36.3 per cent in 1999-2000. Jammu & Kashmir has the lowest share of rural women workers (8 per cent), in 1983. It is further declined to 7.7 per cent in 1999-2000. The share of women workers in rural areas in 1999-2000 ranged from the highest of 42.1 per cent in Maharashtra to lowest of 5.8 per cent in Haryana. The share of women workers in urban areas in 1999-2000 ranged from the highest of 23.3 per cent in Karnataka to lowest of 7.5 per cent in Jammu & Kashmir.

The female workforce in rural areas declined almost all states after 1987-88 except in Andhra Pradesh, Assam and Karnataka. But none of these three States, the improvement did not exceed 3 per cent points. As for urban women, work participation rates improved in ten States, but in their case also the improvement ranged from a higher of 11 per cent in Tamil Nadu to lower of 0.1 per cent in Madhya Pradesh. This table shows the UPS female work participation rates differ from one state to the other, it appears that agriculture is more backward states attracted larger percentage of women than men and at the same time, states which got more prosperous in agriculture have less percentage of women workers.

CONCLUSION

Education is one of the most crutial instruments of empowerment of women. It is only since independence that the importance of education for both the sexes began to be socially recognized. At the time of Independence women literacy rate in India is very low. But after independence the female literacy is rising faster than that of male literacy. This rising trend is more pronounced after globalization era. In all the major states of India male-female gap in literacy is declining gradually from the year 1981 to 2001, but it varies from state to state. Females literacy is higher in the developed states like Kerala, Punjab, Maharashtra, Tamil Nadu and lower in the backward states like Bihar. In both the areas – rural and urban, female literacy rate is in increasing trend. But the rate of increase in literacy in rural areas is faster than that of urban area. Yet the gap between rural/urban literacy is more in India.

Female work participation in rural areas is significantly declined in globalisation era. This declining trend in female workforce is due to excessive depend on agriculture sector itself by women and it is inversely affected by new economic reforms. This declining trend in work participation rate in agriculture sector is because of introduction of technology in agriculture sector after reform period. All the traditional jobs done by women which were more labour intensive have been replaced by machines and that machine now controlled and done by men. As a result of these displacements of women there rural women are engaged in petty household works and they are not receiving subsistence wages. Further, most of them are working as casual labour with no security for their jobs. This casualisation trend supported by the increasing trend of women employment is irregular and temporary.. The usual principal status female participation rates differ from one state to the other and it appears that larger participation of female workers can be seen in agriculturally backward states and less participation in agriculturally more prosperous states.

To conclude, our study revealed a paradoxical observation where female literacy rate is, though gradually increasing in rural areas, employment opportunities in both agricultural and non-agricultural sector is not much visible among rural women folk. This is more so after introduction of reforms and as a result, they are not only suffering from male dominating society but also denying the employment opportunities. Therefore, it is the perquisite of the government to implement employment opportunities exclusively for the benefit of rural women in general and literate women in particular so as to bridge the gap between male and female employment opportunities.

REFERENCES

Adhinarayana, N. (ed.) (2004), “Perspectives on Population, Gender Empowerment and Health in Southern India, etal Published Research Book Centre, Mumbai.

Bhuimali, Anil (ed.) (2004), ‘Education, Employment and Empowering Women, Serials Publications, New Delhi.

Dreeze, Jean and Amartya Sen (1999), ‘India, Economic Development and social Opportunity, New Delhi, Oxford University Press.

Ghosh, Jayathi (1994), Gender-Gender Concerns in Micro-Economic Policy, Economic and Political Weekly, Vol. XII, No. 18, Apirl 30, 1994.

Kishor, Sunita, Kamala Gupta (2004), ‘Women’s Empowerment in India and its states Evidence from the NFHS’, Economic and Political Weekly, Vol. XXXIX, No. 7, February 14, 2004.

Kumar, Utpal D. Bhola Nath Ghosh (ed.) (2004), 'Issues on Empowerment of Women, Mohit Publicaitons, New Delhi.

Nakkeran, N. (2003),'Women Work, Status and Fertility', Economic and Political Weekly, Vol. XXXVIII, No. 67, Sept., 2003.

Renana Jhavvela, Shalini Sinha (2002), 'Liberalisation and the women workers' Economic and Political Weekly, 25-31 May, 2002.

Shanti, K. (2005), 'Women in India, Anmol Publicaitons, New Delhi.

Sen, Amartya (1999), Women's Empowerment Key to Slower Population Growth, The UNDPA Magazine, Vol. 26, No. 4.

Swarna S. Vepa (2005), Feminisation of Agriculture and Marginalisation of their Economic Stake, *Economic and Political Weekly,* 18th June, 2005.

Various Issues of Census of India, Government of India.

13

Analysis of Gender Inequalities in Literacy Rate–A Study in A.P.

Gulam Rabbani and Kunati Raji Reddy

Human resource development places an important role in economic development of any nation. Usually Human Resources Development (HRD) refer to the development of education, health and nutrition and their impact on the size of the population, fertility and mortality in recent years education has been mostly emphasized. According to Human Resource Development (1994) "education is one of the best ways to encourage social integration and to ensure that all sections of society have access to basic educational opportunities that respect diverse cultures and traditions". Education is a means through which a society perpetuates and spreads it own culture it is indispensable for understanding social problems and copying with social stresses and changes.

Educational development may be measurable with the available indicators of development in a country or countries during any specific period of time. The indicators available are school attendance, accessibility to education, availability of schooling facilities per capita income organization and literacy levels etc. of these literacy is considered as one of the basic indicators of education development, which facilities effective discharge of social, cultural, religious and economic responsibilities.

The women related issues are now being strongly discussed in national and international levels. The Indian women are the backbone of the family. Who help in cooking, bringing up children and looking after the members of the family Besides all they also do many jobs of the family education is indispensable for doing such diversified activities efficiently and effectively. Society can not go ahead with lack of women education. It is the mother who imparts the basic education to her children. To educate one woman means to educate whole family. Only educated women can fulfill the all-round development of her children therefore the education of women means to educate the further generation of our country. The liberty, progress and equality of women are helpful for all-round development of any nation in this connection promotion of women's education in particular and education of illiteracy in general has been the major concern of India, since independence.

Studies conducted by Usha Rao 1988 on "Female literacy in Karnataka" and Vaidyanathan and Majundhar (1994), on "Variations in Educational performance in Tamil Nadu" revealed that there are undesirable differences in male and female literacy levels over the years between regions.

The current paper on attempt has been made to analyse Analysis of Gender Inequality in Literacy Rate of Andhra Pradesh.

OBJECTIVES

The main objectives of the study are:

(i) To examine the literacy rates in Andhra Pradesh during different census,

(ii) To study the inter district variations in literacy rates in Andhra Pradesh, and;

(iii) To examine the inequalities in literacy rates between male and female population.

METHODOLOGY

The present study has been taken up on the basis of the secondary data only. The required information on literacy rates were collected from the census of India 1991 and 2001 and statistical abstracts of Andhra Pradesh for different district of Andhra Pradesh. Some statistical techniques are also used for the analysis of literacy rate differentials of the population at the district level.

Literacy rate is an important indicator of the quality of life of the people in a nation and shows the socio-economic development of the country. Literacy means the general ability of the people 'read' and 'write'. The data relating to the literacy rate from 1961 to 2001 have been collected and placed in table 1. The data in table shows that literacy rates were 21.2 per cent in 1961 increased to 60.47 per cent in 2001. During the study period there is a three fold increase in the total literacy rate. Further, the male and female literacy rate breakup revealed that the male literacy rate is higher than female literacy rate in all the years. The male literacy rate increased to 70.32 per cent in 2001, which was only 30.2 per cent in 1961 whereas the female literacy rate increased from 12 per cent in 1961 to 50.43 per cent in 2001 and recorded more than four times during the study period. From the above analysis it can be observed that there is a low literacy rate among female when compared to the male literacy rate. The differentials in literacy rates in rural and urban areas are analysed and placed in table 2. The data shows that 77.4 per cent of urban population are literates whereas 55.5 per cent of the rural only. All literates as per the 2001 census in Andhra Pradesh further the break-up of male and female literacy rates in rural and urban areas are analysed. It shows that 84.4 per cent of male urban population and 66.3 per cent of rural male population are literates the female literacy rate stood at 70.2 per cent in urban areas and 44.4 per cent in rural areas. The analysis clearly shows that the literacy rate is low in rural areas in general and the female literacy rate in both rural and urban areas all found to be low when compared to the male population of the respective area.

Table 1
Literacy Rate in Andhra Pradesh

Year	*Literacy Rate*		
	Total	*Male*	*Female*
1961	21.2	30.2	12.0
1971	24.6	33.2	15.8
1981	29.9	39.3	20.4
1991	44.1	55.1	32.7
2001	60.47	70.32	50.43

The table 3 is presented the district-wise literacy rates in 1991 and 2001 and the change in literacy rate during the same period. The overall literacy rate in 2001 is 60.47 per cent whereas the literacy rate was 44.08 per cent in 1991. The literacy rate showed only

Table 2
Rural-Urban Differentials in Literacy Rates in Andhra Pradesh: 2001

Category	*Literacy Rate*		
	Male	*Female*	*Total*
Rural	66.3	44.4	55.5
Urban	84.4	70.2	77.4

Table 3
District-wise Change in Literacy Rate: 1991-2001

Sl. No.	*District*	*1991*	*2001*	*Variation*
1.	Srikakulam	36.22	55.3	19.08
2.	Vizianagaram	34.19	51.1	16.91
3.	Visakapatnam	45.51	60.0	14.49
4.	East Godavari	48.79	65.5	16.71
5.	West Godavari	53.38	73.5	20.12
6.	Krishna	53.16	68.5	15.34
7.	Guntur	46.35	62.5	16.15
8.	Prakasham	40.30	57.4	17.10
9.	Nellore	47.61	65.1	17.49
10.	Chittoor	49.75	66.8	17.05
11.	Cuddappah	48.12	62.8	14.68
12.	Ananthapur	42.18	56.1	13.92
13.	Kurnool	39.97	53.2	13.23
14.	Mahabubnagar	29.58	44.4	14.82
15.	Ranga Reddy	49.07	66.2	17.13
16.	Hyderabad	71.52	78.8	7.28
17.	Medak	32.41	51.6	19.19
18.	Nizamabad	34.18	52.0	17.82
19.	Adilabad	32.96	52.7	19.74
20.	Karimnagar	37.17	54.9	17.73
21.	Warangal	39.30	57.1	17.80
22.	Khammam	40.50	56.9	16.40
23.	Nalgonda	38.00	57.2	19.20
	Andhra Pradesh	44.08	60.47	16.39

increase of 16.39 per cent during 1991 and 2001. An analysis of district wise literacy rates revealed that the literacy rate is highest in Hyderabad district with 71.52 per cent followed by West Godavari and Krishna districts with 53.38 per cent and 53.16 per cent respectively. The lowest literacy rate was observed in Mahabubnagar district with 29.18 per cent followed by Adilabad and Nizamabad districts with 32.96 per cent and 34.18 per cent respectively during in 1991.

The literacy rate in 2001 have showed an increase of 16.39 per cent over 1991 census and reached 16.47 per cent in 2001 also the Hyderabad district stood at 1st level with 78.8 per cent literacy rate followed by West Godavari with 73.5 per cent. About 10 districts have showed highest literacy rates than the state averages literacy rates. These districts are Hyderabad, West Godavari, Krishna, Chittoor, Ranga Reddy, East Godavari, Nellore, Guntur, Cuddappah (Kadapa) and Visakapatnam. The lowest percentage of literacy is observed in Mahabubnagar districts with 44.4 per cent. The remaining 12 districts have a literacy rate between 50 per cent and 60 per cent. Further, a comparison between 1991 and 2001 literacy rates to find out the improvement (variation) in literacy is made. It is observed that there is 20.12 per cent increase in literacy rates in West Godavari districts followed by Nalgonda (90.2 per cent), Medak (19.19 per cent) and Srikakulam (19.08 per cent). The lowest variation was observed in Hyderabad (7.28 per cent) followed by Kurnool and Ananthapur. It is to be noted that between 1991 and 2001 study period the lowest increase is observed in Hyderabad district which have the highest literacy rate whereas in Kurnool and Ananthapur districts the level of literacy rate is low.

There are significant changes in the overall literacy rate in general and male and female literacy rates in particular during the study period i.e., 1991-2001 the table 4 is presented with the district-wise variations in the male and female literacy rates in two periods it is evident from the table that in 1991 there were only one district (Hyderabad), which have more than 75 per cent of literate male population and four districts namely Cudappah, Chittoor, Krishna and Ranga Reddy have more than 60 per cent literate male population. Whereas in Srikakulam, Vizianagaram, Medak, Nizamabad, Adilabad and Mahabubnagar recorded less than 50 per cent but more than 40 per cent literacy among male population. Further it is observed that the female literacy rate was also high in Hyderabad district (72.5 per cent) followed by West Godavari, Krishna and East Godavari with 46.98 per cent, 45.54 per cent and 42.26 per cent respectively. The lowest was observed in Mahabubnagar district (18.03 per cent) followed by Medak, Adilabad and Nizamabad district with 19.25 per cent, 20.6 per cent and 21.35 per cent respectively.

Table 4
District-wise Change in Literacy Rate among Districts 1991 and 2001

Sl. No.	*District*	*Literacy Rate*					
		Male			*Female*		
		1991	*2001*	*Variation*	*1991*	*2001*	*Variation*
1.	Srikakulam	49.14	67.2	18.06	23.52	43.7	20.18
2.	Vizianagaram	45.93	62.4	16.47	22.47	39.9	17.43
3.	Visakapatnam	56.13	69.7	13.57	34.60	50.1	15.50
4.	East Godavari	55.32	70.0	14.68	42.26	60.9	18.64
5.	West Godavari	59.75	78.0	18.25	46.98	69.0	22.02
6.	Krishna	60.55	74.4	13.85	45.54	63.2	17.66
7.	Guntur	56.54	71.2	14.66	35.85	53.7	17.85
8.	Prakasham	53.14	69.4	16.26	27.06	47.1	18.04
9.	Nellore	58.04	73.7	15.66	36.99	36.4	0.59
10.	Chittoor	62.61	77.6	14.99	36.44	55.8	19.36
11.	Cuddappah	63.14	75.8	12.66	32.35	49.5	17.15
12.	Ananthapur	55.92	68.4	12.48	27.61	43.3	15.69
13.	Kurnool	53.24	66.0	12.76	26.04	40.0	13.96
14.	Mahabubnagar	40.80	56.6	15.80	18.03	31.9	13.87
15.	Ranga Reddy	60.43	75.3	14.87	36.91	56.5	19.59
16.	Hyderabad	78.90	83.7	4.80	63.56	72.5	8.94
17.	Medak	45.15	64.3	19.15	19.25	38.7	19.45
18.	Nizamabad	47.33	64.9	17.57	21.35	39.5	18.15
19.	Adilabad	45.05	65.0	19.95	20.60	40.3	19.70
20.	Karimnagar	50.79	67.1	16.31	23.37	42.7	19.33
21.	Warangal	51.91	68.9	16.99	26.08	45.1	19.02
22.	Khammam	50.04	66.1	16.06	30.53	47.4	16.87
23.	Nalgonda	50.53	69.2	18.67	24.92	44.7	19.78
	Andhra Pradesh	55.12	70.32	15.20	32.72	50.43	17.71

During 2001 the male literate rate was highest in Hyderabad (83.7 per cent) followed by West Godavari, Chittoor, Cuddapah and Ranga Reddy these are recorded more than 75 per cent literate rate. As per as the female literacy rate was concern the highest was recorded in Hyderabad (72.5 per cent) followed by West Godavari, Krishna and East Godavari with 63.2 per cent and 60.9 per cent respectively. The lowest male literacy rate was observed in Mahabubnagar district (56.6 per cent) followed by Vizianagaram Medak and Nizmabad, which recorded are less than 65 per cent but more than 62 per cent. Whereas in female literacy rate in

Mahabubnagar was with the lowest literacy rate of 31.9 per cent followed by Nellore and Medak with 36.4 per cent and 38.7 respectively. Further, the study shows that there are huge variations between the literacy rates during 1991-2001. The Hyderabad district has highest literacy rates in both female and male population; but the variation was lowest between the two periods. The male literacy rate increased by 4.8 per cent and female rate by 8.94 per cent between 1991 and 2001. Whereas, the highest variation in male literacy rate is observed in Adilabad district (19.95 per cent) followed by Medak, West Godavari and Srikakulam with 19.15 per cent, 18.25 per cent and 18.06 per cent respectively. In the case of female literacy rate, West Godavari showed highest improvement of 22.02 per cent between 1991 and 2001 followed by Srikakulam, Adilabad and Ranga Reddy with 20.18 per cent, 19.7 per cent and 19.49 per cent respectively. The Government has taken many policy steps for upliftment of education in Andhra Pradesh which is an important indicator of the development.

There are inequalities in male and female literacy rates during 1991 and 2001. the gender wise inequalities were ascertained and ranks were assigned based on variations in male and female literacy rates are placed in table 5. The table shows that in 1991 the highest gender wise variations were observed in Cuddappah district followed by Ananthapur, Karimnagar and Kurnool districts. While West Godavari showed lowest gender wise inequalities in literacy rates followed by Krishna and Hyderabad districts. In 2001 the highest variation in gender wise literacy rates recorded in Cuddappah district followed by Medak and Nizamabad districts. The lowest variations were recorded in West Godavari followed by East Godavari and Hyderabad.

By and large it is observed that the highest variations are in Cuddappah district and lowest is in West Godavari and East Godavari districts. As per as the gender wise inequalities in literacy rate concern in both 1991 and 2001.

An attempt has been to find the relationship between total literacy rate and male literacy rate, female literacy rate, male and female literacy rate and gender inequalities in the years 1991 and 2001. The correlation between TLR and MLR, TLR and FLR and gender inequalities are calculated and presented in table 6.

It is clear form the table that there exists high positive correlation between total literacy rate (TLR) and male literacy rate (MLR) and male literacy and female literacy rate (FLR) in both 1991 and 2001 census. But medium and high negative correlation were found between TLR, MLR, FLR and gender inequalities in literacy rate in 2001 census as against this low negative and medium correlation was seen to exist between TLR, MLR, FLR and GI in literacy rate in 1991. This relationship between TLR, MLR, FLR and GI indicates that TLR is in favour of reducing gender inequalities. Though MLR in all the districts are higher than FLR, any increase in FLR at present has more positive effect on reducing the gap between male and female literacy rate.

Table 5
District-wise their Ranks and Gender Inequality

Sl. No.	District	1991				2001			
		Total Literacy	Male Literacy	Female Literacy	GI	Total Literacy	Male Literacy	Female Lite racy	GI
1.	Srikakulam	18	18	17	10	16	15	15	11
2.	Vizianagaram	19	20	19	14	22	22	20	12
3.	Visakapatnam	10	9	9	16	10	10	9	15
4.	East Godavari	6	11	4	22	6	9	4	22
5.	West Godavari	2	6	2	23	2	2	2	23
6.	Krishna	3	4	3	21	3	6	3	20
7.	Guntur	9	8	8	18	9	8	8	18
8.	Prakasham	13	13	13	6	11	11	13	9
9.	Nellore	8	7	5	17	7	7	6	19
10.	Chittoor	4	3	7	5	4	3	7	14
11.	Cuddappah	7	2	10	1	8	4	10	1
12.	Ananthapur	11	10	12	2	15	14	16	4
13.	Kurnool	14	12	15	4	18	18	19	13
14.	Mahabubnagar	23	23	23	15	23	23	23	5.5
15.	Ranga Reddy	5	5	6	13	5	5	5	16
16.	Hyderabad	1	1	1	20	1	1	1	21
17.	Medak	22	21	22	8.5	21	21	22	2
18.	Nizamabad	20	19	20	7	20	20	21	3
19.	Adilabad	21	22	21	12	19	19	18	5.5
20.	Karimnagar	17	15	18	3	17	16	17	8
21.	Warangal	15	14	14	8.5	13	13	12	10
22.	Khammam	12	17	11	19	14	17	11	17
23.	Nalgonda	16	16	16	11	12	12	14	7

Table 6
Results of the Rank Correlations

Variables	*R Values*	
	1991	*2001*
TLR and MLR	0.95	0.98
TLR and FLR	0.98	0.97
MLR and FLR	0.91	0.92
TLR and GI	-0.39	-0.70
MLR and GI	-0.15	-0.58
FLR and GI	-0.51	-0.85

CONCLUSIONS

This paper mainly focuses on literacy level in Andhra Pradesh in general and genderwise literacy rate in various districts of Andhra Pradesh in particular 1991 and 2001 Census. It is observed that the rate of literacy increased to 60.47 per cent in 2001 from 44 per cent in 1991. Both male and female literacy rates were shown increased in 2001 over 1991. The urban literacy rate is found to be higher than the rural literacy rate among male and female population in 2001. The highest literacy rate is (both male and female put together) found in Hyderabad and the lowest in Mahbubnagar district in 1991and 2001 Census. The highest variation is found in West Godavari between 1991 and 2001 and lowest in Hyderabad district. Whereas the highest male variation is in Medak district and female variation is in West Godavari. The lowest variation were recorded in Hyderabad district and Nellore districts as per as male and female variations respectively. High positive relationship is found between TLR, MLR and FLR. Whereas Low and Medium negative relationship is found between TLR, MLR FLR and Gender inequalities due to the declining variations between gender inequalities in literacy rates. The gender inequalities are declining due to the active participation of non-government agencies and the State Government programmes in eradication of illiteracy in Andhra Pradesh.

The present educational scenario clearly reveals that educational activities in the state at Andhra Pradesh are mostly confined to few districts only. The planers administrators and implementers involved in literacy and adult education programme must pay greater attention to the present movement with a view to guiding the process of bridging the gender inequalities in literacy and education in this connection non-governmental organization voluntary agencies can play vital role in creating better (good) awareness especially women population towards education and literacy.

REFERENCES

Meera, Seth (2001), Women Development–The Indian Experience, SAGE Publications, New Delhi.

Human Development Report, 1994.

Rao Usha, N.J. (1983), Women in Developing Society, Ashish Publishing House, New Delhi.

Vaidyanathan, A. and Majundar Manabel (1994), Variation in Educational Programme in Tamilnadu, Economic and Political Weekly, Vol. XXIX, No. 25.

UNDP Report, New Delhi, 1994.

14

Girls' Education in India–A Development Imperative

P. Vijayalakshmi Pandit

WHY GIRLS' EDUCATION?

Girls' Education is a development imperative in India. The following reasons explain the necessity and urgency of promoting girl's education.

(a) It is (Elementary education) a Fundamental Right.

(b) There is growing demand for girls education.

(c) For the well-being of the girls/women.

(d) Girl's education promotes social and economic progress.

(e) Enable the girls/women (educated po[1]pulation) political participation.

(f) Brings inter-generational benefits.

(g) It is linked with social justice.

(a) Elementary Education is a Fundamental Right

The 86th Constitutional Amendment Act of 2002 makes elementary education a fundamental right of every child. The constitutional amendment ensuring that all girls and boys receive eight years of good quality education. In India, where gender biases are strong, it is all the more important to ensure that girls receive priority attention and that congenial conditions are created for them to complete eight years of schooling.

(b) Popular Demand

The demand for girls' education is growing. According to the Public Report on Basic Education (1999) survey, for instance, even in the educationally backward states of India, some 89 per cent of parents felt that it was important for a girl to be educated. Failure to fulfil this demand for girls' education amounts to a contempt for popular aspirations of the parents and also.

(c) Individual well-being

Basic education promotes the well-being of girls. More educated women tend to be better informed, enjoy better opportunities for employment, and seek out modern health care and advice much more readily. It is also suggested that educated girls and women respond better to HIV/AIDS prevention messages. Educated women also tend to have a greater say in decision making, enjoy higher self-esteem, and are treated more equally within and outside the household. Moreover, the socialising processes of schooling gives young girls opportunities to make friends, interact and gain a broader perspective of life, gain self-confidence and can think and act critically.

(d) Social and Economic Progress

Education brings benefits to society as well. Educated women are more likely to work in the wage economy, earn higher wages and make better entrepreneurs. Educated women tend to marry late, have fewer children, and ensure longer birth intervals-all of which contribute to improving child and maternal health in society. Consequently for a healthy and quality human resources.

(e) Political Participation

The practice of democracy is strengthened by an educated population. The importance of girls' education assumes special significance in the Indian context because of the 73rd and 74th Constitutional Amendments that make it mandatory for one-third of all seats in local governing bodies to be reserved for women. As more and more young girls get educated and complete eight years of schooling, they will be able to participate more meaningfully in local governance.

(f) Inter-Generational Benefits

There is sufficient evidence to suggest that educated mothers give birth to healthier and better-nourished children than uneducated mothers. Children, especially girls, who have educated mothers, are more likely to escape mortality at a young age than children born to uneducated mothers. An educated mother is more likely to send her own children to school so that benefits are reinforced across generations.

(g) Social Justice

The link between educational deprivation and social inequality is becoming more and more obvious everyday. Basic education is emerging as a powerful tool of empowerment. Ensuring better schooling opportunities for girls is the right step towards ensuring social and gender justice. When educational systems address issues that prevent girls from learning, they simultaneously lower educational barriers for many boys as well. The studies of E.F.A. and UNICEF (Partners of study) revealed that girls' education not only as a means of achieving the equity goals set for education, but also as a means of leveraging overall progress promoting freedom, reducing poverty, and accelerating human development.

TRENDS IN GIRLS' EDUCATION

The 1990's witnessed many positive trends in education in general with slight progress in girl's education.

The perceived positive trends in education are:

(a) Accelerated increases in literacy,

(b) Growing demand for education,

(c) Enrollment rise among children 6-14 years,

(d) Improved physical access,

(e) Increasing school attendance,

(f) decrease in school drop-out.

(a) Accelerated Increase in literacy

The Government progress like Total Literacy Campaign (TLC) of the National Literacy Mission and the measures taken for universalise primary education have led to significant jump in literacy rates in general. The figure 1 gives the literacy rates in India from 1951-2001.

Figure 1
India Literacy Rates 1951-2001*

Literacy rates for 1951-1971 relate to population aged five and above. Those for 1981-2001 related to population aged seven and above.

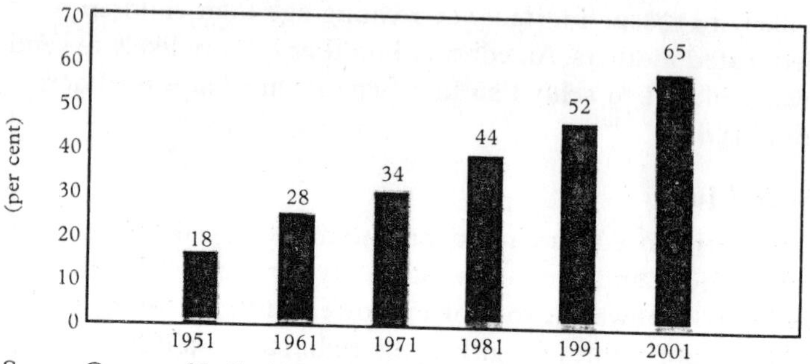

Source: Census of India 2001.

In 1991 around only 52 per cent of the Indian population, aged seven years and over, was literate. This proportion increased to 65 per cent in 2001-a jump of 13 percentage points-the highest recorded in any decade since Independence. However, there are wide disparities among the states-Figure 2 indicates the Literacy rates across the selected Indian States.

Figure 2
literacy Rates Across Selected Indian States

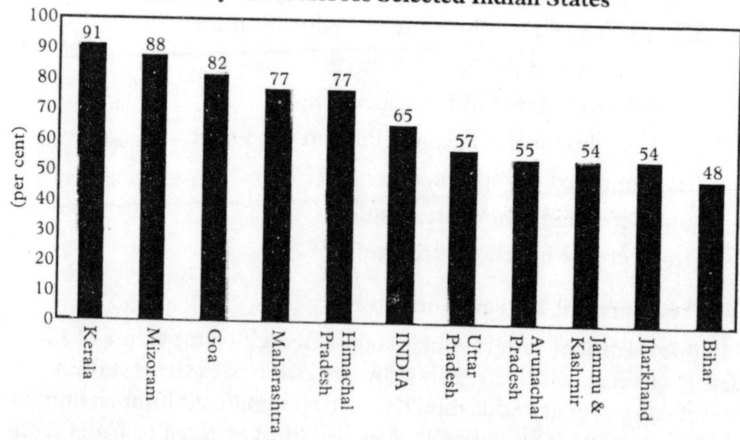

Source: Census of India 2001.

Female literacy though exhibit some progress from 1991 to 2001 the gender differentials in Indian literacy rates of 2001 is considerable. Figure 3 & Figure 4 indicates the same.

Figure 3
Female Literacy in India 1991-2001

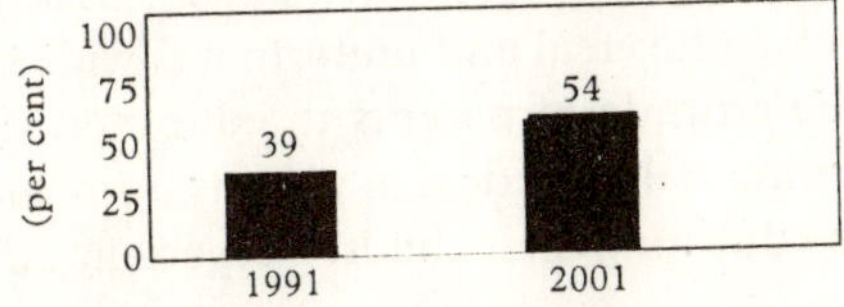

Source: Census of India 2001.

Figure 4
Gender Differentials in India's Literacy Rates 2001

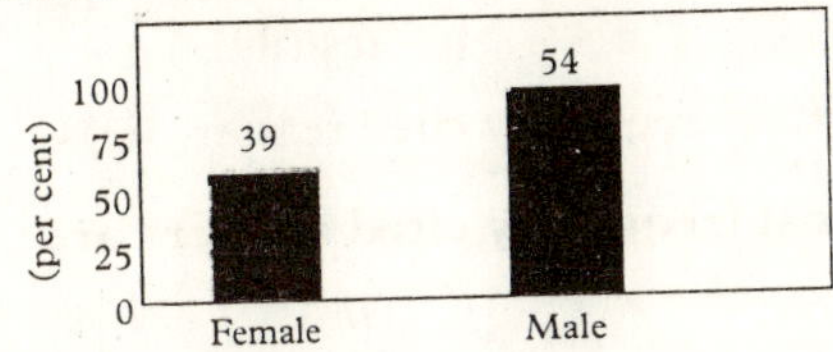

Source: Census of India 2001.

Figure 5
Decadal increase in Female Literacy across selected Indian States 1991-2001

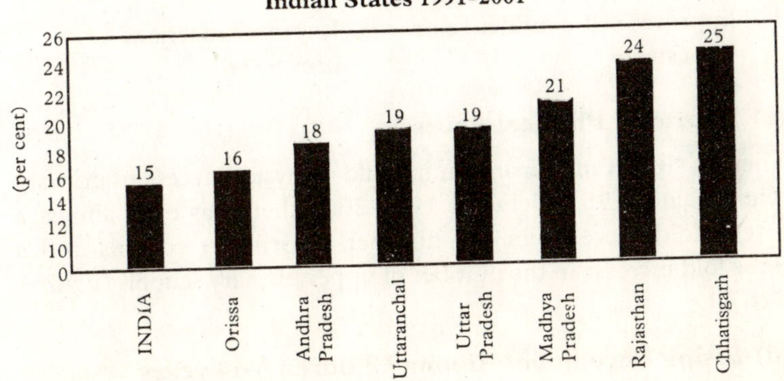

Source: Census of India 2001.

In 2001, female literacy rates fell short of male literacy rates by 22 percentage points. However, between 1991-2001, female literacy went up by 15 percentage points-the largest decadal increase ever. This occurred particularly in the educationally backward states of Chattisgarh, Madhya Pradesh and Rajasthan.

(b) Growing demand for Education

The 1990's have seen an upsurge in the demand for basic education. Though the demand is universal and uniform it is wide spread and growing rapidly. The attitude of parents to education is changing contrary to the conventional attitude that parents from poor families are not interested in educating their children especially girl children.

PARENTS ATTITUDE TO EDUCATION

1. Is it important for boy to be educated?

   Yes (98%)

2. Is it important for girl to be educated?

   Yes (89%)

3. 'If yes, why?' (most frequently cited reasons are)

Most frequently cited answers are

Boys

1. Improves employment and income opportunities.
2. Improves social status. income opportunities.
3. Improves self-confidence or self-esteem

Girls

1. Helps to write letters and keep account.
2. Improves employment and
3. Improves marriage prospects.

(c) Improved Physical Access

There is significant expansion in child's physical access to primary schools since 1951. Between 1951-2001 there has been almost a fifteen-fold increase in the number of primary schools and a three fold increase in the number of upper primary schools (Figures 6 & 7).

(d) Rising Enrollment Among Children 6-14 years

There has been a significant increase in the number of children enrolled in primary schools and a lesser increase in upper primary school. In 2001 114 million children enrolled in primary schools and 43 millions in upper primary schools (Figures 8 & 9).

Figure 6
Increase in Primary Schools

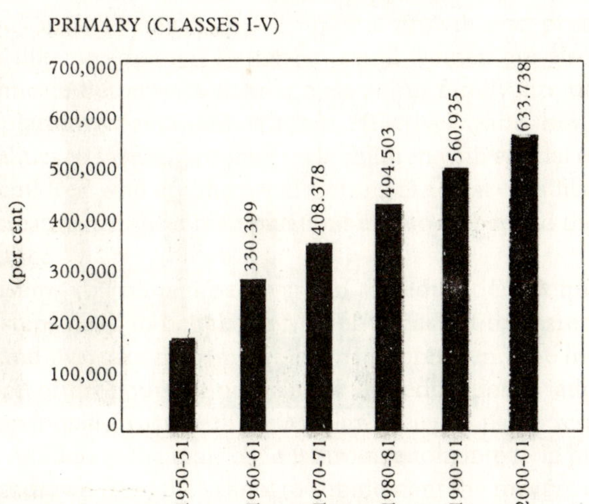

Source: Selected Educational Statistics 2000-2001, Government of India 2002.

Figure 7
Increase in Upper Primary Schools

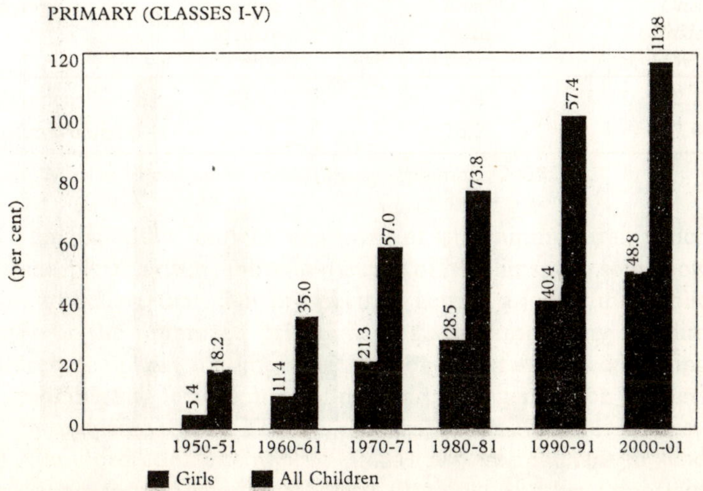

Source: Selected Educational Statistics 2000-2001, Government of India 2002.

Figure 8
Children Enrolled in Primary Schools

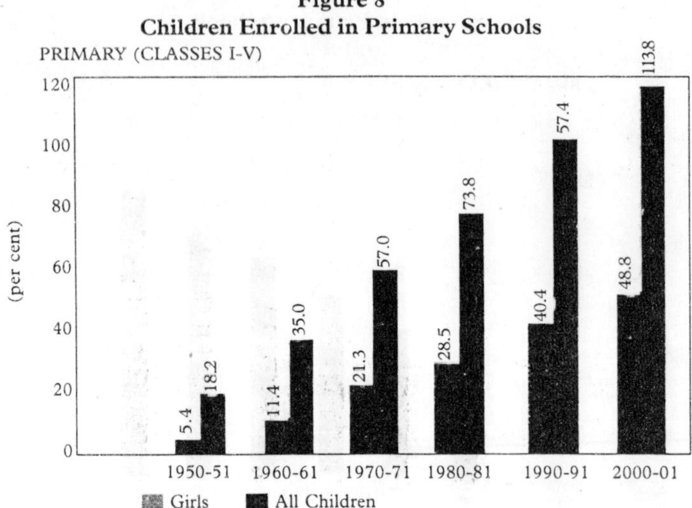

Source: Selected Educational Statistics 2000-2001, Government of India 2002.

Figure 9
Children Enrolled in Upper Primary Schools

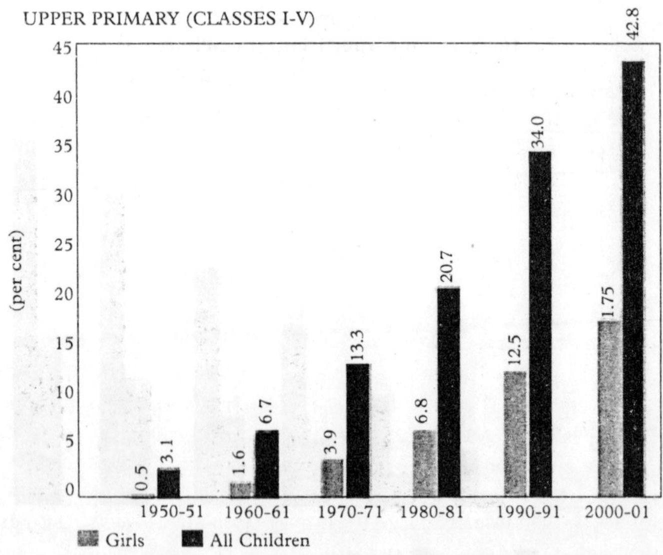

Source: Selected Educational Statistics 2000-2001, Government of India 2002
Enrolment of girls has increased significantly over the years.

PROPORTION OF GIRLS IN ELEMENTARY EDUCATION

Primary Schools (Classes I-V)

1951 - 28 per cent

2001- 44 per cent

In 1951, girls accounted for 28 per cent of all children enrolled in primary school. This proportion went up to 44 per cent in 2001.

Upper Primary Schools (Classes VI-VIII)

1951 - 16 per cent

2001 - 41 per cent

In 1951, girls accounted for 16 per cent of children enrolled in upper-primary schools. This proportion went up to 41 per cent in 2001. Increasing girls' percentage in elementary education has to be given priority.

(e) Increasing School Attendance

As per the National Family Health Survey (1999), India has seen an impressive increase in school attendance for both boys and girls. By 1998-99, close to 79 per cent of children 6-14 years were attending school - up from 68 per cent in 1992-93. But there is gender difference in school attendance (Figure 10).

Figure 10
Gender Differentials in School Attendance
(6-14 years) 1998-1999)

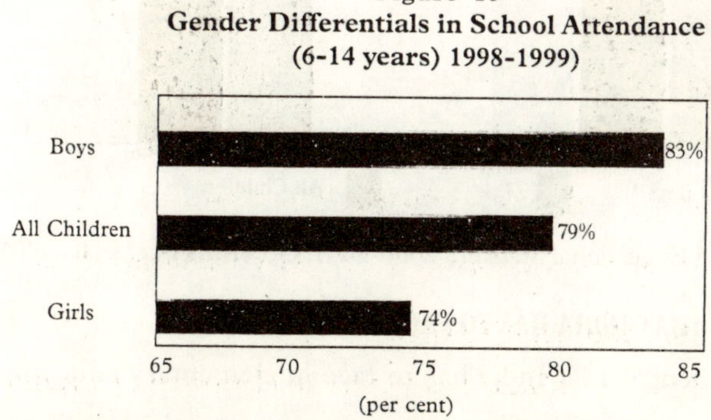

Source: National Family Health Survery-2 (1998-99).

However the school attendance varies across states (1998-99) from more than 90 per cent in Himachal Pradesh and Kerala to 60 in Bihar. In Andhra Pradesh 68 per cent attendance.

(f) Decrease in School Dropout

There has been a gradual decline in dropout rates between 1960-2001. But the level drop-rates are still remain high (Figures 11 & 12).

Figure 11
Dropout rates for Elementary Education (Classes I-VIII)

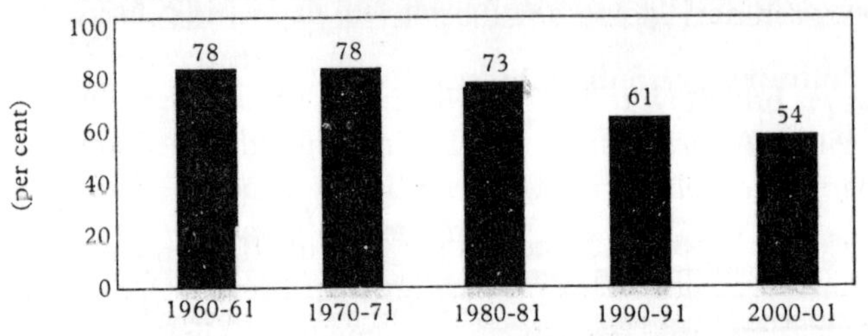

Source: Selected Educational Statistics 2000-2001, Government of India 2002.

Figure 12
Dropout rates for Primary Education (Classes I-V)

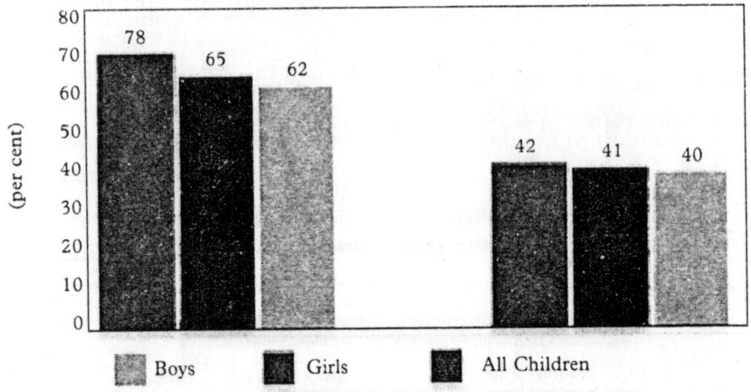

Source: Selected Educational Statistics 2000-2001, Government of India 2002.

CHALLENGES THAT INDIA HAS TO FACE

The key challenges that India has to face in elementary education are:

(a) The backlog of non-literates

(b) Gender gaps in schooling

(c) Learning achievements

(d) School infrastructure

(e) Teacher training and support

(f) Expenditure on education.

(a) The backlog of non-literates

Despite the impressive increase in literacy rates during the 1990s, the backlog of non-literate people remains high. In 2001, close to 296 million people were classified as non-literates. Some 190 million of them are women. (Figure 13).

Figure 13
India's Non-literate Population 1991-2001

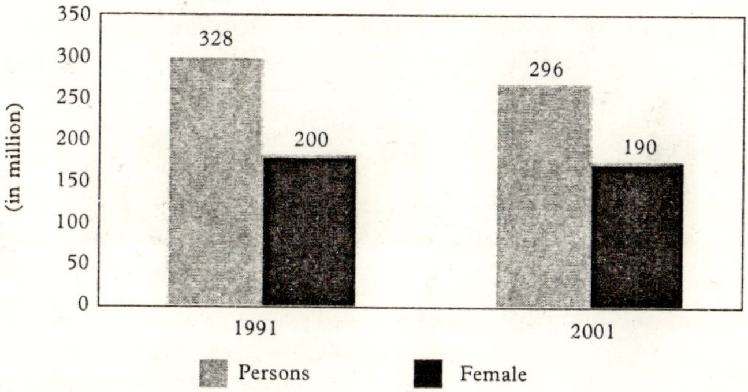

Source: Census of India 2001.

Sixty (60) per cent of the nearly 190 million non-literate girls and women live in six states: Andhra Pradesh, Bihar, Maharashtra, Rajasthan, Uttar Pradesh and West Bengal.

Gender gaps in literacy still persist. In 2001, there was a 22 percentage point difference in literacy rates between women and men- down from 29 percentage points in 1991. Gender gaps in literacy remain particularly high in the more educationally backward states.

The disparities in literacy become all the more striking at the district level data.

District Level Female Literacy, 2001

Lowest	*Highest*
18.5 per cent (Kishanganj, Bihar)	96 per cent (Aizawl, Mizoram)

Gender Gaps in Literacy Across District, 2001

Sawai Madhopur (Maximum)	Rajasthan	Male literacy exceeds female literacy by 41 percentage points.
Jantia Hills (Minimum)	Meghalaya	Female literacy exceeds male literacy by 1 percentage point.

(b) Gender Gaps in Schooling

Barely four out of ten girls who enrol are able to complete the Constitutionally mandated eight years of schooling. Dropout rates especially among girls remain high (Figure 14).

Girls belonging to Scheduled Caste and Scheduled Tribe communities face several more obstacles in attending school.

Figure 14
Gender Differentials in Dropout Rates in Elementary Education (Classes I-VIII)

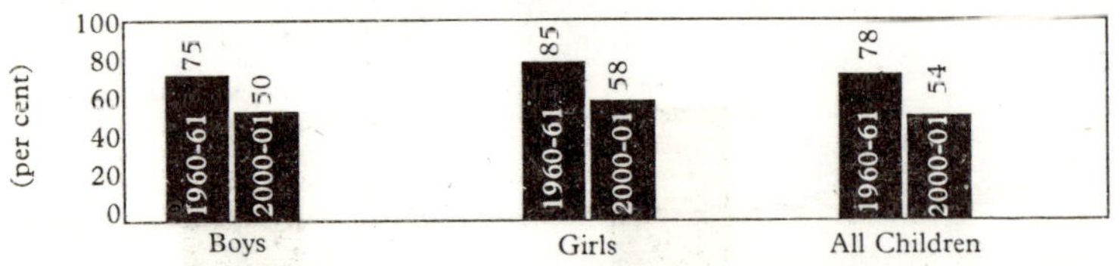

Source: Selected Educational Statistics 2000-2001, Government of India 2002.

'Not interested in studies' is often given as a reason for why most children do not attend school. The response is a reflection of the need to motivate the children to attend the school, improve the quality and delivery of education to make it more attractive, joyful and relevant for children.

Almost twice as many girls as boys are pulled out of school or never sent to school in order to assist in household chores. Main reasons given often are:

(a) never attending school:
- Costs too much
- Not interested in studies
- Required for outside work for payment in cash or kind.

(b) not currently attending school:
- Not interested in studies
- Costs too much

(c) Learning Achievements

A major constraint in assessing India's progress in elementary education has been the lack of specialised and comprehensive data on learning achievements of children. Smaller surveys, however, suggest that even after five years in primary school, many children learn little. A large number of children are not even able to sign their names.

- A learning assessment study conducted in 1997 in Bihar, Karnataka, Maharashtra and Rajasthan revealed that only 40 per cent of students recorded an achievement level of 50 per cent or more in language. The proportion was only 27 per cent of students in mathematics.
- According to a Baseline Assessment Study conducted by the District Primary Education Programme in 1997, the percentage of students in Class II who did not achieve the prescribed 'Minimum Levels of Learning' in language (that is, they failed to score more than 40 per cent marks in the achievement tests) ranges from 59 per cent in Gujarat to 20 per cent in Himachal Pradesh.
- In Class IV, the percentage of students not achieving the prescribed 'Minimum Levels of Learning' in language ranges from 76 per cent (Gujarat) to 41 per cent (Himachal Pradesh) and in mathematics from 90 per cent (Gujarat) to 53 per cent (Himachal Pradesh).

(d) School Infrastructure

The Sixth All India Educational Survey of 1993 brought out the many deficiencies in school infrastructure.

State of school infrastructure in Elementary Education, 1993:

Primary Schools:	*Upper Primary Schools:*
35 per cent have no blackboards.	17 per cent have no blackboards.
35 per cent had no mats or furniture for students.	33 per cent had no mats or furniture for students.
47 per cent had no furniture for teachers.	29 per cent had no furniture for teachers.
985,000 additional classrooms are required.	354,000 additional classrooms are required.

The above survey gives the poor state of school infrastructure.

The Sarva Shiksha Abhiyan (SSA) has been prescribed the following norms for schooling:

Teacher

- One teacher for every 40 children in primary and upper primary schools.

- At least two teachers in a primary school (Classes I-V).
- One teacher for every class in the upper primary school (Classes VI-VIII)

School Alternative Schooling Facility

- Within one kilometre of every habitation.
- Provision for opening of new schools as per State norms or for setting up Education Guarantee Schools in unserved habitations.

Upper Primary Schools

- As per requirement, based on the number of children completing primary education, up to a ceiling of one upper primary school/ section for every two primary schools.

Classrooms

- A room for every teacher or for every grade / class, whichever is lower in primary and upper primary, with the provision that there would be two classrooms with veranda to every primary school with at least two teachers.
- A room for the Headmaster in upper primary school.

Strict implementation of the norms laid down by S.S.A. in providing infrastructure and congenial school atmosphere is essential.

(e) Teacher Training and Support

With expansion of education facilities, the number of teachers has also increased. In 2001, there were close to 1.9 million primary school teachers in India. However, the proportion of female teachers remain low (Figure 15).

Recruitment of School Teachers

Year	*Primary School Teachers*	*Female Primary School Teachers*
1950-51	538,000	82,000
2000-01	1,896,000	675,000

Source: Selected Education Statistics 2000-01, Govt. of India 2002.

Figure 15
Proportion of Female Teachers (2000-01)

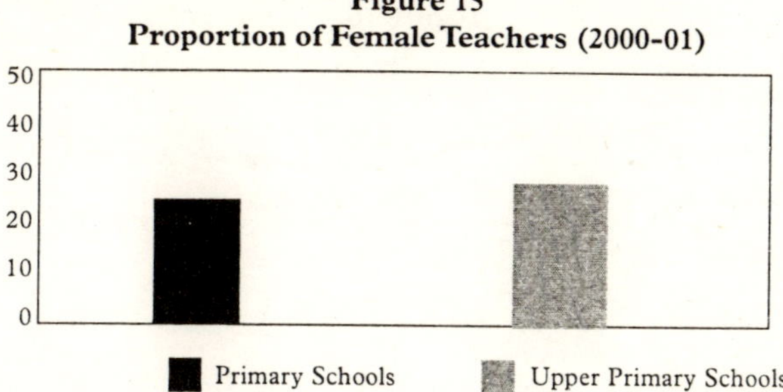

Source: Selected Educational Statistics 2000-2001, Government of India 2002.

Despite the increase in the recruitment of primary school teachers, the pupil-teacher ratio remains high in many states.

Teacher Training

The percentage of trained teachers in primary education is 95 per cent and above in Andhra Pradesh, Gujarat, Himachal Pradesh, Karnataka, Maharashtra, Orissa, Punjab and Tamil Nadu. It is 60 per cent and below in Arunachal Pradesh, Jammu and Kashmir, Manipur, Meghalaya, Nagaland and Tripura.

Source: Selected Educational Statistics 2000-01, Govt. of India 2002.

(f) Expenditure on Education

Government of India has set a goal of allocating 6 per cent of Gross Domestic Product (GDP) towards expenditure on education. By 2000-01, India had spent 4.11 per cent of its GDP on education. The proportion of public spending on elementary education fell from 1.25 per cent of Gross National Product (GNP) in 1990 to 1.08 per cent in 1997 (Figure 16). Investing more on elementary education in general and girl's education in particular will reap more benefits to the family and for the country as a whole.

STRATEGIES FOR ACCELERATING GIRLS' EDUCATION

The Government of India's Sarva Shiksha Abhiyan (SSA) provides the policy frame work to meet education for all. Many efforts in the past to ensure universal schooling for girls have yielded favourable results. Some of the most successful initiates includes.

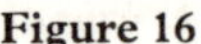

Figure 16

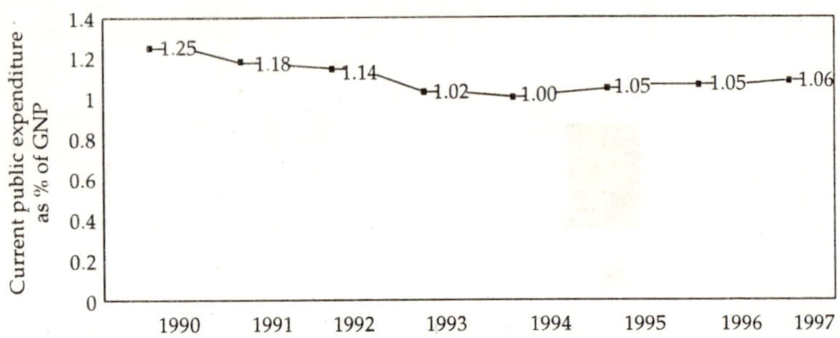

Source: Selected Educational Statistics 2000-2001, Government of India 2002

- Providing regular cooked lunch (mid-day meals) in primary schools.
- Introducing bridging courses to get working children into school.
- Improving the relevance of curriculum for adolescent girls.
- Providing early childhood care.
- Empowering women for local governance.
- Supporting local communities to demand quality education.
- Guaranteeing universal access to primary schools.
- Strengthening planning and monitoring.
- Making the teaching-learning experience joyful.
- Introducing innovative and flexible structures for delivering education.

Mid-day meals in Primary Schools

A recent survey commissioned by UNICEF reveals that school enrolment has shot up after mid-day meals were introduced. Between July 2001 and July 2002, across a sample of schools in three states, Class 1 enrolment rose by 15 per cent-significantly higher than the trend increase of around 2 per cent per year in the 1990s. This surge in enrolment was due mainly to the impressive jumps in female enrolment-17 per cent in Chhattisgarh and 29 per cent in Rajasthan. It was observed that the mid-day meals programme can be effectively implemented by strengthening it in many ways-by providing additional resources, improving the quality of food, maintaining hygienic standards, introducing some variety in the food served, and ensuring minimum disruption to classroom activities.

Getting Working Children into School

Counselling parents/girls and effective community mobilisation and the introduction of bridge schools have proven extremely successful in encouraging working children, particularly girls, to join mainstream primary schools.

The efforts and approach of Mamidipudi Venkatarangaiah Foundation (MVF) to bring the children to schools from child labour particularly girls is commendable. The girl child programme, an integral programmes of MVF took measures to counsel and mobilise the parents of girls, provided buses for transportation, toilets for girls involving the parents and girls in identifying the needs and facilities etc., are some of the initiates to encourage to join school and retain girls in school.

Improving the Relevance of Curriculum

If the parents of girl children perceive education as relevant to the daily struggle for survival, livelyhood and realise the need they may send daughters to school. Some NGO organisations in collaboration could realise such goal through their educational programmes and strategies. 'Nirantar' (Centre for women and education) and 'Mahila Samakhya' (for older and out of school girls in rural areas) combindly established a residential educational programme. The programmes with objectives locally relevant programmes by understanding the aspiration and needs of the students to enhance self-confidence among the girls. Five years later when the trained girls went back to villages many girls started enrolling. This centre continued to attract rural women and girls and long mailing lists wanting to acquire education.

Designing and development of curriculum on nutrition, health and HIV/AIDS as a preventive and awareness building measure at elementary education level is essential.

Empowering Women for Local Governance

Educating and empowering women panchayat representatives in local governments can take measures or adopt strategies to reduce girls dropouts and to retain them in school by bringing about attitudinal changes in villagers. One such initiative is 'Mahila Sansad' (Women's Parliament) of Maa-Beti Mela (Mother-daughter-fair) of Meeton Village, near Lucknow, Uttar Pradesh. The Maa-Beti Mela was considered an effective mechanism in appealing to communities / mothers to mobilise them to send their daughters to school. This is conceived under the DPEP for the state. Encouraging the women panchayathraj members to adopt such creative strategies will increase the girl's enrolment.

Providing Child Care Centres and Education

One reason why many girls are not able to attend schools is to take care of younger siblings. Linking pre-school centres to primary schools is an effective way of ensuring such girls get into primary schools regularly. 'Balwadis' seek to provide quality Early Childhood Care and Education (ECCE) to children between 3-6 years in remote, hilly economically poor communities proved successful in many ways. Community people's involvement worked wonders in some areas by devoting land for pre-schools and primary schools, free labour to build the buildings, honorary services by women groups (WSHG) to act as teachers, ayas, maintaining buildings have made the programme more successful.

Guaranteeing Universal Access

Some state governments introduced Education Guarantee Schemes (EGS) as a strategic accelerating initiative intended to ensure universal access to primary schools. Madhya Pradesh introduced EGS in January 1997 guarantees to provide (within 90 days) a primary schooling facility to any community that does not have one school and put a demand for primary school. Once initiated, the community played a central role in selecting the teacher and providing place and facility for supplementary requirements and resources. Education Guarantee Scheme (EGS) approach appears most practical could be adopted by other states but needs to be strengthened by government and community involvement for better facilities and teacher training and support.

The other acceleration strategies for girls' education are making teaching-learning experience joyful, introducing innovative and flexible structures for realising the teaching/learning objectives.

CONCLUSION

India could have been achieved much progress in 100% literacy, universal education and girl's / women's education during the post independence period if more investment was put in universal elementary education during different 'Five Year Plan periods'.

Even after 58 years of independence the status of basic and elementary education in India in general and girls education in particular is discouraging which is one of the important indicators of the development.

Some Important Suggestions are given below

- Strengthening the education planning and implementation with constant monitoring by allocating more funds for education in general and girls' education in particular.
- A holistic gender sensitive, creative approach to attract the girl children and to retain them in school by community involvement and partnership.
- Involving local panchayats and the representatives to achieve targets and progress in girls' education by training and orienting them to adopt success case studies.
- Encouraging Non-Governmental Organisations (NGO's) to mobilise and sensitise parents and community people about the need for girls to get educated and acquire income generating skills.
- Increasing investment to establish pre-school and primary school especially for girl children with trained women teachers and good infrastructure facilities.
- Integration or convergence of elementary education with other development sectors like health, water, sanitation, food, nutrition and child protection is imperative to realise the Fundamental Right of Child to get free, quality basic education and as well as enabling the girl children to become healthy educated and skilled citizens/human resource for their wellbeing and to contribute for the development of India.

REFERENCES

Education for All: National Plan of Action, India–2003, Department of Elementary Education and Literacy, Ministry of Human Resource Development, Government of India, New Delhi.

Government of Madhya Pradesh, From Your School to Our School: Education Guarantee Scheme, Rajiv Gandhi Shiksha Mission, Government of Madhya Pradesh, 2000.

'Mapping India's Children UNICEF in Action': UNICEF Publication, 2004.

'Acceleration Strategies for Girl's Education' UNICEF Publication, 2003.

Education Initiatives in India, UNICEF Publication, 2003.

15

Promoting Gender Equality through Education in the Indian Context

Mohamed Khaiser Ahmed

INTRODUCTION

> *"The most difficult thing in Life is to discover the obvious"* –Mahabub-Ul-Haq, The Chief Architect of Human Development Index.

Gender relations are important as women constitute nearly half of the human race and their development certainly contributes to human development. Gender inequality is now receiving greater attention. Women and Children represent 67.7% of the country's total population. There cannot be happiness and full development so long as women remain depressed and exploited. No society can be free, fair and just until its women enjoy freedom and justice and opportunities for utilizing their full potential.

The United Nations has been a key forum for the women's advocacy, from the 1975 U.N. International Women's Year through the Decade on Women (1975–1985) and the Global Conference and Summits of the 1990's. The past three decades (1975–2005) have witnessed a steadily increasing awareness of the need to empower women through measures to increase socio-economic equity and broader access to fundamental human rights in evolvements in nutrition, basic health and education along with awareness.

In recognition of the importance of establishing gender equity around the world, the United Nations Development Fund for Women (UNIFEM) was established as a part of UNDP in 1984. The platform of Action resulting from the 1995 Beijing World Conference on Women expanded the concept of women's empowerment calling it gender mainstreaming. As a result of Beijing conference, more than 100 countries announced new initiatives to improve the status of women. In 2000, the follow-up Beijing +5 conference further strengthened the application of the mainstream concept, and used it to highlight the need for more progress in reaching equality worldwide. The year 2005 marks the tenth anniversary of the Beijing World Conference on Women bringing renewed focus and energy to the efforts to empower women.

Pandit Jawaharlal Nehru had said "To awake people it is the women who must be awakened. Once she is on the move, the family moves, the village moves and the nation moves". After Independence the Constitution has given equal opportunities to men and women on paper yet women remain secondary to men.

The concept of empowerment of women is of recent origin. The word empowerment has been given by UN agencies during recent years. It is being increasingly felt that empowerment of women will enable a greater degree of self-confidence, a sense of independence and capability to resist discrimination imposed by the male dominated society.

"Empower' means to make one powerful or equip one with the power to face the challenges of life to overcome the disabilities, handicaps and inequalities. Empowerment is an active, multidimensional process which should enable women to realize their full identity and powers in all spheres of life. It would consist in providing greater access to knowledge and resources, greater autonomy in decision making greater ability to plan their lives, greater control over the circumstances to influence their lives and freedom from the shackles imposed on them by custom, belief and practice.

Empowerment of women can be achieved through education, employment and women's organization. Five important dimensions of female empowerment are 1) Economic Participation, 2) Economic Opportunity, 3) Political Empowerment, 4) Educational attainment, 5) Health and well being.

WOMEN'S EDUCATION

.... there cannot be an educated people without educated women. If general education had to be limited to men or women, that opportunity should be given to women, for them it would more surely be passed on to the next generations.

Dr. S.Radhakrishnan
University Education Commission (1949)

.... the education of girls should receive emphasis, not only on the grounds of social justice, but also be cause it accelerates social transformation.

—National Policyon Education (1968)

........."If you educate a man, you educate an individual, if you educate a women, you educate a family.

Pandit Nehru

Traditionally economists tried to break the shackles of poverty and pave the way for economic development by means of accumulating material capital. But in recent years they have down played the role of physical capital and have attached greater importance to human capital. In the 20th century, more so since the second world war, many industrialized countries witnessed a massive rise in industrial production and productivity per worker. This massive rise was attributed to investment in the form of education and training.

Thus, investment in education contributes to economic growth and economic growth in turn makes it possible for nations to invest in educational development. Education, therefore, in both seed and fruit of economic development. Education alters the attitude to work, consumption preferences, saving propensities, economic rationality, ability to innovate etc.

The interdependence between education and growth is also reflected in the World Education Report 1995 of UNESCO.

We find that developed countries enjoy a very high literacy rate i.e., nearly 99 per cent among males and females. It is disheartening to note that though India is a developing country, its literacy rates are very much lower than all the developing countries i.e, female literacy rate is not even 38 per cent and male is only 65.50 per cent.

Realising the gravity of the situation of gender gap in literacy, the Human Development Report 2001 states "Investing in Women's

Capabilities and empowering them to exercise their choices is not only valuable in itself but also suggests suitable ways to contribute to economic growth and development" The Report affirms that "Human Development is impossible without gender equality. As long as women are excluded from the development process, development will still remain lopsided. Human Development implies endangering the development paradigm. The HD Report further emphasizes" for Human Development Perspective, poverty means the denial of choices and opportunities. And gender equality is essential for empowering women and for eradicating poverty. Thus, Gender equality needs to be a part of each country's strategy for eradicating poverty, both as an end and as a means to eradicating other forms of human poverty.

Table 1
Estimate of Adult Literacy Rate (Percentages)

	1980			*1995*		
	Total	*Male*	*Female*	*Total*	*Male*	*Female*
World	69.50	77.20	61.90	77.40 (7.90)	83.60 (6.40)	71.20 (9.30)
Developing Countries	58.00	68.90	46.80	70.40 (12.40)	78.90 (10.00)	61.70 (14.90)
Least Developed countries	36.50	48.30	24.90	48.80 (12.30)	59.50 (11.20)	38.10 (13.20)
Developed countries	96.60	98.00	95.40	98.70 (2.10)	98.90 (0.90)	98.40 (3.00)
South Africa India	40.80	55.30	25.30	52.00 (1.20)	65.50 (10.20)	37.70 (12.40)

Source: World Education Report 1995 of UNESCO.

Education is an insurance against economic oppression leading to better social status and empowerment ofWomen. Mohanty rightly observed "Education will not only change the lives of women at the personal level by altering the pressure of depending hierarchy and domination through economic autonomy.

The World Bank studies involving 20 countries in the region gave a conclusive support of women's education. The studies indicated that the country with a lower female enrolment rate would have worse indicators of social welfare.

In Asia and Pacific, a number of cultural factors continue to hinder the full participation of girls and women in education. A

World Bank publication shows that in Asia there is a considerable disparity between boys and girls in terms of primary school enrolment this being 77.4% of boys and 59.3% for girls.

The Indian study states that 'in general' the status of women in Indian society has been unequal vis-à-vis men. As a sequel to this, girls suffers from certain social, economic and educational disadvantages when compared to boys. The girls child in India generally suffers from certain age old beliefs and prejudices such as being perceived as being some one who is less useful to family in the long run than her male siblings. As a result she is denied equal access to education. As an educationally disadvantaged group, the girls constitute 48% of the child population, educational disadvantage among girls being visibly greater in rural areas and amongst certain sections of the society.

Women's education of women was confined almost exclusively to urban areas. This is clear from Table 2.

Table 2
Number of Girls per 100 Boys enrolled in School and College

Year	*Primary (I – V) Classes*	*Middle (V-VIII) Classes*	*Secondary (IX – X) Classes*	*Colleges & Universities for general education*
1950-51	39	18	16	11
1955-56	44	25	21	14
1960-61	48	32	23	21
1965-66	57	37	30	25
1970-71	60	41	35	27
1975-76	62	46	39	39
1979-80	62	48	41	42
1980-81	63	49	44	42
1981-82	63	49	43	46
1982-83	64	51	41	46
1983-84	64	51	43	46
1984-85	65	52	44	49
1985-86	67	54	44	51
1986-87	69	54	46	51
1987-88	69	55	47	46
1988-89	70	55	50	46
1989-90	70	56	50	48
1990-91	71	58	50	50

Contd...

Year	*Primary (I – V) Classes*	*Middle (V-VIII) Classes*	*Secondary (IX – X) Classes*	*Colleges & Universities for general education*
1991-92	72	62	52	48
1992-93	72	61	51	50
1993-94P	75	65	55	50
1994-95P	75	64	55	52
1995-96P	76	64	57	56
1996-97P	77	66	59	56

Source: Department of Education, Ministry of Human Resource Development, New Delhi Provisional Excludes professional technical and special courses.

In 1947, girls formed only 23.4% of the total enrolment of 17,750,263 in 218,165 educational institution: 26.7% at the primary stage, 18% at the middle stage, 12.8% in high school, 10.4% in Universities and Colleges of General Education and 6.6% in colleges of professional education. Besides the male/female gap, the system was marked by sharp regional, rural urban and inter-group disparities. Female literacy was 6% compared to 23% for males, (Report of National Committee on Women's Education, 1959).

Presently, India has the second largest educational system in the world after China, with 6,26,737 primary, 1,90,166 upper primary, 79,494 co 79,648 high schools, 28,487 higher secondary school, 7,494 colleges for general education, 540 engineering colleges, 755 medial colleges, 818 colleges of teacher training, 1066 polytechnics, 4,171, TTI's, 1,319 teacher training schools and 308 universities, institutions of national importance and research 308 universities, institutions of national importance and research institutions. In addition, there are, 2,90,000 non-formal center (NFE) for out-of-school children in the age group 6-14 years and a massive volunteer-based literacy programme for adults in the age group 15-35 years. There are 111 million children enrolled in the primary grades Classes 1-V, 40.4 million in classes VI–VIII, 18.5 million in Classes IX-X and 6.98 million students in higher secondary institutions. There are more than six million students enrolled in institutions of higher learning, girls from 43.5% at the primary level, 40.5% at the middle stage, 37.8% at the higher/ higher secondary stage and 38.8% in higher education.

At the college/university level, women's enrolment had also increased steadily from 1.69 million (32%) in 1991-92 to 2.12

million (35.8%) in 1995-96. In the science courses, girls constituted about 35.5% of the total students enrolled in 1995-96. In the MBBS course in the same year 34.50% of the total students enrolled were girls and in Engineering and Architecture courses, 14.25% were girls. Teacher training was the most popular professional course for girls where they constituted 48.47% of those enrolled. The total number of girls in the professional courses was 0.95% lakh in 1995-96. This is clear from Table 3, the Bhaktavatsalam Committee investigated the causes of lack of public support for girl's education, particularly in rural areas, and to suggest measures to secure public co-operation, and the Hansa Mehta Committee, which

Table 3
Number of Females per 100 Males in University Education Disciplines

Year	*Arts*	*Science*	*Commerce*	*Engineering*	*Medicine*
1950-51	15.4	..	0.5	0.3	18.5
1955-56	14.9	..	0.7	0.2	18.9
1960-61	22.3	..	1.1	0.4	25.6
1965-66	36.9	..	4.9	2.2	29.4
1970-71	50.2	21.0	6.2	3.8	25.3
1975-76	44.7	27.1	9.9	5.2	22.0
1979-80	61.0	38.3	15.8	6.8	40.4
1980-81	59.7	38.9	18.5	6.8	40.4
1981-82	64.1	41.4	21.2	6.8	43.1
1982-83	63.0	41.6	22.9	6.8	46.1
1983-84	62.3	42.1	24.1	7.6	47.7
1984-85	66.8	45.8	25.9	8.6	51.4
1985-86	66.7	47.9	28.1	9.2	53.5
1986-87	65.6	47.5	29.2	8.4	43.4
1987-88	64.1	44.3	27.9	8.6+	48.4+
1988-89	63.9	47.1	28.5	8.6+	48.6+
			30.0		
1989-90	63.3	56.8	31.6	11.9	52.6+
1990-91	65.5	58.3	33.8	12.21	52.1+
1991-92	65.3	45.7	35.9	9.5+	53.3+
1992-93	64.7	48.0		11.9	52.4
1993-94P	64.7	49.1	36.5	12.5	57.5
1994-95P	65.5	50.1	38.9	15.1	51.2
1995-96P	70.3	56.8	40.8	16.6	52.7
1996-97P	70.7	54.2	41.4	17.4	54.8

Source: Department of Education, Ministry of Human Resource Development, New Delhi.

recommended co-education as a general pattern with transitional provision for separate schools for girls at the middle stage and common curricula for boys and girls with home science as a common core subject for both boys and girls at the elementary stage. The first comprehensive Education Commission (1964-66) paid special attention to the education of girls and endorsed the recommendation of earlier committees.

According to the 1991 Census, female literacy is 39.29% compared to 64.21% for males. Rural-Urban divide is the sharpest among females themselves. Urban females are twice as well-off in literacy. Scheduled Caste and Scheduled Tribe females are at the bottom.

The programme of Nutritional Support to primary Education which was launched in 1995 in 40 low female literacy blocks provided special programme to the enrolment, retention and attendance of girls.

Universal Primary Education continues to be a priority in the Ninth Plan and simultaneously efforts will be made to ensure both easy and equal access to education for women and girls.

Vocatinalization of secondary education vocational training for women will receive higher priority as one of the ultimate goals of empowering women is to make them economically independent and self reliant. The existing network of National Vocational Training Centre (NVTC), Regional Vocational Training Centre (RVTCs), pre-vocational Training Centres (PVTCs), Industrial Training Institutions (it is) and Craft Training Centres (CTCs) will be further strengthened with necessary improvements in the infrastructure facilities or introduction of up-coming trades, hostels etc. Part time short courses will be started to meet the timings of women and girls. Emerging areas of technical education will also be introduced which have high employment potential like bio-engineering, bio-technology, fabric designing etc.

Due to faster growth of girls educational participation, and persistent efforts, enrolment of girls at the elementary stage has grown steadily over the last five decades. The number of girls at the primary stage has gone up from 5.38 million in 1950-51 to 48.3 million in 1998-99. The number of girls at the middle stage has increased from 0.53% million in 1950-5 to 16.3 million in 1998-99. Between 1990-91 and 1998-99, the strong girl-child focus of EFA programmes and proactive state policies have led to a spurt in the growth of education of girls to a very noticeable extent. In absolute terms enrolment of girls during this period at the primary level has increased by 7.85% million compared to that of boys, whose numbers have increased by 5.75% million.

Education of out-of-school girl is a major chunk of girls in the age group of 10-18. With respect to the UEE, the estimated out of school children in the age group 6-14 years were more than 40 million in 1997-98. Of these 67% were girls. In absolute terms, a total of 27 million girls were out of school, 11 million in the primary age group and 16 million in the upper primary age group. The bulks were rural.

Table 4
Drop out Rate (per cent) at Different Stages of School Education

Year	*Primary (I-V Classes)*		*Middle (I-VIII Classes)*		*`Secondary (I-X Classes)*	
	Girls	*Boys*	*Girls*	*Boys*	*Girls*	*Boys*
1960 - 61	70.93	61.7461.74	-	-	-	-
1665 - 66	70.49	63.17	-	-	-	-
1970 – 71	70.92	64.48	83.40	74.60		
1975 – 76	66.18	60.21	82.80	74.30	-	-
1980 – 81	62.50	56.20	79.40	68.00	86.60	79.80
1981 – 82	57.30	51.10	77.70	68.50	86.81	79.44
1982 – 93	56.30	49.40	74.96	66.04	86.24	78.21
1983 – 84	53.96	47.83	75.27	66.10	84.79	76.41
1988 – 89	49.69	46.74	68.31	59.38	79.46	72.68
1989 – 90	50.35	46.50	68.75	61.00	77.72	70.99
1990 – 91	46.00	40.10	65.13	59.12	76.96	67.50
1991 – 92	44.30	40.30	62.40	56.10	75.87	68.55
1992 – 93P	43.20	40.07	60.06	53.99	74.69	68.51
1992 – 94P	39.05	36.07	56.78	49.95	74.54	68.41.
1992 – 95P	37.79	35.18	56.53	50.02	73.78	67.15
1992 – 96P	41.31	37.92	61.70	54.99	74.07	66.36
1996 – 97P	39.37	38.35	51.89	52.77	66.82	73.04

Source: Department of Education, Ministry of Human Resource Development, Education in India (various years).

Note: Total dropout during a course (Stage) has been taken as per cent of intake in the first course (Stage)

P : Provisional

NA : Not Available.

In recent years, there has been a growing recognition of women contribution to development. This has raised the consciousness of policy makers and planners who issue Policies in favour ofWomen's education.

Evidence abounds that investing in women's education is beneficial to any country's development and experiences confirm the multiplicity of benefits to society when girls and women have access to meaningful education. The benefits include better health for all family members, lower infant mortality rates, longer life expectancy, improved hygiene and better educated children, enhanced productivity improved participation in community life and nation building.

The following are some of the recommendations to promote women education that would ultimately result in better productivity and efficiency.

- More investment to the made in primary education in particular. Quality teachers to be produced by enhancing the salaries of primary teachers. This does not mean that higher secondary and college education should be neglected. Priority should be given in the annual budget (State and Central) to allocate more funds to the women's education and development.
- Compulsory Education to be imparted to female students up to 12th Standard thereby postponing their early marriages.
- Free Education to be imparted to female students. Budgetary allocation should be made for free education. Incentives to be given to these children in the form of free mid-day meals, books, uniforms, cycles etc. and scholarships to meritorious students.
- Government should pass a legislation to implement 33% job reservation to women. If necessary it has to be reviewed once again and conduct debates/seminars/workshops to initiate necessary changes.
- Health Insurance coverage to e given to all the female school going children and women workers.
- Women must be involved in the policy formulation and other decision-making processes relating to their welfare.

Apart from the above, we have to change the social norms and attitudes that result in glaring inequalities in the access to and distribution of resources. Also we have to fight violence be it physical or mental against women. If we can achieve these goals, we shall succeed in removing barriers and opening the doors to a world of opportunities for women.

CONCLUSION

The above analysis clearly reveals that women has a greater role to play in the path of development. In fact, gender equity has no meaning without empowerment of women. Education holds the key. In recognising the importance of gender equality, a number of institutions and organizations have been established by the government. But government alone cannot achieve these goals. For this, active involvement of all women and men, community based organizations, voluntary associations, Panchayat Raj institutions is needed. The issues of gender equality and women's empowerment should be brought to the forefront of public consciousness.

REFERENCES

Ranga, Reddy A. (2002) Ed: Empowerment of Women and Ecological Development.

Hajela, P.D., Goswam P.D. (2000) Ed: Economic Reforms and Employment.

Mohanthy J., Indian Education in the Emerging Society, Sterling, New Delhi.

Shanta N., Returns from Education to Employment Women in Bangalore City Unpublished Thesis, ISEC.

Sharma, Ram (ed.) (1996), Women's Education–A Conceptual Framework, Discovery Publishing House, New Delhi.

Siddlique, M.H. (1993), Women's Education and Occupational Aspirations, Discovery Publishing House, New Delhi.

Swarnalatha E.V. (1993), Women's Education and Occupational Aspirations, Discovery Publishing House, New Delhi.

Sunder, Raj D. (1999), Whither Women's Education, Journal of Social Action, Vol.49, No.4, October-December 1999.

Rajkumar (2000) Ed. Women and Economy Anmol Publications Privte Limited, New Delhi.

Shanthi K., Empowerment of Women, Anmol Publications, New Delhi.

Shylashri C., Social Economic Aspects ofWomen's Education (Unpublished Thesis 2001), Bangalore University.

Human Development Report 1995, 1997, 1999 and 2001 UNDP Oxford University Press, New York.

16

Adolescents and Family Life Education –A Study of College Girls

V. Sreedevi and D. Usha Rani

INTRODUCTION

Sexuality and reproductive health education is an area that generates misconceptions, confusion, fear and unwanted caution. The importance of Reproductive health awareness for adolescents has been recognized, particularly in developing countries, where four out of five of the world's young people live and where more than half of the population was under the age of 25. These young men and women, the parents of tomorrow, must be given an opportunity to develop to their full potential as healthy individuals, to learn how to plan for and rear healthy children and to avoid the dangers to themselves and to society by having children too often, and at an young age. In a traditional society like India, education, guidance and counseling on sexual and reproductive maturity are not available from the parents and the community or from schools and colleges because discussion on sex was a taboo.

However, off late various approaches and strategies were being advocated to meet the requirements of the adolescents. Some of these strategies have worked and some have failed. Some of the strategies were successful in some countries while they failed in other countries. The question that arises is why is the use of an approach in reaching the adolescents very effective in one cultural setting and not in another. In order to understand this, intensive research was needed.

Formulation of suitable programmes and policies for adolescents in different cultural settings requires basic background information and data regarding the fears, misconceptions, concerns and constraints the adolescents were experiencing. With this background in view, the present study "Adolescents and Family Life Education – A Study of College Girls" was undertaken.

METHODOLOGY

The present study examined the perceptions of college going adolescent girls, regarding various reproductive health issues. A total of 200 girls, from Degree Colleges in Tirupati, Chittoor district of Andhra Pradesh were selected randomly for the study.

RESULTS AND DISCUSSION

Each year a large number of women die from complications of pregnancy, child birth and unsafe abortions. Ninety-nine per cent of these deaths occur in developing countries. While not all maternal deaths were predictable, women whose health was already compromised and those who were at the beginning or end of their reproductive lives were at a high risk. Unintended and unwanted pregnancies may also increased women's health risks. About 50 million abortions took place each year. Almost half of these abortions were done in unsafe conditions, resulting in high 75,000 maternal mortality. Helping women and their partners use family planning to avoid risky, as well as unintended and unwanted pregnancies, would save many of their lives. At least 25 per cent of all maternal deaths could be prevented in this way.

In order to prevent complications arising in women, knowledge on reproductive health was essential. To examine the level of knowledge of the respondents of the study on various issues of reproductive health, an attempt was made and the data is presented here under.

STATUS OF MARRIAGE PROPOSALS

Marriage is a social institution. That is why no society allows a couple quietly to pair of and start living as husband and wife. Marriage is too important for such casual arrangements. Marriage brings a number of obligations and privileges effecting a good many people.

Every society has, therefore, developed a pattern for guiding marriages. Though marriage was an individual affair, yet from time to time certain rules have been made to regulate the institution of marriage. In the past, girls were married at a very young age and generally had a child within the year. However, as early marriages and child bearing affected the health of both the mother and the child, later age at marriage was being advocated.

Table 1
Percentage Distribution of Girls by Status of Marriage Proposals

Status of marriage proposals	*No. of respondents*	*Percentage*
Engaged	9	9
Married	3	3
Not yet decided	10	10
Parents yet to decide	78	78
Total	100	100

The data showed that majority of the parents of the respondents were yet to decide. 9 per cent girls were engaged to be married shortly. Only 3 per cent of respondents, were married while one tenth of the girls proposals were not yet decided.

KNOWLEDGE ABOUT SEX DETERMINATION

The data showed that majority of the respondents knew that husband's chromosome determine the sex of a baby. A small per cent of the girls stated that god determined the sex of a baby. One quarter students stated that wife was responsible for the sex of a baby. While higher proportion of girls had correct information, many of the adolescents were misinformed about sex determination.

Table 2
Percentage Distribution of the Girls by knowledge about Sex Determination

Knowledge about sex determination	*No. of respondents*	*Percentage*
God	11	11
Wife's chromosome	25	25
Husband's Chromosome	64	64
Total	100	100

CONTRACEPTION METHODS

The information sought on contraceptive methods was presented in table 3.

Table 3
Percentage Distribution of Girls by knowledge of Different Contraception Methods

Different contraception methods	*No. of respondents*	*Percentage*
Don't know	15	15
Condoms	29	29
Oral pils	41	41
Loops	10	10
Vasectomy	5	5
Total	100	100

The data indicated that less than one sixth of the girls did not have any knowledge about contraception methods. Approximately half of the respondents knew about oral pills. More than one fourth of the girls knew about condoms. One tenth of the respondents knew about loops. 5 per cent of the girls knew about vasectomy. This emphasizes that many students were not aware of contraceptive methods and creation of awareness about these was imperative.

SOURCE OF INFORMATION ON CONTRACEPTIVES

The information collected about source of knowledge on contraceptives was given in table 4.

Table 4
Percentage Distribution of Girls by source of Information about Contraceptives

Source of information about contraceptives	*No. of respondents*	*Percentage*
T.V.	55	55
Books	25	25
Nil	15	15
Sister	5	5
Total	100	100

The data highlights that one sixth of the students had no knowledge about use of contraceptives. One half of the students had information from T.V. 25 per cent of students source of knowledge was books. Only five per cent of the respondents had this information from sisters.

USE ON ADOPTION OF CONTRACEPTION

The data shows that a major proportion of respondents said that they would adopt contraceptives for family planning after marriage. A small proportion of respondents did not want to use any contraceptives for family planning. 18 per cent of adolescent girls did not want to use contraceptives in future.

Table 5
Percentage Distribution of Girls by use on Adoption of Contraceptives for Family Planning

Use on adoption of contraception	*No. of respondents*	*Percentage*
Yes	82	82
No	18	18
Total	100	100

SOURCE OF KNOWLEDGE ON AIDS

The data shows that 73 per cent girls responded that HIV does not develop into AIDS as against one fourth of the girls who stated that HIV developed into AIDS. It is surprising that inspite of T.V. and other A.V. aids continuously advertising the information about HIV/AIDS, still majority of the young subjects were not aware that HIV positive persons would develop AIDS.

Table 6
Percentage Distribution of Girls by source of knowledge on AIDS

Use on adoption of contraception	*No. of respondents*	*Percentage*
T.V.	92	92
Radio	-	-
Films	1	1
Posters	2	2
Teachers	3	3
Awareness programmes	1	1
Others (Doctors, social workers)	1	1
Total	100	100

Table 6 shows the percentage distribution of girl's source of knowledge on AIDS. The data revealed that a major proportion of respondents knowledge on AIDS was T.V., while a small proportion of respondents gained the knowledge on AIDS from teachers and posters. A negligible per cent of respondents learned from others (Doctors, social workers, etc.) and from radio, films and awareness programmes.

SPREAD OF AIDS INFECTION

The data revealed that 2 per cent of the girls stated that kissing can spread AIDS and 2 per cent girls said that breast feeding can spread AIDS. 18 per cent of the girls stated that eating from the same plate also can lead to AIDS. One third of girls rightly stated that sexual intercourse with unwanted persons was the main cause of HIV/AIDS. A quarter of girls said that HIV/AIDS was infected from mother to foetus. 3 girls said hugging as also others who said kissing, playing together and sharing of toilet facilities resulted in AIDS infection. A large number of misconceptions existed about the factors that lead to spread of HIV/AIDS.

Table 7
Percentage Distribution of Girls by Factors Responsible for Spread of AIDS Infection

Factors	*No. of respondents*	*Percentage*
Kissing	5	1.59
Breast feeding	5	1.59
Injected from mother and fetus	80	25.55
Hugging	3	0.9
Sexual inter course	100	31.9
Tabooing	1	0.31
Playing together	62	19.80
Same toilet families	1	0.31
Shaving rajors, needles, others	1	0.48
Eating from the same plate	55	17.57
Total	313	100

FAMILY SIZE ASPIRATIONS

Urbanization and modernization, affected the standard of living of the households which gave way to smaller size families. As such the family size aspirations of the respondents were examined and presented in table 8.

Table 8
Percentage Distribution of Girls by Family size Aspirations

Family size aspirations	*No. of respondents*	*Percentage*
1 Child	25	25
2 Child	71	71
3 Child	3	3
4 Child	1	1
Total	100	100

The data revealed that three fourths (71 per cent) girls preferred two children. Similarly 25 per cent of girls decided to have only one child. A small per cent of respondents preferred three children. 3 per cent of girls preferred family size was three. Only one girl preferred four child family. However, the family size aspirations of majority of girls was one child to two child family.

SON PREFERENCE

The finding of the survey conducted by Health of Family Planning (All India Family Planning Survey) in 1980 revealed people wanted on an average, three children of which at least one must be a son. This study showed that about 30 per cent of the couples having four children, wanted additional children because they were keen to achieve their desired sex composition. The study showed strong son preference.

Table 9
Percentage Distribution of Girls by Son Preference

Son preference	*No. of respondents*	*Percentage*
Until a son is born	8	8
One more chance	12	12
Two more chances	6	6
Three more chances	5	5
Not applicable	69	69
Total	100	100

The data revealed that most of the respondents wanted only one child whether a girl or a boy. 12 per cent girls preferred to take one more chance. 6 per cent girls preferred to take three more chances. 8 per cent of girls stated their preference of son was strong and they would wait until they be get a son.

OPINION ABOUT AGE AT MARRIAGE

Age at marriage has an impact on the health of the women, as it may result in early births, abortions, premature births, still births.

Table 10
Percentage Distribution of Girls by Opinion about their Age at Marriage

Opinion an right age at Marriage	*No. of respondents*	*Percentage*
≥ 21 years	28	28
21+ above years	72	72
Total	100	100

The data revealed that three fourths of the respondents were of the opinion that 21 and above age was the right age for marriage. One fourth of the respondents felt that less than 21 years was the right age for marriage.

FAMILY LIFE EDUCATION

Gaps in knowledge about family planning and reproductive health indicate a need for better family life education in classrooms, beginning at the primary level when most children are still in school. Because young men and women tend to discuss sexual issues with their friends. Programs that provide information through youth organizations might be particularly effective. Family planning and health workers also need to do a better job in providing young men and women with appropriate information and counseling. The data regarding women respondent opinions about family life education was presented in table 11.

It is evident from table 11 that, cent per cent of the respondents opined that family life education is for good reproductive health. Majority of the respondents (81%) expressed that the girl should not conceive immediately after marriage. Rest of the 19% respondents viewed the conception should be immediately after marriage. Among 162 respondents, 96 members opined that one can wait for at least one year after marriage whereas 52 and 14 member's opinion was for two and three years after marriage respectively.

Table 11
Opinion about Family Life Education and Age at Marriage of Girls

Respondents	*F.L.E. is essential for good RH*		*Opinion about marriage after conception*		
	No	*Yes*	*1 yrs.*	*2 yrs.*	*3 yrs.*
No. of respondents	-	200	96	52	14
Percentage	-	100	-	-	-

IMPLICATIONS

In the area of human reproduction and health, various strategies have been used in attempts to develop positive attitudes and encourage responsible and healthy behaviour, help increase community participation in population activities and facilitate acceptance of population programmes in diverse cultural settings.

Primary aim of information, education and communication activities should be to motivate policy makers, programme managers, service providers and communities to translate into action the concept of reproductive rights and reproductive health, including family planning. This will require the strengthening of national capacities to undertake appropriate information, education and communication activities.

Population policies and legislation have a major role to play in the creation of supportive environment of reproductive health and family planning. Information, education and communication activities are facilitated when they are supported by population policies and appropriate legislation. It is also recognized that information, education and communication activities are valuable instruments for facilitating the understanding and acceptances of the goals and objectives of population policies.

Reproductive health and family planning programmes are usually a major component of national population and strategies, and information, education and communication activities provide strong programme support. Strengthening their links will make them mutually supportive and thus enable national programmes to better satisfy unmet demands through the delivery of high-quality reproductive health and family planning services. Many of the programmes include the prevention and control of sexually transmitted diseases and HIV/AIDS, and information, education and communication activities that are valuable tools in reaching groups at risk, especially adolescents, and in raising awareness and promoting behavioural change.

Population education is another common strategy adopted by Governments as part of their population policies. It usually covers such topics as population dynamics, pregnancy and family planning, family life, sex education and more recently, new ways of looking at gender issues, and HIV/AIDS and sexually transmitted diseases. There is increasing evidence that sex and HIV/AIDS education programmes may reduce unsafe practices among sexually active adolescents and reduce early pregnancies.

17

Gender Inequality in Literacy Rates and Education in India

D. Pulla Rao

INTRODUCTION

Gender discrimination or inequality from womb to tomb is a well-known fact in the traditional cultures of the developing countries. In India too, discrimination on the basis of sex often starts at the earliest stages of life. The Vedic era, however, was the golden era as far as equality of status and freedom women are concerned. In this era woman was considered as equal partner and enjoyed equal status and prestige in the society. The couple was called 'Dampati' which means that the husband and wife are the joint owners of the household. The position of the girl child seems to have deteriorated after the first millennia, especially in the north Indian states, due to a change in political equations. Early marriage, low status in marriage due to wide spread polygamy and practice of seclusion among upper class women became rampant. Access to education was also limited. The reforms of the nineteenth century, however, advocated a ban on early marriage of girls, supported widow remarriage and opened schools for girls. This effort was continued more vigorously in the twentieth century with the support from the Indian National Congress, which led the struggle for independence. Though the constitution and a vast body of legislation have promoted gender equality, the status of the girl child continues to be low.

Education is the process that liberates mind. It is liberation from all forms of darkness and ignorance. Women's literacy is essential for economic viability and independence. Acquisition of knowledge is one of the prerequisites for human development. To day all development agencies agree on the importance of educating women in order to promote and maintain family education, health, nutrition and general well being. The aim of education should be to train women in such a way that they apply their acquired knowledge to the pursuits of daily life and fit them for the position they have to fill. Education for women should always be directed towards their holistic development. Education enhances a women's sense of her own health needs and perspectives, and her power to take any health and family planning decisions. This, in turn, helps to reduce child and maternal mortality and morbidity rates. Increased women education leads to greater empowerment of women, to a postponement of the age of marriage and to a reduction in the size of the families etc.

HISTORICAL PERSPECTIVES ON WOMEN EDUCATION IN INDIA

In ancient India women enjoyed a high status in the society. They were provided educational opportunities comparable to men. The social evils like purdah, sati, enforced widowhood and child-marriage crept into the society much later and resulted in the degradation of their status. There were no institutions for education of girls during Muslim period, but girls did receive religious education in the recitation of the Quran in their homes.

Under the British rule, the East India Company was reluctant to take up the responsibility of girl's education for a long time, due to the doctrine of religious neutrality, which was adopted by the Government so as not to offend the natives even on social customs that had nothing to do with religion. The Indian Education Commission (1882) took a serious note of the status and education of women and rated it to be extremely backward, and recommended measures for improvement. But, because of certain socio-political reasons, no noticeable progress could be made. After Independence, the Education Commission (1948-49), set up by the government of India, laid special emphasis on the education of women.

During the Post-Independence period, the main strategy adopted to achieve equalization of educational opportunities has been to make school accessible to every child. It was thought that expansion of educational facilities, as a part of providing universal elementary education for all would make education available to the weaker sections of the society including women.

Gender inequality has become one of the major areas of concern for educationists and policy makers in the developing countries in the 21st century. Gender inequality in India stems from two important sources of differences between men and women i.e. (1) earning capacity that make women utterly dependent upon men and (2) cultural taboos and traditions that greatly restrict the autonomy of women. Biological differentiation has perpetuated a structure, which has deprived women of normalcy of life chances as available to men.

As long as Indian society remains male dominated, the constitutional provisions for legal equality of women with men matters very little. Perhaps, in no area are the laws so openly and widely violated as in the case of women, whether it is a question of education, health, and securing employment or equal wages for equal work. The prevailing mindset of the people of the society is primarily responsible for the gender inequalities, which force women to be submissive.

Women are discriminated against notwithstanding the important role in several aspects of human life and materially contribute significantly for the development of the family, society and the country. Women account for a large percentage of unpaid work, both at home and outside. They actively participate themselves in work on the family farms and in household enterprises. Where they do participate in paid work, their earnings are low employment irregular and insecure, support services inadequate, opportunities for improvement and growth few and collective organization weak.

It is a well-known fact that women play a very important role in agriculture, as it is largely a household enter-prise. They are engaged in agriculture both as main workers and as marginal workers also. Women perform a variety of tasks in agriculture transplantations, such as fertilizer application, weeding harvesting. Their role in the allied activities like management of dairy, poultry, sheep breeding etc is also well known. Indian women are major producers of food in terms of value, volume and hours of work.

Women, of late, have been increasingly involving themselves in work outside agriculture--in the secondary and tertiary sectors. Increasing levels of educational attainments have facilitated such involvement. To carry forward this trend, it is necessary that education of females should continue to be accorded greater and greater priority. Fortunately, the changing norms in the society are now enabling more and more women to actively seek education. Now they can be found in large numbers in the fields of Information Technology, science and space research and in other such fields that demand high level of skills.

As per the National Policy on Education (NPE)–1986, the government of India launched several programmes. One such programme was the Mahila Samakhya. Its main emphasis was on the empowerment of women. The programme endeavours to create a learning environment where women can collectively affirm their potential, gain the strength to demand information and knowledge and move forward to change and take charge of their lives. Following the implementation of programmes specially directed at improving the educational status of women it is possible that women may be fast catching up with men in respect of educational attainments and may also be gaining access to employment in ever increasing numbers. We propose to examine whether this has really been happening. In other words, we propose to examine whether the policies of the government of Andhra Pradesh and of India have contributed to progressive trends–in the sense that they have aided the disadvantaged females more than their counterpart males.

OBJECTIVES

1. To arrive at the index of disparity between males and females in the literacy rate in India using inter-temporal data between 1901-2001.
2. To estimate the growth of educational institutions (from primary to higher education level) in India between 1950-51 and 2001-2002.
3. To analyze the growth of enrollment of females vis-à-vis males in primary, upper primary, secondary and higher education in India between 1950-51 and 1999-2000.
4. To analyze the faculty-wise enrollment of females in higher education during the year 2001-02.

THE DATA

The secondary data relating to the literacy rates of male and female, number of educational institutions from primary to higher levels and enrollment of students by sex in primary, upper primary, secondary and higher education level in India are obtained from the Census reports, Selected Educational Statistics, Ministry of HRD, Government of India and Annual reports, Ministry of HRD, Government of India.

GENDER-WISE DISPARITIES IN LITERACY RATES IN INDIA

The most important characteristic of population is literacy, which is a pre–requisite for the overall development of the country both socially and economically. Female literacy is considered to be a more sensitive index of social development compared to overall literacy rates. Female literacy is negatively related with fertility rates, population growth rates, infant and child mortality rates, and shows a positive association with female age at marriage, life expectancy and participation in modern sectors of the economy. In spite of all the special constitutional provisions and governmental efforts, in the field of education, the disparities between male and female are still large. The gap between the literacy rates of males and females has been presenting since 1901 when the female literacy rate was only 0.60 per cent as against 9.83 per cent among males. The disparity index (ratio of male literacy rate to female literacy rate) in 1901 was 16.38. On the eve of the initiation of planned economic development in 1951 the literacy rate of women was 7.93 per cent. And women education received a phenomenal jerk from 1961. One can notice a double-digit growth rate in that year and it continued to grow at an increasing rate thereafter and even surpassed the cutoff level of 50:50 by the year 2001 (for details please see Table 1).

INTER–STATE DISPARITIES IN LITERACY RATES IN INDIA

Now an attempt is made to analyze the inter-state disparities in the literacy rates for females, males and total persons at census of India, 1991 and 2001. The state wise information on literacy rates for females, males and persons is presented in Table 2.

As can be seen from the table, Kerala retained its position by being on top with a 90.9 per cent literacy rate in the county. The rate among males was 94.2 per cent and among females it was 87.9 per cent. Bihar stood at the bottom with a literacy rate of 47.5 per cent (60.3 per cent for males and 33.6 per cent for females). Among the three new states Uttranchal has the highest literacy rate of 72 per cent for the total population, male literacy rate of 84 per cent and female literacy rate of 60 per cent. Chattisgarh has an overall literacy rate of 65 per cent (males 78 per cent and females 52 per cent); Jharkhand has an overall literacy rate of 54 per cent (68 per cent males and 39 per cent females). Six out of the 28 states in India have a female literacy rate of less than 50 per cent. These states are Rajasthan (44 per cent), Jammu & Kashmir (42 per cent), Jarkhand (39 per cent) and Bihar (34 per cent). The female literacy rate in Madhya Pradesh is 50 per cent.

Table 1
Sex Differences in Literacy Rates in India
(1901 to 2001)

Year	*Male literacy rates*	*Female literacy rates*	*Disparity index*
1901	9.83	0.60	16.4
1911	10.56	1.05	10.1
1921	12.21	1.81	7.6
1931	15.59	2.93	5.3
1941	24.90	7.30	3.4
1951	24.95	7.93	3.1
1961	34.44	12.95	2.6
1971	39.45	18.69	2.1
1981	56.50	29.85	1.9
1991	64.13	39.29	1.6
2001	75.85	54.16	1.4

Source: Census Report, 2001.

The gap between male and female literacy rate is the highest in Rajasthan (32 per cent), followed by Uttar Pradesh (27 per cent), Madhya Pradesh (27 per cent), Jarkhand (27 per cent), Chattisgarh (26 per cent) and Bihar (26 per cent). It is distressing to note that the male–female literacy gap is high in Gujarat (22 per cent). Maharashtra and West Bengal (18 per cent each) including social backwardness.

In terms of progress on the female literacy front during the last decade. Chattisgarh has the best record (the increase in the literacy percentage by 25 points between 1991-2001, followed by Rajasthan (24 per cent), Madhya Pradesh (21 per cent). In the case of males, Rajasthan has the best record (increase of 21.5 points) followed by Chattisgarh (20 points) and Madhya Pradesh (18 points). There is no doubt that special programmes launched by the Government and NGOs in Rajasthan and Madhya Pradesh have succeeded in stepping up literacy rates mostly among males.

Table 2
Literacy Rate in States by Sex: 1991-2001

Sl. No.	*State*	*Females*			*Males*			*Persons*		
		2001	*1991*	*Variation*	*2001*	*1991*	*Variation*	*2001*	*1991*	*Variation*
1.	Andhra Pradesh	51.2	32.7	18.5	70.9	55.1	15.7	61.1	44.1	17.0
2.	Arunachal Pradesh	44.2	29.7	14.6	64.1	51.5	12.6	54.7	41.6	13.2
3.	Assam	56.0	43.0	13.0	71.9	61.9	10.1	64.3	52.9	11.4
4.	Bihar	33.6	22.0	11.6	60.3	51.4	9.0	47.5	37.5	10.0
5	Goa	75.5	67.1	8.4	88.9	83.6	5.2	82.3	75.5	6.8
6.	Gujarat	58.6	48.9	9.7	80.5	73.4	7.1	70.0	61.6	8.4
7.	Haryana	56.3	40.5	15.8	79.3	69.1	10.2	68.6	55.9	12.7
8.	Himachal Pradesh	68.1	52.3	15.8	86.0	75.4	10.6	77.1	63.9	13.2
9.	Karnataka	57.5	44.3	13.1	76.3	67.3	9.0	67.0	56.0	11.0
10.	Kerala	87.9	86.2	1.7	94.2	93.6	0.0	90.9	89.8	1.1
11.	Madhya Pradesh	50.3	29.4	20.9	76.8	58.5	18.3	64.1	44.7	19.4
12.	Maharashtra	67.5	52.3	15.2	86.3	76.6	9.7	77.3	64.9	12.4
13.	Manipur	59.7	47.6	12.1	77.9	71.6	6.2	68.9	59.9	9.0
14.	Mcghalaya	60.4	44.9	15.6	66.1	53.1	13.0	63.3	49.1	14.2
15.	Mizoram	86.1	78.6	7.5	90.7	85.6	5.1	88.5	82.3	6.2
16.	Nagaland	61.6	54.8	6.9	71.8	67.6	4.1	67.1	61.7	5.5
17.	Orissa	51.0	34.7	16.3	76.0	63.1	12.9	63.6	49.1	14.5
18.	Punjab	63.6	50.4	13.1	75.6	65.7	10.0	70.0	58.5	11.5
19.	Rajasthan	44.3	20.4	23.9	76.5	55.0	21.5	61.0	38.6	22.4

Sl. No.	*State*	*Females*			*Males*			*Persons*		
		2001	*1991*	*Variation*	*2001*	*1991*	*Variation*	*2001*	*1991*	*Variation*
20.	Sikkim	61.5	46.8	14.7	76.7	65.7	11.0	69.7	56.0	12.8
21.	Tamil Nadu	64.6	51.3	13.2	82.3	73.8	8.6	73.5	62.7	10.8
22.	Tripura	65.4	49.7	15.8	81.5	70.6	10.9	73.7	60.4	13.3
23	Uttar Pradesh	43.0	24.4	18.6	70.2	54.8	15.4	57.4	40.7	16.7
24.	West Bengal	60.2	46.6	13.7	77.6	67.8	9.8	69.2	57.7	11.5
25.	Chattisgarh	52.4	27.5	24.9	77.9	58.1	19.8	65.2	42.9	22.3
26.	Uttaranchal	60.3	41.6	18.6	84.0	72.8	11.2	72.3	57.8	34.5
27.	Jharkhand	39.4	25.5	13.9	67.9	55.8	12.2	54.1	41.4	12.7
28.	Jammu & Kashmir	41.8	NA	-	65.8	NA	-	54.5	NA	-

Source: Compiled from Population of India 2001. Census Results and Methodology by Ashish Bose.

SPECIAL SCHEMES AND PROGRAMMES FOR PROMOTING EDUCATION OF FEMALES

Several strategies were adopted to promote education of girls in independent India. Theoretically, all formal and non-formal education and training programmes are open to women also along with their male counterparts. However, separate provisions are made for opening of separate institutions or separate wings for women / girls exclusively. Education is free for girls up to the higher secondary stage and several states have made education free for girls right up to the university level as well. Besides, there are other incentives like free noon meals, free books, free uniforms, scholarships for good attendance, bicycles, etc.

In the first three Five Year Plans, girls' education was covered under special component plans with additional allocations. In the Eighth Five Year Plan, a central scheme was introduced to provide funds to the state governments to hire a woman teacher for all single teacher primary schools and also towards cash awards and prizes for villages, blocks and districts with good performance in female education/ literacy. Girls belonging to scheduled castes and scheduled tribes received additional benefits for showing better school attendance. In some states girls/women receive a little high amount of scholarship particularly at the post-metric and technical educational level as a special incentive for promotion of women education. As a result of the protective discrimination policies under constitutional provisions, the enrollment of the SC and ST girl children has considerably improved.

COMMITTEES AND COMMISSIONS ON WOMEN EDUCATION AFTER INDEPENDENCE

After independence, the government of India appointed various committees and commissions to promote the cause of women's education. They are:

1. University Education Commission (1948-49).
2. Secondary Education Commission (1952-53).
3. National Committee on Women Education (1958-59).
4. Committee on differentiation of curricula for boys and girls (1961).
5. Committee to look into causes for lack of public supports for girl's education and enlist public cooperation (1963).

6. Education Commission (1964-66).
7. Committee on status of women (1971-74).
8. National Policy on Education (1986) and Programme of Action (1992).
9. National Perspective Plan for Women's Education (1988-2000 AD).

The above committees and commissions though, differ in their focus, all of them agree on the basic issues like (a) improvement of girl's enrollment in schools, (b) female literacy rate and (c) women empowerment through education.

Despite the near universal and far-reaching benefits through female education, female literacy rates are still low and the school dropout rates are high. There are gender differentials in education at all levels and so are the resulting differentials in employment.

GROWTH OF EDUCATIONAL INSTITUTIONS

After independence, the government took serious steps to establish a large number of primary, upper primary, higher secondary, colleges for general education, colleges for professional education and universities in the country. Table 3 provides data on the number of recognized educational institutions in the country between 1950-51 to 2001-02.

During the last five decades the establishment of educational institutions increased in primary, upper primary, higher/high secondary, colleges for general education, colleges for professional education and universities/deemed universities from 209671 to 664041, from 13596 to 219626, from 7416 to 133492, from 370 to 8737, from 208 to 2409 and from 27 to 272 respectively. The growth rates are calculated for the periods 1950-51 to 2001-02. The rates are 316.7 for primary, 1615.4 for upper primary, 1800.1 for high/high secondary, 2361.4 for colleges for general education, 1158.2 for colleges for professional education and 1007 for universities/deemed universities.

PERCENTAGE SHARE OF FEMALE ENROLLMENT TO TOTAL

Let us now examine the progress of girls' enrollment in primary, upper primary, secondary/higher secondary and higher education stages. As shown in Table 4 in 1950-51, the enrollment of girls was 28.1 per cent at primary school stage, 16.1 per cent at the upper primary stage, 13.3 per cent at secondary/higher secondary level and 10.0 per cent in higher education level compared with the corresponding percentage of 71.9, 83.9, 86.7 and 90.0 per cent among boys. By 1999-2000, the situation has considerably improved at all levels, in favour of females to 43.6 per cent at primary level, 40.4 per cent at upper primary level, 38.9 per cent at secondary/higher secondary level and 39.9 per cent in higher education as against 56.4 per cent in primary stage, 59.6 per cent in upper primary stage, 61.1 per cent in secondary/higher secondary level and 60.1 per cent in higher education stage among boys.

Table 3
Growth of Recognized Educational Institutions from 1950-51 to 2001-02

Year	*Primary*	*Upper Primary*	*High/Hr. Sec/Inter Pre. Jr. Colleges*	*Colleges for general Education*	*Colleges for Professional Education (Engg., Tech., Arch., Medical & Education Colleges)*	*University/ Deemed Univ./ Instt.of National Importance*
1	2	3	4	5	6	7
1950-51	209671	13596	7416	370	208	27
2001-02	664041	219626	133492	8737	2409	272
Growth	316.7	1615.4	1800.1	2361.4	1158.2	1007.0

Source: www.education.nic.in.

Table 4
Percentage of Girls Enrollment to Total Enrollment by Stages 1950-51 to 1999-2000

Year	*Primary Stage (I-V)*	*Upper Primary Stage (VI-VIII)*	*Secondary/Higher Secondary(IX-XII)*	*Higher Education*
1950-51	28.1	16.1	13.3	10.0
1960-61	32.6	23.9	20.5	20.4
1970-71	37.4	29.3	25.0	20.0
1980-81	38.6	32.9	29.6	26.7
1990-91	41.5	36.7	32.9	32.3
1999-2000	43.6	40.4	38.9	39.9

Sources: 1. Selected Educational Statistics, Ministry of HRD, Govt. of India
2. Ministry of HRD, Govt. of India, Annual Report, 2000.

It is evident from the growth rates shown in Table 5, the enrollment of girls has increased at a faster rate than that of boys at primary, upper primary, secondary/higher secondary and higher education level. During our study period (1950-51 to 1999-2000) the Annual Compound Growth Rate of enrollment of girls was 4.53 per cent as against 3.12 per cent of boys in primary stage. The corresponding figures were 7.31 and 4.31 in upper primary stage, 8.34 and 5.30 in secondary/higher secondary stage and 10.66 and 6.87 in higher education respectively. The foregoing analysis shows that during the whole period of 50 years after implementation of our constitution, the growth rate of enrollment of girls has been higher than that of boys.

Table 5
Annual Compound Growth Rate of Enrollment by Stages 1950-2000

Stage	*Annual compound growth rate during 1950-51 to 1999-2000*	
	Boys (%)	*Girls (%)*
Primary	3.12	4.53
Upper Primary	4.31	7.31
Secondary/higher secondary	5.30	8.34
Higher education	6.87	10.66

Note: Computed on the basis of enrollment of boys and girls in different stages.

ENROLLMENT OF FEMALES IN HIGHER, PROFESSIONAL AND TECHNICAL EDUCATION

By 1999-2000 there are 7494 colleges for general education, 540 engineering colleges, 755 medical colleges, 818 Colleges of Teacher Training, and 308 universities including institutions of national importance and research institutions serving more than six million students and scholars in India. There are 1066 Polytechnics, TTIs 4171 and 1319 Teacher Training Schools in 1999-2000.

Though, the share of girls in various faculties has increased very substantially during the last four decades, they continued to be way behind in Arts with 44.7 per cent, Science with 35.6 per cent, Commerce with 31.6 per cent, Education with 47.0 per cent, Engineering and Technology with 19.5 per cent, and Medicine with 38.0 per cent to reach the ideal 50:50 ratio (Please see Table 4).

Table 6
Enrollment of Females as Percentage to Total Enrollment in Higher Education by Faculty

Year	*Arts*	*Science*	*Commerce*	*Education*	*Engg./ Tech.*	*Medicine*
1960-61	18.6	0.0	1.1	32.5	0.8	20.4
1970-71	33.5	18.8	2.8	37.3	1.0	21.3
1980-81	37.5	27.9	15.2	46.7	4.6	23.8
1990-91	39.8	36.8	24.0	44.4	10.9	34.3
1999-2000	44.7	35.6	31.6	47.0	19.5	38.0

Source: Department of Education, Human Resource Development Govt. of India.

CONCLUSIONS AND SUGGESTIONS

The position of the girl child has deteriorated after the first millennia; consequently, access to education was also limited. The most important characteristic of population is literacy, which is prerequisite for the overall development of the country both socially and economically. As per 2001 census, women constitute about 54.16 per cent of the total population in India. In the field of education the disparities between males and females are still larger.

The literacy rate among females has increased at a faster rate than among males. This is evident from the successively decreasing trend of disparity index from 16.4 in 1901 to 1.4 in 2001 in the country. In literacy rate Kerala retained its supremacy position by being on top with a 90.9 per cent literacy rate in 2001 in the country. The rate among males was 94.2 per cent and among females it was 87.9 per cent. Bihar stood at the bottom with a literacy rate of 47.5 per cent (60.3 per cent for males and 33.6 per cent for females).

Several strategies were adopted to promote education of girls in independent India. The Government of India has been appointing various committees and commissions to promote the female education as and when required. Separate provisions are being made for opening of separate institutions or separate wings of women/ girls exclusively. The Government of India had established a large number of educational institutions in the country by 2002.

The enrollment of girls in primary education increased from 28.1 per cent in 1950-51 to 43.6 per cent in 1999-2000; in upper primary education it was increased from 16.1 per cent in 1950-51 to 40.4 per cent in 1999-2000; in secondary education it was increased from 13.3 per cent in 1950-51 to 38.9 per cent in 1999-2000; and in higher education it was increased from 10.0 per cent in 1950-51 to 39.9 per cent in 1999-2000. The enrollment of females has considerably improved at all levels of education in favour of females during the period of our study.

Career counseling is being actively promoted to ensure that the skills acquired by girls are appropriately utilized. These positive initiatives have helped in improving the participation of girls/women at all levels of education especially in higher education since the post-independent period. It is evident that the enrollment of girls/women has increased at a faster rate than that of boys/men at primary, upper primary, secondary/higher secondary and higher education stage.

The foregoing analysis suggests that during the whole period of five decades after implementation of our constitution, the growth rate of enrollment of girls/women in all stages of education has been higher than that of boys/men. The share of girls/women enrollment in various faculties has also increased very substantially during the last four decades. Yet, their share in the educational facilities is less than 50 per cent in the total.

In the above context there is a need for rethinking about the higher education for women. There is a general agreement that the enrollment of women to higher education must be raised at least to cover their share in the total population, which is around 50 per cent. Efforts must be directed to retain the girls in primary and secondary educational levels and enable them to pursue higher studies. And again, in the field of higher education, enrollment into technical, medicine, veterinary sciences and law should be increased through special measures in favour of women.

REFERENCES

Chalam, K.S. (1988), *Education and Weaker sections*, Inter-India Publications, New Delhi.

Chalam, K.S. (1993), *Educational Policy for Human Resources Development*, Rawat Publications, Jaipur.

Chauhan, C.P.S. (2000), 'Contemporary Issues In Higher Education', *University News*, AIU, New Delhi, December 2004.

Chauhan, C.P.S. (1990), *Higher Education In India: Achievements, Failures and Strategies,* Ashish Publishing House, New Delhi.

Government of India. *National Policy on Education* (NPE), 1986 and its Revised Version 1992, MHRD, New Delhi, 1986 and 1992.

Mira Seth (2001), *Women and Development–The Indian Experience*, Sage Publications, New Delhi.

Nurullah, S. and Naik, J.P. (1943), *History of Education in India during the British period*, Macmillan & Co. Ltd., Bombay.

Power, K.B. (2000), 'Higher Education in the Twenty-First Century', *University News*, AIU, New Delhi, December 4.

Sakuntala Narasimhan (1999), *Empowering Women–An Alternative Strategy from Rural India*, Sage Publications, New Delhi.

Sangeetha Purushothaman (1998), *The Empowerment of Women in India–Grassroots Women's Networks and the State*, Sage Publications, New Delhi.

University Grants Commission. *Annual Reports*, 1959-60, 1993-94, 1995-96, 1998-99 and 2001-02, UGC, New Delhi.

PART - III
Women's Employment

18

Gender-Wise Labour Absorption in Agriculture–An Empirical Analysis

G. Mallikarjun, Mohd. Iqbal Ali & T. Papi Reddy

It is widely recognized fact that in many labour surplus economies including India, a significant proportion of the population has to rely on their labour markets only and infact shortage of other cooperating factors such as capital and other production techniques have led to widespread unemployment and under employment. Therefore, the under-utilization of labour has become a crucial factor. The policies which are needed in the present-day Less Developed Countries (LDC)s cannot be derived simply by imitating the historical experience of the developed countries. A development strategy for the LDCs must be designed taking full account of present conditions and future prospects. An important element in such a reconsideration of development strategy is to increase labour absorption in agriculture itself which is the main occupation even today.

It has been argued most notably by Nurkse[1] that the expansion of the industrial sector in the Less Developed Countries (LDC) has been constrained more by a weak inducement to invest due to the limited demand and the actual expansion of the industrial sector has been insufficient to absorb the increment in the labour force in the traditional sectors of the economy. It was this failure of the LDCs to absorb their labour more fully in their industrial sectors which led Ishikawa[2] that the experience of the developed economies may not serve as a lesson to the contemporary developing countries. The most obvious and important difference relates to population pressure. The LDCs at present have a higher density of population on their land than most DCs had when they commended modern economic growth. Further, they are experiencing higher rates of population growth than the DCs even did.

Rural labour markets are characterized by high seasonality resulting in over-and under-utilization of labour in the peak and lean seasons respectively. The inelastic supply of labour in the peak season leading to mechanization and the lack of demand for labour in the lean season is one of the major causes of poverty[3]. Since the peak season is of very short duration, the stress is always on the demand side of the labour market. India is one of the many developing countries where low demand for agricultural labour is coupled with low yield levels[4]. While it is generally argued that crop yield could be improved through increases in per hectare labour input, how to achieve this which is the crux of the problem[5].

Theoretically, the input demand functions are analogous to the usual consumer demand functions in many respects. The major difference is while the consumer demand for a commodity is 'direct' demand, the demand for an input is derived from the demand for the commodity it produces. As in the conventional demand theory, in the case of input demand function also the most important determinants are its price, the prices of other inputs and its output, but this does not exactly operate in the same fashion as in the resource demand function. As far as agricultural labour is concerned, the market forces may not act in the way they do in the case of other inputs or commodities. In the rural labour market, so long as the supply of labour exceeds its demand, reducing wages to equilibrium level may not be effective in reducing under-utilisation of labour. instead, it may reduce the total wage bill due to the inelastic demand for labour in agriculture[6].

NEED OF THE PRESENT STUDY

Most of the earlier research studies had highlighted the impact of irrigation on agricultural development and labour absorption in general, but not bestowed much attention on labour absorption in the case of different types of farmers in the localized areas of the irrigated projects. Even in the mandays required for various agricultural operations like preparation/ploughing of the fields, plucking of sticks, seeding, manuring, applying of fertilizers, spraying of pesticides, irrigation, transporting, marketing etc., has not been much explored. Season-wise analysis of labour absorption in the case of hired and family labour required for various categories of farmers such as marginal, small, medium and big farmers is also not being properly investigated. Particularly, it is necessary to know the labour absorption in on-farm activities in the tract with long experience of irrigation as it only tries to solve the problem of unemployment and under-employment in rural areas. Further, most of the farm management studies of recent times are not stressing much on the Gender-wise analysis of labour absorption.

Keeping the above factors in mind and based on the results of available studies on labour absorption in agriculture, certain objectives are formulated for this study:

OBJECTIVES OF THE STUDY

The main objectives underlying of this study are:

1. To examine the operational-wise labour force absorption in various crops in different types of land.
2. To assess the gender-wise labour absorption among the various categories of farmers.
3. To find out the family and hired labour absorption in selected major irrigations projects.

HYPOTHESES OF THE STUDY

In order to attain the above objectives, following hypotheses are tested:

1. Assured irrigation facilities influences the productivity and generates more mandays in various crops with different intensity.
2. The relationship between farm-size and labour absorption may or may not be inverse as it differs from region to region and season to season.
3. There may be positive association between labour and improved agricultural practices in irrigated areas.
4. Larger the farm size more is the use of hired labour and lesser is the absorption of family labour. On the other smaller the size, higher is the use of family labour and lesser is the hired labour.

RESEARCH DESIGN AND METHODOLOGY ADOPTED IN THE STUDY

The sampling design of the study is a multistage random sampling selection of major irrigation projects as the first stage, selection of the villages was the second stage and then interviewing respondents was the last stage units. The study covered the three important Major Irrigation Projects of Andhra Pradesh-one from Andhra Region (Nagarjuna Sagar Right Canal), one from Telangana Region (Sree Ram Sagar Project) and the third one Rayalaseema Region (K.C. Canal).

SELECTION OF THE RESPONDENTS

The source for selecting the respondents was the village official records and names of those who are categorised as marginal, small, medium and big farmers were taken after consulting the Project and Revenue Officials. Proper care was taken to get representation of all the size group of farmers by adopting random sampling procedures. One hundred and fifty respondents were selected from each project area covering various categories of farmers and thus altogether the survey covered a total number of 450 respondents.

N.S.R.C. areas had the benefits of prolonged irrigation facilities such as continued availability of canal water since the inception of Command Area Development. Major part of the Command Areas of these villages were brought under systematic land developmental activities, such as land levelling, bunding, shaping of land and construction of field channels. Thus, these works helped in proper utilization of water, prevent soil erosion and take the full advantage of irrigated agriculture.

Another set of area is under S.R.S.P. which is receiving water only in recent years. Developmental activities such as levelling, bunding and digging of field channels have not yet been completed to take full advantage or irrigation.

Finally, under K.C. localized areas, though water is made available in all the localised areas, but systematic land developmental work was not initiated to get the irrigation water, most of the field channels are not equipped well to carry the water.

DATA COLLECTION

The primary and secondary data required for the study were conducted by interview schedules specially designed for the purpose using survey methods. Interview method was used as a tool to explore the required information through personal interview with the aid of schedules. In the beginning, schedule was pre-tested in a few villages and on the basis of response, necessary modifications were made in it. After pre-testing, information was elicited from the respondents on their socio-economic background, land particulars such as extent of land owned (wet, irrigated dry and fallow land) and the extent of irrigation available on each type of land. Information on labour absorption on various crops, season wise labour absorption, gender-wise analysis has been collected through a detail interview schedule. Questions were also administered to respondents on their cropping pattern, inputs used and out put produced, land utilization, value of farm and non-farm assets, marketing facilities and other various activities involved in rural areas has also been gathered from various official records ranging from Village Extension Office, Mandal Office and CADA projects.

GENDER-WISE LABOUR ABSORPTION FOR PADDY CROP UNDER SRSP

Under these conditions, we have collected the data to find out labour absorption-gender wise among selected crops and presented in this chapter throws light on the labour absorption-male and female among different categories under S.R.S.P area for raising paddy crop. A number of operations are involved such as preparations and ploughing of fields, sowing, weeding, applying fertilizers, spraying pesticides, harvesting, stocking, threshing, winnowing and transporting. As already mentioned earlier, 39 marginal farms, 60 small farms, 30 medium farms, 15 big farms family and hired labours are put into to raise paddy crop. Particularly family labours are mostly used in small and marginal farmers dependent on family labour itself.

On an average we have seen a large number of female labours involved in sowing and weeding operations whereas male labours are mostly used in ploughing and threshing operations. Category wise observation has shown that on an average per acre marginal farmers used 38 female labourers, 27 male labourers and 7 children for raising paddy crop. Out of 27 mandays, 33 per cent absorbed in ploughing and preparation of the land followed by threshing, winnowing, harvesting, stocking operation in that order. On the other hand nearly 32 per cent female labour absorption took place in sowing and transplanting the seeds, another 26 per cent in weeding operations. It means nearly 58 per cent of female labour force is absorbed in two operations only for raising paddy crops.

GENDER-WISE LABOUR ABSORPTION FOR TURMERIC CROP UNDER SRSP

Labour absorption in turmeric crop has been turmeric is a labour intensive crop and requires more number of man days than that of food crops such as paddy. Particularly in the case of big farms category nearly 100 days were spent by female labours whereas it is 86 in marginal and medium farms category. Even child labour were also found to more visible for raising turmeric cultivation under S.R.S.P area, i.e., 32 days by marginal farms, 34 by small farms, 14 by medium farms and 10 by big farms.

One observation of the study is that almost an equal number of man days were used in marginal, small, medium and big farm categories in the study areas. Particularly provision of irrigation activity absorbs more labour force i.e., 27 per cent in the marginal, small and big farms category and 23 per cent in medium farms category. Female labours were mostly used in weeding, and harvesting operations, i.e. 43 days weeding and 19 days for harvesting and stocking in marginal farms category, 36 and 21 man days for small farmers category, 36 and 25 for medium farms and 42 and 32 each in big farms category.

If we compare category wise labour absorption, except big farms category, that to female labour, there is not much variation in use of labour force among various categories of farms. Intra category wise observation has revealed that male labours in marginal farms category are mostly used in irrigation followed by harvesting, stocking, threshing and winnowing and ploughing in that order. But in the case of female labour, weeding operation occupied first position followed by harvesting, stocking, threshing, and winnowing respectively. In the case of small farms category, after irrigation, harvesting and stocking occupied second position, threshing and winnowing third position. Similarly in the case of medium farms, harvesting, stocking placed first, threshing, winnowing and irrigation occupied second position. In the case of big farms, an equal number of man days was absorbed in the operations like irrigation, harvesting and stocking. Thus labour absorption of turmeric crop in the study area of S.R.S.P has shown that female labours are used more than that of male labours.

GENDER-WISE LABOUR ABSORPTION FOR GROUND NUT CROP UNDER SRSP

Groundnut is another commercial crop preferred by farmers under the S.R.S.P. project area that in marginal, small, medium and big farms in the very first beginning of the operation, tractors were put into use for the preparation of the field-4 hours in big farms, 3 hours by medium farms and 2 hours each by marginal and small farms. Except big farms, others used hired the tractors on the hourly base payments. It is interestingly to note that even for irrigation operation man days were needed even in marginal and small farms.

Further it is to be noted that among the marginal farms category, 23 days were spent by male labours, 47 by female and 18 by children. Particularly large number of male labours in this category are used for irrigation, female and children labour for weeding operation. Even in the case of small farms category also, after irrigation, ploughing occupied second position in the male category and weeding operation in the female labour. However, the similar trend was not observed in the medium farms category where surprisingly female labours have spent 18 days in harvesting and stocking operation and weeding occupied second position.

Another interesting observation is that in the case of big farms category, female labours have spent 16 days each in weeding, harvesting and stocking and threshing and winnowing operations. One shocking observation is that in the big farms category, children have spent 12 days in threshing and winnowing operations of groundnut crop. But in the case of transportation of product only one or two labourers were used. Thus, the analysis on gender-wise labour absorption in the commercial crop like groundnut has revealed that male labours are mostly used on irrigation and ploughing operations, female labours in weeding, harvesting and threshing operations.

GENDER-WISE LABOUR ABSORPTION FOR COTTON CROP UNDER SRSP

Further an attempt was made to find out gender wise labour absorption for cotton crop under S.R.S.P. localized areas of Telangana region that male labourers are used in same number in medium and big farms category and their number is slightly higher than that of small and marginal farms. Most of the male labourers are hired labourers and they are put to use in only two operations such as provision of irrigation, spraying of pesticides and ploughing i.e. in medium farms category 43 per cent in irrigation, 24 per cent in pesticides and 22 per cent in ploughing operations. Similarly in big farms category, irrigation required nearly 38 per cent labour force, pesticides 27 per cent and ploughing 24 per cent.

When we look at female labour composition, medium farms employed more labourers i.e. 65 followed by big, small and marginal farms in that order. Particularly most of the female labours employed in medium and big farms are hired one and they were required for harvesting, stocking and weeding operations. In the case of marginal farms, out of 51 female labourers more than 39 per cent required at the time of harvesting and stocking operation and an other 24 per cent in weeding operation. But in case of small farms category, out of 57 female labourers nearly 32 per cent were used at the time of harvesting and stocking operation. Infact their percentage is still higher in the medium and big farms category i.e., more than 37 per cent female labour force are put to use at the time of harvesting and stocking operations.

As far as child labour is concerned, they were also used in good in number in all the farms, i.e., ranging between 32 to 35. Most of them were used at the time of harvesting and stocking operation itself i.e. 41 per cent in big farms category, 37 per cent by small farms category, 34 per cent by marginal farms and in 33 per cent by medium farms. In other words not only female labourers but also a large number child labourers were used for harvesting and stocking operations itself. Thus, most of the male labours were used for the provision of irrigation facilities, female labourers for harvesting, stocking and weeding operations and child labours at the time of harvesting operation in raising cotton crop under S.R.S.P. localized areas of Telangana region of Andhra Pradesh.

SUM UP

The analysis on gender-wise labour absorption in S.R.S.P. area in the case of paddy crop has shown that a number of operations are involved such as preparation and ploughing of fields, sowing, weeding, applying fertilizers harvesting and ploughing of fields and winnowing and transporting, particularly operations where as a large number of female labourers was involved are sowing and weeding operations and in the male labourers for ploughing and threshing operations. Infact nearly 60 per cent of female labour force is used in two operations it self such as transplanting of seeds and weeding operations. But in the case of turmeric crop, female labourers are mostly used in weeding operations followed by harvesting and stocking, threshing respectively. And labour absorption under S.R.S.P. area has shown that female labourers are mostly used by than that of male labourers. On the other, labour absorption in groundnut crop has shown that male labourers are mostly used for irrigation and ploughing operations and female labourers in weeding, harvesting and threshing operations. One shocking observation is that a large number of children have spent 12 days each in threshing and winnowing operations for raising groundnut crop. In the case of cotton crop, most of the male labourers are hired and are put into use for the major operations like provision of irrigation, spraying of pesticides and ploughing. On the other, a larger number of female labours particularly hired by medium and big farmers are put into use at the time of harvesting and stocking operations in their respective fields. Thus, gender-wise labour absorption in the commercial crop like cotton is quite distinct as male labourers are preferred in certain operations and female labours in others and infact this tendency is observed in all the localised areas under the major irrigation projects of Andhra Pradesh.

NOTES AND REFERENCES

1. Nurkse, Ragner, Problems of Capital Formation in Under Developed Countries, Oxford Basil Blackwell, 1955.
2. Ishikawa, S., Labour Absorption in Asian Agriculture, An Issue paper, ILO, ARTEP, Bangkok, 1978, p. 1.
3. Mellor, J.W., Impact of New Agricultural Technology on Employment and Income Distribution: Concepts and Policy, Cornell University Press, New York, 1976.
4. Ishikawa, S., Labour Absorption in Asian Agriculture An Issues Papers -Bangkok; ILO-ARTEP, 1978, VI, p. 101.
5. Nair, K., Transforming Traditionality: Land and Labour Use in Agriculture in Asia and Africa - New Delhi; Allied, 1983, xiii, p. 168.
6. Booth. A., and Sundrum. R.M., Labour Absorption in Agriculture, Delhi, Oxford University Press, 1984, p. 221.

19

Empowerment of Women Through Employment–A Review

K. Padma Latha

Women's economic empowerment is absolutely essential for raising their status in society. Several studies have indicated that women's employment leads to better education, health and skill development of the family.

Empowerment is a process through which women realize their true potential. The World Bank defines empowerment as 'the process of increasing the capacity of individuals or groups to make choices and to transform those choices into desired actions and outcomes. Central to this process are actions which both build individual and collective assets and improve the efficiency and fairness of the organizational and institutional context which govern the use of these assets'. Thus, empowerment is multi-dimensional and refers to the expansion of freedom of choice and action in all spheres - social, economic and political to shape one's life. For women such freedom is often severely curtailed due to gender inequality in the household as well as in society. Thus, women's empowerment requires a set of assets and capabilities at the individual level and collective level. Economic empowerment is the foremost and basic component in the overall empowerment of women. Therefore, the present paper focuses on need of women's participation in economic activities to achieve empowerment.

The Objectives of the Study are:

1. To present a concrete picture of employment status of women in India.
2. To identify the problems of employed women in various sectors.
3. To suggest measures to overcome these problems so that women employees in India are promoted and strengthened effectively.
4. To review the policies of government under five year plans for the empowerment and employment of women.

The participation of women in income generating activities for the family has been increasing since Independence. Female work participation not only increases their family income but also brings economic independence among women in the household. This helps them to participate more effectively in intra-household decision making and have better access to information. But, economic empowerment of women is possible only when women have full autonomy to spend their income and also control resources.

Traditionally, Indian women have had a dependency syndrome as far as employment is concerned. They were expected to look after the home, help in agriculture, animal care and handicrafts made at home. The woman's status as a wife did not give her control over the family income which remain both the husband who decides the expenditure pattern for the family. In a vast majority of cases the traditional pattern of employment still continues to prevail.

Table 1
Work Participation Rates (in per cent)

Census	*T/R/U*	*Female*	*Male*	*Persons*
1981	Total	19.7	52.6	36.7
	Rural	23.1	53.8	38.8
	Urban	8.3	49.1	30.0
1991	Total	22.3	51.6	37.5
	Rural	26.8	52.6	40.1
	Urban	9.2	48.9	30.2
2001	Total	25.7	51.9	39.3
	Rural	31.0	52.4	42.0
	Urban	11.6	50.9	32.2

Source: Census of India, Govt. of India.

The female work participation rate is considered as the only suitable measure of economic role of women in the society. In India though there has been a slight increase in the female work participation rate from 19.7% in 1981 to 25.7% in 2001, this is still much lower than the male work participation rate in both urban and rural areas. Table 1 gives the details of work participation rates in India.

Moreover, the occupational distribution of women indicates the gender segregation of tasks and the underlying reality of high illiteracy among female workers, which consigns them to low paid, unskilled jobs compared to males. The employment of women is highest of total employment by primary sector. This is followed by the service sector. Table 2 gives details of usual status of female workers in India.

Table 2
Sectoral Distribution of Usual Status of Female Workers in India

(in per cent)

	Sector	*Rural*		*Urban*	
		1983-84	*1999-2000*	*1983-84*	*1999-2000*
I	Primary sector	87.5	85.3	31.5	17.6
II	Secondary sector	8.7	9.0	30.8	29.4
III	Tertiary sector	4.8	5.7	37.7	52.9

Source: Economic Reforms in India, RaviShankar Kumar Singh, p. 402.

The point that female participation in the work force has been declining in India overtime can be highlighted by referring to the comparative situation of the female labour force in three sectors of the economy. In rural India, the female workers' dependence on the primary sector employment witnessed a steady decline until 1983-84, the proportion of workers engaged in the primary sector remained more or less constant. On the otherhand, the proportion of their employment in the secondary and tertiary sectors has witnessed a steady increase. In contrast the inter-sector shifts in case of urban female workers is considerable one and female labour employment is relatively better for the urban areas.

Even though the women are employed and enjoy comforts in life, they still face many problems. The problems of women are multi-dimensional ranging from economic and social problems differ to a considerable extent depending upon level of education, kinds of jobs, social equity, places of work etc. The women working in organized sectors are facing the problems like excessive burden of work, official tensions, discrimination from authorities, problems from co-workers, lack of support from the family members, lack of decision making power, problem of time adjustment for official and household works, transport problems etc. In unorganized sector, the women problems are disparities in wages, long duration of working hours, stagnant and deteriorating working conditions, absence of job security, male domination in the family etc.

SUGGESTIONS

1. Women should have sufficient liberty, freedom, opportunity, and exposure to exhibit their talents in different sectors and fields.
2. The domestic work should be shared by men to eliminate over burdened stress on women. Distribution of home management and child-rearing practices would reduce the number of divorce cases and enhances pleasure in the married life.
3. Common civil code should be implemented.
4. Government and authorities of various institutions should take care to reduce the disparities in wages and to take measures for better working conditions etc.
5. Compulsory women education should be introduced for the equal status of women.
6. The media should respond to the grievances of women as a social responsibility toward society.
7. Government should promote the creative skills of the women who are half of our population.
8. Gender just policies require recognition of the fact that women are child bearers and should strive for suitable working hours designed for them.

Women received attention of the government right from the beginning of the Indian planning. While the thrust of the first four plans was on organizing various welfare activities and giving priority to women's education, the fifth and sixth plans witnessed a shift from 'welfare' to 'overall development of women' with thrust on health, education and employment of women. The stress of the seventh plan was to identifying and promoting beneficiary oriented programmes with a view to extending direct benefits to women.

The eighth plan (1992-97) promised to ensure that benefits of development from different sectors do not by pass women. The Rashtriya Mahila Kosh was setup in 1993 to meet the credit needs of poor and assetless women. The ninth plan (1997-2002) made two significant changes in the strategy of planning for women. Firstly 'empowerment of women' became a primary objective and secondly the plan attempted 'convergence of existing services' available in both women specific and women related sectors. The tenth plan (2002-07) has made a major commitment towards 'empowering women as the agent of socio-economic change and development'. Based on the recommendation of National Policy for Empowerment of Women, the tenth plan suggests a three-fold strategy for empowering women through social empowerment, economic empowerment and gender justice.

In India the Ministries of Agriculture, Rural Development, Industries, Labour, Science and Technology and the Department of Women and Child Development have taken significant initiatives by making specific schemes for enhancing women's employment. Government's biggest effort to give employment to women has been in the rural development sector. The most important programme in this connection was the Integrated Rural Development Programme (IRDP) which was started in 1975. The target under this programme, however, provided coverage to 40% women beneficiaries out of the total beneficiaries. Under the Jawahar Rozgar Yojana, another important initiative of the Rural Development Ministry, 30% of the employment opportunities were reserved for women. Under the Employment Assurance Scheme also a special provision has been made for women. An exclusive programme for women was also being implemented by the Ministry of Rural Development known as Development of Women and Children in Rural Areas (DWCRA). It was started in sixth plan and benefiting lakhs of women. Under this programme the women self-help groups were assisted through a subsidy and loan from IRDP and Training of Rural Youth for self-employment (TRYSEM) and a revolving fund of 25,000 rupees. Besides employment activities, the groups are also motivated to provide greater access for women to basic services like health, education, child care, nutrition, water and sanitation. The Swaran Jayanti Shahari Rozgar Yojana provides for 30% women beneficiaries in all urban employment schemes.

The Prime Minister's Rozgar Yojana launched in 1993 and administered by the Department of Industry provides self-employment opportunities to women entrepreneurs along with men. The Khadi and Village Industries Commissions also provide employment to women. In the village industry sector 45 per cent participation was of women at the end of the eighth five years plan.

The Department of Women and Child Development has planned and executing the 'Support for Training and Employment (STEP), the NORAD scheme with assistance from the Norwegian government for programmes generating income earning activities for destitute women.

The initiative taken by the Department of Women and Child Development was the launching of the Indira Mahila Yozana in 1995. Women are also getting assistance from the National Bank for Agriculture Rural Development (NABARD) and Council for Advancement of People's Action and Rural Technology (CAPART). Mahila Samriddhi Yozana was introduced in 1993 and was evaluated by the Planning Commission in 1996. This scheme aimed to give credit to women for purposes strengthening their economic empowerment.

In some of the states like Andhra Pradesh government gives priority to women for the allotment of Ration Shop dealerships and establishing women co-operative societies for diary forming etc. Employment opportunities under the urban development schemes are still very an adequate and need to be multiplied and strengthened throughout the country. New initiatives through the voluntary sector need to be made for extending skill training to women in the urban slums.

Within the government itself a special effort needs to be made to see that more women are recruited at all levels especially at managerial levels. This has to be done in the Central, State, Local Government, Public and Private sector agencies through a well thought out personnel policy for women. Voluntary organizations have also to be encouraged to run institutions or courses for preparing women for enter into all the services in a very big way.

CONCLUSION

In this era of post-economic reforms, empowerment of women is vital for eliminating poverty. Overall development of the economy, since social empowerment is a long-term phenomenon, emphasis needs to be given for economic empowerment of women. Once women are economically independent they will be able to overcome their dependency on the household as well as the society. Employment is a feasible solution for empowering women. Finally, even though in Indian planning process the efforts were made towards over all development of women, the success of our planning process would finally be judged only when gender equality is achieved.

REFERENCES

Chattopadhyay, Arundhati, 'Women and Entreprenueurship', Yojana, Jan., 2005.

Desai Neera & M. Krishnaraj, 'Women and Society in India'.

Misra, S.K. & V.K. Puri, 'Indian Economy'.

Nirmala, J. & Dhulasi Birundha Varadaraja, 'Empowerment of Women'.

Parvin, M. Razia, 'Empowerment of Women'.

Paul, Devika, 'Gender and Planning', Yojana, Jan, 2005.

Reddy, A. Ranga (ed.), 'Empowerment of Women and Ecological Development'.

Seth, Mira, 'Women and Development'.

Singh, Ravishankar Kumar, 'Economic Reforms in India', Volume-II.

Singh, Bharat, 'Working Women in India'.

20

Gender Disparities in Workforce Participation Rates–A Study in Andhra Pradesh

Gulam Rabbani & M. Ramesh Reddy

In the production process, labour is considered as a primary factoral of production and infact Labour force is the most important factor which influences higher level economic activity in any country, because it is a productive factor and also it activates other factors of production. Thus, the size of the labour force playing an important role in the determinedly the level of its economic activities. The size of laboru force is determining by the number of persons in the age group of 15-60. Children below the 15 years and old people in the age above 60 years are not considered from the labour force. The work force depend upon various factors like sex and age composition, attitude and willingness to work, ability to work job opportunities etc. These factors are different from different regions of countries and periods.

In India, existing different social customs put man and women and on different footings. While men are primary responsible for earning the money necessary for running the households. Whereas women are attached to household activities and women's going out for work is considered to supplement income for house. Even when the woman is employed she has to take full responsibility of the house and family.

In this paper an attempt has been made to analyse availability and utilization of women labour, their workforce participation in the Andhra Pradesh.

OBJECTIVES OF THE STUDY

(i) to study the workforce participation rate in different district of A.P

(ii) to examine variation of the male and female workforce participation rate , and

(iii) to understand the disparities in workforce participation rate between male and female population.

Table 1
District-wise Change in Work Participation Rate of Total Workers to Total Population in Andhra Pradesh: 1991 and 2001

District	*Work Participation Rate*		*Variation*
	1991	*2001*	
Adilabad	44.4	45.0	0.6
Nizamabad	49.7	49.2	0.5
Karimnagar	50.3	49.5	0.8
Medak	47.8	48.5	0.7
Hyderabad	27.4	29.2	1.8
Rangareddy	40.8	39.9	-0.9
Mahabubnagar	50.2	51.8	1.6
Nalgonda	48.3	49.1	0.8
Warangal	47.8	48.2	0.4
Khammam	45.9	48.3	2.4
Srikakulam	48.6	47.5	-1.1
Vizianagaram	50.3	52.2	1.9
Visakapatnam	43.1	41.8	-1.3
East Godavari	38.5	39.6	1.1
West Godavari	43.4	44.2	0.8
Krishna	43.3	44.1	0.8
Guntur	47.9	49.1	1.2
Prakasham	48.6	50.3	1.7
Nellore	45.6	45.5	-0.1
Cuddappah	44.0	44.9	0.9
Kurnool	46.5	49.5	3.0
Ananthapur	46.2	48.9	2.7
Chittoor	45.9	46.9	1.0

Source: Director of Census Operations, Andhra Pradesh, Census of India, 2001.

Table 1 shows district-wise work participation rate of total workers to total population of Andhra Pradesh at two census. Vizianagaram district the highest in work participation rate, smallest in population among 23 districts. In 1991 census it stood highest in the state with 50.3 per cent, in 2001 census the work participation rate increased to 52.2 per cent. With 51.8 per cent Mahabubnagar district, second highest in 2001. In 1991 this district was not for behind and occupied third place with 50.2 per cent, in 2001 improved its work participation rate, Prakasham district with 50.3 per cent third highest in 2001 census, this district too improved its position from fifth highest in 1991 census. This district shared same position in 1991 census with Srikukulam district. In both the districts the work participation rate was 48.6 per cent. Similarly, Warangal and Medak districts shared same with 47.8 per cent in 1991 census. The lowest work participation was observed in Hyderabad district in 1991 and 2001 census. But in interms of work participation rate there is improvement from 27.4 in 1991 to 29.2 in 2001. The next lowest work participation districts are East Godavari and Rangareddy, in 1991 and 2001.

Table 2 reveled that district-wise female work participation rate of female workers to total female population in 1991 and 2001 census and district-wise variation in female work participation rate in two periods. Mahabubnagar district is highest work participation rate among the 23 districts in 2001 census. Whereas In 1991 census too this district was occupied second highest position in the state. With 44.6 per cent Vizianagaram district second highest work participation in 2001 census. In 1991 census this district was occupied fourth highest place work participation with 41.7 per cent, in 2001 census improved its position. Nizamabad district with 44.2 per cent third highest place in 2001 census. Whereas in 1991 census its position was highest work participation in the state it was 45.2 per cent. The fourth and fifth highest work participation rate districts are Karimngar with 43.5 per cent and Nalgonda with 43.1 per cent in 2001 census. While in 1991 census Karimnagar district third highest with 44.3 and Nalgonda district was retained some when it compare to 2001 census. The lowest work participation rate was observed in Hyderabad district in 1991 and 2001 census which was resported 7.4 per cent and 8.8 per cent followed by East Godavari and Rangareddy district with 20.4 per cent and 25.6 per cent in 2001 census respectively. Whereas in 1991 census East Godavari and

Rangareddy districts retained the same position when it compared to 2001 census.

Table 2
District-wise Female Work Participation Rate of Female Total Workers to Total Female Population in Andhra Pradesh 1991 and 2001

District	*Work Participation Rate*		*Variation*
	1991	*2001*	
Adilabad	35.6	37.0	1.4
Nizamabad	45.2	44.2	-1.0
Karimnagar	44.3	43.5	-0.8
Medak	40.3	41.4	1.1
Hyderabad	7.4	8.8	1.4
Rangareddy	28.4	25.6	-2.8
Mahabubnagar	44.9	47.2	2.3
Nalgonda	41.6	43.1	1.5
Warangal	41.0	41.8	0.8
Khammam	35.8	39.5	3.7
Srikakulam	40.9	38.4	-2.5
Vizianagaram	41.7	44.6	2.9
Visakapatnam	29.6	27.8	-1.8
East Godavari	20.2	20.4	0.2
West Godavari	28.6	28.0	-0.6
Krishna	29.1	29.5	0.4
Guntur	38.1	38.7	0.6
Prakasham	41.4	42.5	1.1
Nellore	33.9	32.2	-1.7
Cuddappah	31.7	32.6	0.9
Kurnool	37.9	42.2	4.3
Ananthapur	36.0	39.5	3.5
Chittoor	33.8	35.3	1.5

Source: Director of Census Operations, Andhra Pradesh, Census of India, 2001.

Further, an attempt has been made in changes between two periods in working participation rate, it is revealed that there is a highest increases in work participating rate in Krunool district with 4.3 per cent followed by Khammam with 3.7 per cent, Ananthapuram 3.5, Vizianagaram 2. 9 per cent and Nalgonda with 1.5 per cent, the negative variation was observed in Rangareddy district with 2.8 per cent followed by Srikakulam with -25 per cent Visakapatnam with -1.8 per cent, Nellore with -1.7 per cent,

Nizamabad with -1.0 per cent, Karimangar with -0.8 per cent and West Godavari -0.6 per cent respectively.

Table 3 shows that district-wise male work participation rate and variation to total male population during the 1991 and 2001 census. The overall work participation rate of male with 56.4 per cent in 2001. Whereas, in 1991 census male work participation rate was 55.5 per cent. The work participation rate of male was increased nearly with 1.1 per cent during the above two periods.

Table 3
District-wise Male Work Participation Rate of Male Total Workers to Total Male Population in Andhra Pradesh: 1991 and 2001

District	*Work Participation Rate*		*Variation*
	1991	*2001*	
Adilabad	53.0	52.9	-0.1
Nizamabad	54.2	54.3	0.1
Karimnagar	56.2	55.5	1.3
Medak	55.0	55.5	0.5
Hyderabad	46.0	48.2	2.2
Rangareddy	52.4	53.4	1.0
Mahabubnagar	55.3	56.3	1.0
Nalgonda	54.8	54.9	0.1
Warangal	54.3	54.5	0.2
Khammam	55.5	57.0	1.5
Srikakulam	56.5	56.6	0.1
Vizianagaram	59.0	60.0	1.0
Visakapatnam	56.3	55.6	-0.7
East Godavari	56.8	58.7	1.9
West Godavari	58.0	60.2	2.2
Krishna	57.0	58.4	2.4
Guntur	57.3	59.2	1.9
Prakasham	55.7	57.9	2.2
Nellore	57.1	58.6	1.5
Cuddappah	55.7	56.8	1.1
Kurnool	54.7	56.4	1.7
Ananthapur	55.8	57.9	2.1
Chittoor	57.7	58.3	0.6

Source: Director of Census Operations, Andhra Pradesh, Census of India, 2001.

The district-wise analysis of male work participation rate revealed that, Viziagaram district was highest position with 60.0 per cent followed by the West Godavari 58.0 per cent, Chittoor with 57.7 per cent, Guntur with 57.1 per cent Krishna with 57.0 per cent and East Godavari with 56.8 per cent while the lowest male work participation was observed in Hyderabad district with 46.0 per cent followed by Rangareddy with 52.4 per cent, Adilabad with 53.0 per cent, Nizamabad 54.2 per cent, Warangal 54.3 per cent, Kurnmool 54.7 per cent and Nalgonda with 54.8 per cent.

The male work participation rate during in 2001 census West Godavari District is highest position with 60.2 per cent among 23 districts Vizianagaram district is second position with 60 per cent followed by Guntur with 59.2 per cent East Godavari with 58.7 per cent Nellore with 58.6 per cent, Krishna with 57 per cent Chittoor with 58.3 per cent and Ananthapuram and Prakasham districts are same position with 57.9 per cent.

The lowest percentage of male work participation is observed in Hyderabad district with 48.2 per cent the remaining districts have between 52 percentages and 57 percentage of the male work participation. Further, a comparative analysis of male work participation rate during the two periods or two census Krishna district is increased variation with 2.4 per cent followed by West Godvari, Hyderabad, Prakasham districts have same variation increased with 2.2 per cent, Ananthapuram with 2.1 per cent East Godavari with 1.9 per cent and Nellore, Khammam districts have same variation with 1.5 per cent.

The negative and lowest variation observed in Adilabad with -0.1 per cent followed by Nizamabad, Nalgonda districts have same variation with 0.1 and Warangal districts variation with 0.2.

It is to be noted that during 1991 and 2001 study period the second highest variation increased is observed in Hyderabad district which is the lowest male work participation rate, whereas in Adilabad, Nizamabad and Nalgonda districts have lowest male work participation during the two census.

Table 4 shows that disparities in male and female work participation rate during 1991 and 2001. The Gender wise disparities were ascertained and rankes were assigned based on variations in male and female work participation rate. The table revealed that in 1991 the highest gender wise disparities were observed in Hyderabad district followed by East Godavari, West Godavari, Krishna and Visakapatnam districts. Nizamabad district is lowest gender wise disparities in work participation rate followed by Mahabubnagar, Prakasham, Karimngar, Nalgonda and Warangal. In 2001 the highest variation in gender wise work participation rate found in Hyderabad district followed by East Godavari, West Godavari, Krishna and Rangareddy, Visakapatnam districts are same variation. Whereas in lowest variation in found in mahabubnagar district followed by Nizamabad, Nalgonda, Karimnagar, Warangal and Medak districts.

Table 4
District-wise Male Female Ranks and Gender Disparities

District	*1991*				*2001*			
	Total workers	*Male workers*	*Female workers*	*GD*	*Total workers*	*Male workers*	*Female workers*	*GD*
Adilabad	14	21	14	13	16	21	14	14
Nizamabad	4	20	1	23	6	19	3	22
Karimnagar	2	10	3	20	4	16	4	20
Medak	8	16	9	17	10	16	9	18
Hyderabad	21	23	23	1	23	22	23	1
Rangareddy	19	22	21	6.5	21	20	21	5.5
Mahabubnagar	3	15	2	22	2	14	1	23
Nalgonda	6	17	5	19	7	17	5	21
Warangal	8	19	7	18	12	18	8	19
Khammam	12	14	13	11	11	10	11	13
Srikakulam	5	8	8	16	13	12	13	12
Vizianagaram	1	1	4	14	1	2	2	15.5
Visakapatnam	18	9	18	5	20	15	20	5.5
East Godavari	20	7	22	2	22	4	22	2
West Godavari	16	2	20	3	18	1	19	3
Krishna	17	6	19	4	19	6	18	4
Guntur	7	4	10	12	8	3	12	10
Prakasham	5	13	6	21	3	9	6	15.5
Nellore	13	5	15	9	15	5	17	7
Cuddappah	15	12	17	6.5	17	11	16	8
Kurnool	9	18	11	15	5	13	7	17
Ananthapur	10	11	12	10	9	8	10	11
Chittoor	11	3	16	8	14	7	15	9

Source: Director of Census Operations, Andhra Pradesh, Census of India, 2001.

It interesting to note that the highest disparities are in Hyderabad district and lowest is in Nizamabad and Mahabubnagar district as per as the gender wise disparities in work participation rate concern in both 1991 and 2001.

An attempt has been made to highlight the analysis of gender disparities total work participation rate and male work participation rate, female work participation, male and female work participation rate in the period of 1991 and 2001. The correlation calculated between TWPR and MWPR, TWPR and FWPR and gender disparities are presented in the table 5.

Table 5
Results of the Rank Co-relation

Variables	*Rank Co-efficient*	
	1991	*2001*
TWPR and MWPR	0.16	0.12
TWPR and FWPR	0.94	0.96
MWPR and FWPR	-0.09	-0.04
TWPR and GD	-0.72	-0.88
MWPR and GD	0.28	0.38
FWPR and GD	-0.93	-0.94

The table shows that the relationship between total work participation rate (TWPR) and female work participation rate have high positive correlation, whereas between total work participation rate (TWPR) and male work participation rate have low positive correlative in both 1991 and 2001 census. But low, and high negative correlation were found between male work participation rate and female work participation total work participation rate, female work participation (FWPR) and gender disparities in work participation in both 1991 and 2001, while the correlation between male work participation rate and gender disparities in work participation have median positive in both 1991 and 2001.

The relationship TWPR, MWPR, FWPR and GD indicates that TWPR is in favoru of reducing gender disparities. Though MWPR in all the districts are higher than FWPR and increase in FWPR present has more positive effect reducing the gap between male and female work participation rate. Women in Andhra Pradesh have not been project since beginning as a source of laboru for gainful activity. Their area was mostly confined to household. During the period 1991 census their work participation did not show any significant increase when it compared to 2001 census.

CONCLUSIONS

In this paper an attempt has been made to analyse availability and utilistion of female and male labour workforce participation in A.P. Male participation is predominantly by in these highest in the total workforce as compare to that of female work participation. Male participation shows that Vizianagaram district as the highest (59 percentage) in overall participation of males in this state. Whereas, in female participation Mahabubnagar district as the highest in both 1991 and 2001 census. Only Hyderabad district is very low in male and female work participation. The highest variation is found in Kurnool district between 1991 to 2001 and lowest it means negative variation in the Nellore district. Whereas, the highest male variation is in Krishna district and female variation is in Khammam district. The negative, low, high positive relationship is found between TWR, MWR, FWR whereas, high negative, low positive relationships are found between TWR, MWR, FWR and gender disparities and it is due to the decreasing variations between gender disparities in the workforce participation. In the present work participation in the state of Andhra Pradesh mainly confine to few districts only. The utmost priority by the planners and administrators is to uplift of female work participation rate and should pay greater attention to reduce the gender disparities in the work participation.

REFERENCES

Meera Seth (2001), Women and Development–The Indian Experience, SAGE Publications New Delhi.

Ramesh Chaube and Kalpana Saini (2002), Status of Women in Rural Societies, Adithya Publishers, Madhya Pradesh.

Rao, Usha N.J. (1983), Women in a Developing Society, Ashish Publishing House New Delhi.

21

Impact of the SHGs on Livelihoods, Income and Household Assets: A Study in Karnataka

G. Sreedhar

INTRODUCTION

Self-help groups (SHGs) have been formed all over India during the last one and half decade for the poorer sections, particularly women, with a view to enable them to undertake thrift on a regular basis and access credit and other development inputs/ services so as to come out of the poverty syndrome. Formation and strengthening of SHGs has been perceived as an important instrument/ strategy for poverty reduction in the rural society. In this context, two situations may arise. First, some poorer persons who joined the SHGs may utilize the inputs (notably credit) made available to them under the programme and substantially improve their economic position, and become relatively better-off when compared to other persons who did not join such groups. Second, some persons who were already less poor at the time of their joining the SHGs may further consolidate their economic condition. Even though both these situations are equally possible, it becomes pertinent to delineate the role of SHGs in improving the economic status of their members in order to understand the potential of such groups in poverty reduction. In the absence of information on the economic status of both the members and the non-members at the time of inception of the programme, it becomes difficult to say with reasonable degree of confidence whether the difference in their present economic status is due to the programme benefits. But, their livelihood sources and income as well as their pattern of investment on consumable household assets during the recent past would give us some idea as to what extent their present status could be attributed to the membership with the SHGs and the consequent benefits availed. The qualitative information obtained from the members and non-members on these aspects would also be useful in addressing this issue.

OBJECTIVES AND METHODOLOGY

The present paper attempts to examine the impact of the SHGs on the livelihood sources, income and acquisition of consumable household assets of their members when compared to the non-members in the context of Karnataka state. The study was conducted in 2001, covering Bidar, Kolar and Mysore districts of Karnataka, which represent the average situation in the state in terms of economic development and the progress of SHG movement. The three selected districts also broadly portray the average picture of the state with regard to population density, sex ratio and literacy rates. In terms of economic development, Mysore is well developed, while Bidar is the least developed and Kolar falls in between. All the districts have a fairly well developed bank branch network and the banks are actively involved in the progress of SHG movement.

In Bidar, the DCCB had taken the role of Self-help Promoting Institution (SHPI). It established a training centre called Sahakari Rural Development Academy (SAHARDA) at the district headquarters for providing training to the personnel of cooperatives, banks and NGOs in formation and strengthening of SHGs. In this district, the DCCB, together with the NGOs, formed 1,930 SHGs by March 2001. In Kolar district, 569 SHGs were linked to banks by March 2000. Another 1,200 groups were to be linked by March 2001. A large number of NGOs participated in the SHG-Bank linkage programme. The SHG-Bank linkage programme in Mysore was initiated way back in 1992. By 1999, 809 groups were linked to banks. The Cauvery Grameena Bank (CGB) had taken the role of SHPI in the district, accounting for about 93 per cent of the groups linked up to 1999. There were nine important NGOs through which the linkage programme was implemented. Thus, as far as the SHG-bank linkage programme is concerned, all the three districts are actively involved with Bidar district forging ahead of Kolar and Mysore especially in respect of capacity building and training of bank and NGO personnel engaged in self-help promotion.

For selecting the villages, a few NGOs were chosen in consultation with the Assistant General Manager of NABARD in each district on the basis of criteria such as irrigation and presence of tribal population. In Mysore and Bidar, CGB and DCCB were, respectively, also selected as these were important SHPIs in these districts. From each of these organisations, a list containing the names of SHGs (more than three years old) was collected. Normally, one SHG was selected from the project area of each of the organisation through random sampling method. However, in the case of MYRADA in Mysore, two SHGs were selected as this NGO operates in tribal areas. Similarly, the number of SHGs selected from RORES project area in Kolar was two. Thus, out of 15 SHGs selected for the study, the NGOs facilitated the formation of 13 SHGs, while DCCB in Bidar and CGB in Mysore formed one each. In all, four SHGs were selected from Bidar, six from Kolar and five from Mysore. As many as nine SHGs were formed during the last five years, while the remaining six were formed more than five years back, and interestingly, four of these SHGs were formed nearly a decade ago.

In all the 15 villages, focus group discussions were conducted with members of the SHGs and schedules were canvassed among members and non-members. The methodology followed for selecting the members was to draw lots in the group meeting in order to choose about four members from each group. The views of the members in each group were taken into account for selecting about two non-members from the same village who could be placed on a similar footing when compared to members in terms of socio-economic characteristics. This procedure was adopted to ensure that both the members and the non-members had more or less similar socio-economic background so that whatever differences noticed between them in terms of livelihood opportunities, income and household assets could be attributed to the SHGs. As such, it becomes important to understand the socio-economic characteristics of members and non-members chosen for the study.

SOCIO-ECONOMIC CHARACTERISTICS OF MEMBERS AND NON-MEMBERS

Table 1 presents the socio-economic profile of the member and non-member sample households. It could be seen from Table 1 that over three-fourths of the sample households (both members and non-members) were Hindus, followed by Muslims and Christians. Hindus had greater representation among the sample households from Kolar than among those from Bidar and Mysore. With regard to caste-wise distribution, the households belonging to backward castes accounted for about 37 per cent, followed by scheduled tribes, forward castes and scheduled castes. Thus, over three-fourths (77.5 per cent) of the households belonged to the weaker sections of the society. While the proportion of households belonging to forward castes was relatively higher in Bidar, the backward castes and scheduled castes had taken this place in Kolar and the scheduled tribes in Mysore. The proportion of households belonging to different caste groups is more or less the same between members and non-members in the selected districts. As far as educational levels of members were concerned, nearly two-thirds of them (both members and non-members) were illiterate. Only about 15 per cent had high school education. The proportion of illiterates was highest in the case of Bidar and least in Mysore, with Kolar standing in between. Slightly less than half of the respondents belonged to the age group of 30 to 40 years. About one-fourth each belonged to 18-30 years and 40-55 years respectively, while those aged more than 55 years accounted for 3 per cent. On the whole, nearly three-fourths of the respondents belonged to relatively younger age group of 18-40 years. The proportion of respondents belonging to different age groups is more or less the same between members and non-members in the selected districts with the exception of 40-55 years age group.

HOUSING AND BASIC AMENITIES OF THE SAMPLE HOUSEHOLDS

The most striking aspect is that 90 per cent of the sample households lived in their own houses (Table 2). Nearly two-thirds of them lived in semi-durable houses and about one-fifth in durable houses, with the rest in Kutcha houses. The proportion of respondents living in durable houses was greater in Kolar as compared to the other two districts. More than 90 per cent of the respondents had access to electricity connection; in most of the cases, this was a subsidised connection from the government under Bhagya Jyothi scheme.

Similarly, nearly 95 per cent of the households were in possession of ration card, with which they could obtain subsidised food grains from the Public Distribution System. But only about 60 per cent were in possession of green ration card meant for the households living below poverty line. While about 95 per cent of the respondents had access to safe drinking water, only 15 per cent had individual sanitation facility. The availability of housing and other basic amenities is more or less the same between members and non-members.

Table 1
Distribution of sample Households by Socio-Economic Characteristics

	Bidar		*Kolar*		*Mysore*		*Total*	
	Members (n=16)	*Non Members (n=8)*	*Members (n=24)*	*Non Members (n=12)*	*Members (n=21)*	*Non Members (n=8)*	*Members (n=61)*	*Non Members (n=28)*
Distribution (%) by religion								
Hindu	56.3	62.5	87.5	100.0	76.2	75.0	75.4	82.2
Muslim	18.7	12.5	8.3	0.0	23.8	25.0	16.4	10.7
Christian	25.0	25.0	4.2	0.0	0.0	0.0	8.2	7.1
Distribution (%) by caste								
Scheduled Caste	18.7	25.0	33.4	25.0	0.0	0.0	18.0	17.9
Scheduled Tribe	25.0	25.0	8.3	25.0	33.3	25.0	21.3	25.0
Backward Community	12.5	0.0	50.0	50.0	42.9	50.0	37.7	35.7
Forward Community	43.8	50.0	8.3	0.0	23.8	25.0	23.0	21.4
Distribution (%) by age group (years)								
18 to 30	18.8	25.0	16.7	33.3	42.9	12.5	26.2	25.0
30 to 40	56.2	37.5	50.0	41.7	38.2	50.0	47.5	42.9
40 to 55	25.0	37.5	25.0	25.0	14.3	37.5	21.4	32.1
55 and above	0.0	0.0	8.3	0.0	4.8	0.0	4.9	0.0
Distribution (%) by educational status								
Illiterate	93.8	75.0	70.8	58.3	33.4	75.0	63.9	67.9
Primary	0.0	0.0	4.2	0.0	19.0	25.0	8.2	7.1
Middle school	6.2	0.0	8.3	25.0	23.8	0.0	13.1	10.7
High School	0.0	25.0	16.7	16.7	23.8	0.0	14.8	14.3

Table 2
Distribution (%) of Sample Households by Basic Amenities

	Bidar		*Kolar*		*Mysore*		*Total*	
	Members (n=16)	*Non Members (n=8)*	*Members (n=24)*	*Non Members (n=12)*	*Members (n=21)*	*Non Members (n=8)*	*Members (n=61)*	*Non Members (n=28)*
Distribution (%) of households by type of house								
Durable	12.5	0.0	33.3	25.0	23.8	12.5	24.6	14.3
Semi-durable	75.0	62.5	54.2	50.0	76.2	50.0	67.2	53.6
Kutcha	12.5	37.5	12.5	25.0	0.0	37.5	8.2	32.1
Total (Numbers)	16	8	24	12	21	8	61	28
Households (%) having own house	100.0	100.0	83.3	75.0	90.5	100.0	90.2	89.3
Households (%) having electricity connection	93.8	100	100.0	83.3	81.0	87.5	91.8	89.3
Households (%) having ration card	93.8	100.0	95.8	58.3	100.0	100.0	96.7	82.1
Households (%) having green card (given to the poor)	87.5	87.5	91.7	58.3	90.5	87.5	55.7	67.9
Households (%) having access to protected water supply	81.3	100.0	91.7	100.0	100.0	100.0	91.8	100.0
Households (%) having individual latrines	16.7	0.0	6.3	12.5	23.8	25.0	16.4	10.7

LIVELIHOOD OPPORTUNITIES

Access to different sources of income is an important indicator on the role of SHGs in occupational diversification which improves income security and reduces seasonal fluctuations in income. The household members in a majority of the cases (both members and non-members) derived livelihood from more than one source. However, there is one difference between member and non-member households; a relatively larger proportion of the latter had only one source of income and about two-thirds of them had two or three sources. The pattern is different in the case of member households.

About two-thirds of the member households derived livelihood from three or more sources of income which include cultivation, agricultural wage labour, livestock rearing, sheep rearing, petty business and services (Table 3). There were, however, district-wise variations. The occupational diversification is more discernible among member households in Mysore as compared to the other two districts.

Table 3
Distribution of Members and Non-members by Number of Livelihood Activities

Number of livelihood Activities	*Bidar*		*Kolar*		*Mysore*		*Total*	
	Members	*Non Members*	*Members*	*Non Members*	*Members*	*Non Members*	*Members*	*Non Members*
One	12.4	12.5	16.7	33.3	0	0	9.8	17.9
Two	31.3	25.0	33.3	33.3	19.1	50.0	27.9	35.7
Three	31.3	25.0	33.3	33.4	33.3	25.0	32.8	28.6
Four	25.0	37.5	12.5	0	23.8	0	19.7	10.7
Five	0	0	4.2	0	19.1	25.0	8.2	7.1
Six	0	0	0	0	4.7	0	1.6	0
Total	16	8	24	12	21	8	61	28

Table 4
Proportion of Households Undertaking Different Livelihood Activities

Source	*Bidar*		*Kolar*		*Mysore*		*Total*	
	Members	*Non Members*	*Members*	*Non Members*	*Members*	*Non Members*	*Members*	*Non Members*
One	12.4	12.5	16.7	33.3	0	0	9.8	17.9
Agriculture	50.0	62.5	50.0	33.3	76.2	75.0	59.0	53.6
Livestock	62.5	62.5	37.5	8.3	85.7	50.0	60.7	35.7
Wage Labour	68.8	87.5	79.2	58.3	66.7	75.0	72.1	71.4
Business/ Service	37.5	50.0	37.5	33.3	28.6	0.0	34.4	28.6
Others	6.3	0.0	16.7	33.3	4.8	0.0	9.8	14.3
Total (no. of HHs)	16	8	24	12	21	8	61	28

An analysis of the proportion of households undertaking different livelihood activities also shows that member households were better placed in occupational diversification. Table 4 shows that member households were better placed in respect of livestock, non-farm activities and even agriculture when compared to non-member households. However, not much difference could be noticed between member and non-member households in so far agricultural wage labour is concerned, though the proportion of non-member households undertaking agricultural wage labour was relatively high in Bidar and Mysore.

INCOME FROM DIFFERENT SOURCES

Table 5 shows the annual gross income of the sample households from different sources. It may be noted that the earnings were of the order of Rs. 2,674,275 for member households and Rs. 700,776 for the non-member households. Petty business and services sector accounted for the highest share in the total income of the member households followed by wage labour, agriculture and livestock. In the case of non-members, wages accounted for the highest share in the total income followed by petty business/services, agriculture and livestock. Another important finding is that member households obtained higher income from agriculture, livestock and non-farm activities as compared to non-member households. There were, however, district-wise variations in this regard.

The average annual income per household was found to be higher in the case of members (Rs. 43,841) when compared to non-members (Rs. 25,028) for the state as a whole, the average for all the respondents being Rs. 37,922 (Table 5). Among the districts, the average income was highest in Bidar, followed by Mysore and Kolar – both in the case of members and non-members. A relatively higher income of member households in Bidar could be explained in terms of presence of salary earning members in a few of the sample households from this district.

An analysis of the distribution of households into different income groups revealed that about 39 per cent of both members and non-members belonged to the category of below poverty line with annual income less than Rs. 24,000. Of them, about 15 per cent members and 18 per cent non-members with an annual income of less than Rs.12,000 could be classified as very poor. About 43 per cent of the members and 57 per cent of the non-members

Table 5
Distribution (%) of Income of Households by Different Sources

Sources of income	*Bidar*		*Kolar*		*Mysore*		*Total*	
	Members	*Non-members*	*Members*	*Non-members*	*Members*	*Non-members*	*Members*	*Non-members*
Agriculture	39.5	29.5	12.1	12.4	22.8	20.8	24.5	19.2
Livestock	6.2	5.6	9.5	0.9	10.9	14.4	9.9	6.3
Wage Labour	24.1	29.0	39.5	53.0	26.7	64.8	25.2	44.6
Business / Services	29.8	35.9	36.4	23.9	39.6	0.0	39.8	27.0
Others	0.4	0.0	2.4	9.7	0.1	0.0	0.7	2.9
Total (amount)	980030	216990	551760	212570	880665	211216	2674275	700776
Average Income	61252	27124	22990	17714	41936	26402	43841	25028

belonged to the income group of Rs. 24,000 to Rs. 48,000 per annum. Only 11 per cent members and 4 per cent non-members had an income of greater than Rs.60,000 per annum (Table 6). A relatively larger proportion of member households fell in the higher income categories when compared to non-members.

Table 6
Distribution of Households by Income Categories

	Bidar		*Kolar*		*Mysore*		*Total*	
	Members (n=16)	*Non Members (n=8)*	*Members (n=24)*	*Non Members (n=12)*	*Members (n=21)*	*Non Members (n=8)*	*Members (n=61)*	*Non Members (n=28)*
Less than 12000	0.0	0.0	25.0	33.3	14.3	12.5	14.8	17.9
12000–24000	18.8	25.0	29.2	33.3	23.8	0.0	24.6	21.4
24000–36000	37.5	37.5	25.0	25.0	23.8	62.5	27.9	39.3
36000–48000	6.3	25.0	12.5	8.3	23.8	25.0	14.8	17.9
48000–60000	12.5	0.0	8.3	0.0	0.0	0.0	6.6	0.0
60000 and above	25.0	12.5	0.0	0.0	14.3	0.0	11.5	3.6

Thus, it appears from the above that a majority of the sample households, both among the members and the non-members, belonged to the category of the non-poor. But, this may be true only partially because the average household income does not reflect size of the household and dependency ratio, which varied considerably among these households. Taking into account these factors, higher income does not necessarily mean higher standard of living and hence cannot be concluded that the households are non-poor. This is further corroborated by the distribution of households by income groups and visual impression of the study team on poverty status (Table 7). Most of the households with an annual income of about Rs. 36,000 were felt to be non-poor while conducting the interview. Similarly, most of the households with an annual income of less than Rs. 36,000 were felt to be poor or very poor. Thus, there is a broad correspondence between income categories and visual impressions on poverty status; yet; there is no strict correspondence in the case of a few households.

ACQUISITION OF CONSUMABLE ASSETS

It was found that the proportion of households possessing consumable assets was not very high. Less than one-fifth of member households reported that they possessed bicycle and television, while the corresponding proportion in the case of non-member households was 25 per cent (Table 8). The proportion of households possessing other assets like radio, tape recorder, fan, sewing machine, electric and gas stove was much less among both member and non-members.

Table 7
Distribution of Households by Income Categories and Visual Impression on Poverty Status

Size classes of income (Rs.)	*Members*				*Non-Members*			
	Very poor	*Poor*	*Non-poor*	*Total*	*Very poor*	*Poor*	*Non-poor*	*Total*
< 12,000	22.2	77.8	0.0	100	20.0	80.0	0.0	100
12-24,000	35.3	58.8	5.9	100	33.3	66.6	0.0	100
24-36,000	6.7	80.0	13.3	100	0.0	62.5	37.5	100
36-48,000	10.0	30.0	60.0	100	20.0	40.0	40.0	100
48-60,000	0	33.3	66.7	100	0.0	0.0	0.0	100
60,000>	0	0	100	100	0.0	100	0.0	100
Total	16.4	54.10	29.5	100	17.9	3.57	17.9	100

Table 8
Percentage of Households Possessing Consumable Assets

Name of the asset	*Bidar*		*Kolar*		*Mysore*		*Total*	
	Members	*Non Members*	*Members*	*Non Members*	*Members*	*Non Members*	*Members*	*Non Members*
TV	37.5	50.0	4.2	8.3	19.1	25.0	18.1	25.0
Radio	12.5	0.0	4.2	8.3	14.3	12.5	9.8	7.1
Tape Recorder	25.0	12.5	0.0	8.3	9.5	12.5	9.8	10.7
Bicycle	25.0	25.0	8.3	8.3	28.6	50.0	19.7	25.0
Fan	12.5	0.0	8.3	0.0	4.8	0.0	8.2	0.0
Sewing machine	6.3	12.5	4.2	0.0	4.8	0.0	4.9	3.6
Electric/gas stove	0.0	12.5	4.2	0.0	4.8	0.0	3.3	3.6
Furniture	6.3	12.5	12.5	0.0	33.3	25.0	18.0	10.7

A large number of sample households acquired consumable assets in the last five years. The total amount spent by member households on acquiring all types of assets was Rs. 91,120, while it was Rs. 42,650 for non-members. Interestingly, the main source of investment on consumable assets in the case of member households was their own funds. In contrast, the predominant source of investment for non-member households was hire-purchase (Table 9). The fact that the member households did not resort to hire purchase as compared to non-members suggests that members were placed at an economically advantageous position. The sample households reported that they purchased television and other assets from shop keepers and traders located in nearby towns on hire purchase basis. They were found to be repaying the loan amount in monthly instalments.

Table 9
Distribution (%) of Expenditure on Consumable Assets by Sources

Name of the asset	*Members*				*Non-Members*			
	Own	*Borrowing*	*Hire purchase*	*Total*	*Ownl*	*Borropoor*	*Hire purchase*	*Total*
TV	99.1	0.0	0.9	42,300	12.2	2.0	85.7	24500
Radio	100.0	0.0	0.0	4,650	37.5	62.5	0.0	1600
Tape Recorder	100.0	0.0	0.0	6,400	14.6	36.6	48.8	4100
Bicycle	100.0	0.0	0.0	16,600	100.0	0.0	0.0	5100
Fan	100.0	0.0	0.0	2,900	0.0	0.0	0.0	0
Sewing machine	100.0	0.0	0.0	2,600	100.0	0.0	0.0	1200
Electric/gas stove	59.7	37.3	3.0	6,700	0.0	0.0	100.0	2000
Furniture	66.6	33.4	0.0	8,970	27.7	0.0	72.3	4150
Total	93.3	6.0	0.7	91,120	27.3	7.0	65.7	42,650

As regards the acquisition of household articles, it was found that only very few sample households could do so during the last five years. The main sources of mobilising the funds for this purpose included own savings, hire purchase schemes (on the basis of monthly instalments) and loans from shopkeepers or relatives, and informal cheeti. The compulsory savings made and the loans from the SHG also helped some members to acquire these articles. Further, it was noted that the relatively better-off among the sample households, those having access to more than one source of income and whose incomes are relatively stable due to presence of salaried persons could acquire the articles such as TV, tape recorder, bicycle, gas stove, sewing machine and furniture.

CONCLUSION

From the above discussion, it becomes clear that SHG members were better placed when compared to non-members in term of livelihood sources, income and possession of consumable household assets, even though both had more or less similar socio-economic characteristics. It appears that the savings habit and access to credit enabled the SHG members to diversify their occupational base and contributed to relatively more secured income when compared to non-members who did not have access to such benefits. The SHG - bank linkage programme proved to be a boon to the member households to access higher amounts of credit with the help of which they could take up new occupations or strengthen their existing ones thereby enhancing their livelihood sources and income. As a consequence, the SHGs appear to have contributed to the reduction of poverty to some extent. The role of SHGs also becomes evident in the acquisition of consumable household assets by their members, with only a negligible number of member households depending upon hire purchase schemes as compared to non-members to acquire these articles. Thus, it may be concluded that the SHGs were instrumental in enabling their members to improve their livelihood sources, increase their income base and, to a limited extent, acquire consumable household assets. It follows from the above that whatever differences noticed between members of SHGs and non-members in respect of livelihood sources, income and the pattern of acquisition of household assets could be essentially, though not entirely, attributed to the SHGs.

22

Gender Equality Through Women Entrepreneurship–A Research Perspective

Sita Vanka & N. Linga Murthy

The emergence of the woman entrepreneur–as one who shows enterprise, has an eye for opportunity, a willingness to take risks, a commercial acumen and who through her enterprise creates substantial employment for others–illustrates a new phenomenon in India. Two decades ago, the woman entrepreneur was a species almost unheard of, both policy-wise and in practice. It was only the Industrial Policy Resolution of 1978 which recognized the women entrepreneurs as a special group needing assistance and support in vague terms, and that too as a sequel to the declaration of the International Decade of Women between 1975-85 and the International Conference ofWomen Entrepreneurs held at Delhi in 1984. In about two decades time, women entrepreneurs not only entered business in a small way but ventured into starting and managing large enterprises on professional lines and working hard to sustain and survive in the competing environment.

The significance of this phenomenon must be understood not from the increasing number of women participating in commercial ventures but from the fact that they are entering an arena which was hitherto a "male preserve". Academic debate and research led to a re-examination of a woman's role in society and development and to demand for measures which would help them realize their full potential and transform their ' reproductive role' to a 'productive role' (White, 1984) thus ensuring gender equality, if not as an immediate goal but as a long term realty. The call for "engendering the Human Development paradigm" at the global level (HDR, 1995) and the year of "Empowerment ofWomen" (2000) in India are some examples of recent policy interventions in this direction. Action was initiated on several fronts–Education, health, employment, training etc.–by International, National, and non-governmental organizations. The result is, the conviction among women that it is perhaps the world of entrepreneurship that the recognition and value of women's contribution is the most vital for a better tomorrow (Dhameja, 2002).

WOMEN IN ENTREPRENEURIAL ACTIVITY

Women owned businesses are becoming increasingly important in the economies of almost all countries. It is believed that more than $250 billion is generated by the women annually, control 30% of business and create new businesses at two to three times the rate of their male counterparts (Committee on Small Business, 1984). The surge of entrepreneurship in Britain also evidenced this situation. Women represent one-quarter of self-employed in Britain (Carter and Cannon, 1992). Women's status in the Indian economy as an employer is of recent origin. Literature provides conflicting perspectives but there exists unanimity that women in India should not be the mere recipient of public support, but should don the role of economic agents to enhance their status (Kirve and Kanitkar, 1993). Scholarly literature highlighting interesting insights into the experiences of women entrepreneurs is delineated in the following lines.

RESEARCH–INTERNATIONAL SCENARIO

Women in business have been an emerging theme of scholarly research both in the developed and the developing world. While it is a recent phenomenon in a developing context like India, scholars across the world have exhibited unprecedented interest in the area of women entrepreneurship. Empirical studies conducted in the international arena evidence both qualitative and quantitative evidence on the reasons for starting business, their motivation, profile of women entrepreneurs, opportunities to start businesses, problems and prospects in the field of business experiences and future trends in the area of women entrepreneurship.

Martin & Roberts (1984) documented detailed work histories of women managing business and concluded that the aggregate bi-model profile masks the complex nature of women carrying on business. The study also brought out the fact that women tended to return to paid employment rather than being on their own. On the other hand another study highlights that certain products and services specifically provide opportunities for women to carry on business (Naisbutt, 1985). This according to the study is based on the distinctly 'male' and 'female' imagery associated with certain businesses. That has been supported by Carter (1994) where it was found that women could effectively excel in downstream industries such as service and retail compared to men (Carter, 1994). Some studies concluded that previous experience in the field compared to no experience makes the difference in successfully establishing and manning business (Brush and Hisrich, 1988).

Studies in Sweden (Holnquist & Sundin, 1988) state that the main characteristic of women in business is diversity. In Sweden women are everywhere, every line of business with all kinds of marital status, family backgrounds, children of all ages etc. They seem to be satisfied with entrepreneurship with a sense of independence and self-reliance being very strong for them.

The studies which examined the reasons for starting a business (Kaplan, 1988) have highlighted that creating employment for themselves rather than others, non-economic reason such as autonomy, challenge etc, have been highlighted. On the other hand some studies (Nelson, 1991) reveal that women concentrated in businesses, which required least capital outlay and more in the nature of extending a household activity. Thus household responsibility played a significant role in choosing the activity in business. On the other extreme entrepreneurs in USA converted 'high risk' ventures into sound businesses unlike their counterparts in the other parts of the world. In a country like Great Britain studies (Carter and Cannon, 1992) found out the way women approached starting an enterprise is dominated by the stage they have reached in their life cycle i.e., their age and domestic relationships. This had a bearing on the type of businesses and their individual approach to business ownership. While most of the enterprises where in traditionally female employment sectors like retailing and service sectors, only a few of them had prior experience in non-traditional sectors. The problems experienced as a business owner were very much like those experienced by males (operational problems) and hence had strategies, which were more situational to solve them. Some adopted a deliberate training for remaining in business, as they were skeptical about government promoting women entrepreneurship.

Studies in Hungary (Hisrich & Fuldop, 1993) found the profile of women entrepreneurs as married, belonging to middle and lower social class, mostly a house wife, educated etc. Their interest in business due to frustration in paid employment reportedly drove them to take up new ventures. Gender differences in perceptions of the business environment in general terms and more specific aspects of the environment has revealed interesting results (Kolvereid, 1993). The studies across ventures initiated in Great Britain, Norway and New Zealand found few gender differences in the perception of the influence of the environment on business formation.

Comparative studies (Dolinsky, 1994) revealed entry and stayer status differences of black and white businesswomen. The results reflect the notion that the black women are less likely to enter entrepreneurship than whites, but once they enter they are also marginally less likely to stay in business.

Studies in Holland (Zapalska, 1997) in three big urban centres found that the type of ventures established by women varied widely and included both male dominated and traditional female dominated areas. Businesses related to computers, consulting, sales and advertisement etc with product innovation and product modification has their aims. Though these were relatively new, these were the first to be started by the women entrepreneurs. Their prior experience reportedly helped them to overcome start-up operational problems. This made the Polish women entrepreneurs to initiate a variety of qualitative and quantitative changes in business practices within the industry.

Thus, these studies highlighted some of the issues concerning women entrepreneurs like problems in starting business, profile of women entrepreneurs, opportunities available etc. The studies also evidence that the scholarship did not explore the sustaining of business among women entrepreneurs and the problems and prospects associated with it. The developing context like India where women entrepreneurship is a phenomenon of the recent past, the scenario represents some convergence and some divergence from the international context.

RESEARCH–INDIAN STUDIES

Women starting enterprises got a boost with the international decade of women between the 70s and 80s. Though is about two and a half decades since women have started some form of business and showing their entrepreneurial mettle the very fact that just 5% of business is being carried on by women with almost 50% of them being female in the Indian population speaks of the social cultural and economic distortion in development (Kannitkar & Contractor, 1992). As education levels have grown and compulsions of employment experienced by women also increased the existing economy could not absorb the ever-increasing number of educated men and women, the wage employment options narrowed down. This made some women with business background to enter small businesses (Sethi, 1994). While a fairly large number went out for jobs in wage employment a noticeable phenomenon of their experience in wage employment drove them to look for self-employment. The result is the emergence of women entrepreneurs in small businesses but as experience and the supporting environment changed, women were encouraged to even enter the manufacturing sector, which is supposed to be ultimate in the entrepreneurship movement. This has shown that women are capable of and can successfully establish and manage enterprises on a large scale. The society on the other hand continues to suffer from a variety of misconceptions, apprehensions and suspicion about their capability with the lack of support from lending agencies and policy makers. Added to this, the lack of documentation on successful businesswomen, their success stories experiences also added to the existing disadvantage. Women entrepreneurship thus both in theory and practice was handicapped by literature and also 'role models' for women to push forward with their ideas of making big at the enterprise level. Despite this some studies as evidenced by a large number of women researchers devoted attention to the struggles, obstacles, barriers, frustrations, and experiences of women in business and documented it for scholarly purpose. It is only of late that associations have been formed to voice and discuss the problems and prospects of women entrepreneurs both at the national and the international level.

Singh & Gupta, 1984 found out the reasons for becoming an entrepreneur. The key reason cited was economic gain. Other studies (Singh, 1985) found out that keeping one-self busy, an ambition and pursuing an interest was highlighted as reasons for taking up entrepreneurship. Taking up independent activities was also cited as a reason by some women (Rani, 1986). Research also concentrated on the constraints and limitations for women coming forward to set up enterprises. Lack of confidence with societal barriers, procedural and statutory formalities, limited mobility, discrimination, lack of market exposure, insufficient industrial awareness, apathy of financial institutions etc were highlighted as some constraints for women. Socio-economic studies (Vinze, 1987), psychological characteristics (Azad, 1989) motivational studies (Pillai, 1989), background of women entrepreneurs (Anna, 1990), distinctive features of women entrepreneurs (Shah, 1990) strategies to promote women entrepreneurs (Rao, 1991), problems and perspectives (Srivastava & Chowdhary, 1991) were also conducted in different parts of India. Research on promoting entrepreneurship through training (Rathore & Chhabra, 1991, Nair, 1996) highlighted how women can start business and sustain industry through training. Factors like caste, community and religion also strongly influence the growth of entrepreneurship in rural areas (Jyothi & Prasad, 1993), and face different problems compared to urban societies (Kaur & Prashar, 1993). The role of NGOs in promoting rural entrepreneurship through skill training was also highlighted (Kirve & Kanitkar, 1993). The participation of women with metropolitan urban background is certainly easy and higher according to some scholars (Venkatapathy, 1993).

TRENDS IN RESEARCH

- Women in entrepreneurship have been an emerging theme of scholarly research both in the developed and the developing world. The interest in the area of women entrepreneurship has been a recent phenomenon both in the developed context, more so in the developing context like India, with only two decades of scholarly attention.
- International research evidences both qualitative and quantitative studies on women entrepreneurs.
- The early research at the international level highlighted women preferring paid employment rather than entrepreneurship.

- Studies also evidenced women initially starting ventures, which reflected distinctly *female* imagery.
- Entrepreneurial ventures taken up by women evidenced prior family history of entrepreneurship.
- The reasons for starting businesses were economic in nature, which later shifted to non-economic reasons such as autonomy, challenge, recognition, self-respect etc.
- The profile of women entrepreneurs is typical-married, middle-aged, middle income groups, educated with a few frustrated in wage employment and a few with prior business background.
- Majority of the ventures were located at residence initially and later shifted to business/industrial locations.
- Women faced problems in starting and sustaining business in the nature if social, cultural and economic policy etc.
- Women entrepreneurship was largely seen in small businesses with limited scale of operations, but later shifted to successfully established and managed large enterprises on a large scale.
- A variety of misconceptions, apprehensions and suspicion about their entrepreneurial capability still persists among the lending agencies, policy makers etc.
- Studies on the psychological characteristics, motivation levels, distinctive features and inherent abilities of women entrepreneurs is limited.
- Women entrepreneurship in the rural areas is yet to catch up in a structured way both in terms of the interest of women in rural areas to manage business as also public perception compared to the women entrepreneurs with metropolitan urban background.
- Abundant scholarship is available on the perceptions of women with reference to their problems, constraints both in terms of starting and sustaining business but there is a lack of research in the nature of probing whether the problems are *real* or a matter of *perception* the dearth of experimental designs of research is thus needed

CONCLUSION

Research on women entrepreneurship is a recent phenomenon both at the international level and India. Scholarship evidences research in a unstructured manner with studies conducted more as a matter of convenience. Documentation in terms of the success stories and role models for the next generation is thus limited. There appears some convergence in the nature of research between the developed and the developing context, but the divergence may be attributed to the contextual variations. A formal attempt at conceptualization is also a gray area with the Centers for women studies/Women Cell also taken shape in the recent past. There exists an enormous potential for research in women entrepreneurship more so in the context of liberalization, privatization and globalization to march towards gender equality in the developing context including India

REFERENCES

Azad, G.S. (1989), Development of Entrepreneurship Among Indian Women. SEDME, Vol. XVI (B).

Brush, C. and Hisrich, R. (1988) Women Entrepreneurs: Strategic Origins & Impact on Growth. Frontiers of Entrepreneurship Research. M.A: USA.

Carter, N. (1994), Reducing Barriers between Genders. Academy of Management Meetings, Texas, USA.

Carter, S. and Cannon, J. (1992), Women as Entrepreneurs. London: Acad Press.

Dhameja (2002), Women Entrepreneurs. New Delhi: Deep & Deep.

Dolinsky, A. (1994), Long Tern Entrepreneurship Patterns.JSBM, Vol.32.

Eisenhardt, K.M. (1989), Building Theories from Case Study Research. Academy of Management Review. Vol.14 p. 532-550.

Holnquest,C. and Sunden E.S. (1988), Women as Entrepreneurs in Sweden. Frontiers of Entrepreneurship Research. M.A: USA.

Human Development Report (1995) UNDP, 1995.

International Labor Organization, Geneva, 1982.

Jyothi, V. and Prasad, G. (1993), A Profile of Potential Rural Women Entrepreneurs. SEDME Vol. XX (1).

Kanetkar, A. and Contractor, N. (1992), In Search of Identity-The Women Entrepreneurs in India. Gandhinagar: EDI.

Kaplan, E. (1988), Women Entrepreneurs- Constructing a Framework to Examine Venture Success and Failure. Entrepreneurship Research.M.A: USA.

Kirve, H. and Kanetkar, A. (1993), Entrepreneurship at Grassroots. Job Entrepreneurship Vol. 2(2).

Kolvereid, L. (1993), Is it Difficult to Start Business in All Countries. JSBM, Vol. 31 (4).

Martin, J. and Roberts, C. (1984), Women & Employment. London: HMSO.

Nelson, B.M. (1991), Small Business Opportunities for Women in Jamaica. SEDME Vol. 18(1).

Nousbutt (1985), The Future of Franchising: Looking 25 Years Ahead to The Year 2010. Washington DC-IFA.

Rani, C. (1986), Potential Women Entrepreneurs- A Study. SEDME, Vol. 13 (3) pp. 13-32.

Rao, C.H. (1991), Promotion of Women Entrepreneurship. SEDME Vol. 18 (2).

Sethy, J. (1994), Women Entrepreneurship in India–A Brief Comment. SEDME Vol. 21(4).

Singh, N.P. and Gupta (1984), Potential Women Entrepreneurs-Their Profile, Vision and Motivation. Delhi: NIESBD/MDI.

Srivatsava, A.K. and Choudhary, S. (1991) Women Entrepreneurs-Problems, Perspectives and Role Expectations from Banks. Chandigarh: Punjab University.

Vinze Medha (1987), Women Entrepreneurs in India (1975-85). New Delhi: Mittal.

White, J. (1984), The Rise of Female Capitalism. Business Quarterly Vol. 49, pp. 137-143.

Zapalska, Alina M. (1997), Profile of Women Entrepreneurs & Enterprise in Poland, JSBM, Vol. 35 (4).

23

Gender Discrimination in Agricultural Wages: A Case Study in Kurnool District of Andhra Pradesh

I. Narendra Kumar, V.K. Reddy and G. Chandrasekar Rao

In India, the agricultural sector is providing employment to majority of the population. Directly or indirectly agriculture continues to be the mainstay of livelihood for a majority of the people. The decadal census indicates that 60 per cent of the total population are depending upon agriculture. The reports reveal that 19 to 25 per cent of agricultural labourers were engaged in Agriculture. In briefly, prosperity of the Indian economy depends upon the development of agriculture.

Agricultural labourers are primarily involved in farming. In spite of shifts in the occupational structure during the recent decades, agricultural continues to occupy a pre-dominant place in employment structure, employing about three-fifths of the total workers in India. There has been a spectacular increase in the number of agricultural labourers increasing from a mere 17.26 million at the beginning of the century to 107.45 million in 2001.

The 1951 census report defined agricultural labour as cultivating labourer as an employee or cultivator whose business is merely to perform physical labour in a manner required by the cultivators and the livelihood of cultivating labourer is part of the expenses of the cultivators. Agricultural workers are those who work on others land and who are paid in cash or in kind.[1] The First Agricultural Labour Enquiry defines (1950-51) agricultural labourers are those who are engaged in raising crops on payment of wages. The Second Agricultural Labour Enquiry (1956-57) enlarged the category of agricultural workers to include all those who are engaged in allied occupations like Animal Husbandry, Dairy, Poultry, etc. In its reports the term 'agricultural labourer' was defined as one who followed any one or more of the following agricultural occupations in the capacity of a labourer on hire or on exchange. Whether in cash or kind or partly in cash or partly in kind.

According to the National Commission on labour, "An agricultural labourer is one who is basically unskilled and unorganized and has little for his livelihood other than personal labour. On the basis of mode of work and payment, farm labour can be categorized into family labour, permanent labour, casual labour and contract labour etc.[2] In economic theory wage is the price for labour. The wage rate for agricultural labour is the result of the interaction of demand, for and supply of agricultural labourers. Thus, in the absence of control, they (wages) are determined like all other prices, by supply and demand. The demand for labour varies with endogenous factors and exchange factors. The wage earnings of the agricultural labour house-hold depend on earning strength of a house-hold, number of days on which each member secures agricultural and non-agricultural work and wage rate paid to such work.[3] The structure of wage is a general term for the set of inter relations among a collection of wage rates. It is frequently used in contrast to the concept of wage levels, which refers to an average of the collection. In short, a wage structure is the relation among two or more wages related to one another in some systematic way.[4] The committee on fair wages used the terms minimum wages, fair wages and living wages. As per the committee, the minimum wages should represent the lower limit of fair wage, the next higher level is the fair wage and the highest level of fair wage is the living wage.[5]

A number of empirical studies were conducted both in India and abroad to quantify the extent of wage differential between male and female agricultural labourers. However, there were wide variations among various studies made relating to nature and extent of wage differences. Besides sex, occupation, sectoral, and operational there were regional differences in the level of wages.

The studies made on differential between male and female labour in farm activities in India is presented here.

Subba Rao analyzed that the wage differentials of agricultural labour in East Godavari and West Godavari Districts of Andhra Pradesh. In this study wage differentials exist on the basis of sex, type of land, crop operation, skill etc. The study concludes that with suitable measures, the wage differentials can be minimized.[6]

Parmer in his empirical study of farm wages undertaken in Saurastra region shows that the average daily wage rate of male worker is found to be high at Rs. 11.40 in developed village and it is Rs. 10.23 in less developed villages; whereas female worker is found to earn Rs. 8.02 and Rs. 6.90 in the respective areas, the study also found that the extent of sex wise wage differentials is found to be lower in developed villages 42.12 per cent, when compared 52.91 per cent in less developed areas.[7]

Dhaliwal and Grewal in their analysis of spatial wages of agricultural labourers in Punjab indicates that percentage of agricultural workers per 1000 hectares of cropped area have been found highly significant, explaining 56.36 per cent of the variations in wage rates.[8]

From the various studies on wage discrimination, with regard to sexual division of agricultural work, it is evident that the factors influencing wage differences are: economic, cultural, traditional and social beliefs. Discrimination in wages on the basis of sex is a subject that has long interested the economists but a thorough theoretical and quantitative analysis of it is rather recent phenomena. In this context, it is relevant to refer Richard B. Mekenize and Gardon Tullock views on the lack of study on sex discrimination in labour market. The authors asserted that "as far as we know, no one has done a study on sex discrimination in profit and non-profit organizations".[9]

Keeping in view the need for a region-specific study of wage differentials a humble attempt has been made to study the extent of wage differentials between male and female labourers engaged in agricultural activities in Kurnool District of Andhra Pradesh. The following are the specific objective of the study:

To find out the extent of wage differentials between male and female labourers in agricultural activities. The study was conducted in Three mandal viz., Banaganapalli, Pamulapadu, and Gonegandla of Kurnool District with the objective of examining the wage differentials in particular and the regional variations in wage payments in general. It is felt that there are wide differences in the wage rates between male and female labourers in agricultural sector in the study area. In the study both primary and secondary sources of data were made use of. The primary data were collected from the selected sample mandals and villages through personal interview method. A well designed scheduled was administered to collect data. A multi-stage random sampling techniques was used to collect the data. The total sample size is 216 which include male and female workers in the study area. In order to get correct information a pre-tested structured schedule was administered. The secondary data were collected from books, journals, reports of ministry of labour, census reports etc., the collected data were tabulated and analyzed using simple averages and percentages.

Wage differentials based on sex is one of the important types of wage differences and the principle of 'equal-pay for equal work'. Article 41 of the 1919 constitution of the ILO lain down "the principle that men and women should receive equal remuneration for work of equal value". Wages in agricultural sector differ not only between male and female labourers, but they vary from crop to crop, operation to operation, one type of land to another, one region to another and season to season too. These wage differentials in agricultural sector, up to a certain extent, are desirable and inevitable due to different conditions prevailing in different areas, varying supplied demand conditions of labour during different periods. The present study has been undertaken in the Kurnool District with the objective to examine the extent of wage differential between male and female labourers in farm sector. To identify the factors accounting for wage differentials between male and female labourers, it is necessary to find out the percentage rates of agricultural operations performed by men and women. These percentages are calculated on the basis of number of agricultural operations performed by male and female labourers in the agricultural fields. As there are 13 agricultural operations, if a labourer carries out all these operations, it means that the rate of agricultural operations performed on that particular labourer amount to 100 per cent. If the labourer work in ten operations then the rate of agricultural operations decline and so on. The percentage rates of agricultural operations performed by male and female labourers help one to find out the extent of wage differentials existing between male and

Table 1
Mandal-wise Participation of Male and female Labourers in each Agricultural Operations

(in Percentage)

Sl. No.	Name of the Mandals	Ploughing	Sowing	Seedlings	Transplantation	Weeding	Bunding	Manuring	Spraying	Harvesting	Carrying	Threshing	Winnowing	Total average percentage involvement
1.	Banaganapalli													
	Male	100	100	57	62	48	100	100	100	100	100	100	100	88.91
	Female	–	–	51	38	86	–	–	31	100	81	86	69	45.16
2.	Pamulapadu													
	Male	100	100	58	74	45	100	100	100	100	100	100	100	90.58
	Female	–	–	44	51	96	–	–	34	100	79	89	76	47.42
3.	Gonegandla													
	Male	100	100	65	76	28	100	100	100	100	100	100	100	89.08
	Female	–	–	39	49	95	–	–	24	92	89	94	96	48.16

Source: Field Data.

female labourers swing to differences in the percentage rates of agricultural operations, performed by them. If male and female labourers perform all the operations, the differences in wage rates could be avoided since equal work calls for equal wage. As the percentage rates of agricultural operations performed by male and female labourers differ so the wage rates are also likely to differ. The Table 1 shows the agricultural operations performed both b y the male and female labourers in the study area.

Table 1 shows the agricultural operations performed both by the male and female labourers in the study area. It is observed that there is a clear evidence of gender division of work and the rates of gender division of labour difference from Banaganapalli, Pamulapadu and Gonegandla mandals of Kurnool District. For male labourers the average rate of agricultural operations in Banaganapalli mandal was 88.91, it was 90.58 in the Pamulapadu mandal and 89.08 in the Gonegandla mandal. In Banaganapalli mandal the average rate of agricultural operations performed by women worked out to be 45.16, it was 47.42 in the Pamulapadu mandal and 48.16 in the Gonegandla mandal. Evidently, male labourers are in a better off position as compared to women labourers. Taking into account the gender division of labour we find that the rate of agricultural operations performed by female labourers was less in Banaganapalli mandal as compared Pamulapadu and Gonegandla mandals. The agricultural operations performed by male labourers was less in Banaganapalli mandal as compared to Pamulapadu and Gonegandala mandals. Pressed by the problem of unemployment, the male workers disparately do the operations performed by female labourers and in the bargain they are employed to perform high percentage of agricultural operations. Employers, in order to get the cost of cultivation cut down and reap the profits, employ women in selected operations like transplanting, weeding, etc., paying as minimum wages of they could possible give. For all the other operations male labourers are employed since they accept to work for minimum wages rather than remaining chronically unemployed.

WAGE DIFFERENTIALS IN THE MANDALS

The operation wise and mandal wise average number of days worked per year and wages earned by male and female labourers is indicated in the Table 2.

Table 2
Mandal-wise and Operation wise Average Number of Days Worked in Agriculture

Sl. No.	*Operations*	*Banaganapalli*		*Pamulapadu*		*Gonegandla*	
		No. of days		*No. of days*		*No. of days*	
		Male	*Female*	*Male*	*Female*	*Male*	*Female*
1.	Ploughing	20.45	–	24.31	–	18.97	–
2.	Sowing	18.13	–	20.49	–	17.44	–
3.	Seedling	13.11	11.12	14.39	12.45	10.38	8.31
4.	Transplanting	24.31	18.37	25.18	26.39	22.49	26.49
5.	Weeding	18.95	35.79	16.43	41.16	14.31	38.76
6.	Bunding	10.19	–	12.38	–	8.91	–
7.	Manuring	14.38	–	18.59	–	14.43	–
8.	Spraying	10.79	3.49	13.89	3.17	11.49	3.76
9.	Harvesting	22.71	25.13	20.97	28.39	18.18	26.49
10.	Carrying	17.15	14.74	17.41	15.34	17.74	16.89
11.	Threshing	16.49	14.98	17.37	15.61	15.88	14.85
12.	Winnowing	15.35	13.31	15.84	13.76	15.31	14.39
	Total	202.01	136.93	217.25	156.27	185.53	149.94

Source: Field Data.

Table 2 observed that in Banaganapalli mandal the average number of days the male agricultural labourers worked was 202.01 days per year, and it was 136.93 days by female labourers. In Pamulapadu mandal the average days the male agricultural labourers worked was 217.25 days and 156.27 days by female labourers. Whereas in Gonegandla mandal the average number of days the male labourer worked was 185.53 and it was 149.94 days by female labouers.

In respect of wages in the mandals the average wage rate for male labourers and female labourers are discussed in the Table 3.

Table 3 shows that in respect of wages in Banaganapalli mandal the average wage rate for male labourers was Rs. 38.80 and it as Rs. 33.50 for female labourers. Whereas in the Pamulapadu mandal the average rate of male labour was Rs. 42.48 and for female labourer it was Rs. 34.36, and for female labourer was Rs. 35.75 and for female labourer was Rs. 32.14 in the Gonegandla mandal of the Kurnool District. Obviously, there is among mandals gender division of work gender discrimination in wage payment in the study area. Only eight operations i.e., operations in which both male and female labourers participated alone were taken into account in order to examine the wage differences. For the remaining operations either male or female labourers were participated. Table 4 reveals the operation wise and mandal wise wage differentials between male and female labourers.

Table 3
Average Wages of Agricultural Labourers

(Wages in Rs.)

Sl. No.	Operations	*Banaganapalli*		*Pamulapadu*		*Gonegandla*	
		No. of days		*No. of days*		*No. of days*	
		Male	*Female*	*Male*	*Female*	*Male*	*Female*
1.	Ploughing	38.45	–	42.35	–	32.75	–
2.	Sowing	40.75	–	45.18	–	32.58	–
3.	Seedling	36.48	28.28	38.42	32.99	33.18	28.49
4.	Transplanting	38.13	34.26	38.56	34.98	34.78	30.78
5.	Weeding	36.42	33.09	38.75	36.19	39.79	34.58
6.	Bunding	37.95	–	42.78	–	35.92	–
7.	Manuring	42.91	–	45.62	–	33.49	–
8.	Spraying	39.79	35.25	43.69	34.93	38.61	30.63
9.	Harvesting	38.41	34.42	43.61	34.68	36.75	31.79
10.	Carrying	38.79	36.09	44.79	32.78	36.19	32.98
11.	Threshing	38.49	34.49	42.18	33.45	36.39	34.13
12.	Winnowing	38.98	32.19	43.92	34.91	38.46	33.76
	Total	38.80	33.50	42.48	34.36	35.75	32.14

Source: Field Data.

Table 4 reveals that in the Banaganapalli mandal average percentage of female to male labourers is 87.71 it is 82.67 per cent in Pamulapadu mandal and 87.47 per cent in Gonegandla mandal. It is found that in the Banaganapalli mandal the average percentage of wage differential worked out to be 12.3 per cent, in Pamulapadu mandal 17.32 per cent and in Gonegandla mandal it is 12.53 per cent.

Further in Banaganapalli mandal the percentage of wage differential was higher 22.48 in the case of seedling, followed by winnowing, 17.42 per cent, spraying 11.41 per cent, harvesting and threshing 10.39 per cent, weeding 9.15 per cent and carrying 6.97 per cent. In Pamulapadu mandal the percentage of wage differential was high 26.82 per cent in the case of carrying, followed by threshing

20.7 per cent, winnowing 20.52 per cent, harvesting 20.48 per cent, spraying 20.05 per cent, seedling 14.14 per cent, transplanting 9.29 per cent and 6.61 per cent in the case of weeding. Whereas in Gonegandla mandal the wage differential is high at 20.67 per cent for spraying, followed by for seedling 14.14 per cent, harvesting 13.5 per cent, weeding 13.05 per cent, winnowing 12.22 per cent, transplanting 11.51 per cent, carrying 8.87 per cent and threshing 6.22 per cent. On the whole it was found that the average percentage of wage differential was high in Pamulapadu mandal (82.67 per cent) where as it was low in Gonegandla mandal (87.47 per cent) and Banaganapalli mandal (87.71 per cent).

Table 4
Operation-Wise and Mandal Wise Percentage Wage Differential Between Male and Female Labourers

Operations	*Banaganapalli*		*Pamulapadu*		*Gonegandla*	
	Percentage wage female to male labourers	*Percentage wage differential*	*Percentage wage female to male labourers*	*Percentage wage differential*	*Percentage wage female to male labourers*	*Percentage wage differential*
Seedling	77.52	22.48	85.86	14.14	85.86	14.14
Transplanting	89.85	10.15	90.71	9.29	88.49	11.51
Weeding	90.85	9.15	93.39	6.61	86.91	13.09
Spraying	88.59	11.41	79.95	20.05	79.33	20.67
Harvesting	89.61	10.39	79.52	29.48	86.50	13.50
Carrying	93.03	6.97	73.18	26.82	91.13	8.87
Threshing	89.61	10.39	79.30	20.70	93.78	6.22
Winnowing	82.58	17.42	79.48	20.52	87.78	12.22

Source: Field Data.

In the study area the households viewed that there was no wage discrimination based on caste. The reasons explained by the sample households to become an agricultural labourers were easy accessibility to the job, easy employment and easy to do operations. The sample house-holds stated that the male labourers preferred to perform operations such as ploughing, bunding, manuring, sowing, harvesting, threshing etc., where as the female labourers preferred to perform operations such as transplanting, weeding, harvesting winnowing and seedling.

The above analysis shows that in addition to wage differentials by sex there are regional differences. The main influencing factor for wage differential is gender bias which is against the interests of the female labourers. The demand female labour for exceeds the demand for male labour since the supply of female labour outstrips the supply of male labourers considerably, the female labourers are forced to accept the discriminatory wages for their survival though the efficiency of male and female labourers in the performance of the operations is the same.

SUGGESTIONS

- Awareness building among the agricultural labourers particularly among female labourers is essential. This can be achieved through education regarding equal pay for equal work, gender wage discrimination, etc.
- The National Commission on Rural Labour suggested to set up a separate department at the central and state levels to deal exclusively with rural labour and the payment of minimum wages.
- Implementation of social security measures like group insurance, rural housing, education and health facilities are essential in the rural areas since these measures serve as an economic cushion to the poor, unorganized rural labourers to safeguard against the adverse impact of wage differentials on the living conditions of the rural poor.
- To minimize wage differentials due to landlessness or unevenly distributed land, it is suggested to provide the land to the landless through effective implementation of land reforms, by the state and central government policy.
- To set upon agricultural labourers welfare fund, with the contributions of the employers.

NOTES AND REFERENCES

1. Govt. of India, Census Report 1961.
2. Sarma A.N., Economic Structure of Indian Agriculture, New Delhi, 1989.
3. Fonseka, A.J., Wage issues in Developing Economy: The Indian Experience, Oxford University Press, Delhi, 1985.

4. International Encyclopedia of the Social Sciences, Vol. XV, XVI, XVII, p. 397.
5. Govt. of India, Report of the Committee on Fair wages, New Delhi, 1949.
6. Subba Rao, P., Wage Differentials of Casual Workers in Agricultural Sector, 1982.
7. B.D. Parmar, Rural Labour Market: An empirical study of Farm wages in Saurashtra Region: Indian Journal of Industrial Relations, Oct., 1987.
8. R.S. Dhaliwal and S.S. Grewal: Temporal and Spatial Variations in wage of Agricultural Labourers in Punjab, Indian Journal of Labour Economics, 1981.
9. Richard B., Mekenzie and Garden Tullock, The New World of Economics, Richard D. Irvin Press, 1975.

24

Gender Inequalities among Marginal Farmer and Agricultural Labourer Households–A Study of Two Villages in Khammam District

A. Venkateswarlu & Y. Venkateswara Rao

I

Gender inequalities are reflected in different dimensions eroding the very vitals of social and economic justice throughout the last century. Sex ratio an important dimension of the gender inequalities has come down between 1901 and 2001 census years. At the national level the decrease of number of females for 1000 males is from 972 to 933. At the state level the decrease between 1931 to 2001 is from 987 to 978. At the district level it is increased from 957 to 974 between 1981 to 2001.

On one side voluntary organizations, Mahila Mandals, Women organizations, Women lib movements have striven to create social consciousness on this problem while on other side education, economic progress and media explosion have strengthened the cause of females in social equity. What ever be the movements unfortunately women in this sacred land have been facing inequalities and craving for asserting their status. In some states like Tamilnadu, Rajasthan female children are "Born to die" while in some developed states like Maharashtra, Gujarat and Metropolitan cities modern knowledge in medicine in the form of scanning has been used to give an end to female fetus in the mother's womb. Modern India has forgotten the old saying "Yathra Naryanthu Poojyathe tatra Ramyathe Devatham" and has indulged in different types of atrocities on women.

The objective of this paper is to probe in the gender inequalities among marginal farmer and agricultural labourer households. For this study two villages namely Allipuram and Baswapuram in Khammam district are chosen. The size of the sample is 48 households. As the study is confined to the lower economic sections of the rural society viz. Marginal farmer and Agricultural labourer households are selected at random. 16 households each from Forward Castes, Backward Castes and Scheduled Castes are selected for this study. Questionnaire schedules have been administered and responses have been recorded for data processing.

II

SUMMARY OF FINDINGS

Gender inequalities and bias are analysed by taking the parameters such as duration of work and nature of work, age of marriage, age at first delivery, decision about family planning operations, gender preferences, and education opportunities, contribution of female income and decision making and gender inequalities in other areas.

Duration of work by a female in the household is taken first. 18.75 per cent of the female in the sample households of 48 work 3 to 6 hours as house wives. 37.25 per cent of the female work 6 to 7 hours as casual labour, and take up work in family cultivation in addition to domestic work as house wives. 43.75 per cent of females work 8 to 9 hours as agricultural labourers besides domestic work as house wives. This clearly indicates the typical rural scenario where women are constrained to take up more work than men.

In other words 18.75 per cent of the females in the respondent house holds work as solely house wives while the remaining 81.25 per cent of the females work as house wives besides taking up extra work either as agricultural labourers or as casual labour or labour in own cultivation.

It is a widely known fact that the *average age of marriage of girls* in India more so in rural India is abnormally low despite the prevention of child marriages act. This fact is examined in the area of study and it is observed that 31.25 per cent of girls have been married below 15 years, 58.33 per cent of girls have been married between 15-18 years and 10.42 per cent of girls have been married between 18-21 years. No respondent married female in the area of study has been married after 21 years and the inference is that the maximum age of marriage is just 21 years. With limited or zero education and total economic dependence on the parents give no scope to the rural females to decide their age of marriage, not to speak of the selection of the spouse. It is the males in the family to decide the age and select the groom. Gender bias is extremely felt in the context of marriages of girls in the area of study. The respondents opined that from the moment a girl child is born family members especially males think about her marriage.

Age at first delivery in view of the early marriages is comparatively low in rural India. This fact is also analysed by taking the 48 respondent females of the sample. 4.17 per cent of the females have their first delivery between 13-15 years, 25 per cent of the respondent females have their first delivery between 15-17 years, 47.92 per cent between 17-19 years, 16.67 per cent between 19-21 years and the remaining 6.25 per cent of females have their first delivery between 21-23 years. In other words 75 per cent of the respondent females have become mothers at a tender age of below 19 years. Females are neither physically nor mentally mature to give child births during such an early period. Their health is affected and no wonders that some of them become grand mothers before 35 years of age.

Family planning or family welfare has captured the attention of the rural people under the thrust given by the government of India and the state Governments over the period since the first five year plan. The sex of the spouse under going family planning operation is also an indicator of decision taking on a vital issue. It is found that only 12.5 per cent of males against 87.5 per cent of females have undergone family planning operation. Here also male domination is clear in forcing the females to undergo operation. The reasons for more number of tubectomy operations as revealed by the female respondents are;

(a) Males should take up hard work regularly.

(b) Males have to lift and carry heavy loads.

(c) Males cannot find more rest periods.

The opinions reflect special treatment towards males or gender bias. They also reflect the ignorance of rural people with regard to family planning operations to some extent.

However, at the time of family planning the sex of the child as analysed throws an interesting point. 26 (54.17%) households have opted for family planning with a male child where as 22 (45.83%) families have opted family planning with a female child. These figures show a clear bias towards male child. 10 (20.83%) respondents have opted for family planning with two children in the study area. In this, 7 (70%) house holds have male children and 3 (30%) have female children. 22 (45.83%) households have stopped with the third child. Among them 13 (59.09) households have male children and 9 (40.91) have female children. 11 (22.92%) households have stopped child birth with fourth child. Of them 4 (36.36%) house holds have male babies and 7 (63.64%) households have female babies. 5 (10.42%) households have opted for family planning with 5 children. Two (40%) of them have boys and three (60%) of them have girls. Households with more male children have opted for family planning with two or three children. But households with more girls have waited for male children and postponed family planning operations upto four to five children. The mind set with regard to child birth is totally towards males in the Indian context for which different social, economic, cultural and religious factors can be attributed.

In order to analyse the sex ratios further children below one year age are taken in Allipuram a sample village as a whole. There are 14 male children against 10 female children below one year of age in the village. Again from the same village children between one to five years are taken. Their number is 68 male children and 61 female children. This data clearly shows a bias towards male children and this fact is very much alarming at the national level. Indian society, perhaps for different socio, cultural reasons is moving more towards "son stroke".

The data on the percentage of female income in the total household income presented in table 1.

Of the total 48 respondent households 18.75 per cent of females have 20 per cent of income in the total households income. 27.08 per cent of females have 30 per cent, 41.67 per cent of females have 40 per cent, 8.33 per cent of females have 50 per cent, and 4.17 per cent of females have 60 per cent of income in the total house hold income. It indicates that most of the females have contributing considerable share in the total household income.

Table 1
Percentage of Female Income in Total Household Income

Household Income range	*Percentage of female income in the total household income*					
	20%	*30%*	*40%*	*50%*	*60%*	*Total*
0 - 5000	3	3	7	2	2	17
5001 - 10000	2	4	9	2	–	17
10001 - 20000	4	6	4	–	–	14
Total	9 (18.75)	13 (27.08)	20 (41.67)	4 (8.33)	2 (4.17)	48 (100.00)

The gender preferences in providing education opportunities to children among sample households is also gathered. The respondent households have expressed willingness to educate both boys and girls. But they stop the education of the girl child if the educational institutions are above 4 kilometers of distance. They apprehend safety and security of the girls if they go by bus or on foot to far of places for studies. Meanwhile most of the respondents states that they stop the education of a girl when a proper match is likely to be fixed. It is marriage even in tender age which is more important than the education of the girl child in the opinion of a majority of respondents. Moreover the elder ladies in the house give training in domestic activities to the girl child with a view to perform early marriage at the cost of education. Some times they keep the girls to take care of young babies in the household and are prepared to discontinue the education of the girls. The rural culture is such that a girl is to be groomed to become a housewife irrespective of her education. All these facts and the rural compulsions convert most of the girls in to school dropouts.

Specific areas of gender inequalities are analysed by collecting the opinions of the respondents. A clear bias between boys and girls surfaces in the following areas.

(a) Boys are free to spend by demanding from the parents from out of family incomes. But even for necessity girls have no such freedom and they should account for any expenditure. The requirements of the girls are provided materially by the male members of the household.

(b) With regard to food the Indian custom, especially in rural areas is such that the male members and the boys are served first what ever food that is available. Girl children are to be satisfied with the left overs while the elderly females and the house wives eat what ever that is remaining. There is clear cut discrimination towards boys in providing qualitative and nutritious food. As the Nobel Lauret *Prof. Amartyasen* has pointed out once that this practice is changed largely in the middle and upper middle sections with the dinning table concept. That too in the urban centers and also among the educated.

(c) With regard to social respect a female in the Indian society should cover her total body, shrink and look downwards in her public appearance in rural India. Education and media explosion have brought radical changes in this aspect but within limitations. The females in the rural set up should not sit on cots or chairs when in-laws or male guests are in the house. They should not interfere in any discussions openly. In some cases a female should not talk to a male even if he is a close relative like son-in-law. But there are no restrictions on the male members of the household to move, talk or interact with anyone.

(d) The average expenditure in the rural set up on the education of the girls is extremely low when compared with the expenditure on the education of boys this is mostly responsible for gender inequalities as age advances.

(e) Customs and traditions in the Indian society are also responsible to a great extent for gender inequalities. A male child carries the family burden whereas a female child goes to the in-law's house after marriage. This mindset is at the base for gender inequalities.

(f) With regard to luxuries, pleasure trips or school excursions or movie goings boys are free. Girls face so many restrictions and in most cases refusals. This discrimination gets strengthened in the social system as boys and girls grow in to adults.

(g) Males and male children are free to claim the family savings and family assets. When a house hold purchases any immovable property it will be in the name of males. Equal rights to the girls in the family property is just on paper. As girls leave the family to the in-laws house family properties are always in the name of boys to facilitate sales or loan raising when the family needs. It is throughout India that a female child is always considered an alien with regard to family properties.

(h) Even for small mistakes or slipouts in the day to day household maintenance most of the ladies are harassed and in most cases physically beaten. The male psyche always takes advantage of the dependency component of the female personality. Even trivial issues like the taste of a curry or inability to provide the curries ordered for or a small delay in fetching hot water for a bath, males are ready to accuse, abuse and manhandle the females mostly partners as revealed by most of the respondents. For any failure in the socio-economic set up out side the household the male pin points and accuses the partner in some form or other.

(i) Males may have different addictions like alcohol, gambling, extra marital relations etc. They may commit any mistakes like losing money while travelling due to carelessness, disrespect to the parents of the partner, lavish spending etc. But the spouses should never question them. The male igo in the Indian set up always expects the stoic silence from the females. Most of the respondent females have given their experience on the promise of secrecy.

(j) Respondent households give more importance to the health and well being of male children. Medical checkups, followup medicines, medical care, nutritious food during illness are all the areas in which the girls are neglected to some extent.

This is a micro study and it is confined to the weaker sections of the rural society. So the conclusions of this study have their own limitations. However, they too reflect the national scenario of gender in-equalities widely prevalent in the country.

Drastic changes are taking place under the influence of the media, expanding transport and communication facilities and education. But these changes are easily discernible in the urban educated sections of the Indian society. But rural India still groans under the gender bias. It is often lamented that it is better to be a tree in a forest than to be a girl child. Gender inequalities are widely prevalent in rural India in different dimensions as analysed above. The socio, cultural, religious, economical aspects of the Indian society need drastic changes to end the gender bias. Education particularly women education is powerfull instrument towards this direction. Sexual imbalances in the population which may lead to biological issues can be reduced by improving the status and dignity of the girl child in India. The governments both of the center and at states should come forward with different schemes to improve the conditions of the females in India. A social awareness that the girl child is not born only to get married with dowry offerings should be created. A re-vibrating India an India emerging as a global force should honour and appreciate the role of females who constitute half of the population.

REFERENCES

Malathi Ramanathan (2004), "Women and Empowerment: Shri Mahila Griha Udyog Lijjiat Papad", EPW, VOL XXXIX No. 17 and 24.

Sunita Kishor, Kamala Gupta (2004), "Women's Empowerment in India and in its States Evidences from the NFHS' EPW. VOL. XXXIX No.7, Feb.14.

Rehana Jhavvala, Shalini Sinha (2002), 'Liberalisation and the Women Workers', EPW, May 25-31, 2002.

25

Gender Issue in Watershed Programmes–A Study

K. Ramanuja Rao & Manduva Narasimha Rao

The Preamble of Indian Constitution refers to the guarantee of social justice. Right to equality has been preserved as a Fundamental Right under Chapter III of our Constitution, which also has a provision for optimistic action in favour of women. Despite these Constitutional provisions, special laws enacted to promote gender justice; the condition of women continues to be a cause of anxiety.

Though we moved to a new millennium, we have still doubts to pride ourselves a society where there is total gender equality. At the international level, for the first time, the United Nations Charter in the year 1945, discussed about the gender discrimination, which was later reiterated in the Universal Declaration of Human Rights of 1948. Since then, almost all human rights tools have reinforced and extended protections against discrimination of women. The International Covenant on Civil and Political Rights adopted in 1966 guarantees equal protection of the law to both the sexes. The International Covenant on Economic, Social and Cultural Rights also adopted in 1966 Promises women equality of status. The most significant conceptual move forward in the international law of women's rights is the *Convention on the Elimination of All Forms of Discrimination Against Women* (CEDAW), effect from 1981, provides that women be given equal rights on par with men. The Preamble of CEDAW maintains that "*the full and complete development of a country, the welfare of the world and the cause of peace require the maximum participation of women on equal terms with men in all fields.*" The *'Fourth World Conference on Women'*, held at Beijing in September 1995, the year of the fiftieth anniversary of the founding of the United Nations, reaffirming gender equality as a fundamental pre-requisite for social justice.

In this context, this paper tries to focus on the role of women in Indian agriculture with special emphasis on gender issue in watershed programme. Indian rural women are very much involved in agricultural and its allied activities. However, the nature and degree of their participation differs with the variations in agro production systems. The contribution of female in agricultural production varies with the landowning status of farm households and community too has its role. Their roles range from managers to landless labourers. In over all production, women's average input is estimated at 55 per cent to 66 per cent of the total labour, much higher in certain regions. It is amazing to note that in the Indian Himalayas a pair of bullocks works 1064 hours, a man 1212 hours and a woman 3485 hours in a year on a hectare farm, a figure that exemplifies women's significant contribution to agricultural production. (Shiva FAO, 1991).

Swaminathan, the famous agricultural scientist opined that, some historians believe that it was *'woman'* who first cultivated crop plants and thereby began the art and science of farming. While men went out for hunting in search of food, women started gathering seeds from the native flora and began cultivating for collection of food, fodder, fiber and fuel. Women have played and continue to play a significant role in the preservation of basic life support amenities such as water, land, flora and fauna. Therefore, without the total physical participation of women, it will not be possible to search for alternative systems of land management and shifting cultivation, arrest gene and soil erosion, plants and farm animals. (Prasad & Singh 1992). Women play a significant and crucial role in agricultural development and allied fields including main crop production, livestock production, horticulture, post harvest operations, agro/ social forestry, fisheries. It is a fact long taken for granted but also ignored. As above said, the nature and extent of women's involvement in agriculture, no doubt, varies greatly from region to region, community to community and social status. Even within a region, their contribution some times found different. But regardless of these variations, there is hardly any activity in agricultural production, except ploughing in which women are not actively involved. In some of the farm activities like processing and storage, women outnumbered men. (Aggarwal 2003) Studies on women in agriculture conducted in India and other developing and under developed countries are also arrived at the conclusion that women contribute to a great extent in agricultural production. Acknowledgment of their vital role in agriculture should not obscure the fact that farm women continue to be concerned with their primary role as wives, mothers and homemakers. Hence, women play multi-dimensional roles as here under.

MULTI-DIMENSIONAL ROLE OF WOMEN

(i) **In Agriculture:** Sowing, transplanting, weeding, irrigation, fertilizer application, plant protection, harvesting, winnowing, storing etc.

(ii) **In Domestic:** Cooking, child rearing, water collection, fire wood gathering, household maintenance etc.

(iii) **In Allied Activities:** Supervision of Cattle, fodder collection, milking, grazing etc.

Mainly the rural women are engaged in agricultural activities in three different ways depending on the socio-economic status of their family and regional factors.

(i) Paid Labourers

(ii) Working on their own lands

(ii) In agricultural production by way of labour supervision and the participation in post harvest operations.

Women are also actively participating in newly introduced watershed programmes.

Watershed is defined as a geo-hydrological entity or an area that drains at a common point on the drainage system. It is bounded by the ridge line, which starts from and closes at the same common draining point duly encircling the watershed area. It is a process to achieve sustainable development of natural resources like soil, water and vegetation. It also helps in understanding the relationship among soil, water and plants and linkages between uplands and downstream stress.

A watershed generally consists of three physical sectors:

(i) Non-arable land which includes forest land, grazing and barren land.

(ii) Arable or cultivated land, and cultivable waste.

(iii) Drainage area, comprising network of natural drainage lines and water bodies.

These three components are hydrologically intercepted and would have to be treated as one geo-hydrological entity for planning and implementation of watershed development programmes, in order to ensure optimal use of natural resources, higher production and socio-economic development on a sustainable basis.

By realizing the maxim "*better late, than never*" Government of India while designing guidelines for Watershed Programmes have provided significant platform for women to participate, involve and also to make decisions in Natural Resource Management. For the active participation of community, emphasis laid on involvement of women and weaker sections as far as possible in all the stages of the programmes. The representation of women in watershed committees made mandatory and employment in the project should be provided on priority to women and members of target groups. A provision is also made to the target groups and women groups (SHGs), financial assistance in the form of loan is ensured through revolving fund for economic activities. Thus, the watershed programme has become a pro-women scheme, where women are expected to benefit more than men. These are land and water conservation and recharging programmes which also deals with socio-economic aspects. The women are participating actively in watershed programmes because of its combination such as drinking water, fodder development, fire wood and rearing of livestock etc., As most of these sectors are manned by women, they are experiencing immediate results because of their participation and decision making in such programmes.

Not only government but also men have changed their mind set and slowly realizing the fact that women ought to be involved in every activity of watershed programme. We have conducted a field study very recently in five villages of Warangal district namely Shalapally of Dharmasagar Mandal, Goparajupally of Jangaon Mandal, Bonthagattu Nagaram of Narmeta Mandal Sripathipally of Ghanpur Mandal, Pochannapet of Bachannapet Mandal, where we found a positive sign of men for involvement of women in watershed programmes. We have interviewed 200 farmers by administering interview-schedule. To understand various factors which influence women participation, we have gathered the information on different parameters. Their opinions have been elicited and presented in the following tables.

Table 1
Opinion of the Respondents about the Need for Participation of Women in Watershed Programmes

Opinion about need for women participation	*Number of Respondents*	*Per cent*
Participation is required	125	62.5
Participation is not required	40	20.0
Did not express any opinion	35	17.5
Total	200	100.0

Source: Field data.

This table throws light on the women participation in the watershed programmes as women empowerment in all spheres of life is being focused by the government. Women participation is needed in not only political arena but also in economic spheres to bring gender equality and also to remove the gender discrimination. A modest attempt has been made in our study on the need for participation of women in watershed programmes and opinion of the male respondents has been presented in this table. It is happy to note that more than 62 per cent respondents, all of them are male, favoured that women should also participate in watershed programmes and further opined that there should not be gender inequality in the development activities under taken by the government or by any agency for that matter. 20 per cent of the respondents strongly opposed the women participation as most of them, probably, is orthodox in their nature. Further, caste also acting as barrier and hindrance for women participation in some cases. Another observation of the study is that nearly 18 per cent of the respondents did not come out openly to elicit their opinion on the need of women's participation. Anyway, this study has focused the need of the women participation in developmental activities including watershed programmes which is praise worthy one.

In order to get some more information about the extent of women participation in watershed programmes, we have collected the opinions of beneficiaries and presented their opinions in the table. The opinion has been classified into four categories. Such as; (i) involving fully, (ii) involving partially, (iii) involving satisfactorily and (iv) involving neutrally. This table denotes nearly 53 per cent of the beneficiaries opined that women should be fully involved in watershed programmes, another 15 per cent had an opinion that women participation should be in a limited way. On the other, 10 per cent of the respondents did not feel much happy about their participation. Another 46 respondents have not expressed their opinion. Surprisingly, only one respondent openly expressed his opinion that women should not involve in watershed programmes.

Table 2
Opinion of Respondents about level of Participation of Women in Watershed Programmes

Opinion of Respondent	*Male Respondents*	*Per cent*
Involving fully'	105	52.5
Involving partially	29	14.5
Involving satisfactorily	19	9.5
Involving neutrally	46	23.0
Not involving	1	0.5
Total	200	100.0

Source: Field data.

Table 3
Extent of Usefulness of Participation of Women in Watershed Programmes

Extent of usefulness of participation of women in Watershed Programmes	*Number of Respondents*	*Per cent*
To a great extent	47	23.5
To a large extent	25	12.5
To a moderate extent	83	41.5
To some extent	18	9.0
To negligible extent	27	13.5
Total	200	100.0

Source: Field data.

The extent of usefulness of the participation of women in watershed programmes is also gathered. Some questions were specially designed on women empowerment and participation level. Table discloses that 23.5 per cent of the respondents have opined that women participation in watershed programmes have helped them a lot. Out of 200 respondents, 83 said that their level of participation is only to a moderate. A minority i.e., 13.5 per cent respondents expressed that participation of women in these programmes did not fetch them much.

Table 4
Type of Family and Opinion about Women Participation

Type of Family	*About women participation*			*Total*
	Participation is required	*Participation is not required*	*Did not express any opinion*	
Joint Family	22 (28.20)	49 (62.8)	07 (8.97)	78 (100)
Nuclear Family	85 (69.67)	28 (22.95)	9 (7.37)	122 (100)
Total	107 (53.50)	77 (38.50)	16 (8.0)	200

Source: Field data.
Note: The figures in parenthesis indicate percentage.

In Indian social system women participation in social, economic and political activities is mostly depends on the type of family in which women live i.e., Joint Family or Nuclear Family. Particularly, in joint family system there will be close knit among various members of the family and head of the house. The role of the head of the house plays an important role in decision making process. There will be always less mobility of women labour in joint family system as the decision either to participate is mostly depends upon elder members' decision. However, in case of Nuclear family system some of the above observations may not be visible and decisions mostly taken either by husband or wife. Table denotes the opinion of the respondents about women participation. It is interesting to note that nearly 70 per cent of the respondents who are from nuclear family have strongly opined that women should actively participate in all activities including watershed programmes, whereas in the joint family system we could observe only about 29 per cent favoured women participation. In other words, nearly 63 per cent of the respondents living in joint family system did not prefer women participation in watershed programmes. Another exciting observation is that the per centage of respondents who did not express any opinion is almost same both in joint and nuclear family types i.e., seven and nine respondents in our sample. Thus, it has been proved right that the orthodox nature of joint family system is still dominating.

Table 5
Annual Income and Opinion about Women Participation

About women participation	*Annual Income*				*Total*
	Rs. 15,000/-	*>15,000 to 20,000*	*>20,000 to 25,000*	*Above 25,000/-*	
Participation is required	28 (22.4)	51 (40.8)	30 (24.0)	16 (12.8)	125 (100)
Participation is not required	11 (27.5)	17 (42.5)	3 (7.5)	9 (22.5)	40 (100.0)
Did not express any opinion	3 (8.6)	14 (40.0)	11 (31.4)	7 (20.0)	35 (100.0)
Total	42 (21.0)	82 (41.0)	44 (22.0)	32 (16.0)	200 (100.0)

Source: Field data.
Note: The figures in parenthesis indicate percentage.

As it has already been mentioned earlier that due to the development of watershed programme in drought prone and rain fed areas both male and female participation is visible. It is hypothesized that women participation is found to be different depending upon the economic status. Hence, we have collected the opinion of the beneficiaries on women participation based on their annual income. Table denotes that women participation is necessary at the various stages of watershed programmes and surprisingly we could see out of 200, forty members i.e., 20 per cent opposed the women participation. In fact 35 members did not express any opinion which also indirectly supporting the argument of the 20 per cent who opposed the women participation.

Out of 125 respondents who supported the women participation nearly 63 per cent were earning annual income to the extent of Rs. 20,000/- and another 24 per cent up to Rs. 25,000/-. We could also observe more than 12 per cent of the respondents were earning annual income above Rs. 25,000/-. Similar trend is observed when we enquired about respondents' annual income who opposed women participation. In the sense, out of 40 respondents, nearly seven respondents had their annual income up to Rs. 20,000/-. Another interesting observation is that more than 22 per cent respondents who opposed women participation in watershed programmes are earning more than Rs. 25,000/-. It means, a large number of respondents whose annual income is in the range of above 15,000/ -and 20,000/- have expressed positive opinion as well as negative opinion about women participation in watershed programmes. The above table also reflects that a large number of respondents who are earning more than Rs. 25,000/- annual income did not prefer women participation. One important point worth to be mentioned here that when annual income of respondents is taken, it does not include only their agricultural income but also income earned from other sources such as through traditional occupations, business, etc., Therefore, the study suggests that a large number of middle income group respondents have favoured women participation whereas higher income group did not like it. One of the strongest reasons might be that most of the higher income people may belong to higher caste and the social customs and traditions did not encourage women to participate in the watershed programmes along with their male counter parts.

Table 6
Marital Status and Women Participation

Marital Status	*About women participation*			*Total*
	Participation is required	*Participation is not required*	*Did not express any opinion*	
Married	89 (62.2)	31 (21.7)	23 (16.1)	143 (100)
Never married	2 (18.2)	0 (.0)	9 (81.8)	11 (100)
Divorcee	8 (20.5)	31 (79.5)	0 (.0)	39 (100)
Widow	1 (14.3)	3 (42.9)	3 (42.9)	7 (100)
Total	125 (62.5)	40 (20)	35 (17.5)	200 (100)

Source: Field data.
Note: The figures in parenthesis indicate percentage.

Having come to know that a large number of respondents preferred women participation in watershed programmes, we have collected the opinion of the respondents to find out whether participation is required or not in case of women married, never married, divorcee and widow. Table shows that out of 200 respondents 143 respondents have expressed their opinion whether married women can participate in these programmes. Out of which 62 per cent suggested that married women can participate in watershed programmes and 21 per cent did not support this view. Another 16 per cent respondents did not express any opinion. It means, a large number of respondents opined that married women can participate in various stages of watershed programmes. But on the other, 31 respondents strongly objected the divorce women in participation in any activities including watershed programmes and it is purely social compulsion prevailing in rural areas even in to day. Most of the divorce women are in pitiful condition as they are not earning even subsistence income for the maintenance of their livelihood and due to the declining of the joint family system, as our study also reveals, most of the divorced women's socio-economic conditions are deplorable. The same tendency we could observe in case of widow women. Therefore, most of the respondents preferred only married women's participation in watershed programmes and objected the participation of women who are never married, divorcee and widow in any social activity and watershed programmes. This might be due to illiteracy, ignorance and social customs that are still prevailing in rural areas.

Table 7
Community wise Opinion about Women Participation

Community	*About women participation*			*Total*
	Participation is required	*Participation is not required*	*Neutral*	
Other Caste	25 (100.0)	0 (.0)	0 (.0)	25 (100.0)
Backward Caste	49 (55.7)	24 (27.3)	15 (17.0)	88 (100.0)
Scheduled Caste	14 (45.2)	6 (19.4)	11 (35.5)	31 (100.0)
Scheduled Tribe	37 (66.1)	10 (17.9)	9 (16.1)	56 (100.0)
Total	125 (62.5)	40 (20.0)	35 (17.5)	200 (100.0)

Source: Field data.
Note: The figures in parenthesis indicate percentage

However, the above opinion may not be same among all caste groups as it is usually hypothesized that the response from forward and backward castes would be quite different to that of scheduled castes and tribes. In order to test the above notion, we have collected the data and presented in the table. It shows that all the forward caste respondents strongly opined that women irrespective of their socio-economic status should actively participate in the programmes. And surprisingly, after forward castes, we could see percentage wise, scheduled tribes respondents opined the same opinion and occupied second position followed by backward class and scheduled class. The reasons to get such response from forward castes are that most of their lands are near to watershed areas and closely observe the benefits of such programmes. Further, most of the forward caste women do not have subsidiary occupations compare to that of other community women and excessively depend only on agriculture. In the case of scheduled tribe women also, most of them preferring to work in agriculture related activities including watershed programmes and did not choose other subsidiary occupations unlike other community women. In fact, they are not only hard working but also accustomed to expose to rough whether. Compare to other women, scheduled tribe women have strong physique due to which they are preferred mostly in constructional activities. On the other, we could see out of 88 backward class respondents, only 55 per cent of respondents preferred women participation and assumed that women as well can participate in their traditional occupations instead of excessively depend upon agriculture or watershed programmes. In case of respondents belonging to scheduled castes, out of 31 only 14 respondents i.e., 45 per cent favoured women participation and 35 per cent did not react to the statement. Hence, the study suggests that different caste people opined differently due to their different socio-economic and cultural background on women participation.

Intra village wise opinion of the respondents on the women participation in Watershed programmes has been gathered and presented in the table. In altogether the opinion was gathered from the five villages representing five mandals in Warangal District. The villages are Pochannapeta, Sripathipally, Goparajupally, Shalapally and Bonthagattu Nagaram. Out of 200 respondents, 125 respondents in the selected villages have expressed their opinion that participation of women is required at different stages of watershed programmes. Particularly, large number of respondents ie., more than 62 per cent living in nuclear family preferred this opinion. In fact once we move from Pochannapeta to Shalapally, Shalapally to Sripathipally, Sripathipally to Goparajupally and Goparajupally to Bonthagattu Nagaram response on the participation of women in the nuclear family is found to be 86.2 per cent, 71 per cent, 61.9 per cent, 44.4 per cent and 38.5 per cent respectively. In other words large number of respondents in Pochannapeta preferred women participation in watershed programmes. On the other more than 60 per cent farmers of joint family living in Bonthagattu Nagaram agreed with this opinion.

Table 8
Village and Family Type wise Opinion on Women Participaiton

About women Participation	*Name of the village*	*Type of family*		*Total*
		Joint family	*Nuclear family*	
Participation is required	Pochannapeta	4 (13.8)	24 (86.2)	29 (100.0)
	Shalapally	9 (29.0)	22 (71.0)	31 (100.0)
	Sripathipally	8 (38.1)	13 (61.9)	21 (100.)
	Goparajupally	10 (55.6)	8 (44.4)	18 (100.0)
	Bonthagattunagaram	16 (61.5)	10 (38.5)	26 (100.0)
	Total	47 (37.6)	78 (62.4)	125 (100.0)
Participation is not required	Pochannapeta	4 (80.0)	1 (20.0)	5 (100.0)
	Shalappally	6 (85.7)	1 (14.3)	7 (100.0)
	Sripathipally	0(.0)	7 (100.0)	7(100.0)
	Goparajupally	10 (71.4)	4 (28.6)	14 (100.0)
	Bonthagattunagaram	5 (71.4)	2 (28.6)	7 (100.0)
	Total	25 (62.5)	15 (37.5)	40 (100.0)
Did not express any opinion	Pochannapeta	6 (100.0)	0 (.0)	6 (100.0)
	Shalapally	0 (.0)	2 (100.0)	2 (100.0)
	Sripathipally	9 (75.0)	3 (25.0)	12 (100.0)
	Goparajupally	6 (75.0)	2 (25.0)	8 (100.0)
	Bonthagattunagaram	7 (100.0)	0 (.0)	7 (100.0)
	Total	28 (80.0)	7 (20.0)	35 (100.0)

Source: Field data.
Note: The figures in parenthesis indicate percentage.

When we look at the views of the respondents who are not in favour of women participation in watershed programmes, all these respondents i.e., 62.5 per cent who are reluctant for women participation belong to joint family. Particularly in Shalapally and Pochannapeta villages, the respondents from joint family have opposed women participation. It means, the family members who are living in nuclear families in the villages of Shalapally and Pochannapeta have preferred women participation in watershed programmes whereas joint family members were unwilling for women participation. Thus, the responses of women participation differ from village to village and irrespective of their socio-economic back ground and also family type. In other words, it is not same in all the study villages.

CONCLUSIONS

Regularly we come across the buzzwords like women *empowerment, emancipation and gender equality* mostly in almost all government welfare programmes and in seminars, workshops and symposia from academic side. However, a woman is considered as not only the first teacher of a child but also the first agriculturist, age old patriarchal society did not allow women to come out of four walls to articulate and participate in developmental programmes. But, this was prevailed in the past. With the fast growing social needs, advancement of technology along with rapid industrialization and urbanization women are now provided opportunities everywhere. Under Liberalization policy and in the era of privatization and globalization, the role of women is being changed. These latest changes made women to grab the job market, proved better in some areas by acquiring, and attained through their merit, perseverance and decision-making. Still women are neglected and are not given proper recognition in the developmental programmes like watershed etc.,

REFERENCES

Shah, Amita (1998), *Watershed Development Programmes: Emerging Environment Pespectives.* Economic and Political Weekly, Vol. XXVIII, No. 26: A66-80.

Reddy, C. Bakka and A. Ravinder (2004), *Watershed development programmes; understanding the impacts.* WASSAN, Hyderabad and A.P. Water Conservation Mission.

Central Research Institute for Dryland Agriculture, Hyderabad. Field Manual on Watershed Management. 1995, Hyderabad.

Crispino Lobo, *Rain decided to help us*. Economic Development Institute of the World Bank and Social Centre, 1995. Pimpalgaonwagha, Maharashtra.

Ed. Setty, *Janmabhoomi-Rural Development*. Dr. M.C.R. Human Resources Development Institute of Andhra Pradesh, Hyderabad, 2000.

Gupta, Tirath and Mohan Deepinder (1982), *Technology Options and Economic Policy for Dry land Agriculture: Potential and Challenges*. Concept Publishing House, New Delhi.

National Institute of Rural Development, Hyderabad. *Journal of Rural Development*. Volume 17, No. 3, July-Sept. 1998. P. 465.

R.C. Chowdary, O.N. Srivastava, *Field Manual on Planning and Management of Watershed Projects*, 2002 National Institute of Rural Develoment, Hyderabad.

R.S. Deshpande, A. Narayanamoorhty, *Artha Vignana*. December, 1999. Journal of Gokhale Institute of Politic & Economic. P. 384.

Shiva Vandana & Gitanjali Bedi (2002), Globalization of Agriculture, Food Security and Sustainability in Sustainable Agriculture and Food Security Sage Publications, New Delhi.

Shiva Vandana & Ritu Singh (2003) Biopiracy of Indian Wheat Navdanya/ RFSTE, New Delhi.

Shiva Vandana, Afsar Jafri, Ashok Emani, Seeds of Suicide, The Ecological and Human Costs and Manish Pande, 2002 of Globalisation of Agriculture, RFSTE, New Delhi.

Shiva Vandana and Kunwar Jalees (2004),Farmerís Suicide in Indiaî RFSTE, New Delhi.

Shiva Vandana, Radha Holla Bhar, Corporate Hijack of Food How World Bank and Afsar H. Jafri and Kunwar Jalees, 2003 WTO are pushing The Poor To Starvation, RFSTE, New Delhi.

Shiva Vandana, Afsar H. Jafri and Kunwar Jalees (2003), The Mirage of Market Access: How Globalization is Destroying Farmers Lives and Livelihood, Navdanya/RFSTE, New Delhi.

Shiva Vandana (2001), The Violence of Green Revolution, The Other India Press (Goa) and RFSTE, New Delhi.

26

Working Women in the Organised Industrial Sector

C. Swarajyalakshmi

"Woman is the companion of man, gifted with equal mental capacities. She has the right to participate in minutest details of the activities of man, and she has the same right of freedom and liberty as he. She is entitled to a supreme place in her own sphere of activity as man is in his. Man and woman are equal in status, but are not identical. They are a peerless pair being complementary to one another; each helps the other, so that without the one, the existence of the other cannot be conceived, and, therefore, it follows as a necessary corollary from these facts that anything that will impair the status of either of them will involve the equal ruin of both."

— **M.K. Gandhi (1918)**

WOMEN IN INDUSTRIES

Since times immemorial, women have constituted an effective part of the working force in India. They worked along with the male members of the household in sowing seeds, weeding, transplanting, watering the fields, harvesting the crops, tending cattle, poultry, and also helping in family enterprises such as beedi-making, rope-making, pottery, etc. They do all this in addition to their normal domestic work as house wife and thus women always played a dual role in the society.

In the earlier stages, only male workers predominated in the working force in the factories. But, now women workers have increasingly taken into industrial work both skilled and semiskilled. Formerly, they were mostly confined to plantation and the textile industry. Now young girls from middle class families are working in factories in increasing numbers.

ORGANISED SECTOR

The organised sector is characterised by the modern relations of production and is regulated and governed by laws that are meant to protect the security and working conditions of workers and also supported by the labour organisations that can look after their interests.

WORKING WOMEN

Working women are those women who are earning full or part of their livelihood by engaging themselves in any occupation or work for pay or profit.

Women begun to work with different motives. The mechanisation of household work leaves ample time to women for out-door remunerative work. Moreover, the changes in industrial and technological processes have resulted in a marked increase in the range of occupations open to women. Apart from the desire to escape from monotony and dullness of home life, the economic conditions drive quite a number of women into employment.

WHY WOMEN WORK?

A very careful, well thought out and planned effort in connection with her work and at her home including paying attention and catering to all the needs of her husband and children, and attending to all the details of the job outside her home are essential, if she wants to be a successful wife, mother and worker. Women are accepting jobs and are continuing in their jobs purely on account of economic compulsions; just to while away their time and to build up their careers; to have an independent source of income and to be aloof from tensions, conflicts and unpleasant atmosphere of home; to have a proper utilisation of their spare time, knowledge, skills, experience and professional and academic qualifications; to get some relief from routine and drudgery of the domestic work; habituated to work and cannot keep quite; working just to while away time after marriage. The causes behind the employment of working women are-to help themselves, their respective families, serve the society and make good use of knowledge they gained for economically and otherwise gainful purposes.

Working women are subjected to all sorts of humiliation, ill-treatment, harassment, injustice, victimisation discrimination and are not treated on par with men in several matters like pay and allowances, working conditions, incentive wage payments, professional growth, etc., by their employers, in spite of all the tall talk we are hearing day-in and day-out about the women's liberation movement and salvation of women from exploitation and perpetration of injustice on them by men. It is a fact that women are always looked down as weaker sections even tough they invest same energies and efforts etc., in their work along with their men-folk. The result is that they are very often paid lesser wages than men. The slogan of 'Equal Pay for Equal Work' remains a slogan only and not practiced still on a wider scale in several parts of the world. Apart from this injustice and humiliation, etc. women workers are very often looked down by their fellow men workers with suspicion, jealousy, misunderstandings and envy at several places. Apart from this, they have to live and work under great stress and strain, tensions, conflicts and perpetual agony. They have to subdue their interests and future well being according to the wishes, whims and fancies and dictates from their parents, husbands, colleagues, bosses and some times even their own family members and members in the society. Women workers are the worst victims of the traditional, social conflicts, taboos, beliefs and all sorts of conservative notions and thinking. This is particularly so in the case of women employed in industrial sector.

In this paper an attempt has been made to discuss the various problems of the women workers working in the organised industrial sector. The problems of working women are in fact multifarious and of a multi-dimensional nature.

EMPLOYMENT OF WOMEN

Other things being equal, there is still discrimination. Women are not accepted in higher posts unless they are atleast 20 per cent superior to men in qualifications and experience. Therefore, women are not recruited to the higher posts for they are considered incompetent.

RESERVATION OF CERTAIN CATEGORIES OF JOBS FOR WOMEN

Employers had a policy of reserving certain categories/light works and types of jobs for women in some organisations. The reasons for the reservations are women are not fit for heavy work because of their weak physique, women workers do not like manual work, and women workers always like lighter jobs and more leisure.

PAYMENT OF REMUNERATION

The wages of women generally lag behind as compared to their male counter parts. The net wage earnings of women are less than those of men even if the wage rates are the same. The law forcing the employers to given maternity and other benefits, which raise their labour cost, is one of the reason for the discrimination of wages between men and women.

PROMOTIONS

Domestic commitments will lead women to reject or not seek or not be offered promotion than the case or men.

TRANSFERS

Most of the women are not accepting promotions due to the fear of transfers. A working women may be a wife, a mother and an employee in the organisation. Frequent transfers will create more problems to her. If he goes away to some other place on transfer, the husband, children etc. will suffer due to lack of proper caretakers. Most of the working women are not accepting transfers thereby, in most of the cases transfers are standing in the way of professional growth or promotion and sometimes leads to the resignation of the job.

TRAINING

The Indian women has for long been, by and large wedded to tradition and has generally confined herself to household chores. Nevertheless, women have, played a vital role in our industrial growth and overall socio-economic development. In the wake of rapid industrialisation, the development of educational and training facilities for women have also assumed greater importance. Due to economic stress and strains, an increasing number of women out of necessity, become active participants in the labour force. In order to meet their aspirations of the youth as well as to meet the fast changing skill needs of industry, training programmes are necessary. These programmes were not properly arranged for women.

WELFARE PROGRAMMES FOR WOMEN

Most of the Acts make special provision regarding health and safety of women workers and promote their welfare. In most of the organisations working women have reported that there are no facilities for storing and drying clothes, no shelters, rest rooms & lunch rooms, no creches, no separate canteen facilities, no spittoons provided, no washing facilities, first-aid-appliances are not available, no separate toilets for women and no resting facilities for women. There are no separate welfare officers and medical officers appointed in the organisations. Sickness benefits under Employee State Insurance Scheme are not extended to them. Also Disablement benefit, maternity benefit, medical benefit, aid for cremation expenses, recreation and cultural activities etc. are not extended to the working women.

PROBLEMS WITH REGARD TO LEAVE AND HOLIDAYS HOURS OF WORK ETC.

The statutory obligation in respect of hours of work is not properly fulfilled in many of the industries, women workers are experiencing lots of problems. Maternity leave facility is not extended in many cases.

CONFLICT BETWEEN DOMESTIC AND OFFICIALS DUTIES

Women's job have been affected due to problems of care of youngsters and difficulty in management of home and they are overburdened with both at home and job.

Carrying out almost single-handedly all the duties and responsibilities of home overstrains a working- women and makes her tried and irritable which in turn is liable to make her an unpleasant and un-enjoyable company for her husband and children. Most of the working women were experiencing substantial difficulty in carrying out their household duties and the duties of this 'wife role' adequately including- the care and attention given to the husband along- with their jobs. Most of the working women are ignoring their domestic responsibilities on account of taking up a job, not-able to find adequate leisure in their domestic life, getting to much tired, irritated indifferent etc. in their domestic life, they were not extended any help, sympathy, co-operation etc. in their domestic life, there is criticism from the members of the family on account of their spending comparatively lesser time with them. Therefore working women undergo a constant struggle to look after the office duties and keep a happy home.

SHARING OF EARNING

Most of the working women divert their earning to meet the domestic expenditure. Some utilised their earning to purchase labour saving household devices, few others reserve them for giving dowry, purchase of jewellery, buying costly dresses and cosmetics. Most of the working women does not have surplus balance to save and invest in the purchase of property.

Working-women were not allowed to sped even their own earnings the way they felt like spending, but have to hand over their pay to their parents or husbands or in-laws. Whenever she assert her right over her earnings they were invariably involved in friction, and bickerings with their husbands and other family members.

TRANSPORT

Lack of transportation or conveyance facilities and accommodation facilities to the employees by their employers involve the working-women in several problems.

JOB ENVIRONMENT

Working-women sometimes do not like their jobs due to the environmental problems like no proper prospects of promotion, too much of work, they are not paid adequate remuneration, there is too much of bossism, ill-treatment by bosses, unhealthy atmosphere, not congenial for good health, and there is discrimination against women in the matter of providing amenities by the management for women workers.

OTHER PROBLEMS

The attitude of the boss, treatment by superiors, relation with male colleagues, relations with female colleagues and problems from neighbours, non-working women, treatment of working women by husbands, attitude of other family members, housing problems, delay in returning from company, recreational and cultural activities, marriage, economic problems, child rearing, difference in temperament, problem of sex, problems of separation, participation in union etc. are some of the other problems experienced by women workers.

PROBLEM FROM THE VIEW POINT OF THE MANAGEMENT

Employer's prejudice against the working women or against women employed in and carrying out "male professions" or "male occupations" was also found to be a hindrance in their way to progress officially or non-officially and in achieving an equally high official status as that of men.

The gate keepers of the professional world view these women with amusement, suspicion and hostility even when they are well-qualified for entering into the professions or jobs. Some private firms had stopped recruiting women for training as mangers, because they money invested did not payoff. Some of the factories had stopped employing women because most of the intelligent young and small girls, get married and leave the job.

Some of the complaints the managements have against the working women are;

They are jealous of each other, they are incapable of facing tension and strains of executive decision-making, they occupy posts which in a country with so much of unemployment rightfully belong to men, they work for fun and they do not really need their jobs, with the growth of education the concept of wife and mother has changes but that of husband and father remains unchanged which must be changed, more and more women are looking at marriage as a means to develop their personalities.

SUGGESTIONS

A number of suggestions are given below to overcome the various problems that working women are facing in the organised industrial sector.

The employer should come forward readily to employ women in larger numbers.

Employers of the industrial and business units in the organised sector should adopt a more liberal policy in the matter of employing women in as many categories of jobs as possible.

The employers should give a serious thought in the matter of equal remuneration for equal work and wipe out the discrimination in the matter of payment of remuneration to women. The principle of equal remuneration for equal work should be rigidly followed.

The policy of discrimination in the matter of assignment of tasks to women workers should be avoided forthwith.

It is suggested that whenever an opportunity arises for promotion of any employee in the organisation, women should also be considered equally along with men and under any circumstances, no impression should be created that they are discrimL1lated against men in this matter. For this purpose there should be more enlightened managements who can understand the aspirations and ambitions of women in their right perspective in the matter of building up careers and professional growth.

The working women employed in the organised sector may be deputed to some training programmes to acquire fresh skills, knowledge, experience and understanding with the help of which they can take up better job and strive their best for further professional growth.

Incentive wage payment schemes such as, productivity linked bonus or exgratia payments schemes should be evolved for the benefit of working women. This will have its own impact on the efficiency, productivity and levels of performance of the working women.

The working women are to be provided with separate toilets, separate spittoons, separate drinking water facilities, washing facilities, facilities for storing and drying their clothes, facilities for sitting, separate canteen, shelters, rest rooms and lunch rooms, creches for the benefit of the children of the women workers, a separate welfare officer, extend sickness benefits, benefits prescribed under the maternity benefit act of 1961, disablement benefit, funeral benefit, superannuation benefits like pension, provident fund, gratuity, employee benefit fund. Recreational and cultural activities should be arranged to the women workers.

The women workers employed in the industrial units should work for not more than 48 hrs in a week, they should be allowed atleast one day as a holiday in every week, intervals for rest for all the women workers in the industrial units should be fixed and they should not work on the night shifts.

The family members should understand the problems of working women with more sympathy and should try not to rub them on the wrong shoulders, but give a patient hearing to their problems and extend their wholehearted cooperation in making their life happy, contented and fruitful. They should be allowed to set apart a reasonable portion of their earnings to save and invest on which they can fall back upon in times of crisis, contingencies, emergency etc.

Company should make suitable arrangements of transport for their women workers along with other workers and if possible exclusively for women.

The managements and employees of the industrial units can jointly organise some cultural and recreational activities on Sunday and other holidays and induce the working women to participate in these activities.

CONCLUSION

Any number of suggestions can be given in this direction but what is required at the moment is a wholehearted implementation of these various suggestions can be given in this direction but what is required at the moment is a wholehearted implementation of these various suggestions by all concerned people, let them be their officials, husbands, family members, neighbours, male and female colleagues etc. The problems of working women are interwoven with a number of intricate socio-economic and cultural problems in a country, apart from the traditional set up, the habits, the conventions, the philosophy of life and the approaches to various problems facing in a society. Hence, the problems of working women are of a multi-dimensional character. It is only a multipronged attack on the problems that can help the working women to come out of the several ;ills, woes from which the working women are suffering. The UNO has also celebrated with all the fanfare at its command throughout the world an International Women's Year and also dedicated an entire decade (1975-1985) for the promotion of welfare and prosperity of women and recognising their status in society. Alas! the working women in many parts of the world are still the worst sufferers. In a developing economy like that of India, the role that is assigned to women is a far from satisfactory. Women are not treated on par with men in several spheres of activities. It is time they would be given their due share, put a stop to their exploitation, wipe out all traces of injustice, discrimination, harassment, humiliation and insults etc. Every conceivable effort has be made to treat them on par with men and strive our best for all their overall prosperity and happiness. Workers are the backbone and nerve centre of all activity in any industry. The plight of the women workers should not be lost sight of under any circumstances.

REFERENCES

Boserup Ester (1970), Womens Role in Economic Development, St.Martin's Press, New York.

Desai, Neera (1957), Women in Modern India, Vora and Company Publishers Private Ltd., Bombay.

Ghosh, S.K. (1984), Women in a Changing Society, Ashish Publishing House, New Delhi.

Kathryn M. Borman, Women in the Work place Effects on Families. Ablex Publishing Corporation, Norwood, New Jersey.

Marilyn J. Davidson (1984), Working Women-An International Survey, John Wiley Publications, New York.

Zaheeruddin (1987), Labour Welfare Laws and Employment Conditions in India, International Book House, Delhi.

Swarajyalaksmi, C. (1992), Women at Work Insights from Indian Organisations, Discovery Publishing House, New Delhi.

27

Role of Micro Finance & Changing Socio–Economic Conditions of Women

K. Harathi

> *"Indeed, the test of orderliness in a country is not the number of millionaires it owns, but the absence of starvation among its masses."*
>
> —**Mahatma Gandhi**

Women constitute half the world's population and make up one-third of the labour force. In India, although literacy levels have registered an increase, majority of women are still illiterate, without any access to property and credit.

Banks realised that women need not only a wide spectrum of financial services, but also adequate and timely access to them. Women tend to be much more prompt in repayment of loans as compared to men. Hence, they desperately require support and help, particularly in the form of credit to enable them to set up income generating projects, which will enable them to make a living on a sustainable basis.

The Banking Division of the Ministry of Finance in consultation with the Reserve Bank of India (RBI) and other institutions ascertained the problems faced by women entrepreneurs in order to help overcome the hurdles being faced by them in access to bank credit and credit plus services.

As Kofi Annan, Secretary General of the United Nations, rightly put it: "When the poorest, especially woman receive credit, they become economic actors with power. Power to improve not only their own lives, but in a widening circle to impact the lives of their families, their communities and their nations." Several steps have been initiated at the Indian Government and other banking institutional levels for strengthening women entrepreneurial capabilities, skill training and making available counselling and consultancy services so as to help them to settle in income generating activities. If this is implemented well, women's empowerment would soon become a reality leading to gender parity in a few years.

Hence, the proposed paper is mainly focused to examine the role of Micro finance through various Central Government sponsored poverty alleviation and self–employment schemes in the reduction of women's poverty. It is also to study the changing socio-economic conditions of women. Therefore, the study aims to analyse the impact of the Micro finance on the women especially in the empowerment process in Khammam District of Andhra Pradesh.

In the era of globalisation, micro finance has become an important player in poverty alleviation and empowerment of women in the developing world. Micro Finance includes small credit programmes ranging from Rs. 2000 to Rs. 5000.

NEED FOR THE PROGRAM

Research suggests that equity and efficiency argument for targeting credit to women remain powerful: the whole family is more likely to benefit from credit targeting to women, where they control income, than when it is targeted to men.

METHODOLOGY

The present study being secondary data based, it exclusively depended on the DRDA & Velugu reports of Khammam Dist, from 2003–4 March to 2005 July.

DATA COVERAGE

The information required for the purpose collected directly from DRDA, Khammam & different successful stories of women from Velugu and APMAS magazines and news papers.

PROFILE

State: Andhra Pradesh

Population 2001 census

(a) Males	:	3,82,86,811
(b) Female	:	3,74,40,730
Total	:	7,57,27,541
Sex Ratio	:	1000 : 978
Growth Ratio	:	13.86%
Literacy		
Male	:	2,38,36,077 70.85%
Female	:	1,67,28,688 51.17%
Total	:	4,03,04,765 61.11%
Rural & Urban Population		
Rural Population	:	5,52,23,944 (72.92%)
Urban Population	:	2,05,03,594 (27.08%)
District: Khammam		
Area in Sq KM	:	16029
No. of Mandals	:	46
No. of Villages	:	1095
No. of Towns	:	10
Population	:	25,65,412
Density	:	160
Literacy % 7 years and above		57.72

Andhra Pradesh, the fifth largest state in India with a population of 7,57,27,541 Corers. Over an area of 2.75 lakh Sq. Kms. Andhra Pradesh state consists of three natural sub divisions namely: the developed Costal Andhra region with 9 Districts, the developing Telangana region with 10 Districts and the Rayalaseema with 4 Districts. Telangana region was identified by the World Bank as 'drought prone area' and agency area in 1976 and has been receiving Government attention and assistance under various employment generating and rural development programs.

Khammam District in AP over an area of 16,029 Sq. Kms., with a population of 25,65,412. According to 2001 census there are 978 women per every 1000 men in Andhra Pradesh. Their share being 49.50% in AP. The working population constitutes about 36% in AP. A major working women are employed in the unorganised sector. This indicates deprivation of women in employment.

At present Government of Andhra Pradesh is implementing two programmes:

1. DWCRA
2. VELUGU

The supporting agency for both is DRDA. Both programmes are supporting self help groups in Andhra Pradesh.

SHGS

SHGS are micro enterprises. They are increasingly and gainfully run by rural women for their empowerment. Theses are in fact have reinforced the Gandhiji concept of "Production by the mass". These programmes are supported by UNICEF, Central and state Governments with 50% matching fund.

Its features: Identification and classification of rural poor women into self–help groups with 10–15 members. Government sanctions Rs. 25000 revolving fund to each group. Each group should save Rs. 90 per month. Members should have annual income of Rs. 11,000. Government will create bank linkage to SHGS. All groups should repay savings, revolving fund and bank loan. SHGS should invest on quick income generating activities. Qualitative and quantitative production is must. These activities should remove economic exploitation.

DWCRA

Development of women and children in rural areas (DWCRA) implemented in the year 1980. For the first time this programme was implemented in 500 Districts in India. In the second phase in the year 1993–94 the programme encouraged self help groups (SHGS) and employment oriented development strategy.

VELUGU (SHGS) IN AP

SAARC meeting at Colombo in 1991 & in 1993 at Dhaka declaration for eradication of poverty by the year 2002 which urged for the empowerment approach to poverty elevation in which the poor are give support to develop and fully utilise there productive capacities.

AP District poverty initiative project (DPIP) commenced in AP in June 2000 is now operational in 6 of the most backward Districts of AP. AP government established an independent support organisation by the name of Society for Elimination of Rural Poverty (SERP). The objective of scheme is to bring assistance by providing income-generating assets through a mix of Bank credit and Government subsidy for self help groups (SGHS).

At present Government of AP is implementing Indira Kranthi Padhakam (IKP).

INDIRA KRANTHI PADHAKAM (IKP)

In the year 2004–05 Government of AP merged both DWCRA & VELUGU programmes and implementing as *INDIRA KRANTHI PADHAKAM (IKP)* through DRDA.

MICRO CREDIT, FEMINISATION OF POVERTY AND WOMEN'S EMPOWERMENT:

The Society for Alleviation of Poverty in Andhra Pradesh (SAPAP) felt that poverty is feminised. Micro credit is the panacea for poverty reduction and women's empowerment. The development agencies should focus on the inter linkage between gender, women and poverty. Policy makers and planners of other poverty reduction programmes should focus on micro credit, social capital, poverty reduction and women's empowerment.

In June 2002 the project started in 16 Districts in 500 mandals. Now total 860 mandals in the state are in Velugu project. The meaning of Telugu word 'VELUGU' is focus or light. It aims to provide minimum facilities and requirements to every family by the year 2020.

IMPLEMENTATION OF SHGS (DWCRA & VELUGU) THROUGH DRDA IN KHAMMAM DISTRICT:

The SHGS are assisted by the following schemes:

1. Integrated Rural Development Programme (IRDP)
2. Swarna Grama Swarajya Yojana (SGSY)
3. State revolving fund
4. SHG Bank linkage

MICRO FINANCE

The SHGS of 22 mandals have accessed bank linkage to a tune of Rs.3010.55 lakhs till 2003–04 for Velugu (DRDA) programme. Micro credit plans were prepared by the each SHGS to convince the banker for a higher amount of loan justifying the need of every member of SHG.

The Government of India conducted two days conference on Micro finance at New Delhi in the month of April 2005. The Conference stressed the role of NABARD regarding the Micro finance and Women empowerment.

The following Banks links the SHGS:

1. Commercial Banks - 48
2. Regional Rural Banks -196
3. Co-operative Banks -316

Total -560

SHG BANK LINKAGE

Previous achievements up to 2004 – 2005

(Rs. In lakhs)

Financial Year	Physical Groups	Finance
2001 – 02	16,147	917.07
2002 – 03	10,563	2127.73
2003 – 04	17,436	3342.43
2004 – 05	17,035	4181.92

Source: DRDA Khammam (reports enclosed).

At present there are nearly 33,000 SHGS are functioning in the District. Bank linkage up to 31/07/05 was Rs. 947.50 Lakhs for 5,541 groups.

The above table revels the fact that there is an increasing trend in the bank linkage (micro finance) in Khammam District. Micro credit increased by 4.56 times. In the year 2001-02 the finance was Rs. 917.07 lakhs, it raised to Rs. 4181.92 lakhs in the year 2004-05.

The Bank Linkage used for the following Activities:

1. Paper glass, cups making 2. Flour mills 3. Poultry 4. Pottery 5. Iron shop's 6. Carpentry 7. Banian making 8. Tailoring 9. Mat knitting 10. Cross cultivation 11. Fish stall 12. Fruit juice stall

13. Vegetable shop 14. Bangle shop 15. Provision shop 16. Procurement of forest products 17. Leaf plates 18. Jute bags 19. Wormy compost 20. Fancy goods 21. Chappal making 22. Cattle taming 23. Hotel 24. Cycle shop's 25. Printing press 26. Cotton mattress 27. Lace knitting 28. Pickles 29. Spices packing 30. Papad making 31. Plant nursery 32. Paper covers 33. Lambada embroidery 34. Cement bricks 35. Wire baskets 36. Dairy farm 37. Selling steel goods 38. Saree business 39. Plastic flowers 40. Vegetable cultivation 41. Old iron buying 42. Fruit stall 43. Food processing 44. Pop corn 45. Potato chips 46. Bakery items 47. Bamboo baskets 48. Soft toys 49. Saree rolling 50. Candle making .

IMPACT OF MICRO FINANCE (BANK LINKAGE)

Total SHGS A/c are 31,277 with a total bank linkage of Rs. 4181.92 lakhs for 17,035 groups up to March 2005. On the basis of the above data (DRDA), successful stories of women published in VELUGU, Indira Kranthi Pathakamam(IKP) and APMAS magazines and news papers it is observed that Feminisation of credit is implemented through Micro finance which changed the Socio–Economic conditions of women.

POSITIVE IMPACT

Impact on access of household Members to basic needs

1. Food, health and nutrition condition improved
2. Shelter and amenities like electricity, drainage, toilets, gas and safe water are developed.
3. Education–Members are sending their children to school, there is a lot of improvement in attendance.
4. No seasonal migration

Impact on Gender based access to basic needs

1. Access to delivery with trained personnel
2. No disparity in special food distribution
3. Female infant child and adult death rates are reduced
4. Girl child education, women respondents being able to sign
5. Women are able to buy new cloths

Impact on causes of household Poverty

1. Members purchasing productive asserts, land, livestock, shop and equipments.
2. Bonded labour shifted as self employed.
3. Greater proportion of members shift from low growth agriculture to growth services and trade which increased employment to their husbands also.
4. Consumption of alcohol reduced, unnecessary household expenditure on alcohol is curtailed, which also had impact on domestic violence.

Gender specific cause of Poverty

1. Women perceived rights over livestock's, legal ownership of new land and the ability to have a say over use of husband's income.
2. The very poorest member who have joined groups have not been able to access as much number and quantum of loan amounts as other members.

Impact on Women's Empowerment

1. Power of individual women members (and their female foetus/ infant/children) to firstly survive, and then have control over their labour, mobility, resources, reproduction, body and decision making process has indeed improved since formation.
2. The practice of female feticide maybe lower among SHG members. Over all female foetus, infant and children in member household may have a greater chance to survive.
3. More women members reported that their husband did house work and took care of children when they went to meeting and banks.
4. Member's access to and control over land, livestock, shop and income is higher and has slightly improved. Savings as a household asset created in last 5years. Savings are legally theirs as it was on their name. Though jewel is a non-productive asset women perceive it as their own to greater extant then land and immoveable asset.
5. Loans: 15% of loans were for consumption purpose and 85% for production purpose. Most members are not mere pupates

channelling loans to men, but play a significant role in decision making on credit.

6. Repayment: During months when work is available all group members save out of their own income. However during lean seasons they saved out of their own household income to repay the loans.
7. Women freedom to move and interact: The new places visited by members were DRDA office, bank, collector office, MRO and MDO office. Members reported that they went without their husband or men.
8. Contesting in the elections charged women permanently. All SHGS have leaders, which developed leadership position.
9. Reproductive rights: Improvement in reproductive rights(how many children to have, spacing between children, decision on abortion, place of delivery, age of marriage of daughters).
10. Women's control over body: (Women's ability to live life free of violence at home, work place and broader public) Domestic violence was significantly low, and violence at work place in public reduced.

Impact on Empowerment at the Collective and Wider Level

1. Collective interventions at community level: Village organisation and SHG members are able to challenge anti women and anti dalit social practices, child marriages, dowry system, window marriages, untouchability, caste discrimination and atrocity.
2. Collective intervention in market organisation: SHGS reported having intervened directly in some kinds of marketing organisation or the other labour commodity and financial collective intervention with state and local bodies. Women contested in the resent elections. Members attending Gramashaba meetings, which developed the infrastructure facilities in the village. Members developed collective interventions with Government organisations, health sub centres, schools, Anganwadi centres, MDO office, literacy programs, DWCRA markets, Agriculture and Sericulture department and legal aid cell.

Impact on Strategic Gender Awareness

1. An indicator of gender awareness at individual level is the ability of women to challenge gender related attitudes and social norms in the own personal lives. Son preference is very high in India. Now among the members son preference was lower and freedom given to adolescent girls was high.

NEGATIVE IMPACT

Loan Management

Many women are merely post-boxes passing on full amount of their loans directly to their husband, sons or son-in-laws, with little or no access to the income generated and receiving back only enough money to make loan repayments. Some women keep part of their loan for their own enterprises and passing on the remainder to men.

Access and Control over Assets

Many women continue to register land and productive assets in their husbands name because of inheritance laws.

Impact on Marriage Practices

Dowry price maybe rising due to women's increased access to credit. Credit provider here was an alternate provider of dowry. Some husbands were beating women threatening to ask for further dowry payments if she did not bring more credit.

Self-respect and self worth

Micro finance designed for poor or poorest: Micro credit programme do not and cannot reach the poorest people.

Poorest women will never be able to meet monthly repayment rates so the group members exclude them. So long grace period loans, interest free loans, less interest and group loans required for this women.

Concluding Remarks

The banks need to significantly improve the design and monitoring of micro finance programmes to support the empowerment of women. Financial sustainability must be balance against the need to ensure the same credit packages are accessible to the poorest.

Close monitoring by the banks in different aspects of control over credit and other aspects of empowerment is essential. Proper education and technical training inputs which support women to manage and use the loans themselves.

More investment needed in activities, which help to change men's attitude to women. Banks should increase female staff and field workers regarding micro finance.

The Government of India is thus responsible for using the hard earned savings of general public, particularly of the lower and middle –income groups on social banking and poverty alleviation programmes. On Government's own admission, as much as 60% of these funds are misappropriated by the higher income groups, the bank officials, the middlemen and the politicians and do not reach the poor for whom they are meant. Even the balance 40% of bank advances that really reach the poor does not return to the banks, because of collision between the borrowers and the corrupt and inefficient bank staff. The ultimate sufferers are the bank and the saving public who entrust their savings to safe custody of bank and hope to earn a decent interest income.

The remarkable success of the Government Bank in Bangladesh is a good example for social changes. Micro credit movement has constantly aimed at removing the disadvantages, which women suffer in the rural marketing by making a special effect to provide credit to women borrowers with very high rate of repayment.

REFERENCES

DRDA and VELUGU (Khammam) Reports.

VELUGU, APMAS magazine and Newspapers.

Towards women empowerment and poverty reduction-Rajani.K.Murthy, K.Raju, Amitha Kamath.

Reflections on Micro finance–Nalini Kasinathan.

Banks to the fore–Dr. Deepali Pant Joshi.

Indian Economy–Datt & Sunderam.

Welfare, choice & development–Biswanth Roy.

Development as Freedom–Dr. Amartya Sen.

Economic Reforms & Employment–P.D. Hajela & M.P. Goswami.

2003-04

Mandal Wise SHG Bank Linkage Performance Report Upto 31-03-2004

Sl. No.	Mandai Name	SHG Nc s. in the Branch as on 31.03.04	Bank Linkage during 01-04-2003 to 31-03-2004					
			Fresh		Renewal		Total	
			Groups	Amount	Groups	Amount	Groups	Amount
1.	Aswapuram	448	160	26.34	77	30.76	237	57.10
2.	Aswaraopeta	670	249	23.15	162	62.67	411	85.82
3.	Bayvaram	501	139	28.15	227	156.33	366	184.48
4.	Bhadraoialam	1022	407	26.65	204	63.62	611	90.27
5.	Bonakal	612	214	14.47	96	28.09	310	42.56
6.	Burgampadu	876	295	28.52	189	79.70	484	108.22
7.	Chandrugonda	669	178	15.93	117	39.73	295	55.66
8.	Cherla	484	124	17.80	103	35.18	227	52.98
9.	Chinthakani	778	357	33.22	170	65.99	527	99.21
10.	Chintur	361	81	8.53	23	7.21	104	15.74
11.	Dammapeta	710	296	32.40	174	48.61	470	81.01
12.	Dummugudem	615	220	13.16	183	42.10	403	55.26
13.	Enkur	575	133	8.61	102	30.85	235	39.46
14.	Garla	485	132	11.72	41	12.31	173	24.03
15.	Gundala	342	50	5.00	8	2.00	58	7.00
16.	Julurpad	542	196	11.81	201	50.49	397	62.30
17.	Kallur	841	329	31.18	182	64.67	511	95.85
18.	Kamepalu	562	180	9.93	78	32.23	258	42.16
19.	Khammam (U)	805	317	45.02	201	72.74	518	153.76
20.	Khammam(r)	1067	467	46.19	243	98.86	710	145.05
21.	Konderla	744	367	25.82	263	83.24	630	109.06
22.	Kothagudem	1332	482	69.30	260	102.59	742	171.89
23.	Kukunur	402	228	8.34	84	24.76	312	33.10

Sl. No.	Mandai Name	SHG Nc s. in the Branch as on 31.03.04	Bank Linkage during 01-04-2003 to 31-03-2004					
			Fresh		Renewal		Total	
			Groups	Amount	Groups	Amount	Groups	Amount
24.	Kunavaram	410	200	12.21	26	11.30	226	23.51
25.	Kusumanchi	877	278	19.80	417	138.08	695	157.88
26.	Madhira	765	297	27.74	190	57.45	487	85.19
27.	Manuguru	558	169	15.56	33	13.69	202	29.25
28.	Mudigonda	789	229	19.83	171	77.56	400	97.39
29.	Mulakalapalli	543	113	6.51	34	8.92	147	15.43
30.	Nelakondapalu	786	177	8.54	129	48.48	306	57.02
31.	Paloncha	409	155	43.35	66	33.98	221	77.33
32.	Penubaw	598	197	17.39	83	29.27	280	46.66
33.	Pinapaka	654	272	30.32	150	51.10	422	81.42
34.	Sathupaw	917	400	36.64	245	66.45	645	103.09
35.	Singareni	782	370	23.64	89	24.05	459	47.69
36.	Tekulapalu	420	200	21.64	30	6.32	230	27.96
37.	Thallada	987	479	64.25	241	101.58	720	165.83
38.	Thirumalayapalem	878	353	23.15	172	55.56	525	78.71
39.	V R Puram	426	57	3.26	64	30.04	121	33.30
40.	Velairpad	335	198	10.00	98	14.75	296	24.75
41.	Vemsur	657	197	23.28	149	44.97	345	68.25
42.	Venkatapuram	384	140	8.16	61	14.95	201	23.11
43.	Wazeedu	380	193	26.34	80	8.69	273	35.03
44.	Wyra	662	305	27.79	195	88.02	500	115.81
45.	Yellandu	602	243	37.12	122	39.15	365	76.27
46.	Yerrupalem	638	278	17.49	102	42.09	380	59.58
	Grand Total ==>	29900	11101	1065.25	6335	2241.18	17436	3342.43

Mandal Wise SHG Bank Linkage Performance Report From 01.04.04 to 31-03-2005
2004-05

(Rs. In Lakhs)

Sl. No.	Mandai Name	Total SHG A/Cs	Target 2004-05.		Linkage up to 31.03.05					
					Fresh		Renewal		Total	
			Groups	Amount	Groups	Amount	Groups	Amount	Groups	Amount
1.	Aswapuram	474	230	63.05	130	17.40	183	88.56	313	105.96
2.	Aswaraopeta	742	327	89.31	109	10.70	302	117.77	411	128.47
3.	Bayyaram	528	241	66.18	136	14.25	295	145.94	431	160.19
4.	Bhadrachalam	1040	500	138.26	241	20.17	274	65.69	515	85.86
5.	Bonakal	627	277	75.78	125	9.97	223	50.71	348	60.68
6.	Burgampadu	876	461	125.55	175	15.54	168	61.18	343	76.72
7.	Chandrugonda	688	330	90.25	258	17.15	156	41.44	414	58.59
8.	Cherla	490	260	71.32	154	19.72	212	74.79	366	94.51
9.	Chinthakani	941	377	102.83	129	8.87	326	71.09	455	79.96
10.	Chintur	366	175	48.33	88	7.23	87	11.13	175	18.36
11.	Dammapeta	728	368	100.53	172	15.22	284	94.13	456	109.35
12.	Dummugudem	641	303	82.82	129	12.76	304	111.64	433	124.40
13.	Enkur	581	281	77.00	118	11.48	152	41.38	270	52.86
14.	Garla	495	240	65.91	121	12.90	40	23.17	161	36.07
15.	Gundala	342	171	47.62	109	21.42	48	3.11	157	24.53
16.	Julurpad	545	264	72.27	66	12.16	152	68.39	218	80.55
17.	Kallur	858	435	118.52	207	19.16	431	145.32	638	164.48
18.	Kamepalli	568	280	76.60	72	5.37	179	49.32	251	54.69
19.	Khammam (U)	954	401	109.32	326	45.94	398	229.85	724	275.79
20.	Khammam(R)	1120	557	151.65	123	8.14	282	99.93	405	108.07
21.	Konderla	771	363	99.04	49	4.74	342	100.51	391	105.25
22.	Kothagudem	1373	495	134.88	237	31.12	424	112.51	661	143.63

Sl. No.	Mandai Name	Total SHG A/Cs	Target 2004-05.		Linkage up to 31.03.05					
					Fresh		Renewal		Total	
			Groups	Amount	Groups	Amount	Groups	Amount	Groups	Amount
23.	Kukunur	409	203	55.7.7	128	10.15	152	47.57	280	57.72
24.	Kunavaram	413	215	59.15	73	5.44	56	11.66	129	17.10
25.	Kusumanchi	905	446	121.49	97	7.12	342	133.97	439	141.09
26.	Madhlra	771	399	103.91	180	15.56	368	91.63	548	107.19
27.	Manuguru	572	278	76.05	204	25.01	164	37.00	368	62.01
28.	Mudigonda	902	436	118.92	139	15.44	221	81.88	360	97.32
29.	Mulakalapalu	579	285	78.08	189	14.51	58	13.60	247	28.11
30.	Nelakonoapalu	788	398	108.65	102	8.71	272	79.21	374	87.92
31.	Paloncha	488	213	58.61	180	36.95	188	84.29	368	121.24
32.	Penubalu	613	306	83.63	86	9.25	215	43.24	301	52.49
33.	Pinapaka	654	350	95.66	240	15.52	210	40.67	450	56.19
34.	Sathupalli	944	455	101.06	218	20.77	359	88.12	577	108.89
35.	Singareni	782	394	107.56	153	11.45	196	36.94	349	48.39
36.	Tekulapalu	420	275	75.38	102	13.19	40	10.40	142	23.59
37.	Thallada	996	527	143.54	145	15.11	475	216.01	620	231.12
38.	Thirumalayapalem	950	429	114.03	107	13.57	360	128.95	467	142.52
39.	V.R. Puram	446	250	68.62	110	6.98	120	44.69	230	51.67
40.	Velairpad	338	170	47.98	36	2.24	35	5.06	71	7.30
41.	Vemsur	681	350	95.93	178	24.42	305	97.24	483	121.66
42.	Venkatapuram	497	234	50.29	125	12.31	173	35.80	298	48.11
43.	Wazeedu	380	193	53.06	140	10.65	176	42.73	316	53.38
44.	Wyra	669	354	96.61	117	12.01	310	143.17	427	155.18
45.	Yellandu	651	323	87.37	175	32.53	135	62.63	310	95.16
46.	Yerrupalem	681	340	91.63	143	13.07	202	104.53	345	117.60
	Grand Total=>	31277	15159	4100.00	6641	693.37	10394	3488.55	17035	4181.92

Mandal Wise SHG Bank Linkage Performance Report From 01.04.05 to 31-07-2005
2005-06

(Rs. In Lakhs)

Sl. No.	Mandai Name	Total SHG A/Cs	Target 2004-05.		Linkage up to 31.03.05					
					Fresh		Renewal		Total	
			Groups	Amount	Groups	Amount	Groups	Amount	Groups	Amount
1.	Aswapuram	474	220	97.05	5	0.70	41	19.17	46	19.87
2.	Aswaraopeta	742	392	190.65	2	0.20	97	51.85	99	52.05
3.	Bayvaram	528	425	213.15	23	3.42	86	37.37	109	40.79
4.	Bhadrachalam	1040	479	226.80	35	3.60	67	15.45	102	19.05
5.	Bonakal	627	257	114.30	5	0.66	63	20.38	68	21.04
6.	Burgampadu	876	298	153.15	0	0.00	29	13.92	29	13.92
7.	Chandrugonda	688	308	136.80	21	1.50	91	29.45	112	30.95
8.	Cherla	490	270	126.30	62	26.00	126	44.50	188	70.50
9.	Chinthakani	941	534	225.15	17	1.84	143	54.06	160	55.90
10.	Chintur	366	359	200.40	12	1.25	12	1.91	24	3.16
11.	Dammapeta	728	424	217.80	7	0.60	103	25.03	110	25.63
12.	Dummugudem	641	362	166.80	25	11.00	28	25.50	53	36.50
13.	Enkur	581	339	175.95	6	0.60	129	33.63	135	34.23
14.	Garla	495	195	89.10	1	0.10	19	5.70	20	5.80
15.	Gundala	351	119	67.95	25	2.92	11	2.92	36	5.84
16.	Julurpad	545	203	106.80	0	0.00	172	49.99	172	49.99
17.	Kallur	876	375	172.50	11	1.53	172	58.28	183	59.81
18.	Kamepalli	568	182	99.75	8	1.00	124	49.33	132	50.33
19.	Khammam (U)	1028	718	324.45	68	9.21	190	77.17	258	86.38
20.	Khamnam	1120	560	275.60	29	2.87	158	81.72	187	84.59
21.	Konijerla	771	428	234.00	1	0.10	282	119.69	283	119.79
22.	Kothagudem	1377	630	329.25	101	9.71	316	95.27	417	104.98

Sl. No.	Mandai Name	Total SHG A/Cs	Target 2004-05.		Linkage up to 31.03.05					
					Fresh		Renewal		Total	
			Groups	Amount	Groups	Amount	Groups	Amount	Groups	Amount
23.	Kukunur	409	177	78.00	8	0.79	129	51.11	137	51.90
24.	Kunavaram	413	125	61. 50	7	1.20	21	6.18	28	7.38
25.	Kusumanchi	905	373	204.00	5	0.57	187	78.33	192	78.90
26.	Madhira	771	294	142.20	2	0.28	73	29.84	75	30.12
27.	Manuguru	572	279	108.30	2	0.20	42	10.65	44	10.85
28.	Mudigonda	904	454	228.90	15	2.23	73	17.35	88	19.58
29.	Mulakalapalli	579	255	115.65	1	0.10	17	5.90	18	6.00
30.	Nelakondapalli	812	287	150.75	29	4.50	113	55.27	142	59.77
31.	Paloncha	489	246	91.35	29	6.24	131	64.23	160	70.47
32.	Penuballi	615	279	146.70	12	1.22	102	26.44	114	27.66
33.	Pinapaka	654	294	15.90	15	1.48	57	14.53	72	16 01
34.	Sathupalli	944	363	206.10	7	1.20	71	23.53	78	24.73
35.	Singareni	782	307	164.25	0	0.00	6	2.10	6	2.10
36.	Tekulapalli	420	157	94.35	15	1.50	114	24.25	129	25.75
37.	Thallada	995	460	251.70	9	1.20	263	147.55	272	148.75
38.	Thirumalayapalem	950	380	205.20	48	5.56	187	69.20	235	74.76
39.	VR Puram	446	248	124.20	10	0.80	20	6.50	30	7.30
40.	Velairpad	338	147	80.10	40	1.98	64	10.20	104	12.18
41.	Vemsur	681	393	176.40	45	35.34	216	95.27	261	130.61
42.	Venkatapuram	497	370	139.95	5	0.94	53	12.60	58	13.54
43.	Wazeedu	414	267	125.70	31	3.90	34	16.11	65	20.01
44.	Wyra	719	386	221.85	10	1.40	170	76.67	180	78.07
45.	Yellandu	651	373	140.25	8	1.10	37	18.27	45	19.37
46.	Yerrupalem	685	342	162.00	21	3.07	64	17.52	85	20.59
	Grand Total ==>	31499	15333	7500.00	838	166.61	4703	1791.89	6641	1947.50

PART - IV
Women's Health

28

Prevalence of Chronic Energy Deficiency and Obesity among Rural Women–An Analysis of Nutrient intakes in Relation to Plane of Nutrition

D.L. Kusuma and B. Babitha

INTRODUCTION

The lives of women in developing countries differ from those of men for cultural, biological and socio-economic reasons. These differences place women at significantly higher risk than men of malnutrition and mortality. The importance of women's nutritional status to their own health, productivity and quality of life and to the survival and healthy development of their children and other family members who depend on women's domestic and market work, warrant serious efforts to reduce malnutrition among women (Leslie, 1991).

Women are members of the households in which they acquire, cook, serve consume and store food and their nutritional profile is also part of the household's nutritional profile. However, what sets these dimensions apart and makes them particularly interesting is the apparent contradiction that while *women are in a commanding position, over the household resources that determine individual nutrition, they are themselves quite malnourished, often more so than other family members* (Meera Chattarjee, 1989).

Thus, women's health has emerged as both a powerful political platform and a dynamic public health issue. Women suffer more acute symptoms, chronic conditions and short and long term disabilities resulting from health problems. Women are vulnerable to several weight related health risks associated with being overweight, loosing weight and being underweight by choice or by circumstances. They have shorter life expectancy, experience high maternal mortality and have a higher incidence of chronic diseases and conditions such as chronic energy deficiency, obesity, nutritional anaemia, osteoporosis, diabetes, hypertension and other cardiovascular diseases. Women's overall health status is further diminished by higher rates of poverty, lack of education and limited or non-existent access to medical care.

Women constitute half of the countries population, in other words half of the country's human resource. Women in the Indian society are traditionally the providers of nutrition to the family. In India nearly 70 per cent constitute rural area and remaining is urban and semi-urban areas. The life style of rural women reveals that 90-95 per cent of the women work for the economic support in addition to the responsibility of attending to the household chores. If one looks at the picture of any rural area it is evident that it comprises of 5 – 10 per cent elite families and the remaining major chunk of families belong to middle, low and very poor income groups. This picture is true throughout India. An examination of work and nutritional and health status of women in relation to the conditions prevailing in the rural areas will throw light on not only the nutritional and health risk of women but also those of the future generations.

CED and obesity are the two conditions, which are the two models for chronic energy deficiency and chronic energy excess respectively in the study of nutrition. CED, according to Norgan (1994), refers to an intake of energy less than the requirement for a period of several months or years. He also stated that CED is the most widespread nutritional deficiency. It is observed to affect half the world's children and recent evidence reveal that as much adult population suffer from this nutritional deficiency. Waterlow, Ferro-Luzzi and James (1987) defined the use of definition of CED as a steady state which can be maintained but at a level at which certain functions of health are impaired, using as indicators the body mass index and the ratio of energy turnover to basal metabolic rate in adults, and the deficit in weight for height in children. The steady state will change when either energy supply is reduced or demands for energy output increase and this change is not counter balanced on the other side of the equation. In response to this change, there is a fall in body weight but not in essential energy output. Monitoring of individuals has shown that body weight does change as soon as energy imbalance occurs (Ferro-Luzzi, 1990).

While CED continues to be a problem in India, annual data provided by NNMB (1994) shows that 3.6 per cent of the rural population had a BMI exceeding 25 indicating the prevalence of obesity. Considering the populations covered by NNMB surveys that comprise of predominantly low-income groups, these figures must be considered significant. *There has been rapid increase in the proportion of middle-income group in recent years. The incidence of obesity in these section may be expected to be much higher than the values reported for the low-income group by the NNMB.*

CED has been proved to be a disorder strongly associated with economic deprivation. There is evidence both in the western and Indian contexts that obesity is positively correlated with income. However, several research works done in India (Gupta et. al., 1983; Dua and Seth, 1988) focus on the fact that obesity among women is not uncommon even in the low and middle income groups. The recent National Family Health Survey reveals that 5.9 per cent of rural women suffer from obesity. The only community based study carried out in northern India revealed the prevalence of obesity to be as high as 33 per cent in adults of more than 30 years of age (NFHS-2, 2000).

It is widely accepted that obesity is detrimental to health (Bray, 1985; Kissbah et. al., 1989). Prospective studies have confirmed the significant association between obesity and mortality related to cardio-vascular diseases (Terry et. al., 1992).

There is a threshold at which risk dramatically increase. Obesity is highly reversible, and if it is corrected in time, some of its risk too are corrected. Mortality rates are no higher for the formerly obese than for the never obese. Prevention is desirable, but where it has failed, treatment is needed (Whitney et. al., 1987).

Developing countries as compared to the rich countries must rely much more heavily on prevention rather than on therapeutic management of these diseases; their national health systems can just not afford the massive cost of the therapeutic care of these diseases on large scale. Research in prevention would mostly consist in the identification of factors in diets and lifestyle, which would favour the control of these degenerative diseases (Gopalan, 1994).

The International Conference on Nutrition (ICN) reaffirmed that practical, accurate and cost-effective methods to identify nutritionally at risk populations are essential to the design and implementation of effective policies and programmes to promote nutritional well being and to monitor the impact of such programmes. After examining a wide range of possible monitoring tools, FAO selected the Body Mass Index (BMI) as a potentially valuable monitoring approach (Shetty and James, 1994).

The FAO/WHO/UNU reported the use of BMI in the assessment of nutritional status of the community. The scope of BMI was described as: BMI is a simple but objective anthropometric indicator of the nutritional status of the adult population and seems to be closely related to their food consumption levels. It is relatively inexpensive easy to collect and to analyze. Collection of data on weight and height from which BMI is derived can readily be incorporated into regional and national surveys that are presently being conducted. It could be used for the purpose of nutritional surveillance or for the purpose of monitoring since this allows for inter regional or inter-country comparisons as well as longitudinal comparisons within the same region or country.

In this background the present investigation was carried out with the objective to project the prevalence of nutritional problems of Chronic Energy Deficiency and Obesity among rural women. The purpose was to examine their food and nutrient intakes, to be able to provide guidelines for our rural women groups, in view of the detrimental consequences of both the states of malnutrition.

METHODOLOGY

Selection of the Study Area

Chittoor District comprises of rural areas that have striking socio-cultural and economic differences. Therefore, to minimize the socio-cultural variations, the Chandragiri Mandal, Chittoor District of Andhra Pradesh state South India was purposively chosen for the present investigation.

About the Study Area

The villages in chandragiri Mandal of Chittoor district are 15-20 Kilometers away from the Chandragiri town, which is a semi urban area and 10-40 Km away from Tirupati, which is the nearest Urban area. It was observed that the proximity to these two urban areas does influence the lifestyle of the inhabitants, in the socio-cultural and economic contexts. Though, the main occupation of a majority was agriculture, the crop pattern reflected the needs of the urban areas. Further, a majority of the high-income group families had business as another important occupation contributing significantly to the total family income. Each habitat was composed of a main village and small hamlets, where only scheduled caste families were the inhabitants. For a cluster of villages there was one hamlet inhabited by only scheduled tribes.

All villages had the facilities provided by the government such as electricity, roads and transport, protected water supply and primary schools. The total number of villages was 23 in the southeast, southwest, northeast and northwest areas of Chandragiri Mandal. From among them six villages approximately covering 1/4th–1/5th of the total number were selected randomly for the present study.

Selection of Sample

It was observed that several research works done in the rural areas that the life style of the women belonging to the HSL (High Standard of Living) groups were significantly different form there of MSL (Medium Standard of Living) and LSL (Low Standard of Living) groups of women. The HSL women were not directly involved in the forming activities and a majority and only very sedentary life style. Whereas, the MSL and LSL groups of women were directly involved in the different farming activities and were performing moderate to heavy categories of physical work and their life styles were observed to be more or less similar. Therefore, to minimize the variation in the group due to differences in the physical activity and food intake patterns the HSL group was purposively omitted and the households having 18-50 year old women from the MSL and LSL groups only were chosen for the present study.

Thus, the total number of women eligible for the present study was 600 distributed as 310 in the LSL and 290 in the MSL group. These women were further stratified into two groups on the basis of age as 18-30 and 30-50 years. The height and weight of all the 600 women were measured and the Body Mass Index (BMI) was calculated. Based on this parameter the women in each SL (Standard of Living) and age group were divided into different categories of nutritional sates as CED, Normal and Obese groups using the BMI cut-off points proposed by James et. al., (1989). Later from the above grades three groups of women belonging to extreme nutritional states viz., a) CED Grade III b) Obesity Grade II and c) Normal representing the plane of nutrition were selected. The sample size in each group was 40.

Tools for Collection of Data

A general information survey schedule was administered to collect data on age and SL of the subject (Schedule-I). A nutrition survey schedule was used to collect information related to different nutritional status parameters such as anthropometry (Schedule-II) and diet survey (Schedule-III) and physical activity assessment (Schedule-IV).

Assessment of Standard of Living

The summary household measure called the standard of living index (SLI) used in the National Family Health Survey-II (2000) was used in the present study. The SLI is calculated by adding the scores obtained for type of house, toilet facility, source of lighting, main fuel for cooking, source of drinking water, separate room for cooking, ownership of house, agricultural land, irrigated land, live stock and durable goods. Based on the total index scores the households were classified into three SLI categories as follows (Table 1).

Table 1
The Index Scores for Standard of Living of Households

Range of Index score	*SLI Category*
0-14	Low
15-24	Medium
25-27	High

Anthropometric Measurements and Techniques:

It has been shown that nutritional anthropometry is a simple and reliable index of nutritional status. The somatic measurements chosen were height, weight.

Weight/Height Index–The Body Mass Index (BMI)

As a measure of body composition, in fact body fat, a weight/height index has to have both high correlation with the amount of body fat, as well as a low correlation with body height, or else in short and tall people body composition would be systematically over or under estimated. The most frequently used index today is the Quetlet or body mass index (BMI). The correlation of body mass index with body fat is relatively high (ranging from 0.6 to 0.8, depending on age) and the correlation with body height is generally low (Khosla and Lowe, 1967, Keys et. al., 1972, Womersley and Durnin, 1977; Garrow and Webster, 1985, Deurenberg, Westrate and Seidell, 1991). The BMI is a simple but objective anthropometric indicator of the nutritional status of the adult population and seems to be closely related to their food composition level. It is relatively inexpensive, easy to collect and to analyse. The BMI is sensitive to socio-economic status and to seasonal fluctuations in food consumption relative to the level of physical activity. In the present context the BMI was calculated using the formula wt/ht$^{2.}$ The following cut-off points (Table 2) were used to classify the subjects into different nutritional states.

Table 2
Cut-off Points of BMI

BMI Class	*Presumptive Diagnosis*
< 16.0	CED – Grade III Severe
16.0 - 17.0	CED – Grade II Moderate
17.0 – 18.5	CED – Grade I Mild
18.5 – 20.0	Low Weight Normal
20.0 – 25.0	Normal
25.0 – 30.0	Obese Grade I
>30.0	Obese Grade II

Diet Survey

Diet surveys are essential part of all nutrition surveys. They provide useful information to interpret the existing nutritional situations in any community. To elicit information pertaining to the quality and quantity of diets consumed by the rural women subjects a schedule (Schedule III) was formulated. The diet survey was conducted for 3 days in a week, selecting two week days and one weekend day.

The data was collected in the combination of 24 hour recall and weightment method. The researcher herself measured the cooked food consumed by the subjects in randomize meal sessions, so that for each subject during the three day period all the meal sessions that would occur in a day were covered by the researcher. Prior to the investigation the subjects were provided with a set of standardized cups and the use was demonstrated. The subjects were instructed to record the amount of food consumed by them at all the meals, which were not attended by the researcher. Both the subjects and the investigator measured the food using the standardized cups. Illiterate women were attached to literate subjects of the study or other members in the family or neighbours to record the dietary intake information.

Statistical Analysis

Appropriate statistical analysis was conducted to examine the differences between the CED, Normal and Obesity groups.

RESULTS AND DISCUSSION

The per cent prevalence of different grades of CED and obesity and the normal group is presented in table 3 and represented diagrammatically in fig. 1. Among the 600 subjects, while 50.3 per cent of the women belonged to normal group, 34.8 and 14.83 per cent of women belonged to CED and obesity groups respectively.

The distribution of subjects as per income reveal that a high per cent of LSL women were in grade I CED (14.52) when compared with MSL women (12.76). There was very little difference for the other grades of CED between the LSL and MSL groups; the per cent of women in low weight normal group was 15.81 and 14.48 respectively and an equal per cent from both groups were in normal group (35.16 and 35.17 respectively). With regard to obesity a slightly higher per cent (7.24) of women of MSL where in Grade-II obesity when compared with that of LSL (6.45). Whereas in Grade-I the percentage was more in LSL (8.06) when compared with MSL (7.93).

The data as related to age reveal that, in the LSL group of women; the per cent in the three grades of CED was grater in the 18-30 years age group than 30-50 years age group. With regard to MSL age groups such a definite trend was not observed. It was observed that in this group the per cent in Grade-II CED was similar

Table 3

Distribution of the per cent Prevalence of Different Nutritional States among Rural Women as per Standard of Living and Age

Nutritional state	*BMI Cut off values*	*Nutritional grade (Gr)*	*Standard of Living*						*Grand total % (No)*	*% Prevalence (No)*
			18-30Yrs % (No)	*30-50 yrs % (No)*	*Total % (No)*	*18-30 yrs % (No)*	*30-50 yrs % (No)*	*Total % (No)*		
CED	< 16	Gr-III-Severe	12.86(18)	9.41(16)	10.96(34)	11.68(16)	12.42(19)	12.07(35)	11.5(69)	
	16-17	Gr-II-Moderate	9.28(13)	8.82(15)	9.03(28)	10.22(14)	10.46(16)	10.34(30)	9.67(58)	34.8
	17-18.5	Gr-I-Mild	15.71(22)	13.53(23)	14.52(45)	15.33(21)	10.46(16)	12.76(37)	13.67(82)	(209)
Normal	18.5-20.0	Low weight	17.14(24)	14.71(25)	15.81(49)	15.33(21)	13.73(21)	14.48(42)	15.17(91)	
	20.0-25.0	Normal								50.3
		Normal	29.28(41)	40.0(68)	35.61(109)	31.39(43)	38.56(59)	35.17(102)	35.17(211)	(302)
Obese	25.0-30.0	Gr-I-Over weight	8.57(12)	7.65(13)	8.06(25)	8.76(12)	7.19(11)	7.93(23)	8.0(23)	14.83
	>30.0	Gr-II-Obese	7.14(10)	6.88(10)	6.45(20)	7.29(10)	7.19(11)	7.24(21)	6.83(41)	(89)
Total	140	170	310	137	153	290	600	600		

for both age groups while those in Grade-III CED was higher in the 18-30 years age when compared with 30-50 years. With regard to Grade-I CED the percentage was higher in the 30-50 years when compared with the 19-30 years.

With regard to normal nutritional state the trend observed was similar for the 18-30 and 30-50 years age group of LSL and MSL groups. It was evident that the percentage of 'low weight normal' was higher in 18-30 years group when compared 30-50 years group. With regard to 'normal' group, the percentage of women were greater in the 30-50 years when compared with the 18-30 years group. However, there were slight differences in the percentage of low weight normal and normal group for the 18-30 and 30-50 years age of MSL and LSL categories.

In both LSL and MSL group the 18-30 years age group registered a high percentage of overweight and obese subjects when compared with the 30-50 years age group. In both the age groups with the exception of MSL 30-50 years, the per cent of overweight Grade-I were greater than the obese Grade-II women.

DISCUSSION

Periodic survey carried out by NNMB of the National Institute of Nutrition, Hyderabad and the recent National Family Health Survey (NFHS, 2000) initiated by the Ministry of Health and Family Welfare, Government of India focus on the trends pertaining to CED and obesity among rural women.

The findings for India based on two separate series of National Nutrition Monitoring Bureau surveys conducted between 1974-79 and 1988-90 showed that India had a high proportion of adult males and females with BMI < 18.5, even in 1989-1990. It was observed through NNMB reported that the prevalence of CED among the rural women was 47.1 per cent, 6.6 per cent were obese and 46.3 per cent were normal (NNMB Report, 1996). This reveals the increasing trend in the prevalence of obesity even among the rural groups. In the present study the per cent of rural women having BMI <16 and belonging to GIII CED was 11.5 which is in close agreement with that of NNMB data (1988-1990) of 10.2 per cent.

NFHS–2 surveys (2000) revealed that the prevalence of CED was 40.6 per cent and that of obesity was 5.9 per cent among rural women. These figures pertaining to CED were greater than those observed for the urban counterparts. When compared with data of the present investigation the percentages were lower for the rural women. The differences may be attributed to the nature of the sample.

NNMB collects data from 10 states and the agreement of this data with that of the present data, which is from a micro level investigation, reveal that the nutritional issues of Indian adults call for an indepth investigation.

Focusing on the recent trends as observed from the NFHS and NNMB surveys Sachdev (1997) in his analysis on nutritional status of women in India, commented that inspite of a distinct shift of the distribution to the right even now CED is prevalent in 37-47 per cent of the women with the severe from being documented in 10 per cent. Further, obesity is beginning to emerge (7 to 12 per cent) as another end of the spectrum of malnutrition.

Several other researchers globally have focused that the problem of obesity is on the increase. Further, a few of them reveal that obesity is on the increase not only among the elite group but also among middle and low socio-economic groups (Stene et. Al., 2001; Misra, 2001; Hakeem,2001; Filozof et. Al., 2001).

The observations of the present study reiterate the findings of the above surveys and research works. However, the relatively higher percentage of over-weight/obesity (14.83 per cent) observed in the present context may be because of the fact that women aged >50 years were excluded for the assessment of BMI. Even if the total women population is considered the prevalence of both CED and obesity still remain strikingly high in the present rural community.

In the present study slight differences were observed between the LSL and MSL groups and the 18-30 and 30-50 year age groups for the prevalence of different states and grades of malnutrition. BMI closely correlates with body weight. And it is a well-established fact that slight increments in weight are associated with age. The increments may be possible with the normal groups in the per cent context.

Several studies have proved the effect of income on the nutritional status. The differences in nutritional status related to income may be immediately and clearly evident probably as related to other nutritional status parameters rather than in the body composition which is a consequence of long term nutrition input.

Weight status of Subjects

In the present context weight (wt) height (ht) were the nutritional anthropometric measurements done for the rural women belonging to the three nutritional states viz., chronic energy deficient (CED), obese and normal.

The CED group recorded a mean weight of 36.23 kg. The mean weight registered by the obese was 71.46 kg. The mean weight of normal group was 50.01 kg. The weight recorded by the obese is twice that of the CED group. The mean difference between CED and normal was about 14kg; between obese and normal was about 21 kg and between obese and CED was 35 kg. The difference in weight between the groups were found to be significant at 1 per cent level (P<0.01).

The data on weight segregated in relation to standard of living and age of the subjects revealed that mean weights recorded by women of MSL were higher when compared with those of the LSL. With regard to age the mean weight of 30-50 years women registered were higher than those of the 18-20 years age group. However, the differences observed were not significant.

The trends pertaining to the distribution of weight in relation to BMI of the subjects is depicted in (Fig. 2). It was observed that the weights ranged from 30-49 kg for the CED, 56-96 for the obese and 39 to 71 for the normal group.

Discussion

The mean differences in weight are visibly striking as both CED and obese nutritional states chosen belong to the extreme levels. In the present context grade III CED and Grade II obese women were chosen for purposes of comparison. The data reveals that the women with a BMI > 18.5, BMI ranging from 18.5 to 25, which is considered to be 'Normal' group, registered a mean weight of 50.0 kg which is the value of weight recommended for reference Indian women.

NNMB (1980) reported the mean weight of women aged between 25 and 44 years living in rural areas of ten States. The rural Indian women weighed 42.4 kg. Regional variations were observed, but were not very striking. Weights ranged from a low 39.9 kg in West Bengal, to a maximum of 44.4 kg in Madhya Pradesh. The mean weight for Andhra Pradesh rural women was reported to be 42.7 kg. ICMR (1991) showed the mean weight of rural Indian women as 44.3 kg. That, weight is closely associated with socio-economic status was clearly focused from the data of NNMB collected for men and women belonging to different levels of socio-economic status. The data however, were not segregated for women.

Table 4
Anthropometric Profiles of CED, Obese and Normal Groups of Women Subjects

Parameter	*CED*		*OBESE*		*Normal*		*'F'Value*
	Mean±SD	*Range*	*Mean±SD*	*Range*	*Mean±SD*	*Range*	
Weight (Kg)	36.22± 4.15	30-49	71.46± 7.76	56-96	50.01± 6.28	39-71	321.958*
Height (cm)	153.18± 7.80	140-187	149.67± 5.99	130-163	150.90± 5.67	138-170	2.958^{NS}
BMI (wt/ht^2)	15.34± 0.59	13.07-16	31.81± 2.71	30-42.6	21.90± 1.82	18.5-24.8	746-992*

NS - Not Significant
* 'F' - Significant at P < 0.01–1% level

It is evident from the range of values in each nutritional state that the weights were in a continuum while the BMI chosen was in close range. Weights of CED encroached into the weights of normal group and that of the normal heavily encroached into obese / overweight group and vice-versa. Between the normal and Grade-II, CED Grade-I and Grade-II should occur in between, may be very close to either CED or the normal group. In such a situation the other metabolic and biochemical correlates also may be distributed into the adjacent nutritional categories.

Height Status

The data on heights were segregated in relation to standard of living and age of the subjects (Table 5). It was observed that the values registered by LSL women in all the three groups were lower than that of MSL group. The differences however, were not statistically significant. Within each nutritional state the differing levels of deprivation or affluence might have influenced the stature to some extent.

Discussion

According to NNMB surveys conducted during 1975 and 1994 the mean height recorded by adult women was 149.9 and 151.5

Table 5
Mean Nutrient Intakes of the Rural Women Subjects

Nutrients	*CED*		*OBESE*		*NORMAL*		*'F'Value*
	Mean ±SD	*Range*	*Mean ±SD*	*Range*	*Mean ±SD*	*Range*	
Energy (k.cal)	1680.8±141.8	1432.1-2000	2458.8±286.3	2053-3043	2143.7±172.9	1724.8-2448	139.23*
Protein (gm)	44.9±4.7	35.7-56.6	52.6±7.6	35-70.5	53.7±7.8	31.2-68.7	19.530*
Fat (gm)	29.2±7.9	20.0-53.35	44.9±9.6	25-68.5	49.7±7.4	35.5-60.5	66.150*
Carbohydrate(gm)	283.1±47.4	216.3-370.4	431.3±67.4	300.5-578.1	436.8±76.2	250.5-640	72.380*
Calcium (mg)	363.9±62.7	300.5-500	576.1±108.3	265.8-720.5	522.9±91.1	325.5-700.2	40.500*
Iron (mg)	13.3±5.1	7.0-25.8	23.2±4.9	15-35	23.1±7.3	7.0-35.0	37.930*
Vit 'A' (ig)	1692.3±353.0	549.6-2300	1987.6±6287	600.3-3200	2148.9±362.7	1500-3250	9.890*
Vtt 'B' (mg)	0.8±0.2	0.2-1.05	1.0±0.2	0.6-1.5	1.1±0.2	0.7-2.0	28.810*
Vit 'C' (mg)	34.3±7.7	25.0-69.0	34.2±12.8	16-75.5	40.3±12.6	16.0-75.0	3.830**

cms respectively. The height increments tended to be higher than past years, probably due to health and nutrition interventions.

ICMR (1991) reported that the mean height of rural Indian women was 154 cms. The NFHS-2 survey (2000) recorded the mean height of the rural women as 141.1 cms. The values varied only slightly between 150 and 155 cms. for different population groups. Thirteen per cent of women were under 145 cms in height when compared with the mean height values reported by the above studies the present group of rural women is observed to be in the similar status for height.

The women when classified according to BMI those who are tall but in lower weight range appear to be classified in the CED group. At lower values of height they may have a BMI, which categorizes them as normal. Similarly in the other extreme of obesity / overweight if the statures are improved the women again may shift into the Normal grade. Thus, in this classification of BMI those who are tall and those who are short to some extent may not truly belong to the nutritional grades, attributed to them.

With regard to age however no definite trends related to height were observed; which is expected, because height in growth ceases around 18 years of age while muscle mass and fat accretion can occur through life span. Thus, adult height may be regarded as a consequence of past nutrition. In the developing countries and in the rural areas no dramatic changes occur in the socio-economic status of the rural households. The deprivations continue over generations. Thus, the better status in height for the rural women in the present study may be understood in the light of genetic potential being realized because of the health and nutrition inputs provided through health and welfare programs.

In the present context as height and weight profiles are being focused for the extreme conditions of malnutrition it may be interpreted that while tall people are at risk pf CED, the short statured are at risk of obesity.

The Nutrient Intake of the Subjects

Nutrient intakes usually are a reflection of food intake, as cooked food is translated into raw ingredients and their nutrient composition is focused as nutrient intakes. However, the variety of foods included contributes significantly to the variation in the nutrient intakes particularly with regard to vitamins and minerals. The food intake usually closely reflects the calorie and protein intake.

The data on nutrient intakes is presented in table 5. The analysis of variance conducted reveals that there is a significant variation in the intakes. Nutrient intakes of CED group women was lower than obese and normal groups. The 't' test revealed that difference was lower than obese and normal groups and the difference was significant ($p<0.01$). With regard the obese and normal groups however, for a majority of nutrients the difference between the groups was not significant. The mean intake of fat by the obese was observed to be lower than that of the normal group. The difference was significant ($P < 0.05$). A similar trend was observed in the case of intakes of Vitamin 'C'. However, a distinct and significant ($P < 0.01$) difference was evident between the above two groups for caloric intakes; the intake of calories of obese was greater than the normal women group.

The mean nutrient intakes were compared with the RDA (ICMR, 1991). The mean deficits observed with regard to calories were 25 per cent for the CED group. All 40 members in the group showed deficits of varying level. Nearly 70 per cent of the subjects in this group had per cent deficit ranging from 20 to 35.

In the case of obese 57 per cent of the subjects had intakes exceeding the RDA for calories. However, the remaining 43 per cent subjects showed deficits of varying degrees. Among the 17 subjects 13 showed deficits in the range of 1–10 per cent while for 4 subjects the deficits ranged from 15–25.

With regard to normal subjects, 50 per cent of the subjects were having caloric intakes above the RDA. The remaining 50 per cent showed deficits ranging from 1-20 per cent.

The per cent contribution of carbohydrate to calories was 67.3, 70.16 and 81.5 for CED, obese and normal groups respectively. The recommended intake of cereals is around 300 g/day. The women were observed to be using high amount of cereals. In addition, even if the pulse intakes were low, it would make additional contribution to the total carbohydrate intake. Thus in this context the contribution to the total calories is dominated by carbohydrate calories. As per balanced diets 75 per cent of the total calories should come from carbohydrates. This indicates an imbalance in the food intake, which may significantly affect other nutrient intake profile.

The mean protein intake was found to be satisfactory for the obese and normal groups. When compared with the RDA, CED group showed 10 per cent deficit for protein. It is clear from the discussion in the preceding section that these women consumed cereal food in large quantities. This implies that the major contribution to the protein intake is from cereal food alone as the intakes of other food items that contribute to protein such as pulse, milk and milk products registered inadequate intakes.

With regard to fat while the recommended intake was 20g per day all groups including CED registered higher intakes than the RDA. The intakes of fat by obese and normal were 40 per cent higher than that observed for the CED group. The visible fat intake was only 6-7 g/day. A daily Indian diet which provides 2400 calories will contain about 40 g of fat a day out of which 25 g will be invisible fat and 15 g visible fat (ICMR, 1995). Therefore, in the present context also it may be inferred that though the visible fat is minimum the rest is being contributed by invisible fat. Further, the dietaries of the women showed liberal consumption of groundnut, which can make a substantial contribution of fat to the diets.

The mean Vit 'C' intake of CED and obese women was similar (34 mg) and had deficit of 15 per cent when compared with that of RDA. The intakes were satisfactory for the normal women (40 mg).

Discussion

The actual intakes of women subject's in the present context were higher for a majority of households than those observed by the NNMB surveys. In the present study utmost care was taken in recording and translating the food intakes into nutrient intakes. Further, India has experienced a dramatic increase in the food production particularly that of the cereal grains. The public distribution system (PDS) supplies cereal grains at subsidized rates. This and the measures taken by the government in ensuring equal wages for women might have shown some visible changes in the food intakes in the recent years. The higher intakes observed for the present group may be a consequence of these improvements.

Protein intakes based on NNMB (1980) survey data showed that the mean protein intake was 48.79 g/day in females of Andhra Pradesh. The protein intake by women was below 75 per cent of RDA in all states, several investigators (Phansalker et al., 1959, Apte and Venkatachalam, 1962 and Narasinga Rao, 1989) have stated that in India the diet of a large majority of the population consists predominantly of cereals and lacks protein rich and protective foods.

The iron content of several commonly consumed foods as reported in earlier food composition tables has been showed rather high. Re-evaluation has yielded much lower figure for so called iron rich foods, like green leafy vegetables.

Recent studies have also shown that iron contents based on analysis of food as purchased are higher due to contaminant iron. Washing the foods free of contamination lowers the iron content by about 20-30 per cent. The true iron intakes in India are about 20-30 per cent lower than those assessed earlier (ICMR, 1995). The preparation procedure followed like mincing the green leafy vegetables and then cleaning is still most prevalent inspite of continuous community education efforts. Some greens like drumstick and Agathi were boiled and the cooked water is drained off. Such procedures may lead to substantial loss of the nutrient. Thus, most probably the intakes focused may be still lower in view of the facts stated above. Further, the three day dietary intake recorded the frequency of intake of green leafy vegetables at least once and also has the advantage of the iron contribution from the consumption of animal sources of food from a week end day. However, the intakes spread out for 7 days may still be lowered.

The per cent iron content of greens, which were the main source, varies from 0.3 to 38.5 mg. Therefore, the type of greens added is significant in meeting the iron content. It was observed that the green leafy vegetables 'Sirikeerai' was grown as a cash crop and consumed by a majority. But, at other times when this vegetable is not available the dietaries may show different levels of iron intakes in these subjects.

Milk is rich source of calcium. Calcium intake is fairly high being in the range of 1 g or more a day in communities that consume plenty of milk as in the west. However, in developing countries where milk intake is low, most dietary calcium comes from cereals. Since these are only a moderate source, the daily intake of calcium in such communities is in the low range of 300–500 mg a day. Other rich sources of calcium among plant foods are the millet, ragi and green leafy vegetables (ICMR, 1995).

In the present study though quantitative judgment is used, in the case of milk intake, it is a well known fact that milk is diluted at varius levels; at the time of milching, at the time of transferring from one vessel to another (rinsing), while preparing curd, while preparing buttermilk, while preparing coffee etc. Therefore, the intake may be influenced by these dilutions, which could not be objectively assessed. However, the milk consumption has increased particularly because of the 'operation flood' or 'white revolution' programmes aiming at the increase in milk production. In the rural areas the farmers, and women groups were supplied with milching cows or loans are given to purchase milching cows at subsidized rates. Sale of milk has become one of the additional occupation for a majority. Therefore, only some amount of the milk was observed to be utilized for household consumption. Thus, deficiency of calcium is observed only among CED group for which all the foods consumed were found to be inadequate when compared with the standards.

β-Carotene forms a major source of dietary Vitamin 'A' in many developing countries including India. The major plant sources of β-Carotene are green leafy vegetables. The absorption of carotene from greens was found to be much higher than carrots and papaya, ranging from 50-99 per cent. Among factors, which can influence the absorption and utilization of β-Carotene, levels of dietary protein and fat are believed to be important. At recommended levels of dietary protein and fat, absorption of β-Carotene has been shown to be satisfactory in Indian subjects.

In the present context the intake of both protein and fat were lower than the recommended levels for the CED group. This situation may aggravate the already existing deficiency. A moderate level deficiency was observed for the obsess and normal groups. It is to be noted that though green leafy vegetables were the main source of the Vitamin 'A' precursor, the β-Carotene, their composition for the same shows a wide range. The β-Carotene content of greens popular in these areas ranged from 14,000 to 120 μg. This implies that the type of green leafy vegetables included in the diet is crucial to meeting the need for Vitamin 'A'.

The diet survey was undertaken during the months of June and July when the monsoon should begin. But, in the recent years there are some changes observed in the seasons and many a times summer is extending upto June and July with one or two episodes of rain. With the result fruits like mango and papaya are available in plenty and the consumption of the same is high. The same adequate intake levels may not be uniformly maintained although the year.

In habitual Indian diets cereals from the major source of thiamine. In the rice eating population, this is the single most important dietary article, which provides thiamine. Since the vitamin is both water-soluble and heat labile in alkaline solution, considerable amounts are lost during cooking. Retention of thiamine has been found to vary between 30 and 80 per cent of the original amount in several Indian preparations. From rice, loss of thiamine is much higher during washing than cooking (ICMR, 1995). If calculated on this basis all groups including the normal group too may be expected to be experiencing some degree of thiamine deficiency and the already existing deficiency of obese may be increased and in the case of CED the condition may be aggravated further reaching severe degree of deficiency.

Vitamin 'C' is present in high concentrations in leafy vegetables and citrus fruits. Many other commonly consumed fruits such as tomatoes and bananas and vegetables such as potatoes contain useful amounts. The vitamin is readily destroyed by oxidation during storage and cooking at high temperatures. As practiced in Indian households, cooking losses from vegetables have been found to vary widely ranging from negligible quantities to as high as 80 per cent that originally contained. Vitamin 'C' in Indian diets is contributed to a very large extent from cooking vegetables and only a small proportion is derived from raw vegetables and fruits.

In the present context the procedures observed to be followed during preparation and cooking of the vegetables certainly would lead to some losses of this nutrient. However, the intake of several seasonal wild fruits and berries which could not be quantified may be significantly contributing to the need for the vitamin.

SUMMARY AND CONCLUSIONS

The results of the present study reveal that the chronic rates of energy deficiency and excess are widely prevalent among our rural women groups.

The empirical evidences related to dietary intakes reveal that several socio-economic, biological and environmental factors influence the food intake behaviour and thus nutrient intakes of population in general and women in specific. Further, the present nutritional state, which is a consequence of both past and present nutrition, also is shown to influence the food and the subsequent nutrient intakes.

Thus, it is evident from the findings of the study that inspite of all the above mentioned influences the women in CED, obese and normal groups showed distinct differences for several nutrients. This indicates that the under nutrition and over nutrition situations are being sustained by the food and nutrient intakes observed.

The results imply the need and urgency to address the problem of malnutrition, which have several detrimental consequences, to women in particular.

The distribution of height in relation to BMI is presented in table. The data reveal that unlike the trends observed for weight, the height values of CED not only encroached into both obese and normal height values but also in some instances exceeded them.

The trends evident in the contribution of calories to the total calories by the proximate principles CHO, protein and fat in different nutritional states is presented in table. It was clear that irrespective of the nutritional states is carbohydrate dominated in satisfying the calorie needs, followed by fat, both visible and invisible making a combined contribution. The contribution from protein was lower than that of fat.

29

Menarche and Related Problems–A Comparative Study of Inter and Degree Students

D. Usha Rani and V. Sreedevi

INTRODUCTION

Throughout the ages, menstruation in women has been the subject of much speculation and superstitious belief on the part of both laymen and medical men. Only within the last hundred years has any reliable scientific information been available about this function. Research continues to add answers to some of the baffling questions that have existed about this function. In general, however, it may be said that menstruation is the result of failure of conception to occur.

Certain changes in emotions and in physical functioning are commonly seen in women during the menstrual cycle. But menstruation is not an illness and usually is not accompanied by serious pain, although about half of the women experience uneasiness of some kind or other during menstruation. The present study deals with the attitudes of adolescent girls towards menarche and associated problems there on.

METHODOLOGY

In the present study an attempt is made to examine the perceptions of adolescent girls regarding menarche and related problems. The study was undertaken in various colleges of Chittoor district of Andhra Pradesh. The respondents were girls aged between 17-20 years. 200 girls, 100 from Junior Colleges and 100 from Degree Colleges in Chittoor were selected using random sampling technique.

RESULTS AND DISCUSSION

The reproductive health of adolescents, who from a significant and important group, have unfortunately received little or no attention either from the health or educational authorities. These young people are the future of the country, and therefore, their health and well-being becomes an important national concern. During adolescence growth is rapid, disorganized and confusing compared to the relatively stable earlier period of childhood. It is a turbulent period of development when the changes of puberty occur significantly the growth and maturation of the sex organs and emergence of the powerful sex drive. Adolescents require time to get used to their changing bodies and the new body image. In the present study an attempt was made to examine the various concerns associated with menarche and related problems.

LEARNING ABOUT MERARCHE

Learning occur within the learner. People learn through their experiences that is through their activity. By the process of learning, the individual experiences a change in her behaviour through her own efforts. The following table explains the distribution of adolescent girls with respect to them learning about menarche.

Table 1
Percentage Distribution of Adolescents by their Learning about Menarche

Learning about menarche	*Intermediate*		*Degree*	
	No.	*%*	*No.*	*%*
Before Menarche	24	24	30	30
After Menarche	76	76	70	70
Total	100	100	100	100

Table 1 indicates the percentage of intermediate and degree girls with respect of their learning about menarche. Data shows that majority of girls studying intermediate learnt about menarche only after attaining puberty (76%) when compared to those who learnt before attaining the puberty (24%). A high percentage of girls studying degree also learnt about menarche only after attaining their puberty (70%) and nearly one-third of the girls learnt about menarche before attaining their menarche (30%). The research highlight that 3/4th of both the respondents had no knowledge about menarche before they attained their period. The respondents irrespective of their educational levels reported that they were frightened when menstruation occurred first. This itself necessitates that providing knowledge about various issues of reproductive health is very much essential for adolescents so as to prepare them for future parenthood.

SOURCE OF KNOWLEDGE

Knowledge is something that is acquired by the individual through various sources. The adolescent girls should have thorough knowledge about menarche, as they were prone to many psychological and physiological changes during this period. The data regarding source of knowledge about menarche was provided in table 2.

Table 2
Percentage Distribution of Adolescent Girls by their Source of knowledge

Source of Knowledge	*Intermediate*		*Degree*	
	No.	*%*	*No.*	*%*
Mother	61	61	52	52
Sister	2	2	9	9
Friends	23	23	23	23
Relatives	1	1	-	-
Books	4	4	7	7
Grandmother	9	9	9	9
Total	100	100	100	100

It is evident that a greater percentage of girls studying intermediate (61%) and degree (52%), had their source of knowledge from their mothers. But an equal percentage of (23%) intermediate and degree girls had their source of knowledge from their friends whereas for a small percentage of girls studying intermediate the source was their sister (2%) and books (4%). An equal percentage of intermediate and degree girls (9%) had information from their grandmothers.

PLACE OF ATTAINING MENARCHE

The distribution of adolescent girls by place of attaining menarche was presented in table 3.

Table 3
Percentage Distribution of Adolescent Girls by the Place of Attaining Menarche

Place of attaining menarche	*Intermediate*		*Degree*	
	No.	*%*	*No.*	*%*
At home	82	82	91	91
At class	18	18	9	9
Total	100	100	100	100

The data in table 3 reveals that majority of girls from Intermediate (82%) and Degree (91%) attained their menarche at home while a lesser percentage of girls of Intermediate (18%) and Degree girls (9%) attained their menarche in the class which were very traumatic.

SOURSE OF INFORMATION

Adolescence was the crucial period of bodily changes. Adolescents, particularly girls feel shy to express their personal feelings. They share mostly with the persons with whom they are very much attached.The following table provides information about the source who first informed them about menarche.

Table 4
Percentage Distribution of Respondents by who Informed them First about Menarche

Source	*Intermediate*		*Degree*	
	No.	*%*	*No.*	*%*
Teacher	6	6	2	2
Mother	84	84	79	79
Sister	6	6	13	13
Grandmother	4	4	6	6
Total	100	100	100	100

Table 4 presents the percentage distribution of Intermediate and Degree girls with respect to source of first information, about menarche. Data reveals that majority of the girls studying Intermediate were first informed about menarche by their mothers (84%) followed by sister (6%) Teacher (6%) and grandmother (4%). Similar trend was observed among the Degree students also who were informed by Mother (79%) followed by sister (13%) grandmother (6%) and teacher (2%).

GAP BETWEEN MENSTRUATION CYCLES

The information regarding the gap between the menstruation cycles of the adolescent girls was given in table 5.

Table 5
Percentage Distribution of Respondents by Gap between Menstruation Cycles

Gap between Menstruation Cycle	*Intermediate*		*Degree*	
	No.	*%*	*No.*	*%*
Yes	37	37	52	52
No	63	63	48	48
Total	100	100	100	100

The data in table 5 reveals that nearly two thirds (63%) of girls studying intermediate expressed that the gap between the menstruation cycle was not correct and the cycles were very irregular, whereas for one third of the respondents (37%) the cycle was regular and there was correct time gap between cycles. Coming to the students studying degree, almost an equal percentage of the students expressed that the gap between cycles (52%) was correct while 48 per cent reported that the gap between cycles was either more or less.

DURATION OF PERIODS

Duration of periods depends upon one's own physiology. It may last from days to a week. The following table shows the distribution of intermediate and degree girls with respect to the number of days their periods lasted.

The date in the table 6 shows that 2/3rd of intermediate girls (66%) and nearly half of degree girls (45%) had the duration of period for about 5 days whereas one third of degree girls (34%)

and nearly above one tenth of intermediate girls (13%) had 3 to 4 days of duration. The remaining Inter (21%) and Degree girls (15%) had more periods than 6 days.

Table 6
Percentage Distribution of Respondents by Number of Days their periods Lasted

Duration of periods	*Intermediate*		*Degree*	
	No.	*%*	*No.*	*%*
2 days	-	-	6	6
3 or 4 days	13	13	34	34
5 days	66	66	45	45
6 days & above	21	21	15	15
Total	100	100	100	100

ATTITUDE TOWARDS MENARCHE AND RELATED PROBLEMS

Throughout the ages, menstruation in women has been the subject of much speculation and superstitious belief on the part of both laymen and medical men. Only within the last hundred years has any reliable scientific information been available about this function. Research continues to add answers to some of the baffling questions that have existed about this function. In general, however, it may be said that menstruation is the result of failure of conception to occur.

Certain changes in emotions and in physical functioning were commonly seen in women during the menstrual cycle. But menstruation is not an illness and usually is not accompanied by serious pain, although about half of the women experience uneasiness of some kind or other during menstruation. The present study deals with the attitudes of adolescent girls towards menarche and associated problems there on.

FEELINGS BEFORE MENSTRUATION

Some adolescent girls experience a measure of discomfort just preceding or during menstruation, as the body tissues tend to retain fluids. This retention of fluids may cause a temporary weight gain with accompanying feeling of pressure and tension. Therefore, there is a tendency toward emotional unevenness and feeling of depression at this time. However, they are not prolonged or seriously uncomfortable. The following table shows the feelings of adolescent girls before menstruation.

Table 7
Percentage Distribution of Respondents by Feelings before Menstruation

Feelings before menstruation	*Intermediate*		*Degree*	
	No.	*%*	*No.*	*%*
Tension and irritation	5	5	10	10
Back pain, Stomachache, Headache and giddiness	18	18	30	30
Comfortable	52	52	49	49
Uncomfortable	25	25	11	11
Total	100	100	100	100

Table 7 presents the feelings of the respondents before menstruation. Majority of the sample population showed that they were normal before mensus and did not feel any discomfort. The data shows that more than half of the girls studying intermediate (52%) and a little less than half of the girls studying degree (49%) were quite comfortable before menstruation and did not feel any uneasiness. However, in both the groups, considerable number of adolescent girls experienced uneasiness, discomfort, pain and other such associated problems before menstruation. A quarter of intermediate girls (25%) as also one tenth of degree girls (11%) reported that they were uncomfortable before menstruation. Headache, stomachache, backache and giddiness were experienced by one third (30%) and one fifth (18%) of the degree and inter girls respectively. Tension and irritation were experienced by 5 per cent of inter and 10 per cent of degree girls. They stated that during this period they lost their temper easily. The data shows that significant number of adolescents in both the groups were experiencing a number of problems and physical discomfort before menstruation.

FEELINGS DURING MENSTRUATION

Feelings of the adolescent girls during menstruation were presented in table 8.

The data in table 8 shows that an overwhelming majority of the adolescents in both the groups were experiencing problems during menstruation. The picture was striking when compared to the data on 'feelings before menstruation'. Even the girls who were comfortable and normal just before menstruation, suffered with various problems during menstruation. The proportion of girls feeling uncomfortable was higher among the Intermediate girls as compared to the Degree girls. Nearly 60 per cent of the Inter girls and half of the Degree girls (50%) stated that they were very uncomfortable during menstruation. This feeling of discomfort was reported by majority of the girls followed by backache, stomachache, and pain. Restlessness and anxiety were reported by 6 per cent inter and 14 per cent degree girls. Tension and short temperedness was experienced by an equal proportion of girls in both the groups (8% each). The data shows that majority of the adolescent girls experienced physical and emotional difficulties during menstruation.

Table 8
Percentage Distribution of Intermediate and Degree Girls by Feelings During Menstruation

Feelings before menstruation	*Intermediate*		*Degree*	
	No.	*%*	*No.*	*%*
Short tempered and Tension	8	8	8	8
Back pain, Stomachache and pain	13	13	19	19
Uncomfortable	57	57	50	50
Normal	16	16	7	7
Restlessness and anxiety	6	6	14	14
Weakness	—	—	2	2
Total	100	100	100	100

COLLEGE ATTENDANCE DURING MENSTRUATION

During menstrual periods, girls frequently experienced headaches, backaches, cramps and abdominal pain, accompanied by fainting, vomiting, skin irritations and swelling of the legs and ankles. As a result, they feel tired, depressed and irritable at the time of their periods resulting in loss of College days/working days.

From the table 9, it was evident that a large proportion of the respondents attended college during menstruation. Majority of the sample population studying inter (87%) and degree (93%) attended college during menstruation. However nearly one tenth of the respondents studying degree (7%) and 13% of girls studying inter did not go to college during menstruation as they experienced severe physical discomfort.

Table 9
Percentage Distribution of Respondents by College Attendance During Menstruation

College attendence during menstruation	*Intermediate*		*Degree*	
	No.	*%*	*No.*	*%*
Yes	87	87	93	93
No	13	13	7	7
Total	100	100	100	100

COLLEGE ATTENDANCE DURING HEAVY BLEEDING

The girls menstrual periods generally occurred at regular intervals but very markedly in length of the first year or so. The flow of menstrual bleeding also varied.

Table 10
Percentage Distribution of Respondents by College Attendance During Heavy Bleeding

College attendence during heavy bleeding	*Intermediate*		*Degree*	
	No.	*%*	*No.*	*%*
Yes	37	37	53	53
No	63	63	47	47
Total	100	100	100	100

Table 10 presents the data of adolescent girls by attendance to college in case of heavy bleeding during periods. The data showed that a high per cent of girls studying intermediate (63%) did not go to college during heavy bleeding as compared to 47% of girls studying degree. Compared to this, majority of girls studying degree (53%) attended college even during heavy bleeding as against one third of the girls studying intermediate (37%). Put together, it may be observed that majority of the adolescents experienced problems during menstruation and there was considerable loss of college days.

NUMBER OF COLLEGE DAYS LOST

Number of college days lost during menstruation of adolescent girls was presented in table 11.

Table 11
Percentage Distribution of Respondents by the Number of College Days Lost During Menstruation

Feelings before menstruation	*Intermediate*		*Degree*	
	No.	*%*	*No.*	*%*
Don't Stop	41	41	56	56
1 Day	31	31	20	20
2 Days	11	11	15	15
3 Days	17	17	9	9
Total	100	100	100	100

Table 11 shows the distribution of adolescent girls with respect to the number of college days lost during menstruation. A large number of students in Inter (41%) and Degree (56%) said that they went to college during menstruation. However, majority of the students, especially those in Inter were absenting from college at least for a day. Nearly one third of respondents studying Inter (31%) and one fifth studying Degree (20%) did not go to college for one day. 11% of Inter and 15% of Degree girls lost two days and for 17% of Inter and 9% of Degree girls it was three days. It was clear from the data that there was significant proportion of loss of college days which would definitely have an adverse effect on the studies of the adolescent girls.

SITUATION DURING MENSTRUATION

Physical discomfort due to frequent headache, backache, cramps and abdominal pain experienced by the adolescent girls, they could not do their work efficiently, they had difficulty in studying with concentration and were irritated easily. Table 12 shows the situation of girls during menstruation.

Table 12 presents the situation of adolescent girls during menstruation. Majority of the respondents studying Inter (27.2%) and Degree (28.7%) were not able to work properly during menstruation. A small per cent of girls studying Inter (20.6%) and degree (23.3%) lost their temper during menstruation. Similarly one fourth of adolescent girls studying Inter (27.6%) and Degree (23.4%) had difficulty in studying, because their concentration was affected due to physical and psychological stress generated during menstruation. The data clearly shows that physical problems associated with mental stress adversely affected the productive efficacy of the adolescents.

Table 14
Percentage Distribution of the Respondents by Situation During Menstruation

Situation during menstruation	*Intermediate*				*Degree*			
	Yes		*No*		*Yes*		*No*	
	No.	*%*	*No.*	*%*	*No.*	*%*	*No*	*%*
Not able to work properly	62	27.2	38	22.2	76	28.7	24	17.6
Find difficulty to study	63	27.6	37	21.5	62	23.4	38	27.9
Find difficulty in studying	56	24.6	44	25.5	65	24.6	35	25.7
Get more anger	47	20.6	53	30.8	61	23.3	39	28.8
Total	228	100.00	172	100.00	264	100.00	136	100.00

SUM UP

Information and knowledge about menstrual cycle, its associated problems and natural process should be given to adolescent girls before menarche itself. Majority of the respondents studying Intermediate (63%) and Degree (81%) wanted to know about menstrual cycle in detail. Cent per cent of the girls studying Degree and 95% of girls in Inter opined that family life education was imperative for the growth and well-being of the adolescents.

With respect to the attitudes of adolescent girls about various issues on reproductive health, only a few percentage of girls studying Inter (15.40%) and Degree (17.66%) knew information correctly on various reproductive health issues but a major proportion of the respondents were not aware of the right concepts of the issues. Hence, a well planned educational programme is very much essential to educate the adolescent girls on the issues of reproductive health.

IMPLICATIONS

The findings of the study show that women respondents are plagued with various concern and uncertainties. Their needs and aspirations are hampered by various socio-cultural constraints. Hence, any programmes formulated for their benefit should have in integrated multi-dimensional approach aiming at building up of awareness of health care. The programmes should facilitate for a holistic development of women.

The following programmes may be undertaken for attaining quality reproductive health.

POPULATION INFORMATION, EDUCATION AND COMMUNICATION STRATEGIES FOR GOOD REPRODUCTIVE HEALTH

Population policies and legislation have a major role to play in the creation of a supportive environment for reproductive health and family planning. Information, education and communication activities are facilitated when they are supported by population policies and appropriate legislation. It is also recognized that information, education and communication activities are valuable instruments for facilitating the understanding and acceptance of the goals and objectives of population policies.

Population education is another common strategy adopted by Governments as part of their population policies. It usually covers such topics as population dynamics, pregnancy and family planning, family life, sex education and more recently, new ways of looking at gender issues, and HIV/AIDS and sexually transmitted diseases. There is increasing evidence that sex and HIV/AIDS education programmes may reduce unsafe practices among sexually active adolescents and reduce early pregnancies.

GENDER EQUALITY AND EQUITY

The programme of Action affirms that the full participation and partnership of both women and men is required in reproductive life. Education and information that promote such aims, along with responsible sexuality and respect for women, are also fundamental to improving the status and role of women in society. Increasing the education given to girls and women contributes to their empowerment and to improved family health. Expanding women's knowledge of reproductive health and expanding their choices enables them to meet their reproductive goals. Information, education and communication activities can contribute to eradicating harmful practices against women and girls, such as female genital mutilation; drawing attention to the health needs of the girl-child; eliminating nutrition practices that discriminate against girls; involving men and reproductive health and family planning programmes; removing barriers to women's rights and enforcing legislation on early marriage, sexual exploitation and violence; and ensuring that women have equal access to education, are guaranteed equal opportunity to work an deceive equal pay for equal work.

PARTICIPATION OF PROGRAMME USERS

The participation of programme users in the design, implementation and evaluation of information, education and communication programme interventions increases the likelihood of success. Different population group have their own perspectives, ideas and opinions in many areas, particularly about sexual and reproductive health. Communicating effectively with them requires their direct participation.

30

Nutritional Status and Dietary Profile of Married Pregnant Adolescent Girls and Young Women

Baby Depur and G. Nagamani

Adolescence is a period of rapid growth and development. Nutritional requirements in relation to body size are more during adolescence. Majority of the girls do not achieve their full height and weight potential on account of their dietary insufficiencies during growing periods. Most of the girls in rural areas are married at an early age and bear children. Hence, they are likely to under go greater nutritional stress if they fail to receive adequate nourishment during adolescence.

Mothers having body weights less than 38 Kgs and heights less than 145 cms during their reproductive period are likely to be at risk during delivery and give birth to babies of low birth weight (Gopalan, 1989). Adolescent girls constitute about 7 per cent of the population in India and 2.3. Per cent of them get married before the age of 18 years. Early marriage was followed by early maternity which increased mortality among women. These cultural attributes have left a deep mark on women's health in India. These cultural compulsions are more pronounced in rural areas and in families of low socio economic groups.

Keeping this factors in view, this study was conducted with an objective to asses the nutritional status of rural married pregnant, non pregnant adolescent girls and pregnant and non pregnant young women by anthropometry, Dietary intake and haemoglobin levels.

MATERIAL AND METHODS

The study was conducted in Tirupati Rural Mandal of Chittoor District (A.P). Purposive random sampling was adopted in the selection of respondents. A total of hundred families were randomly selected. A group of married pregnant adolescent girls (n = 25), married non pregnant adolescent girls (n = 25) and pregnant young women (n = 25), non pregnant young woman (n = 25) of reproductive age covering 15-21 years from each family was the main subject of the study.

Anthropometric measurements were recorded for height, weight and mid upper arm circumference (MUAC) by using standard techniques (Jelliffe, 1966). BMI was calculated by using the formula wt (kgs)/Ht (m^2). Dietary survey of all the households and intakes by the subjects selected was carried out to get food intake data for 3 alternate days in a week by 24 hours recall method and one day intakes by weighment. Thus, a mean of three days intake was considered. Accordingly, nutritive value of diets were calculated using food values book of ICMR, India and compared with ICMR RDA's (Gopalan et al., 1993). Cyanmethaemoglobin method (Dacie and Lewis, 1995) was employed for estimation of haemoglobin (Hb) in the blood samples of the subjects. The level of Hb was compared with the standard values suggested by WHO (1989) for grades of anaemia.

RESULTS AND DISCUSSION

The socio-economic characteristics of the study adolescent girls and young women showed that 64.6 per cent of girls and young women belonged to scheduled caste followed by 35.4 per cent in backward class. The mean age, attainment of menarche, income and educational status of girls and young woman are presented in Table 1.

ANTHROPOMETRY

The mean height, weight, MUAC and calculated BMI scores of married adolescent girls and young woman are given the Table 2. The data showed that all the married pregnant and non pregnant adolescent girls and young women were far below (87-94%) the

Table 1
General Information of Adolescent Girls and Young Women

General information	*Adolescent girls (15-18 years)*		*Young woman (19-21 years)*	
	Pregnant	*Non Pregnant*	*Pregnant*	*Non Pregnant*
Mean age	17.23	16.78	21.23	20.50
Mean age of menarche	13.54	13.78	14.01	13.95
Income (Rs.)	800-1000/-	1000-1200/-	1200-1500/-	1400-1600/-
Education Illiterate	5%	-	-	-
Upto Primary Education	90%	65%	75%	85%
Upto Secondary Education	5%	35%	25%	15%

Table 2
Mean Heights, Weights, BMI and MUAC of Married Pregnant, Non-Pregnant Rural Adolescent Girls and Pregnant, Non-Pregnant Young Women

Group	*Height (cm)*	*Weight (Kg)*	*BMI (wt/ht^2)*	*MUAC (cm)*
ICMR (R_1) (Non Pregnant)	156	50	20.55	23.24
Pregnant	-	50+12	-	-
Married-non pregnant girls (15 to 18 years) (n=25)	148 ± 2.05	43.5 ± 2.25	19.85	19.5 ± 2.15
Pregnant adolescent (15 to 18 years) (n = 25) Ist trimester	148 ± 2.10	45 ± 2.25	20.54	20.00 ± 1.15
IInd trimester	148.5 ± 2.25	47 ± 2.25	20.54	20.5 ± 1.20
IIIrd trimester	148.0 ± 2.15	49 ± 3.05	22.37	21.50 ± 2.00
Non pregnant Young women (19-21 years) (n=25)	151 ± 2.10	45 ± 2.50	19.95	21 ± 2.25
Pregnant young woman Ist trimester	150.50 ± 2.15	47 ± 2.25	20.88	21.75 ± 2.00
IInd trimester	150.15 ± 2.50	53 ± 3.00	23.55	21.90 ± 2.15
IIIrd trimester	150 ± 3.15	55 ± 2.50	25.33	21.95 ± 2.25

ICMR standards for heights and weights. The mean heights of all the married girls (aged 15-18 years) was found to be less than 150 Cm, and mean weights were found to be les than 45 Kg and mean

MUAC was less than 20 cm, respectively. The mean heights, weights and MUAC of young women was 151 Cm, 45 Kg, and 21.50 cm, where the expected means for height 156 Cm, weight 50 Kg and MUAC 23 Cm, for the said age groups to ICMR standards are clearly seen. The adolescent married girls and young women could not reach to the given ICMR standard height & weights. The means of rural girls were significantly low for the three measurements made. However in the present study pregnant adolescent girls fail to gain in weight as well as MUAC in the three trimesters. It is clear that pregnant adolescent girls had weight less than 45 kg and gain in weight i.e., 6 kgs than expected weight of 12 kgs indicating slow growth process and poor fetal growth in adolescent pregnant mothers. Weight gain at 28 and 32 weeks of pregnancy was better among pregnant young women, i.e., 10 Kg. Mean BMI of all the married adolescent girls was very low than compared to young women. This indicates that even prior to pregnancy and during pregnancy the adolescent mothers would not have an optimum nutritional status.

Similar findings have been reported by National Nutrition Monitoring Bureau (NNMB, 1972–97) which shows that heights, weights and growth rates of adolescents of low income groups, in both rural and urban areas are about 70-80 per cent of those of well-to-do adolescents in India. Similarly in other studies girls belonging to low socio economic groups have been found to be shorter and lighter as compared to well–to-do girls. Pushpamma et al., (1982); chaturvedi et al., (1994); Pallavi et al., (2002).

DIETARY INTAKE

The nutrient intakes of married pregnant, non pregnant adolescent girls and young women are presented in Table 3. It is observed that all the nutrient intakes were far below the ICMR RDA. The intake of body building and protective foods by the adolescent girls was very low than young women. They hardly consume 100 – 200 ml of milk or 50 g of pulse items and 100 g of any other vegetables. Once a week or once in fortnight, they consume flesh foods. Even if they consume, a very low amount is given to girls. This gross inadequacy in the diets is clearly seen in the form of nutrient intakes. The nutrient intakes are lower than the recommended dietary allowances. This pattern of dietary intakes is observed in all age groups and it is continuously prolonged throughout the reproductive period and is almost a regular feature of the diets of slum, rural scheduled caste girls and young women. From the table 3, it is clear that both groups of girls and young women met only 60 to 70% of RDA. It is therefore evident that teenage mothers who are already at lower than optimum nutritional status before pregnancy also had lower intake of nutrients during pregnancy compared to young women aged 19–21 years. The above findings can be explained by the fact that girls belonging to low socio economic group have inadequate diets both qualitatively and quantitatively compared to well to do adolescent girls.

Table 3
Mean Nutrient Intakes of Married Pregnant and Non-Pregnant Rural Adolescent Girls and Young Women

Parameters	*RDA*	*Pregnant adolescent girls (15-18 years)*	*Pregnant Young women (19-21 years)*	*RDA*	*Non-pregnant adolescent girls (15-18 years)*	*Non Preganant Young Women (19-21 Years)*
Energy (Kcal)	2175	1668. 78 ± 12.22	1758.65 ± 11.58	2060	1568.48 ±12.46	1628.28 ±12.21
Protein (gm)	60	33.23 ± 7.7	35.23 ± 7.78	60	29.23 ± 2.45	30.23 ±4.45
Calcium (mg)	500	317.43 ±15.9	350.43 ±15.45	500	259.36 ±12.46	274.35 ±10.46
Iron (mg)	30	23.4±6.7	25.4±7.8	30	20.4±4.4	21.4±7.7
Vitamin C (mg)	40	26.34 ± 3.34	30.25 ± 13.30	40	24.58 ± 2.58	25.58 ±3.58
Vitamin A (mg)	600	314.8 ±19.43	317.87 ± 19.43	600	279.13 ± 19.53	299.13 ±15.53

HAEMOGLOBIN LEVELS

Based on Haemoglobin levels, as suggested by WHO the per cent of girls and young women suffering from different degrees of anaemia was tabulated in Table 4. The mean haemoglobin levels ranged from 6.46 to 11 gm per 100 ml of blood. The number and per cent of girls and women suffering were denoted. Majority (60 per cent) of the pregnant adolescent girls had severe anemia hb < 7 g/dl followed by moderate anaemia hb< 8- 9 g/dl. From the table-4, it is observed that young women had lower degree of anaemia than compared to the pregnant adolescent girls. The lesser haemoglobin level among girls and young women may be due to the fact that the dietary intake of iron was found to be very low than the ICMR RDA. Besides this, the major share of iron was contributed by cereals and pulses and the presence of phytic substances in cereals and pulses reduce the biological availability of iron.

Table 4
The Number and Per cent of Girls and Young Women Suffering from Different Degrees of Anaemia

Hb level gm/dl	*Number of Subjects*				
	Degrees of anaemia	*Pregnant adolescent girls (n = 25)*	*Non-pregnant adolescent girls (n = 25)*	*Pregnant young women (n=25)*	*Non pregnant young women (n = 25)*
< 12	Anaemic	–	–	–	–
< 7	Severe	15 (60)	10(40)	6 (24)	2 (8)
8 to 9.00	Moderate	6 (24)	9 (36)	10 (40)	11 (44)
10 to 10.9	Mild	4(16)	6 (24)	7(28)	9 (36)
11 to 11.9	Marginal	–	–	2 (8)	3 (12)

• Figures in parenthesis indicate percentages.

In the present study, adolescent pregnant mothers had height less than 150 cm which is indicative of incomplete skeletal development and weight less than 45 kgs indicates poor nutritional status. It is therefore evident that teenage mothers who are already at a lower than optimum nutritional status before pregnancy also had lower intake of nutrients resulted in poor growth and aneamia. The adolescents mothers showed poor weight gain generally considered to be indicative of not only poor obstetric risk but also of greater chances of abortions, still births and low birth weights of the offspring.

The findings of the study reveal that there is an urgent need to initiate nutrition supplementary intervention measures as well as nutrition education programmes to improve the health and nutritional status of girls from deprived communities. The situation calls for nutritional educational programmes immediately to educate teenage girls and mothers on the consequences of early marriage, followed by early maternity and provide them special nutritional inputs and better monitoring facilities especially before pregnancy and during pregnancy in rural areas. This would ensure the health and well being of mothers as well as their children and to strengthen the cycle of mothers to be, mothers and their children to go and grow in a healthy way.

REFERENCES

Dacie, J.V. and S.M. Lewis (1995), (Eds): "Practical Hematology Churchill, Livingston, Vth edition, 132.

Gopalan, C., Rama Shastri, B.V., Balasubramanyam S.C. (1993), Nutritive Value of Indian Foods, NIN, ICMR, Hyderabad.

Gopalan, C. (1989), Women and Nutrition in India. Some Practical Consideration, NFI Bulletin, 1989. 10:1-4.

Jelliffe, D.B. (1966), The Assessment of Nutritional Status of the Community. World Health Organisation, WHO Monograph Series No. 583.

Kamala Krishnaswamy and Rameshwara Sharma, K.V. (2000), Health and Nutritional Status of Women Adolescent Girls in India. Workshop on Empowerment of Women with Special Reference to Women's Health. National Commission for Women, Nov. 25-26, S.V. University, Tirupati.

National Nutrition Monitoring Bureau, Report of Survey (1972-97): National Institute of Nutrition, ICMR, Hyderabad.

Pallavi, P. Kharade and Usha Antony (2002), Nutritional Status and Outcome of Pregnancy in Young and Older Mothers in Mumbai. The Ind. J. Nutr. Dietet., 39, 26.

Pushpamma, P., Geervani K.P. Lakshmi Devi, N. (1982), Food intake Nutrient Adequacy and Anthropometry of Adolescents in Andhra Pradesh. Indian Journal of Medial Research, 75; 61-67.

Swapna Chaturvedi, Kapil, U. Bhati, T., Gnanasekaram, N. and R.M. Pandey (1994), Nutritional Status of Married Adolescent Girls in Rural Rajasthan. Indian J. Paediatr, 61, 695-70.

WHO Report (1989), Iron Deficiency Anaemia: Preventing and Controlling Iron Deficiency Anaemia through Primary Health Centre. World Health Organisation, Geneva, 25.

31

Mainstreaming Gender in Health, Nutrition & Population Stabilization

Padma

The mainstream refers to an inter-related set of dominant ideas, values, practices, institutions and organizations that determine "who gets what" within a society. The ideas and practices within the mainstream tend to reflect and reinforce each other and thus provide a rationale for any gives allocation of societal resources and opportunities.

Being part of the mainstream means that women and men have equitable access to resources, including opportunities and rewards. It implies equal participation in influencing what is valued in shaping options within society. Becoming part of the mainstream means sharing equitably in the benefits of development. Becoming part of the mainstream offers the opportunity to influence who does what in a society, who owns (and can own) what, who has access to jobs and incomes, who controls the society's resources and institutions, who makes decisions, who sets priorities.

CHANGING ATTITUDES

Gender mainstreaming requires gender-responsive public policy. When gender equality considerations are incorporated into policy-making, the concerns and needs of both women and men become integral parts of the design, implementations, monitoring and evaluation of policies and programmes in all sectors of society. Mainstreaming is more than an "add women and stir" approach to policy making. It goes beyond requiring an equal mix of men and women in the decision-making process. Equal participation is important, but an awareness of the changes that will be needed to make women full functioning partners in the development process is just as important.

Gender mainstreaming often involves challenging the status quo. It means changing policies and institutions so that they actively promote gender equality. It will involve adjustments to the attitudes of individuals, organisations and systems. It is a transformative process that involves rethinking social values and development goals. In the end, the fairness, justice and intelligent use of resources inherent in gender mainstreaming must therefore be understood as a complex, multi-dimensional and long-term process that focuses on the needs of both women and men in order to achieve the optimal development of their society.

GENDER MAINSTREAMING

- Gender mainstreaming is a process or strategy to work toward the goal of gender equality. It is not an end in itself.
- It is an approach to governance that makes men's and women's concerns and experiences an integral part of the design, implementation, monitoring and evaluation of policies and programs in all sectors of society.
- It involves changing policies and institutions so that they actively promote gender equality.
- It is a long-term, transformative process that involves rethinking socio-cultural values and development goals.

WHY IS GENDER MAINSTREAMING IMPORTANT

Gender mainstreaming is an important aspect of good governance. It seeks to ensure that institutions, policies and programs responds to the need and interests of women as well as men, and distribute benefits equitably between women and men. It contributes to social, economic and cultural progress. It leads to greater fairness, equality and justice for women and men, thus enhancing the accountability of governments to achieve results for all citizens. Biology and

Physiology are two of the few ways in which men and women irrefutably differ; health policies and programmes are logical entry points for the integration of a gender perspective.

At the same time, we know that health is not simply the lack of physical infirmity, nor is it a simple question of bodily parts and functions – it is a holistic state of well-being, and is thus profoundly influenced by psychological and social factors. For this reason, an analysis of health must go beyond male and female bodies to the institutions, traditions and attitudes that play a crucial role in determining quality of care, and root cause of poor health. As many of these institutions and factors are premised upon the different roles of men and women in society, a gender perspective here is critical.

WHAT IS THE ISSUE? WHAT IS THE GOAL

Life expectancy at birth is one of the few health-related statistics that is widely available and gender disaggregated. Gender plays an important and irrefutable role in life expectancy. Worldwide and as a group, women tend to live longer than men, and Eastern Europe maintains the highest gap between male and female life expectancy in the world.

Some important causes and factors of low male life expectancy include:

- Deaths in armed conflicts and street violence;
- High mortality rates from accidents, including traffic accidents in particular;
- Occupational hazards and accidents;
- High rates of suicide;
- Alcoholism-related death.

Thus while biology may play a role, it is evident that male life expectancy can be dramatically affected by different environments in which men and women operate, by their different choices of coping mechanisms–all related to the social and economic gender roles assumed by men and women assume throughout their lifetimes.

The reason for examining life expectancy from a gender perspective is to provide important insight into gender disparities in the health and well-being of the population. The ultimate goal in regards to life expectancy is:

- 59 Research has shown women to be at a slight biological advantage in terms of life span (World Bank Consultation Draft, Chapter 1, pg. 10).
- To close the gap between male and female life expectancy at birth, aiming for maximum life expectancy whereby both men and women can enjoy healthy and productive lives.

Justice: The ultimate human right is the right to life. It is therefore a human rights imperative to address factors that systematically deny one gender or the other the right to enjoy a full and healthy life.

Efficiency: Healthy national demographics require a roughly balanced male: female ratio. In transition countries, low average life span in men is largely affected by death from unnatural causes in working-age males. This has an obvious impact on the productivity of the labour force, and can thus affect the economic growth of the nation as a whole.

Quality of Life: High death rates among working age males affects not only men, but women and families as well. For example, poverty rates among pension-aged windows tend to be very high, as they are unable to cover basic costs of rent and utilities from a single pension. Living conditions of families with children are also likely to deteriorate, particularly if the man was the main breadwinner (women's disadvantage in the labour market is also a factor here).

CONCLUSIONS

Impacting mortality rates is a long-term process and effects of any policies or measures to reduce male mortality will not be evident for some time to come. Ensuring high quality mental and physical health care for men, targeting preventive care at men and reducing external risks (i.e. removing occupational hazards, reducing traffic fatalities) are directions in which policies should move to tackle this issue.

- Provide adequate and correct information to the community, particularly the women about MTP services at health centres. Include this information along with other actives so that women have easy access to it. For examples when women come for immunization of their children.
- Place adequately trained health staff at convenient times. Ensure equipment and facilities for abortion and dealing with complication.

- Provide gender sensitive training to health staff on how to deal with women needing abortion services.
- Introduce a programme for post abortion follow up so that women are given adequate treatment and care. This information will spread to others.
- Initiate a more proactive approach for identifying and referring women needing abortion services.
- Review MTP act and abortion policy to enable menstrual regulation and to involve midlevel providers so that a greater number of women are reached.

Conduct a series of meetings or workshops with stake holders (Ob/gyn specialists, health service providers, private practitioners, consumers, NGOs and opinion.

PART - V
Gender Equality

32

Empowerment of Women and Moving Towards Equality –Some Conceptual Issues

C. Sivaramakrishna Rao, N. Linga Murthy and K. Mohan Reddy

Over the last two decades of the women's movement across India, there is an increasing emphasis on the promotion of gross-root level organisation for women's development and discussions take place on women's status and empowerment. It is important than to look at the context in which discussions over empowerment and indeed women's empowerment have arisen. On the whole, the context is one where there is a contradiction between a hierarchical social order and a democratic political system. Where the rights of citizenship and democratic constitution founder against entrenched tradition and prejudice (Malavika Karlekar, 2004). The traditional disabilities due to caste and gender were social and not just economic. Deep-rooted ideas of purity and pollution governed the social standings of different castes and sexes; men and women were deemed to be of unequal moral worth as were the different 'Varnas' and the social hierarchy was underpinned by a legal order in which privileges and disabilities were carefully modulated according to caste and gender. The law has now changed; social attitudes have also changed though to a much smaller extent. Despite the changes, women and persons of inferior caste continue to suffer from many disadvantages (Andre Beteille, 1999).

There are systematic disparities in the freedoms that men and women enjoy in different societies, and these disparities are often not reducible to differences in income or resources. While differential wages or payment rates constitute an important part of gender inequality in most societies, there are many other spheres of differential benefits, e.g., in the division of labour within the household, in the context of care or education received, in liberties that different members are permitted to enjoy. There is a lot of indirect evidence of differential treatment of women and men, and particularly of girls vis-à-vis boys, in many parts of the world e.g. among rural families in Asia and North Africa (Amartya Sen, 1992).

It is in this context, empowerment of women awareness greater significance. Citing various dictionary meanings of empowerment, which can range from 'give power to' and 'give capacity to perform some mental or physical activity to 'delegate authority,·to give legal rights', Banerjee (1993) parts out that these meanings encapsulate both economic empowerment as well as its more wide ranging ramifications, while empowerment may be invoked in virtually any context, be it human rights, basic needs, capacity building, skill promotion or overall economic security. Banarjee argues that of all the components, capacity building is the only one that is not with reference to others, or in relation to them, but rather puts the onus for self-development on women. Malavika Karlekar argues that it is this meaning of empowerment that is the most relevant in the present context. At the same time, however one looks at empowerment, its operationalisation means a change in social and power relations as it seeks to change society through a rearrangement of power'.

The notion of capacity building stresses individual growth as much it not more than an expand adjustment in the sharing of power and authority. Nonetheless, as enhancing individual capacity involves new skills as well as new ways of viewing oneself, the process may cause a woman to reflect on her situation including a sense of autonomy or lack of it; it may also help her to work towards a better adjustment to domestic power relation as well as her attitude to the wider environment. At the same time at the inter-personal level, empowerment of some may lead to the disempowerment of others– or at any rate, a perception that they are being disempowered. This is particularly true of men within families who often feel threatened when women organise. Empowerment clearly leads to a better sense of self-worth, often through collective action, which aims at, among other things, economic improvement. For as Beteille argues, empowerment is largely about 'ordinary, common people, rather than politicians, experts and other socially or culturally advantaged persons', an improvement in the quality of life is integral to the understanding of the term (Malavika Karlekar, 2004).

Arguing that increasingly, empowerment is being used pervasively, not only by government/international agencies, but by NGOs, activists and researchers as well, Narayana Banarjee goes on to draw attention to the fact that the process often involves participation in and through organisations. Grassroots women organisations act as pressure groups as well as agencies for conscienstisation, combining both agitational and developmental approaches they are expected to negotiate the distributional aspects of power and resources. Decision making is to be decentralised and the role of collective leadership emphasized.

Since the 1990's, the Welfare approach that viewed women as beneficiaries or recipients of benefits, services and concessions has been modified by the developmental approach. The latter emphasises methods of enabling and empowering women to become independent in all aspects of their lives rather than merely availing relief dispensations. According to Srilatha Battiwala NGOs usually focus on one of three approaches–integrated development, economic empowerment or consciousness–rising, while these three are not discrete and mutually exclusive, organisations tend to focus on one approach more than the other. Today most NGOs believe in a developmental orientation that stresses capacity building for its members where assistance is limited to a defined period to equip the poor with literacy, skills, tools and so forth. Other with a more radical ideology stress the need to restructure societies through organised action. For, while empowerment may be at the cost of a growing sense of disempowerment among the once powerful to be meaningful and effective, capacity building has also to inculcate the skills of role–sharing and participatory behaviour among the new elite.

But one should recognise that power is a social relationship that involves people, whether as individuals or groups. Conflict is the defining projects of power. (Joy Deshmukh, Ranadive) Feminists have had varied responses to the issue of power. According to Hooks, radical feminists challenged the prevailing notion of power as domination and attempted to transform its meaning and in vain. Chelser and Goadman argues in favour of women working to obtain power within the existing social structures. But the authors basic some interesting questions:

(i) Is there some possibility that once in power women would overcome the established economic and social system and be more humanist?

(ii) Do women lust for Power?

(iii) Do they really resist the pressure of ambition?

(iv) Do they nor care about working for themselves, for society?

(v) Do women possess greater moral values, more substantial values than men do, or one they just as conditioned to relate to short range personal goals, or do they just lack information?

(vi) Do women nor want the control in same way of human beings by other human beings?

(vii) Do women resist job promotion because of their understanding of the moral compromise?

(viii) Do women question the moral justification, if any, for such control of power?

Many participants in feminist movements sincerely believe that women are different from men and would exercise power differently. According to Hooks, though they are assigned different sex - gender based roles to play in society, women are not taught a different value system. Although they do not have the power that ruling groups of men exert, they do not conceptualise power differently. Like most men, most women are taught from childhood that dominating and controlling others is the basic expression of power. They would organise it differently only if they had a different value system. Feminist activists now realise that women are likely to exercise power in the same manner as men when they assume the same positions in social and political arenas (Joy Deshmukh Ranadive, 2005).

At the same time attempts have been made by other feminists to redefine power positively with new organisational strategies and an emphasis on internal democracy. Power need not be understood only in the negative sense of a relation between the exploited and exploiter. Feminist writing has now began to see that as much as there is power over, there is also power to, power with and power within. Power over involves an either/ or relationship of domination/ subordination. It is based ultimately on socially sanctioned threats of violence and intimidation, and requires constant vigilance to maintain. It also invites active and passive resistance. Power to relates to having decision-making authority and power to solve problems, and can be creative and enabling. The third, power with involves people organising with a common purpose or common understanding to achieve collective goals. The fourth, power within refers to self-confidence, self-awareness and assertiveness. By analysing their experience and through this power, individuals can recognise how power operates in their lives and gain the confidence to act to influence and change this. Empowerment can not be seen as separate from power.

The first interpretation of power–power over–offers the rationale to begin the process of empowerment. The second interpretation–power to–refers to the ultimate stage of empowerment, when a person has achieved the capacity to take action. The third dimension, power with, reflects on the methods that such a process can initiate and set in motion that is institutions such as purposeful collections. The fourth interpretation of power within can be interpreted as sustenance of the process where by empowerment does not remain limited to intermittent actions, but can be conceived as the building of capacities to carryout future action in a sustained manner. Power can not be reconceptualised and reinterpreted unless one pays attention to alteration of value systems. If value systems can be altered, say to that of human rights, then power can be sought in the understandings of power alluded to earlier (Joy Deshmukh–Ranadive, 2005).

Amartya Sen views development as freedom. Freedom can be sustained only through equal participation. In the context of development, empowerment can not be given to anyone; it is a process whereby an inequality–of participation in the various processes of development–moves towards becoming an equality. Empowerment is thus a process where constraints that impede equal participation are reduced. Empowerment can also be understood as an expansion in spaces–physical spaces, economic, socio-cultural and political spaces.

Physical space is of two kinds–geographical space and body space. The limited mobility of women over geographical distance restricts their access to opportunities in education, health and employment. A woman's ownership and control of her own body is often limited. Many cultures views women's bodies as property owned by men. Sexuality and reproductive behaviour are also controlled. On the one hand, women have limited control over their bodies; on the other, there are restrictions about the geographical spaces that their bodies can inhabit or move across. Hence, there are restrictions both within and outside the house applicable to women (Joy Deshmukh Ranadive, 2005).

Economic spaces represent opportunities for livelihoods, employment, property and acquisition of assets. Though they do a lot of household work, their economic contribution has been hidden from view, unless their work translates into monetary incomes, it is rarely regarded as work. Even if we argue that poverty alleviation programmes often see the generation of livelihoods and incomes as the panacea to pull households out of poverty traps, to what extent they can empower women is a moot point. The employment guarantee Act in rural areas should have an equal coverage for generating work to rural women.

Socio-cultural space is determined by class, caste, race, region and ideological frameworks in which a society operates. Socio-cultural environment and spaces and the most stubborn and difficult to alter. The cost of an expansion in this space is often high for an individual woman. That is why collectives and collective actions are seen as most effective vehicles for empowerment. To a certain extent a greater access to political space can trigger some change in socio-cultural space. Political space has also two dimensions to it the public political space and private political space. Public political space is achieved through access to public office and processes of political activity. It can also be interpreted as the promotion of social capital. The expansion of these spaces in one of the most important constituents towards lending voice to the problems of poor and marginalised groups. A greater participation of women in Panchayati Raj system can be viewed as step in the empowerment though some would argue that it is of nominal significance. One has to view the long-run changes that can take place by their increased participation as it would lead to changes in socio-cultural space. Private political space consists of hierarchies and placements within families and households, which are determined by age, relationship and gender. Kinship, lineage, ideology and socio-cultural norms determine these placements and consequently the status of member within the households. Interventions such as micro credit succeed in affecting the macro and domestic environments, particularly the economic dimension, since they enhance opportunities for livelihoods. They also expand the political dimension by facilitating the promotion of self-help group (Jon-Deshmukh Ranadive, 2005). Through these interventions can lead to an expansion in mental space, for an expansion of socio-cultural space, the logic has to be turned on its head. Thus, there has to be an expansion of mental space for there to be an expansion in socio-cultural space. For this to happen, there is need for outside interventions that supplement economic interventions. What are needed are interventions that seek to alter value systems so that information then gets transformed into knowledge that empowers.

But the new value system that tries to replace the old should not be inimical to women empowerment. The trap lies here in the nature of values that are being transmitted. In the case of the sweep of globalization, where the value system hinges upon competitiveness and consumerism, a mere demonstration effect of more market oriented life styles through fast paced information technology and the media makes for a transformation of values that is necessarily democratic. On the other hand, they are necessarily removed from values of justices. These transitions are taking place world wide. In some countries an attempt to preserve the local heritage, customs and traditions in the face of such global change have led to more rigid structures for women. The need today for awareness of human rights and democracy is far more acute than ever before. The grip of injustice based upon consumerism is different to perceive since it is a abetted within the models of new life styles that appear to embody progress (Joy Deshmukh, Ranadive).

In India, as in South Asia, the family and the community are considered to be the most natural of all relationships. They provide emotional security, material support, a sense of belongingness status, legitimacy and social identity. Hence, it is indeed relevant to talk of the right to be human in the context of the family and household. A woman has the right to be first recognised as a human being before various roles are expected of her in the domestic and public arenas. For this happen, everyday patterns of gender discrimination that are usually accepted justified as socially legitimate have to be questioned and placed at a centre stage. In the context of the values of democracy and existing discriminatory social norms, feminist ideology should attempt to change current understandings of power and empowerment in such as manner that men are not isolated from the processes leading to equality. There is immense advantage to be gained by both men and women where gender discrimination is effectively countered. Though, this process will take some time for realisation, it is the same pattern for moving towards equality.

REFERENCES

Malavika Karlekar, "A Note on the Empowerment of Women", *Indian Journal of Gender Studies,* 11:2 (2004), SAGE Publications, New Delhi.

Andre Beteille (1999), "Empowerment", *Economic and Political Weekly,* March 6-13.

Amartya Sen (1992), "Inequality Re-examined", Oxford University Press, New Delhi.

Joy Deshmukh--Ranadive, "Are Democracy and Human Rights Valid within Domestic Units? Some Theoretical Explorations", *Indian Journal of Gender Studies,* 12:1 (2005), SAGE Publications, New Delhi.

Sunny Jose, "Gender bias in Resource Allocation in India: Where do Household Models and Empirical Evidence Interest", *Indian Journal of Gender Studies* 10:3 (2003), SAGE Publicaitons, New Delhi.

Jo-Anne Everingham, "Mahila Sanghas as Feminist Groups: The Empowermernt ofWomen and Coastal Orissa", *Indian Journal of Gender Studies,* 9:1 (2002), SAGE Publications, New Delhi.

33

Gender Equality: New Opportunities for Moving Ahead

B. Ratna Kumari, Tara Kumari & A. Rajani

Gender equality and women's empowerment are critical to all areas of development, and gender experts are urging that they be fully integrated into the implementation and monitoring of all eight Millennium Development Goals (MDGs). This would entail having a broader set of priorities and actions at the national level.

At the same time, a goal specifically geared toward gender equality and women's empowerment is seen as crucial. Work is therefore under way to ensure that MDG 3 (Promote gender equality and empower women) is grounded in a broad framework that seeks to take action in spheres beyond education and spheres including health and political and economic decision-making.

To this end, the UN Millennium project which is making recommendations to help countries achieve the MDGs, has adopted a framework for MDG 3 that has three dimensions: improving women's capabilities (as measured by education, health and nutrition): increasing women's access to economic and political opportunities: and ensuring women's security (by reducing women's vulnerability to violence and conflict). Within this framework, the Project's Task Force on Education and Gender Equality has outlined a series of priority actions for countries *(www.unmillennium project.org)*.

The status of women in India has gradually changed from pre independence period to post modernity. Hence there is a need to take up research regarding women development and gender empowerment in India so that one can assess the gender equality in our Country. In this context, the present study has made an attempt to define the term gender equality in a broader sense with a patriarchal perspective and to analyze Gender Development Index in India and challenges in achieving gender equality and to suggest some policy implications for gender equality.

OBJECTIVES

The objectives of the study are:

1. To define and debate patriarchy and gender equality and how it dominates the issue of gender equality.
2. To analyze the Gender Development Index in India.
3. To study the challenges in the empowerment process and;
4. To suggest some policy implication for gender equality in India.

WHAT IS PATRIARCHY?

The word patriarchy literally means the rule of the father. It is used more generally to refer to male domination, to the power relationships by which men dominate women and to characterize the system whereby women are kept subordinate in a number of ways.

Patriarchy may defined as a system where men control women's lives, bodies, labour and experiences (Kamal Bhasin, 1994). Patriarchy is deeply rooted in the society because all social institutions-the family, religion, the legal system, the economic system system and economic institutions, political systems and institutions, media, educational institutions and knowledge systems are patriarchal in nature.

Men and women both contribute to the sustenance of this system. Women support the rule of men for a variety of complex reasons, the most important being class privileges to men who confirm. In order to return their privileges, women are continually renegotiating for their bargaining power, some times at the cost of other women.

The belief of the existence of matriarchal communities in some regions in Kerala and the north east is a misconception.

Matrilineality and matrilocality have existed among the Naris of Kerala and in Garo and Khasi tribes of north–east India, and have been confused with matriarchy anywhere in the world except in Greek and Hindu mythology.

The three terms were clarified:

- Matriarchy is a system where decisions and all social institutions are under women's control
- Matrilienality refers to transfer of property from mother to daughter
- Matrilocality means relocation of a women's husband to her place of residence after marriage.

Thus Power and gender are terms so commonly conjoined that their combined invocation has almost cease to be indexical. Feminism initially altered us to the fact that gender inequality is not natural, that women speak from unique worlds, and that their gender is (at least to a large extent) a cultural incarnation. Power is both the source of oppression in its abuse and the source of emancipation in its use.

Gender is a term which should be treated with care. There is a tendency to employ it as a synonym, not to say euphemism for sex. This entails a regrettable loss of the distinction between the two terms, a distinction which may be defined briefly as follows. A person's gender, however, is a social and historical construct and is the consequence of various kinds of conditioning. Gender, however, is something much more flexible. There is also a tendency to use gender as a synonym for women. A gender analysis implies reading facts and social processes in the light of their differential effection gender roles. Basically, it means recognizing that cultural, social, political and economic systems and institutions are not gender neutral. The end purpose of adopting a gender analysis is to redefine the basic assumptions of dominant cultural, social and economic structures in order to promote and secure women's basic human rights, needs and aspirations. Gender equality means an equal visibility, empowerment and participation of both sexes in all spheres of public and private life. It means giving women and men, girls and boys, the same opportunities to participate fully in the development of their societies and to achieve self fulfillment. Gender equality represents an essential component of human rights and a key to development. It requires a new partnership between women and men, girls and boys. One that is based on mutual respect, dialogue and the sharing of public and private responsibilities.

Gender equality does not mean that men and women become the same, but that their opportunities and life changes are equal. Gender and development (GAD) approach grew from the analysis of the social relations between women and men to explain why women were still marginally benefiting from development processes despite the fact that their specific contributions were being recognized.

DEBATES ABOUT GENDER

Debate 1

The term 'gender' is now the dominant coverall one for analysis of sexed identities and practices–that is, for discussing social relations within and between groups identified as men and women (Kemp and squires, 1997:11). This dominance is comparatively recent: the shift from focusing on particular identities, such as occurs in women's studies, to focus on Gender studies has been disputed by many feminists on the grounds that this involves conveniently moving attention away from women's subordination.

Debate 2

The term 'gender' has also been criticized on the basis that it sets up too sharp a divide between social and natural/bodily. Gender has been used to indicate that nature (bodies) do not necessarily tell you much about human social organization of sexed identities and practices. In short, a male body does not necessarily result in social masculinity, in a personal identity deemed 'masculine' gender in this setting was seen as a reference to 'social construction'. The word implied a radical critique of conservative views that asserted biological determination. Gender in other words, suggested a critique of the wide range of views that assumed that bodily 'sex' determinants the self and that biological sex difference explains human social arrangements. Gender was a term that enabled a questioning of biological presumptions, such as that biological sex difference explains human social arrangements. Gender was a term that enabled a questioning of dialogistic presumptions, such as that made bodies are naturally more aggressive, women are less mathematical thinkers, and so on.

Debate 3

Writers who justify the usage of the term 'gender' as against 'sex' or sexuality do so as a means of indicating that the differentiation of men and women is not a simple direct expression of external nature. By contrast those who dispute its usage reject the biological social division this seems to imply and relatedly refuse to demarcate (bodily) sex, sexuality and gender. Biological (reproductive) sex differences, sexuality (exotic, sometimes reproductive) and gendered social arrangements (typically linked to sex differences and reproduction) are considered interconnected in this analysis. Hence gender mainstreaming is an important tool to achieve gender equality according to the UNIFEM.

GENDER MAINSTREAMING

Gender mainstreaming is a process to achieve greater gender equality and overcome the costs of women's marginalization. The costs of gender inequality are particularly need in indicating development in terms of more poverty, increased deprivation and chronic failure in satisfaction of social needs (nutrition, health, education, dignity, social prestige and self esteem). Thus the term of "gender mainstreaming" has been referred to as a comprehensive strategy that involves the integration of women oriented programmes and gender issues into development institutions by allotting social budget.

AN ANALYSIS–GENDER DEVELOPMENT INDEX IN INDIA

The impact of the various developmental policies, plans and programmes implemented by the Government over the last few years has brought forth a perceptible improvement in the Socio-economic status of women, which is clearly shown in the table 1 selected Gender Development Index. There has been a slight increase in the total female population and the sex ratio has registered a marginal improvement from 927 in the year 1991 to 933 in 2001. There has been a decline in the birth, death and maternal mortality rates. The birth rate has declined from 35.6 in 1981 to 25 in 2002: the death rate has declined from 12.5 in 1981 to 8.1 in 2002. The female literacy rate shows an increase from 29.85 per cent in 1981 to 53.67 per cent in 2001. Besides there is an increase in the enrolment rate, a decrease in the drop out rate, an increase in the work participation rate of women both in urban and rural areas, a marginal increase in the representation of women in decision making bodies such as the Indian Administrative Service, Indian Police Service, etc., and in the electoral bodies. See the below Table for more details.

Selected Gender Development Index

Sl. No.	*Indicators*	*1991*			*2001*		
		Women	*Men*	*Total*	*Women*	*Men*	*Total*
	Demography and vital statistics						
1.	Population million 1991 & 2001	407.1	439.2	846.3	496.4	532.2	1028.6
2.	Decimal Growth (1981 & 2001)	23.37	24.30	23.85	21.96	21.16	21.54
3.	Sex Ratio (1991 & 2001)	927			933		
4.	Life expectancy at birth(in years in 1991 & 2001)	58.1	57.1		65.3	62.3	
5.	Mean Age at marriage (1981 & 1991)	18.3	23.3		19.5	23.9	
	Health and Family Welfare						
6.	Birth Rate (per 1000 in 1981 & 2002)			35.6			
7.	Death Rate (Per 1000 in 1981 & 2002)	12.7	12.4	12.5	7.7	8.4	8.1
8.	Infant Mortality Rate (per 1000 live births in 1990 & 2002)	81	78	80	6.5	62	64
9.	Child Mortality Rate (per 1000 live births under 5 yrs of age in 1985 & 2001)	40.4	36.6	38.4	71.6	70.5	71.1
10.	Maternal mortality rate (per 10000 live births in 1997 & 1998)	408			407		
	Literacy and Education						
11.	Literacy Rate (1991 & 2001) in percentage	39.29	64.13	52.21	53.67	75.26	64.84
12.	Gross Enrolment Ratio (1990-1991 & 2002-2003)						
	Class I-V	85.5	114.0	100.1	93.1	97.5	95.3
	Class VI-VIII	47.0	76.6	62.1	56.2	65.3	61.0

Sl. No.	*Indicators*	*1991*			*2001*		
		Women	*Men*	*Total*	*Women*	*Men*	*Total*
13.	Dropout Rate 1990-91 & 2002-03) in percentage						
	Class I-V	46.0	40.1	42.6	33.7	35.8	34.9
	Classes I-VIII	65.1	59.1	60.9	52.3	53.4	52.8
	Work and Employment						
14.	Work participation rate (1991 & 2001) in percentage	22.3	51.6	37.5	25..6	51.7	39.1
15.	Organized sector (number in millions in 1981 & 1999) (DGE & T)	2.80 (12.2%)	20.5	22.85	4.83	23.20	28.11
16.	Public Sector (number in millions in 1981 & 1999) (employment review)	1.5 (8.7%)	14.0				
17.	Government (number in millions in 1981 & 1997)	1.2 (11%)	9.7	10.9	1.61 (4.6%)	9.1	10.1
	Decision Making						
18.	Administration (no in IAS & IPS IN 1997 & 2000)	608	7347	7955	645	7860	8505
19.	PRIs (No in figures in 1985)	318 (33.5%)	630	948	725	1997	2722
20.	Parliament (No in 1991 & 2004)	7.7 (9.7%)	712	789	72 (9.2%)	712	784
21.	Central council of minister (no in 1985 & 2001)	4 (10.5%)	36	40	8 (10.5%)	66	74

Source: X Plan, Government of India: Sample Registration System.

Significant gains have been made in the life expectancy of women, literacy and representation of women in local self- governing institutions. Despite the growing sensitivity with regard to the elimination of discriminatory laws, the shift in the planning process from 'welfare to 'development' and to 'empowerment' the constitutional and legal provisions for affirmative action, the institutional mechanisms and increased investment, gender discrimination continues to be a daunting challenge and there is much to be accomplished in translating the dejure rights into defacto enjoyment of rights and equal results.

CHALLENGES

Access to benefits of development has been conditioned by the prevailing social discrimination that women face. The socio-cultural norms, traditional practices and prejudices, patriarchal values are major obstacles towards achieving defacto equality for women. The process of liberalization has exacerbated existing regional disparities creating pockets of prosperity amidst poverty and deprivation, as investment generally tends to flow to regions that have taken a lead in infrastructure development. The Government has taken note of these regional disparities and has taken steps to correct these imbalances by providing more resources, improving infrastructure and providing incentives to promote and develop the under developed regions also.

Certain critical areas of concerns viz., increasing burden of poverty, unequal access to primary health care, under nutrition, high rates of illiteracy and lack of training, lack of access to and control over assets and resources, inequalities in sharing power and decision making, lack of access to information and media, increasing violence against women, adolescents and girl children and persisting discrimination against the girl child, require immediate attention in order to ensure defacto equality and practical realization of rights for women. The Government is addressing these concerns through the National policy for empowerment of women, 2001 and the planning strategies which will enhance the social gains in terms of education, health and employment capabilities, which will enhance the social gains in terms of education, health and employment capabilities, which will in turn enable empowerment of women.

Lack of desegregated data on various development indicators both at the State and District levels has been a major problem in monitoring the progress made in improving the status of women towards achieving equality on par with men. Hence there is a need to take up separate measures in order to achieve gender equality in our Country.

SPECIAL MEASURES

The policy of the Hindu Succession (Amendment) Bill 2004 is significant not only because it gets women equal rights in all property, including ancestral one, but also because it gives them equal rights on agricultural land did not figure in the original Bill and was included only after women's groups in the country lobbied for its inclusion. Significantly, it also gives daughters right equivalent to sons in joint family property.

The Prohibition of Domestic Violence Act, 2005 aims to provide more effective protection to women who are victims of violence of any kind within the family and for mattress end, the UN Millennium Project, which is making MDGs, has adopted a framework for MDG 3 that has three dimensions such as:

1. Improving women's capabilities (as measured by education, health and nutrition).
2. Including women's access to Economic and political opportunities, and
3. Ensuring women's security by reducing women's vulnerability to violence and conflict.

Thus gender equality has outlined a series of priority actions for Countries: They are:

1. Strengthening post primary scholarship for girls.
2. Special attention is being paid to 146 districts identified as low female literacy districts. Under this scheme, 100 per cent financial assistance is given to state governments and voluntary organizations for the establishment of new primary/upper primary schools and multi-stream residential higher secondary schools for girls belonging to these groups. The scheme covers 325 blocks in 13 states, 3 UT s and 4 districts in Assam.
3. Provide free textbooks, uniforms, stationary, school bags, etc. to these students.
4. Reservation of seats for SC/ST in the central Government institutions of higher education.
5. Relaxation in the minimum qualifying cut-off percentage for admission to Universities, colleges and technical institutions.
6. Reservation of scholarships exclusively for SC/ST students under the National Talent Search Scheme.
7. Improving reproductive health.
8. Investing in infrastructure to reduce women's and girls time burdens.

9. Granting property and inheritance rights for women and girls,
10. Eliminating gender inequality in employment.
11. Increasing women's seats in governance.
12. Combining violence against girls and women.

The Initial Report has highlighted the special measures adopted by Government to ensure that women are able to exercise and enjoy fundamental rights and freedom. Realizing the low status of women and the historical discrimination faced by women, the constitution of India not only prohibited discrimination against women but also provided scope for special measures in favors of men (Article 15(13)). It also further guarantees equality in opportunities in employment (Article 16(4)). Applying this principle the state has provided affirmative action to improve the status of women.

One of the important special measures adopted by the state was the 73rd and 74th Amendments of the constitution, which provides for reservation of seats and the posts of chairpersons for women in institutions of local governance. To ensure effective participation of tribal women in the process of planning and decision making, these amendments have been extended to the scheduled areas through the panchayats (Extension to the Scheduled Areas) Act, 1996. Our constitution declares India to be a sovereign and a secular country and prohibits discrimination on the basis of caste, creed or sex. Certain groups of women suffer multiple forms of discrimination based on caste, religion and disability ways than on men.

CONCLUSION

However, to influence policy discussions at the local and international levels, women's groups and other NGOs need to become familiar with the MDG process and with key international legal instruments and other agreements that commit Governments to action. The challenge is to bring about changes against to patriarchy, and in policies, programs and spending priorities on a scale that benefits the most disadvantaged populations. Therefore laws alone will not help better for the lot of Indian women, a large number of women endure ill-treatment, oppression and abuse, what is needed is a change in the mindset: this has happen not only among the masses but among our law-makers.

REFERENCES

Chris Beasley (2005), Gender and Sexuality–Critical Theories Critical Thinkers Sage Publications, New Delhi.

Gender Planning (1994), Gujarat Institute of Development Research.

Government of India's II and III Periodic Report on the Convention on the Elimination of all forms of Discrimination against Women (CEDAW) (1997-2005) (Department of Human Resource Development Government of India 2005).

Lorraine Radttke H. and Henderins J. Stam Power/Gender Social Relations in Theory and Practice by Sage Publications, New Delhi.

Parthasarathy G. & Ratna Kumari B. (2002), Gender and Poverty, The Indian case by Andhra University, Visakhapatnam.

Population Reference Bureau 2005.

Ratna Kumari (2005), Gender Mainstreaming in Trade Policies in BIMSTEC. Paper Published in National Seminar on BIMSTEC. Towards a Bay of Bengal Economic Community: Organized by Centre for SAARC Studies, Visakhapatnam.

34

Discrimination Against Girl Child: A Study of Two Villages in Guntur District

D. Srilatha and B. Sambasiva Rao

The sex ratio in India has been tilted against women. The sex ratio continuously declined over a period of time. In 1981 it was 935, but it fell to 927 in 1991. However, it increased to 933 in 2001. China and other South Asian countries with the exception of Srilanka are also experiencing the problem of declining female male ratio. The causes for this problem have been identified as under enumeration.

Sex selective migration, sex ratio at birth as well as sex differential in mortality. Under- enumeration, especially of child brides in certain regions where such a custom is observed is accepted as a key factor accounting for deficit of girls in the 10-14 age group. On the other hand, there is no evidence to support the likelihood of sex differentials in migration i.e. greater out migration of women. Similarly there is no evidence to support high male to female child at birth. In Indian, girl child as well as women's mortality rate is relatively higher.

The sex ratio at birth is biologically determined and globally ranges between 102 and 107 male births to 100 female births. Unless there is conscious effort at intervention by human beings, the sex ratio at birth is most unlikely to change significantly over a long period of time. Despite overall improvements in the mortality situations and aggregates increase in the life expectancy of women, FMR is on the decline.

DISCRIMINATION AGAINST GIRL CHILD

Even to day women have been the worst suffering of the quaint tradition prevailing in many forms, which also vary from place to place. Our Indian society is completely male dominated; women are exploited, oppressed and deprived in every sphere of life. In our country, every year 12 millions girl are born. But despite being biologically stronger than boys, 3 millions girls do not survive till their 15th birthday. About 1/3rd of these deaths are in the first year of life. It is estimated that every sixth female death is due to gender discrimination.

Female foeticide and infanticide are the most hideous outcome of sex discrimination. Son preference, a deep rooted social value combined with poverty, illiteracy and low status of girls are among the few of the factors associated with female mortality before and after birth. Son preference, in other words, also means an unconscious neglect of the girl child.

A girl child runs the risk of female infanticide or the denial of life by deliberate killing or neglect at the time of birth and during the vulnerable period of infancy. Female infant mortality rate has declined substantially during the last 15 years from 111 in 1981 to 72 in 1995. Still one in every 13 children dies before completing the 5th year. Sex-bias in health care prevails in the country, which accounts for higher female mortality and poor girl child survival. Studies indicate that girls do not receive timely and adequate health care. When chances of survival are reduced, fewer resources are invested on the treatment of girls.

Girls are often treated as inferior undermining their self-esteem. Discrimination and neglect in child hood can lead to a life long downward spiral of deprivation and exclusion from the social main stream. Gender bias in educational processes, including curricula, educational materials and practices reinforce existing gender inequalities. Girls are less encouraged than boys to participate in and learn about the social, economic and political functioning of the society. They are not offered the same opportunities as boys to take part in decision-making process.

Among educated families, adoption of small family norm of either having one or two off spring has been a special advantage for proper bringing of girl child. This ideology is deeply rooted in the North India, particularly in the BIMARU states (Bihar, Madhya Pradesh, Rajasthan, Uttar Pradesh).

Attitudes and Beliefs towards Girl Child and Son Preference

- Sons are definitely preferred over daughter.
- Sons are necessary for the material and spiritual advancement of their parents.
- Sons are considered ritually and economically desirable, essentially for lighting the funeral pyres of the parents and release of their souls.
- Sons continue the family tree.
- Son is 'Kul Ka Deepak'.

Girl Child is a Liability

- Bringing up a girl child is like watering a neighbor's plant.
- Girls are "*Parayadhan*".
- Girl Child is drain on family resources because of the dowry custom.
- Girls are liability as the rituals that are associated with a girl or a women demand expenditure from parents throughout life.

OBJECTIVES AND METHODOLOGY

Keeping in view of the importance of the issue, the study is intended to analyze the following objectives:

1. To analyze the girl child discrimination in terms of literacy in the study villages.
2. To find out the age at marriage of girl child in the study area.

METHODOLOGY

For the purpose of intensive investigation, two villages are selected in the Repalle area of Guntur District. A sample of 100 households from each village were selected from different categories of households viz. Forward Castes, Backward Castes and SCs/STs in the village. Data were collected on educational status, family background, community patterns, social customs etc. A pre-tested and well-designed schedule was administered among the households to get the information. The reference period for the study is 2004-2005.

ANALYSIS

For centuries, women have been asking for a dignified life, a life where they will be treated as equals, where they can enjoy freedom on par with men, where they will feel that they also matter for society and for families. The time has come to make this human beings and they must enjoy all the privileges and rights of human beings. As a human being, a woman has the same nature as a man and both are rational, social, free, equal, rights and duties and both have complementary roles to play in society..No one is superior or inferior. Hence, male-domination must give way to equality of status between the two sexes and women must have an equal share of power in all aspects of life. But, in reality, there is discrimination in terms of educational status and also age at marriage among different families in rural areas.

DISCRIMINATION IN THE CASE OF AGE AT MARRIAGE

Female foeticide and infanticide are the most hideous out come of sex discrimination. Son preference, a deep rooted social value combined with poverty, illiteracy and low status of girls are among the few of the factors associated with female mortality before and after birth. Son preference in other words also means an unconsciousness neglect of the girl child. It is evident from the Table 1 that there are only a few girls i.e. 3 girls married between the age 11 and 13, who belongs to SC category in Aduvuladeevi village, whereas in case of other castes such as ST, BC and OC, there are no girls who married between this age group. 10 per cent of the total SC girls and 5 per cent of the total BC girls in the study area married between the age group 14 and 16. All girls of ST category in the study area married between the age 17 and 19, whereas most of the SC, BC and OC category girls also married between this age group, i.e. 54 per cent of the SC girls, 78 per cent of the BC girls and 88 per cent of the OC girls married between the age group 17 and 19. There are no ST girls married between the age group 20 and 25, while 30 per cent of the SC girls, 17 per cent of the BC girls and 13 per cent of the OC girls married between this age group.

Table 1
Age at Marriage of Girls Among Different Castes in Aduvaladeevi Village

Age at Marriage	*ST*	*SC*	*BC*	*OC*	*Total*
11-13	-	3 (5.40)	-	-	3 (3.00)
14-16	-	6 (10.70)	1 (5.60)	-	7 (7.00)
17-19	10 (100.00)	30 (53.60)	14 (77.80)	14 (87.50)	68 (68.00)
20-25	-	17 (30.40)	3 (16.70)	2 (12.50)	22 (22.00)
Total	10 (100.00)	56 (100.00)	18 (100.00)	16 (100.00)	100 (100.00)

Source: Field Study.

Table 2
Age Atmarriage of Boys Among Different Castes in Aduvaladeevi Village

Age at Marriage	*ST*	*SC*	*BC*	*OC*	*Total*
No Boys	1 (100.00)	5 (8.90)	2 (11.10)	3 (18.80)	11 (11.00)
11-13	-	-	-	-	-
14-16	-	-	-	-	-
17-19	-	1 (1.80)	-	-	1 (1.00)
20-25	1 (10.00)	10 (17.90)	1 (5.60)	-	12 (12.00)
25-28	8 (80.00)	35 (62.50)	12 (66.70)	11 (68.80)	66 (66.00)
After 28	-	5 (8.90)	3 (16.70)	2 (12.50)	10 (10.00)
Total:	10 (100.00)	56 (100.00)	18 (100.00)	16 (100.00)	100 (100.00)

Source: Field Study.

It is observed from the Table 2 that 11 respondents belonging to all categories have no male children in the study area as the study is mainly concentrated on the female child discrimination. No boys belonging to all categories in the study area married below the age of 16 years old. Only one boy belonging to SC category married between the age group 17 and 19, in which group, there are no boys belonging to other categories like ST, BC and OC married between this age group. None of OC category boys married between the age group 20 and 25, while the 12 boys belonging to ST, SC and BC married between this group. A high percentage of boys in the study area married between the age group 25 and 28. There are no ST boys married after 28 years, whereas 9 per cent of the total SC boys, 17 per cent of the total BC boys and 13 per cent of the total OC boys in the Aduvuladeevi village, married after 28 years. If we compare the age at marriage of boys and girls in Aduvuladeevi village, it is found that most of the girls are taken marriages timely between the age group 17 and 19, while most of the boys are taken marriages lately between the age group 25 and 28.

Age at marriage of girls in Nakshtra Nagar is showed in Table 3. BC got married early years as compared to other caste groups. It is noticed that above 50 per cent of the all caste groups got married before legal age. Only BCs and OCs (44.40 per cent of BCs and 33.30 per cent of OCs) got married in the age group of 20-25 years.

Table 3
Age at Marriage of Girls Among Different Castes in Nakshtra Nagar Village

Age at Marriage	*ST*	*SC*	*BC*	*OC*	*Total*
11-13	-	-	-	-	-
14-16	4	6	9	1	20
	(13.80)	(26.10)	(33.30)	(4.80)	(20.00)
17-19	25	17	6	13	61
	(86.20)	(73.90)	(22.20)	(61.90)	(61.00)
20-25	-	-	12	7	19
			(44.40)	(33.30)	(19.00)
Total	10	56	18	16	100
	(100.00)	(100.00)	(100.00)	(100.00)	(100.00)

Source: Field Study.

Age at marriage of boys in Nakshtra Nagar village is showed in the Table 4. No boys belonging to all categories in the study area married below the age of 16 years old. In Nakshtra Nagar village, most of the boys are got married in the age group of 25-28 years. It shows that 39.10 per cent of SCs and 7.40 per cent of the BCs are got married later ages. From the Table, it is observed that in Nakshtra Nagar village boys are got married later ages as compared to girls.

Table 4
Age at Marriage of Boys Among Different Castes in Nakshtra Nagar Village

Age at Marriage	*ST*	*SC*	*BC*	*OC*	*Total*
No Boys	8 (27.60)	2 (8.70)	2 (7.40)	7 (33.30)	19 (19.00)
11-13	-	-	-	-	-
14-16	-	-	-	-	-
17-19	-	-	-	-	-
20-25	4 (13.80)	1 (4.30)	6 (22.20)	4 (19.00)	15 (15.00)
25-28	17 (58.60)	11 (47.80)	17 (63.00)	10 (47.60)	55 (55.00)
After 28	-	9 (39.10)	2 (7.40)	-	11 (11.00)
Total	10 (100.00)	56 (100.00)	18 (100.00)	16 (100.00)	100 (100.00)

Source: Field Study.

Table 5
Educational Status of Girls Among Different Castes in Aduvaladeevi Village

Educational Status	*ST*	*SC*	*BC*	*OC*	*Total*
Illiterate	3 (30.00)	46 (82.10)	14 (77.80)	14 (87.50)	77 (77.00)
Primary Education	-	4 (7.10)	-	-	4 (4.00)
Secondary	3 (30.00)	-	-	-	3 (30.00)
Intermediate	4 (40.00)	2 (3.60)	4 (22.20)	2 (12.50)	12 (12.00)
Above Degree	-	4 (7.10)	-	-	4 (4.00)
Total	10 (100.00)	56 (100.00)	18 (100.00)	16 (100.00)	100 (100.00)

Source: Field Study.

DISCRIMINATION IN TERMS OF LITERACY

Level of education of girls in Aduvuladeevi village is showed in the Table 5. Illiterate girls are very high in Aduvuladeevi village in all caste groups i.e. 30.00 per cent are STs, 82.10 per cent are SCs, 77.80 per cent are BCs and 87.50 per cent are OCs. It shows clearly that illiterates are very high among SCs when compared to other caste groups. Most of the STs are studied intermediate when compared to other caste groups.

Educational status of the girls among different castes in Nakshtra Nagar village is presented in the Table 6. About 51.70 per cent of STs and 65.20 per cent of the SCs, about 55.60 per cent of the BCs and 47.60 per cent of the OCs are illiterates. Illiteracy rates are very high among SCs as compared to other caste groups. Above 27.60 per cent of the STs studied above Degree as against 4.30 per cent of SCs, 11.10 per cent of BCs and 4.80 per cent of OCs. It is observed that illiterates are very high among girls in Nakshtra Nagar Village.

Table 6
Educational Status of Girls Among Different Castes in Nakshtra Nagar Village

Educational Status	*ST*	*SC*	*BC*	*OC*	*Total*
Illiterate	15	15	15	10	55
	(51.70)	(65.20)	(55.60)	(47.60)	(55.00)
Primary Education	-	-	-	-	-
Secondary	-	-	3	-	3
			(11.10)		(3.00)
Intermediate	6	7	6	10	29
	(20.70)	(30.40)	(22.20)	(47.60)	(29.00)
Above Degree	8	1	3	1	13
	(27.60)	(4.30)	(11.10)	(4.80)	(13.00)
Total	29	23	27	21	100
	(100.00)	(100.00)	(100.00)	(100.00)	(100.00)

Source: Field Study

CONCLUSION

The analysis reveals that in the case of age at marriage, the parents perform early marriages to girls compared to boys in all the social groups in the study area. The parents are showing lot of interest to complete the marriages of their daughters (before 18) in order to relieve the burden. So, the girl is considered to be a burden to the family in all the groups in the two villages. In dealing with the literacy level also, most of the girls are denied of minimum education. So, it is the need of the hour to create awareness in regard to ideal age of marriage of girl as well as significance of girls education.

35

Declining Child Sex Ratio in Andhra Pradesh: Causes and Consequences

A. Rajani

INTRODUCTION

Decline in Sex ratio is considered as an indicator of the lower status of Women than men and discrimination of females existing in the country (James 2004). The deficit in the female population vary by region, by social group, age group and levels of development (Agnihotri 1995; Mari Bhat 2002, Premi 2001, Ashish Bose 2001). One of the disturbing demographic trends recorded by the 2001 census is the decline in Juvenile Sex Ratio across the country including that of Andhra Pradesh.

The main focus of the study is to analyse factors affecting the Juvenile sex ratio in Andhra Pradesh. The issue of analyzing decline in the Juvenile sex ratio is undoubtedly by a diverse and complex phenominon. There are a number of studies to analyse the problem after the census (2001) results were announced.

The main features of this analysis include the use of sex ratio data in the Juvenile age group population in the different states of the country, and different districts of the state of Andhra Pradesh. Andhra Pradesh scenario reveals a different phenomenon because less developed districts ofTelangana (Mahabubnagar, Rangareddy, Medak, Nizamabad, Adilabad, Karimnagar, Warangal, Khammam, Nalgonda), experience higher decline in Juvenile Sex Ratio during 1991–2001.

Objectives

1. To analyse the trends and inter–regional variations in Juvenile sex ratio in Andhra Pradesh as well as India.
2. To review the recent studies on the declining the Juvenile sex ratio.
3. To examine the factors contributing to the decline in the Juvenile sex ratio, in A.P.
4. To examine the implications of the decline in sex ratio for social policy.

   Centre for Women's Studies, Andhra University, Visakhapatnam.

Methodology

The study is based on the census 2001 data as well as other sources like National Family Health survey (NFHS), publications of the Directorate of economics and statistics and commissionerate of family welfare, and Reproductive and Chilled Health Survey (RCHS).

We have used statistical techniques like means, standard deviations, and Co-efficient of variation as well as multiple regression analysis. We have also used t–ratios and F–ratios, for testing the hypothesis and the validity of the model that is estimated.

TRENDS IN SEX RATIO

Child Sex Ratio in India and Andhra Pradesh

Table 1 shows that Child Sex Ratio (0-6) in India and Andhra Pradesh. In Andhra Pradesh the decline is to the tune of 11 points from 975 in 1991 to 964 in 2001. Considering Census years 1981-2001, the decline amount to around 28 points. In India 945 girls per 1000 boys in 1991 to 927 in 2001 a decrease of 18 points.The child sex ratio is higher in Andhra Pradesh compared to India for all the 5 census years i.e., from 1961–2001.

Inter District variations in Child Sex Ratio in Andhra Pradesh

Table 2 examines the decline in sex ratio in the age group 0-6 between 1991 and 2001 in the State of Andhra Pradesh. The decline is to the tune of 11 points from 975 in 1991 to 964 in 2001. Considering Census years 1981-2001, the decline amounts to around 28 points. The decline is observed in almost all the districts except Nellore and Anantapur. The sharpest decline is observed in the districts of Mahabubnagar, Adilabad and Warangal. Interestingly, Mahabubnagar and Adilabad are some of the poorest districts in the State.

Table 1
Child Sex Ratio (Girls per 1,000 boys aged 0-6): 1961-2001

Year	*India*	*Andhra Pradesh*	*Rajasthan*	*Madhya Pradesh*	*Maharastra*
1961	976	1002	951	982	978
1971	964	990	933	976	978
1981	962	992	954	978	956
1991	945	975	916	941	946
2001	927	964	909	929	917

Source: Census of India 1991 (1993: 13); Census of India 2001 (2001:92-94).

Table 2
Sex Ratio of Child Population (0-6) by Districts in Andhra Pradesh: 1991 & 2001

Districts	*1991*	*2001*	*(2001-1991)*
Adilabad	986	964	-22
Nizamabad	979	966	-14
Karimnagar	981	977	-3
Medak	981	964	-17
Hyderabad	963	950	-13
Rangareddy	972	970	-2
Mahabubnagar	981	957	-24
Nalgonda	981	962	-19
Warangal	977	955	-22
Khammam	981	968	-12
Srikakulam	986	976	-11
Vizianagaram	996	981	-15
Visakhapatnam	985	973	-12
East Godavari	994	978	-16
West Godavari	984	977	-7
Krishna	964	959	-5
Guntur	970	955	-14
Prakasam	969	966	-4
Nellore	937	955	19
Cuddapah	968	952	-16

Districts	*1991*	*2001*	*(2001-1991)*
Kurnool	955	944	-11
Anantapur	962	963	1
Chittoor	970	959	-10
A.P.	975	964	-11
Average	974.87	963.96	
STDEV	13.23	9.99	
CV	1.36	1.03	

Source: As Ex Ante.

Inter State variations in Child Sex Ratio In India

Table 3 presents Inter State variations in Child Sex Ratio in India. At the state level the Child Sex Ratio is declined by 38 points in Rajasthan, 33 points in Punjab, 28 points in Orissa, and 26 points in Madhya Pradesh between 1981 and 1991. In fact all the major states and Delhi showed a decline in Child Sex Ratio by various points between 1981 and 1991.

Table 3
Sex Ratio of Child Population (0-6) by States in India: 1991 & 2001

India/States Union Territories	*Child Population (aged 0-6)*		
	1991	*2001*	*2001-1991*
India	945	927	-18
J & K	NA	937	-
Himachal Pradesh	951	897	-54
Punjab	875	793	-82
Chandigarh	899	845	-54
Uttaranchal	948	906	-42
Haryana	879	820	-59
Delhi	915	865	-50
Rajasthan	916	909	-7
Uttar Pradesh	927	916	-11
Bihar	953	938	-15
Sikkim	965	986	21
Arunachal Pradesh	982	961	-21
Nagaland	993	975	-18
Manipur	974	961	-13

Contd...

India/States Union Territories	*Child Population (aged 0-6)*		
	1991	*2001*	*2001-1991*
Mizoram	969	971	2
Tripura	967	975	8
Meghalaya	986	975	-11
Assam	975	964	-11
West Bengal	967	963	-4
Jharkhand	979	966	-13
Orissa	967	950	-17
Chhattisgarh	984	975	-9
Madhya Pradesh	941	929	-12
Gujarat	928	878	-50
Daman and DIU	958	925	-33
Dadra and Nagar Haveli	1013	973	-40
Maharshtra	946	917	-29
Andhra Pradesh	975	964	-11
Karnataka	960	949	-11
Goa	964	933	-31
Lakshadweep	941	974	33
Kerala	958	963	5
Tamil Nadu	948	939	-9
Pondicherry	963	958	-5
A and N Islands	973	965	-8
Average	951.41	930.67	
STDEV	30.78	48.80	
CV	3.24	5.25	

Source: Census of India 2001 (2001: 92,94).

In the 2001 Census child Sex Ratio has declined further by 18 points–from 945 in 1991 to 927 in 2001.This decline is found in all the states and union territories except Kerala (5 points increase), Sikkim (21 points increase,Tripura (8 points increase) and Mizoram (2 points increase). But it is a matter of serious concern that the child sex ratio declined by 82 points to mere 793 in Punjab, by 59 points in Haryana, 54 points in Himachal Pradesh and Chandigarh, 50 points in Gujarat and Delhi, and 42 points in Uttarachal.

A Review of Literature

In this section we have presented a review of some recent studies pertaining to the trends in sex ratio and factors associated with the declining the trends in over all sex ratio and Juvenile Sex Ratio.

Ashish Bose (2001) has examined the most alarming finding namely, the sharp decline in the female/male ratio, among the children in the 0 - 6 age group, in the face of an increase in the sex ratio of the total population. In 1991 the sex ratio for the total population was 927 (females per 1000 males), it increased to 933 in 2001, an increase of 6 points, In contrast, the sex ratio of the child population (0-6 age group) which was 945 in 1991 decrease to 927, a decrease of 18 points. He explained in short the girl child (below 6 years) has lost out badly in spite of numerous projects and programmes, seminars and conferences focusing attention on the girl child for over a decade. He explained the decline in the sex ratio of the child population is a secular trend. In 1961, the sex ratio in the 0-6 age group was 976, it declined to 964 in 1971, to 962 in 1981 and to 945 in 1991. But the sharpest decline has been during 1991-2001.

He explained in 1980's the demographically backward states classified as BIMARU States (Bihar, Madhya Pradesh, Rajasthan and Uttar Pradesh), an acronym which is now generally accepted.

In 2001 he introduced another acronym –DEMARU where D stands for daughters, and "MARU" stands for killing, E will denote elimination. He stated that on the basis of a statistical cut off point of 50 points decline in the juvenile sex ratio Punjab, Haryana, Himachal Pradesh and Gujarat classified as DEMARU states.

He examined the causes for decline of the sex ratio of the child population. They are:

- Neglect of the girl child resulting in their higher mortality at younger ages.
- Higher maternal mortality
- Sex selective female abortion
- Female infanticide
- Change in sex ratio at birth

He explained that there is no doubt that increasing use of pre-natal sex determination tests and female feticide must have contributed significantly to the significant decline in the sex ratio in the last two decades.

K.S. James (2002) has explained in his article, sex ratio is a useful indicator to understand women's health and position in any society. He explained that India has distinction along with China and a few other South Asian Countries having a deficit of females for a long period. He found that four reasons are often mooted to as plausible reasons for such a secular decline in sex ratio.

- Differential mortality between males and females
- Different undercount of females than males
- Drop in the female birth leading to adverse sex ratio at birth.
- Large scale surplus emigration of females over males.

He explained in his article that the district level sex ratio of the population in Andhra Pradesh in 1997 and 2001(census) most of the districts in the state recorded in increase in the sex ratio. Some districts in the south coastal (Andhra) one of the developed regions of the state portray a decline in sex ratio.

He explained that the increase in overall sex ratio in Andhra Pradesh could be seen as the result of improvement in mortality among females compared to males in different age groups. The life expectancy of females is higher than males in all the periods since 1970.

He also observed that a decline in sex ratio in the age group 0-6 between 1997 and 2001 in the Andhra Pradesh. The decline is to the tune of 11 points from 975 in 1991 to 964 in 2001. The decline is observed in almost all the districts except Nellore and Anantapur. The sharpest decline is observed in the districts of Mahabubnagar, Adilabad and Warangal.

He concluded that, of the four reasons mooted for the decline in sex ratio, Viz., Sex differentials in mortality, migration, undercount and change in sex ratio at birth, the improvement in the overall sex ratio can be explained by the fact that female death rates have become lower and survival chances of females are more than males in most of the ages. This is particularly true in the adult ages where male mortality is not only higher than females but tended to stagnate. However, for the 0-6 age group, there is no reason to believe a worsening mortality for females. The other reason often suggested is the relative undercount of females. The undercount of females in the 0-4 and 5-9 age groups has not been very different from males in the earlier two census. Sex selective migration is unlikely in the younger age groups as both male and female children move together with parents. Hence, one would suspect increasing incidence of female feticide in the state through the use of available modern techniques.

Mari Bhatt P.N. (2002) in a two part article has examined the plausible factors that are causing declining overall sex ratio as well as Juvenile sex ratio using the census data.

In the first part of his article he observed that over a time there have been convergences of the sex ratios of adults and children. Female-Male ratios decline in the regions and social groups where the adult sex ratios were substantially higher than the child sex ratios. He concluded that in the first half of the last century the overall sex ratio declined because of the decline of adult ages especially at age 40 and over. After independence the decline has been more concentrated at ages under 15.

In the second part of his article, evidence is presented to show that the fall in the adult sex ratio was mainly because of the control of the famines that used to take heavy tool of older women. The accelerator fall in the child sex ratio after 1981 seems to be largely due to the diffusion of pre-natal sex selection techniques in regions with well enriched gender bias.

He concluded that although the declines were marginal it is not entirely clear why the child sex ratio decline during 1951-81. It could be because of expansion of medical services in rural areas that brought gender bias in provision of health care are from century long trend of fall in female-male ratio at birth, as a result of improvements in nutritional status and midwifery practices.

Mahendra K. Premi (2001) has examined the overall improvement in sex ratio in favour of females may be explained by the fact that female death rates have become lower than the male death rates. But the sex ratio at birth (SRB) becoming more favourable to males has, however, influenced the overall sex ratio in the opposite direction, which is reflected in the adverse child sex ratio. The under count of females in the 0-4 and 5-9 age groups has not been very different from male undercount and cannot explain the decline in child sex ratio between 1981 and 1997 or between 1991 and 2001. In 1991 census the net omission rate of girls in the age group 0-4 was 23.5% per 1000 as against 24.0 per cent of boys. He expected that the female under count in child population has not deteriorated in the 2001 census.

He analysed that the state level data on infant mortality rate and age specific mortality rates for 0-4 and 5-9 age groups. Five year moving averages have been computed to discern the pattern.

Satish B. Agnihotri (2003) has examined the factors behind decline in the juvenile sex ratio in India. He observed that the sex ratio decline was sharp in Urban area (32 points) than in rural areas (16) during 1991-2001. He explained that the traditional wisdom regarding the determinants of declining child sex ratio (migration, under-count or biologically ordained adverse sex ratios at birth) using extensively the census data, he estimated regression coefficients with regard to determinants of declining the sex ratio. The author recommended several suggestions to enhance the juvenile sex ratio:

- Creation of Employment for women.
- Prevention of Crime against Women.
- Enforcement of anti dowry law and old-age securities.

Amartya Sen Points out (June 9, 2003) in his cover story essay in Frontiline, "Taking together all the evidences that exists, it is clear that sharp fall in child sex ratio reflects not a rise in female child mortality, but a fall in female births via-a-vis male births, and is almost certainly connected with increased availability and use of gender determination of fetuses".

Secondary level data from Tamil Nadu, Karnataka and Andhra Pradesh points to some disturbing trends. First, sex determination and sex selective abortions appear to be widely practiced in the urban as well as in the rural areas. Secondly, the practice of sex determination and sex selective abortion seem to cut across caste, class and occupation, moving from only certain pockets to the general population. Third, there appears to be a sharp rise in the number of Scan centers and there is evidence of the existence of illegal mobile scan machines that make the rounds of villages. Fourth, the pre-conception and pre-natal Diagnostic Techniques (Prohibition of Sex Selection) Act, 2003, that prohibits sex selection and regulates the use of the techniques, seems to be flouted with impunity.

The reasons for underlying the low and falling sex ratios are:

1. Son preference appears to be a strong reason for sex selective abortion or neglect of girls within the household.
2. The various programmes by the State Governments to address female infanticide and sex selective abortion seem to have had no impact on the practices.

A comprehensive programmes such as creating mass awareness –among men and women-on the importance of girl children, developing schemes to increase the employment potential of women, counseling pregnant women and their families and training girl children in specific skills that would eventually increase the status of women by making them independent, socially economically and politically may help to address the problem in the short run. It is in this context that institutions such as the State, Women's groups, non-governmental organizations and mass media have a crucial role to play.

The Times of India reported that the design for a male child at all costs in India has now resulted in an alarming scenario. The child sex ratio for the stands at 927 in 2001, down from 945 in 1991. The main cause of decline in sex ratio is female foetus in India. The discovery of the Ultra sound technique has proved to be the nemesis of the female fetus in India. All the techniques can be used to detect the sex of the fetus with in 4-6 weeks of pregnancy, making abortion serious business than the usual methods that come into only 14 weeks after pregnancy. There after abortions become medically dangerous for the mother but acquired entirely different dimensions. The recent technologies automatically lend themselves to this heinous practice of sex selection. The Pre-Natal Diagnosis Test (PNDT) act allows pre-natal diagnosis chromosomal abnormalities, genetic metabolic disorders and congenital abnormalities. Similarly, PNDT techniques on women are allowed only in certain conditions if she is more than 35 years old exposed to certain drugs, radiation, or has a history of mental retardation on.

The Indian council of Medical Research has now issued guidelines on regulation of genetic and assisted reproductive facilities. But since such facilities are not used across the board for sex selection, it remains to be seen if this has an appreciable on the sex ratio. The preferred methods will obviously remain the cheaper and more dangerous ones such as ultrasound amniocentesis in the second trimester of pregnancy. Beyond the culture of deliberate neglect also contributes to deaths of older girl children.

In the Article 'Girl Child' Mira Seth Explained, The position of the girl child seems to have deteriorated after the first millennia, especially in the north Indian states, due to wide spread polygamy and practice of seclusion among upper class women became rampant. Access to education was also limited.

The reformists of the nineteenth century, however, advocated a ban on early marriage of girls, supported widow remarriage and opened schools for girls. This effort was continued more aggressively in the twentieth century with support from the Indian National Congress leading the struggle for independence. Though the Constitution and a vast body of legislation has promoted gender equality, the status of the girl child continues to be low. One indication is the low sex ratios of women.

One reason for the declining sex ratio also appeared to be the paradox of development characterized by smaller family size and culturally determined notions of sex preference. The nurturing of girl children was different from that of male children. Parents did not want daughters to continue studying after the tenth standard as it would make the search for a groom more difficult. They also felt that investment in girls' education was unrewarding and the money so invested should instead be saved for their dowries. The need to pay a heavy dowry in the future was, infact, the main reason for feticide and infanticide. Females did not enjoy any property inheritance rights which passed on to males and hereditary land often had to be sold to accumulate dowries for daughters.

According to hearsay evidence, infanticide was carried out by giving the girl child milk poisoned with insecticide or by suffocating her by covering her nose and mouth or giving her a locally grown poisonous plant in her milk.

Leela Visaria (2004) explained, in India, the deficit of girls or a decline in the sex ratio has recently become much more evident in the younger age groups. The juvenile sex ratio for the country as a whole dropped by 4.5 per cent between 1981 and 2001 or from 971 to 927 girls per 1000 boys. At the same time, the deficit of young girls, which was not al all evident in 1981 except in the traditionally and historically masculine states of Haryana and Punjab, became quite stark by 2001 in other neighbouring states such as Himachal Pradesh, Gujarat, and also in parts of Rajasthan and Maharashtra. In fact, according to the 2001 Census there were 49 districts in India where, for every 1000 male children 0-6 years of age, there were less than 850 female children. A majority (38) of these districts were located in the 3 northern and western states of Punjab, Haryana and Gujarat (Census of India, 2001). The decline of 60 to 83 points in the juvenile sex ratio between 1991 and 2000 a span of just one decade – observed in many of these districts cannot be explained solely by the discrimination against girls that has been practiced in this region for several decades because at no other time, since the Census taking of the region commenced, has the sex ratio of children declined so drastically.

Factors influencing Child Sex Ratio–A Regression Analysis

The regression model chosen is as follows:

Y = $b_0 + b_1 x_1 + b_2 x_2 + b_3 x_3 + b_4 x_4 + b_5 x_5 + b_6 x_6 + u$

Where Y = Child Sex Ratio (No. of girls per 1000 boys in the age group of 0–6 years).

x_1 = Poverty Ratio (% below poverty line)

x_2 = Primary Health Care (Number of primary health centers).

x_3 : Family Planning (No. of acceptors of vasectomy and Tubectomy)

x_4 = Infant Mortality Rate (No. of children dying below age One for 1000 live births)

x_5 = Female Literacy Rate (% of females who know how to read and write).

x_6 = Overall Sex Ratio (Number of females per 1000 males)

u = Error term.

b_0 = Intercept.

b_1 to b_6 = Regression Coefficients.

We hypothesis that the couples above poverty line, may discriminate children by sex, and on the contrary poor people do not discriminate. So we expect the regression coefficient to be positive.

We hypothesis that the more the primary health care services provide better care and counseling to the couples and thus leads to less child mortality and higher juvenile sex ratio.

We expect that the higher family planning acceptance, leads to lesser birth spacing and less birth rate that causes lower child mortality and hence higher child sex ratio.

Infant mortality rate is supposed to be the root cause of lower child sex ratio through girl child discrimination. Hence these two are relatively correlated.

We hypothesis that the educated parents would not discriminate the children by sex. So we expect that the regression coefficient to be positive.

The overall sex ratio is of course the direct influencing factor that determines the juvenile sex ratio. Hence we expect these two are positively correlated.

All the regression results show that all the independent variables have expected signs. However four out of six variables are statistically significant in Andhra Pradesh model, only three variables are significant in All India model.

In Andhra Pradesh the significant variables are poverty ratio, Infant mortality rate, literacy rate and overall se ratio. In All India Model only Infant Mortality rate, Literacy rate and overall sex ration are found to be statistically significant.

R bar square is 0.57 for Andhra Pradesh and 0.45 for all India. F – value is 173.18 for A.P. and 12.36 for all India. These values show that the model is the best fit.

Table 4
Regression Results

Sl. No.	*Variable*	*A.P. Model*	*All India Model*
1.	Poverty Ratio	1.33* (3.25)	0.25 (1.01)
2.	Primary Health Care	0.01 (1.20)	0.21 (2.96)
3.	Family Planning	1.35 (1.02)	1.12 (0.91)
4.	Infant Mortality Rate	-11.22* (2.52)	-10.96* (3.01)
5.	Literacy Rate	1.02* (3.74)	1.03* (3.04)
6.	Overall Sex Ratio	0.92* (10.42)	0.84* (5.62)
	F – value	173.18	12.36
	R Bar Square Value	0.57	0.45

Figures in brackets are the respective t–values and
* Statistically Significant.

CONCLUSIONS AND POLICY IMPLICATIONS:

In Andhra Pradesh, the Child Sex Ratio decline is to the tune of 11 points from 975 in 1991 to 964 in 2001. Considering census years 1981-2001, the decline amounts to around 28 points. In India the decline was from 945 Girls per 1000 Boys in 1991 to 927 in 2001 a decrease of 18 points.

Most of the districts in the state recorded in increase in the over all sex ratio. Some districts in the south coastal Andhra, recorded a decline in sex ratio. These districts are East Godavari, West Godavari and Krishna. Other than these three districts,

Mahabubnagar also recorded a one point decline, its overall sex ratio is favourable to female both in 1991 and 2001 census years.

The decline in sex ratio in the age group 0-6 between 1991 and 2001 in the Andhra Pradesh. The decline is to the tune of 11 points from 975 in 1991 to 964 in 2001. Considering census years 1981-2001, the decline amount to around 28 points. The decline is observed in almost all the districts except Nellore and Anantapur. The sharpest decline is observed in the districts of Mahabubnagar, Adilabad and Warangal. Interestingly, Mahabubnagar and Adilabad are some of the poorest districts in the State.

The factors influencing sex ratio as per literature available are:- Son preference, sex selected abortions, under enumeration of females, drop in the female birth leading to adverse sex ratio at birth, high infant and child mortality, female infanticide, also we have made an attempt to estimate the impact of certain selected socio-economic and demographic variables using regression analysis, based on inter district variations in Andhra Pradesh, and inter state variations in all India.

In such scenario the effort of the government has been sectoral, especially since the nineties. A plan of action for the improvement of the status of the girl child has been made by the department of women and child development.

Government of India has been implementing several schemes for protecting women and children. The Integrated Child Development Services (ICDS) is the World's largest publicity funded program for early child hood. It was first launched in 33 selected blocks in 1975, and continuous to be flag ship scheme towards promoting the overall development of the young children (0-6 years) especially the girl child, and expectant and nursing mothers all over the country through its holistic package of six basic services. Health checkup, immunization, referral services, supplementary nutrition, pre-school education and health and nutritional education through a single window delivery.

A bill to constitute the national commission for children was framed and laid in Lok Sabha in December, 2003. Similarly the National Charter for children highlighting the roles and responsibilities of both the government and community towards children and duties of children towards their families societies and country has been notified in the official gazette of Indian on February, 2004.

Both the Central and State Government are implementing a number of programmes for the development of women and children, in the last five years.

- Integrated Child Development Services.
- Child welfare Institutions.
- Nutrition.
- Women Education.

Under the vision 2020 programme, women empowerment policy has been formulated. The main thrust of the policy is to convergence of all activities pertaining to women in order to improve education, health nutrition for women and children. The policy also calls for the setting up of a women development agency at the district levels of focus on women and child development activities and for gender sensitization.

The government of India formulated and announced its national plan of action for the SAARC decade of the girl child (1991-2000 AD) in 1992. "It would help sustain the consciousness aroused all over the country during the SAARC year of the girl child and achieve its goals set for a brighter future of the girl child in India within its decade.

The government launched Balika Samridhi Yojana on 2nd October, 1997. The specific objective is to change female and community attitudes towards the girl child. This scheme encourages enrolment and retention of girls in schools.

After Independence, the Government of India has taken several measures to hoist the status of women. The different Plans, programmes and Policies have laid emphasis on women empowerment and raising the economic, educational, health and political participation of women to match that of men.

The Anganwadi Workers provide supplementary food to children under 6 years of age, pregnant and nursing women, pre-school education to children between 3 and 6 years of age and health and nutrition education. Health and family welfare workers (ANM) deliver a package of services including immunization, health check-up, and organize referral services.

The Government of Andhra Pradesh with a view to increase the enrolment of the Children in the age group of 6-11 has started the Mid-Day Meal Programme in all the recognised Elementary Schools from 14-11-1982. Tamil Nadu was the first state to initiate a massive noon meal programme to children. Under the scheme children between the ages of 2-14 years offending Balwadies/Schools are fed daily through 63,000 Noon meal programme centers, at an expense of 0.44-0.90 per beneficiary. This programme has been sustained by the state for marks two decades. Andhra Pradesh initiated a similar Mid Day Meals Programme (MDM) in 1980 which was extended to cover an school children in the stat in grade 1 to 5 in 1982-83.

The National Nutrition Policy adopted in 1993 advocates a comprehensive inter-secteral strategy for all aviating the multi-faceted problem of malnutrition and achieving an optimal state of nutrition for all sections of the society. The policy seeks to strike a balance between the short terms measures like direct nutrition interventions and the long term measures like institutional/ structural changes, and thus create and enabling environment and necessary conditions for improving nutritional and health status.

A National creche fund was set up by the Government of India in the year 1993-94 as a workers fund with a view to meet the growing need for opening more crèches. Assistance under the scheme is being made available to registered voluntary organizations/mahila mandals to convert existing Anganwadi Centers into Anganwadi-Cum-Creche Centers out of the interest earned plat the corpus fund. The scheme covers 4,286 general crèches and 599 Anganwadi-Cum-Creche Centres beneficing 1.22 Lakh Children.

REFERENCES

Ashish Bose (2001), "Fighting Female Feticide" Growing Greed and Shrinking Child Sex Ratio, *Economic and Political Weekly* Vol. 36 (36) pp. 3427–3429.

Ashish Bose (2002), 'Census of India–2001 and After'. *Economic and Political Weekly* Vol. 36 (20) pp. 1685 to 1687.

Ashish Bose (2002), "Curbing Female Foeticide" Doctors, Governors and Civil Society Ensure Failure. *Economic and Political Weekly* Vol. 37(8) pp. 696–697.

James.K.S. (2004), "A Note on Sex Ratio from 2001 Census Results in Andhra Pradesh" in G. Ramachandrudu & M. Prasada Rao (eds.) *Census 2001 & Human Development of India.* Serials Publications, New Delhi.

James.K.S. (2004), "A Note on Sex Ratio from 2001 Census Results in Andhra Pradesh" in G. Ramachandrudu & M. Prasada Rao (eds.)

Census 2001 & Human Development of India. Serials Publications, New Delhi.

Mahendra K. Premi (2001), "The Missing Girl Child" *Economic and Political Weekly* Vol. 36 (21) pp. 1875–1880.

Mari Bhat P.N. (2002), "On the Trail of Missing Indian Females–I: Search for Clues. *Economic and Political Weekly* Vol. 37(51) pp. 5105–5118.

Mari Bhat P.N. (2002), "On the Trail of Missing Indian Females–II: Search for Clues. *Economic and Political Weekly* Vol. 37(52) pp. 5244–5262.

Ramachandrudu, G. & Rajani A. (2005), "Declining Juvenile Sex Ratio in Andhra Pradesh–Some Reflections on Social Policy." Paper presented at the, APEA, 23rd Annual Conference Organised by School of Economics, Andhra University, Visakhapatnam (12–13 Feb., 2005.

Satish Balaram Agnihotri (2000), *"Sex Ratio Patterns in the Indian Population"*, Sage Publications, Delhi.

36

Gender Related Development Index and Gender Empowerment Measure in India and ASEAN Region –A Comparative Study

P. Tara Kumari and P. Vijaya Prakash

The Human development paradigm, which puts people at the centre of its concern, is now a universally acknowledged strategy for the development of a nation. The real wealth of a nation is in its people, both men and women, and the purpose of development is to create an environment to enable them to enjoy, healthy and creative lives.

All over the world, women have been occupied as power agents of social change. Investing in women's capabilities and empowering them to exercise their choices is not only valuable in itself but is also the surest way to contribute to economic growth and over all development.

Gender equality is a core development issue and is a development objective because; in no region of the developing world are women equal to men in legal social and economic rights. Gender gaps are widespread in access to and control of resources, in economic opportunities in power and political voice.

Gender equality we define in terms of equality under law, equality of opportunities including access to human capital and other productive resources and equality of reward of work and equality of voice. In simple terms gender equality means in terms of equality of outcomes.

Gender relations are important as women constitute not only half of the human race but their development certainly constitute to human development. The gender related development index (GDI) thus supplements the basic indicator of human development, the human development index (HDI).

The GDI concentrates on the same variables as the HDI but focuses on inequality between women and men. This index too is supplemented by the gender empowerment index (GEM). The GEM focuses on three variables that reflect women's participation in political decision–making their access to professional opportunities and their earning power. The GDI focuses on components like women's life expectancy, female adult literacy and gross enrolment ratio and female per capital income. The GDI and GEM are developed in the UNDP's HDR (1991).

Inequality between men and women is found to be universal, but it is fast declining in ASIAN region comparing to India. Further, ASEAN region has emerged as an important region in the world with a significant improvement in their growth. India lagged behind the ASEAN region in GDI and GEM particularly in women's life expectancy, female adult literacy, female per–income, women participation in political and earning power etc. In the light of this background, this paper examines the women's development in India and ASEAN region.

The concept of Gender: Gender is once referred exclusively to an aspect of language for (for instance the pronouns he and she). But latter it has been appropriated by feminists and scholars to refer to the social organizations of the relationship between the sexes. In many societies for example, women traditionally were expected to take care of children while men earned a living. Note that gender is used to, refer to biologically determined characteristics such as women's capacities for bearing children. Gender arrangements are not the result of natural difference between men and women but of social and cultural choices.

The GDI measures: To estimate the GDI, a measure is constructed for the overall achievements of women and men in three dimensions of HDI; life expectancy, educational attainment and adjustment in real income after taking rote of in equalities between women and men. In other words, the GDI is adjusted to the HDI for gender equality in life expectancy, educational attainment and income. For life expectancy, allowance is made for the biological edge that women enjoy in living longer than men. In adjusting this component for gender difference in the new GDI calculations, women's actual life expectancy relative to its maximum value and men's actual life expectancy relative to its maximum value are separately calculated and then combined in equality sensitive way. For educational attainment, the GDI gives two third weight to adult literacy and one third to combined primary, secondary and a tertiary enrolment as in the HDI. In respect of the GDI's third dimension, income rises serious issue of estimation, as there is substantial disparity between men and women in earned income. The share of earned income for women and men are derived by shares of earned income. If there is a gender disparity between these two proportional shares of earned income, average real GDP per capital is adjusted down words accordingly.

The Gender Empowerment Measures: The GDI development in the UNDP's HDR (1995) concentrates on participation of economic, political, and professional forms.

Like HDI and GDI, the GEM focuses on few selected variables, even though participation can take many forms. It uses indices pertaining to three variables. They are power over economic resources based on earned income in per capital terms, that is PPP dollars, unadjusted. Access to professional opportunities and participation in political decision making, are represented by the share of parliamentary seats. It differs from the GDI, which is primarily concerned with basic capabilities and living standards. In both GDI and GEM, income variables reflects on family members earning power, an important factor economic recognition, independence and reward.

The GDI and Gem treat the income variable differently. In the GEM, income is evaluated not for its contribution to basic human development such as longer life, literacy and freedom from poverty but it is evaluated as a source of economic power that frees the income earner from a wider set of possibilities and exercises a broader range of options. For access to professional opportunities and participation in economics decision making the variable chosen is women's share of jobs classified as administrative or managerial jobs which lie closer to decision making. But professional and technical jobs represent opportunities for carrier development.

Table 1
Gender Related Development Index

Sl. No.	Country	GDI		Life expectancy at birth year 2003		Adult literacy rate % age 152 above 2003		Combined enrolment ratio for primary school and tenting school		Estimated		HDI rent GDI Rank
		Rank	Value	F	M	F	M	F	M	F	M	
1.	Singapore	-	-	80.6	76.7	88.6	96.6	-	-	16,489	32,089	-
2.	Malaysia	50	0.791	75.6	70.9	85.4	92.0	73	68	6,075	12,869	0
3.	Thailand	57	0.774	73.8	66.3	90.5	94.9	72	72	5,784	9,452	1
4.	Philippines	63	0.755	72.5	68.3	92.7	92.5	83	83	3,213	5,409	3
5.	Indonesia	87	0.691	69.8	63.4	98.9	99.6	74	74	1,385	2,099	1
6.	India	98	0.586	65.0	61.8	47.8	73.4	56	56	1,569	4,130	0

Source: Human Development Report 2005.

Women often acquire specialization in higher education but are prevented by cultural or economic barriers from taking jobs that will be valuable. Their potential is thus underused. The third variable is access to political opportunities and participation in political decision making. No gender specific training is required to be a parliamentarian. Neither public speaking, nor the ability to represent the opinions of the electorate, nor the art of winning public confidence requires exclusively masculine traits. But political factors on obstruct women. One of the best indicators of political participation would be women's share of representation in local bodies such as municipal councils, but these data are rarely available. So the variable chosen for the GEM is representation in parliament, in both upper and lower houses. The three dimensions are valued equally in constructing the gender empowerment measure. In computing the index, the parameter of equality aversions (e) chosen is 2, the same as the gender–related development index.

The GEM is not intended to be a prescriptive index, with the intent of setting universal cultural norms. What is crucial is not achieving a certain percentage representation in selected political and economic arenas, but proving equality of choice to both women and men. The GEM examines the out come in economic and political participation. Structural barriers to women's access to these arenas could be the results of choices by both women and men one their desired roles in society. This is a matter of concern for the people of every country.

The data on gender related development index are shown in table 1. As can be seen from the table the GDI Rank is highest in Malaysia where as it is lowest in India. The life expectancy at birth for females is highest in Singapore whereas it is lowest in India: The adult literacy rate for females is highest in Indonesia, whereas it is lowest in India. The combined enrolment ratio for females is highest in Philippines whereas it is lowest in India. Estimated earned income for females Is highest in Singapore while in India it is slightly higher than Indonesia. On the whole the GDI is better for ASEAN region when compared to India.

The data on GEM are shown in Table 2. As can be seen from table, the percentage of seats held by women in parliament is higher in Singapore, followed by Philippines, Malaysia, Indonesia, India, and Thailand. The ratio of estimated female to male earned income is highest in Thailand, followed by Philippines, Indonesia &

Table 2
Gender–Empowerment Measures

Sl. No.	Country	Gender empowerment measures GEM		Seats in parliament held by women % of total	Female legislature senior officials and measures % of total	Female professional and technical workers % of total	Ratio of estimated female to male earned income
		Rank	Value				
1.	Singapore	22	0.654	16.0	26	45	0.51
2.	Malaysia	51	0.502	13.1	23	40	0.47
3.	Thailand	63	0.452	8.1	26	52	0.61
4.	Philippines	46	0.526	15.4	58	62	0.59
5.	Indonesia	-	-	11.3	-	-	0.52
6.	India	-	-	9.3	-	-	0.38

Singapore, Malaysia and India. The GEM is found to be better in ASEAN region when compared to India.

The table 3 shows gender inequality in education. It is evident from this table that the adult literacy rank, and value are highest in Philippines and lowest in India. In the case of youth literacy, the female rate per cent age 15-24 is highest in Singapore and lowest in India. Female rate as per cent of male rate is highest in Philippines, and lowest it in India. Net primary enrolment female ratio to male is more are less the same in ASEAN & India. Gross tertiary enrolment in female rate percentage is highest in Philippines and lowest in India, while the ratio of female to male is highest in Thailand and lowest in India. Thus Gender inequality in education is less in ASEAN Region and more in India.

The statistical information on gender inequality in economic activities is presented in table 4. It can be observed from the table that the female economic activity for ages 15& above as per cent of male rate is highest in Thailand and lowest in India. In the employment by economic activities in agriculture sector, women are observed to be more in Thailand, followed by Indonesia, Philippines & Malaysia. Women are found to be more in industrial sector in Malaysia compared to Singapore, Thailand, Philippines and Indonesia. Women are found to be more in service sector in Singapore followed by Philippines, Malaysia, Indonesia and Thailand. Thus, Gender inequality in economic activities is more felt in India compared to ASEAN region.

Women's political participation is shown in table 5. It is evident from the table that Women exercised the right to vote much earlier in Thailand and Philippines when compared to India. Contesting in elections by women also has come much earlier in Thailand and Philippines when compared to India. Women were elected to parliament since 1941 in Philippines, while in India they were elected from 1952. Women were appointed to parliament since 1948 in Thailand and in Indonesia from 1952. Women in government at ministerial level is higher in Philippines (25 per cent) followed by Indonesia (10.8 per cent), Malaysia (9.1 per cent), and Thailand (7.7 per cent) and India (3.4 per cent). Seats in parliament held by women as per cent of total in lower house is higher in Singapore (16.0 per cent), followed by Philippines (15.3 per cent), Indonesia (11.3 per cent), Thailand (10.6 per cent) Malaysia (9.1 per cent) and India (8.3 per cent). In higher house, seats in parliament held

Table 3
Gender Inequality in Education

Sl. No	Country	*Adult Literacy*		*Youth literacy*		*Net primary enrolment*		*Net secondary enrolment*		*Gross tertiary enrolment*	
		Rank	*Value*	*Female rate % age 5-24*	*Female rate as % of male rate*	*Female ratio % 2002-03*	*Ratio of female to male*	*Female ratio % 2002-03*	*Ratio of female to male 2002-03*	*Female rate % 2002-03*	*Ratio of female to male*
1.	Singapore	88.6	92	99.3	100	-	-	-	-	-	-
2.	Malaysia	85.4	93	97.3	100	93	1.00	74	1.11	33	1.28
3.	Thailand	90.5	95	97.8	100	84	0.98	78	1.02	21	1.78
4.	Philippines	92.7	100	95.7	101	95	1.02	65	1.19	34	1.28
5.	Indonesia	83.4	90	97.6	99	92	0.98	54	0.99	15	0.80
6.	India	47.8	65	67.7	80	85	0.94	-	-	10	0.68

Table 4
Gender Inequality in Economic Activities

Sl. No.	*Country*	*Female economic activities age 15 and above*			*Employment by Economics activities %*						*Contributing family works*	
		Rate % 2003	*A Index 1990=100 2003*	*As % of male rate 2003*	*Agriculture*		*Industry*		*Services*		*Women 1995-2002*	*Men 1995-2002*
					Women	*Men*	*Women*	*Men*	*Women*	*Men*		
1.	Singapore	50.0	99	64	-	-	18	31	81	69	76	24
2.	Malaysia	49.2	110	62	14	21	29	34	57	45	-	-
3.	Thailand	72.9	97	85	48	50	17	20	35	30	66	34
4.	Philippines	50.1	107	62	25	45	12	18	63	37	—	-
5.	Indonesia	56.3	112	69	43	43	16	19	41	38	-	-
6.	India	42.5	105	50	-	-	-	-	-	-	-	-

Table 5
Women Political Participation

Sl. No.	Country	Year women received rights		Year first women elected (E) or appointed (A) to parliament	Women in Government at Ministerial level % of total 2005	Seats in parliament held by women (% of total)		
		Total	To stand for election			Lower House		Higher house
						1990	2005	2005
1.	Singapore	1947	1947	1963E	0	5	16.0	-
2.	Malaysia	1957	1957	1959E	9.1	5	9.1	25.7
3.	Thailand	1932	1932	1948A	7.7	3	10.6	10.5
4.	Philippines	1937	1937	1941E	25.0	9	15.3	16.7
5.	Indonesia	1945	1945	1950A	10.8	12	11.3	-
6.	India	1950	1950	1952E	3.4	5	8.3	11.6

by women as per cent of total seats accounted for 25.7 per cent in Malaysia, 16.7 per cent, in Philippines, 11.6 per cent in India and 10.5 per cent in Thailand, thus, the Women's political participation is higher in ASEAN region when compared to India. When, India is lagging behind the ASEAN region in both GDI and GEM. Life expectancy is one of the indicators of health status of women. By improving health facility, Life expectancy can be improved. The gross female tertiary enrolment is relatively low in India as well as in the ASEAN region. Hence, appropriate steps should be taken to improve this. By increasing the employment opportunities and through self-employment programms empowerment of women can be increased. The number of seats in parliament held by women is relatively low in India. In order to increase the seats in parliament, reservation of seats for women has to be made statutorily.

Thus, it is to be concluded that with the increasing recognition for human capital formation as a catalyst for development, gender related index in India is to be improved and gender empowerment is to be sustained in India.

37

Progress of Gender Equality–A Study of the Saarc Region

P. Leela

INTRODUCTION

The first Human Development Report points out that "the real wealth of a nation is its people, and the purpose of development is to create an enabling environment for people to enjoy long, healthy and creative lives" (U.N.D.P 1990). The U.N. Report prepared at the time of the International Development Decade ofWomen (1975–85), pointed out that women constituted half of the world's population, did two-thirds of the World work hours, but received only a tenth of the World's income and owned less than a hundredth of the World property (Mahajan 1989). Inferiority in the status of women is one of the characteristics of underdevelopment (Leibenstein 1957). The International Women's Year in 1975 and the Fourth World Conference on Women at Beijing in 1995 brought to the fore the importance of gender dimension in respect of the overall development of a nation. "socially, economically, culturally and legally, women world-wide face gender linked handicaps."(S. Narasimhan 2000).

In 1995, the UNDP has put forward two gender-linked measures of human development. These are the Gender-related Development Index (GDI) and the Gender Empowerment Measure (GEM). The GDI helps in taking note of inequalities in the basic health status between men and women, besides education and incomes. The GEM helps to access the political and economic participation of women in the progress of a nation. In this context, the object of the present paper is to examine the progress of gender in the SAARC region, which includes India and the neighbouring countries, namely, Bangladesh, Bhutan, Maldives, Nepal, Pakistan and Sri Lanka.

TRENDS IN GDI AND GEM IN THE SAARC COUNTRIES

Table 1 shows the data relating to the Gender Related Development Index for the SAARC countries. It is evident from Table 1 that among the SAARC countries, Sri Lanka has the highest GDI rank, followed by India, Bangladesh, Nepal and Pakistan, based on the GDI value of 0.747 for Sri Lanka, 0.586 for India, 0.514 for Bangladesh, 0.511 for Nepal and 0.508 for Pakistan. Life expectancy at birth is one of the important variables taken in the construction of the GDI. Life expectancy at birth for females, is found to be highest at 76.8 years in Sri Lanka, followed by 66.1 years in Maldives, 65 years in India, 64.2 years in Bhutan, 63.7 years in Bangladesh and 63.2 years in Pakistan. Nepal has the lowest female life expectancy at 62 years. Adult literacy rate for females which is also one of the determinants of the GDI, is found to be highest at 97.2 per cent in Maldives, followed by 88.6 per cent in Sri Lanka. The other countries of SAARC are far behind Maldives and Sri Lanka. Female adult literacy is found to be 47.8 per cent in India (almost less than half that of Maldives), followed by 35.2 per cent in Pakistan and 34.9 per cent in Nepal. Female adult literacy rate is lowest at 31.4 per cent in Bangladesh. Combined gross enrolment ratio for primary, secondary and tertiary schools for females is found to be highest in Sri Lanka (69 per cent), followed by India (56 per cent), Nepal (55 per cent), Bangladesh (54 per cent) and Pakistan (31 per cent). It is found to be lowest in Bhutan at 14 per cent. Estimated earned income for females is found to be highest at $2579 in Sri Lanka, $1245 for Bangladesh and $1050 for Pakistan and lowest at $949 in Nepal. The GDI rank is found to be much higher than the HDI rank in Sri Lanka and slightly higher than the HDI in Bangladesh. HDI and GDI ranks are found to be the same in respect of India. GDI rank is found to be less than HDI rank in the case of Nepal and Pakistan.

On the whole, among the seven SAARC countries, the Gender-Related Development Index (GDI) is found to be highest in Sri Lanka, compared to the other countries.Data relating to Gender

Table 1
Gender Related Development Index (GDI)

	Gender Related development index (GDI)		*Life Expectancy at birth (years) 2003*		*Adult Literacy rate (% ages 15 and above) 2003*		*Combined gross enrolment ratio for primary secondary and tertiary schools (%) 2002/03*		*Estimated earned Income (PPP US $) 2003*		*HDI Rank minus GDI Rank*
	Rank	*Value*	*Female*	*Male*	*Female*	*Male*	*Female*	*Male*	*Female*	*Male*	
Bangladesh	105	0.514	63.7	62.1	31.4	50.3	54	52	1245	2289	2
Bhutan	..	..	64.2	61.7	..	..	14	16	..	..	..
India	98	0.586	65.0	61.8	47.8	73.4	56	64	1569	4130	0
Maldives	..	..	66.1	67.1	97.2	97.3	..	..	..	..	..
Nepal	106	0.511	62.0	61.2	34.9	62.7	55	66	949	1868	-2
Pakistan	107	0.508	63.2	62.8	35.2	61.7	31	43	1050	3082	-4
Sri Lanka	66	0.747	76.8	71.5	88.6	92.2	69	67	2579	5009	7

Source: UNDP, Human Development Report 2005.

Empowerment Measure are not available for India for purposes of comparison. But, in terms of the seats in Parliament held by women, Pakistan seems to be better placed than India, as shown in Table 2.

Table 2
Gender Empowerment Measure (Gem)

HDI Rank Country	*Gender Empowerment Measure (GEM)*		*Seats in Parliament held by women (% of total)*	*Female Legislators senior officials & managers % of total*	*Female Professionals & technical workers % of total*	*Ratio of Estimated female to male earned income*
	Rank	*Value*				
139 Bangladesh	79	0.218	2.0	8	25	0.54
134 Bhutan	–	–	8.7	–	–	–
127 India	–	–	9.3	–	–	0.38
96 Maldives	–	–	4.8	15	40	–
136 Nepal	–	–	6.4	–	–	0.51
135 Pakistan	71	0.379	20.6	2	26	0.34
93 Sri Lanka	72	0.370	4.9	21	46	0.51

Source: UNDP, Human Development Report 2005.

Table 3
Gender Inequality in Education

HDI Rank Country	*Adult Literacy*		*Youth Literacy*	
	Female Rate (% ages 15 and above) 2003	*Female Rate as % of male rate 2003*	*Female Rate (% ages 15 –24) 2003*	*Female Rate as % of male rate 2003*
139 Bangladesh	31.4	62	41.1	71
134 Bhutan	–	–	–	–
127 India	47.8	65	67.7	80
96 Maldives	97.2	400	99.2	100
136 Nepal	34.9	56	60.1	75
135 Pakistan	35.2	57	53.9	72
93 Sri Lanka	88.6	96	96.0	101

Source: UNDP, Human Development Report 2005.

There are considerable gender inequalities in respect of education. These are shown in Table 3. It is evident from Table 3 that the female adult literacy rate (for ages 15 and above) is highest at 97.2 per cent in Maldives, followed by 88.6 per cent in Sri Lanka. As pointed out earlier, female adult literacy rate is very much lower in the other SAARC countries (including India) ranging from 31.4 per cent in Bangladesh to 47.8 per cent in India. In Maldives the female adult literacy rate as percentage of male literacy rate is 100 per cent , followed by 96 per cent in Sri Lanka, but only 65 per cent in India, 62 per cent in Bangladesh, 57 per cent in Pakistan and 56 per cent in Nepal. Female youth literacy rate (for ages 15-24 years) is highest at 99.2 per cent in Maldives, followed by 96 per cent in Sri Lanka but much lower in other countries at 67.7 per cent in India, 60.1 per cent in Nepal, 53.9 per cent in Pakistan and lowest at 41.1 per cent in Bangladesh.

Thus, the female adult literacy rate is quite low in the SAARC region, except in Maldives and Sri Lanka. Female youth literacy rate in the age group 15-24 years, is very low in Bangladesh.

There are gender inequalities in economic activity in the SAARC Region. These are shown in Table 4. It is evident from the Table that the female rate of economic activity is higher at 66.5 per cent in Bangladesh and at 65.4 per cent in Maldives, but lower in Bhutan at 57.1 per cent, in Nepal at 56.9 per cent in Sri Lanka at 43.5per cent, India at 42.5 per cent and lowest at 36.7 per cent in Pakistan. Female economic activity as a percentage of male rate is also considerably high at 80 per cent in Maldives, 76 per cent in Bangladesh but lowest at 44 per cent in Pakistan. A high percentage of women in the SAARC Region are employed in the agricultural sector. During 1995-2002, 77 per cent of women in Bangladesh and 73 per cent of women in Pakistan are employed in agriculture. However in Maldives only 5 per cent of women are employed in the agricultural sector.

Table 5 shows the position of political participation of women in the SAARC region. It is evident from the Table that women received the right to vote as early as 1931 in Sri Lanka and 1932 in Maldives, compared to 1947 in Pakistan, 1950 in India, 1957 in Nepal, 1953 in Bhutan, and 1972 in Bangladesh. There are more women in Government at Ministerial level 11.8 per cent in Maldives and 10.3 per cent in Sri Lanka compared to 8.3 per cent in Bangladesh, 7.4 per cent in Nepal, 5.6 per cent in Pakistan and 3.4 per cent in India. The percentage of seats held by women in the lower house of the Parliament is higher at 21.3 per cent in Pakistan, compared to 12 per cent in Maldives, 8.7 per cent in Bhutan, 8.3

Table 4
Gender Inequality In Economic Activity

HDI Rank	Country	Female economic activity (ages 15 and above)			Employment By Economic Activities (%)					
					Agriculture		Industry		Services	
		Rate (%) 2003	Index (1990=100) 2003	As % of male Rate 2003	Women 1995-2002	Men 1995-2002	Women 1995-2002	Men 1995-2002	Women 1995-2002	Men 1995-2002
139	Bangladesh	66.5	101	76	77	53	9	11	12	30
134	Bhutan	57.1	100	65	–	–	–	–	–	–
127	India	42.5	105	50	–	–	–	–	–	–
96	Maldives	65.4	101	80	5	18	24	16	39	35
136	Nepal	56.9	101	67	–	–	–	–	–	–
135	Pakistan	36.7	129	44	73	44	9	20	18	36
93	Sri Lanka	43.5	108	56	49	38	22	23	27	37

Source: UNDP, Human Development Report 2005.

per cent in India, 5.9 per cent in Nepal, 4.9 per cent in Sri Lanka and only 2 per cent in Bangladesh. Similarly, the percentage of seats held by women in the upper house of the Parliament is found to be higher at 18 per cent in Pakistan, compared to 11.6 per cent in India and 8.3 per cent in Nepal.

Table 5
Women's Political Participation

HDI Rank	*Country*	*Women Received*		*Women in government at ministerial level (% of total) 2005*	*Seats in Parliament Held by Women (% of total)*	
		Right to Vote	*Right to stand for election*		*Lower House 2005*	*Upper House 2005*
139	Bangladesh	1972	1972	8.3	2.0	–
134	Bhutan	1953	1953	0	8.7	–
127	India	1950	1950	3.4	8.3	11.6
96	Maldives	1932	1932	11.8	12.0	–
136	Nepal	1951	1951	7.4	5.9	8.3
135	Pakistan	1947	1947	5.6	21.3	18.0
93	Sri Lanka	1931	1931	10.3	4.9	18.0

Source: UNDP, Human Development Report 2005.

CONCLUSION

There is much variation in the progress and development of women in the seven countries of the SAARC Region. In terms of the GDI, Sri Lanka is in a better position while Pakistan is in a lower position. Female life expectancy at birth, is highest in Sri Lanka while female adult literacy rate and female youth literacy rate are relatively high in Maldives and Sri Lanka. Female estimated earned income is high in Sri Lanka. Political participation of women has started much early in the 1930's in Sri Lanka and Maldives. Percentage of seats held by women in the lower house of the Parliament, which is the decision-making body, is relatively better in Pakistan and Maldives in the SAARC Region.

In the light of the above, steps have to be taken to bring down the gender disparities that exist in the countries of the SAARC Region. Measures should be taken to create awareness regarding maintenance of good health. Policies should be implemented to improve health facilities in the rural areas, where most of the women live. This will increase the life expectancy at birth. Both adult and youth literacy rates have to be improved by increasing the enrolment of girls in schools and colleges. Literacy plays a strategic role in improving health, in providing better employment opportunities and in increasing earned incomes. Better earning capacity will in its turn improve the decision making capacity of women and enhance the status of women in the society, Gender disparities have to be brought down considerably to improve the GDI and thereby the relative HDI rankings of the member countries of the SAARC Region.

REFERENCES

Leibenstein (1957), *Economic Backwardness and Economic Growth.*

Mahajan, V.S. (Ed.) (1989), *Women's Contribution to India's Economic and Social Development,* Deep and Deep Publications, New Delhi.

Narasimhan, S. (2000), "Reflections on Indian Economic Development and Poverty Eradication Development as if People Mattered", in R.V.R. Chandrasekhara Rao, A. Prasanna Kumar and K.C.Reddy (ed), *Perspectives on Indian Development: Economy, Polity and Society,* (Essays in Honour of Prof. B. Sarveswara Rao), Sterling Publishers Pvt. Ltd., New Delhi.

U.N.D.P (1990), *World Development Report.*

38

Gender Discrimination in Domestic Sphere and Place of Work – A Study

M. Pushpa Latha and B. Sudhakar

Women are not accorded equal status with men practically in all countries of the world. In the new conceptualisation of development, building capabilities, eliminating of poverty and equality of gender became one of the integral process of development. Gender justice and equality are not mere outcome of development policy but are simultaneously instruments of balanced development for both male and female. The World Conference on Women, at Beijing platform expressed the concern at the incidence of violence against the women. As long as there is a gender bias, violence and inequalities, it is difficult to claim progress in human development in the economy. Family structures in developing countries like India manifest and perpetuate the subordinate status of women. There are several hidden social constraints that inhabit women's free choice of what they want to do. The focus of the study is to examine the forms of gender inequalities prevail among working women. For this teachers and nurses in Khammam district are interviewed. The main objective of this study is to examine the extent of control over income earned by the respondent, level of participation in household decision making, the disputes at domestic level and prevalence of gender inequalities at work place.

METHODOLOGY

For this study, 40 women teachers and nurses have been chosen randomly in Khammam urban mandal and interviewed with the help of a structured questionnaire. In this sample, the women respondents who are holding their positions in Medical and Health departments as Public Health Nurses, Health Visitors, General Nurses and ANM's, and the teacher respondents who have TTC, BA, BSc, BEd and MA, MSc, BEd, qualifications. Out of 40 respondents, nurses are in between 41–60 age group and 30–50 age group are teacher respondents. Out of the selected respondents, 87.50 per cent of nurses and teacher are working in government institutions and remaining 12.50 per cent are working in private institutions. The selected women who are working in the government institutions are working at a distance of 5 to 10 kilometers away from the head quarters and remaining are working in private institutions of Khammam district.

SOCIO-ECONOMIC BACKGROUND

Out of the total sample, 50 per cent of the sample belonged to Schedule Caste and remaining 50 per cent of them belonged to Backward Classes. Further, 90 per cent of the sample belonged to nuclear family and 10 per cent belonged to the joint family. It is to be noted that 25 per cent of the respondents are having one child and the remaining 75 per cent have 2-3 children. Out of the sample 40 per cent of the respondents are living in rented houses and 60 per cent of them have own houses.

GENDER DISCRIMINATION IN DOMESTIC SPHERE

Table 1 gives the details as to the nature of marriage arrangement of the selected respondents. It is to be seen that 17.50 per cent of the total respondents could select this life partners individually and 22.50 per cent took individual decision but have taken the acceptance from their elders but 60 per cent of the respondents have accepted arranged marriages. This clearly states the fact that majority of women are not in a position to choose their own life partner.

The analyses in regard to the share of the income of the women respondents in maintaining the family indicates that 97.50 per cent of the sample respondents who are earning their income between

Rs. 4,001–Rs. 10,000 above could contribute to the tune of 50 per cent of household income and 2.50 per cent who are earning below Rs. 2,000-4,000, could contribute to the extent of 25 per cent.

Table 1
Marriage Particulars

Settlement	*Nurse*	*Teacher*	*Total*
Individual settlement	06 (15.00)	01 (2.50)	07 (17.50)
Individual settlement acceptance taken by the elders	05 (12.50)	04 (10.0)	09 (22.50)
Arranged marriages	09 (22.50)	15 (37.50)	24 (60.00)
Total	20 (50.00)	20 (50.00)	40 (100.00)

Source: Field Work.

Table 2 reveals the decision making power of the women respondents towards their income earning, saving, purchasing the fixed assets/gold, household things, husband wearings and the respondents health care etc.

We can see that there is a vast difference between the nurse and teacher women respondents in decision making power on the above said issues. Most of the nurses have right to earn and spend when compared to teachers. It is observed that some of the teachers who have settled their life with the persons who hail from the same profession are working in the same institutions are unable to enjoy their fruits of labour because their entire salary is being taken away by their husbands as soon as they sign on the aquittance. More over, they cannot even maintain friendly relationship with their colleagues to speak or share their views freely, because at each and every step they are controlled by their husbands. Very few of them are depending on the family members in purchasing the things. It shows that the decision making power of the nurses are independent with regard to their salary, saving, purchases of household things, husband wearings, and also regarding their personal health care etc. where as the teachers are parasites in taking the decision making power as they give full financial responsibility to the men.

Table 3 gives the particulars of gender preference or interest of the sample women respondents. 40 per cent of the respondents are interested towards the male child, 30 per cent of them showed interest towards female child, and remaining 30 per cent showed their interest towards both the male and female child.

Table 2
Personal Level Decision Making of Working Women Respondents

Particulars 1	*Expenditure of salary*	*Savings*	*Fixed assets/ gold*	*House hold things*	*Husband wearings*	*Health*
1. NURSES						
a. Respondent	10 (25.00)	11 (27.50)	6 (15.00)	6 (15.00)	8 (20.00)	14 (35.00)
b. Husband	3 (7.50)	6 (15.00)	4 (10.00)	1 (2.50)	4 (10.00)	3 (7.50)
c. Both	7 (17.50)	3 (7.50)	5 (12.50)	6 (15.00)	6 (15.00)	1
d. Family members	-	-	4 (10.00)	7 (17.50)	2 (5.00)	3 (7.50)
Total	20 (50.00)	20 (50.00)	20 (50.00)	20 (50.00)	20 (50.00)	20 (50.00)
2. TEACHERS						
a. Respondent	5 (12.50)	6 (15.00)	4 (10.00)	3 (7.50)	3 (7.50)	6 (15.00)
b. Husband	8 (20.00)	9 (22.50)	10 (25.00)	7 (12.50)	17 (42.50)	11 (27.50)
c. Both	7 (17.50)	5 (12.50)	6 (15.00)	8 (20.00)	-	-
d. Family members	-	-	-	2 (5.00)	-	3 (7.50)
Total	20 (50.00)	20 (50.00)	20 (50.00)	20 (50.00)	20 (50.00)	20 (50.00)
Grand Total (1+2)	40 (100.00)	40 (100.00)	40 (100.00)	40 (100.00)	40 (100.00)	40 (100.00)

Source: Field Work.

Mzost of the respondents preferred the male child because the expenditure of the male is less when compared to female with regard to their dress, education, employment, and marriage. In a patriarchal society, the male child has been given much more importance because as he is the heir of the family, and will take care of the parents even after his marriage.

However, 30.00 per cent of the respondents expressed that, due to increase in the level of education and employment, the male or female children are leaving their parents alone and are settling themselves in other places. Therefore, the respondents have no bias on the gender issue.

Table 3
Preference of Children

Preference	*Male*	*Female*	*Both*	*Total*
1. Nurse	7 (17.50)	7 (17.50)	6 (15.00)	20 (50.00)
2. Teacher	9 (22.50)	5 (12.50)	6 (15.00)	20 (50.00)
Total (1+2)	16 (40.00)	12 (30.00)	12 (30.00)	40 (100.00)

Source: Primary data

Table 4 gives the particulars and causes of gender disputes in the family. Though the women are working, earning, and sharing the expenditure of the family, they are still facing problems and disputes with their husbands.

Table 4
Causes of Disputes in the Family

Sl. No.	*Cause of disputes*	*Nurse*	*Teacher*	*Total*
1.	Dishonoring of In-laws	2 (5.00)	3 (7.50)	5 (12.50)
2.	Decision to go to the parents house	1 (2.50)	2 (5.00)	3 (7.50)
3.	Economic issues	6 (15.00)	5 (12.50)	11 (27.50)
4.	Children issues	2 (5.00)	4 (10.00)	6 (15.00)
5.	Preparation of food	-	1 (2.50)	1 (2.50)
6.	Earned income	5 (12.50)	6 (15.00)	11 (27.50)
7.	Inter-caste	1 (2.50)	-	1 (2.50)
8.	Other issues	3 (7.50)	1 (2.50)	4 (10.00)
9.	Total	20 (50.00)	20 (50.00)	40 (100.00)

Source: Primary data.

One of the teacher respondents who settled her life individually with a low level educated unemployee reported that though she is earning, spending, and saving for her family, there are still small disputes with the husband in regard to the care of children, like feeding, sending them to school. These disputes turned to a big issue with the involvement of her in-laws and compelled him to re-marry and as a result he gave birth to another child. Even now if she raises her voice against this issue, the in-laws treated it as dishonoring them because they have given house as a property therefore they encouraged their son to take recourse in violence against her and thrown out her belongings so ruthlessly along with her male and female children who are in 6th and 8th standards. Therefore, it is observed that the male domination is being encouraged by in-laws as he carries the name of their family.

It has been observed that 7.5 per cent of respondents are not even enjoying their freedom of taking decision to go either to their parent's house or to their relative's house though they are earning and sharing their income for the welfare of the family. Some of the respondents reported that they don't even have freedom to go out or even to speak with others with out husband's permission.

Regarding the economic issues 27.50 per cent of the respondents reported that their husbands are wasting their money in gambling and in taking the liquor and 15.00 per cent of them expressed that the disputes regarding children's issues like educating, petting the male child and neglecting the female child by giving less priority towards her education, suppressing her views and showing no interest towards her future. In case of food items 2.50 per cent of them are also having petty disputes like cooking the food, and serving the food on time, while 27.50 per cent reported that in spite of earning they have no economic liberty even to spend a few amount of money on their own as their entire salary is being taken away by their husbands. One of the respondent who has done *inter-caste marriage* reported that she is being suppressed by him because of her low caste, and the other issues like unable to bring the expected dowry or any other property from the parents, lack of understanding among relations, disputes among the children at play time, negative thinking between them are also causes for the disputes in the family.

GENDER DISCRIMINATION AT WORK PLACE

Table 5 narrates the causes of gender discrimination at work place of the sample women respondents. Out of the total sample, 25 per cent opined that there is more male domination especially in terms of decisions, 22.50 per cent said that during the distribution of work, the women are being appreciated not for her work but in order to make her to do even the work of the other men while 22.50 per cent are facing problems with the men while granting the leave at their work places whereas,12.50 per cent of the nurse respondents have reported that they are facing male domination and sexual abusement at the work place though they are working and serving to the (patients)/society with lot of dedication. Thus, working women are subjected to gender discrimination at the work place.

Table 5
Causes of Gender Inequalities at Work Place at Work Place

Sl. No.	*Nature of work*	*Per-mission*	*Perfor-mance of duties*	*Work distri-butions*	*Sexual abuses*	*Other problems*	*Total*
1.	Nurses	3 (7.50)	6 (15.00)	4 (10.00)	5 (12.50)	2 (5.00)	20 (50.00)
2.	Teachers	6 (15.00)	4 (10.00)	5 (12.50)	-	5 (12.50)	20 (50.00)
	Total	9 (22.50)	10 (25.00)	9 (22.50)	5 (12.50)	7 (17.50)	40 (100.00)

Source: Primary data.

The discrimination against women at domestic level and at work places have to be removed by creating awareness among the women to fight against the guilty.

REFERENCES

Ashish Bose, "Missing Men and Lonely Women." E.P.W. Vol. XXXV, No. 27, p. 2361-62.

Govind Kelker, "Gender Equality and Poverty Reduction in South Asia" E.P.W. Vol. XL, No. 4709-4718.

Meena Acharya, Puspa Ghimire, "Gender Indicators of Equality, Inclusion and Poverty Reduction", E.P.W. Vol. XL No. 44 and 45 Oct. 29, 2005.

Rita Manchanda, "Gender Relations in Post-conflict Reconstruction" E.P.W. Vol. XL No. 44 and 45, p. 4737-4745.

Radhika Coomaraswamy, "Human Security and Gender Violence" E.P.W. Vol. XL, No. 4737-4745.

39

Gender Equality Through Empowerment of Women in India

S. Vijaya Kumar

"Yathra nariyasthu pujyathe ramanthe thathra devathaha", the meaning of this Snaskrit sloka is, where women are respected, there angels will reside. This shows that in olden days (Age of Vedas) women were given high status in society. They were treated equal to men. It is evident from the ancient scripts that the women like Vishwavara, Gosa, Gaargi, and Mythreya leamt Vedas and participated in Vedanta discussions. But, in the later stages, gradually male domination increased in the society.

In India, according to 2001 census nearly half of the population constitutes women. In the world's population also half of the populations are women. They are working on par with men in all sectors like administration, teaching, medical, commercial, banking, industry and even in defense. It is notable that they are contributing to 10per cent of world's productivity. Though, in all sectors on an average out of three hours, women are working for two hours, but they are getting only 10per cent income out of total income from labour.

Though women are contributing equally to men in the annual global productivities, they are not getting equal wages on par with men. Thus they are subject to "labour robbery". This shows clear gender discrimination. According to I.L.O, out of every six women subjected to gender bias and negligence, one women in living in absolute poverty. In one survey, I.L.O. mentioned that out of three, one women is participating in global economic development and productive activities. But, for this they are earning only 1/10th of the global income.

In India, there is gender bias preference to male child. The girl child is subjected to discrimination in all respects–education; marriage employment etc., According to UNDP report, in Punjab, the male child is given preference when compared to female child. The people of this state are spending nearly double amount on male child when compared with female child for their brought up. Female literacy is less in our country when compared to male literacy. According to 2001 census male literacy is 75.85 per cent and female literacy is 54.16 per cent.

The research was done by Prabhat Jha and his colleagues at St. Michael's Hospital at the University of Toronto and Rajesh Kumar of the Postgraduate Institute of Medical Education and Research, Chandigarh. "They discovered that the "girl deficit" was more common among educated families, especially in homes where the first born was a girl. The desire to have a male heir was found to drive families to sex-determination tests and termination of pregnancy if the foetus was female.

Highlighting the continuing trend of falling female birth rate in India, the study said. "Prenatal sex determination followed by selective abortion of female foetus is the most plausible explanation for the low sex ratio at birth in India". The study is based on a national survey of 1.1 million Indian households further claims that nearly five lakh female babies are lost in India every year because of selective abortions.

The principle of gender equality is enshrined in the Indian Constitution in its Preamble, Fundamental Rights, Fundamental Duties and Directive Principles. The Constitution not only grants equality to women, but also empowers the State to adopt measures of positive discrimination in favour of women.

From the Fifth Five Year Plan (1974-78) onwards there has been a marked shift in the approach to women's issues from welfare to development. In recent years, the empowerment of women has been recognized as the central issue in determining the status of women. The National Commission for Women was set up by an

Act of Parliament in 1990 to safeguard the rights and legal entitlements of women. The 73rd and 74th Amendments (1993) to the Constitution of India have provided for reservation of seats in the local bodies of Panchayats and Municipalities for women laying a strong foundation for their participation in decision making at the local levels.

India has also ratified various international conventions and human rights instruments committing to secure equal rights of women. Key among them is the ratification of the Convention on Elimination of All Forms of Discrimination Against Women (CEDAW) in 1993.

The women's movement and a wide-spread network of non-Government Organizations which have strong grass-roots presence and deep insight into women's concerns have contributed in inspiring initiatives for the empowerment of women.

However, there still exists a wide gap between the goals enunciated in the Constitution, legislation, policies, plans, programmes, and related mechanisms on the one hand and the situational reality of the status of women in India, on the other. This has been analyzed extensively in the Report of the Committee on the Status of Women in India, "Towards Equality", 1974 and highlighted in the National Perspective Plan for Women, 1988-2000, the Shramshkti Report, 1988 and the Platform for Action, Five Years After-An assessment".

Gender disparity manifests itself in various forms, the most obvious being the trend of continuously declining female ratio in population in the last few decades. Social stereotyping and violence at the domestic and societal levels are some of the manifestations.

The underlying causes of gender inequality are related to social and economic structure, which is based on informal and formal norms, and practices.

Consequently, the access of women particularly those belonging to weaker sections including Scheduled Castes/Scheduled Tribes/ Other backward Classes and minorities, majority of whom are in the rural areas and in the informal, unorganized sector – to education, health and productive resources, among others, is inadequate. Therefore, they remain largely marginalized, poor and socially excluded.

ECONOMIC EMPOWERMENT OF WOMEN

Since women comprise the majority of the population below the poverty line and are very often in situations of extreme poverty given the harsh realties of intra-household and social discrimination, macro economic policies and poverty eradication programmes will specifically address the needs and problems of such women. There will be improved implementation of programmes which are already women oriented with special targets for women. Steps will be taken for mobilization of poor women and convergence of services, by offering them a range of economic and social options, along with necessary support measures to enhance their capabilities.

Women's perspectives will be included in designing and implementing macro-economic and social policies by institutionalizing their participation in such processes. Their contribution to socio-economic development as producers and workers will be recognized in the formal and informal sectors (including home based workers) and appropriate policies relating to employment and to her working conditions will be drawn up. Such measures could include: Reinterpretation and redefinition of conventional concepts of work wherever necessary e.g. in the Census records, to reflect women's contribution as producers and workers.

Globalization has presented new challenges for the realization of the goal of women's equality, the gender impact of which has not been systematically evaluated fully. However, from the macro-level studies that were commissioned by the Department of Women & Child Development, it is evident that there is a need for reframing policies for access to employment and quality of employment. Benefits of the growing global economy have been unevenly distributed leading to wider economic disparities, the feminization of poverty, increased gender inequality through often deteriorating working conditions and unsafe working environment especially in the informal economy and rural areas. Strategies will be designed to enhance the capacity of women and empower them to meet the negative social and economic impacts, which may flow from the globalization process.

The provision of support services for women, like child care facilities, including crèches at work places and educational institutions, homes for the aged and the disabled will be expanded and improved to create an enabling environment and to ensure their full cooperation in social, political and economic life. Women-friendly personnel policies will also be drawn up to encourage women to participate effectively in the3 developmental process.

SOCIAL EMPOWERMENT OF WOMEN

There is considerable evidence for the claim that access to education can bring about changes in cognitive ability which is essential to women's capacity to question, to reflect on, and to act on the conditions of their lives and to gain access to knowledge, information, and new ideas. A study from Tamil Nadu found that better-educated women scored higher than less educated women on a composite index measuring their access to, and control over, resources, as well as their role in economic decision-making. Educated women also appear less likely to suffer from domestic violence. A study by Sen in West Bengal noted that educated women were better able to deal with violent husband: 'access to secondary stages of education may have an important contributory role in enhancing women's capacity to exercise control in their lives....through a combination of literacy and numeric skills, and enhanced self-esteem". The widely document3ed anti-liquor movement mounted by members of Mahila Samakhya, a literacy programme for women in India, was sparked off by images of collective action against alcoholism in their literacy primer. The design of educational curricula has not yet taken account of the fact that many more women are entering the labour market around the world, making critical contributions to household income Policy makers often continue to see the benefits of educating girls and women in terms of improving family health and welfare, rather than preparing women for a more equal place in the economy and in society.

Women's lack of skills partly explains why they continue to be confined to the poorer paid and more casualties forms of paid work. These limitations to education as a route to empowerment do not negate the earlier positive finding, but they suggest the need for caution in assuming that the effects of education can be taken for granted or that they will be uniform across all contexts. They point to the various aspects of educational provision that militate against not only its empowerment potential but even its ability to attract and retain girls in school, particularly those from poor backgrounds. Equal access to education for women and girls will be ensured. Special measures will be taken to eliminate discrimination, universalize education, eradicate illiteracy, create a gender-sensitive educational system, increase enrolment and retention rates of girls and improve the quality of education to facilitate life-long learning as well as development of occupation/vocation/technical skills by women. Reducing the gender gap in secondary and higher education would be a focus area. Sectoral time targets in existing policies will be achieved, with a special focus on girls and women, particularly those belonging to weaker sections including the Scheduled Castes/ Scheduled Tribes/Other Backward Classes/Minorities. Gender sensitive curricula would be developed at all levels of educational system in order to address sex stereotyping as one of the causes of gender discrimination.

Women's equality in power sharing and active participation in decision making, including decision making in political process at all levels will be ensured for the achievement of the goals of empowerment. All measures to be taken to guarantee women equal access to and full participation in decision making bodies at every level, including the legislative, executive, judicial, corporate, statutory bodies, as also the advisory Commissions, Committees, Boards, Trusts etc. Affirmative action such as reservations/quotas, including in higher legislative bodes, will be considered whenever necessary on a time bound basis. Women-friendly personnel policies will also be drawn up to encourage women to participate effectively in the developmental process.

POLITICAL EMPOWERMENT OF WOMEN

As half of the population are women, they are entitled to at least half of the seats in parliament. Such an achievement would led to women's empowerment. A review of the relevant statistics suggests that, regardless of political systems, the proportion of women in national parliaments around the world is extremely low, averaging 13.8 per cent in 2000.

There is some debate about whether greater participation and influence in local government structures are more relevant goals for poor women than increasing women's seats in national parliaments. The former, after all, make the decisions that most directly affect the lives of poor people. In recognition of this, a number of states in India, where there is now 33 per cent reservation of seats for women in local government, have added further inducements to local communities to encourage women's participation. Madhya Pradesh and Kerala, for example, require that one third of participants in the regular open village meetings are female before there is considered to be a quorum. Kerala also allocate 10 per cent of development funds received by local councils from the state to be used for women's development and to be managed by representatives of female groups of the village assembly. Clearly all these measures, including the reservation policy itself, are open to abuse. There has been much discussion in India about the possibility that women are merely proxies for husbands or powerful men within their family or caste. Objections are raised on the grounds that only supporters of parties in power attend village meetings; or that women are being harassed to spend funds in ways that do not benefit poorer women. While these are valid concerns, they may also alter over time, as women become more experienced in the political arena. Studies in India, for example, showed that many of the elected women were gaining self-confidence. They questioned the priorities of panchayat (local government) development programmes, emphasized issues affecting women such as fuel and water, and had begun to build broad alliances among themselves. One study showed that women representatives were likely to allocate resources differently from men, suggesting that their presence allowed a different set of priorities to be expressed.

HEALTH AND NUTRITION

A holistic approach to women's health which includes both nutrition and health services will be adopted and special attention will be given to the needs of women and the girl at all stages of the life cycle. The reduction of infant mortality and maternal mortality, which are sensitive indicators of human development, is a priority concern. This policy reiterates the national demographic goals for infant Mortality Rate (IMR), maternal Mortality Rate (MMR) set out in the National Population Policy 2000. Women should have access to comprehensive, affordable and quality health care. To effectively meet problems of infant and maternal mortality, and early marriage the availability of good and accurate data at micro level on deaths, birth and marriages is required. Strict implementation of registration of births and deaths would be ensured and registration of marriages would be made compulsory.

In view of the high risk of malnutrition and disease that women face at all the three critical stages viz., infancy childhood, adolescent and reproductive phase, focused attention would be paid to meeting the nutritional needs of women at all stages of the life cycle. This is also important in view of the critical link between the health of adolescent girls, pregnant and lactating women with the health of infant and young children. Special efforts will be made to tackle the problem of macro and micro nutrient deficiencies especially amongst pregnant and lactating women as it leads to various diseases and disabilities.

In recognition of the diversity of women's situations and in acknowledgement of the needs of specially disadvantaged groups, measures and programmes will be undertaken to provide them with special assistance. These groups include women in extreme poverty, destitute women, women in conflict situations, women affected by natural calamities, women in less developed regions, the disabled widows, elderly women, single women in difficult circumstances, women heading house holds, those displaced from employment, migrants, women who are victims of marital violence, deserted women and prostitutes etc. All forms of violence against women, physical and mental, whether at domestic or societal levels, including those arising from customs, traditions or accepted practices shall be dealt with effectively with a view to eliminate its incidence. Institutions and mechanisms/schemes for assistance will be created and strengthened for prevention of such violence, including sexual harassment at work place and customs like dowry; for the rehabilitation of the victims of violence and for taking effective action against the perpetrators of such violence. A special emphasis will also be laid on programmes and measures to deal with trafficking in women and girls.

All forms of discrimination against the girl child and violation of her rights shall be eliminated by undertaking strong measures both preventive and punitive within and outside the family. These would relate specifically to strict enforcement of laws against prenatal sex selection and the practices of female feticide, female infanticide, child marriage, child abuse and child prostitution etc. Removal of discrimination in the treatment of the girl child within the family and outside and projection of a positive image of the girl child will be actively fostered. There will be special emphasis on the needs of the girl child and earmarking of substantial investments in the areas relating to food and nutrition, health and education, and in vocational education. In implementing programmes for eliminating child labour, there will be a special focus on girl children.

The UN Secretary-Generals report concludes that 'more work needs to be done at every level, to create the enabling environment envisioned in the Platform for Action, in which women's rights are recognized as an indispensable part of human rights and women as well as men have the opportunity to realize their full potential'.

SUGGESTIONS

1. Creating an environment through positive economic and social policies for full development of women to enable them to realize their full potential.
2. The de-jure and de-facto enjoyment of all human rights and fundamental freedom by women on equal basis with men in all spheres-political, economic, social, cultural and civil.
3. Equal access to participation and decision making of women in social, political and economic life of the nation.
4. Equal access to women to health care, quality education at all levels, career and vocational guidance, employment, equal remuneration, occupational health and safety, social security and public office etc.
5. Strengthening legal systems aimed at elimination of all forms of discrimination against women.
6. Changing societal attitudes and community practices by active participation and involvement of both men and women.
7. Mainstreaming a gender perspective in the development process.
8. Elimination of discrimination and all forms of violence against women and the girl child.
9. Building and strengthening partnerships with civil society, particularly women's organizations and
10. In every district, measures to be taken to eradicate prostitution and they should be properly rehabilitated.

CONCLUSION

If the above said suggestions are implemented in our country, we can achieve the goal of Gender Equality and Empowerment of Women.

REFERENCES

UN (1979), Convention on the Elimination of All Forms of Discrimination Against Women.

Institutions, Organization and Gender Equality in an era of Globalization-Aruna Rao and David Kelleher.

Fundamentalisms, Globalization, and Women's Human Rights–Fatou Sow.

The Women's Movement in the Era of Globalization: Does it Face Extinction?–Andrea Medina Rosas and Shamillah Wilson.

Using the Master's Tools: Feminism, Media and Ending Vilence Against Women-Sanya Sarnavka.

Trafficking and Women's Human Rights in a Globalize World-Pamela Shifman.

The Hindu: 10-01-2006.

40

Gender Discrimination in India

K. Narasimhulu

INTRODUCTION

The position of the girl child seems to have deteriorated after the first millennia, especially in the North Indian states, due to a change in political equations. Early marriage, low status in marriage due to widespread polygamy and practice of seclusion among upper class women became rampant. Access to education was also limited.

The reformists of the nineteenth century, however, advocated a ban on early marriage of girls, supported widow remarriage and opened schools for girls. This effort was continued more aggressively in the twentieth century with support from the Indian National Congress leading the struggle for independence. Though the constitution and a vast body of legislation has promoted gender equality, the status of the girl child continues to be low. One indication is low sex ratios of women.

LOW SEX RATIO

This is revealed through a study of the sex ratios existing in our country from 1901 onwards. Strangely enough, inspite of the advances in medical sciences, the drop in death rate from 42.6 per cent in 1901-1911 to 9.2 per cent in 2001, the tremendous advances made in the eradication of malaria and control of infectious diseases like tuberculosis, as well as, an increase in life expectancy for women from 23.3 years in 1901-11 to 61.7 in 1991-96, the sex ratios of our population continue to be adverse for women. In 1901, the sex ratio was 972 females per 1000 males. This ratio has been continuously declining from 1951 onwards and it has come to 933 in 2001.

Every census figure has recorded this fall with the exception of the 1981 census which may be due to the fact that it did not include the sex ratios of the states of Assam and Jammu and Kashmir as their population was recorded on the basis of projected figures given in the report of the Standing Committee of Experts on population projections. The cataclysmic trauma of the partition of India in 1947 and the consequential mass migrations of population did not seem to have affected the tendency of the sex ratios to decline. The change in the religious complexion of the country's population has not stopped this decline. The development process of independent India at a pace never achieved before have also not succeeded in stopping the decline of sex ratios.

It is also seen from the data that the sex ratio in urban is less than the sex ratio in rural areas. The differentials in sex ratio on the basis of religion and caste also indicate that sex ratios are declining more in the case of Hindus, including Scheduled Castes, than in the case of other communities. It is strange that the sikhs, representing one of the most progressive communities in the country, show a very adverse sex ratio, compared to other communities. This has happened inspite of the migration of a large number of Sikh males abroad. A possible explanation for this seems to be in the concentration of Sikhs in the Indo-Gangetic cultural region. The decline in the case of Scheduled Tribes is much less.

The incidence of poverty is not as important and determining a factor in the declining sex ratios as that of a predominant culture. High per capita incomes of Punjab and Haryana have not given them higher sex ratios, nor has the incidence of poverty levels increased the sex ratios among Scheduled Castes, Scheduled Tribes and Muslims. It is a contagion they have caught from the predominant culture of the places in which they are located.

An important concern of demographers, policy makers, planners, administrators and health functionaries is the possibility of female foeticide of the existences of infanticide in some rare cases contributing to adverse female sex ratios.

From the preliminary surveys conducted so far in different parts of the country, it appears that the main cause of adverse female sex ratio is the practice of universal infanticide or amniocentesis.

EMPIRICAL STUDIES

Infact, from the information available till now, these practices may be considered as not very important statistically in the context of 28 million annual births in the country. The causes appear to be more cultural, related to the lowest status of women in the Indo-Gangetic basin compared to the South and the North-East. The cultural norm is the reluctant acceptance of the birth of a girl child, perceived as an economic burden, leading to her neglect in infancy, childhood and adolescence, early age of marriage, early pregnancy, poor nutrition and poor pre and antenatal health care.

Once the child is born, the Infant Mortality Rate in the first year of life is often adverse as far as female children are concerned. The data available through the SRS (Sample Registration System) conducted by the Registrar General of Census from the year 1972 onwards shows. This, the total infant mortality rate in 1972 was 139, for males it was 132 and for females 148 per thousand births. This adverse relationship of female IMR with male IMR continued rise upto 1987. Since then, after the introduction of the Universal Immunization Programme at the end of 1985, the gap between male and female mortality rates narrowed down and from 1988 onwards, except from 1990, the female IMR has been lower than the male IMR. It may also be noted that females in urban areas have generally had lower IMR than their counterparts in rural areas (see Table 1).

Table 1
Infant Mortality Rates* by Sex-All India

Year	*Rural*			*Urban*			*Total*		
	Males	*Females*	*Persons*	*Males*	*Females*	*Persons*	*Males*	*Females*	*Persons*
1972	141	161	150	85	85	85	132	148	139
1973	141	144	143	88	90	89	132	135	134
1976	133	146	139	78	82	80	124	134	129
1977	136	146	140	80	82	81	126	135	130
1978	132	143	137	74	75	74	123	131	127
1979	129	131	130	73	71	72	119	12	120
1980	123	125	124	65	65	65	113	115	114
1981	119	119	119	63	62	62	110	111	110
1982	114	114	114	70	60	65	106	104	105
1983	113	114	114	69	63	66	105	105	105

Contd...

Year	Rural			Urban			Total		
	Males	Fe-males	Per-sons	Males	Fe-males	Per-sons	Males	Fe-males	Per-sons
1984	113	114	113	68	64	66	104	104	104
1985	106	107	107	56	62	59	96	98	97
1986	104	106	96	64	60	62	96	97	96
1987	103	106	104	63	57	61	95	96	95
1988	103	102	102	65	59	62	96	94	94
1989	100	98	91	100	98	58	92	90	91
1990	54	88	86	50	49	50	78	81	80
1991	87	87	87	53	52	53	81	80	80
1992	84	86	85	54	52	53	79	80	79
1993	81	84	82	47	44	45	73	75	74
1994	NA	NA	80	NA	NA	52	75	73	74
1995	NA	NA	80	NA	NA	NA	49	NA	74
1998	NA	NA	77	NA	NA	45	9.8	73.5	72

Source: Sample Registration System, Registrar General and Commissioner, Census Operations, Government of India, New Delhi, various years.
Note: *Per 1,000 live births.

The significant drop in IMR is largely due to the grand success of the Expanded Programme of Immunization started in 1978 and the universal immunization launched in 1985 which was succeeded in getting more than 845 per cent children immunised., Although, sex wise data is not maintained, practical experience and surveys conducted indicate no significant differences in the coverage of girls and boys. It remains to be seen whether this improvement in Female IMR will result in higher sex ratios in the next census (2011).

The child mortality rates in the age group of 0-4 based on SRS figures for male and female have been adverse as far as females are concerned in the data available for 1972 onwards right upto 1993. This phenomenon can only be attributed to the lower health care towards girl children, where delay often takes place in taking the girl child to the hospital, as also her lower nutrition status leading to poor health.

An analysis of total mortality rates shows that 30 per cent of the mortality rates are contributed by child mortality. Here, as figures of girl child mortality are higher than boys, this factor contributes to lower sex ratio.

Girl child's health is largely determined by her nutrition status. This is shown in Table 2.

As far as the nutrition standard of children from the age of 1-6 is concerned, there is disparity in the nutrition available to male and female children, both as far as calories and proteins are concerned.

Table 2
Daily Average Intake of Energy and Protein against Allowance by Age Group-1990

Age Group	*Energy kilocalories/day*				*Protein, gram/day*			
	Recommended		*Intake*		*Recommended*		*Intake*	
	Female	*Male*	*Female*	*Male*	*Female*	*Male*	*Female*	*Male*
1-3	1,050	1,200	773	780	22.5	23.5	21.9	22.0
4-6	1,500	1,700	1,097	1112	28.5	30.0	30.9	31.5
7-9	1,800	2,050	1320	1325	43.0	43.0	36.0	39.0
10-12	1,950	2,150	1483	1550	62.0	59.0	41.0	42.9
13-15	2,050	2,400	1620	1773	65.0	76.0	42.9	49.1
16-18	2,050	2,600	1721	1937	66.0	81.0	47.7	58.6
>18	1,800	2,350	1789	2169	50.0	60.0	50.4	62.0

In 1993, the Drugs Country Report sponsored by the Govt. of India and UNDCP (United Nations Drug control Programme) revealed that 93 per cent of girls in rural areas of Rajasthan suffered from first to third degree chronic energy deficiencies. The calorie intake of nutrients for girls in the age groups of 10-18 years was deficient by 26-36 per cent, while protein deficiency amounted to 23-32 per cent. Iron deficiency and anaemia rates were also higher among girls compared to boys.

It is a said reality that girls constitute a fair percentage of street children in India. Drug abuse is rampant among these children. Girls who are drug addicts are liable to be sexually exploited and exposed to diseases which follow from such abuses.

A phenomenon which was quite rare but is now causing concern for young girls is the increase in the incidence of violence against them. The annual reports of the National Crime bureau confirm the rise in the incidence of rape of young girls in the age group of 10 to 16 years. It has gone up by 28 per cent between the years 1991 and 1995. Girls are also subjected to sexual abuse as indicated in a study conducted by the National Mental Health Institute, Bangalore in 1994.

The exploitation of girls is also indicated by the fact that the incidence of girl prostitution is on the increase a survey conducted by the Central Social Welfare Board in 1991 in six metropolitan cities showed that 40 per cent of the prostitutes covered by the survey took to their profession when they were under 18 years of age. The incidence of sexually transmitted diseases and aids among this group is high. The family planning association of India's sex education counseling centres has reported an increased attendance of girls in the 15 to 25 years age group visiting these centres with such diseases.

The Department of Women and Child Development wanted to get information on the status of the girl child from an independent intellectual source having empathy for girls and hence a special study was sponsored on the girl child and the family through the UGC centres for women development studies in the university system in India in 1990.. This study had many interesting aspects related to the girls in our country. As far as their education is concerned, according to the sample taken, 61 per cent of the girls attended schools. The dropped out rate is 17 per cent and 21 per cent never attended the school. There were rural urban variations as far as attendance of girls in schools is concerned. 54 per cent of the rural girls in the underdeveloped areas going to schools compared to 82 per cent among the urban middle class areas. It is also noticed that as far as girls who had never attended school are only 4 per cent are brahmins, 15 per cent from other forward castes and 41 per cent from the Scheduled tribes.

There are inter-religion variations also. Nearly 97 per cent Sikh girls were going to schools, whereas among the christians it was 93.4 per cent, 71.5 per cent among Muslims and 75.2 per cent among Hindus. There was a 23 per cent drop-out rate from co-educational schools as compared to only 17 per cent from girls schools. If the school was within the village or locatify, 75 per cent of the girls attended, whereas if the school was more than 2 kilometers away 18 per cent dropped-out. Less than 20 per cent of the girls stayed with relatives or friends or in hostels to facilitate school attendance.

REASONS FOR NOT ATTENDING SCHOOLS

The reasons for not attending school were varied. Economic reasons were cited for 8.6 per cent, 4 per cent did not attend school because the family did not value education and 3 per cent because girls were required at home to look after younger siblings or to do household work. Of the total sample of girls who had dropped out, 45 per cent dropped out in the age group of 7-11 years, that is, in the first three or four years of schooling, and 22 per cent dropped out at the age of 12-13 years. The number of girls attending school decreased as the age level increased. Of the 14-15 year old, 18.6 per cent were attending school but only 9 per cent of 16-18 years old were still in school. The study also indicated that as far as girls' education was concerned, the higher the caste, the less the objection to it. Of the families surveyed in the study, only 1.3 per cent were Brahmins, 15.6 per cent were Forward Caste, 13.3 per cent Scheduled Castes and 39.7 per cent were Backward castes. Social cultural reasons are important among the backward classes where family as well as society does not value girls' education. The higher level of education of the mother and the father also promoted girls' school attendance. The study also indicated that the higher the occupational level of the father, the higher the attendance of girls in school. Higher income groups laid greater emphasis on girls' education. Fewer girls (52 per cent) attended school when the income was between 330-500 rupees per month compared to 70 per cent of the girls attending school when the income was between 1,500-3,000 rupees and 85 per cent girls in school if the income is between 3,000-5,000 rupees per month. Household tasks also affected the attendance in school. Of the 8.6 per cent girls who had to fetch water for the household, 80 per cent were in school but out of the girls looking after younger children, only 61.4 per cent were in school. The study made the unique discovery that about 71 per cent of the girls attending school said there was no problem in walking to school. Altogether only 7 per cent of the girls mentioned problems of bad weather, their own ill health or a feeling of insecurity as reasons for not attending school. Residing a reasonable distance from school was not in itself a factor in determining the number of girls who attended school. It appears that poverty and economic marginality tended to be the strong determinants in all major outcomes, including the attendance of girl children in schools. Most girls did not take part in extra-curricular activities but 49.3 per cent did take part in games and 21.8 per cent in dance and music. It is significant that among the aspirations of the girl child, the most important seemed to be to become a teacher, followed by the desire to be a good housewife and third in aspirations came the adoption of the vocation of a doctor or a nurse. As far as the level of education up to which the girl child herself thinks she should study, 31.4 per cent of the sample surveyed thought that they would like to study upto graduation; followed by high schooling, 26.7 per cent; post graduate or professional, 21.0; and no specific level was the response of 11.4 per cent.

Studies also revealed that as far as the health status of the girl was concerned, the higher the father's education, larger the percentage of girls being immunised. Of the non-literate fathers, 46 per cent did not immunise their child but only 6 per cent of the fathers in the technical/professional categories failed to do so. As far as nutrition was concerned, the study did not indicate the level of nutrition reaching the girls except breast feeding but it did indicate that one-third of the families surveyed ate together, in one-third of the families there was no specific order of eating whereas, in another one-third, female members were the last to eat and the males of the family were the first to eat.

The study also investigated the question of the employment of girl children. It was found that 87.3 per cent of the girls did not perform any economic activity towards supplementing the family income. This percentage did not take into account all girls who contributed to the household occupation. In the total sample, 12.8 per cent of the girls did contribute towards the family income out of which 4.7 per cent earned between 100-300 rupees per month. The girls did not keep any earned income for themselves. It was further clear that out of the girls employed, 51.6 per cent were employed as agricultural labourers and in related activities, 17.2 per cent in home-based establishments or family business, 9.4 per cent as piece-rate workers in crafts, 7.8 per cent in domestic and personal services and 4.7 per cent were self employed. Of the employed girls, 39 per cent were employed by businessmen, contractors or landlords, 12.5 per cent by individuals and households and 14 per cent by others. About 54.7 per cent of the girls were satisfied with their work, around 17.2 per cent said they were not satisfied, 19.5 per cent liked working because it made them economically independent and 11 per cent disliked the drudgery and the long hours of work. These 13 per cent of girls never employed should not be expected to contribute to family budget but be put in schools.

This comprehensive study, conducted by he UGC, impartially and under the leadership of women professors, has come up with a most significant insight: that the girl child across the country is conscious and aware of the fact that she should be educated. A large percentage of the girls have expressed a desire for a career after education. The study also brings out a fact, confirmed by government data, that the caste of the girl, parents' educational levels and economic condition affect her access to health and educational opportunities and also compel her to work. We will see later on how the development processes are meeting this need.

The status of the girl child in India, as compared to other South Asian countries, is somewhere between the very low status in Pakistan and Nepal and the high achievements of Sri Lanka and the Maldives. We have adverse sex ratios compared to Sri Lanka and higher fertility rates compared to Sri Lanka and Pakistan. The age of marriage is among the lowest and contraceptive prevalence rates are lower than Sri Lanka and the Maldives in the 15-19 year age group. the percentage of girls giving birth in this age group is also the highest in our country. The literacy rate for Indian girls in the age group of 10-19 is highest after Sri Lanka and the maldives. Labour force participation rates in the age group of 10-14 are about 5 per cent compared to 6.6 per cent in Bangladesh and 28.5 per cent in Nepal. In the age group of 15-19 years, these rates are 26.2 per cent in India compared to 59.5 per cent in Bangladesh, 49.3 per cent in Nepal and 33.4 per cent in Pakistan.

In such a scenario, the effort of the government has been multi sectoral, especially since the nineties. A plan of action for the improvement of the status of the girl child has been made by the Department of Women and Child Development. It lays down the objectives to be achieved by various development departments of the government to improve the girl child's share of developmental efforts. Specific goals have been laid down for improving her health, education and awareness status. The nodal department of women and child development has prepared several awareness generation programmes on this issue. There has been a media blitz, especially over the national television networks, on the advantages of having a girl child and the need for gender equality in her upbringing in the family. Her need for nutrition, access to health and education and future employment is stressed. The need for giving attention to the needs of girl children is also emphasised through training modules for the orientation of government officials in the executive and judicial branch. Parliamentarians and workers of voluntary organisations are also given such courses. Funds are specifically given to NGOs for running awareness generation campaigns in the community. A marvelous process of sanitisation on this issue has already taken place and the process will have to be a continuous effort.

The Integrated Child development Scheme (ICDS) centres spread throughout the country, both in urban and rural areas, give nutrition, immunisation, health care and pre-school education to children up to 6 years of age and will be covering 264.86 lakh children at the end of 1999-2000 and 55.9 lakh nursing and expectant mothers. The national evaluation of this programme conducted by the National Institute of Public Cooperation and Child development, in 1992, showed no gender discrimination in nutrition in its centers.

The Food and Nutrition Board of the Department of Women and Child Development conducts nutrition education, training and awareness work throughout the country, and also monitors the quality of food supplied by the ICDS. According to the Census of 1991, there were 9.418 crore boys in the age group of 10-19 and 8.355 crore girls in the same age group. They represented 26.61 per cent of the total male population and 20.7 per cent of the total female population of the country at the time of the census. The awareness of the low status of adolescent girls as far as nutrition is concerned and the fact that parents are very keen to marry off girls soon after puberty induced the government to make an integrated adolescent girls programme as a component of selected blocks of the ICDS. As a result of this 507 blocks constituting 3.51 lakh girls have been covered to date under this programme. This programme aims at giving supplementary nutrition to the girls in the age group of 6 to 11 years and basic health and nutrition and non-formal literacy to the girls belonging to the age group of 11-15 years. In addition to health and nutrition education, they are also imparted vocational training in simple crafts based on local resources and availability of local kill for training. The scheme now covers 3.57 lakh beneficiaries.

The Department of Woman and Child Development, besides introducing the adolescent girls programme in the ICDS which, it run for about 160 lakh children, also gives assistance for training of such girls through NORAD, the programme funded by the Norwegian Development Agency and the schemes of the Central

Social Welfare Board. The Balika Samriddhi Scheme, 1997 of this department gifts the mother of a girl child by providing the girl scholarships to attend middle and high school, and if she remains unmarried till the age of 18, it provides facilities for pursuing higher studies or self-employment. The Ministry of Health has introduced special schemes for the health of the girl children, especially to counter-act anaemia, and gives attention to their reproductive health and population education. The introduction of the micro-nutrient programmes is also helping in improving their health. The Ministry of education' efforts in promoting the girl child's share of education are very comprehensive. The efforts to ameliorate child labour including that of girls is receiving special attention in the Ministry of Labour. Voluntary effort has not been lagging behind in the sphere of sensitising the girl child. The state governments are also taking interest in improving the status of the girl child. Rajasthan, through its scheme 'Rajya Lakhsmi'; Haryana through 'Apni Beti, Apna Dhan' and Haryana Integrated Women's Empowerment and development Project; Karnataka through 'Namana Magalu'; and Tamil Nadu give bonds to some parents at the time of the birth of a girl child in an effort to enhance her status.

The Mahila Samakhya sensitises the community and women's groups on the girl child's needs in seven states. The Lok Jumbish of Rajasthan promotes her education. The Pariwar Sewa Sansthan, the Family Planning Association of India, works on health and family welfare issues, Sakshi in Delhi and Samvad in Bangalore along with Vimochana work in the field of girl child abuse, child custody and rape, Satya Shodan Ashram in Madhya Pradesh helps to prevent tribal girls from being sold into prostitution. Adithi in Bihar has taken several initiatives for the girl child. Numerous other voluntary organisations spread all over the country are trying to improve the life of the girl child in significant ways.

CONCLUSION

A review of the status of the girl child indicates that it is the people's perception, in general, that the birth of a girl child is less desirable than that of a baby boy. It is ingrained in the Indian psyche, cutting across religious, caste and regional barriers, that the birth of a girl child evokes less happiness than that of a boy. If the first child born to parents is a girl, she is less unwelcome than her subsequent sisters. The phenomenon of aborting female foetuses is occasionally recorded to in cities as well as in rural areas if girl children are already present in a family. The passing of the Prevention and Regulation of Amniocentesis Act, 1993, has not been a great hindrance as doctors still use the procedure of ultrasonography to predict the sex of a foetus.

The awareness campaign about the need of having girl children and giving them great care needs to be strengthened through the use of the multi-media as well as making it obligatory for all voluntary organisations receiving grants from the government to propagate this message. The Integrated Child development Programme's nutrition component has to be strengthened by the Planning Commission by giving 100 per cent allocations for it to the states and tying it down for use only for this purpose. Adolescent girls' entry into the ICDS has to be strengthened through better vocationalisation of her training. Parents of those girl children who send them out to work have to be compensated for releasing her for school as in the case of the Haryana Development Project. The provision of creches in rural areas should be strengthened through greater involvement of voluntary organisations and public funding for this cause so that girls can be released from the burden of rearing siblings. It is important that a greater vocationalisation of girls' education takes place so that society views them as an important productive economic resource and not a burden to be married off. Reproductive health care programmes for young girls need to be strengthened so that they become healthier creators of the future generation. The responsibility of the nation's future is on their frail shoulders and they need our best and devoted care.

REFERENCES

Viji Srinivasan, Female Infanticide in Bihar, Adithi, Patna, Bihar, 1994. Unpublished.

Declining Sex Ratio and the Problems of Female Infanticide–A Study in Salem District of Tamil Nadu, Department of Women and Child, Government of India and Madras School of Social Work, 1994, Unpublished.

B. Devi Prasad, A Study of the Declining Sex Ratio in Andhra Pradesh, Andhra University, Visakhapatnam, 1994, Unpublished.

Usha S. Nayar and K. Anil Kumar, Declining Sex Ratio in Gujarat. Unit for Child and Youth Research, Tata Institute of Social Sciences, Bombay, 1995, Unpublished.

Mahendra K. Premi and Saraswati Raju, Imbalance in Child Sex Ratio in Madhya Pradesh and Rajasthan, Centre for the Study of Regional Development, Jawaharlal Nehru University, New Delhi, May 1996, Unpublished.

Usha Nayar, Doomed Before Birth, Study of Declining Sex Ratio in the Age Group 0-6 Years in Selected Districts of Punjab and Haryana. Department of Women's Studies, National Council of Educational Research and Training, New Delhi, Unpublished.

Evaluation of Pulse Polio 1995-1996 and 1996-1997, Ministry of Health and Family Welfare, Department of Family Welfare, Government of India, New Delhi, Unpublished.

World Drug Report (1997), UNDCP, Vienna, 1997.

Country Paper, India Paper for UNFPA Conference on Adolescents in Delhi on 21-24rd July, 1998, p. 5.

The National Family and Health Survey, International Institute of Population Studies (IIPS), Bombay, 1993.

S. Anand Laskhmy (Comp. aided). The Girl Child and the Family. An Action Research Study, sponsored by the Department of Women and Child Development, Government of India and executed by the UGC Centres for Women, New Delhi, 1994.

41

Gender Inequality: In Retrospect and Prospect

V.V. Reddy and G.Bhaskar

This paper is based on the assumption that gender inequality is the result of the socio-economic discrimination against women. This discrimination has made women a 'weaker sex'. Therefore, gender equality can be achieved only by a radical change in the existing socio-economic structure, specially property relations, which condition the overall status of men and women. Reforms in the present socio-economic structure by legislation or building public opinion, as experience proved, cannot bring about gender equality.

This paper is divided into three sections. The first section discusses the historical evolution of gender inequality; section two examines the Indian tradition of gender inequality, and the third section focuses on liberal and radical view of gender problem in India.

SECTION – I

Gender inequality might be traced back to pre-history, i.e., unrecorded history of humankind. It has evolved over a period of thousands of centuries, particularly with the emergence of the institutions of marriage and family in the civilized society. Before these two institutions have attained their modern form, they have gone through various stages and different forms.

In the horay past, in the primitive society, men and women of the same tribe lived in promiscuity for generations. In other words, men lived in polygamy and women in polyandry. The children born out of promiscuity were, therefore, regarded as common children to all men and women.

The children born out of group marriages were regarded as before as common children of a given group of men and women. It was the duty of women to look after children. Naturally, the children were attached to their mother and stood by her in prosperity as well as in adversity. The solidarity between the children and the mother gave upper hand to women, and this established 'mother's right which was recognized by custom. Mother's right was a natural corollary to mother's lineage by which sons and daughters were identified by the mother. This was the only period in history during which women were revered, and therefore, enjoyed a status higher than that of men.

Later, after the elapse of a long time, marriage, and therefore, family took the form of single pairs, in which man and woman enjoyed equal status, and were free to walk out of the marriage in case of incomparability. They paired again with the man and woman of their choice. This free separation of the couple was possible because private property had not yet originated and settled habitats were not developed to bind the couple in marriage and the family.

The downfall of women's status began with the emergence of patriarchal family in ancient society and the transformation of women into the status of semi-slaves. This family was based on private property and the inheritance of the family property by the male children.

The origin of private property was traced by Frederick Engels to the domestication of wild animals and cattle breading. With the domestication of animals, food gathering and hunting as a regular occupation had disappeared, and agriculture, plant cultivation for food and grass growing for fodder, become the main occupation of the people. This development not only marked the institution of private property but also the settled habitat in the form of small villages. The development of agriculture naturally led to the growth of crafts mainly connected with farm tools and implements needed for ploughing land and threshing crops.

In the patriarchal family only man owned and managed the family property. Hence, he became the head of the family and exercised unquestionable authority over the family members in matters like rituals and ceremonies, including fixing marriages. The role of women was confined to domestic work and rearing of children. Thus, mother lineage was converted into father's lineage. With father's lineage women were degraded in their status, with no rights but only obligations to the family. It was demanded absolute fidelity of woman to her husband to ensure the paternity of the children so that male children born out wedlock inherited the family property. Men still lived in polygamy.

The development of productive forces was very slow in the ancient society because little or no surplus product was available after meeting the consumption needs of the patriarchal family and its slaves. Further, the antagonism between the oppressed slaves and their masters often led to slave revolts and the consequent loss of life and property. One of the classic examples of slave revolts was the one led by Spartacus, which shook the slave society, and the subsequent face of slave society.

The birth of Christianity and its spread in Europe provided sinews to the struggle of the slaves for liberation from servitude. The new religion opposed to slavery and preached universal brotherhood. Therefore, Christianity became a rallying point and a saviour for all the oppressed people. The inability of the Roman Empire to hold together the outlaying territories led to the decay and the final disintegration of the empire. The fall of the Roman Empire paved the way for the transition of the ancient slave society to the feudal society where in the basic family was still the patriarchal family.

Feudal society made no difference to the status of women: they remained subordinate to men and men dominated home and the external world, though feudalism emerged in a new epoch of development by releasing productive forces from the oppressive master-slave production relations.

Feudalism transformed the former slaves into bonded tenant formers, who were allotted small plots of land for their personal cultivation in return to labour –rent by which they were obliged to work some days in a week on the estate of the lord. This arrangement was a sea change when compared with the slave labour. Now, in contrast to the slave, the tenant farmer had material incentive to work hard and raise crop yields on his plot as well as on lord's estate for he could retain his plot as long as he raised higher yields on the estate too. This system of agriculture produced a surplus since the lord need not feed the slaves or the tenant farmers. The surplus product now was exchanged to the products of craftsmen and traders such as clothing, furniture and farm implements. Therefore, the larger the surplus produced in agriculture, the greater the scope for the growth of crafts and other trades. This laid the basis for the evolution of an exchange economy and therefore, to commodity production.

The development of commodity production had its impact on the agrarian system. Labour-rent was gradually replaced by rent in kind or cash. The latter form of rent was more convenient, for, the landlords could buy with cash consumption goods directly from the traders and pay taxes, as the government did not accept taxes in kind. This system of rent was also in the interests of the tiller as he now need not work freely on the lord's estate and could; therefore, devote his entire working time on his plot.

In feudal society Christianity became a dominant religion in Europe, and the Church itself acquired estates through the charities of the kings and the faithfuls. It also collected rents from the tenants, thus becoming the biggest institutionalized landlord and a biggest patriarch. Therefore, it adopted a patriarchal attitude towards women and had no word against their oppression.

The growth of commodity production, and in its wake, the sharp class struggle between the rising bourgeoisie and landed interests on the one hand, and on the other, between peasants and the landlords had eventually led to the downfall of feudalism, and the rise of capitalism to both economic and political power.

Capitalist production, as we know, is not meant for the self-consumption of the producers but for exchange to make a profit. Therefore, profit motive or monetary gain pervades both social and personal relations. As a result, a new eithic is born, the eithic of money-nexus. In the new eithic all values once treasured as secred became profane, and every thing is measured in terms of money.

The money-nexus also entered the bourgeois monogaman family. Because, as Marx and Engels wrote in the Communist Manifesto, that the bourgeoisie see in their wife as instruments of production, i.e., as objects of production' of their children Marriages in bourgeois families are mostly arranged marriages for a consideration, for monetary gain. There may not be a dowry in the Indian sense either in cash or kind, but the main consideration is whether the bride brings or not productive assets or economic power to the groom's family.

The bourgeois monogaman family inherited patriarchal tradition of extra-marital relations. Therefore, Engels noted that monogamy in bourgeois family had not reached its ideal of single couple bonded to each other. This is because of the fact that monogaman family is based on contradictory foundation of private property. In this context, Engels gave the example of proletarian family. This family has no private property of worth the name, and both the husband and the wife earn their livelihood by wage-labour. In case of incompatibility, they separate of their own free will without formal divorce. It is not so with bourgeoisie couple, property or business considerations come in the way of separation.

It should be noted, however, that Engels has stated a fundamental problem of the monogamy-the relation between private property and gender inequality. Therefore, Engels was of the opinion that the abolition of private property, and the transition to communist property, which in any case, takes a long period of time to shed behind all the vestiges associated with private property, including private property mentality. Therefore, the abolition of private property is an important step forward to gender equality[1].

SECTION – II

GENDER INEQUALITY-INDIAN TRADITION

The Indian tradition and custom has never treated women equal to men. Although there are many mythological stories and references in Vedas and Puranas wherein women are revered and put them on high pedestal, in practice, women in general are accorded a low status, by assigning them the role of bearing children and homemaking.

Women are called and their salvation, it is said, lies in life long service with devolution to male members of the family. This tradition avers mainly to *Manu Smriti*, whose author Manu, is regarded by Hindus as the supreme law-giver.

Manu Smiriti starts with the dictum: "Women are created (by god) in order to bear children[2]".

Manu Smriti ordained absolute control of man over women. "In childhood a girl should be under the will of her father, in her youth of her husband's; her husband being dead, of her son; a women should never enjoy her own will". Says Manu further: "Day and night should women be kept by the male members of the family in a state dependence."Thus, Manu distrusts women, and Hindu men have taken full advantage of Manu Smriti to keep women in thralldom. Manu, however, kind enough to women by ordering men to take care of them because women are needed to propagate the humankind.

The concept *pativrata* is an invention of men to force women into absolute loyalty and subordination to the husband so that the paternity of the children is ensured. Manu ordained absolute fidelity of women to the husband by saying:" Though of bad conduct or debauched, or even devoid of good qualities, a husband must always be worshiped like a god by a good wife". Stories abound in Indian mythology about the power of *pativratyam.* Thus, Savitri brings back her dead husband, Satyavan, to life, and Sumathi carries her leper husband willingly to a woman of his desire, and it is said that by this act she became endeared to gods.

More henious was the tradition of *Sati* whereby the Hindu widow was burnt on the pyre of her husband. The followers of Manu Smriti justified *Sati* by saying that women must follow their husbands in death. The real reason behind *Sati* is something different, it related to socio-economic factors. First, the Hindu widow became economically a burden to the family, and second, she might bring bad name to the family if she commits adultary in a moment weakness when lured by men. During the Mogul period thousands of Rajput women burnt themselves so that the conquers did not abuse them. Even today, in some parts of the country some women follow the tradition of *Sati* either voluntarily or by force. (Ms. Kanwar in the 1980's in Rajastan was drugged and thrown into her husband's pyre). Of course, such cases are rare today.

Until the Hindu Code Bill was enacted in 1956, Hindu widow had no right to her husband's property, and with the recent Central Act daughters got the right to father's property along with the sons. But given the patriarchal tradition, most of the women do not assert their Constitutional rights to property.

Today Hindu widow, although not forced to *Sati,* she is ill treated and is assigned the role of a maid servant. She gets up early in the morning, does all the household work, eats the leftovers and retires to bed late in the night.

Inspite of Reformist movement, which was carried forward in 1940's by the left parties, widow remarriages, not withstanding the law, are prohibited by custom which is more powerful than formal law. Where the Hindu widow wants remarriage, the family and relatives put all kinds of pressures against it in order to retain her property with the family. In case the widow is bold enough to defy the family and remarried, it is often on considerations of widow's property.

Another ignoble custom of Indian tradition is the system of dowry. Dowry amounts to buying the groom by paying cash or kind. Even then, the husband's family subjects the bride to physical and mental harassment and thereby drives her to suicide or burnt her to death to get the son married again for dowry. Such cases are daily reported in the newspapers.

Dowry system is more common in the rural and urban middle class families. The former insist on landed property, while the urban families want the dowry in cash. The husband may be a petty government officer or a clerk whose monthly income is barely sufficient to maintain an urban family. So, marriage provides an occasion to get consumer durables from the bride's parents. Today, the dowry system spread even among the lower classes. Even a wage-labourer demands a dowry[3].

The anti-dowry Act of 1961 had prohibited giving and accepting dowry. But to the authors' knowledge no dowry giving and accepting cases are reported to the law enforcing authorities. The anti-dowry Act does not take cognizance of reporting of such cases by other than the parents of the bride and the groom. Therefore, filing a dowry case by the bride's father amounts to wrecking the marriage of his daughter. Thus, the law-makers are clever to perpetuate the dowry system.

The dowry system is the main reason why the parents prefer a son to a daughter. The sons are regarded as assets, while the girls are looked upon as a financial burden to the family. If it is known, by scanning that the foetus is a girl, the woman opts for an abortion either voluntarily or by the pressure of her family. Preference to male child naturally leads to the neglect of female child. In most of the families the parents compare a girl to a oven on the chest of the parents. Therefore, they try to marry off the girl as early as possible. This is the main reason for the child marriages in the Indian society. Thousands of child marriages are preformed every year against the law, but no parents, are prosecuted.

SECTION – III

GENDER EQUALITY: LIBERAL VIEW

In spite of strong patriarchal tradition in India, social reformers and nationalist leaders fought against discrimination and cruelty to women.

The first among them was Raja Ram Mohan Roy who was a crusader against the practice of *Sati*. He compared *Sati* with murder, and made several representations to the government, and successfully got the practice banned.

Swami Vivekananda held a liberal view of women's status, although he insisted that a woman should be first a mother and last a mother. He advocated women's education, which was a toboo those days, for, an educated mother could play better the role of motherhood. He complemented American women for their participation in public affairs, and endorsed the same for the Indian women provided their main focus remained on motherhood. Strangely the Swamiji preferred arranged and early marriages for Indian girls. Because, to quote him:" If they have to be married anyway without their consent, it is better they are married very early, before they fall in love, if they (boys and girls) are allowed to grow up apart, the boy may like some other girl, and the girl some other boy, and some evil will happen".

Sri Aarobindo, who was a revolutionary in his youth, but who renounced the worldly avocations and retired to Mother's asram in Pondicherry, advocated gender equality. Says he: "To reduce women's role solely to interior and domestic occupations, and men's part exclusively to exterior and social occupations, thus separating what could be united, would be to perpetuate the present sad state of things, from which both are equally suffering". Therefore, Aarobindo advocated the breaking of the traditional division of labour between men and women–breadwinning and home keeping, and suggested that gender equality could be achieved through participation in each other's domain. He wanted the participation of women in politics because their involvement would bring human touch to politics on account of their characteristic of motherhood.

Mahatma Gandhi did not agree with Tulasidas' dictum: 'Drum, fools and women are fit to beatn'. He wrote:" whatever Tulasidas' view may have been about women, there is no doubt that if man treats his wife like an animal, and considers her as his property he cuts himself from his better half". But he was conservative regarding economic independence and higher education for women. He wrote: "Women should not have to earn her living. A state of affairs in which women have to work as telegraph clerks, typists or compositors, can be, I think, is no good.." As to women's education, he wrote:" There must be, therefore, separate arrangements for the education of women after their attainment of certain age. They should be taught the management of the house, the things they should do or do not do during pregnancy and nursing and caring of children". Thus, Gandhiji had not distinguished himself much from the traditional view of women in respect of education and employment.

When it comes to the question of women joining Salt Satyagraha, Gandhiji dissuade women, and restricted their activities to picketing of liquor shops and the shops selling foreign-made cloth. But we know that despite these restrictions thousands of housewives had joined the freedom movement and went to jail. This showed that women were capable of heroic deeds and could excel men outside home.

Although Gandhiji believed in Varna, he ruled out any connection between Varna and marriage, and thereby implicitly approved inter-caste marriages.

GENDER EQUALITY: RADICAL VIEW

Jawaharlal Nehru had a better understanding of the gender problem, and set the tone for a radical view of the problem. He wrote: That the root cause of women's plight was their economic dependence upon men. For, Nehru wrote: "All the good legislation in the world will not make a man or woman a free agent as long as he or she is economically under another's bondage. It is the economic bondage that is the root cause of the trouble of the Indian woman and to the removal of this our energies must be directed." True to his belief, after Independence, he got the Hindu Code Bill passed by the parliament, inspite of opposition in his own party and orthodox Hindus. Next to Raja Ram Mohan Roy, it was Nehru who had contributed to the advancement of Indian women- the former saved the Hindu widow from *Sati* and the latter liberated the Hindu widow from the patriarchal bondage.

Some writers oppose the radical view of the status of women. For example, the authors of *Indian Approach to Women's Empowerment*

(2004) refer to the so-called biological and psychological differences between men and women, and therefore they conclude men remain men, women remain women. They suggest that women can uplift themselves by developing their psychic power, which is alleged to be stronger than physical power. But Hans Enoksson says that biological difference exist but there are no psychological differences, because if boys and girls are brought up in the same social environment their mental make-up would be more or less the same. Seema Mustafa, a well-known columnist, supports Enoksson when she wrote:" There is no difference between man and woman other than biological...It all depends on the bring up. We make these roles. We bring up women as weaker sex. Therefore, their role is confined to housework." Long ago Karl Marx remarked "It is not the consciousness that determines the being. On the contrary, it is the being that determines the consciousness". By being Marx meant human being in a historically determined socio-economic formation.

History is replete with examples of women who proved their merit in politics, social service (Mother Therisa). Literature and fine arts, not withstanding their biology or psychology. We are familiar with the saying: 'that behind the success of a man there is a woman'. Men would not be men without the advice and support of women.

Another harmful trend to women's advancement is radical feminism. This trend originated in the West, and concentrates on the criticism of men and attributes that all the woes of women are due to male domination at home and outside, and ignores the kind of socio-economic conditions of subjugation of women to men.

Women began organizing in India after Independence. All India Women's Federation, of left orientation, was organized to advance the cause of women. But with the split of the Communist Party of India, it also split into two. There are also independent women organizations and groups fighting for women's rights. These organizations are not based on regular membership and the leadership is mainly urban elitist. They conduct demonstrations on specific issues like atrocities against women, and meet in annual conferences to pass resolutions on advancing women's rights. Of late, women's organizations, along with political parties, are demanding one-third political reservations to parliament. Those political parties who demand one-third reservations for women in parliament have not even one per cent women in their decision-making bodies. This shows that political parties, including left parties, have not broken from the patriarchal tradition.

Women's organizations at this stage must concentrate more on the education of girls from the elementary to higher education. For, we consider the spread of education among girls, the future women, is a step forward in the process of achieving gender equality. Women must of necessity have political reservations in the legislative bodies because their presence shall have a sobering effect on legislative proceedings. At the same time, they should campain in favour of reservations for girls in professional courses. We may recall here when N.T. Rama Rao was the Chief Minister of Andhra Pradesh, the government provided 30 per cent representation for girls in educational institutions and employment. As a result, women in large numbers got employment in highly paid jobs at home and abroad. Women's employment and associate economic independence, gives them self confidence. Therefore, what is required is to build a broad based political and social movement to advance the cause of women as the patriarchal tradition in India is still strong.

NOTES

1. The first author of this paper who was in the U.S.S.R. in 1983 observed that male superiority still existed there. The husband, although the wife contributed to family income because of right to employment, takes major decisions regarding major household purchases and the places to go during vacation. The author was told by well-meaning Indian residents in Moscow that wife-beating and harassment of women at work-place was not uncommon dasis, the first author is reminded of a saying in Telugu to the effect that even if the tamarind tree dies the taste to sourness does not die.
2. All the quotes of Manu Smriti are from K.B. Archak (Ed) Manu Smriti and Women, Dharwad, 1998.
3. Some time ago the first author met a professor in a university who explained the logic behind the dowry system. Since the husband has to maintain his wife and children life long she has to pay dowry. A strange logic indeed.

BOOKS CONSULTED

Federick Engels, The Origin of Family, Private Property and the State (1894), Progress Publishers, Moscow, 1972.

K.B. Archak (ed.), Manu Smriti and women, Dharwad, 1998.

Manu Smruti, Translated by Pt. Jwala Prasad Chaturvedi, Haridwar, 1992.

Chanakhaya Niti, Translated by Pt. Jwala Prasad Chaturvedi, Haridwar, undated.

Swami Vivekananda, Women of India, in Collected Works, Vol. 8, Advaita Ashrama, Calcultha, 1963.

Sre Aurobindo, on Women, Mother's Ashram Trust, Pondicherry, undated.

Pushpa Joshi (ed.), Gandhi on Women, Ahmedabad, 1988.

Jawaharlal Nehru, Discovery of India, Bombay, 1946.

Bharat and Madhu Jahunjhunwala, Indian Approach to Women's Empowerment, 2004, New Delhi.

42

Women and Law: Towards Gender Justice

Vijaya Chandra Tenneti & T. Yadagiri Rao

INTRODUCTION

Women constitute about one half of the global population, but they are placed at various disadvantageous positions due to gender difference and bias. They have been the victims of violence and exploitation by the male dominated society all over the world. The exploitation against the women goes unabated from times immemorial, some times in the name of religion, some times on the pretext of writings, in the scriptures and some times by the social sanctions[1].

For centuries past, women all over the world have not only been denied full justice, social economic and political but also as a weaker sex. They have been used, abused, exploited and then discarded to lead immoral, street, vagrant and destitute life till their death.

CRIMES AGAINST WOMEN: THE PRESENT SCENARIO

The equality of status guaranteed by the Constitution is only a myth to millions of women for whom life is stalked by various kinds of violence within their homes, at work place and in educational system. Women becomes the victims torture, domestic violence in every 10 minutes, one molestation in every 22 minutes, one kidnapping and abduction I every 40 minutes, one connected with prostitution every

70 minutes and one dowry death inevery 106 minutes in India. Thus, every five minutes one women is victimized by crime in India.

GENDER EQUALITY: THE CONSTITUTIONAL MANDATE AND THE LEGISLATIVE FRAME WORK

The Constitution of India, in categorical terms, prohibits gender discrimination in what so ever manner or of what so ever nature. The Constitution of India guarantees both rights and privileges to women through fundamental rights and Directive Principles of State Policy. Article 14 confers on men and women equal rights and opportunities in political, economic and social spheres. Article 15 prohibits discrimination against any citizen on grounds of religion, race, caste, sex, etc. alike. Article 15 (3) makes a special provision enabling the State to make affirmative discrimination in favour of women. Similarly, Article 16 provides for equality of opportunities, Article 39(a) mentions that the State shall direct its policy towards securing for both men and women, equally, the right to a means of livelihood, Article 39(c) ensures equal pay for equal work. Article 42 directs the State to make provision for ensuring just and humane conditions of work and maternity relief. Above all, the Constitution imposes a fundamental duty on every citizen through Article 51(A)(e) to renounce practices derogatory to the dignity of women.

In order to safeguard the various constitutional rights, the State has enacted many women-specific and women-related legislation's some of such legislations are: Equal Remuneration Act of 1976. The Hindu Marriage Act of 1955 as amended in 1976. The Immoral Traffic (Prevention) Act of 1956 as amended and renamed in 1986. Dowry Prohibition Act of 1961. An amendment brought in 1984 to this Act made women's subjection to cruelly a cognizable offence. The second amendment brought in 1986 makes the husband or in-laws punishable, if a woman commits suicide within seven years of her marriage and it has been proved that she has been subjected to cruelly. Also, a new criminal offence of 'Dowry Death' has been incorporated in the Indian Penal Code. The Child Marriage Restraint Act of 1976 raises the age for marriage of a girl to 18 years from 15 years and that of a boy 21 years and makes offences under this Act cognizable. The Factories Act of 19 provides for establishment of a creches where 30 women a employed (including casual and contract labourers). The Medical Termination Pregnancy Act of 1971 legalizes abortion by qualified professional on humanitarian or medical grounds. The latest to the roster are Prevention of Domestic Violence Act 2005.

GENDER JUSTICE: THE JUDICIAL RESPONSE

It is significant to note that, the Indian judiciary, has been playing the role of a catalyst in protecting and promoting the human rights of women The judiciary has been working as epitome in protecting the rights of women At a time when the legislature has failed to perform its duty of promptly responding to the needs of the women, in the changing socio-economic scenario and when the executive has become lethargic towards the problems of women, the judiciary has step in to fill this vacuum and through its activist role, has passed several land mark judgements, of far reaching implications for the emancipation of women. Some the rights articulated by the judiciary pertaining to the women need a special mention:

1. Right to live with human dignity: The apex court has held that, the fundamental right to personal liberty mean, not merely confined to physical existence but it includes within its ambit the right to live with human dignity[3].
2. Right to privacy of women: The courts have held that, fundamental right to life under Article 21 of the constitution also includes, the right to privacy[4].
3. Mothers as equal guardians : Though father is considered to be the natural guardian of a minor child, through its historic judgement, the supreme court has held that, even at times, mother can also act as the natural guardian of a minor child, where the welfare of the child is the paramount consideration[5].
4. Rights to seek divorce and maintenance: The courts have declared that under Section 125 of the criminal procedure code, every women is entitled for maintenance[6].
5. Right to Stridhana and right against dowry : The courts have also declared that, women will have absolute rights over the property which she receives as 'stridhana' and that a women is entitled to receive back the dowry amounts paid by her[7].
6. Protection against illegal arrests and detentions and right to compensation. The right to compensation is yet another significant right declared by the judiciary, wherein, women as a victim of a crime has a right to seek compensation from the wrong doers[8].

7. Protection of women from prostitution and rehabilitation of their children[9].
8. Right to economic empowerment : The supreme court in a number of cases held that right to economic empowerment of a women is a human rights of women[10].
9. Right against sexual harassment : The courts have held that, it is the duty of the employer or other responsible persons in work places or other institutions, whether public or private, to prevent sexual harassment of working women[11].
10. Right to equal remuneration

GENDER JUSTICE: THE FUTURE STRATEGIES

The status of women in our country stems from their less economic liberty and consequent dependence and lack of decision making power. They do not have control over the resources for lack of access to the decision making structures in the country. The legislators can play a pivotal role in empowering the women by making reservations in various decision making structures. The bill for reservation of 33 per cent seats for women folk in Parliament and State Legislative Assemblies has not yet been passed for lack of unanimity between various political parties of the country. This reservation is the prime need of the hour.

The other measures which are necessary to provide effective protection of women against gender based violence, interalia are:

1. Effective legal measures, including penal sanctions, civil remedies and compensatory provisions to protect women against all kinds of violence, including violence and abuse in the family, sexual assault and sexual harassment in the workplace;
2. Preventive measures, including public information and education programmes "gender sensitive training of judicial and law enforcement officers and other public officials" to change attitudes concerning the roles and status of men and women;
3. Protective measures, including refuges, counseling, rehabilitation and other support services for women who are the victims of violence or who are at risk of violence.

The police officers, prosecutors and judges at all levels of hierarchy need to be exposed to the gender equality education which would enlighten them on existing assumptions, myths and realities about women. There is urgent need to training of the persons involved in the criminal justice system, nature of violence against women, domestic violence etc.,The participation of victims, NGOs, lawyers and social activists in such training programs may help in sensitizing the gender based violence by the law enforcement agency.

To conclude in the words of the great saint Guru Nanak

> *"It is from women, the condemned one, that we are conceived and it is from her that we are born. It is to woman that we are engaged, and married. It is to women who is our life long friend. And it is she who keeps our race going. It is women through whom we establish our socialites. Then why denounce her from whom even kings and great men are born."*

NOTES AND REFERENCES

1. R.K. Bag, "Domestic Violence and Crime Against Women–Criminal Justice Response in India", Criminal Law Journal, January 1999, p. 1.
2. Ibid.
3. Maneka Gandhi Vs. Union of India, AIR SC 1976.
4. T. Saritha Vs. Venkatasubbaiah, AIR 1983 AP 356.
5. Githa Hari Haran Vs. RBI and Vandana Shiva Vs. J. Badhopadhyaya, 1999 AIR SCW, 811.
6. Mohd Ahmed Khan Vs. Shahabanu Begum and others, AIR 1985 SC 1945.
7. Prathiba Rani Vs. Suraj Kumar, AIR 1985 SC 628.
8. Rudalshah Vs. State of Bihar, AIR 1983, SC 1086.
9. Gourav Jain Vs. Union of India, AIR 1997, SC 3021.
10. Maslimani Mudaliar Vs. Idol of Swamy Nathan Thukkoli, AIR 1996, SC 1967.
11. Vishaka Vs. State of Rajasthan, AIR 1997, SC 3011.
12. Quoted in Mohd. Wasim Ali, "Crimes Against Women: An Appraisal of Judicial Trends in India, Cr.L.J. February, 1999, P. 17.

43

Gender Dimensions among Adivasis of Eastern Ghats (Sharing the experience of Jana Chetana, an NGO)

M. Sankara Reddi, M. Chandrayya and M. Sundara Rao

INTRODUCTION

Development planning involving viewing situations through different lenses. A gender perspective adds to such a holistic approach. Development institutions recognize that the gender component forms an important aspect of the design, implementation and evaluation of development projects. The major objective of this paper was to at an understanding of gender dimensions among the Adivasis of Eastern Ghats. This required gender sensitive participatory tools and techniques.

Women's issues have been receiving considerable attention since the UN Declaration of 1975 as *International Women's Year* and the period between 1975-1985 as have been receiving considerable attention since the UN Declaration of 1975 as *InternationalWomen's decade*. The changed stance of International bodies was necessitated by women's secondary position and a high level discrimination against women. It was clearly felt that a social equality could remain as a dream without ending the discrimination against more than 50 per cent of world's population, who are basically responsible for all domestic chores, food preparation and child rearing in addition to formal and informal economic activities. Women suffer from hunger and poverty in greater numbers and to greater degree than men, more so, in rural areas. The government of India appointed a National Committee on the status of Women in India in 1972 and the committee published its report in 1975. This was the first ever official attempt to study the status of Indian women and recommend changes to improve their position. The report highlighted that despite constitutional guarantees, the roles, rights and participation of women in all spheres of life were limited.

Women's weaker position made Government of India to accommodate women in development activities due to which changes were happening in the society. The changes have created opportunities for women of some classes and often-created problem like displacing women from the labour force, forced women to migrate and did not reduce the drudgery in traditional women's work. It was due to the super imposition of the pattern of development on a pre-existing system with social structures severely in disfavour of women. In fact the development planning itself is highly male biased and has not been conducive to the creation of a much-needed ideological and institutional change. It is to be noted that the demographic-statistical profile confirms the disadvantaged position of women in India. The women themselves have felt helpless and overwhelmed by the problems they face by virtue of simply being women. This pervasive sense of powerlessness forced many women to seek succor from welfare agencies, social organisations and Government. The issues and problems regarding the empowerment and development of women are complex, yet specific areas and its relevance from the perspective of women is not clearly identified. It is not easy to work out a strategy for providing solutions to the process of women development and gender aspects.

WHAT IS GENDER?

"It is not a question of seeking some new universal model, but of innovating indigenously and devising local answers to community needs, drawing on the skills and energy of women in full equality with men, benefiting from valuable traditions as well as new technologies" ...the Oslo Fjord Declaration, Feb. 1995. The term 'gender' is often used as synonymous with 'sex', male and female. Though the two are indeed synonymous according to English language dictionaries, the term 'gender' has over the past three decades evolved into a concept different from 'sex'. Ann Oakley and others used the term gender in the 1970s to describe those characteristics of men and women, which are socially determined, as against 'sex', which describes biologically determined characteristics. This distinction between sex and gender provides a useful analytical tool for focusing attention on differences between women and men, which are socially constructed. Many of the differences in men's and women's roles and responsibilities, norms and values guiding appropriate behaviour and access to and control over resources, have less to do with the fact that they were born male or female or that women alone can be impregnated and bear children, and more with how society expects women and men to behave. These in turn are derived from patriarchal ideology – a system of ideas based on a belief in inherent male superiority. This ideology typically includes the belief that male control over property is 'the natural order of things'.

Gender analysis was then used to emphasise aspects of gender differentiation in relation to:

- Sharing work.
- Sharing resources and Benefits.
- Human Rights; and
- Culture and Religion.

Harvard suggested four interrelated components:

- Activity Profile. (Productive-Reproductive-Community Role).
- Access-Control Profile. (Position-Status)
- Determinant factors for access and control; and
- Project Cycle Analysis.

The integration of anthropological methods and the development of new and innovative qualitative methods for research thus become critical to the exploration of gender and other structural issues in social research.

QUALITATIVE TOOLS FOR GENDER ANALYSIS

- Time Allocation Study.
- Activity Profile.

5. Is reversal of roles on the agenda of gender?
6. How does gender differ from Women in Development?

It is to be noted that gender is not a synonym for the word 'women' nor is it an abbreviation for 'men and women'. It is more a concept that attempts to look at and understand the distinctions between men and women that are externally influenced and conditions imposed on the naturally given biological sexes. Gender does not convey that all women are alike. While social and economic structures disrupt homogeneity, women share experiences, strengths, and obstacles that bind them together as a group. Gender is all about reconciling growth with equitable distribution of benefits among men and women, equality of power-relations between men and women, and most of all to highlight the interdependence and partnership between men and women in any area of development. More so, their fullest participation is needed to achieve sustainable development. Thus, it is necessary to ensure that women have: Equality of access, Equality of participation and Equality of control.

Who is a tribal?

The definition may vary with the purpose for which it is required. A politician in India with a palatial bungalow, car, colour television, video set, and a fat bank balance could still claim to be a tribal, just because his fore-fathers happened to belong to a government recognized tribe. He might have used that humble origin of his to amass enormous wealth by exploiting the system. His entire family, including the women, may pretend to be ultra-modern and display much artificial sophistication in their dealings with others. Since such neo-tribals are increasing in number, it becomes very difficult to study genuine tribals who from time immemorial have been true to the nature.

The tribals of India have been in contact with other people for a very long time and have been greatly influenced by them. The degree of influence is proportional to the intermingling with outsiders. Tribes like the Bills, Gonds, Gadaba, Koya, Konda Reddy and Jatapu almost live like Hindus. After independence, due to various developmental and welfare projects executed by government and Non Government Organisations, it has become extremely difficult to distinguish between the tribal and the non-tribal way of life. Some other tribes have taken to mining and hence it is almost impossible to find pure tribals who have remained unchanged for centuries. Fortunately for historians, anthropologists and sociologists there are still some tribes in Eastern Ghats are totally unaffected by any developmental programme and therefore we conducted a empirical study to assess the "Status of Women in Tribal of Eastern Ghats". Some of the tribes are restricted to the Andhra-Orissa boarder which is totally cut off from the rest of the country by mountains, hills, rivers, springs and a total lack of roads and communications.

SHARING OF EXPERIENCE OF JANA CHETANA

Jana Chetana's present intervention is a Sustainable Tribal Empowerment Programme (STEP) under the assistance of CARE INDIA, which envisages transformation in adivasi women's lives and alters the relationship between adivasi men and adivasi women. It is working in 199 Adivasi Village belongs to Seethampeta, Palakonda and Veeraghattam Mandals of Srikakulam District of Andhra Pradesh. Jana Chetana believe changes will be occurring in the shared space for collaborative relationship while women and men pursue action within their separate spaces which are essential and conductive for the development of the full potential of both women and men.

Towards the above transformative process to take place, Jana Chetana has analysed the gender issues prevalent in the Adivasis and clarifies the gender related power relations maintained in adivasi society. A coherent policy and action plan to address the various prevailing gender issues are developed by Jana Chetana which we believe would lead to a collaborative relationship between men and women as well as would provide space for women's autonomy. In a community based sustainable tribal empowerment of adivasi to ensure their livelihood security. While pursuing this programme with gender sensitivity, Jana Chetana cannot address all the identified 22 gender issues within a period of 3 years for practical reasons. Based on the consensus of women and men, we have agreed to focus on a few and we have developed an action plan to address five of the twenty two gender issues during this project period of 3 years.

PROFILE OF SRIKAKULAM

Srikakulam District of Andhra Pradesh is the extreme North Eastern district, situated within the geographic coordinates of 18-20' and

19-10' of northern latitude and 83-5' and 84.50' of eastern longitude the total area of the district is 5,837 Sq. Kms, with a seacoast of 193 Kms. The Srikakulam District Tribal Sub-Plan Area is consists of 20 Mandals, distributed over 102 Pachayats. There are 606 Revenue Villages in Tribal Sub Plan Area. The tribal population living in the Tribal Sub Plan Area is 13.40 lakhs. It covers 7.02 per cent of the total area, covering an area of 819 square kilometers. According to 2001 census, the total Scheduled Tribe population in Srikakulam is 1,51,249, which constitute 5.96 per cent. The literacy rate of Scheduled Tribe of Srikakulam is 19.70 per cent, of which female is 10.41 per cent.

These tribals are mostly confined to Seethampeta, Kotturu, Bhamini, Pathapathanam, Meliaputti and Mandasa Mandals of Srikakulam District. Savara, Jatapu, Gadaba, Konda Dora are predominant tribes in Srikakulam. Anthropologists have classified Savaras as "Konda Savaras or "Kapu Savaras", based on their geographical distribution, attire and costumes employed in their dances. They live in small villages consisting of not more than twenty to sixty houses. Their everyday activities are so well coordinated and inter-linked. It is tempted to view the entire village as a super-family. Irrespective of one's gender, every person has a vital role to play in the welfare of the community. A housewife is the nucleus of domestic activity. She rises early in the morning, fetches water from a distant spring, prepares a breakfast of *"Pakala"* or "Ambali", cleans the house, cooks the other meals, accompanies her husband to the forest, and gathers fruits, leaves and firewood. During the monsoon season, she assists in all agricultural activity and this includes hard labour. She can walk fifteen to twenty kilometers in a day, can carry a heavy-load on her head through difficult mountains and can go without food for an entire day. How many of us can even think of choosing such a life?

Compared to modern women a tribal woman has very little wealth of her own. She has just a piece of coarse cloth to cover her womanhood. She is very fond of ornaments, yet has just one or two strings of red, blue or white beads. In addition, she may have some bangles, earrings and necklaces made of cheap metal. That materialistic comforts and riches are not the indices of happiness is well illustrated by the tribal woman. She is always very cheerful and light-hearted, often laughing and joking with members of her family or with the neighbours. She is truthful and honest. She never denies any offence she might have committed and willingly faces the consequences. These are some of the sterling qualities of Tribal women. We the modern people have to learn from our tribal sisters. It is true that the tribal woman avoids outsiders, but once she gets over her natural shyness, she is extremely frank and communicative. Considering her utter poverty and her constant struggle to maintain the barest minimum standard of life, her light-heartedness is amazing.

Women-libbers of the outside world may feel ashamed if they come to know how. Tribal women have acquired a dominant role of partnership in married life. The tribal woman fondles her man like she would a child, loves him like a paramour (lover), keeps him company like a companion would and works with him like an equal partner. While she will do everything for him, she will never be his subordinate. She has gained this status by sheer hard work and not by being demanding. There is nothing she will not or cannot do. She even attends to the funerals of her near and dear ones, something so called 'refined' Hindus do not allow for a woman. The tribal woman also assists in erecting a memorial for the dead. The birth of a son is not a special cause for joy as boys and girls are considered equal to the tribals. The modern mother, who undergoes an abortion after learning from latest clinical techniques, that her foetus is that of a girl, should learn from her tribal sister, to accept the children of either gender, as a gift of God Almighty. A tribal woman declares her pregnancy with pride and does not welcome her husband till she is willing to conceive again. Delivery is without the assistance of a midwife and mother herself cuts the umbilical chord. The mother nurses the baby with her milk, carries it everywhere in a piece of old cloth hanging from her shoulder. She puts her child to sleep in a bamboo cradle. Older sisters attend to their younger siblings. The young girls are of fair colour, graceful and pretty, but as they grow older this gloss diminishes because of frequent child bearing, long journeys to markets and fairs, and heavy domestic and field labour. The tribal woman does not fight the aging process but becomes a grandmother gracefully.

THE INSTITUTION OF GHOTUL

Tribal houses are too small to accommodate a large family. Therefore, they have adapted a special institution called "Ghotul" to solve their accommodation problem. The Ghotul are predominantly found among Murias, Bondas and Khonds. Boys and girls of six years of age are entitled to membership. The female workers of the Ghotul are known as "Motiyaris or Boya" and they are assigned important administrative duties at the Ghotul. They are responsible for the general cleanliness of the building and premises, the punctual arrival of members, the taking of the attendance, the supervision of sitting arrangements, and the assurance of liberal supply of fire wood, mustard oil, tobacco etc. Each girl has to attend to a male member of the Ghotul. If he is extremely tired after a day's work, she massages his body and applies oil. If the boy is pleased, he presents her with a wooden comb and perhaps a plum. When activities for the night commence, the girls have to intermingle with the boys and distribute themselves around the fire. Together they gossip or make fun of each other. More serious discussions, group singing, playing of musical instruments and dancing follow this. When it is time to retire for the day the girls share beds with boys. This is perhaps the tribal way to inculcate the habit of community living amongst youngsters. These tribals have perfected the art of co-existence from time-immemorial whereas the most advanced countries such as U.S.A. United Kingdom, France, Germany and Sweden have had to introduce such a system of co-education very recently. Nobody should be under the impression that Ghotul life is permissively vulgar or immoral. Residents are expected to play the game of love by strictly adhering to all the rules and regulations. It is our belief that the mothers train their daughters to the extent they can go at the Ghotuls. Any lapse on anybody's part attracts very severe punishment from the authorities. Therefore, premarital pregnancies are very rare. If it does happen, then the girl names the father and a wedding is quickly arranged.

A VERY FASHIONABLE STUDENT AT THE TRIBAL CO-ED INSTITUTION OF GHOTUL

Marriage is a very serious matter for the tribals. A clan and a set of clan-gods identify each group. No marriages are permitted within a given clan, as all the members of a clan are considered brothers and sisters ("Anna Chelalu"). When a woman marries outside her clan, she is considered a part of her husband's clan. A girl has the right to select her father's sister's son as her life partner. Similarly, a girl can marry her maternal uncle. A woman has a free hand to select her groom and is never compelled to marry a man against her choice.

Child marriage is not permissible and pre-puberty marriages are quite unheard of.

Tribal brides are in great demand and therefore the groom's party has to pay the "Bridal Price" or "Oli" which is determined on the basis of the bride's age, socio-economical status of both parties. In the event the prospective son-in-law is not in a position to bear such an expense then he has to work in the bride's house for a number of years before the wedding is arranged. The bridal price is not paid in cash but in kind, such as grains, fowls, pigs and wines, to meet the marriage expenses and host a grand dinner and a drinking bout that follows the wedding. All the members of the village are invited to participate in the wedding by singing, dancing and drinking. If at any time in the past, the groom happened to misbehave with any of the Motiyaris or Boya then the entire female fraternity boycotts the wedding. This is a great deterrent, because it is very hard to think of a wedding without the cheering and loud laughing of Motiyaris or Boya.

Each tribe follows its own custom after the wedding. The bride may go to her in-laws' house or the groom may join the bridal family and in some cases the couple may start a household of their own. All the members of the groom's family, especially the bride's brothers-in-law, treat her with great respect and kindness. A tribal woman faces sickness, accidents, calamities and even death of near ones with calm and resolve. In the event the husband prematurely dies, it is his younger brother who has the first right to marry her. The bereaved widow also has an equal right to refuse him and marry anyone she takes fancy to. But no one is allowed to have more than one wife, and a widower or a divorcee is not allowed to marry a virgin. A widow's new husband has to pay the bridal price to her former husband's family.

At times the tribals also run into marital problems. If a husband turns out to be brutal, crude, insane, impotent, unfaithful, criminal or diseased, then the wife has every right to complain about him to the tribal head *Gomango or Naidu or Patel.* He in turn assembles his advisory council and gives an opportunity to the couple to plead their cases. If the council is convinced of the husband's guilt, the wife is allowed to get a separation and marry anybody she chooses. In some instances the former husband has tried to disturb the wife's new household and in the scuffle that ensued the wife has killed the former husband. In such an event the council has no hesitation in pardoning them all. What a down-to-the-earth system of justice this? Of course, after the tribal court's decision to acquit, civilized people outside have sometimes dragged them to criminal courts where they were found guilty and imprisoned for life. In tribal society women are not treated as inferior or second-class citizens. Although they are on par with the men, they complement rather than compete with each other. This status of the tribal women has existed from ancient times, as can be seen from Savara Wall Painting or Pictographs or Eedisung. These paintings were executed as early as five to fifty centuries before the birth of Christ. Most of these paintings represent hunting scenes, fighting sequences, animal sacrifices, rituals to ward off evil spirits and so on. The scenes that depict every day life, women are shown to be involved in food gathering, basket weaving, singing and dancing. Pregnant women, women giving birth, and nursing mothers are also depicted. This special status for women might have given rise to the mother-goddess cult. Even today most of the tribals of the area are the worshippers of the goddess like Adamma, Yellamma, Mukkudamma, Malliamma, Neelamma, Polamma, Majji Goramma, Modukondamma, Sammakka-Sarakka and Danteshwari. It seems as though inequality among modern men and women is a curse of the civilized world and the women's fight for equal right with men is the luxury of educated, city bred women. These modern women are at cross roads; while enjoying their special status, they also want equal rights?

All their problems do not arise out of inequality alone. "Women in Tribal Society" gives some insight into how some of the modern woman's problems can be solved. Tribal women themselves are increasingly subjected to the stress associated with the developmental activities. The tribal women were free from sexually transmitted diseases as they have healthy sex. On the other the establishment of Industries in tribal areas a large number of tribal men and women rushed to the construction site in search of a better way of life. Unfortunately, the women became the victims of lust and rape and hence had to take to prostitution to earn their living. They used even those who were employed as cooks and maidservants in the houses of the officers as mistresses. If they conceived, the employers did not hesitate for a moment to caste aspirations on their character and drove them out of the house. In this way, men without any character became the judges of morality of the tribal women. If something is not urgently done to save these women from the clutches of these unscrupulous men then a day will come when there will be nothing to talk about the "Women in Tribal Societies".

DIMENSIONS OF GENDER AMONG ADIVASIS OF EASTERN GHATS:

Sl. No.	*Issues*	*Causes*	*Problem Level*
1.	Dowry	Traditional value, societal pressure, family Prestige, Convention, Compulsion (or) Demand, less economic value of women.	50%
2.	Rape	Non-acceptance of sexual advances, Peer Pressure, jealousy, revenge, anger, land lords domination, lack of moral value, Alcoholism, perception of women as sexual objects.	20%
3.	Domestic Violence	Irresponsible behaviour questioned, sexual infidelity and lack of trust / mutual understanding, economic instability, patriarchal values, breaching of traditional norms, non payment of dowry, women blamed for men's infertility, suspicious nature of husband, difference in value and opinion.	70%
4.	Sex pre selection	Believe that girl child will not be economically supportive, economic burden/dowry, misconception that girls are dispensable.	60%
5.	Sexual harassment as work	Women considered being biologically inferior, men take advantage of women's poverty, Lack of moral vales, women seen as possession, lack of social support.	50%
6.	Prostitution	Prior sexual abuse, poverty, lack of food security. need to supplement income, dowry, domestic violence against women, hungry siblings.	25%
7.	Women not allowed to decide whether to have a child or not	In-grained perception that man is the deciding authority. Women considered being men's property. Women's view not socially accepted, under estimation of women's capacity to take appropriate decision, belief and practice that women are subordinate to men, perception of women's role and obligation to reproduce.	50%
8.	Health negligence and deprivation	Priority for male's health, lack of financial freedom for women to seek help, low income, ignorance, illiteracy women's traditional low priority for themselves. Insensitive healthcare system.	50%

Sl. No.	*Issues*	*Causes*	*Problem Level*
9.	Women discrimination	Racially considered inferior. Misconception of women's role as domestic workers socially stigmatised. Less societal value for women, no access to education, culture and tradition, poor decision making power among women.	60%
10.	No right to property	Patriarchal values men are traditionally inherit property. Unfavourable laws. Daughters will leave homes after marriage and hence cannot govern father's property. Social belief that son should look after parents and therefore son is the deciding authority on property rights.	80%
11.	Domestic labour	Patriarchal society prescribed role for women to cook, clean home, provide sexual services to husband, bear and rear children, clean, collect water, fuel, wash, look after elders, relatives, cattle.	100%
12.	Sterilization/ family planning	State family planning policy and targets, men believe that they would be impotent and incapable of hard work, family pressure, poverty, ignorance, women's frustration over irresponsible husbands.	80%
13.	Women discriminated against public worship	Social stigma, customs and tradition, women considered impure during menstruation, domination by men, social belief that something evil will happen to the village if women, sit in religious places. Inferior position for women by religions.	60%
14.	Male domination in village decision making	Patriarchal values, women considered to be biologically inferior, less intelligent, women prevented exposure to social governance and denied leadership, wives are considered not native to village, as they are born elsewhere, desire to suppress women.	100%
15.	Early marriage	Feeling of insecurity of parents, fear of sexual abuse, fear of evil spirit, misconception that marriage is the ultimate and after puberty, avoid parental responsibility, no access to education, social and family pressure, tradition, village traditions, large family.	60%
16.	Deserted women	Infertility, increase no of girl children for which she is blamed, dowry, forced marriage, ill-health, extramarital relationships, violence.	50%

Sl. No.	*Issues*	*Causes*	*Problem Level*
17.	Widow discrimination	Custom and tradition, belief that widow is ill women, religious norms, widow held responsible by religious for early death of husbands, widow is not a part of the society, sanction of sexual violence against widows.	30%
18.	Heavy physical burden/work for low wage/ income	Illiteracy, lack of skills, unequal wage distribution, lack of marketing facilities.	70%
19.	No power over food production	Male preference, male dominated society, less/no decision-making power, attitude of women themselves as submissive to their husband, lack of farm property.	60%

CONCLUSION AND RECOMMENDATIONS

This study has shown that gender roles and responsibilities interact at every stage. Although there seems to be established gender roles and responsibilities, there is a tendency for them to shift and change under different circumstances. The study also shows that access to and control over assets (land, house, etc) enhances the bargaining power of women in the intra and extra-household circumstances. It is also noticed that women participation in decision-making in and out of household affairs is greater as we go down in the social stratification. Therefore, the interventions should focus on the following aspects to enable women to move in the right direction.

1. Involving women in institutional credit process.
2. Enhancing bargaining power of women by building their capacity and confidence level.
3. Promote bargaining power of women.
4. Training on basic accounts, marketing, quality management etc.
5. Imparting knowledge of best collection, storage and local value addition processes.
6. Bringing awareness of different products and the economic value of the local value addition.
7. Children should be placed in Bridge schools.
8. Providing medicines, precautionary measures to prevent sun stroke.

GENDER POWER RELATIONS AMONG ADIVASIS OF EASTERN GHATS:

Sl. No.	*Issues*	*Causes*	*Power Relations*	*Result*
1.	Dowry	Traditional value, societal pressure, family prestige, Convention, Compulsion (or) Demand, less economic value of women	Male is considered a superior race, and therefore is eligible for high expectation if dowry, can demand it, it a sign of male worthiness/women seen as a liability and her contributions to family and society go unnoticed.	Women ill treated, subjected to torture, leads to suicide/murder, dignity loss, psychological stress, She becomes a victim to slander. Parents become badly indebted furthering poverty; women's status remains low.
2.	Rape	Non-acceptance of sexual advances, peer pressure, jealousy, revenge, anger, landlords, domination, lack of moral vale, alcoholism, and perception of women as sexual objects.	Social power is with men, men view women as object of sexual pleasure, affected women, become a target of publicity by media, women develop a feeling of inferiority, justice controlled by men and Police. Women victim not to voice out injustice.	Suicide/death stigmatised, abandoned, gain in society, burden to parents, ill health, bears the child of unknown father, victimised by other men in society will not be eligible for marriage, psychologically affected.
3.	Domestic violence	To maintain male dominance when his irresponsible behaviour is questioned, sexual infidelity and lack of trust/mutual understanding, economic instability patriarchal values, breaching of traditional norms, non payment of dowry, women blamed for men's infertility, suspicious nature of husband, difference in value and opinion.	Man considered to be bread winner and head of the family, man is the ultimate decision making authority, social belief that husbands are equal to god, female accepts certain degree of violence, religious sanctions, male takes all rights to control his wife as it is accepted in the community. No social support and society refuses to interfere.	Material and physical injures, ill health, suicide/death, less attention to children, women not able to contribute to the well being of family, income loss, insecure children.

Sl. No.	*Issues*	*Causes*	*Power Relations*	*Result*
4.	Sex pre selection	Belief that girl child will not be economically supportive. Avoid future economic burden, poverty based priority for few children. Social system and belief. Religious importance for sons to perform funeral rites.	Husband decides over continuation of pregnancy. Private doctors perform abortion. Cry of women ignored. Belief that male is prosperity and female is burden.	Ill health, mental depression inability to overcome guilt of female feticide, chronic pelvic infection, deaths, and women men ration lowered low status of women institutionalised.
5.	Sexual harassment at work	Women considered being biologically inferior, men take advantage of women's poverty, lack of oral values, woman seen as possession, lack of social support.	Men socio economically and physically more powerful and hence, exploit women. Vulnerability of women and corrupt legal support/ action.	Living with mental stress, pushed to live in poverty, victim of gossip in her work place, physical and mental depression, suspicious husband.

ACCESS-CONTROL AND DECISION MAKING AMONG ADIVASIS OF EASTERN GHATS

Issues	*Adivasis of Easteren Ghats*					
	Access		*Control*		*Decision Making*	
	Male	*Female*	*Male*	*Female*	*Male*	*Female*
Food	✓	✓	–	✓	–	✓
House Hold Assets	✓	✓	–	✓	–	✓
Production	✓	–	✓	–	✓	✓
Education	✓	–	✓	–	✓	✓
Health	✓	✓	✓	✓	✓	✓
Children's Marriage	–	–	–	–	–	✓
Birth Day of Child	–	–	–	✓	–	✓
Income	✓	✓	✓	–	✓	✓

REFERENCES

Elwin, Verrier: Leaves From the Jungle: Life in a Gond Village, Oxford University Press. 1936.

Elwin, Verrier: The Tribal World of Verrier Elwin; An Autobiography. Oxford University Press. 1964.

Chauhan, Abha (1990), Tribal Women and Social Change in India. Etawah: A.C. Brothers.

Daspande W.R., K.K. Awasthi and D.K. Srivastava (1988), "Travails of Tribals in Jhabua, "Indian Farming, 38 (No. 8, Nov.).

Gender Considerations in Summary Projects Outlines (SPROUTS) and Programmes Documents, ILO Programmes.

44

Women Empowerment–A Socio-legal Approach

K. Sudhakar and M. Ravinder

Empowerment of women involves many things – economic opportunity, property rights, political representation, social equality, personal rights and so on. The Indian society is a patriarchal system in which women's position within the structure and duties towards the family precede their rights as individuals. Many who argue for empowerment of women do so either with or without a full understanding of the conflicts between the historical and contemporary status of women in the patriarchy and the goals of empowerment. Certainly we may track a grate many changes that have occurred in the direction of change in the status of women in India but women have yet to achieve or realize many of the ideal stages of social, psychological, economic and political empowerment. Hence it is certainly more appropriate to define empowerment as a process rather than an end-point.

Empowerment by means of education, literacy, modest income-generating projects is clearly insufficient to ameliorate the prospects for a higher quality of the life for women. The process or empowerment is taking place at so many levels that it is quite difficult to gauge the actual nature and extent of empowerment in improving status of women. Certainly, the process is entangled in the struggle of civil society against the state and under the weight of historical practice and ongoing debates over the appropriate role of ideologies.

property, productive resources and benefit of development irrespective of gender difference. Political empowerment, of course, impels equal role in decision-making process sin power structure from grass root level to national level. All these dimensions of empowerment are inter related with each other.

Amendment to the Constitution in 1992 to strengthen the sharing of power by women at local level has opened a new chapter in the history of women's struggle for empowerment. The enactment of the 73rd an and 74th Constitutional amendment i.e. Panchayat Raj and Nagara palikas in India , no doubt a land mark event in this regard. It is important because of revolutionary measures by reserving 33 per cent sates for women at all levels in the local governance. Economic empowerment through Panchayat Raj and Municipalities (Nagara Palikas).

The impact of reservation on women in Panchayat and Municipalities bodies is instructive. Initially the criticism was made that women were merely proxies for some male member of the family. The subsequent field study found that in a few months of a year, the actual policies followed by the Panchayats and Municipalities have been much more sensitive to economic need of the poor. In so far as the economic impact of such policies as family planning and conservation tend to be differently felt by the women, human resource development being one of the major agenda in the plan of Panchayats, all the development efforts were directed to empower women besides mainstreaming them into the national development. The emphasis in respect of women was to make them economically independent and self –reliant. It is observed that women is targeted after she attained one economic independence. Women surpanches in several areas paid special attention to the problem of violence against women both at demotic and societal arenas.

Women both in traditional and modern social structure have always been the victims of exploitation. In third world economics like India , they are at the bottom of every hierarchy, oppression has further magnified as they toil under the double burden of gender. Now there has been tremendous effort for giving one-third reservation to women in local self government institutional framework. Soon or later this step will be proved as a milestone in the direction of not only women's development but all round development of India as a whole.

SUGGESTIONS

Training should be given to women for capacity building among them. Women should be taught not to keep undue pressure of their family members. Workshops and seminars should be organised by the Government for regular interaction among women representatives across districts and states. Such interaction would help them to exchange their ideas on performance and failure of local self-government institutional frame work. Adequate information relating to various programmes and activities including economic incentive oriented schemes promoted by the Government should be made available to women for their knowledge and involvement and implementation of such schemes, programmes etc. Majority of women had no independent source of earning. . It is suggested that the Government should run programmes of such kind wherein the programmes generate independent income earning status of women.